FREDERIK PEETERS

LUPUS

TOP SHELF

LUPUS © 2019 Frederik Peeters.

Editor-in-Chief: Chris Staros.

Lettered and Designed by Chris Ross.

Translation by Edward Gauvin.

Previously published by Les Éditions Atrabile.

Rights arranged through Nicolas Grivel Agency.

Published by Top Shelf Productions, PO Box 1282, Marietta, GA 30061-1282, USA. Top Shelf Productions is an imprint of IDW Publishing, a division of Idea and Design Works, LLC. Offices: 2765 Truxtun Road, San Diego, CA 92106. Top Shelf Productions®, the Top Shelf logo, Idea and Design Works®, and the IDW logo are registered trademarks of Idea and Design Works, LLC. All Rights Reserved. With the exception of small excerpts of artwork used for review purposes, none of the contents of this publication may be reprinted without the permission of IDW Publishing. IDW Publishing does not read or accept unsolicited submissions of ideas, stories, or artwork.

Visit our online catalog at www.topshelfcomix.com.

ISBN 978-1-60309-459-7

Printed in China.

23 22 21 20 19   5 4 3 2 1

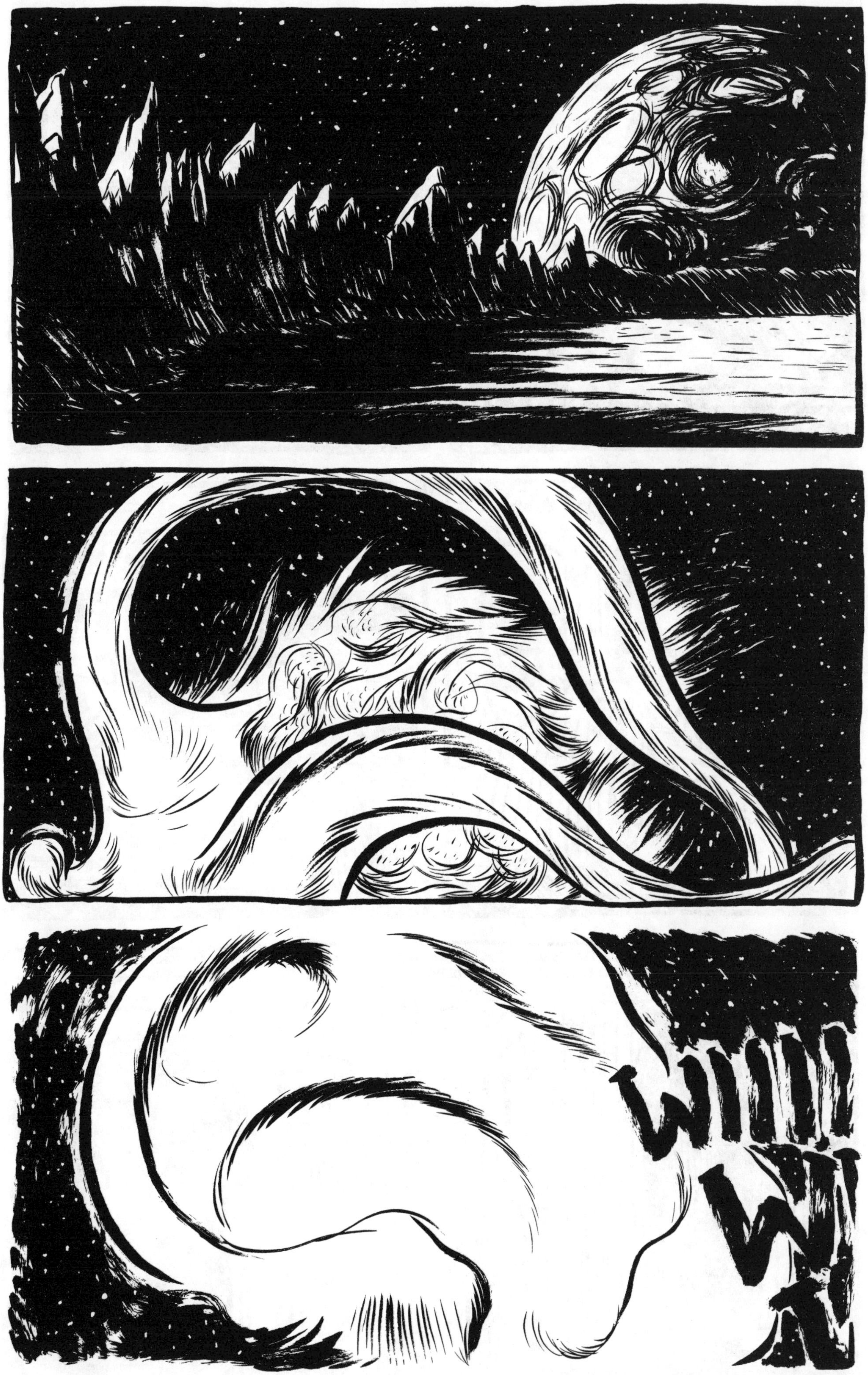

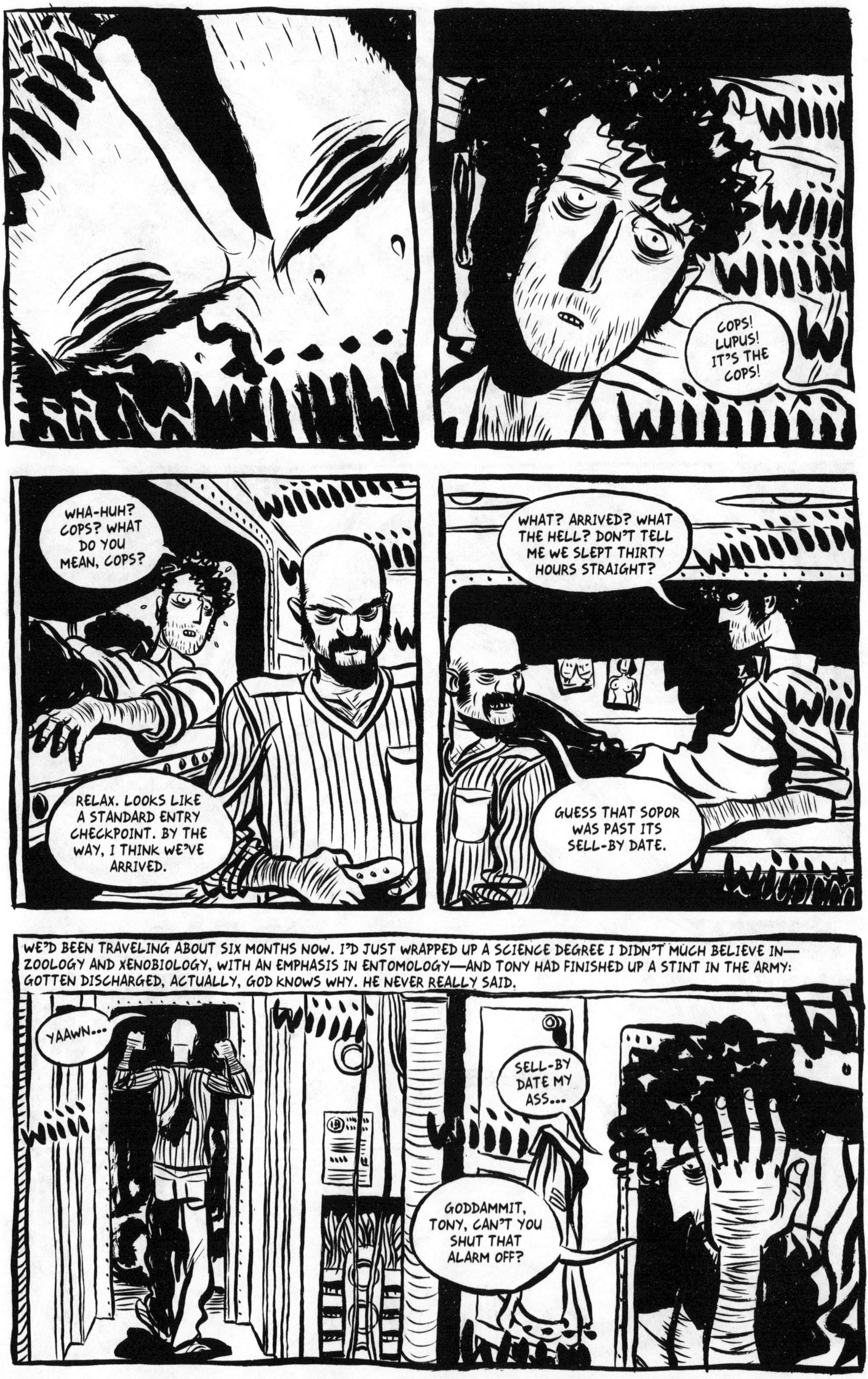
COPS! LUPUS! IT'S THE COPS!
WHA-HUH? COPS? WHAT DO YOU MEAN, COPS?
RELAX. LOOKS LIKE A STANDARD ENTRY CHECKPOINT. BY THE WAY, I THINK WE'VE ARRIVED.
WHAT? ARRIVED? WHAT THE HELL? DON'T TELL ME WE SLEPT THIRTY HOURS STRAIGHT?
GUESS THAT SOPOR WAS PAST ITS SELL-BY DATE.
WE'D BEEN TRAVELING ABOUT SIX MONTHS NOW. I'D JUST WRAPPED UP A SCIENCE DEGREE I DIDN'T MUCH BELIEVE IN—ZOOLOGY AND XENOBIOLOGY, WITH AN EMPHASIS IN ENTOMOLOGY—AND TONY HAD FINISHED UP A STINT IN THE ARMY: GOTTEN DISCHARGED, ACTUALLY, GOD KNOWS WHY. HE NEVER REALLY SAID.
YAAWN...
SELL-BY DATE MY ASS...
GODDAMMIT, TONY, CAN'T YOU SHUT THAT ALARM OFF?

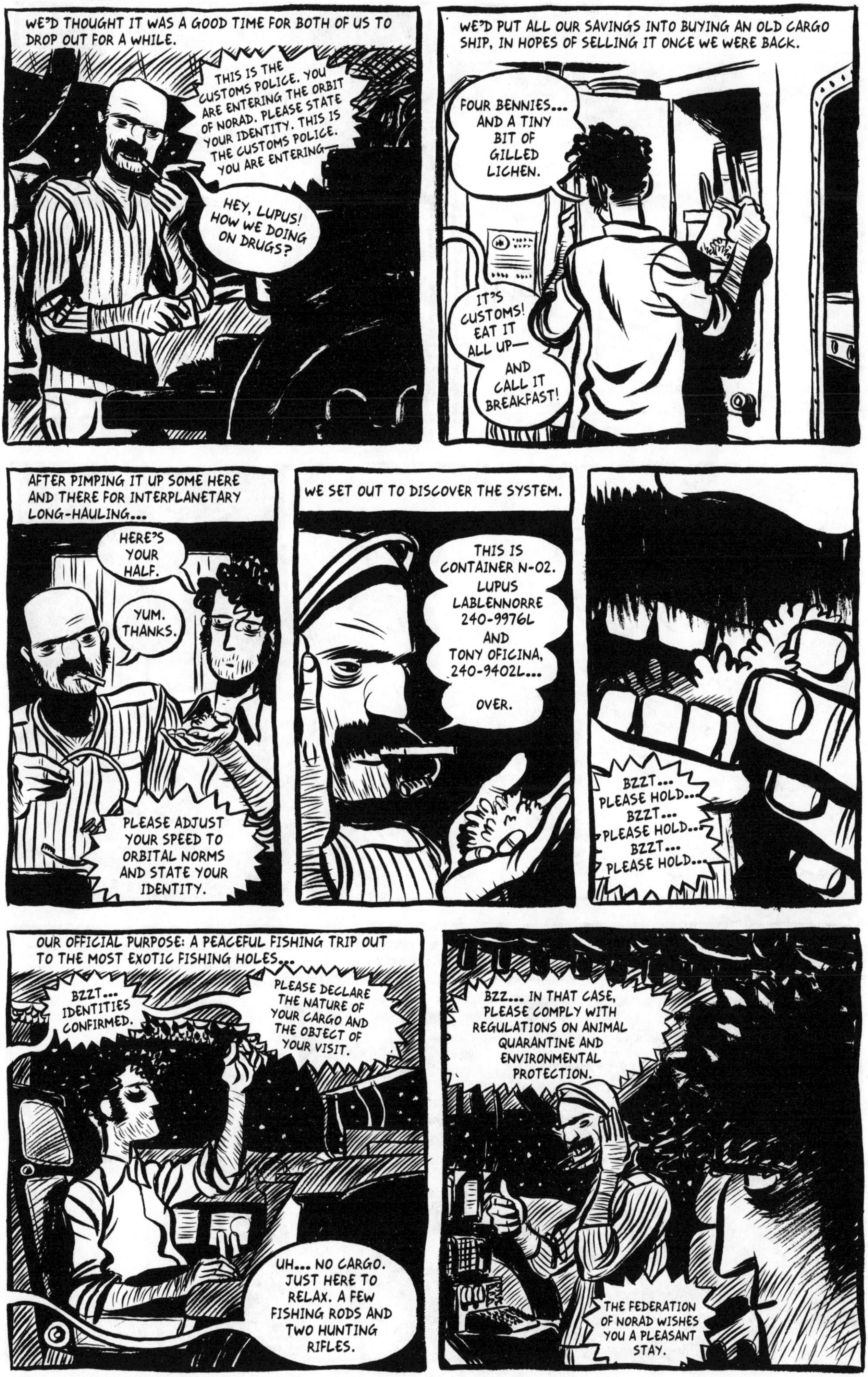

WE'D THOUGHT IT WAS A GOOD TIME FOR BOTH OF US TO DROP OUT FOR A WHILE.
THIS IS THE CUSTOMS POLICE. YOU ARE ENTERING THE ORBIT OF NORAD. PLEASE STATE YOUR IDENTITY. THIS IS THE CUSTOMS POLICE. YOU ARE ENTERING—
HEY, LUPUS! HOW WE DOING ON DRUGS?
WE'D PUT ALL OUR SAVINGS INTO BUYING AN OLD CARGO SHIP, IN HOPES OF SELLING IT ONCE WE WERE BACK.
FOUR BENNIES... AND A TINY BIT OF GILLED LICHEN.
IT'S CUSTOMS! EAT IT ALL UP—
AND CALL IT BREAKFAST!
AFTER PIMPING IT UP SOME HERE AND THERE FOR INTERPLANETARY LONG-HAULING...
HERE'S YOUR HALF.
YUM. THANKS.
PLEASE ADJUST YOUR SPEED TO ORBITAL NORMS AND STATE YOUR IDENTITY.
WE SET OUT TO DISCOVER THE SYSTEM.
THIS IS CONTAINER N-02. LUPUS LABLENNORRE 240-9976L AND TONY OFICINA, 240-9402L... OVER.
BZZT... PLEASE HOLD... BZZT... PLEASE HOLD... BZZT... PLEASE HOLD...
OUR OFFICIAL PURPOSE: A PEACEFUL FISHING TRIP OUT TO THE MOST EXOTIC FISHING HOLES...
BZZT... IDENTITIES CONFIRMED.
PLEASE DECLARE THE NATURE OF YOUR CARGO AND THE OBJECT OF YOUR VISIT.
UH... NO CARGO. JUST HERE TO RELAX. A FEW FISHING RODS AND TWO HUNTING RIFLES.
BZZ... IN THAT CASE, PLEASE COMPLY WITH REGULATIONS ON ANIMAL QUARANTINE AND ENVIRONMENTAL PROTECTION.
THE FEDERATION OF NORAD WISHES YOU A PLEASANT STAY.

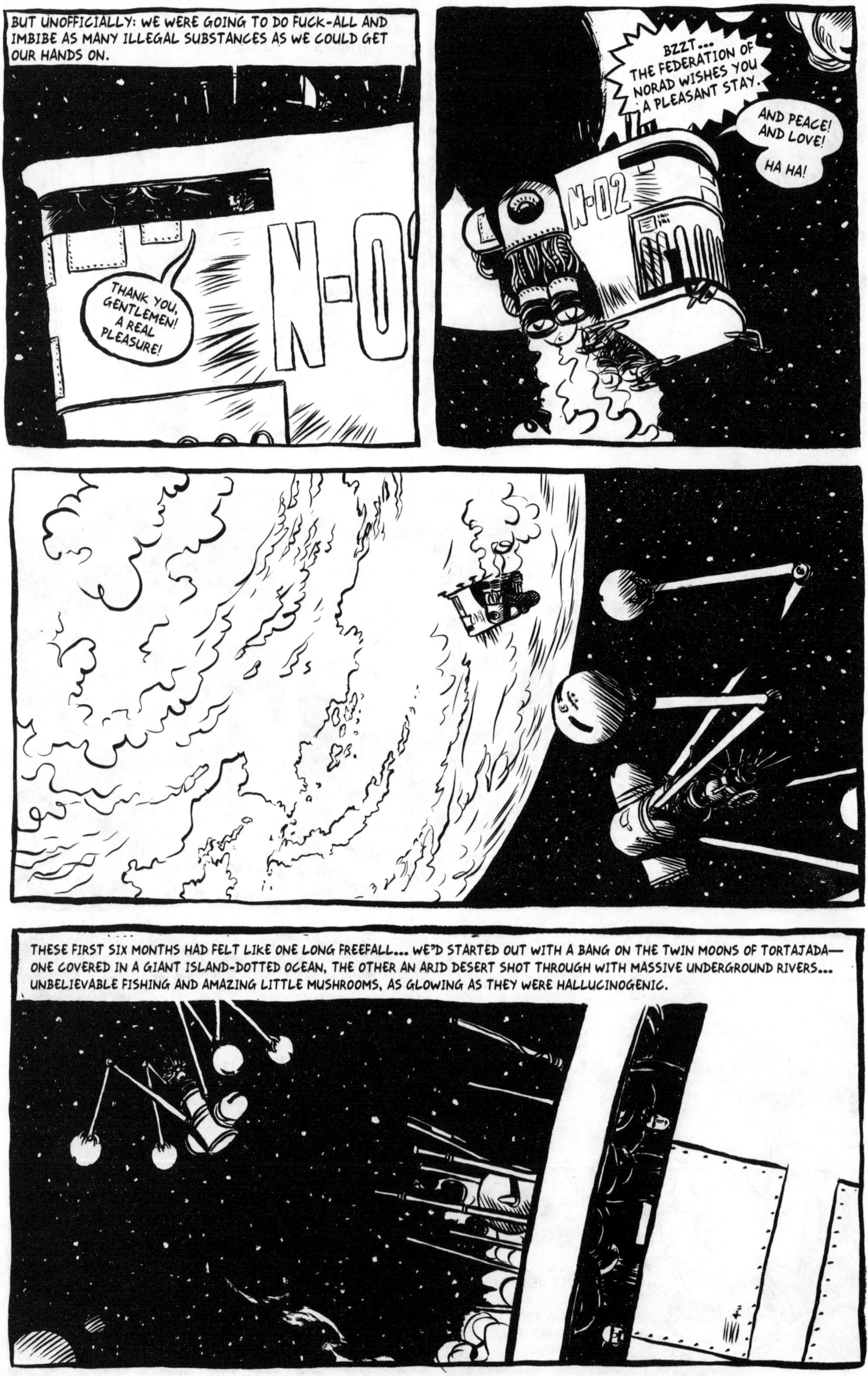
BUT UNOFFICIALLY: WE WERE GOING TO DO FUCK-ALL AND IMBIBE AS MANY ILLEGAL SUBSTANCES AS WE COULD GET OUR HANDS ON.
N-O
THANK YOU, GENTLEMEN! A REAL PLEASURE!
BZZT... THE FEDERATION OF NORAD WISHES YOU A PLEASANT STAY.
AND PEACE! AND LOVE!
HA HA!
N-02
THESE FIRST SIX MONTHS HAD FELT LIKE ONE LONG FREEFALL... WE'D STARTED OUT WITH A BANG ON THE TWIN MOONS OF TORTAJADA— ONE COVERED IN A GIANT ISLAND-DOTTED OCEAN, THE OTHER AN ARID DESERT SHOT THROUGH WITH MASSIVE UNDERGROUND RIVERS... UNBELIEVABLE FISHING AND AMAZING LITTLE MUSHROOMS, AS GLOWING AS THEY WERE HALLUCINOGENIC.

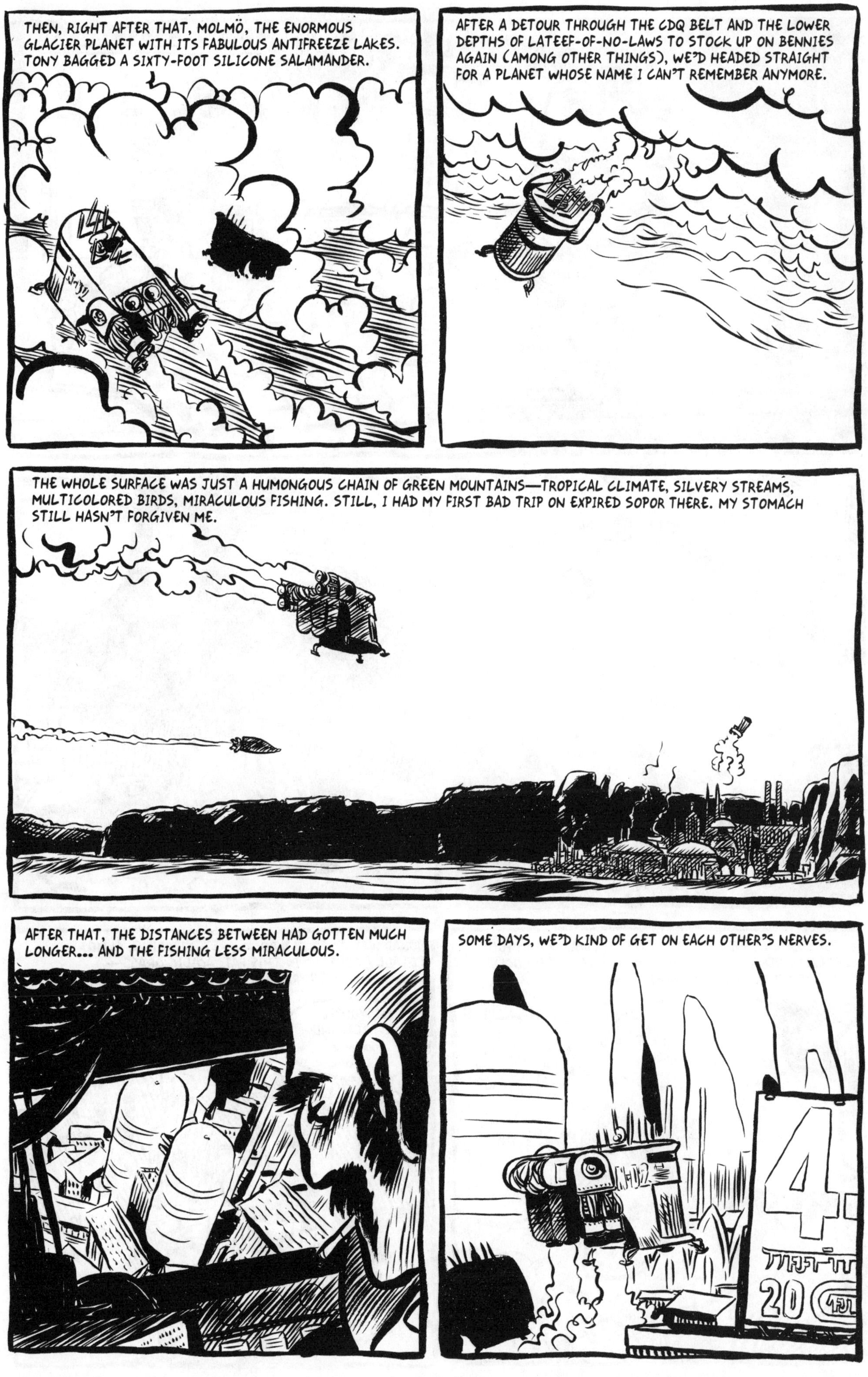
THEN, RIGHT AFTER THAT, MOLMÖ, THE ENORMOUS GLACIER PLANET WITH ITS FABULOUS ANTIFREEZE LAKES. TONY BAGGED A SIXTY-FOOT SILICONE SALAMANDER.
AFTER A DETOUR THROUGH THE CDQ BELT AND THE LOWER DEPTHS OF LATEEF-OF-NO-LAWS TO STOCK UP ON BENNIES AGAIN (AMONG OTHER THINGS), WE'D HEADED STRAIGHT FOR A PLANET WHOSE NAME I CAN'T REMEMBER ANYMORE.
THE WHOLE SURFACE WAS JUST A HUMONGOUS CHAIN OF GREEN MOUNTAINS—TROPICAL CLIMATE, SILVERY STREAMS, MULTICOLORED BIRDS, MIRACULOUS FISHING. STILL, I HAD MY FIRST BAD TRIP ON EXPIRED SOPOR THERE. MY STOMACH STILL HASN'T FORGIVEN ME.
AFTER THAT, THE DISTANCES BETWEEN HAD GOTTEN MUCH LONGER... AND THE FISHING LESS MIRACULOUS.
SOME DAYS, WE'D KIND OF GET ON EACH OTHER'S NERVES.

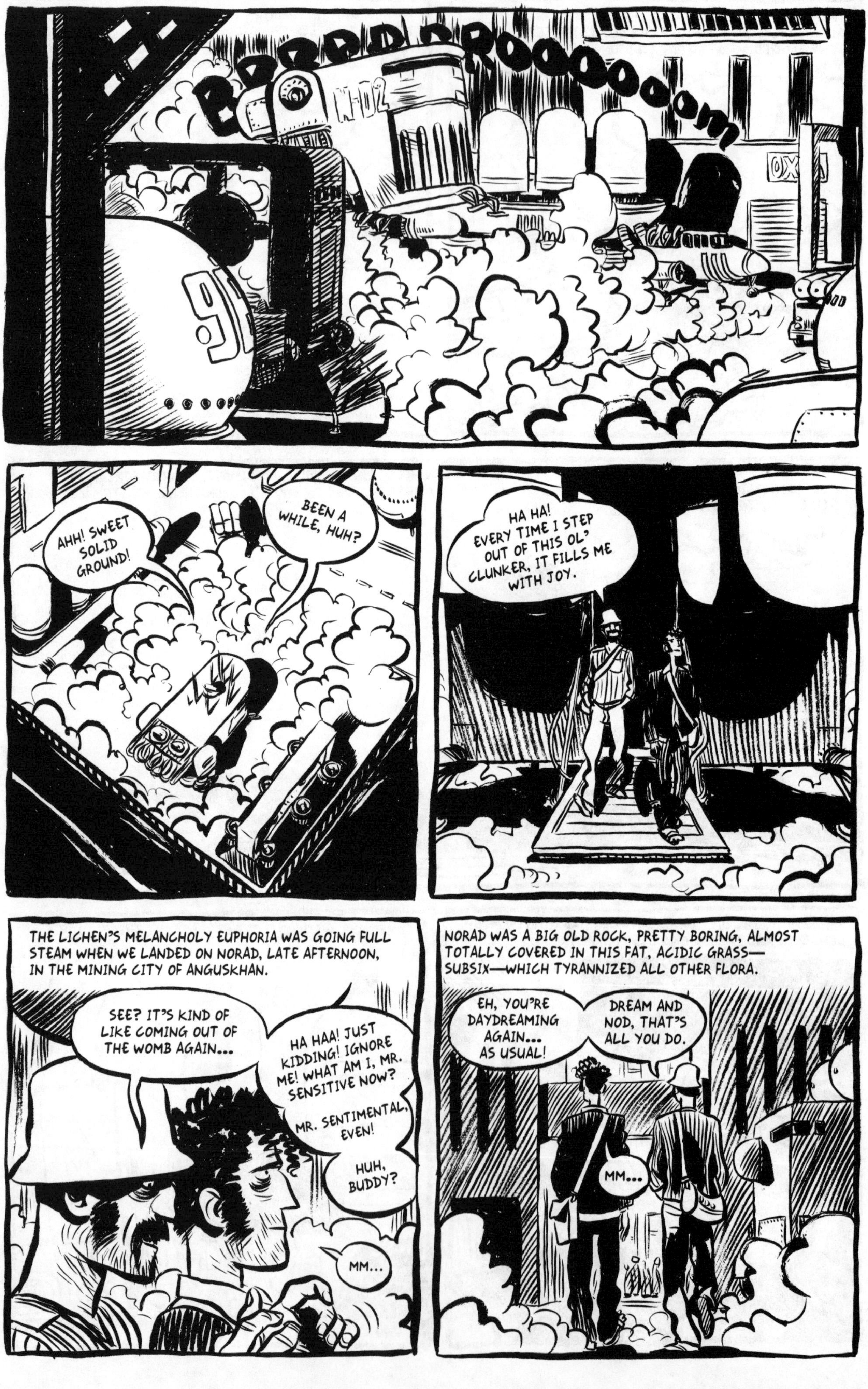
BRRRRRROOOOOOOOM
N-02
AHH! SWEET SOLID GROUND!
BEEN A WHILE, HUH?
HA HA! EVERY TIME I STEP OUT OF THIS OL' CLUNKER, IT FILLS ME WITH JOY.
THE LICHEN'S MELANCHOLY EUPHORIA WAS GOING FULL STEAM WHEN WE LANDED ON NORAD, LATE AFTERNOON, IN THE MINING CITY OF ANGUSKHAN.
SEE? IT'S KIND OF LIKE COMING OUT OF THE WOMB AGAIN...
HA HAA! JUST KIDDING! IGNORE ME! WHAT AM I, MR. SENSITIVE NOW?
MR. SENTIMENTAL, EVEN!
HUH, BUDDY?
MM...
NORAD WAS A BIG OLD ROCK, PRETTY BORING, ALMOST TOTALLY COVERED IN THIS FAT, ACIDIC GRASS—SUBSIX—WHICH TYRANNIZED ALL OTHER FLORA.
EH, YOU'RE DAYDREAMING AGAIN... AS USUAL!
DREAM AND NOD, THAT'S ALL YOU DO.
MM...

WHICH WAS WHAT GAVE IT ITS NICKNAME, THE "PLANET OF GRASS." GOTTA ADMIT, IT HAD A NICE RING. ITS TRADE INTERESTS LAY UNDERGROUND, IN ENORMOUS ALUMINUM DEPOSITS. WE WERE MORE INTO WHAT WAS HAPPENING UNDERWATER, DEEP IN ITS HYDROCHLORIC SEAS, WHERE MONSTERS FROM ANOTHER TIME WERE SAID TO HOLD SWAY...

THERE! 350! BE A NICE GUY AND FILL'ER UP TOO, WILL YA?

AND ALSO IN THE LOANSHARK DISTRICT, WHERE EVERY DRUG BELOVED BY MINERS COULD BE HAD BY THE WAGONFUL.

AIR'S PRETTY OXYGEN-RICH, DON'T YOU THINK?

DOES ME A WORLD OF GOOD!

YEAH, YEAH, SURE, THAT'S PROBABLY IT.

TONY WAS ALWAYS REAL NERVOUS WHEN HE KNEW WE HAD NO DRUGS LEFT. HIS MIND WOULD HONE IN ON JUST ONE THING: RESUPPLY.

SAY, LITTLE MAN, YOU KNOW WHERE THE LOANSHARK DISTRICT IS? YOU KNOW? LOANS? YOU KNOW?

YES... !LINGAM... LOANS...

BEFORE LEAVING, A FRIEND OF HIS, AN ARMY BUDDY, I THINK, HAD MADE HIM A LIST OF EVERY DEALER IN THE SYSTEM. SO WE WERE NEVER AT A LOSS. I'D EVEN SAY A GOOD PART OF OUR ROUTE WAS PLANNED AROUND THAT LIST.

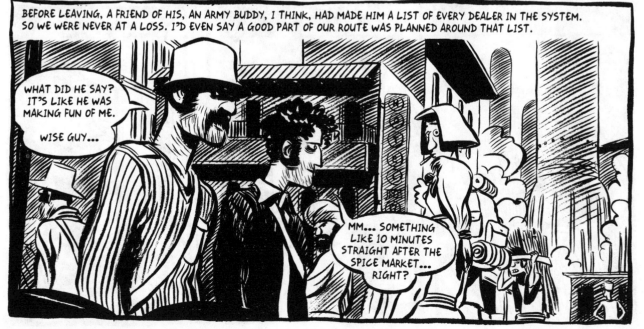

WHAT DID HE SAY? IT'S LIKE HE WAS MAKING FUN OF ME.

WISE GUY...

MM... SOMETHING LIKE 10 MINUTES STRAIGHT AFTER THE SPICE MARKET... RIGHT?

9

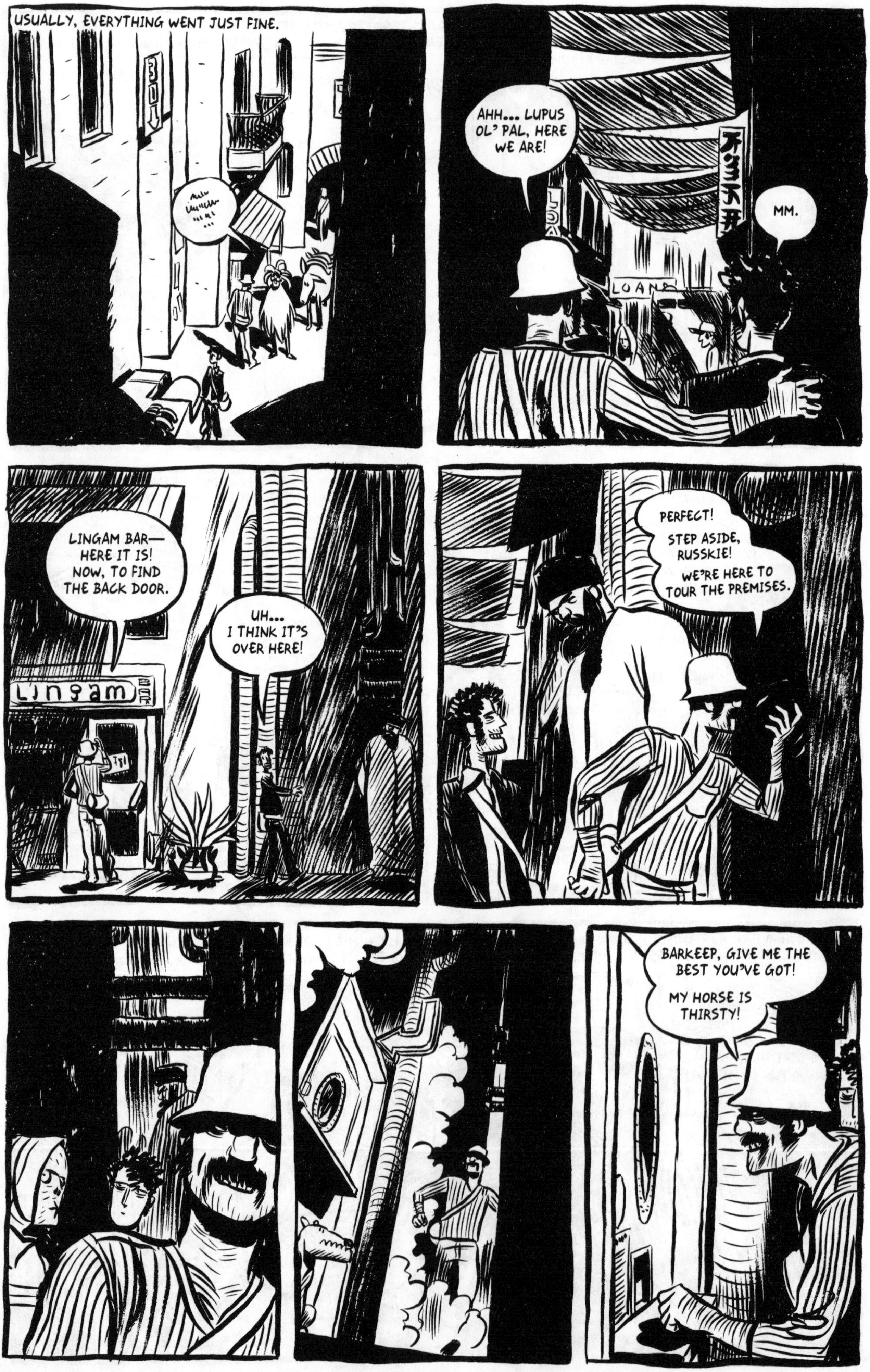
USUALLY, EVERYTHING WENT JUST FINE.
AHH... LUPUS OL' PAL, HERE WE ARE!
MM.
LOANS
LINGAM BAR— HERE IT IS! NOW, TO FIND THE BACK DOOR.
UH... I THINK IT'S OVER HERE!
LINGAM BAR
PERFECT!
STEP ASIDE, RUSSKIE!
WE'RE HERE TO TOUR THE PREMISES.
BARKEEP, GIVE ME THE BEST YOU'VE GOT!
MY HORSE IS THIRSTY!

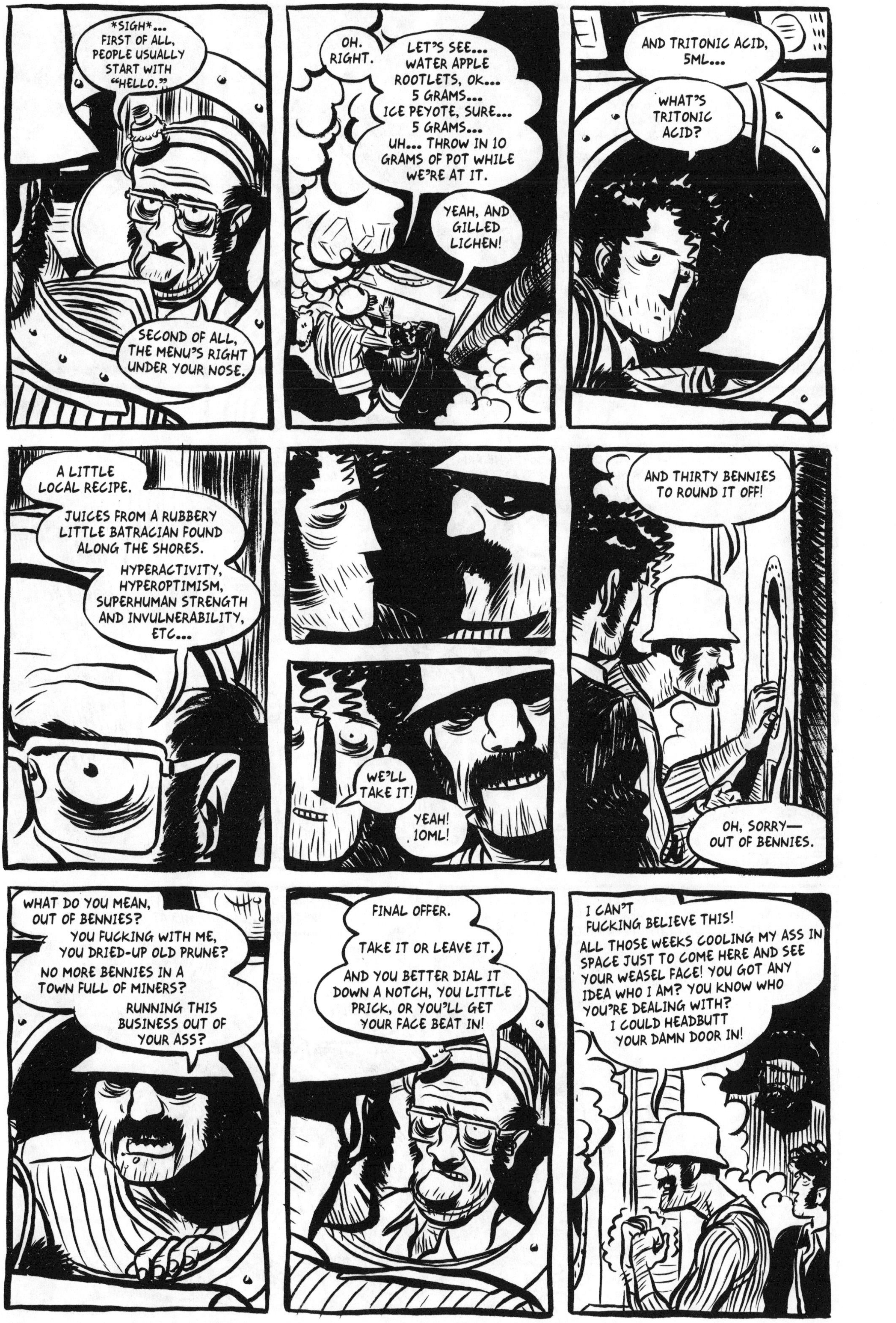
SIGH... FIRST OF ALL, PEOPLE USUALLY START WITH "HELLO."
SECOND OF ALL, THE MENU'S RIGHT UNDER YOUR NOSE.
OH. RIGHT.
LET'S SEE... WATER APPLE ROOTLETS, OK... 5 GRAMS... ICE PEYOTE, SURE... 5 GRAMS... UH... THROW IN 10 GRAMS OF POT WHILE WE'RE AT IT.
YEAH, AND GILLED LICHEN!
AND TRITONIC ACID, 5ML...
WHAT'S TRITONIC ACID?
A LITTLE LOCAL RECIPE.
JUICES FROM A RUBBERY LITTLE BATRACIAN FOUND ALONG THE SHORES.
HYPERACTIVITY, HYPEROPTIMISM, SUPERHUMAN STRENGTH AND INVULNERABILITY, ETC...
WE'LL TAKE IT!
YEAH! 10ML!
AND THIRTY BENNIES TO ROUND IT OFF!
OH, SORRY— OUT OF BENNIES.
WHAT DO YOU MEAN, OUT OF BENNIES?
YOU FUCKING WITH ME, YOU DRIED-UP OLD PRUNE?
NO MORE BENNIES IN A TOWN FULL OF MINERS?
RUNNING THIS BUSINESS OUT OF YOUR ASS?
FINAL OFFER.
TAKE IT OR LEAVE IT.
AND YOU BETTER DIAL IT DOWN A NOTCH, YOU LITTLE PRICK, OR YOU'LL GET YOUR FACE BEAT IN!
I CAN'T FUCKING BELIEVE THIS!
ALL THOSE WEEKS COOLING MY ASS IN SPACE JUST TO COME HERE AND SEE YOUR WEASEL FACE! YOU GOT ANY IDEA WHO I AM? YOU KNOW WHO YOU'RE DEALING WITH?
I COULD HEADBUTT YOUR DAMN DOOR IN!

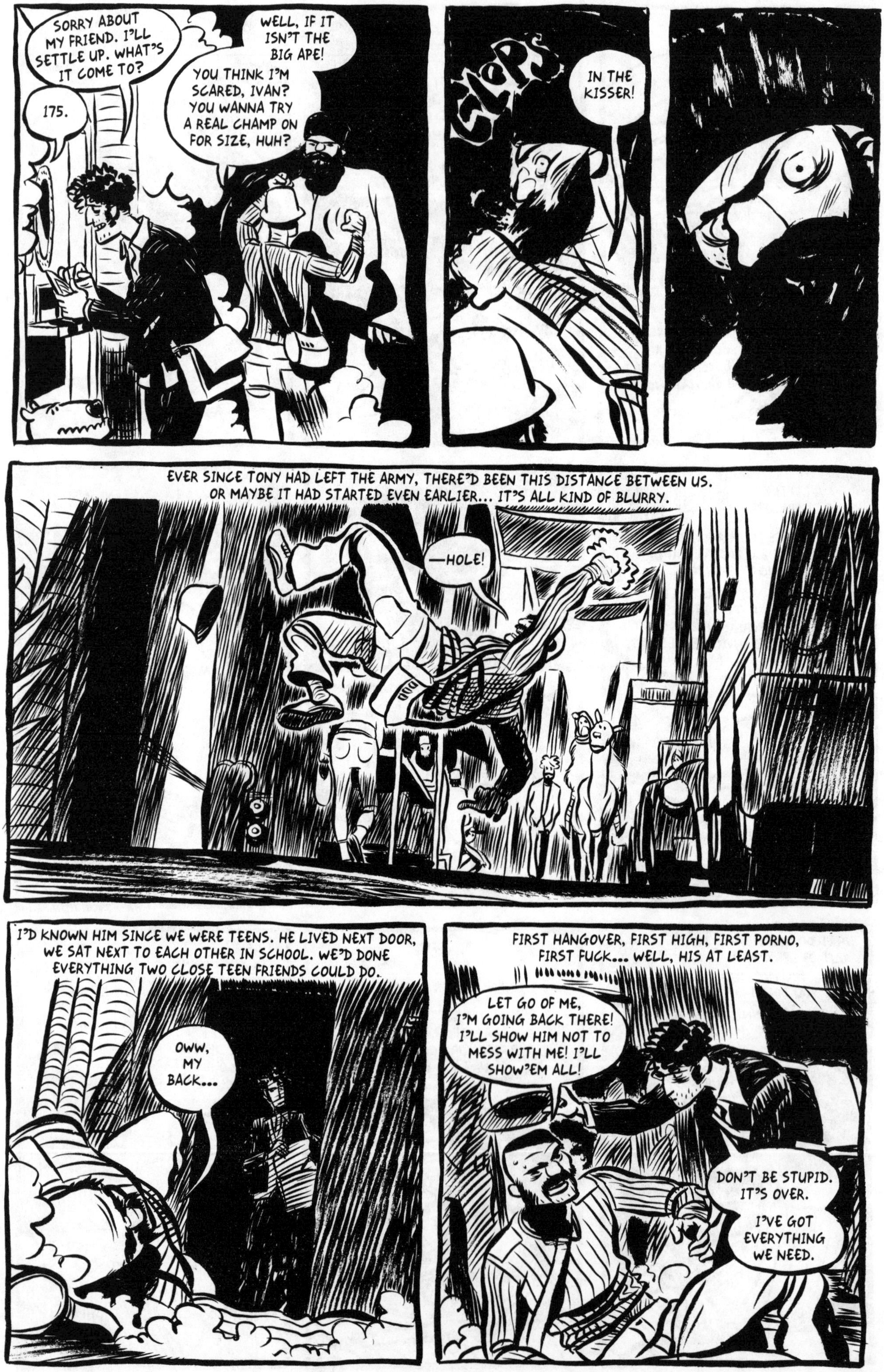

SORRY ABOUT MY FRIEND. I'LL SETTLE UP. WHAT'S IT COME TO?
175.
WELL, IF IT ISN'T THE BIG APE!
YOU THINK I'M SCARED, IVAN? YOU WANNA TRY A REAL CHAMP ON FOR SIZE, HUH?
SLOPS
IN THE KISSER!
EVER SINCE TONY HAD LEFT THE ARMY, THERE'D BEEN THIS DISTANCE BETWEEN US. OR MAYBE IT HAD STARTED EVEN EARLIER... IT'S ALL KIND OF BLURRY.
—HOLE!
I'D KNOWN HIM SINCE WE WERE TEENS. HE LIVED NEXT DOOR, WE SAT NEXT TO EACH OTHER IN SCHOOL. WE'D DONE EVERYTHING TWO CLOSE TEEN FRIENDS COULD DO.
OWW, MY BACK...
FIRST HANGOVER, FIRST HIGH, FIRST PORNO, FIRST FUCK... WELL, HIS AT LEAST.
LET GO OF ME, I'M GOING BACK THERE! I'LL SHOW HIM NOT TO MESS WITH ME! I'LL SHOW'EM ALL!
DON'T BE STUPID. IT'S OVER.
I'VE GOT EVERYTHING WE NEED.

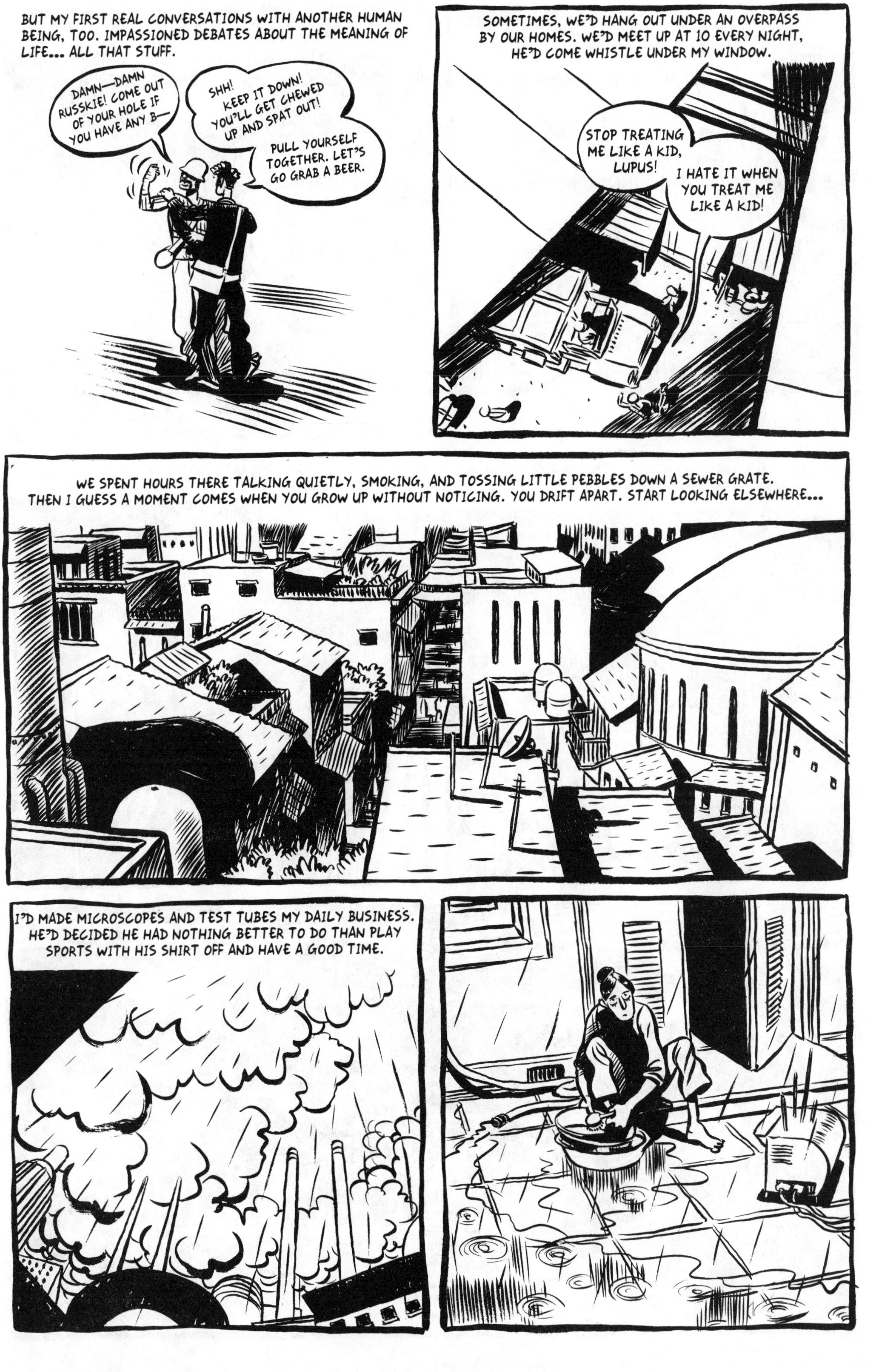
BUT MY FIRST REAL CONVERSATIONS WITH ANOTHER HUMAN BEING, TOO. IMPASSIONED DEBATES ABOUT THE MEANING OF LIFE... ALL THAT STUFF.
DAMN—DAMN RUSSKIE! COME OUT OF YOUR HOLE IF YOU HAVE ANY B—
SHH! KEEP IT DOWN! YOU'LL GET CHEWED UP AND SPAT OUT!
PULL YOURSELF TOGETHER. LET'S GO GRAB A BEER.
SOMETIMES, WE'D HANG OUT UNDER AN OVERPASS BY OUR HOMES. WE'D MEET UP AT 10 EVERY NIGHT, HE'D COME WHISTLE UNDER MY WINDOW.
STOP TREATING ME LIKE A KID, LUPUS!
I HATE IT WHEN YOU TREAT ME LIKE A KID!
WE SPENT HOURS THERE TALKING QUIETLY, SMOKING, AND TOSSING LITTLE PEBBLES DOWN A SEWER GRATE.
THEN I GUESS A MOMENT COMES WHEN YOU GROW UP WITHOUT NOTICING. YOU DRIFT APART. START LOOKING ELSEWHERE...
I'D MADE MICROSCOPES AND TEST TUBES MY DAILY BUSINESS. HE'D DECIDED HE HAD NOTHING BETTER TO DO THAN PLAY SPORTS WITH HIS SHIRT OFF AND HAVE A GOOD TIME.

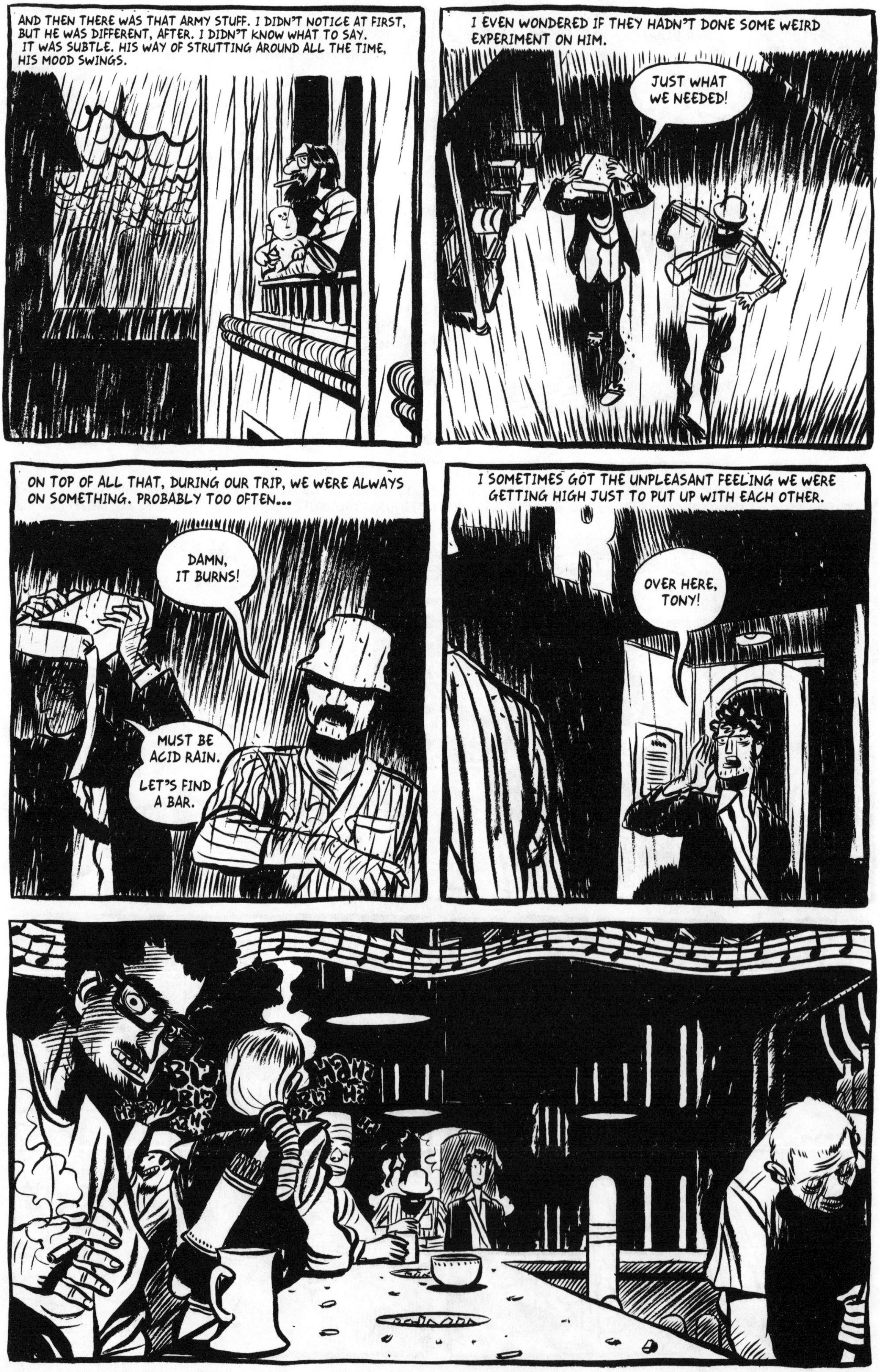
AND THEN THERE WAS THAT ARMY STUFF. I DIDN'T NOTICE AT FIRST, BUT HE WAS DIFFERENT, AFTER. I DIDN'T KNOW WHAT TO SAY. IT WAS SUBTLE. HIS WAY OF STRUTTING AROUND ALL THE TIME, HIS MOOD SWINGS.
I EVEN WONDERED IF THEY HADN'T DONE SOME WEIRD EXPERIMENT ON HIM.
JUST WHAT WE NEEDED!
ON TOP OF ALL THAT, DURING OUR TRIP, WE WERE ALWAYS ON SOMETHING. PROBABLY TOO OFTEN...
DAMN, IT BURNS!
MUST BE ACID RAIN.
LET'S FIND A BAR.
I SOMETIMES GOT THE UNPLEASANT FEELING WE WERE GETTING HIGH JUST TO PUT UP WITH EACH OTHER.
OVER HERE, TONY!

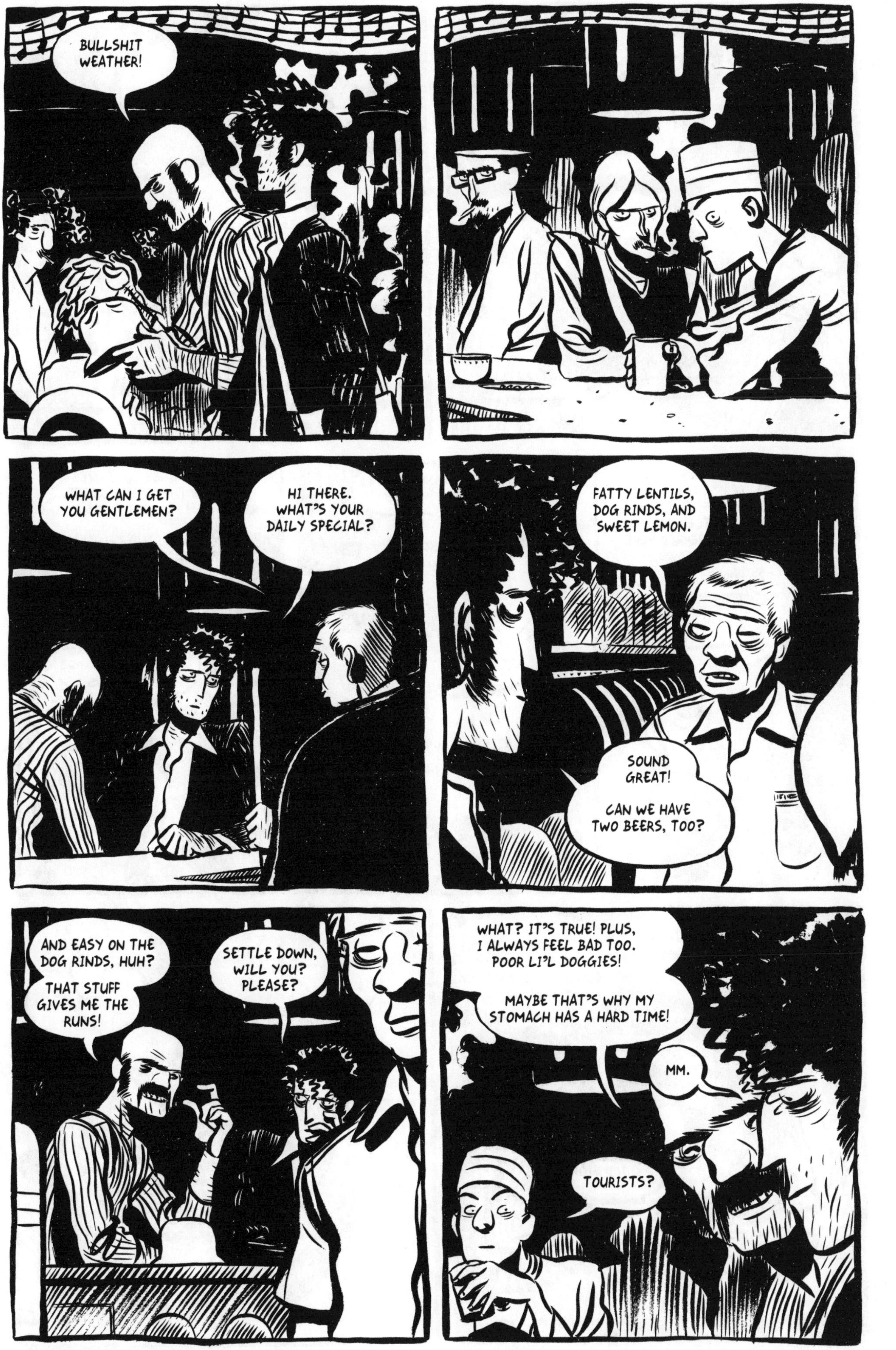
BULLSHIT WEATHER!
WHAT CAN I GET YOU GENTLEMEN?
HI THERE. WHAT'S YOUR DAILY SPECIAL?
FATTY LENTILS, DOG RINDS, AND SWEET LEMON.
SOUND GREAT!
CAN WE HAVE TWO BEERS, TOO?
AND EASY ON THE DOG RINDS, HUH?
THAT STUFF GIVES ME THE RUNS!
SETTLE DOWN, WILL YOU? PLEASE?
WHAT? IT'S TRUE! PLUS, I ALWAYS FEEL BAD TOO. POOR LI'L DOGGIES!
MAYBE THAT'S WHY MY STOMACH HAS A HARD TIME!
MM.
TOURISTS?

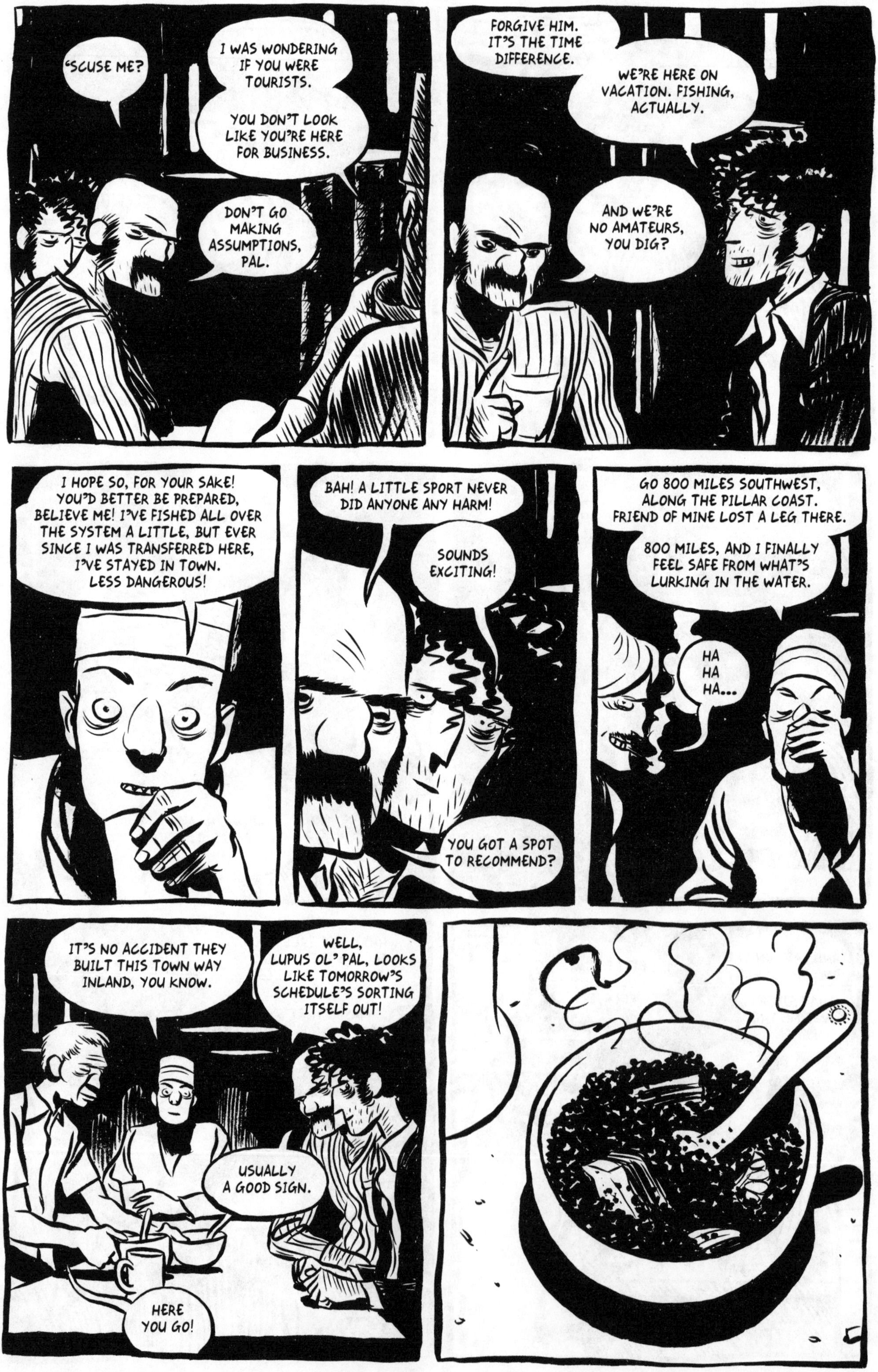
'SCUSE ME?
I WAS WONDERING IF YOU WERE TOURISTS.
YOU DON'T LOOK LIKE YOU'RE HERE FOR BUSINESS.
DON'T GO MAKING ASSUMPTIONS, PAL.
FORGIVE HIM. IT'S THE TIME DIFFERENCE.
WE'RE HERE ON VACATION. FISHING, ACTUALLY.
AND WE'RE NO AMATEURS, YOU DIG?
I HOPE SO, FOR YOUR SAKE! YOU'D BETTER BE PREPARED, BELIEVE ME! I'VE FISHED ALL OVER THE SYSTEM A LITTLE, BUT EVER SINCE I WAS TRANSFERRED HERE, I'VE STAYED IN TOWN. LESS DANGEROUS!
BAH! A LITTLE SPORT NEVER DID ANYONE ANY HARM!
SOUNDS EXCITING!
YOU GOT A SPOT TO RECOMMEND?
GO 800 MILES SOUTHWEST, ALONG THE PILLAR COAST. FRIEND OF MINE LOST A LEG THERE.
800 MILES, AND I FINALLY FEEL SAFE FROM WHAT'S LURKING IN THE WATER.
HA HA HA...
IT'S NO ACCIDENT THEY BUILT THIS TOWN WAY INLAND, YOU KNOW.
WELL, LUPUS OL' PAL, LOOKS LIKE TOMORROW'S SCHEDULE'S SORTING ITSELF OUT!
USUALLY A GOOD SIGN.
HERE YOU GO!

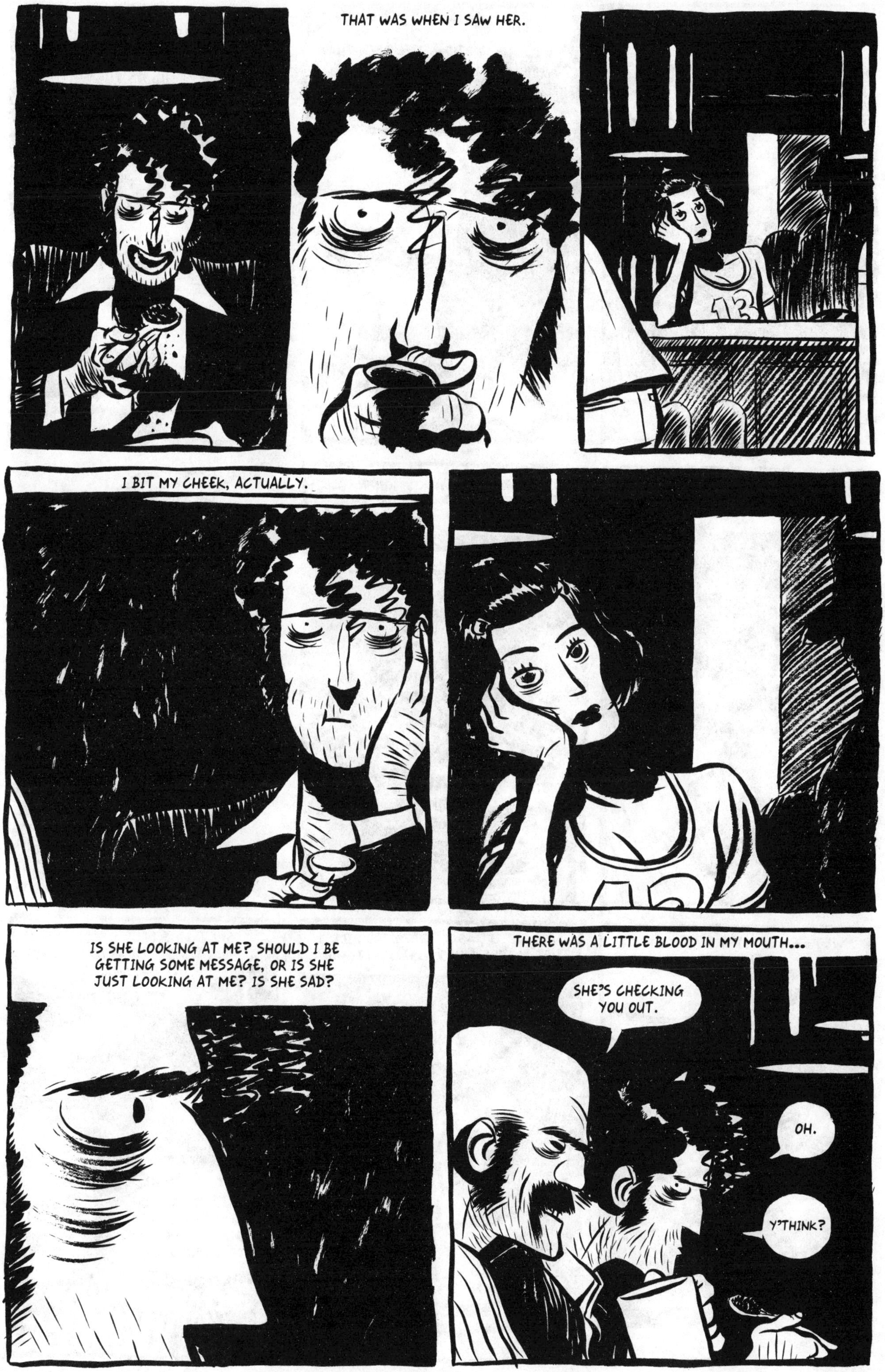
THAT WAS WHEN I SAW HER.
I BIT MY CHEEK, ACTUALLY.
IS SHE LOOKING AT ME? SHOULD I BE GETTING SOME MESSAGE, OR IS SHE JUST LOOKING AT ME? IS SHE SAD?
THERE WAS A LITTLE BLOOD IN MY MOUTH...
SHE'S CHECKING YOU OUT.
OH.
Y'THINK?

I EVER TELL YOU WHAT I THINK ABOUT YOU AND WOMEN? YOU LITTLE CHICKENSHIT.

OH, CAN IT! WE JUST DON'T SEE THINGS THE SAME WAY, IS ALL.

IT'S BEEN TEN YEARS SINCE WE EVEN TALKED ABOUT IT.

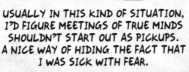

GO ON!

Y'KNOW, I'VE BEEN THAT LITTLE VOICE INSIDE YOU FOR TEN YEARS, AND YOU'VE BEEN IGNORING ME!

GO TALK TO HER!

USUALLY IN THIS KIND OF SITUATION, I'D FIGURE MEETINGS OF TRUE MINDS SHOULDN'T START OUT AS PICKUPS. A NICE WAY OF HIDING THE FACT THAT I WAS SICK WITH FEAR.

OH, WHAT'S THE POINT?

WE'RE LEAVING TOMORROW, RIGHT?

BUT THAT NIGHT, IT WAS SOMETHING ELSE...

WE'RE FREE, LUPUS.

MY MIND WASN'T RACING, IMAGINING ALL THE WAYS IT COULD GO WRONG. I WAS COMPLETELY DETACHED—BLISSED OUT, EVEN.

"WE'RE FREE." IT HAD A NICE RING, I THOUGHT.

SO I GOT UP, AS IF THAT GIRL DIDN'T EXIST... LIKE I WAS JUST STRETCHING.

SHE LOOKS DRUNK. WATCH OUT! ALWAYS GOTTA WATCH OUT FOR DRUNK CHICKS!

YEAH... I'D SAY YOU GOTTA WATCH OUT FOR GUYS WHO'RE TRIPPING LIKE YOU!

18

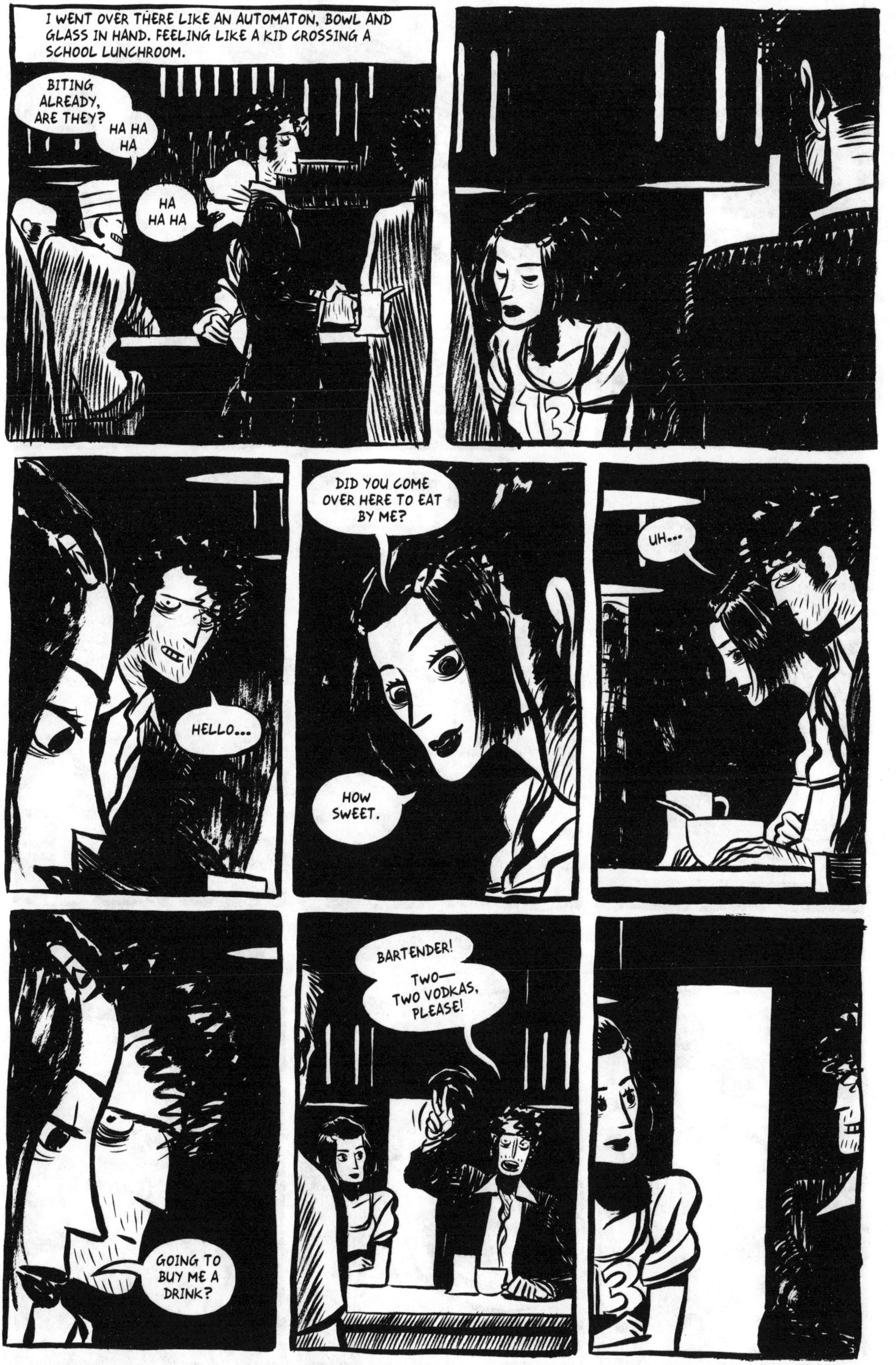
I WENT OVER THERE LIKE AN AUTOMATON, BOWL AND GLASS IN HAND. FEELING LIKE A KID CROSSING A SCHOOL LUNCHROOM.
BITING ALREADY, ARE THEY?
HA HA HA
HA HA HA
HELLO...
DID YOU COME OVER HERE TO EAT BY ME?
HOW SWEET.
UH...
GOING TO BUY ME A DRINK?
BARTENDER!
TWO— TWO VODKAS, PLEASE!

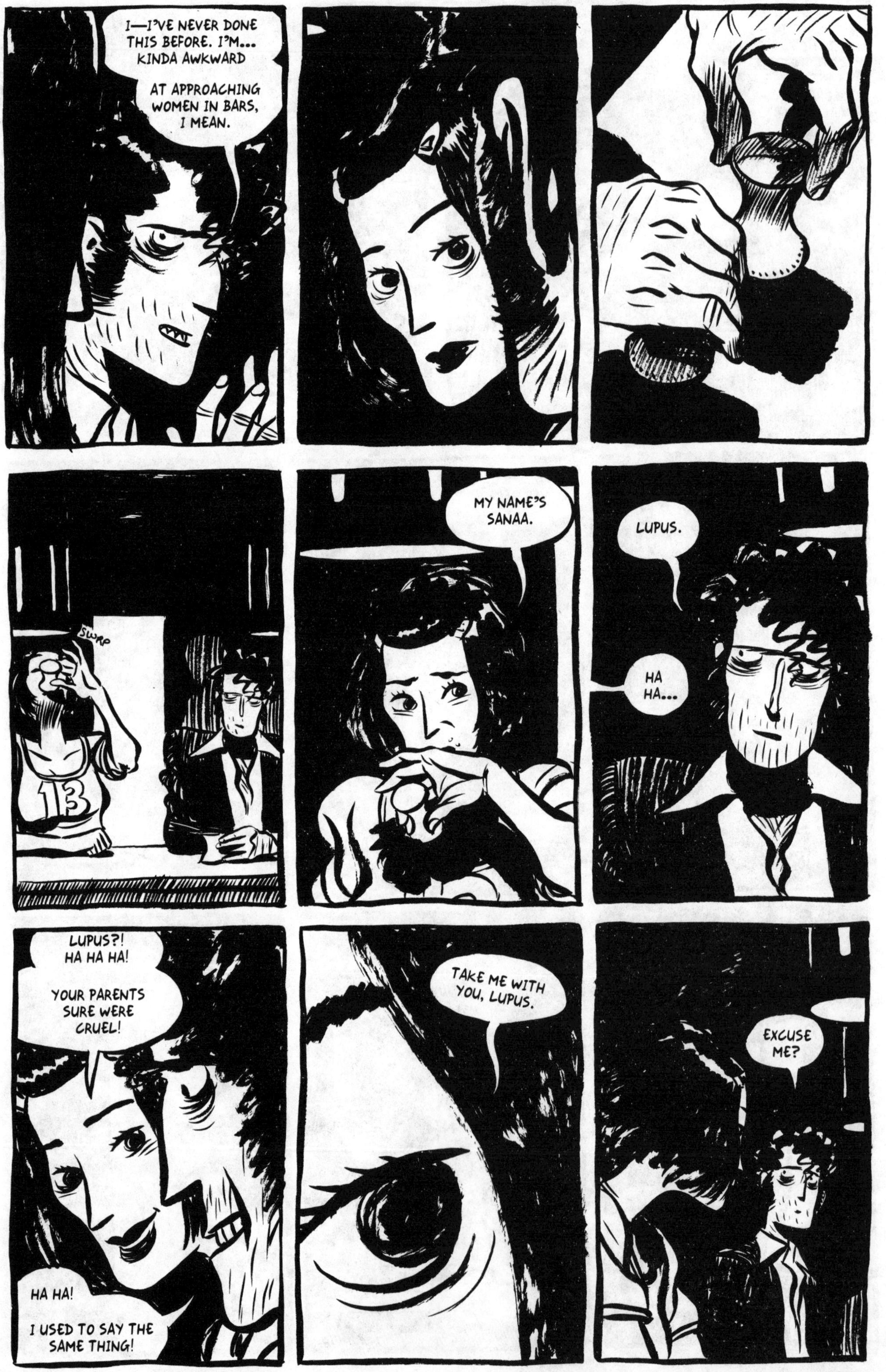
I—I'VE NEVER DONE THIS BEFORE. I'M... KINDA AWKWARD
AT APPROACHING WOMEN IN BARS, I MEAN.
SWRP
MY NAME'S SANAA.
LUPUS.
HA HA...
LUPUS?! HA HA HA!
YOUR PARENTS SURE WERE CRUEL!
HA HA!
I USED TO SAY THE SAME THING!
TAKE ME WITH YOU, LUPUS.
EXCUSE ME?

YOU'RE TRAVELING WITH YOUR FRIEND, RIGHT?

TAKE ME WITH YOU!

I'LL PAY MY WAY.

SHE WAS AS RADIANT AS THE SUN... KIND OF ALOOF, BUT NOT AT ALL INTIMIDATING.

AFTER SEVERAL MONTHS OF LIVING DAY IN AND DAY OUT WITH ANOTHER GUY, I'D COMPLETELY FORGOTTEN HOW INTENSE A HUMAN CONNECTION COULD BE.

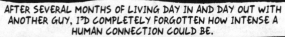

SHE'D BEEN BORN HERE, THE DAUGHTER OF A MAJOR MINING CONTRACTOR. SHE DODGED MY QUESTIONS, SKETCHING OUT A BRIEF, UNFLATTERING PORTRAIT OF HER FAMILY. SHE WAS 26. SHE SAW HER CHOICES AS BEING: GROW OLD OR GET AWAY...

I ASKED HER WHY SHE LOOKED SAD ALL THE TIME. EVEN WHEN SHE LAUGHED, I THOUGHT SHE LOOKED SAD. SHE SAID SHE OFTEN FELT LIKE A BLACK HOLE, A BALL OF ANTIMATTER. I SHOULD'VE LISTENED TO HER, BELIEVED HER, INSTEAD OF GRINNING LIKE AN IDIOT.

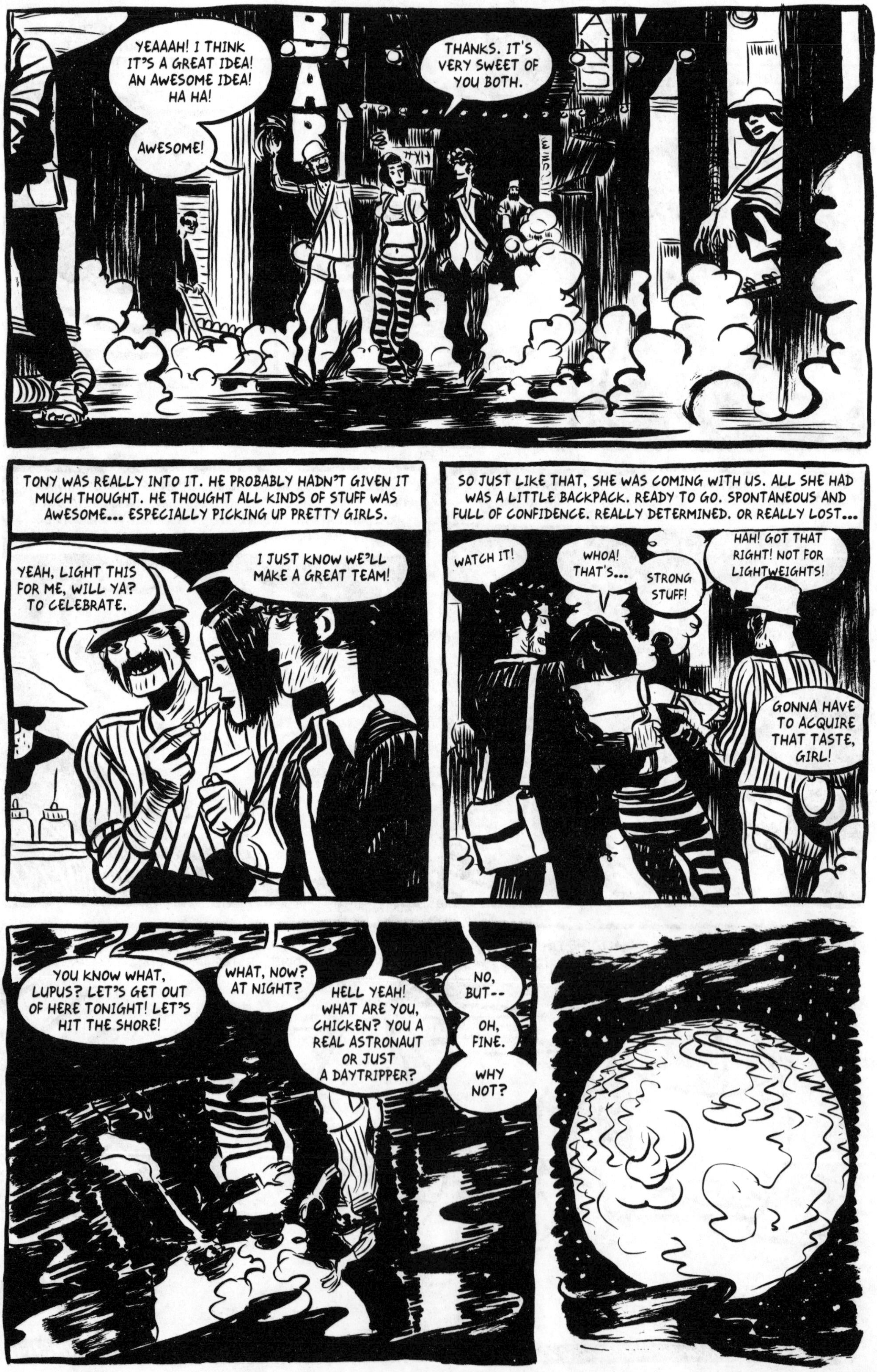
YEAAAH! I THINK IT'S A GREAT IDEA! AN AWESOME IDEA! HA HA!
AWESOME!
THANKS. IT'S VERY SWEET OF YOU BOTH.
TONY WAS REALLY INTO IT. HE PROBABLY HADN'T GIVEN IT MUCH THOUGHT. HE THOUGHT ALL KINDS OF STUFF WAS AWESOME... ESPECIALLY PICKING UP PRETTY GIRLS.
YEAH, LIGHT THIS FOR ME, WILL YA? TO CELEBRATE.
I JUST KNOW WE'LL MAKE A GREAT TEAM!
SO JUST LIKE THAT, SHE WAS COMING WITH US. ALL SHE HAD WAS A LITTLE BACKPACK. READY TO GO. SPONTANEOUS AND FULL OF CONFIDENCE. REALLY DETERMINED. OR REALLY LOST...
WATCH IT!
WHOA! THAT'S...
STRONG STUFF!
HAH! GOT THAT RIGHT! NOT FOR LIGHTWEIGHTS!
GONNA HAVE TO ACQUIRE THAT TASTE, GIRL!
YOU KNOW WHAT, LUPUS? LET'S GET OUT OF HERE TONIGHT! LET'S HIT THE SHORE!
WHAT, NOW? AT NIGHT?
HELL YEAH! WHAT ARE YOU, CHICKEN? YOU A REAL ASTRONAUT OR JUST A DAYTRIPPER?
NO, BUT--
OH, FINE.
WHY NOT?

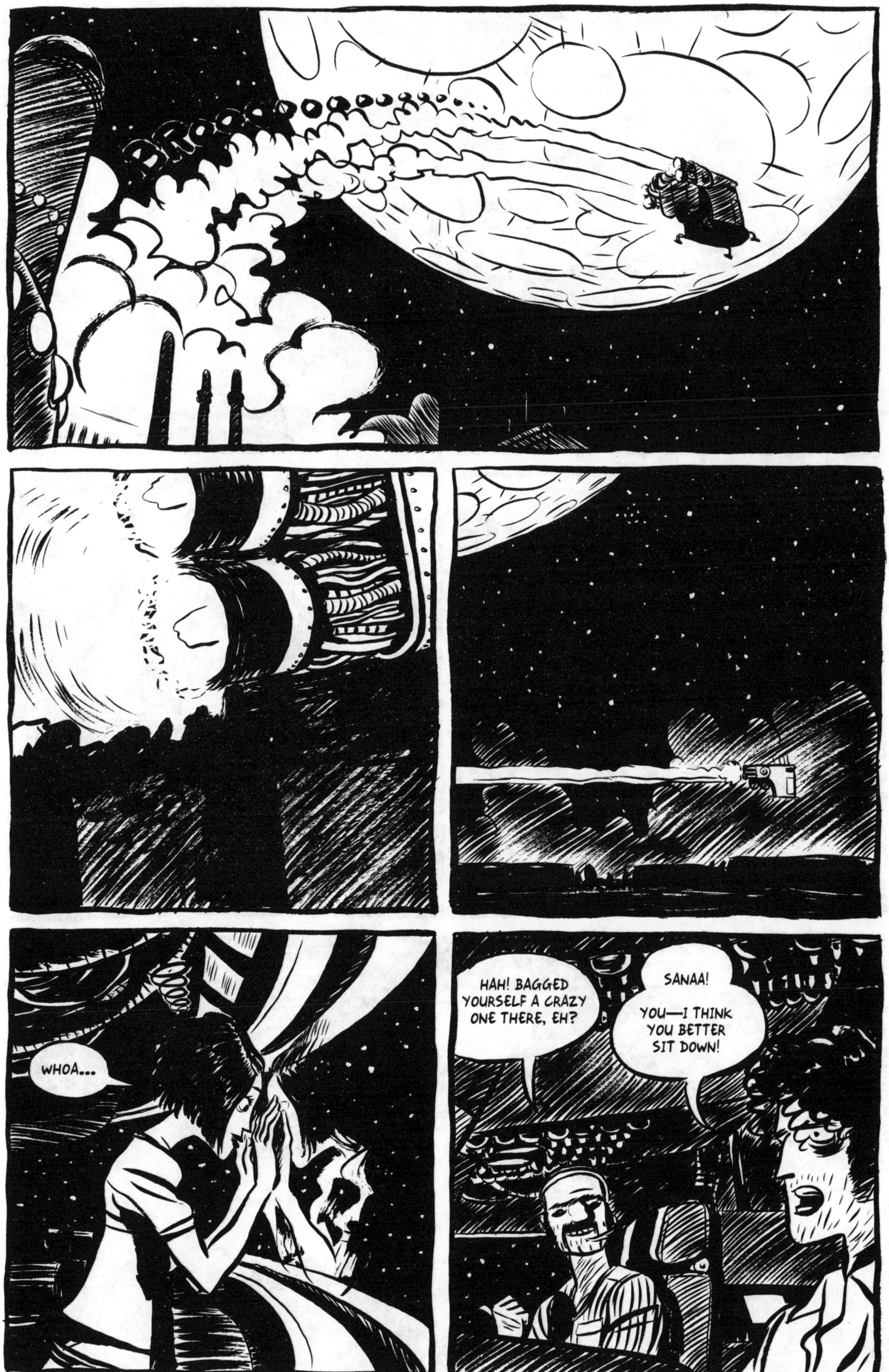
WHOA...
HAH! BAGGED YOURSELF A CRAZY ONE THERE, EH?
SANAA!
YOU—I THINK YOU BETTER SIT DOWN!

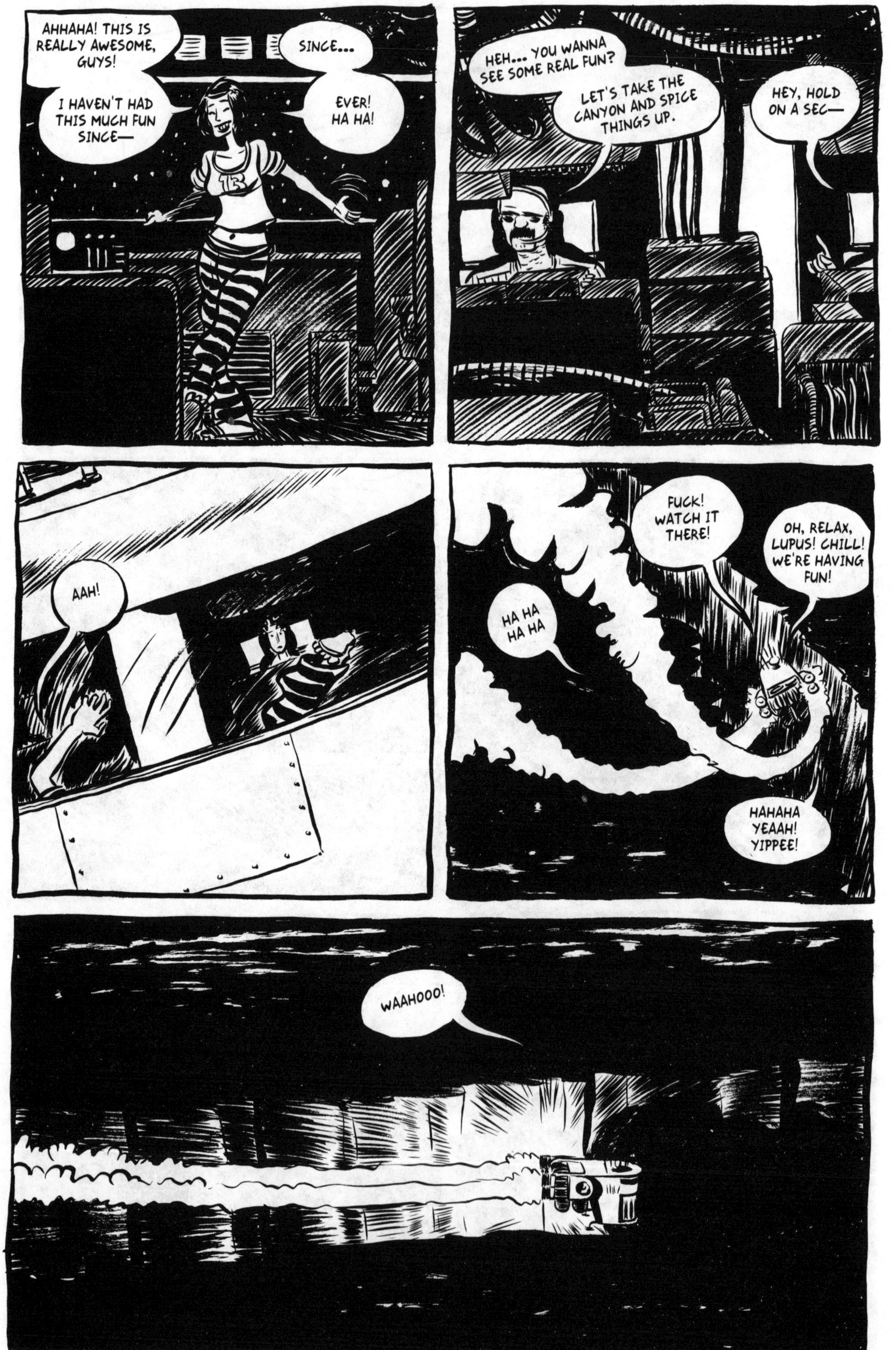
AHHAHA! THIS IS REALLY AWESOME, GUYS!
I HAVEN'T HAD THIS MUCH FUN SINCE—
SINCE...
EVER! HA HA!
HEH... YOU WANNA SEE SOME REAL FUN?
LET'S TAKE THE CANYON AND SPICE THINGS UP.
HEY, HOLD ON A SEC—
AAH!
FUCK! WATCH IT THERE!
OH, RELAX, LUPUS! CHILL! WE'RE HAVING FUN!
HA HA HA HA
HAHAHA YEAAH! YIPPEE!
WAAHOOO!

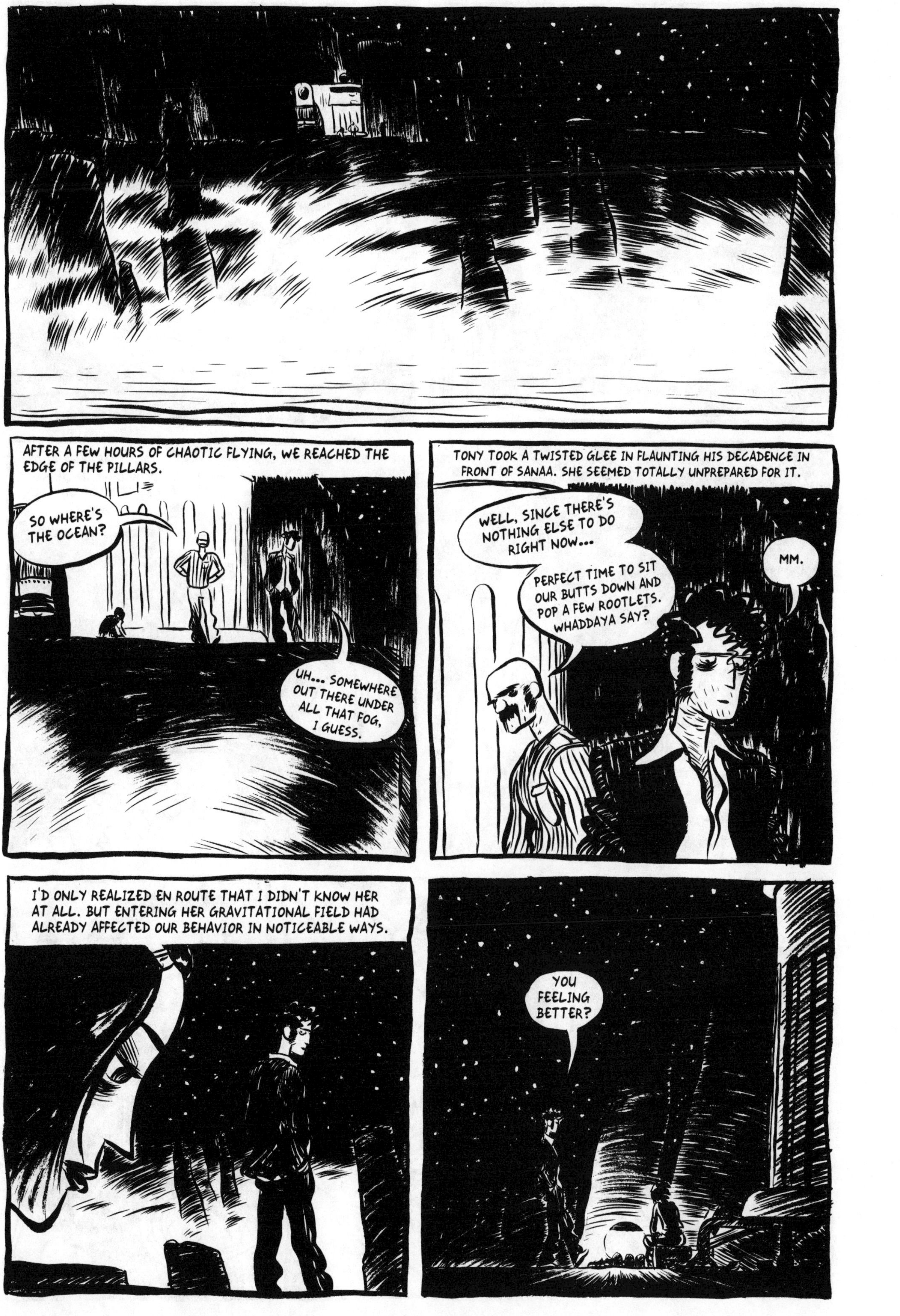
AFTER A FEW HOURS OF CHAOTIC FLYING, WE REACHED THE EDGE OF THE PILLARS.
SO WHERE'S THE OCEAN?
UH... SOMEWHERE OUT THERE UNDER ALL THAT FOG, I GUESS.
TONY TOOK A TWISTED GLEE IN FLAUNTING HIS DECADENCE IN FRONT OF SANAA. SHE SEEMED TOTALLY UNPREPARED FOR IT.
WELL, SINCE THERE'S NOTHING ELSE TO DO RIGHT NOW...
PERFECT TIME TO SIT OUR BUTTS DOWN AND POP A FEW ROOTLETS. WHADDAYA SAY?
MM.
I'D ONLY REALIZED EN ROUTE THAT I DIDN'T KNOW HER AT ALL. BUT ENTERING HER GRAVITATIONAL FIELD HAD ALREADY AFFECTED OUR BEHAVIOR IN NOTICEABLE WAYS.
YOU FEELING BETTER?

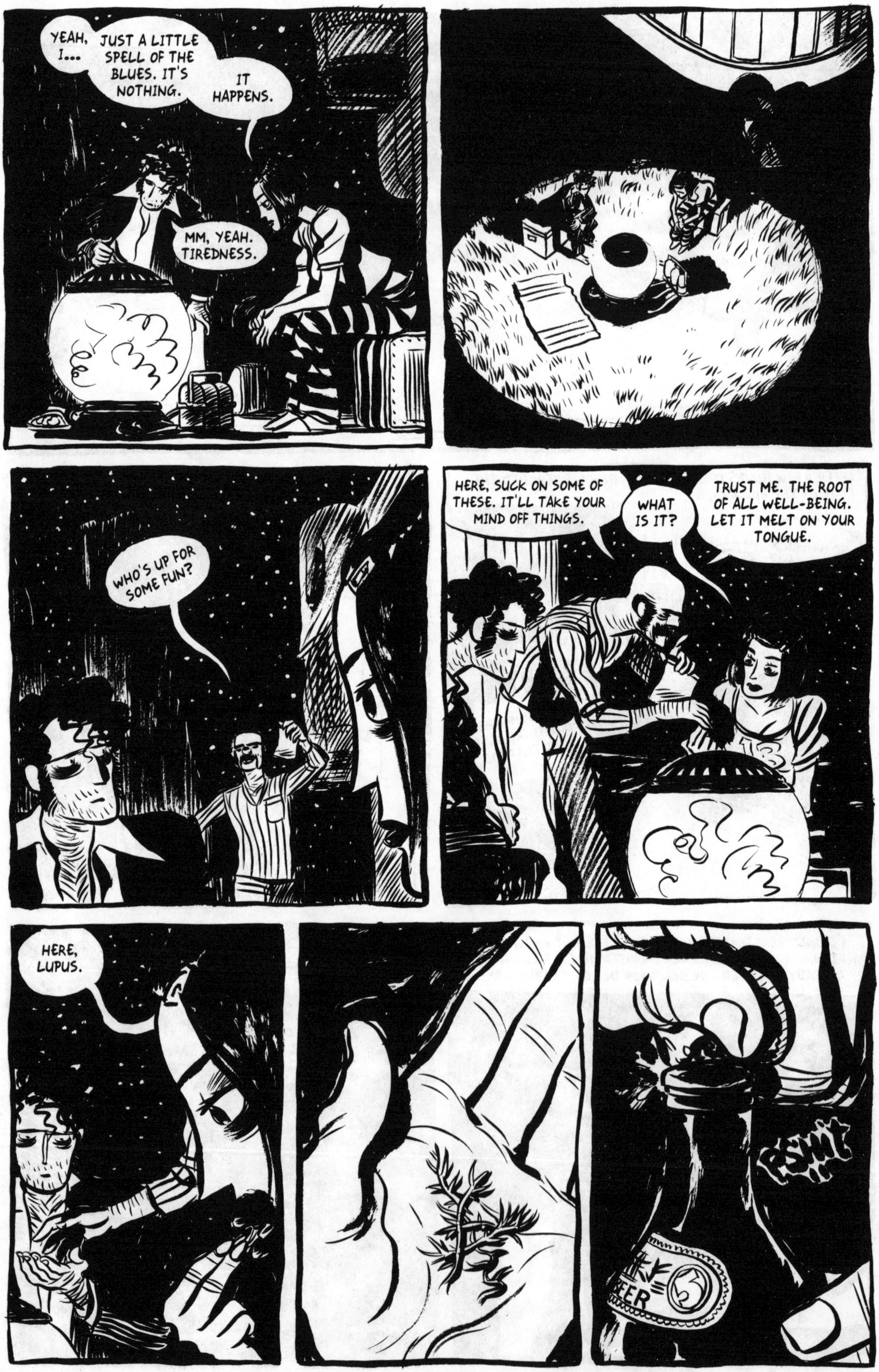
YEAH, I...
JUST A LITTLE SPELL OF THE BLUES. IT'S NOTHING.
IT HAPPENS.
MM, YEAH. TIREDNESS.
WHO'S UP FOR SOME FUN?
HERE, SUCK ON SOME OF THESE. IT'LL TAKE YOUR MIND OFF THINGS.
WHAT IS IT?
TRUST ME. THE ROOT OF ALL WELL-BEING. LET IT MELT ON YOUR TONGUE.
HERE, LUPUS.
PSHT
BEER

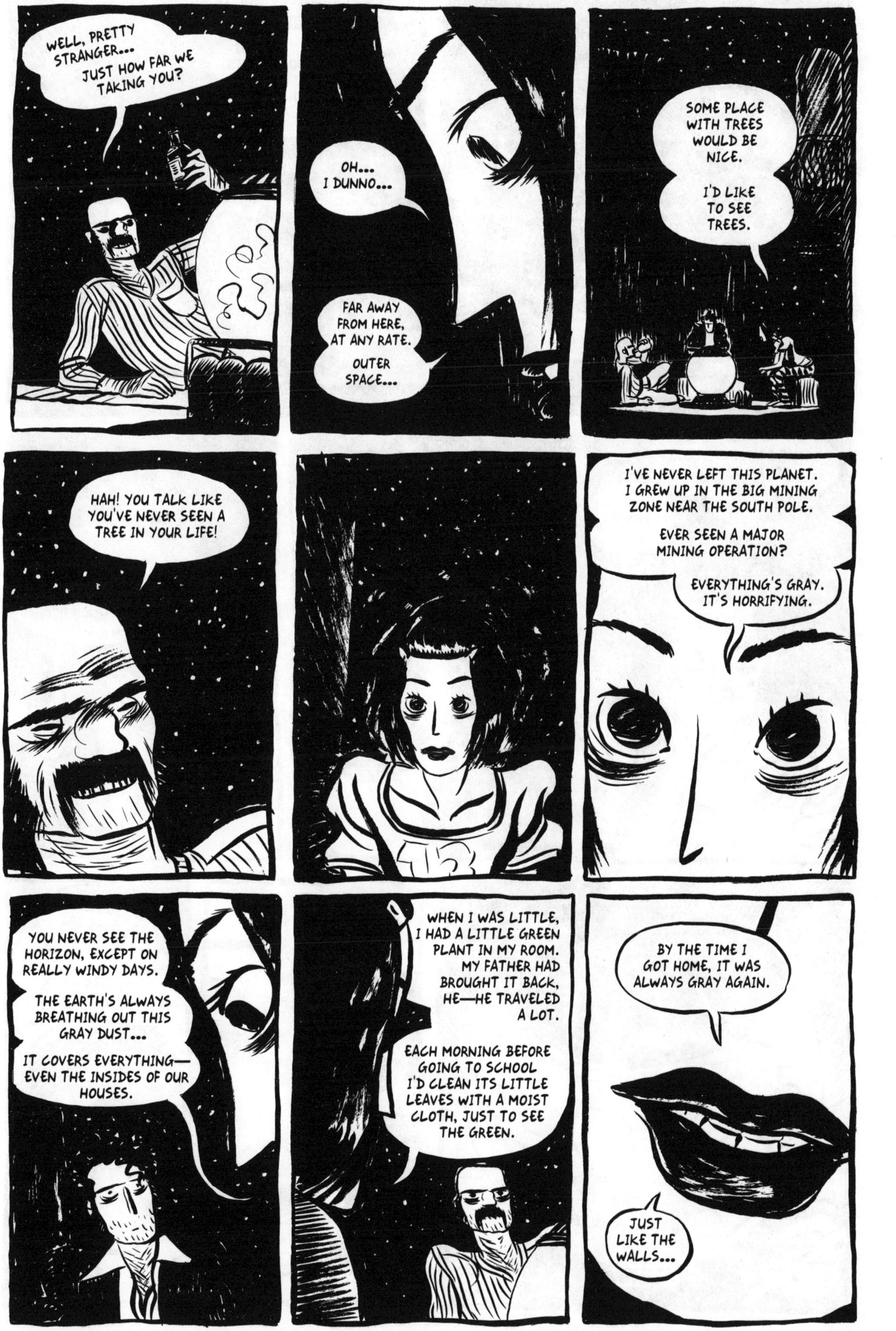
WELL, PRETTY STRANGER... JUST HOW FAR WE TAKING YOU?
OH... I DUNNO...
FAR AWAY FROM HERE, AT ANY RATE.
OUTER SPACE...
SOME PLACE WITH TREES WOULD BE NICE.
I'D LIKE TO SEE TREES.
HAH! YOU TALK LIKE YOU'VE NEVER SEEN A TREE IN YOUR LIFE!
I'VE NEVER LEFT THIS PLANET. I GREW UP IN THE BIG MINING ZONE NEAR THE SOUTH POLE.
EVER SEEN A MAJOR MINING OPERATION?
EVERYTHING'S GRAY. IT'S HORRIFYING.
YOU NEVER SEE THE HORIZON, EXCEPT ON REALLY WINDY DAYS.
THE EARTH'S ALWAYS BREATHING OUT THIS GRAY DUST...
IT COVERS EVERYTHING— EVEN THE INSIDES OF OUR HOUSES.
WHEN I WAS LITTLE, I HAD A LITTLE GREEN PLANT IN MY ROOM. MY FATHER HAD BROUGHT IT BACK, HE—HE TRAVELED A LOT.
EACH MORNING BEFORE GOING TO SCHOOL I'D CLEAN ITS LITTLE LEAVES WITH A MOIST CLOTH, JUST TO SEE THE GREEN.
BY THE TIME I GOT HOME, IT WAS ALWAYS GRAY AGAIN.
JUST LIKE THE WALLS...

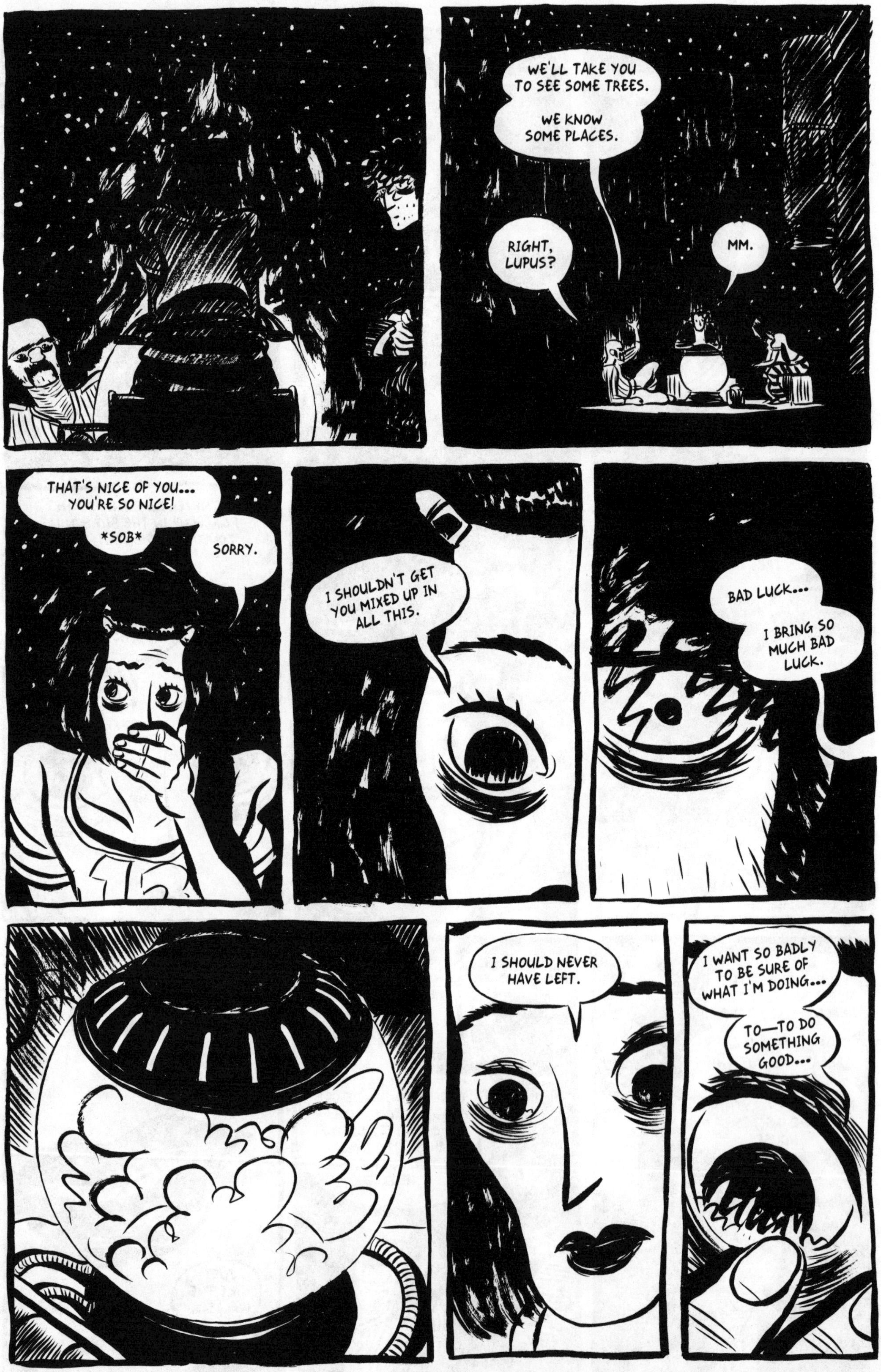
WE'LL TAKE YOU TO SEE SOME TREES.
WE KNOW SOME PLACES.
RIGHT, LUPUS?
MM.
THAT'S NICE OF YOU... YOU'RE SO NICE!
SOB
SORRY.
I SHOULDN'T GET YOU MIXED UP IN ALL THIS.
BAD LUCK...
I BRING SO MUCH BAD LUCK.
I SHOULD NEVER HAVE LEFT.
I WANT SO BADLY TO BE SURE OF WHAT I'M DOING...
TO—TO DO SOMETHING GOOD...

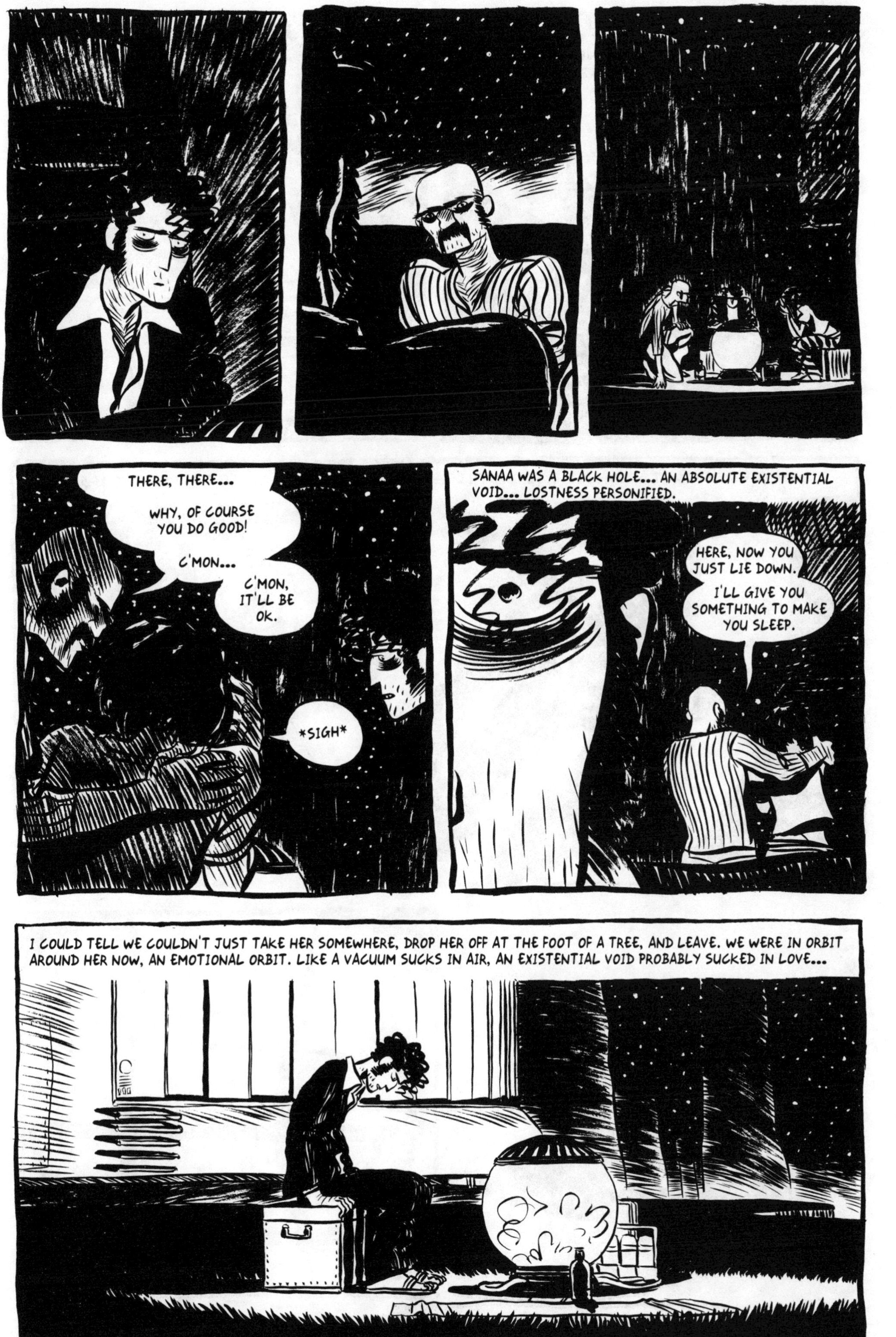

THERE, THERE...
WHY, OF COURSE YOU DO GOOD!
C'MON...
C'MON, IT'LL BE OK.
SIGH
SANAA WAS A BLACK HOLE... AN ABSOLUTE EXISTENTIAL VOID... LOSTNESS PERSONIFIED.
HERE, NOW YOU JUST LIE DOWN.
I'LL GIVE YOU SOMETHING TO MAKE YOU SLEEP.
I COULD TELL WE COULDN'T JUST TAKE HER SOMEWHERE, DROP HER OFF AT THE FOOT OF A TREE, AND LEAVE. WE WERE IN ORBIT AROUND HER NOW, AN EMOTIONAL ORBIT. LIKE A VACUUM SUCKS IN AIR, AN EXISTENTIAL VOID PROBABLY SUCKED IN LOVE...

AND I REALIZED THAT BESIDE HER, I COULD FEEL POWERUL, SOLID, ABLE TO CHANGE THE COURSE OF THINGS. JUST THEN, I WAS PETRIFIED. THE FEELING FRIGHTENED ME. IT'D BEEN A LONG TIME SINCE ANY DRUG HAD BEEN ABLE TO MAKE ME FEEL LIKE THAT.

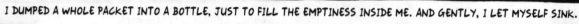

I DUMPED A WHOLE PACKET INTO A BOTTLE, JUST TO FILL THE EMPTINESS INSIDE ME. AND GENTLY, I LET MYSELF SINK.

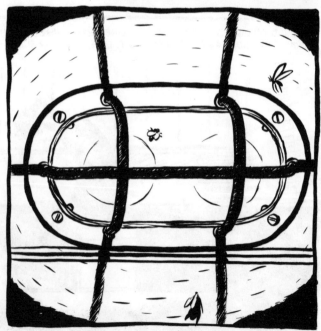

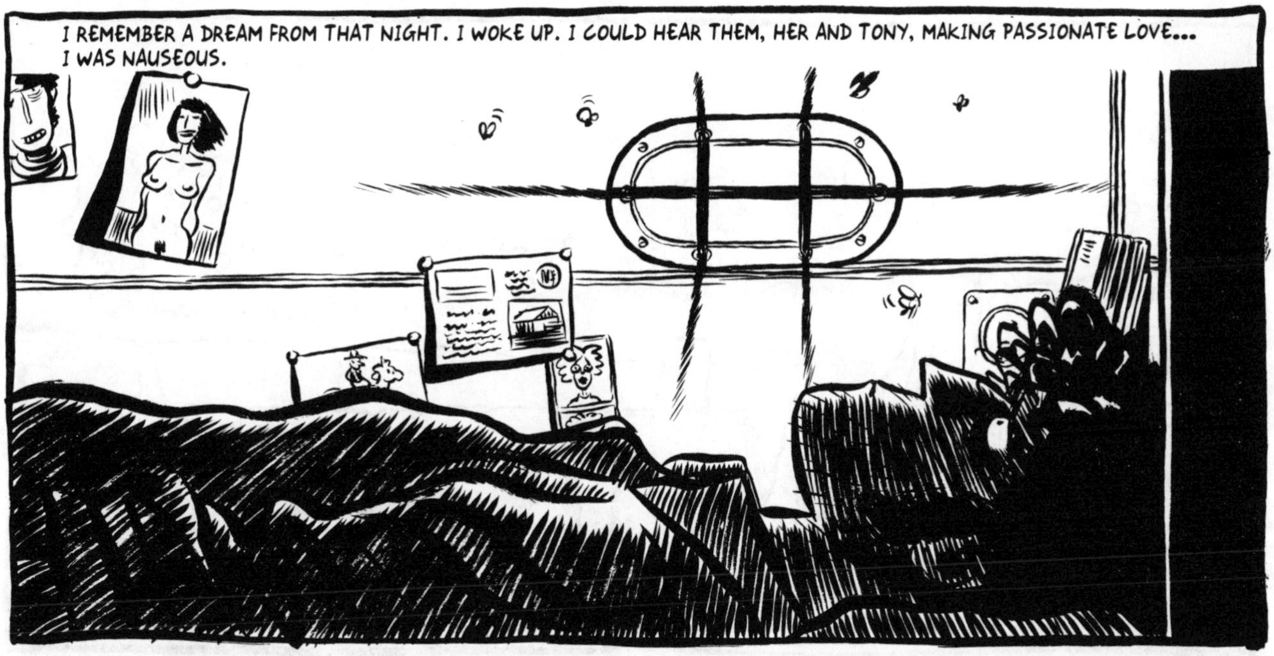
I REMEMBER A DREAM FROM THAT NIGHT. I WOKE UP. I COULD HEAR THEM, HER AND TONY, MAKING PASSIONATE LOVE... I WAS NAUSEOUS.

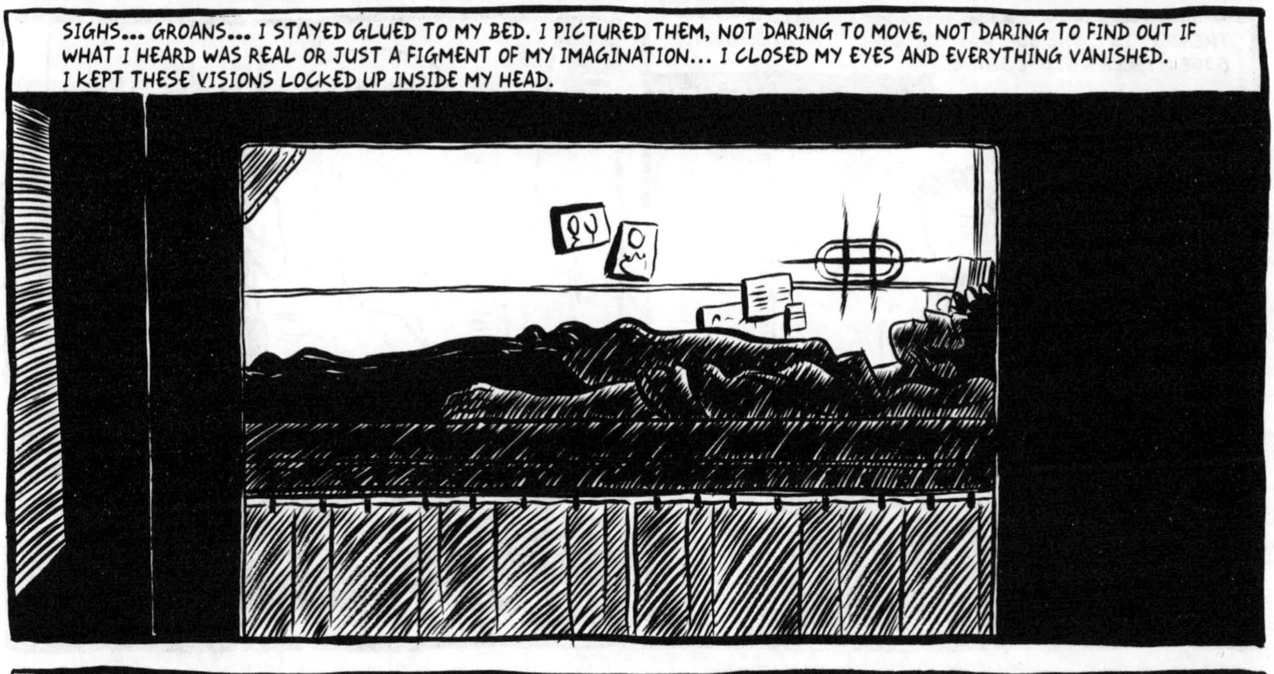
SIGHS... GROANS... I STAYED GLUED TO MY BED. I PICTURED THEM, NOT DARING TO MOVE, NOT DARING TO FIND OUT IF WHAT I HEARD WAS REAL OR JUST A FIGMENT OF MY IMAGINATION... I CLOSED MY EYES AND EVERYTHING VANISHED. I KEPT THESE VISIONS LOCKED UP INSIDE MY HEAD.

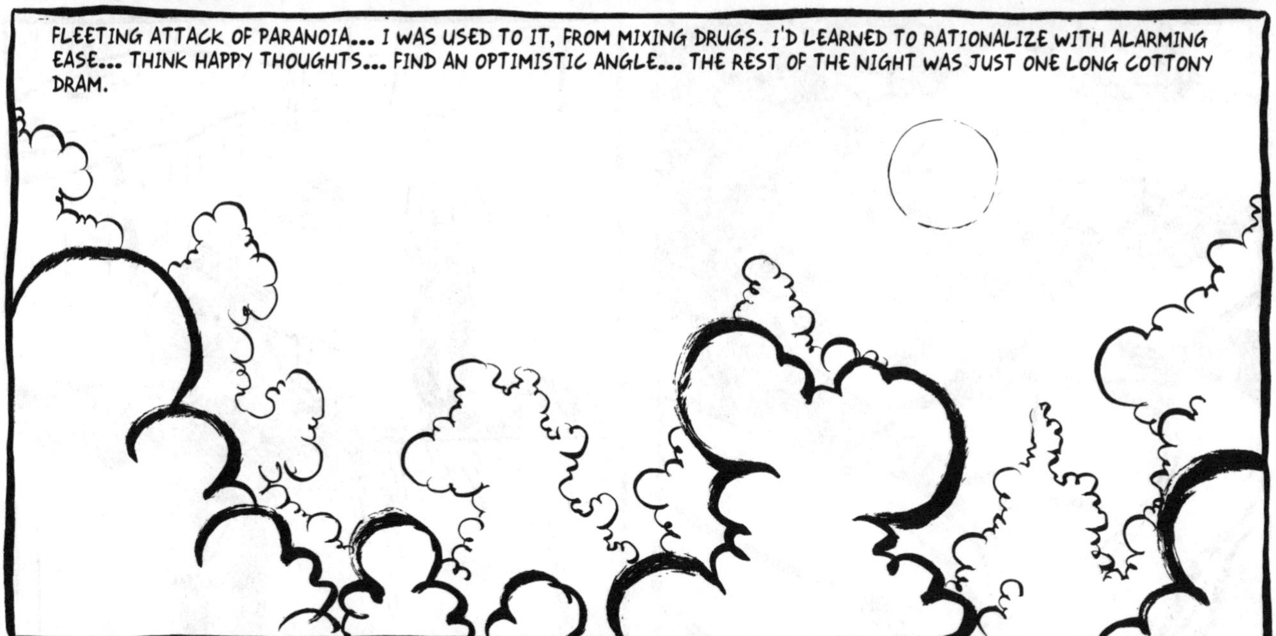
FLEETING ATTACK OF PARANOIA... I WAS USED TO IT, FROM MIXING DRUGS. I'D LEARNED TO RATIONALIZE WITH ALARMING EASE... THINK HAPPY THOUGHTS... FIND AN OPTIMISTIC ANGLE... THE REST OF THE NIGHT WAS JUST ONE LONG COTTONY DRAM.

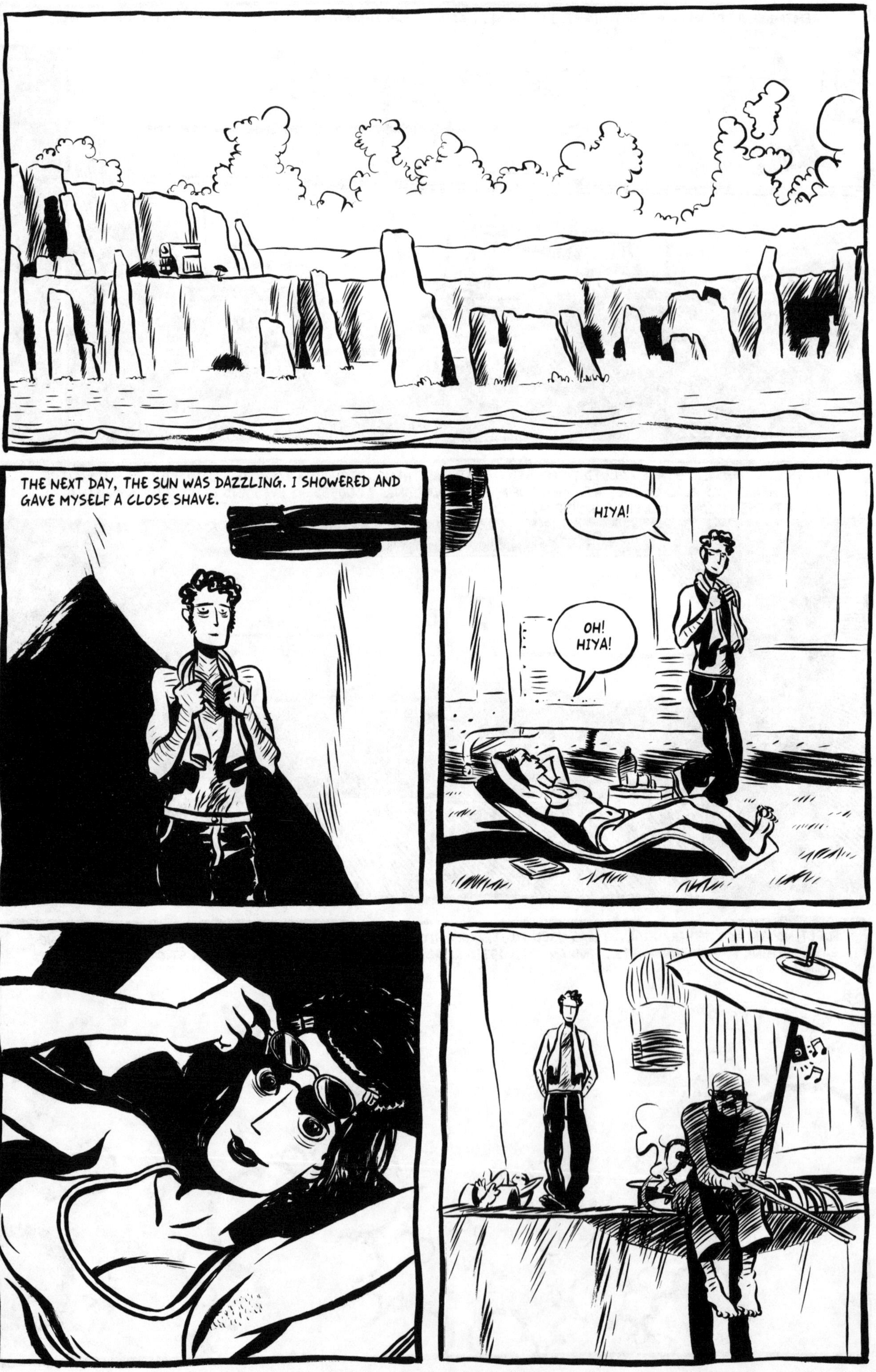
THE NEXT DAY, THE SUN WAS DAZZLING. I SHOWERED AND GAVE MYSELF A CLOSE SHAVE.
HIYA!
OH! HIYA!

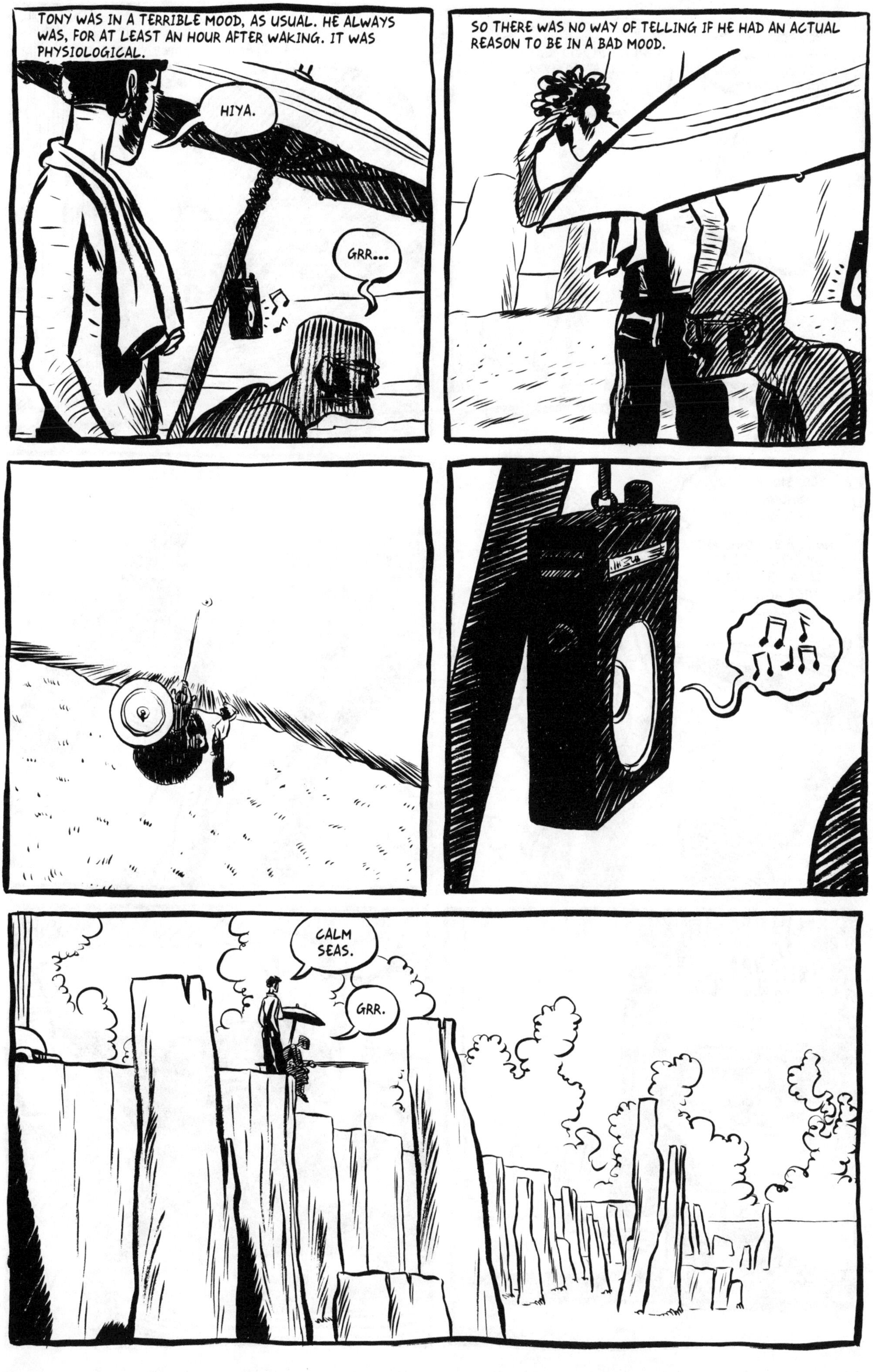
TONY WAS IN A TERRIBLE MOOD, AS USUAL. HE ALWAYS WAS, FOR AT LEAST AN HOUR AFTER WAKING. IT WAS PHYSIOLOGICAL.
HIYA.
GRR...
SO THERE WAS NO WAY OF TELLING IF HE HAD AN ACTUAL REASON TO BE IN A BAD MOOD.
CALM SEAS.
GRR.

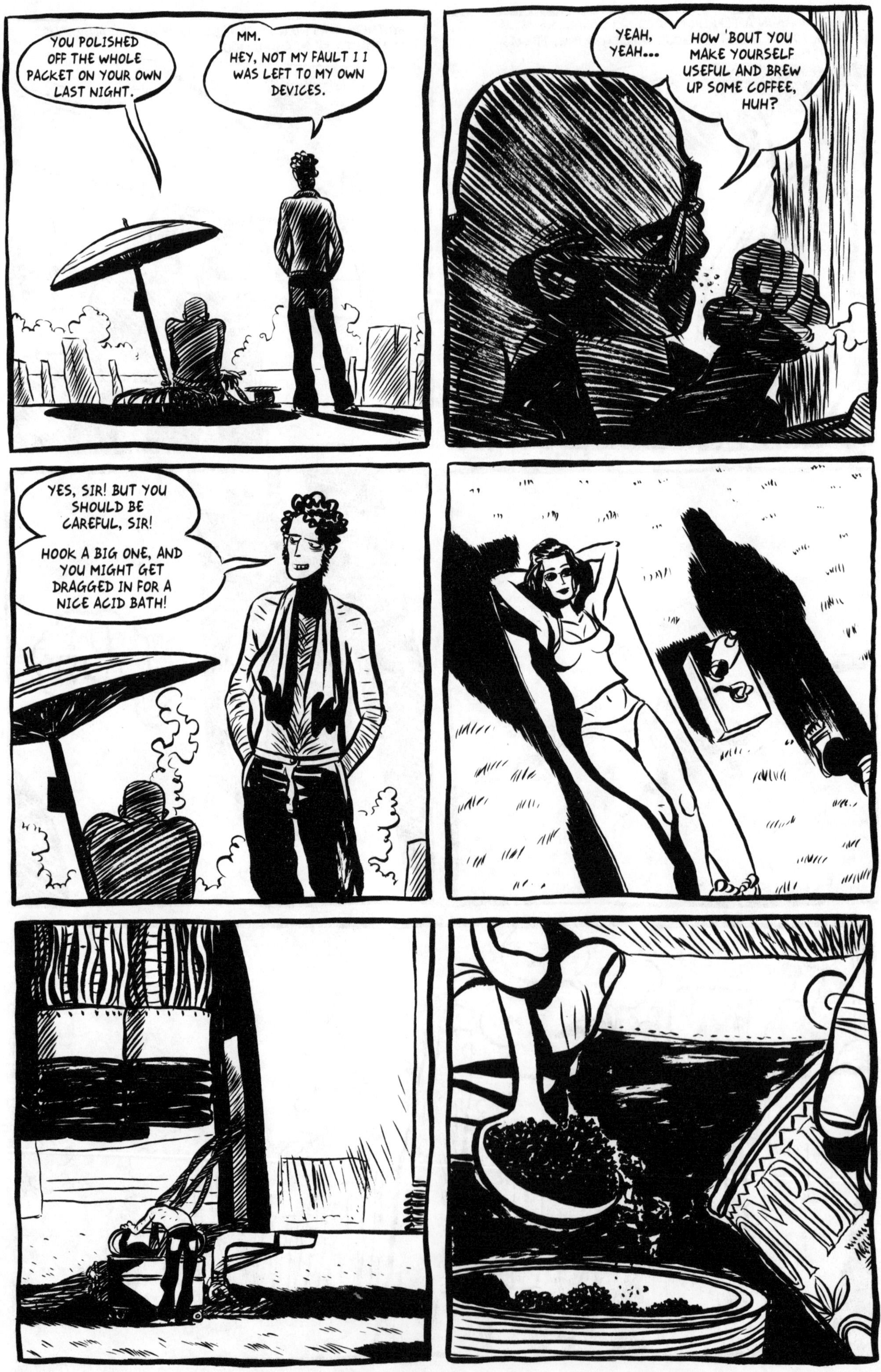
YOU POLISHED OFF THE WHOLE PACKET ON YOUR OWN LAST NIGHT.
MM.
HEY, NOT MY FAULT I I WAS LEFT TO MY OWN DEVICES.
YEAH, YEAH...
HOW 'BOUT YOU MAKE YOURSELF USEFUL AND BREW UP SOME COFFEE, HUH?
YES, SIR! BUT YOU SHOULD BE CAREFUL, SIR!
HOOK A BIG ONE, AND YOU MIGHT GET DRAGGED IN FOR A NICE ACID BATH!

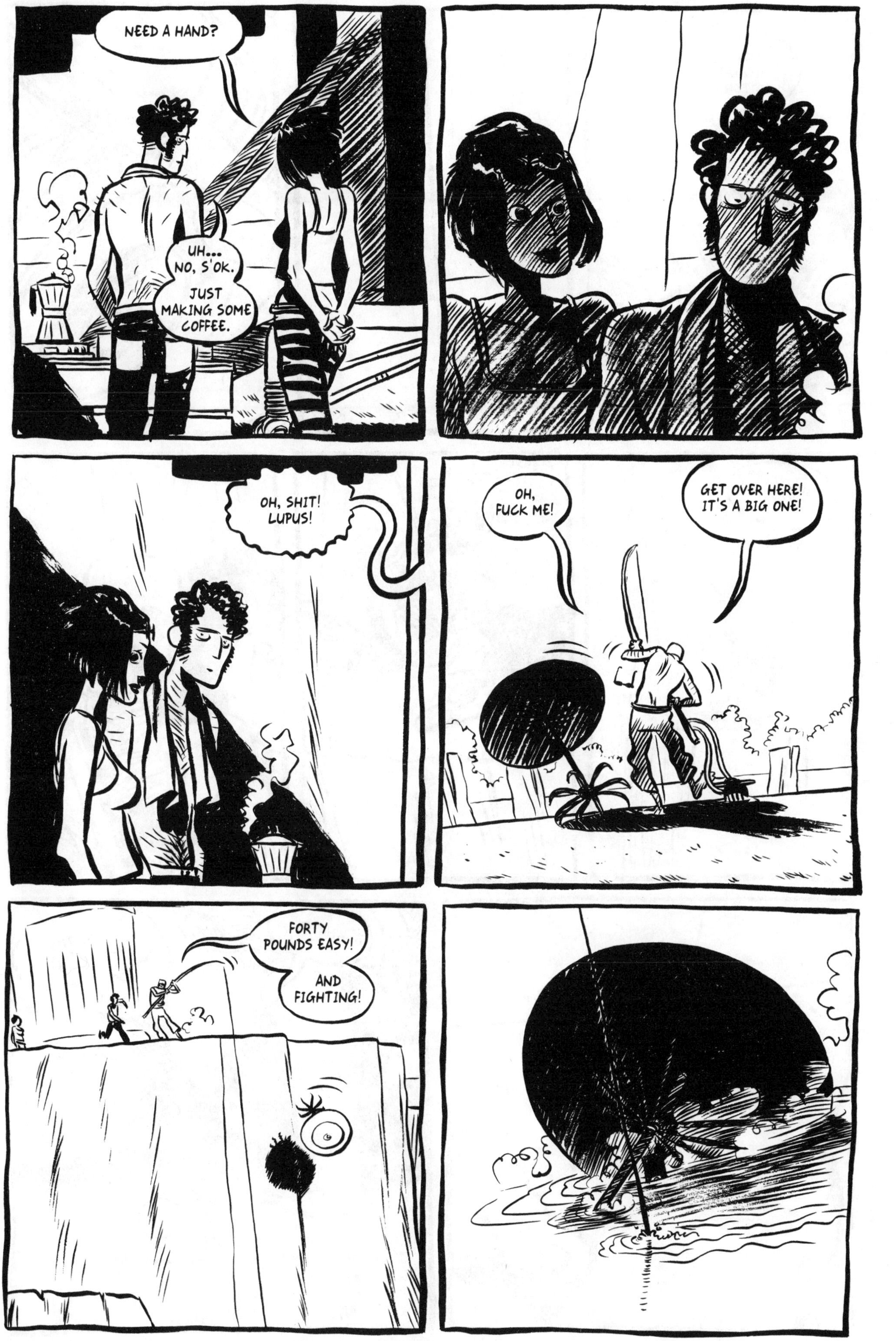
NEED A HAND?
UH... NO, S'OK.
JUST MAKING SOME COFFEE.
OH, SHIT! LUPUS!
OH, FUCK ME!
GET OVER HERE! IT'S A BIG ONE!
FORTY POUNDS EASY!
AND FIGHTING!

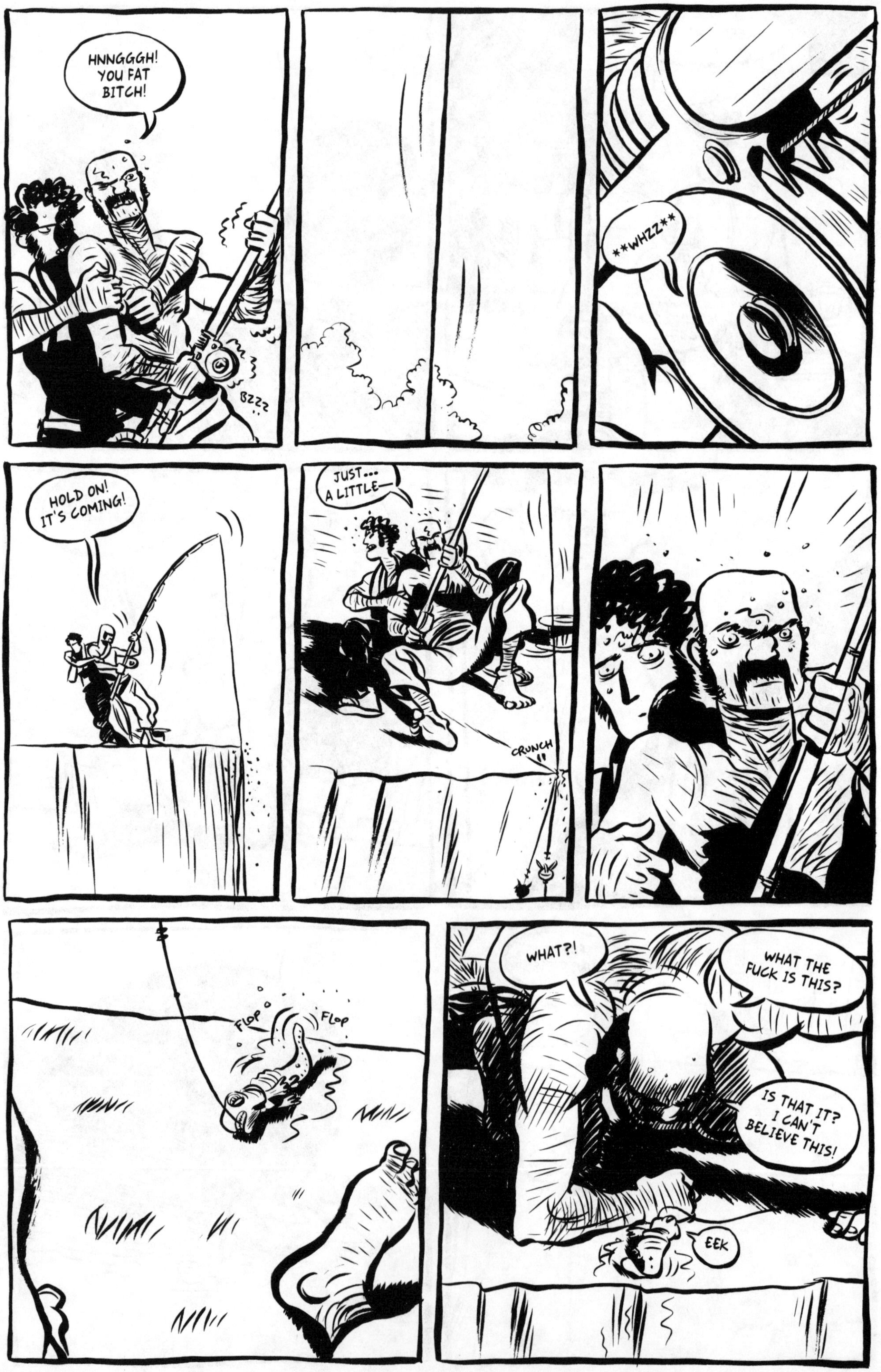

HNNGGGH! YOU FAT BITCH!
BZZZ
WHZZ
HOLD ON! IT'S COMING!
JUST... A LITTLE—
CRUNCH
FLOP
FLOP
WHAT?!
WHAT THE FUCK IS THIS?
IS THAT IT? I CAN'T BELIEVE THIS!
EEK

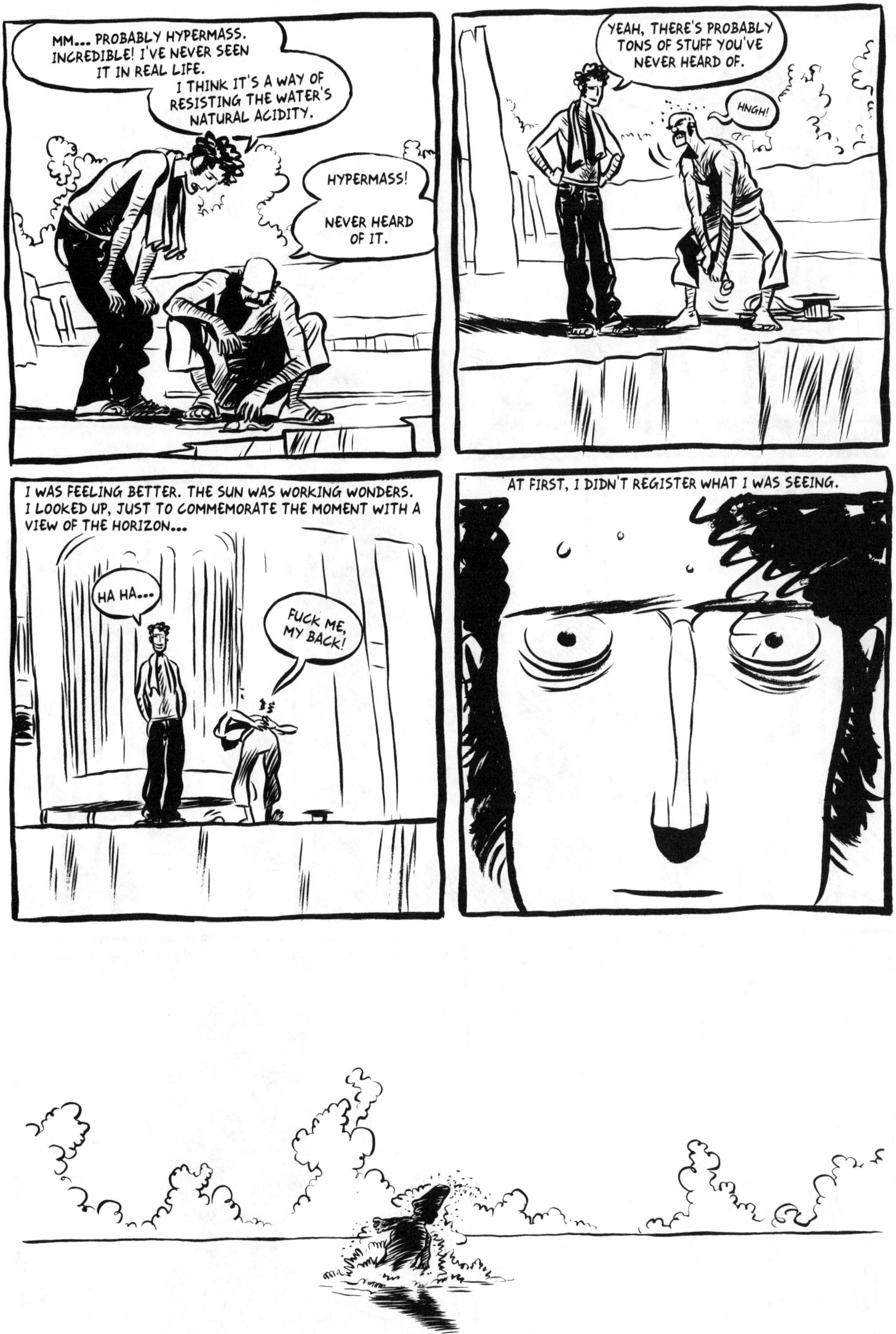
MM... PROBABLY HYPERMASS. INCREDIBLE! I'VE NEVER SEEN IT IN REAL LIFE.
I THINK IT'S A WAY OF RESISTING THE WATER'S NATURAL ACIDITY.
HYPERMASS!
NEVER HEARD OF IT.
YEAH, THERE'S PROBABLY TONS OF STUFF YOU'VE NEVER HEARD OF.
HNGH!
I WAS FEELING BETTER. THE SUN WAS WORKING WONDERS. I LOOKED UP, JUST TO COMMEMORATE THE MOMENT WITH A VIEW OF THE HORIZON...
HA HA...
FUCK ME, MY BACK!
AT FIRST, I DIDN'T REGISTER WHAT I WAS SEEING.

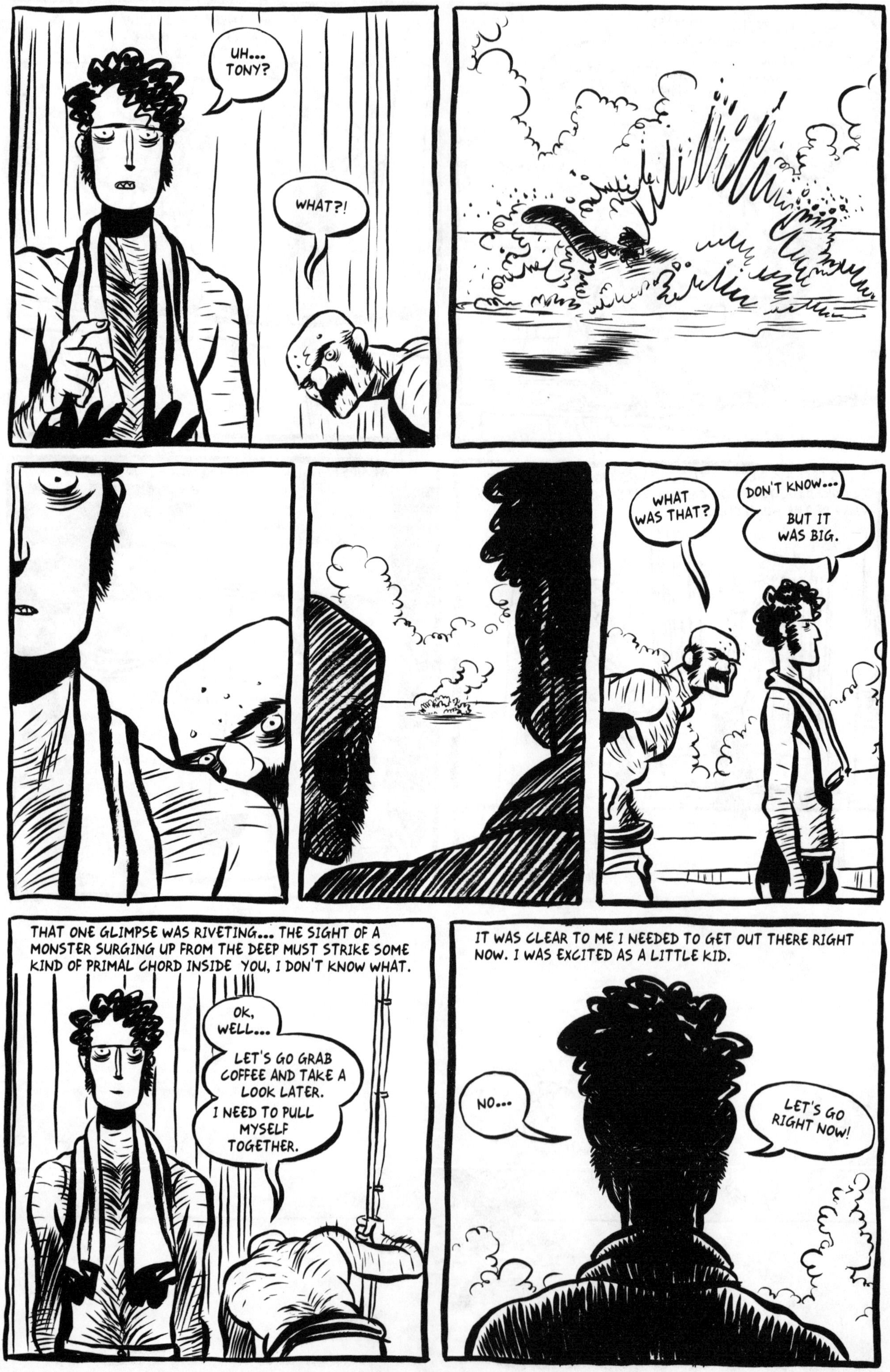
UH... TONY?
WHAT?!
WHAT WAS THAT?
DON'T KNOW...
BUT IT WAS BIG.
THAT ONE GLIMPSE WAS RIVETING... THE SIGHT OF A MONSTER SURGING UP FROM THE DEEP MUST STRIKE SOME KIND OF PRIMAL CHORD INSIDE YOU, I DON'T KNOW WHAT.
OK, WELL...
LET'S GO GRAB COFFEE AND TAKE A LOOK LATER.
I NEED TO PULL MYSELF TOGETHER.
IT WAS CLEAR TO ME I NEEDED TO GET OUT THERE RIGHT NOW. I WAS EXCITED AS A LITTLE KID.
NO...
LET'S GO RIGHT NOW!

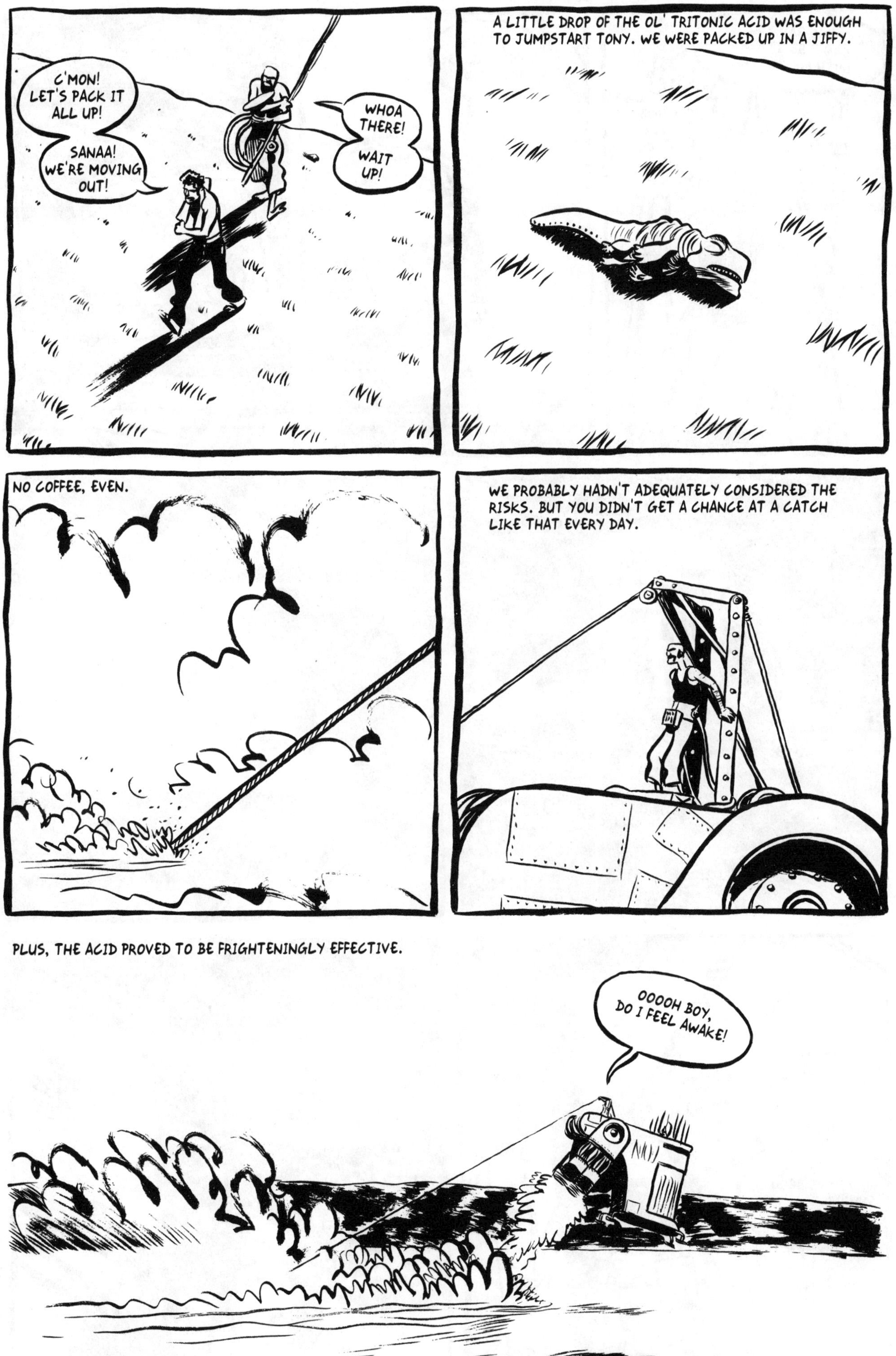
C'MON! LET'S PACK IT ALL UP!
SANAA! WE'RE MOVING OUT!
WHOA THERE!
WAIT UP!
A LITTLE DROP OF THE OL' TRITONIC ACID WAS ENOUGH TO JUMPSTART TONY. WE WERE PACKED UP IN A JIFFY.
NO COFFEE, EVEN.
WE PROBABLY HADN'T ADEQUATELY CONSIDERED THE RISKS. BUT YOU DIDN'T GET A CHANCE AT A CATCH LIKE THAT EVERY DAY.
PLUS, THE ACID PROVED TO BE FRIGHTENINGLY EFFECTIVE.
OOOOH BOY, DO I FEEL AWAKE!

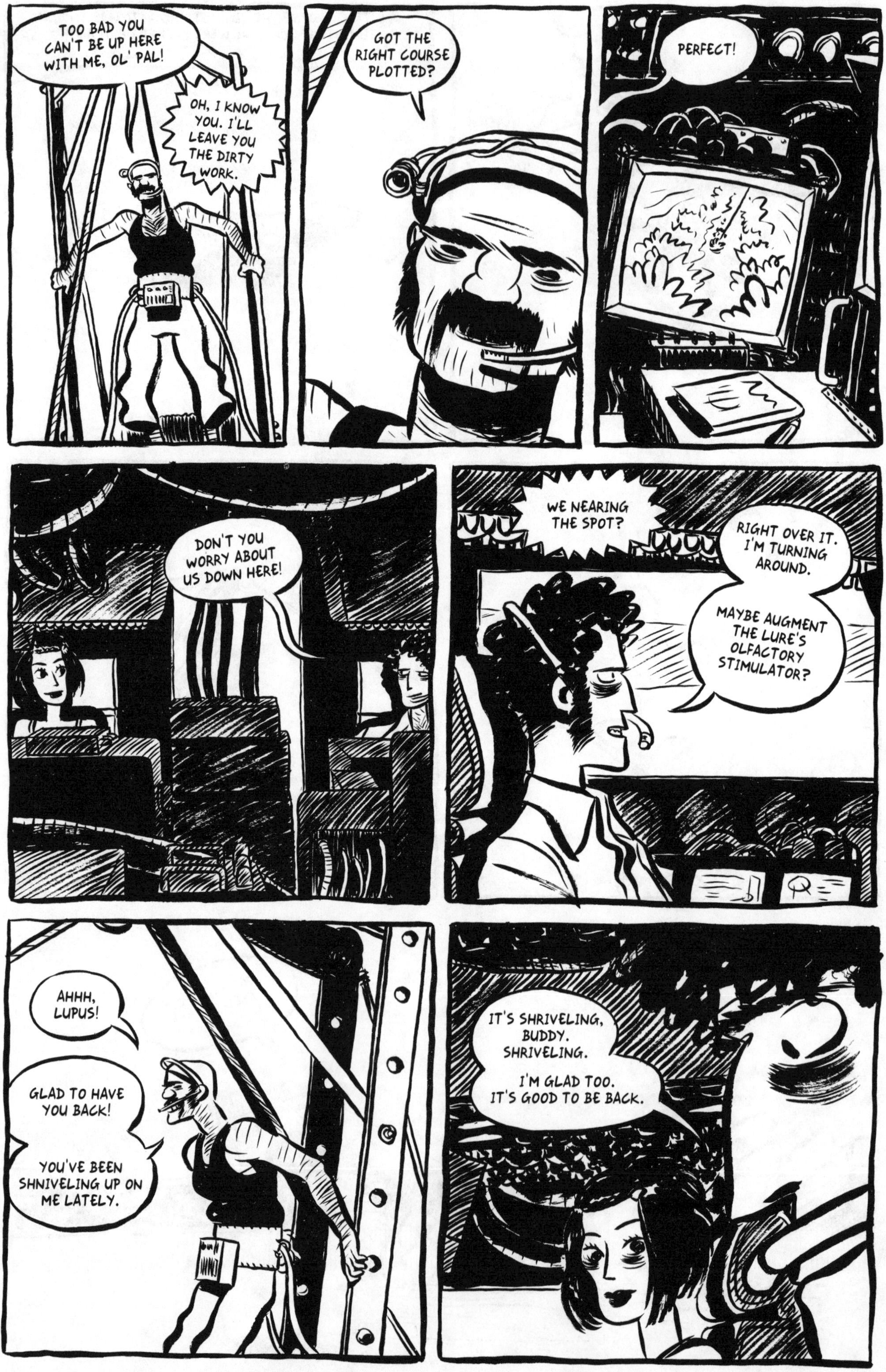
TOO BAD YOU CAN'T BE UP HERE WITH ME, OL' PAL!
OH, I KNOW YOU. I'LL LEAVE YOU THE DIRTY WORK.
GOT THE RIGHT COURSE PLOTTED?
PERFECT!
DON'T YOU WORRY ABOUT US DOWN HERE!
WE NEARING THE SPOT?
RIGHT OVER IT. I'M TURNING AROUND.
MAYBE AUGMENT THE LURE'S OLFACTORY STIMULATOR?
AHHH, LUPUS!
GLAD TO HAVE YOU BACK!
YOU'VE BEEN SHNIVELING UP ON ME LATELY.
IT'S SHRIVELING, BUDDY. SHRIVELING.
I'M GLAD TOO. IT'S GOOD TO BE BACK.

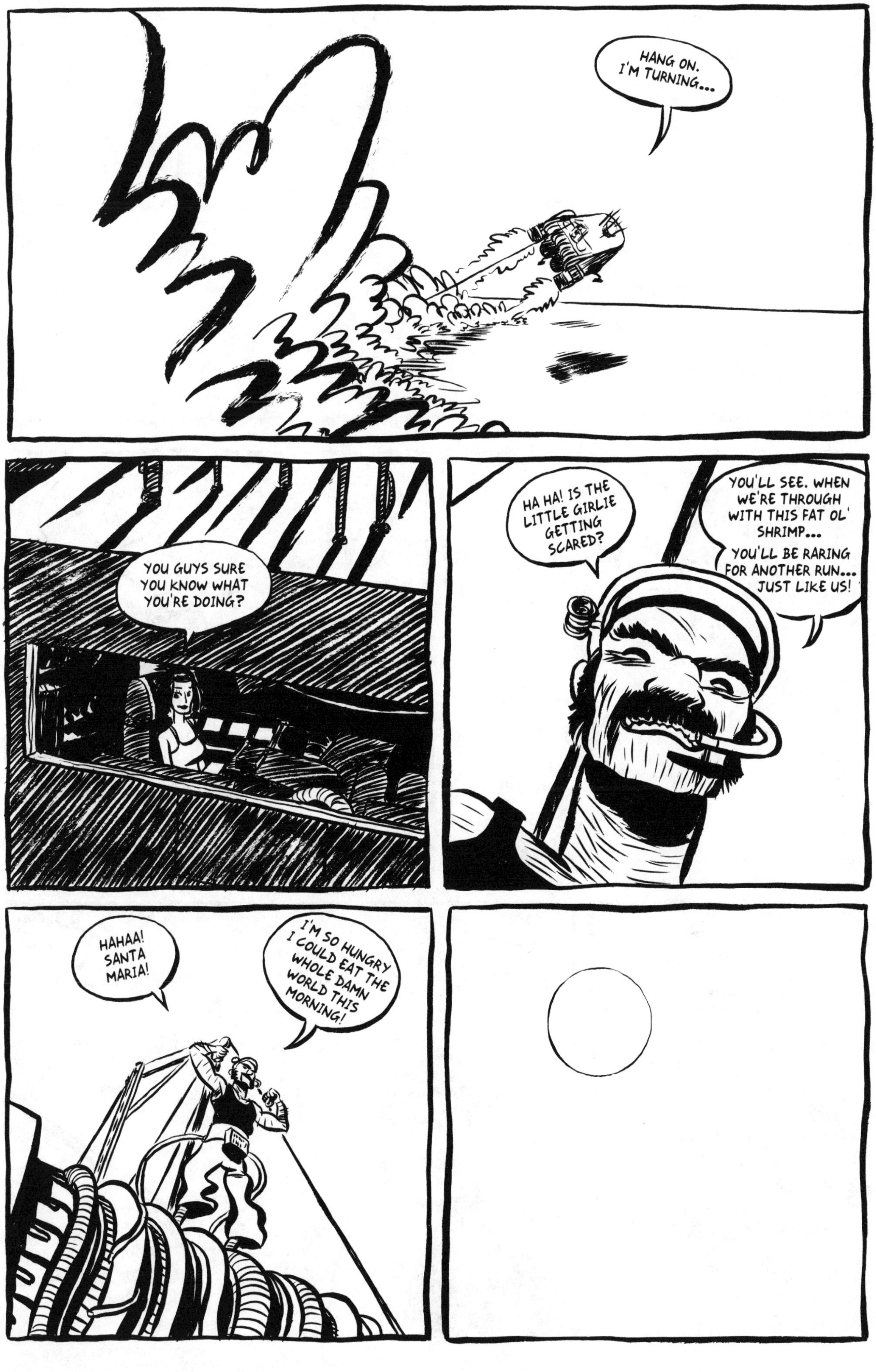
HANG ON. I'M TURNING...
YOU GUYS SURE YOU KNOW WHAT YOU'RE DOING?
HA HA! IS THE LITTLE GIRLIE GETTING SCARED?
YOU'LL SEE. WHEN WE'RE THROUGH WITH THIS FAT OL' SHRIMP...
YOU'LL BE RARING FOR ANOTHER RUN... JUST LIKE US!
HAHAA! SANTA MARIA!
I'M SO HUNGRY I COULD EAT THE WHOLE DAMN WORLD THIS MORNING!

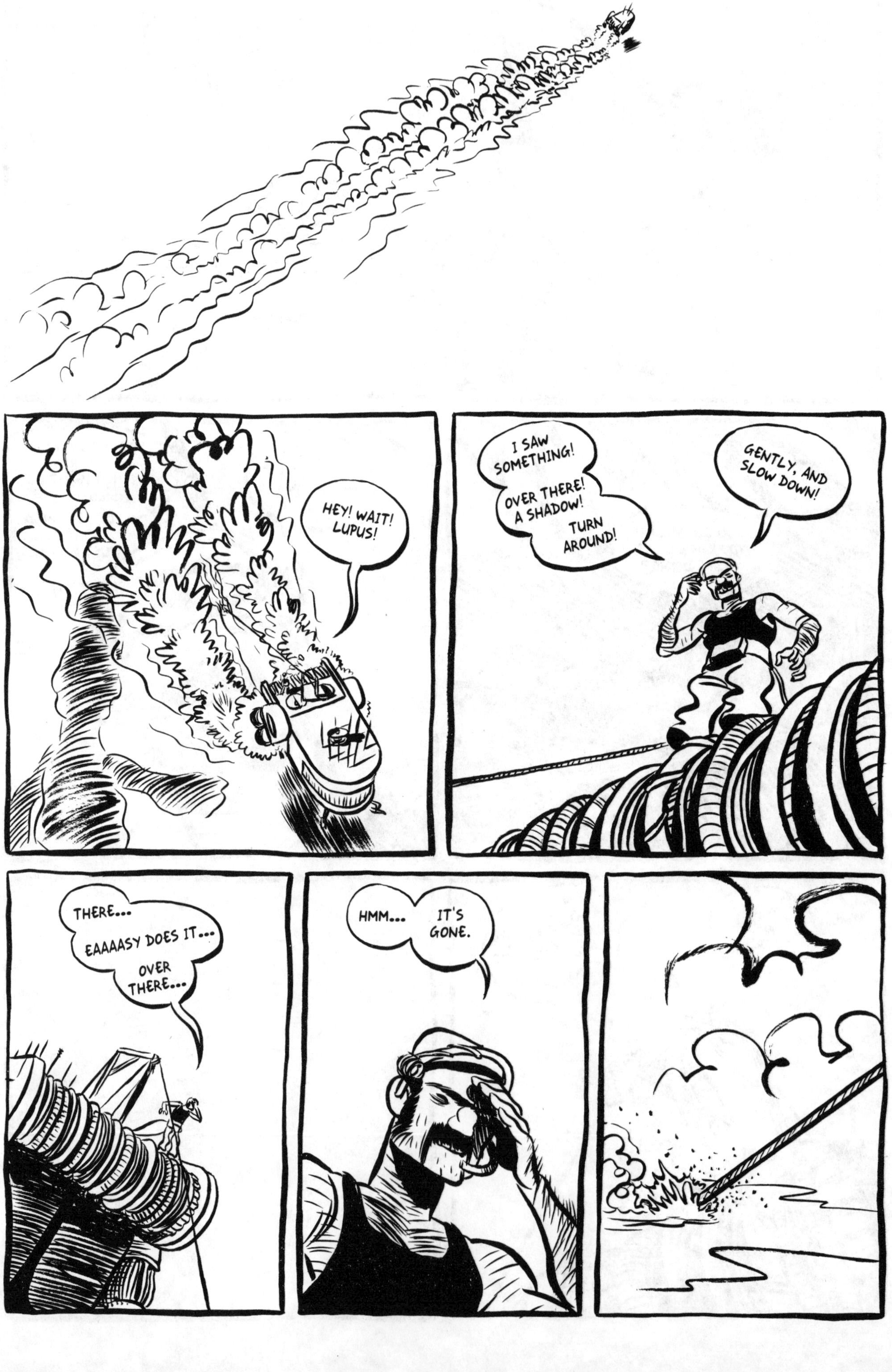
HEY! WAIT! LUPUS!
I SAW SOMETHING!
OVER THERE! A SHADOW!
TURN AROUND!
GENTLY, AND SLOW DOWN!
THERE...
EAAAASY DOES IT...
OVER THERE...
HMM...
IT'S GONE.

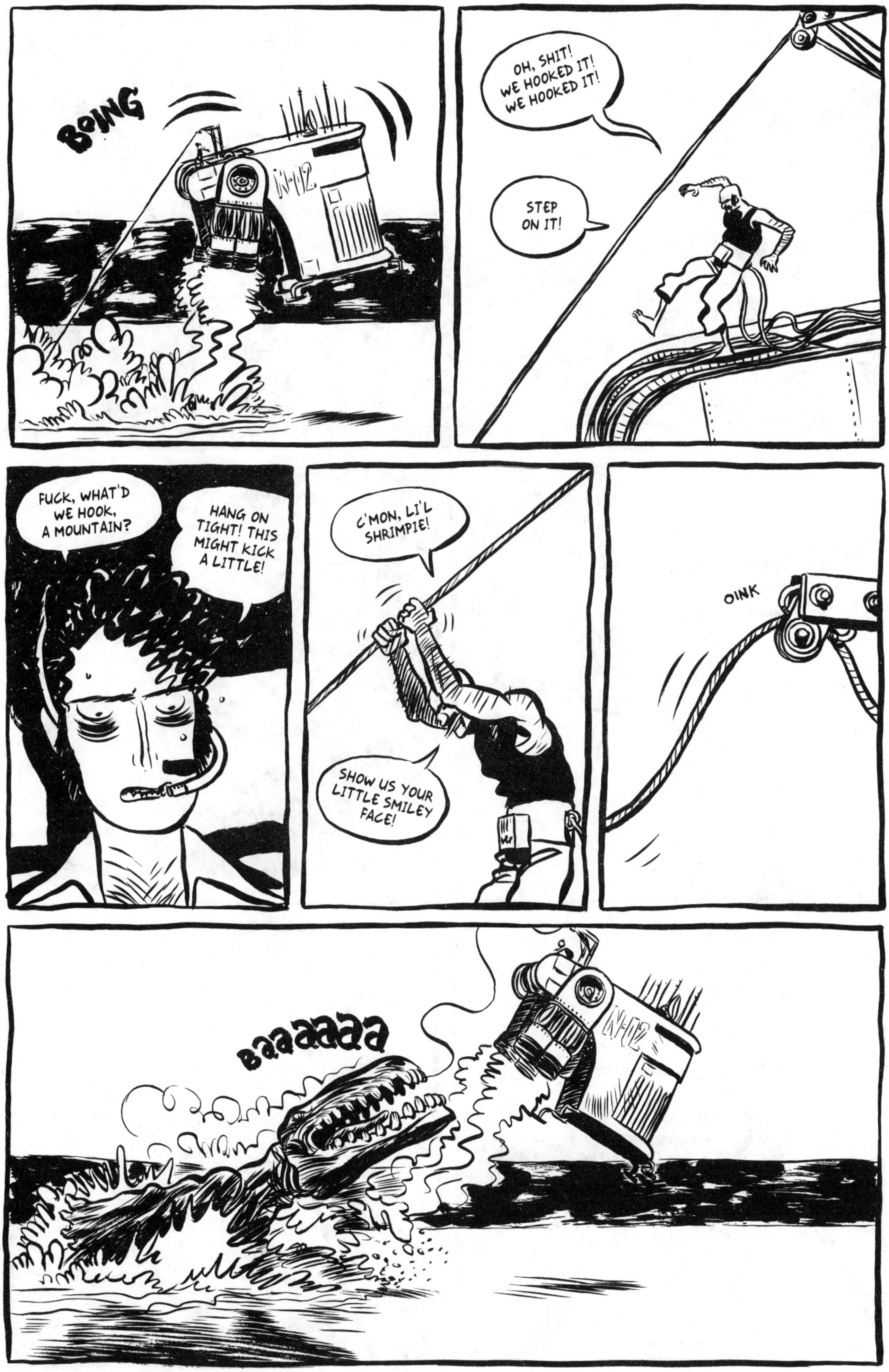
BOING
OH, SHIT! WE HOOKED IT! WE HOOKED IT!
STEP ON IT!
FUCK, WHAT'D WE HOOK, A MOUNTAIN?
HANG ON TIGHT! THIS MIGHT KICK A LITTLE!
C'MON, LI'L SHRIMPIE!
SHOW US YOUR LITTLE SMILEY FACE!
OINK
BAAAAAA

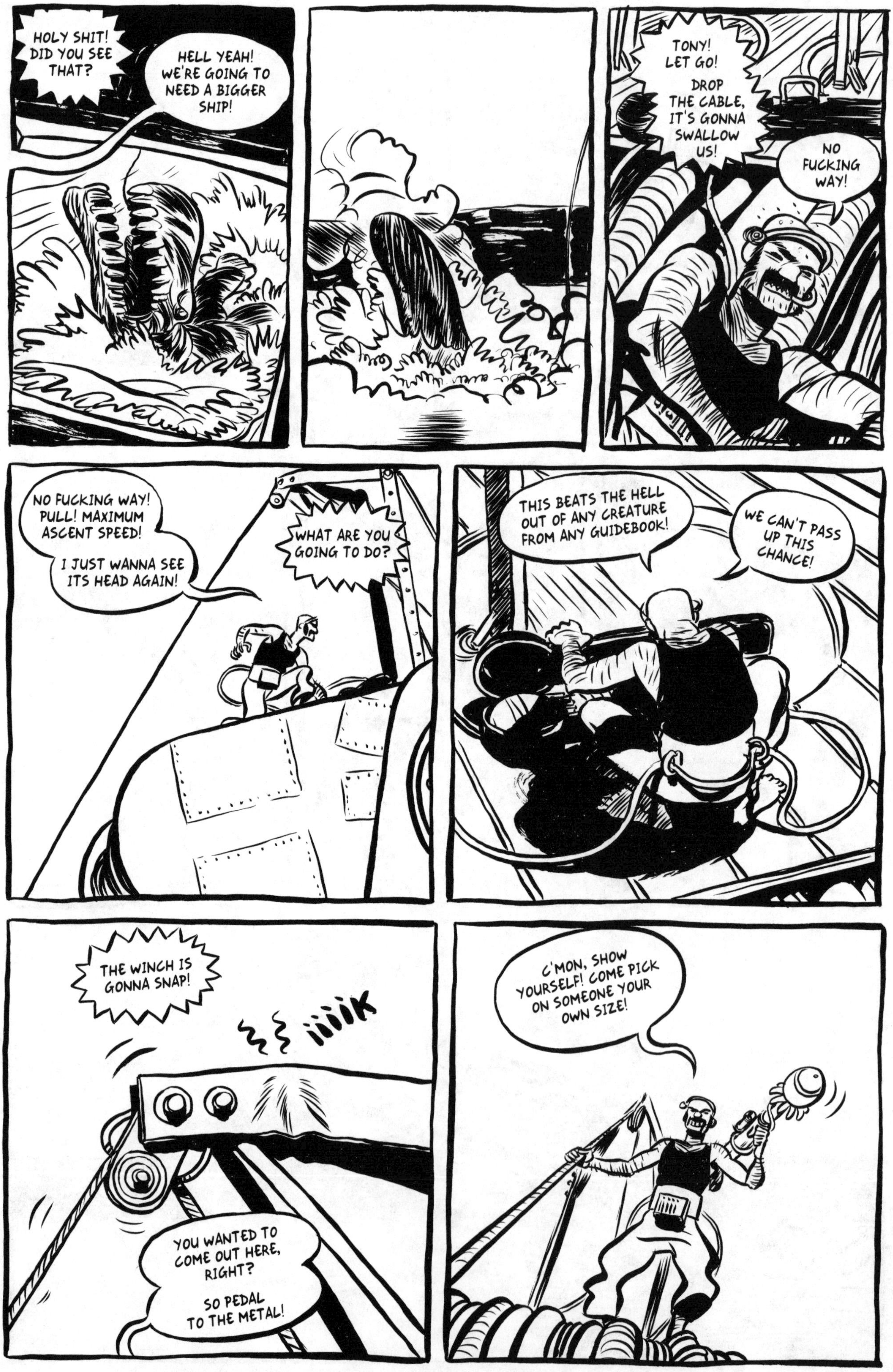
HOLY SHIT! DID YOU SEE THAT?
HELL YEAH! WE'RE GOING TO NEED A BIGGER SHIP!
TONY! LET GO!
DROP THE CABLE, IT'S GONNA SWALLOW US!
NO FUCKING WAY!
NO FUCKING WAY! PULL! MAXIMUM ASCENT SPEED!
I JUST WANNA SEE ITS HEAD AGAIN!
WHAT ARE YOU GOING TO DO?
THIS BEATS THE HELL OUT OF ANY CREATURE FROM ANY GUIDEBOOK!
WE CAN'T PASS UP THIS CHANCE!
THE WINCH IS GONNA SNAP!
iiiiiK
YOU WANTED TO COME OUT HERE, RIGHT?
SO PEDAL TO THE METAL!
C'MON, SHOW YOURSELF! COME PICK ON SOMEONE YOUR OWN SIZE!

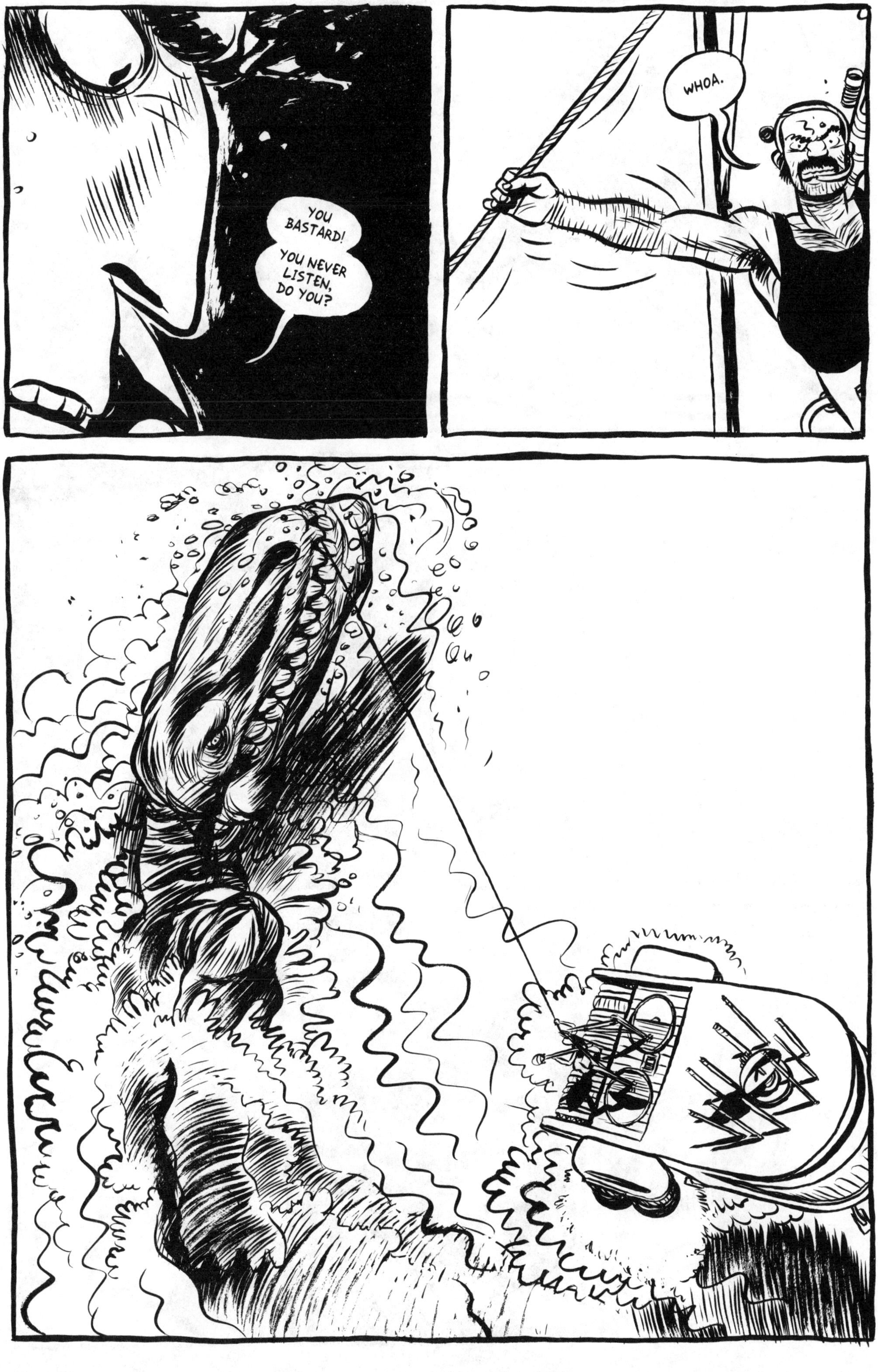
YOU BASTARD!
YOU NEVER LISTEN, DO YOU?
WHOA.

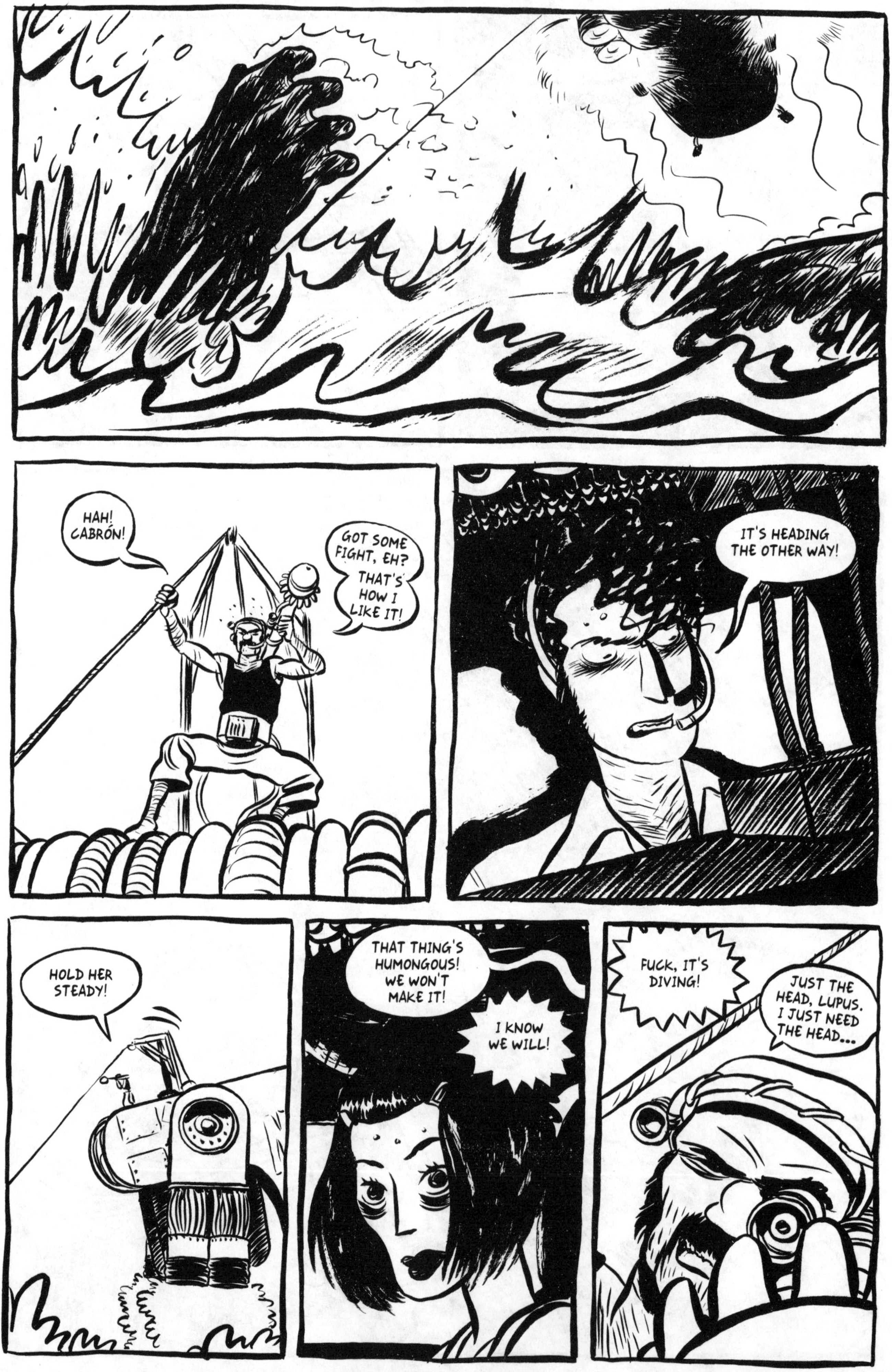
HAH! CABRÓN!
GOT SOME FIGHT, EH? THAT'S HOW I LIKE IT!
IT'S HEADING THE OTHER WAY!
HOLD HER STEADY!
THAT THING'S HUMONGOUS! WE WON'T MAKE IT!
I KNOW WE WILL!
FUCK, IT'S DIVING!
JUST THE HEAD, LUPUS. I JUST NEED THE HEAD...

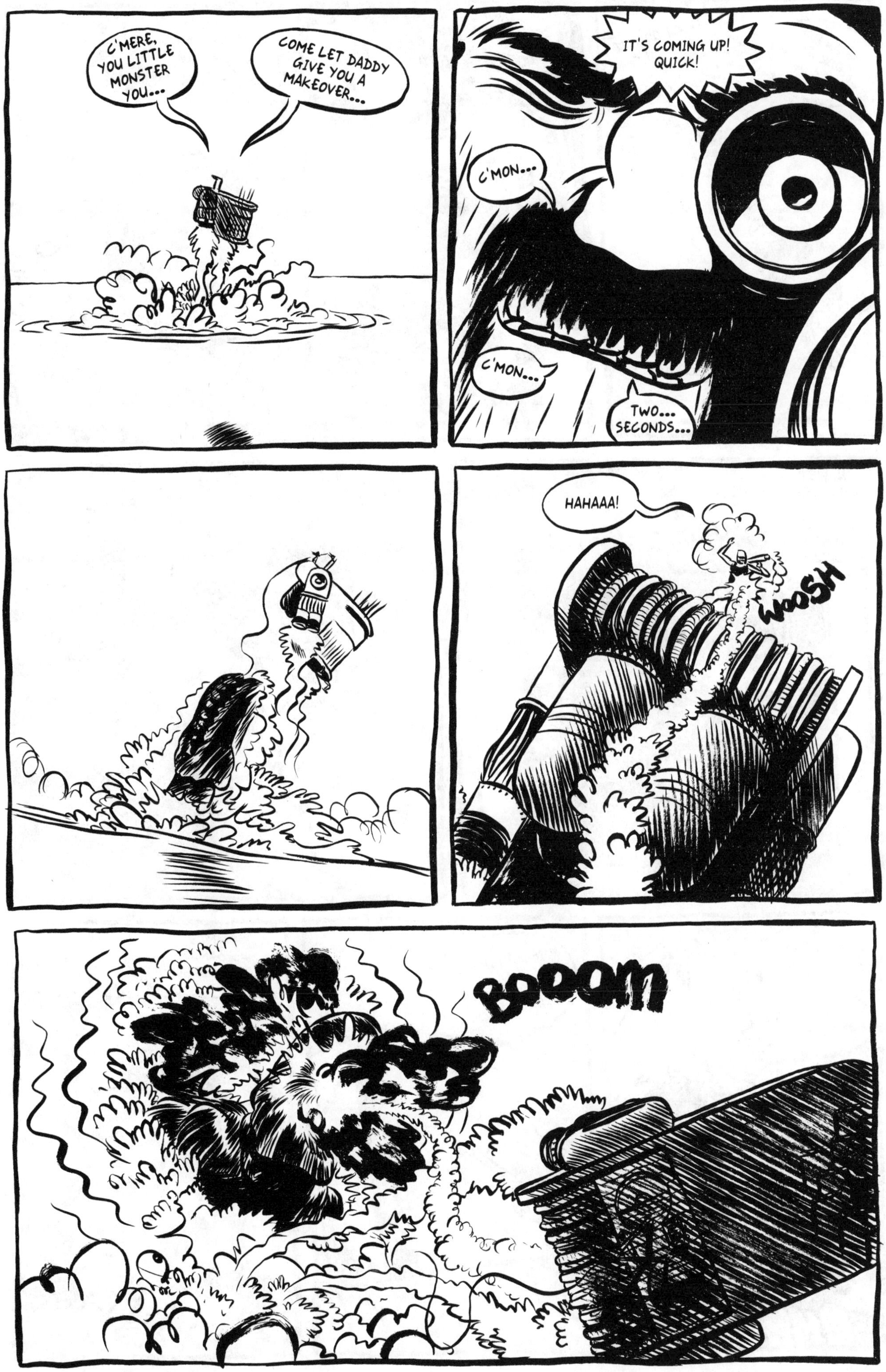
C'MERE, YOU LITTLE MONSTER YOU...
COME LET DADDY GIVE YOU A MAKEOVER...
IT'S COMING UP! QUICK!
C'MON...
C'MON...
TWO... SECONDS...
HAHAAA!
WOOSH
BOOOM

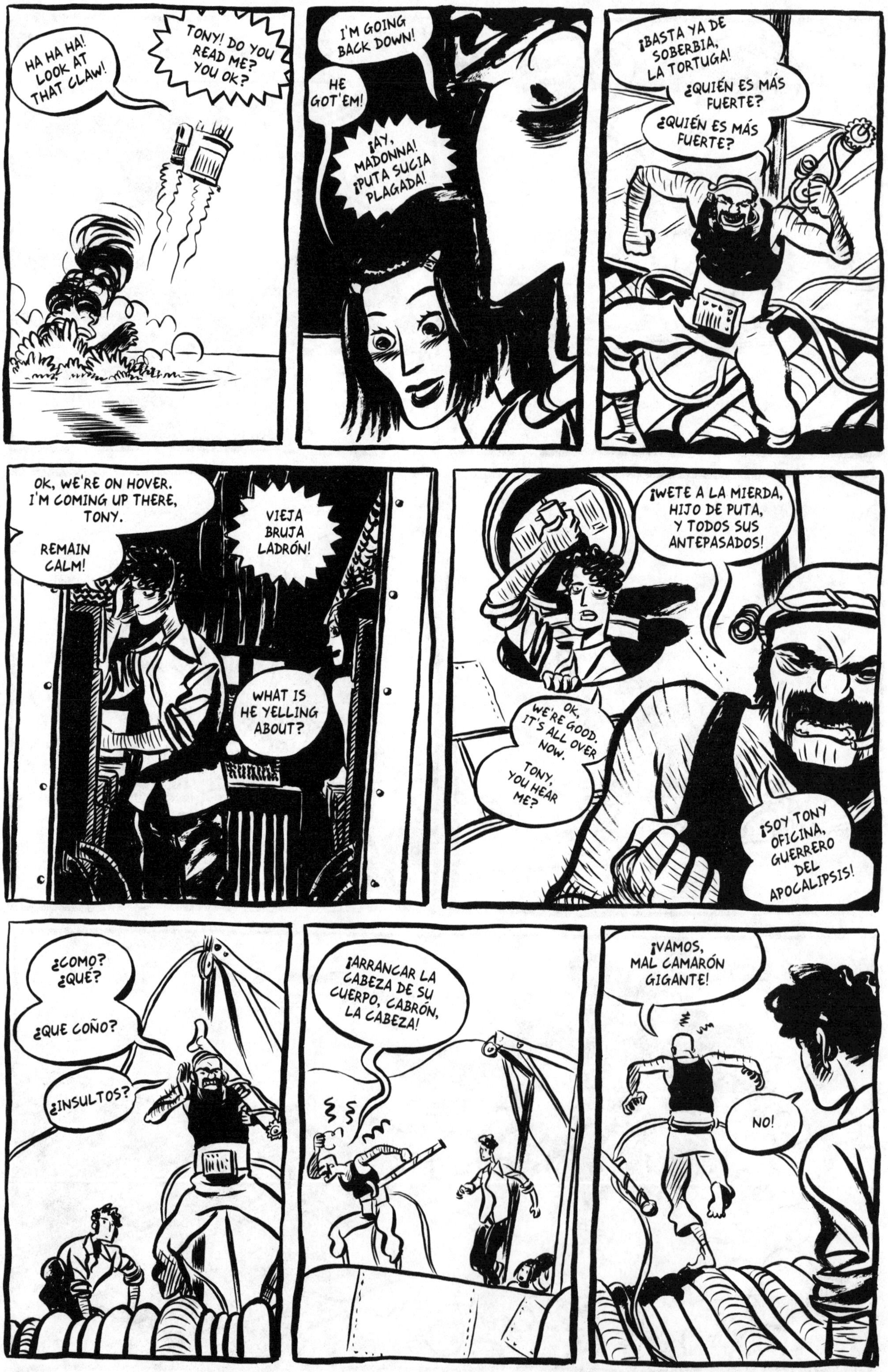
HA HA HA! LOOK AT THAT CLAW!
TONY! DO YOU READ ME? YOU OK?
I'M GOING BACK DOWN!
HE GOT'EM!
¡AY, MADONNA! ¡PUTA SUCIA PLAGADA!
¡BASTA YA DE SOBERBIA, LA TORTUGA!
¿QUIÉN ES MÁS FUERTE?
¿QUIÉN ES MÁS FUERTE?
OK, WE'RE ON HOVER. I'M COMING UP THERE, TONY.
REMAIN CALM!
VIEJA BRUJA LADRÓN!
WHAT IS HE YELLING ABOUT?
¡WETE A LA MIERDA, HIJO DE PUTA, Y TODOS SUS ANTEPASADOS!
OK, WE'RE GOOD. IT'S ALL OVER NOW.
TONY, YOU HEAR ME?
¡SOY TONY OFICINA, GUERRERO DEL APOCALIPSIS!
¿COMO? ¿QUÉ?
¿QUE COÑO?
¿INSULTOS?
¡ARRANCAR LA CABEZA DE SU CUERPO, CABRÓN, LA CABEZA!
¡VAMOS, MAL CAMARÓN GIGANTE!
NO!

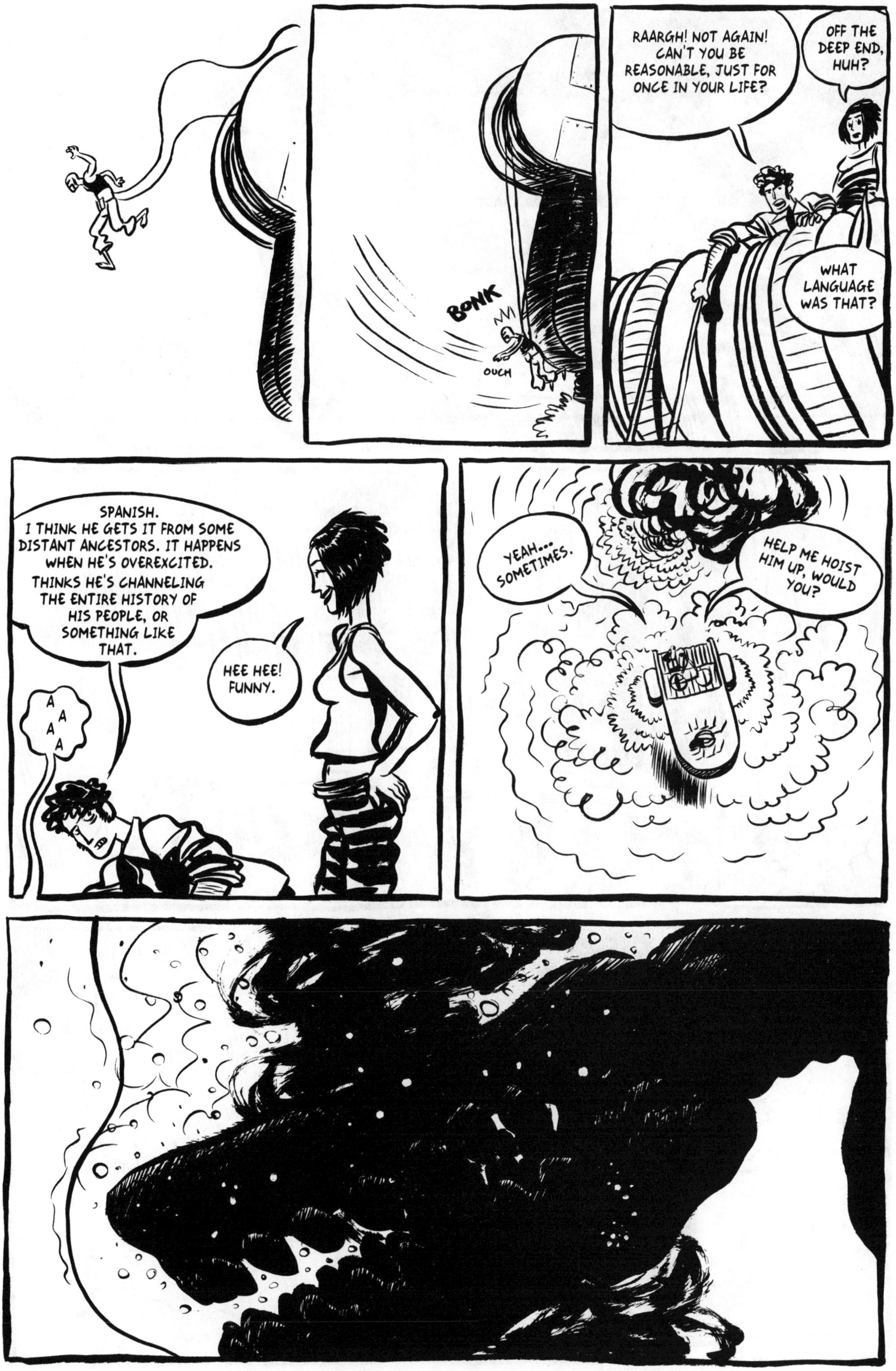
BONK
OUCH
RAARGH! NOT AGAIN! CAN'T YOU BE REASONABLE, JUST FOR ONCE IN YOUR LIFE?
OFF THE DEEP END, HUH?
WHAT LANGUAGE WAS THAT?
SPANISH. I THINK HE GETS IT FROM SOME DISTANT ANCESTORS. IT HAPPENS WHEN HE'S OVEREXCITED.
THINKS HE'S CHANNELING THE ENTIRE HISTORY OF HIS PEOPLE, OR SOMETHING LIKE THAT.
A A A A
HEE HEE! FUNNY.
YEAH... SOMETIMES.
HELP ME HOIST HIM UP, WOULD YOU?

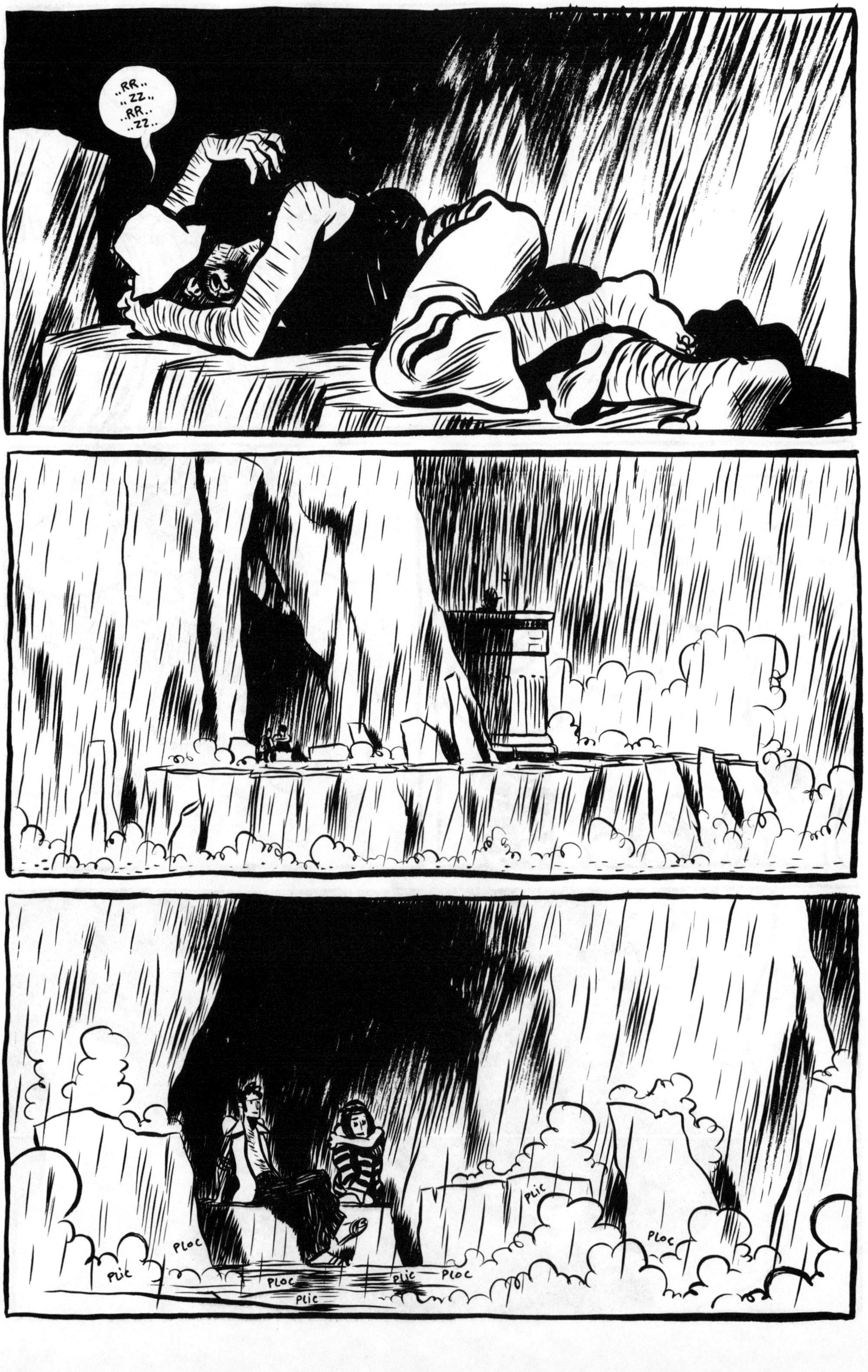
..RR.. ..ZZ.. ..RR.. ..ZZ..
PLIC
PLOC
PLOC
PLIC
PLOC
PLIC
PLIC
PLOC
PLOC

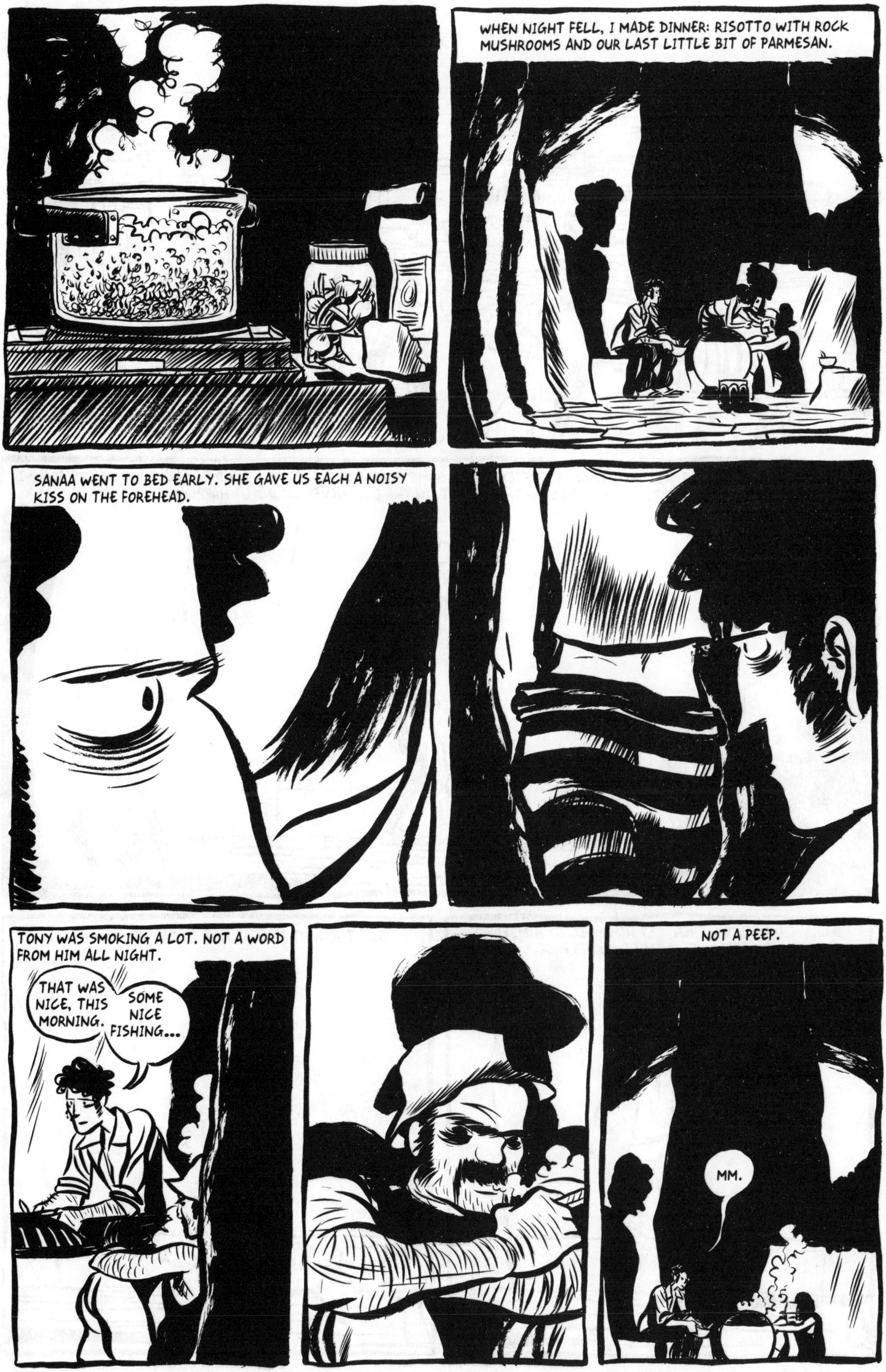
WHEN NIGHT FELL, I MADE DINNER: RISOTTO WITH ROCK MUSHROOMS AND OUR LAST LITTLE BIT OF PARMESAN.
SANAA WENT TO BED EARLY. SHE GAVE US EACH A NOISY KISS ON THE FOREHEAD.
TONY WAS SMOKING A LOT. NOT A WORD FROM HIM ALL NIGHT.
THAT WAS NICE, THIS MORNING.
SOME NICE FISHING...
NOT A PEEP.
MM.

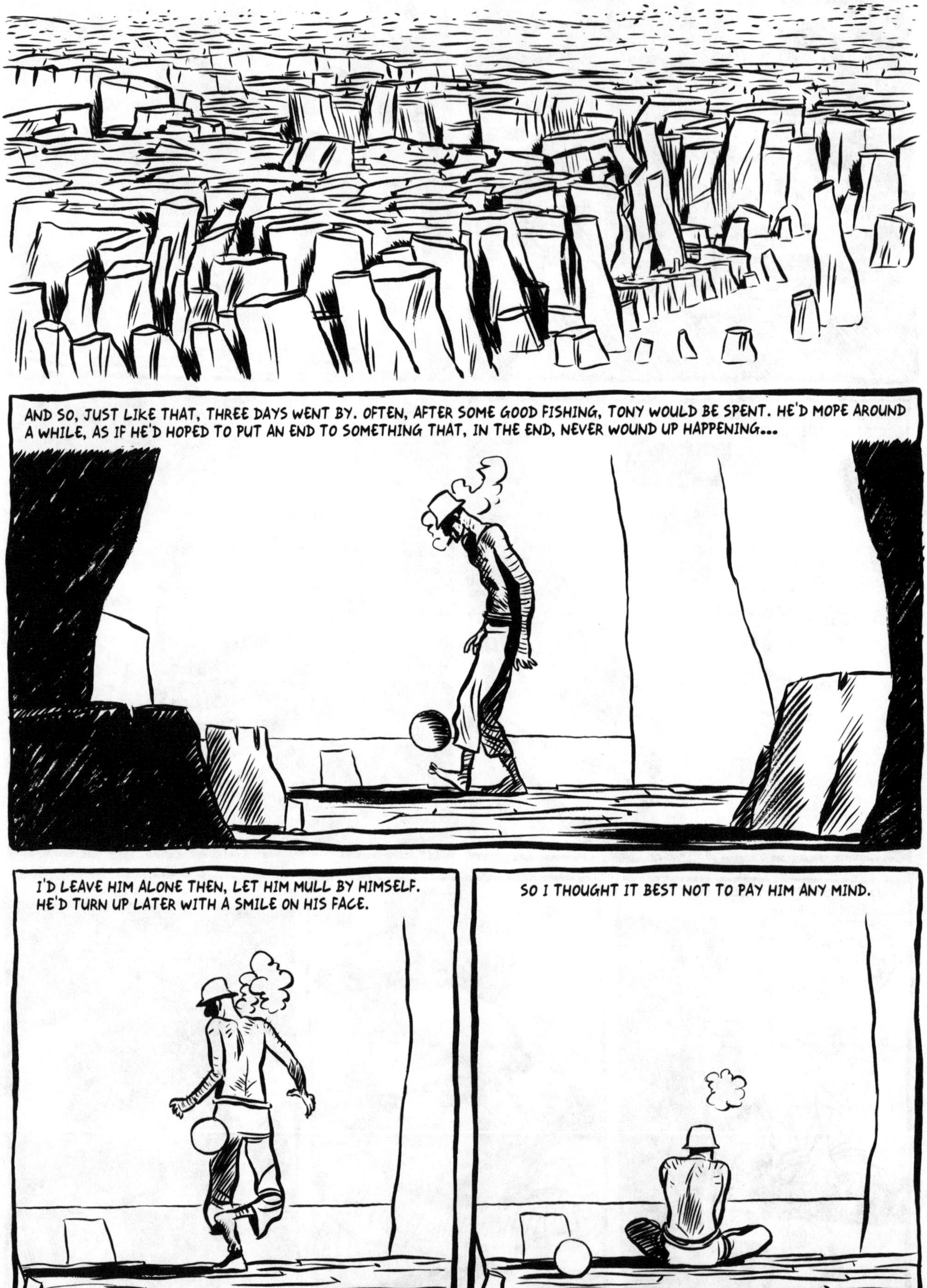
AND SO, JUST LIKE THAT, THREE DAYS WENT BY. OFTEN, AFTER SOME GOOD FISHING, TONY WOULD BE SPENT. HE'D MOPE AROUND A WHILE, AS IF HE'D HOPED TO PUT AN END TO SOMETHING THAT, IN THE END, NEVER WOUND UP HAPPENING...
I'D LEAVE HIM ALONE THEN, LET HIM MULL BY HIMSELF. HE'D TURN UP LATER WITH A SMILE ON HIS FACE.
SO I THOUGHT IT BEST NOT TO PAY HIM ANY MIND.

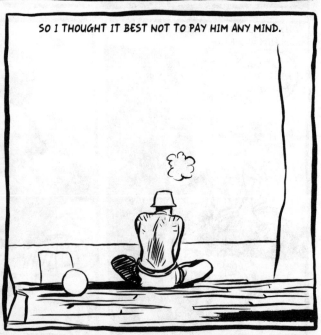

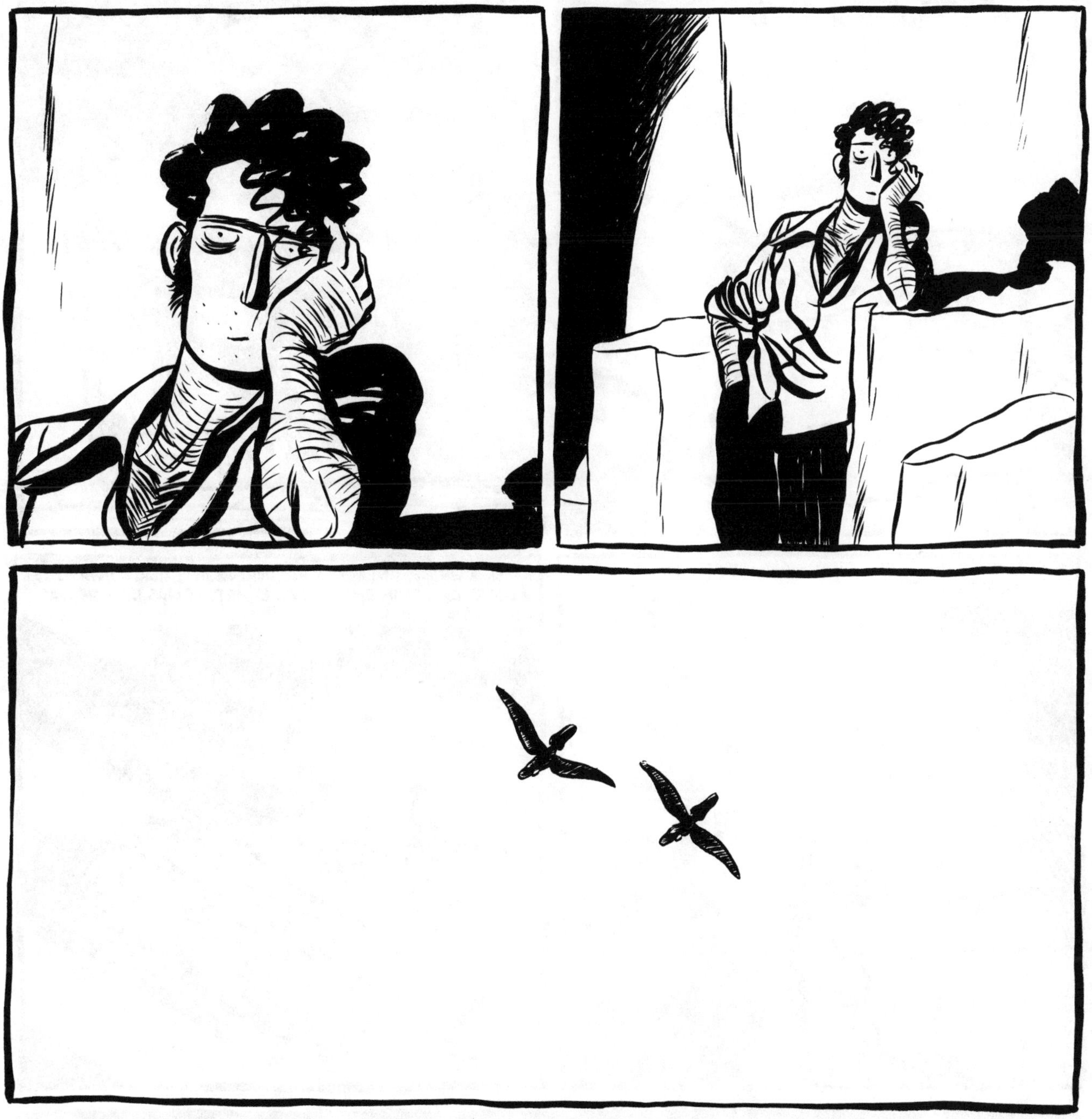

WE HEADED OUT FAITHFULLY A FEW TIMES, BUT IN VAIN. IT WAS OBVIOUS WE'D LUCKED OUT ONCE, AND COULDN'T COUNT ON IT AGAIN. ALL WE HAD TO SHOW FOR THREE DAYS WAS A GOOEY OLD PAIR OF CRUSTACEANS THAT WEREN'T EVEN EDIBLE.

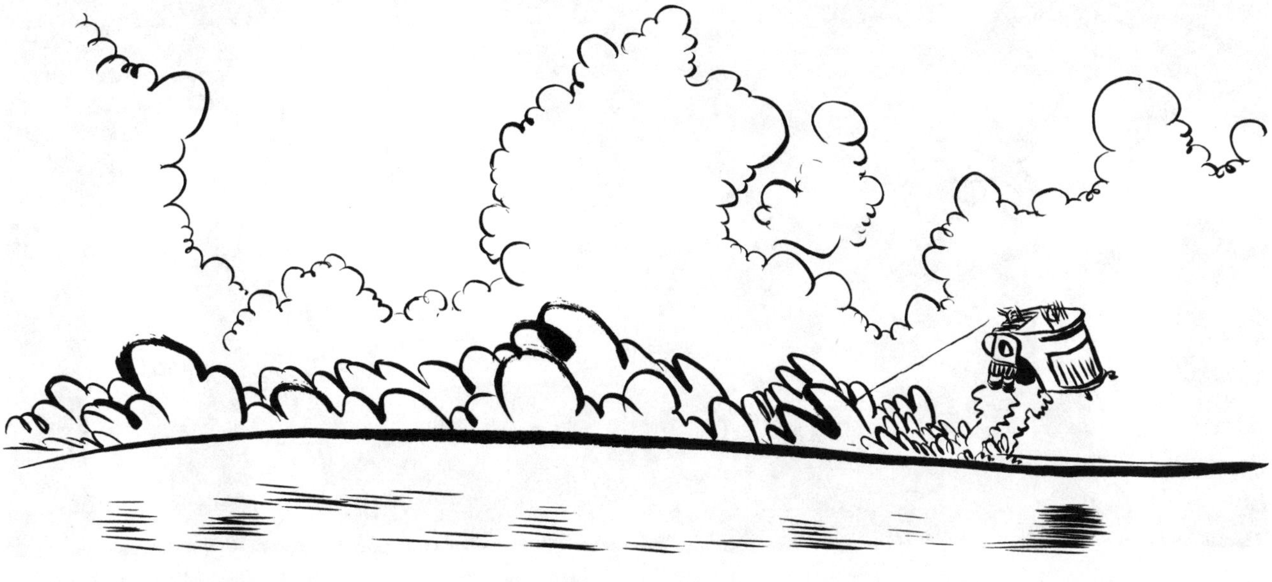

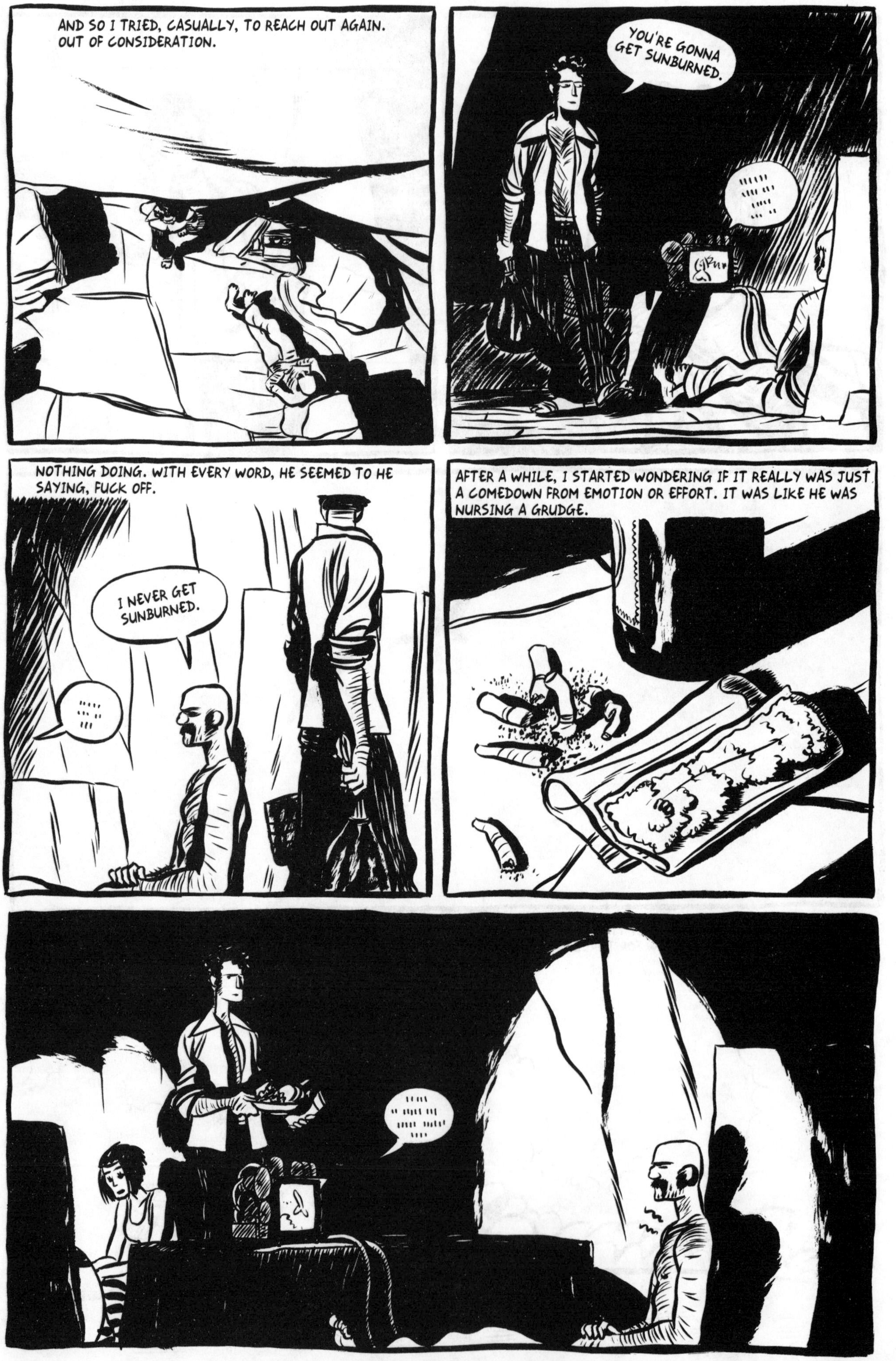
AND SO I TRIED, CASUALLY, TO REACH OUT AGAIN. OUT OF CONSIDERATION.
YOU'RE GONNA GET SUNBURNED.
NOTHING DOING. WITH EVERY WORD, HE SEEMED TO HE SAYING, FUCK OFF.
I NEVER GET SUNBURNED.
AFTER A WHILE, I STARTED WONDERING IF IT REALLY WAS JUST A COMEDOWN FROM EMOTION OR EFFORT. IT WAS LIKE HE WAS NURSING A GRUDGE.

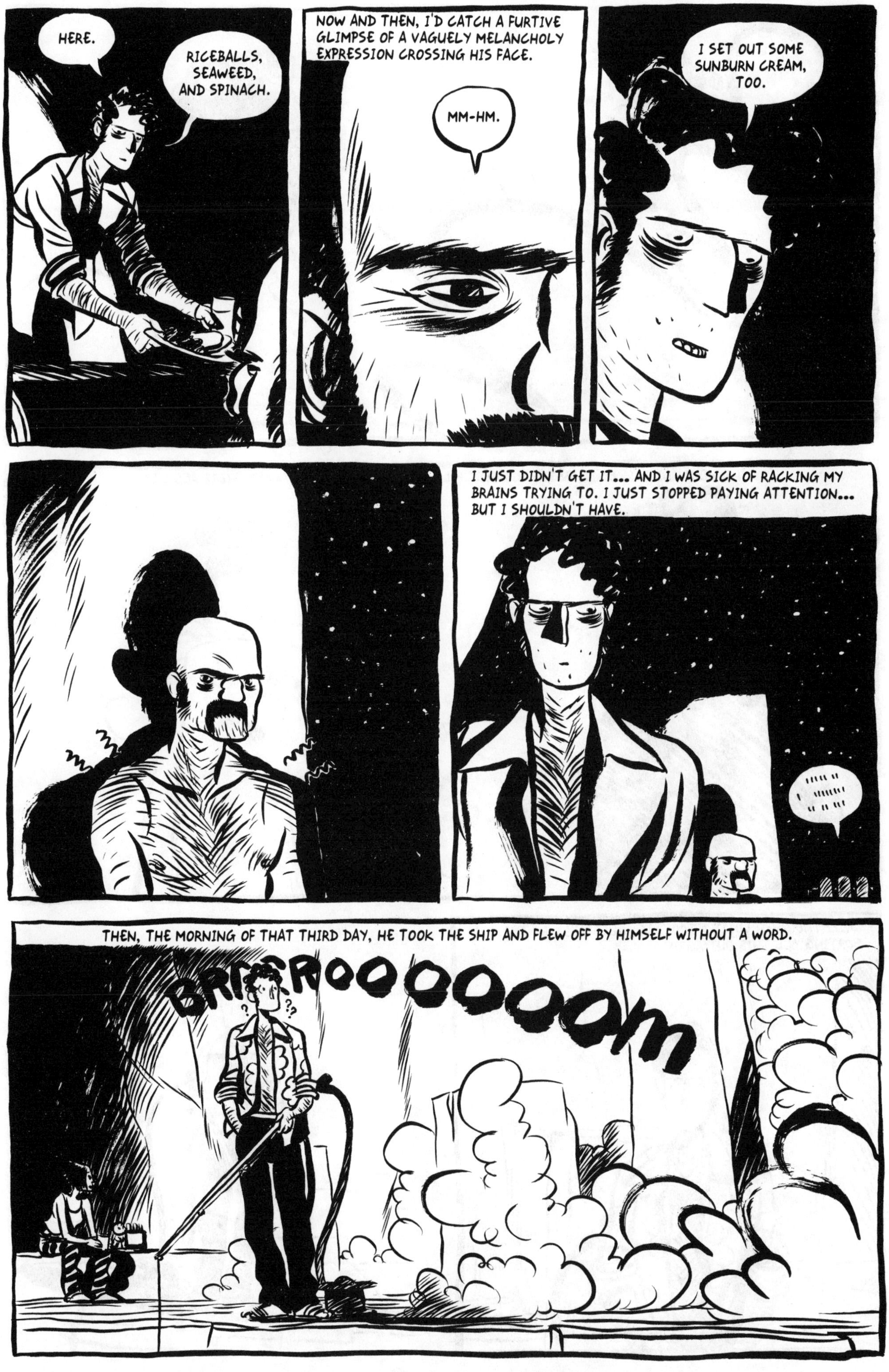
HERE.
RICEBALLS, SEAWEED, AND SPINACH.
NOW AND THEN, I'D CATCH A FURTIVE GLIMPSE OF A VAGUELY MELANCHOLY EXPRESSION CROSSING HIS FACE.
MM-HM.
I SET OUT SOME SUNBURN CREAM, TOO.
I JUST DIDN'T GET IT... AND I WAS SICK OF RACKING MY BRAINS TRYING TO. I JUST STOPPED PAYING ATTENTION... BUT I SHOULDN'T HAVE.
THEN, THE MORNING OF THAT THIRD DAY, HE TOOK THE SHIP AND FLEW OFF BY HIMSELF WITHOUT A WORD.
BRRROOOOOOOM

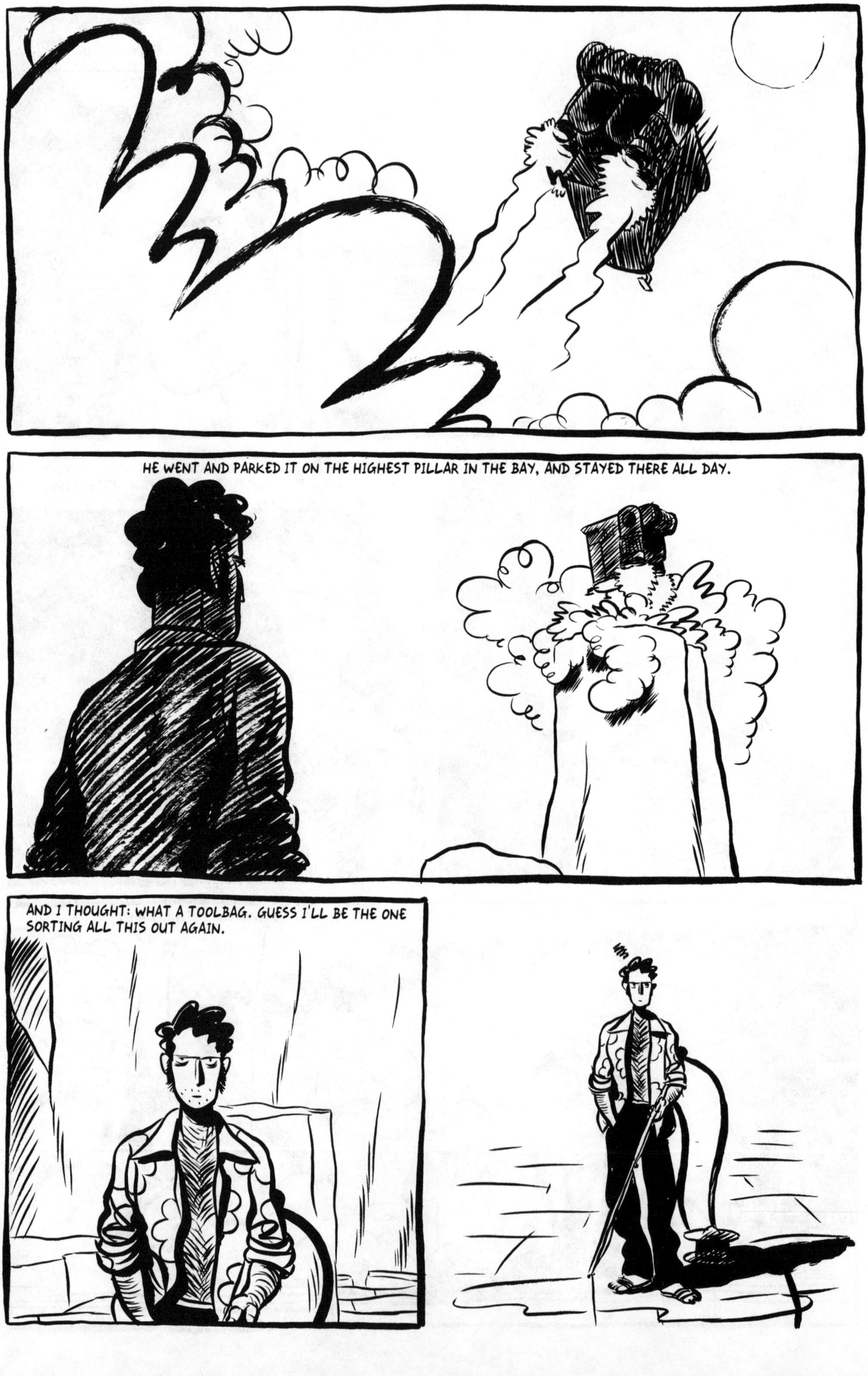
HE WENT AND PARKED IT ON THE HIGHEST PILLAR IN THE BAY, AND STAYED THERE ALL DAY.
AND I THOUGHT: WHAT A TOOLBAG. GUESS I'LL BE THE ONE SORTING ALL THIS OUT AGAIN.

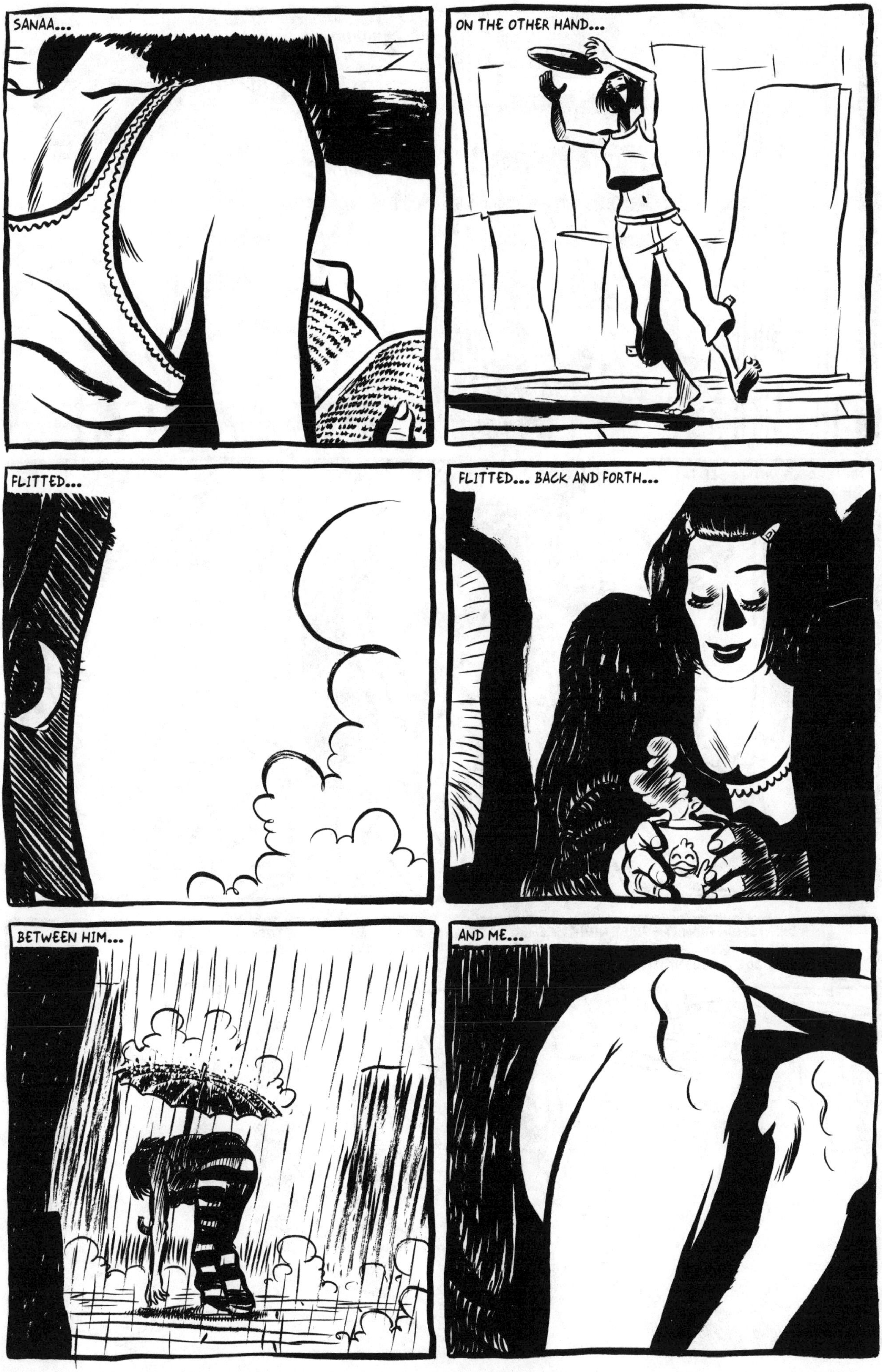
SANAA...
ON THE OTHER HAND...
FLITTED...
FLITTED... BACK AND FORTH...
BETWEEN HIM...
AND ME...

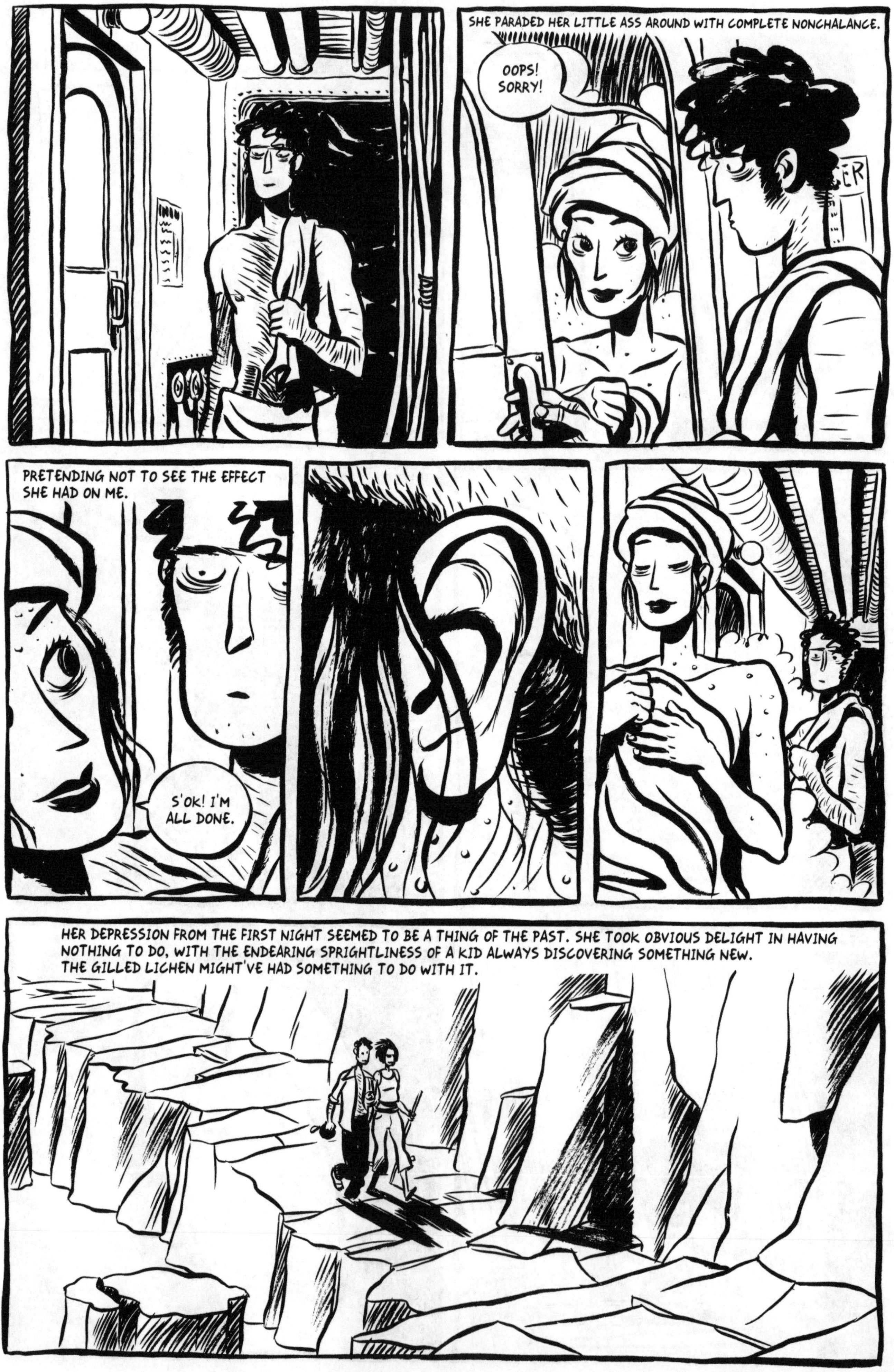
SHE PARADED HER LITTLE ASS AROUND WITH COMPLETE NONCHALANCE.
OOPS! SORRY!
PRETENDING NOT TO SEE THE EFFECT SHE HAD ON ME.
S'OK! I'M ALL DONE.
HER DEPRESSION FROM THE FIRST NIGHT SEEMED TO BE A THING OF THE PAST. SHE TOOK OBVIOUS DELIGHT IN HAVING NOTHING TO DO, WITH THE ENDEARING SPRIGHTLINESS OF A KID ALWAYS DISCOVERING SOMETHING NEW. THE GILLED LICHEN MIGHT'VE HAD SOMETHING TO DO WITH IT.

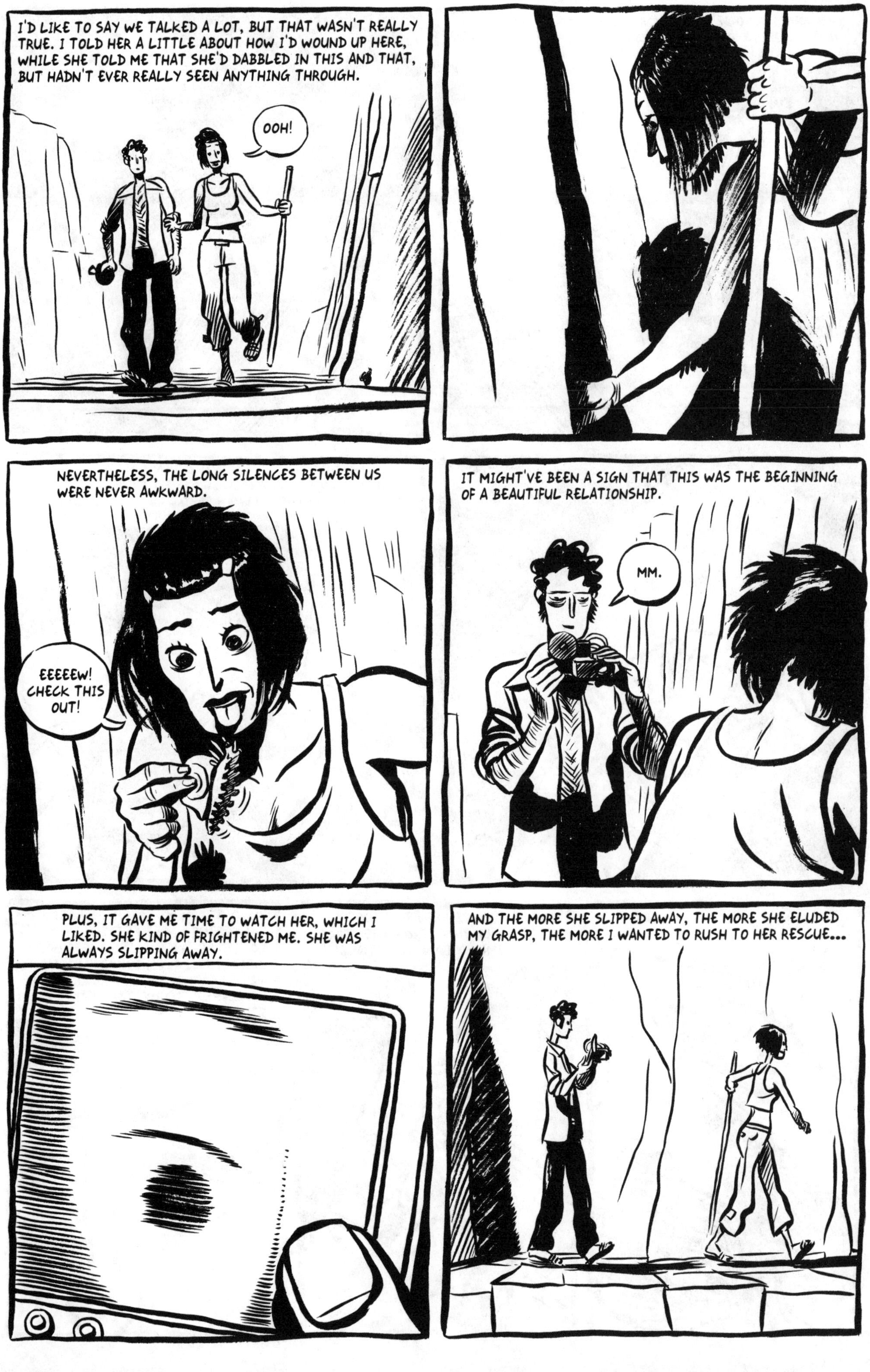
I'D LIKE TO SAY WE TALKED A LOT, BUT THAT WASN'T REALLY TRUE. I TOLD HER A LITTLE ABOUT HOW I'D WOUND UP HERE, WHILE SHE TOLD ME THAT SHE'D DABBLED IN THIS AND THAT, BUT HADN'T EVER REALLY SEEN ANYTHING THROUGH.
OOH!
NEVERTHELESS, THE LONG SILENCES BETWEEN US WERE NEVER AWKWARD.
EEEEEW! CHECK THIS OUT!
IT MIGHT'VE BEEN A SIGN THAT THIS WAS THE BEGINNING OF A BEAUTIFUL RELATIONSHIP.
MM.
PLUS, IT GAVE ME TIME TO WATCH HER, WHICH I LIKED. SHE KIND OF FRIGHTENED ME. SHE WAS ALWAYS SLIPPING AWAY.
AND THE MORE SHE SLIPPED AWAY, THE MORE SHE ELUDED MY GRASP, THE MORE I WANTED TO RUSH TO HER RESCUE...

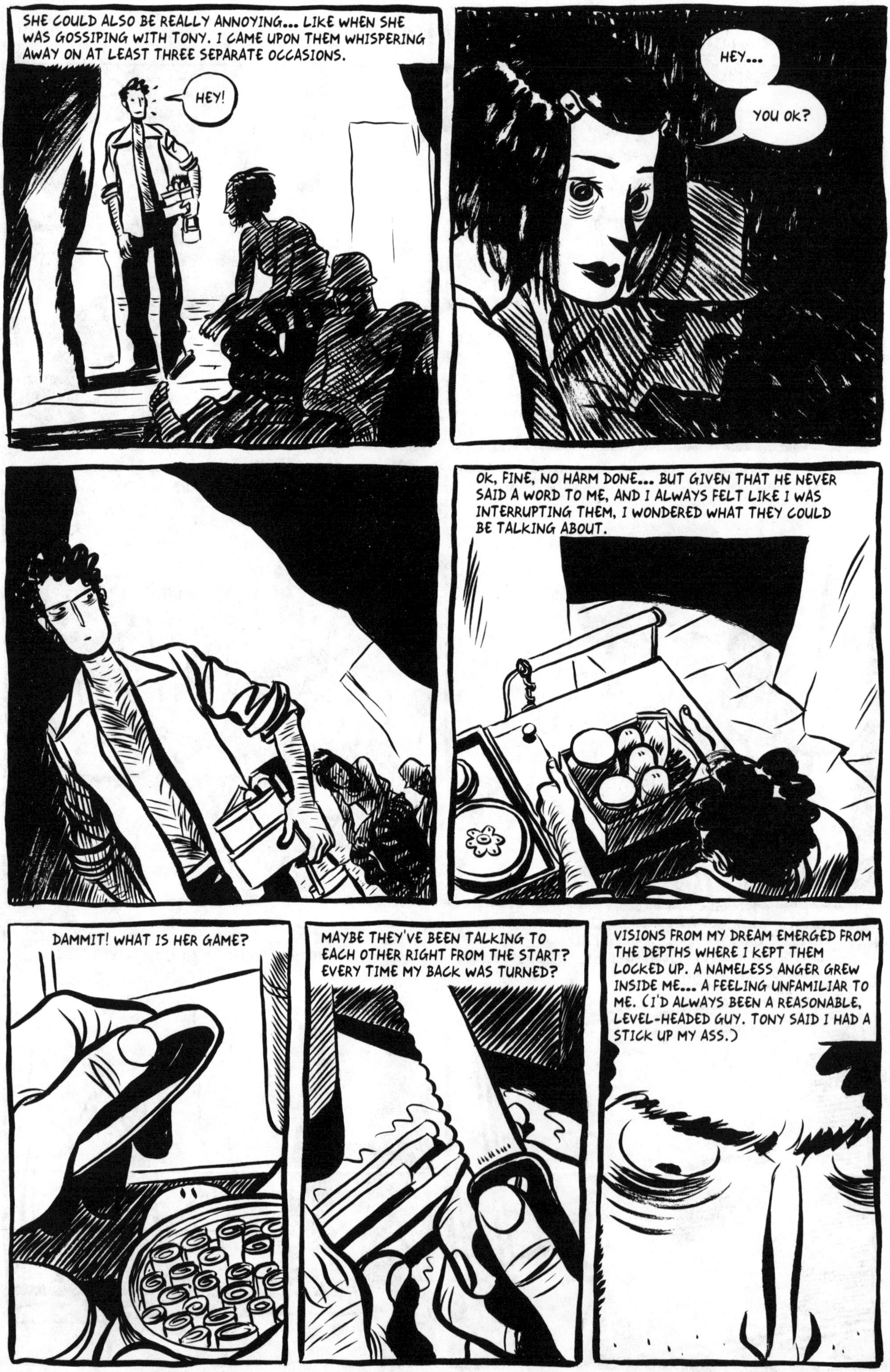
SHE COULD ALSO BE REALLY ANNOYING... LIKE WHEN SHE WAS GOSSIPING WITH TONY. I CAME UPON THEM WHISPERING AWAY ON AT LEAST THREE SEPARATE OCCASIONS.
HEY!
HEY...
YOU OK?
OK, FINE, NO HARM DONE... BUT GIVEN THAT HE NEVER SAID A WORD TO ME, AND I ALWAYS FELT LIKE I WAS INTERRUPTING THEM, I WONDERED WHAT THEY COULD BE TALKING ABOUT.
DAMMIT! WHAT IS HER GAME?
MAYBE THEY'VE BEEN TALKING TO EACH OTHER RIGHT FROM THE START? EVERY TIME MY BACK WAS TURNED?
VISIONS FROM MY DREAM EMERGED FROM THE DEPTHS WHERE I KEPT THEM LOCKED UP. A NAMELESS ANGER GREW INSIDE ME... A FEELING UNFAMILIAR TO ME. (I'D ALWAYS BEEN A REASONABLE, LEVEL-HEADED GUY. TONY SAID I HAD A STICK UP MY ASS.)

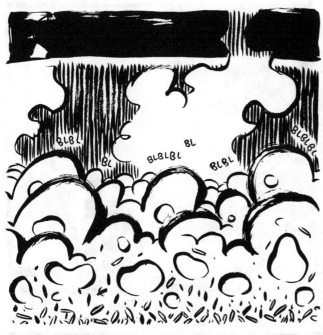

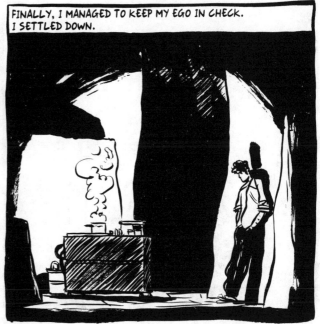

BLBL
BL
BLBLBL
BL
BLBL
BLBLBL
FINALLY, I MANAGED TO KEEP MY EGO IN CHECK.
I SETTLED DOWN.
THERE'S NOTHING GOING ON BETWEEN THEM...
NOTHING GOING ON BETWEEN ANY OF US,
IN FACT.
PEOPLE TALK. THAT'S WHAT THEY DO.

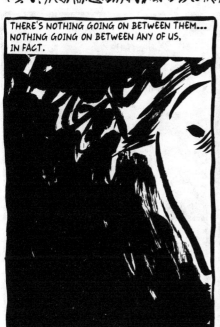

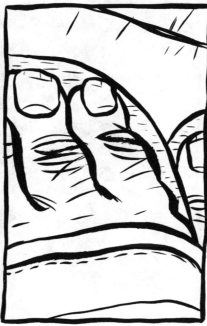

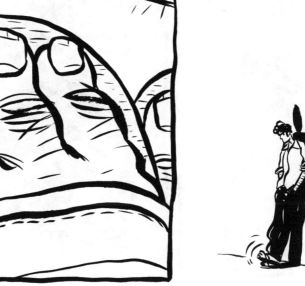

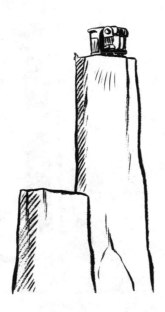

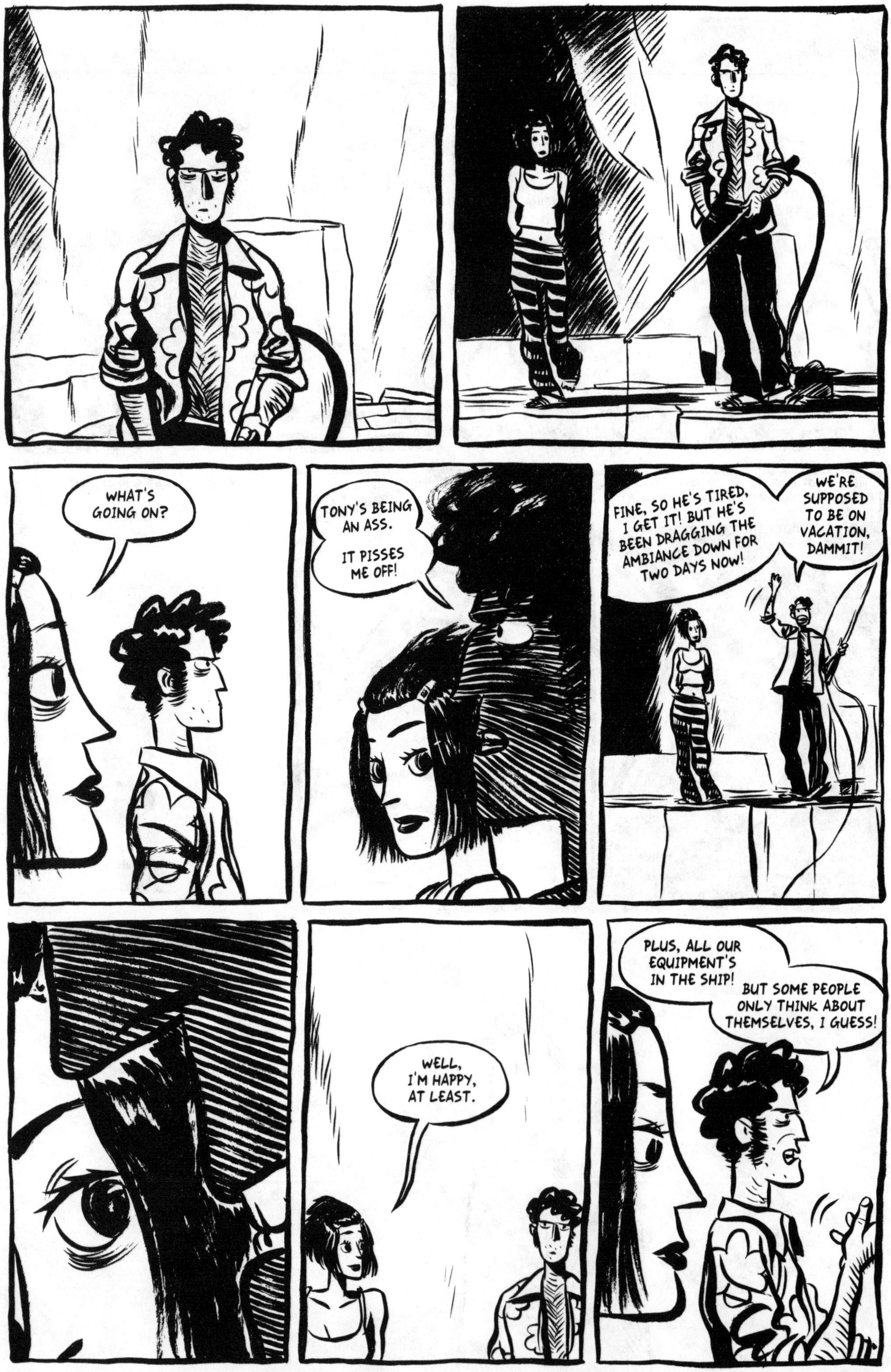
WHAT'S GOING ON?
TONY'S BEING AN ASS.
IT PISSES ME OFF!
FINE, SO HE'S TIRED, I GET IT! BUT HE'S BEEN DRAGGING THE AMBIANCE DOWN FOR TWO DAYS NOW!
WE'RE SUPPOSED TO BE ON VACATION, DAMMIT!
WELL, I'M HAPPY, AT LEAST.
PLUS, ALL OUR EQUIPMENT'S IN THE SHIP!
BUT SOME PEOPLE ONLY THINK ABOUT THEMSELVES, I GUESS!

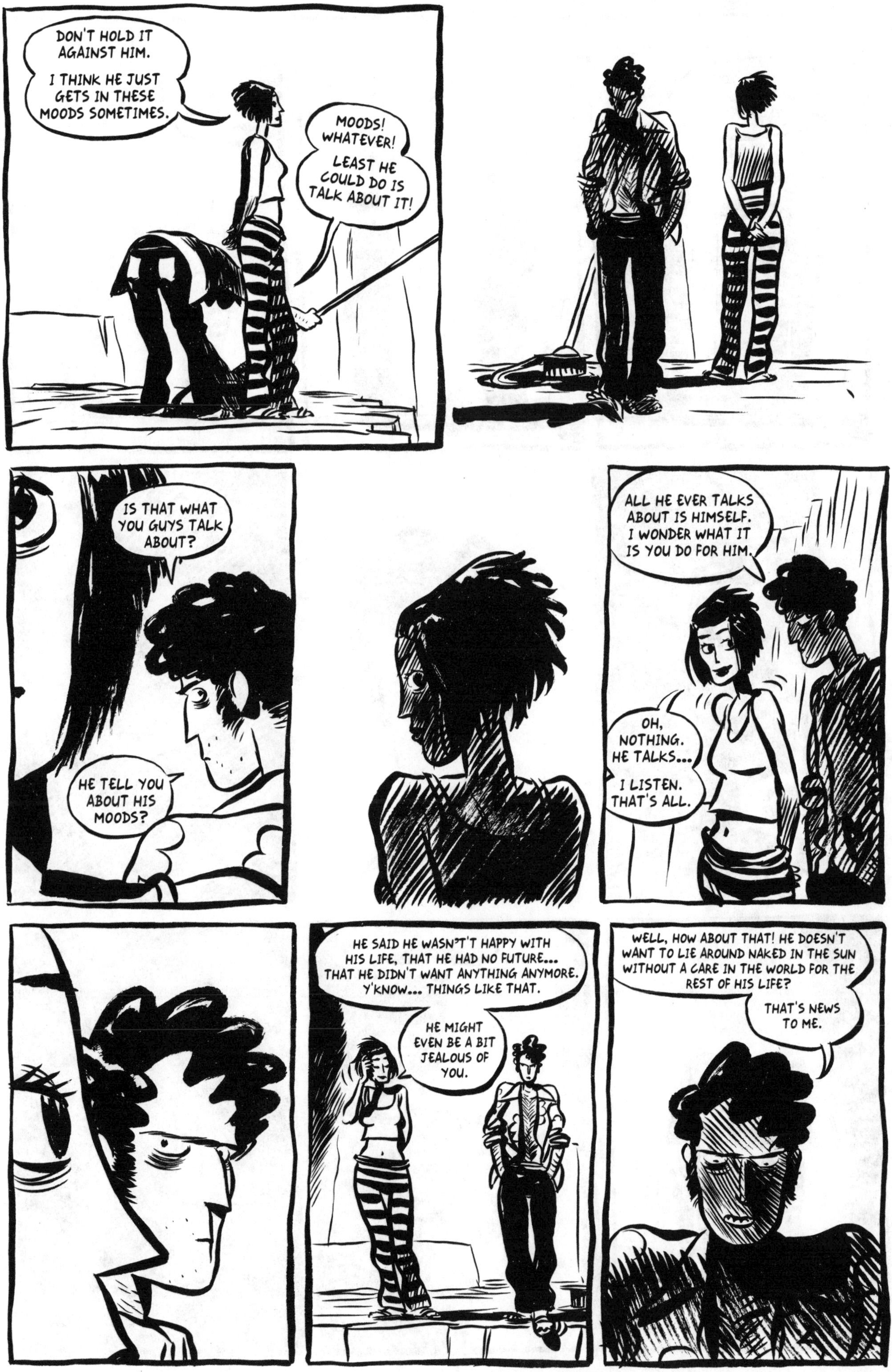
DON'T HOLD IT AGAINST HIM.
I THINK HE JUST GETS IN THESE MOODS SOMETIMES.
MOODS! WHATEVER!
LEAST HE COULD DO IS TALK ABOUT IT!
IS THAT WHAT YOU GUYS TALK ABOUT?
HE TELL YOU ABOUT HIS MOODS?
ALL HE EVER TALKS ABOUT IS HIMSELF. I WONDER WHAT IT IS YOU DO FOR HIM.
OH, NOTHING. HE TALKS... I LISTEN. THAT'S ALL.
HE SAID HE WASN'T'T HAPPY WITH HIS LIFE, THAT HE HAD NO FUTURE... THAT HE DIDN'T WANT ANYTHING ANYMORE. Y'KNOW... THINGS LIKE THAT.
HE MIGHT EVEN BE A BIT JEALOUS OF YOU.
WELL, HOW ABOUT THAT! HE DOESN'T WANT TO LIE AROUND NAKED IN THE SUN WITHOUT A CARE IN THE WORLD FOR THE REST OF HIS LIFE?
THAT'S NEWS TO ME.

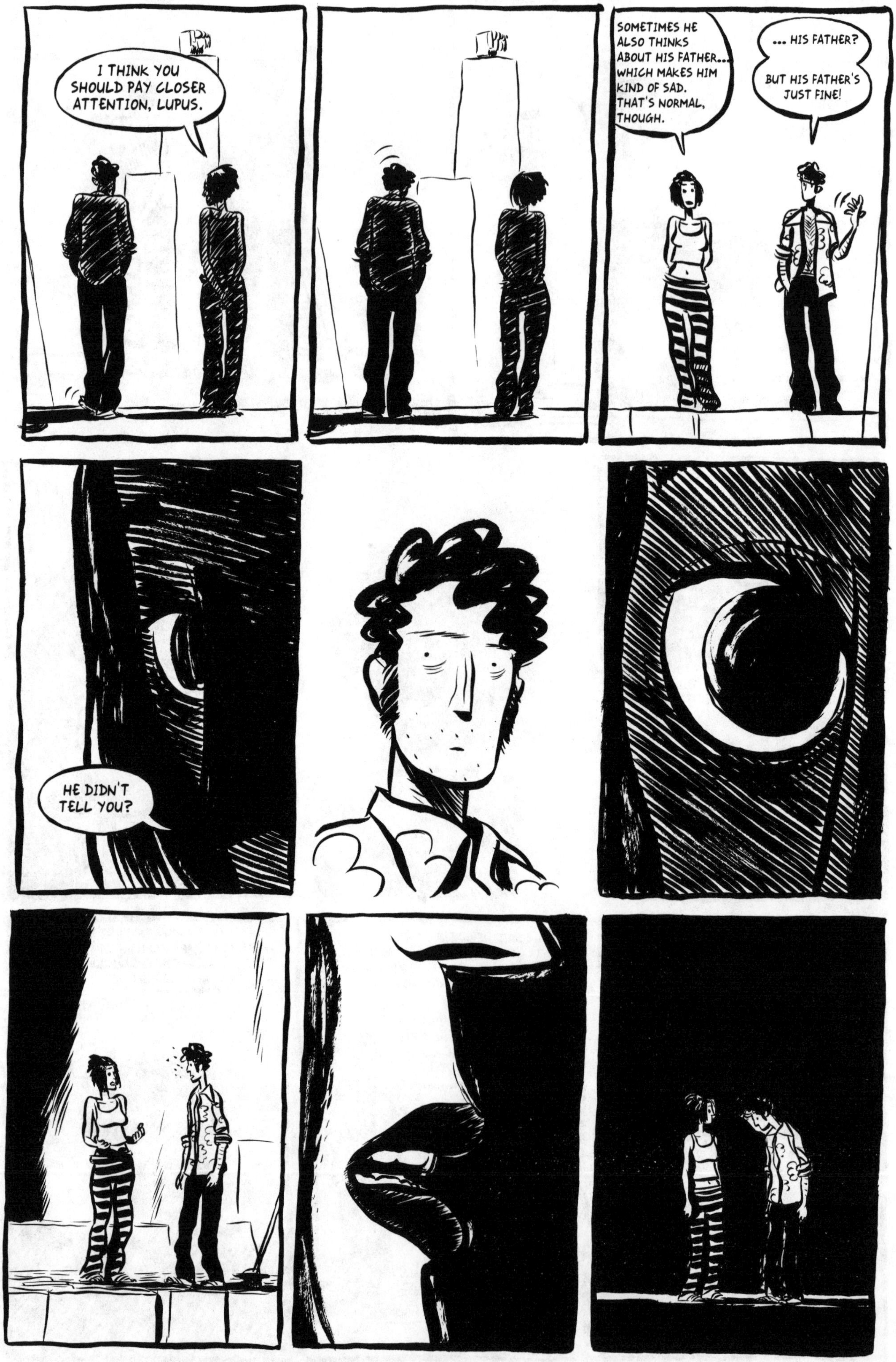
I THINK YOU SHOULD PAY CLOSER ATTENTION, LUPUS.
SOMETIMES HE ALSO THINKS ABOUT HIS FATHER... WHICH MAKES HIM KIND OF SAD. THAT'S NORMAL, THOUGH.
... HIS FATHER?
BUT HIS FATHER'S JUST FINE!
HE DIDN'T TELL YOU?

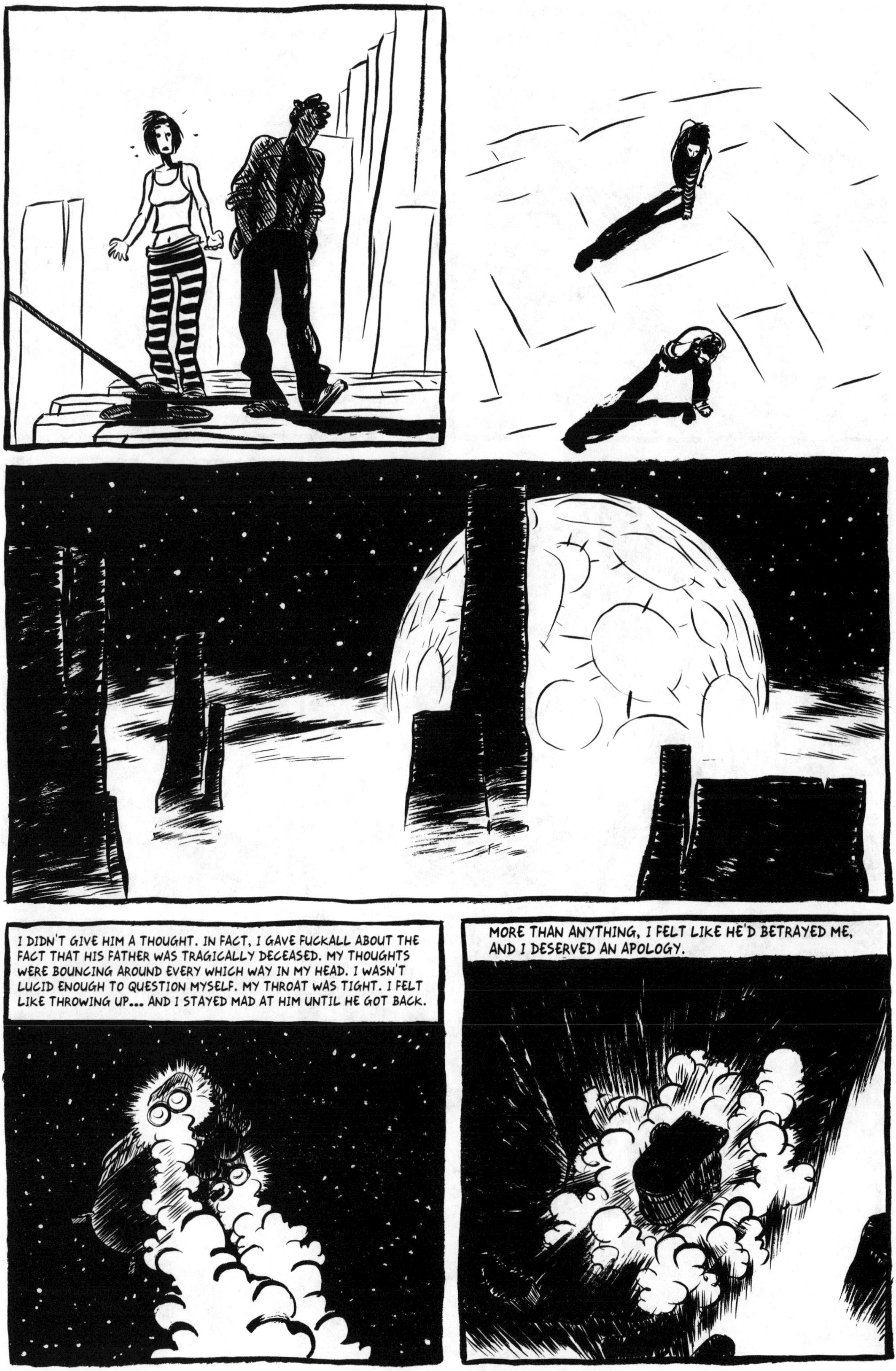
I DIDN'T GIVE HIM A THOUGHT. IN FACT, I GAVE FUCKALL ABOUT THE FACT THAT HIS FATHER WAS TRAGICALLY DECEASED. MY THOUGHTS WERE BOUNCING AROUND EVERY WHICH WAY IN MY HEAD. I WASN'T LUCID ENOUGH TO QUESTION MYSELF. MY THROAT WAS TIGHT. I FELT LIKE THROWING UP... AND I STAYED MAD AT HIM UNTIL HE GOT BACK.
MORE THAN ANYTHING, I FELT LIKE HE'D BETRAYED ME, AND I DESERVED AN APOLOGY.

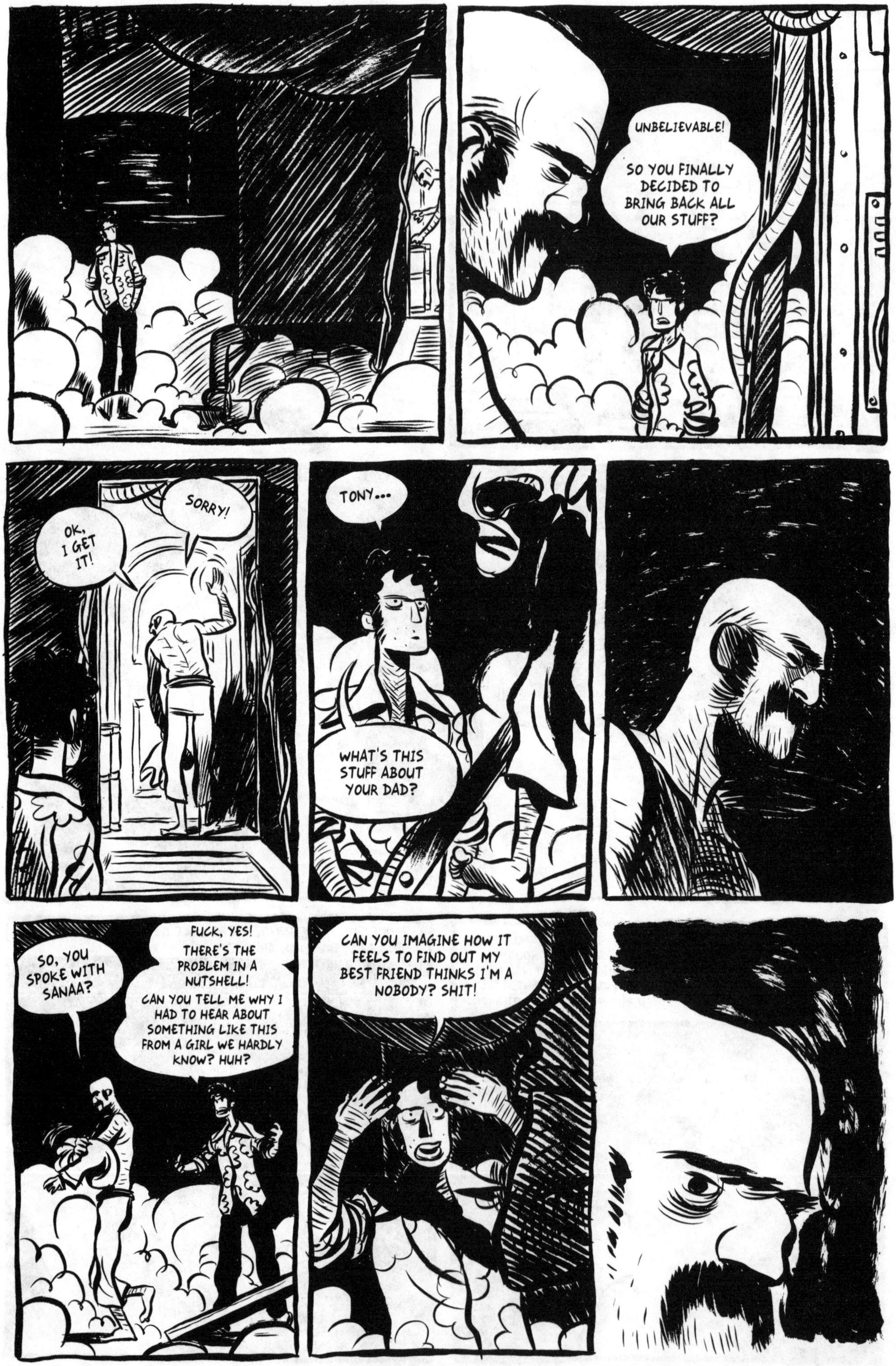
UNBELIEVABLE!
SO YOU FINALLY DECIDED TO BRING BACK ALL OUR STUFF?
OK, I GET IT!
SORRY!
TONY...
WHAT'S THIS STUFF ABOUT YOUR DAD?
SO, YOU SPOKE WITH SANAA?
FUCK, YES!
THERE'S THE PROBLEM IN A NUTSHELL!
CAN YOU TELL ME WHY I HAD TO HEAR ABOUT SOMETHING LIKE THIS FROM A GIRL WE HARDLY KNOW? HUH?
CAN YOU IMAGINE HOW IT FEELS TO FIND OUT MY BEST FRIEND THINKS I'M A NOBODY? SHIT!

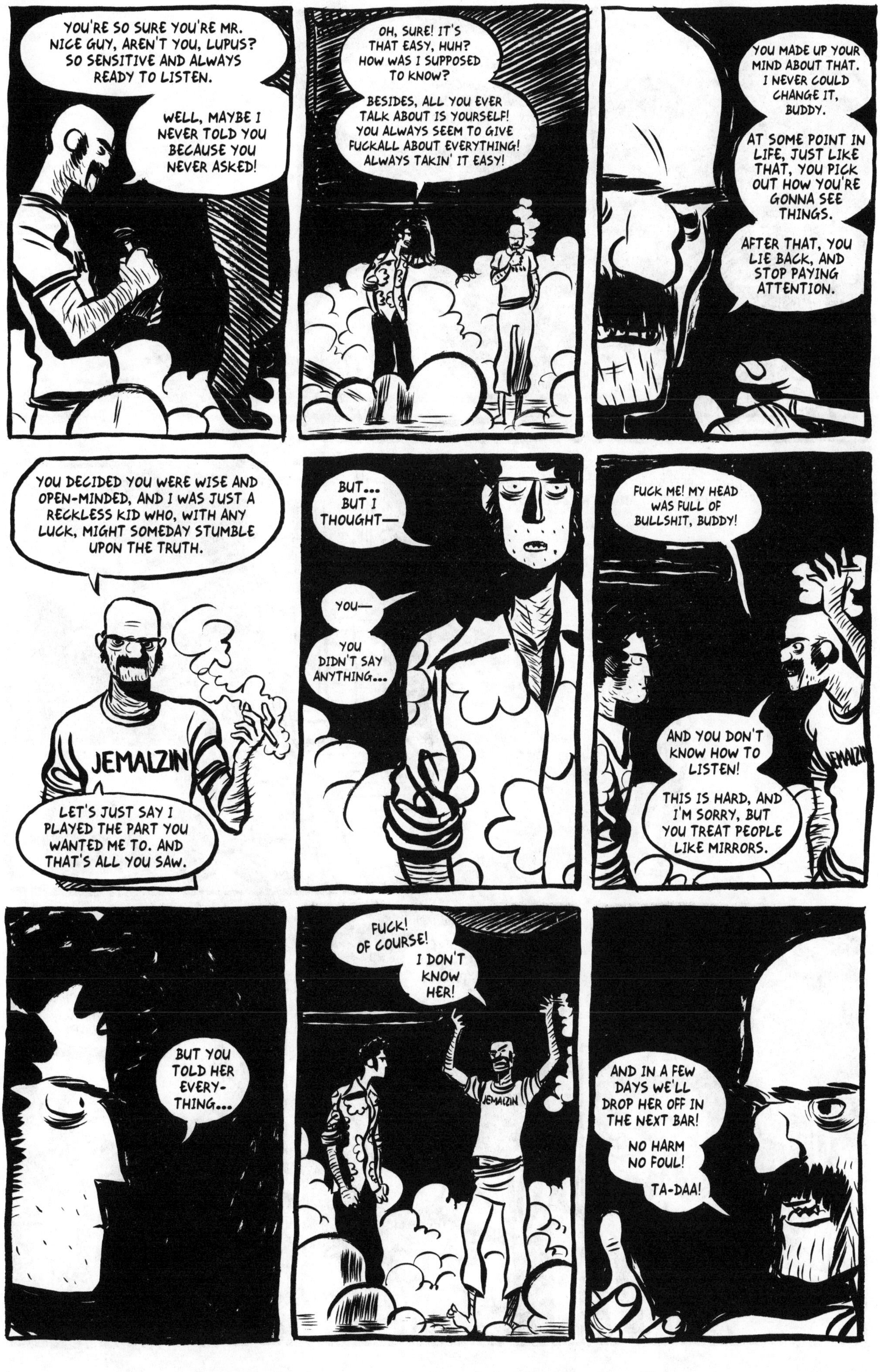
YOU'RE SO SURE YOU'RE MR. NICE GUY, AREN'T YOU, LUPUS? SO SENSITIVE AND ALWAYS READY TO LISTEN.
WELL, MAYBE I NEVER TOLD YOU BECAUSE YOU NEVER ASKED!
OH, SURE! IT'S THAT EASY, HUH? HOW WAS I SUPPOSED TO KNOW?
BESIDES, ALL YOU EVER TALK ABOUT IS YOURSELF! YOU ALWAYS SEEM TO GIVE FUCKALL ABOUT EVERYTHING! ALWAYS TAKIN' IT EASY!
YOU MADE UP YOUR MIND ABOUT THAT. I NEVER COULD CHANGE IT, BUDDY.
AT SOME POINT IN LIFE, JUST LIKE THAT, YOU PICK OUT HOW YOU'RE GONNA SEE THINGS.
AFTER THAT, YOU LIE BACK, AND STOP PAYING ATTENTION.
YOU DECIDED YOU WERE WISE AND OPEN-MINDED, AND I WAS JUST A RECKLESS KID WHO, WITH ANY LUCK, MIGHT SOMEDAY STUMBLE UPON THE TRUTH.
JEMALZIN
LET'S JUST SAY I PLAYED THE PART YOU WANTED ME TO. AND THAT'S ALL YOU SAW.
BUT... BUT I THOUGHT—
YOU—
YOU DIDN'T SAY ANYTHING...
FUCK ME! MY HEAD WAS FULL OF BULLSHIT, BUDDY!
AND YOU DON'T KNOW HOW TO LISTEN!
THIS IS HARD, AND I'M SORRY, BUT YOU TREAT PEOPLE LIKE MIRRORS.
JEMALZIN
BUT YOU TOLD HER EVERY-THING...
FUCK! OF COURSE!
I DON'T KNOW HER!
JEMALZIN
AND IN A FEW DAYS WE'LL DROP HER OFF IN THE NEXT BAR!
NO HARM NO FOUL!
TA-DAA!

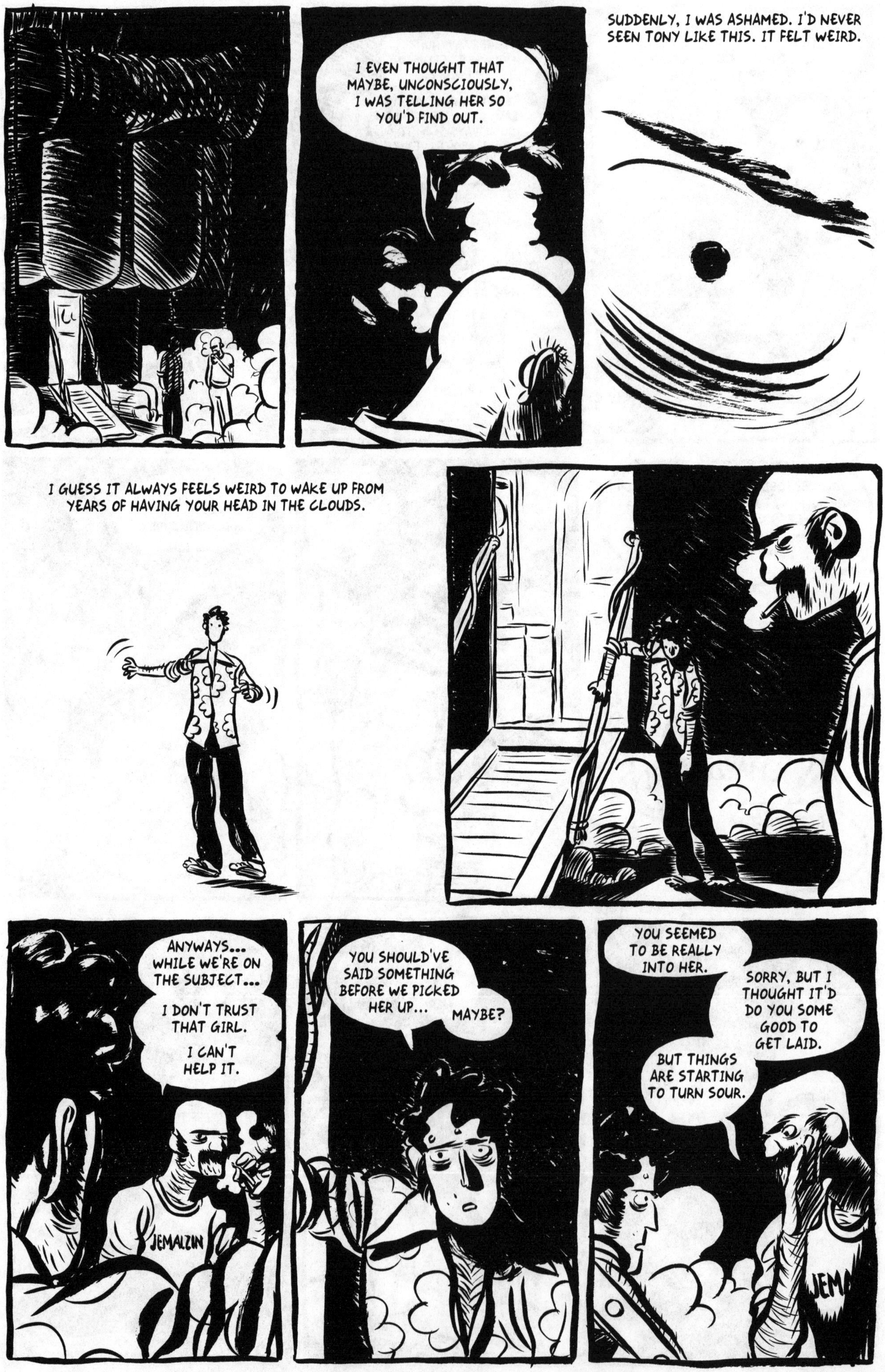
I EVEN THOUGHT THAT MAYBE, UNCONSCIOUSLY, I WAS TELLING HER SO YOU'D FIND OUT.
SUDDENLY, I WAS ASHAMED. I'D NEVER SEEN TONY LIKE THIS. IT FELT WEIRD.
I GUESS IT ALWAYS FEELS WEIRD TO WAKE UP FROM YEARS OF HAVING YOUR HEAD IN THE CLOUDS.
ANYWAYS... WHILE WE'RE ON THE SUBJECT...
I DON'T TRUST THAT GIRL.
I CAN'T HELP IT.
JEMALZIN
YOU SHOULD'VE SAID SOMETHING BEFORE WE PICKED HER UP...
MAYBE?
YOU SEEMED TO BE REALLY INTO HER.
SORRY, BUT I THOUGHT IT'D DO YOU SOME GOOD TO GET LAID.
BUT THINGS ARE STARTING TO TURN SOUR.
JEM

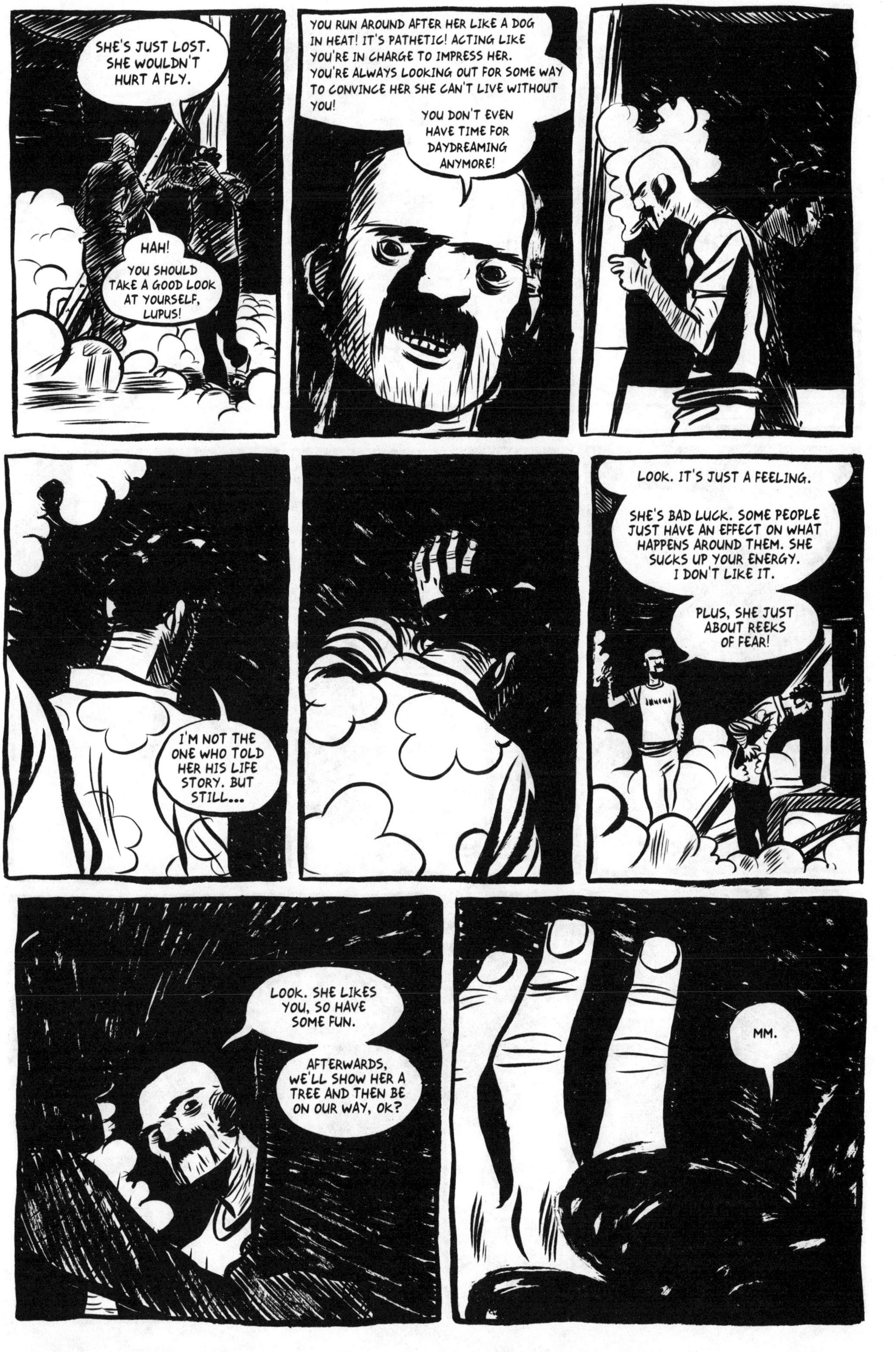

SHE'S JUST LOST. SHE WOULDN'T HURT A FLY.
HAH! YOU SHOULD TAKE A GOOD LOOK AT YOURSELF, LUPUS!
YOU RUN AROUND AFTER HER LIKE A DOG IN HEAT! IT'S PATHETIC! ACTING LIKE YOU'RE IN CHARGE TO IMPRESS HER. YOU'RE ALWAYS LOOKING OUT FOR SOME WAY TO CONVINCE HER SHE CAN'T LIVE WITHOUT YOU!
YOU DON'T EVEN HAVE TIME FOR DAYDREAMING ANYMORE!
I'M NOT THE ONE WHO TOLD HER HIS LIFE STORY. BUT STILL...
LOOK. IT'S JUST A FEELING.
SHE'S BAD LUCK. SOME PEOPLE JUST HAVE AN EFFECT ON WHAT HAPPENS AROUND THEM. SHE SUCKS UP YOUR ENERGY. I DON'T LIKE IT.
PLUS, SHE JUST ABOUT REEKS OF FEAR!
LOOK. SHE LIKES YOU, SO HAVE SOME FUN.
AFTERWARDS, WE'LL SHOW HER A TREE AND THEN BE ON OUR WAY, OK?
MM.

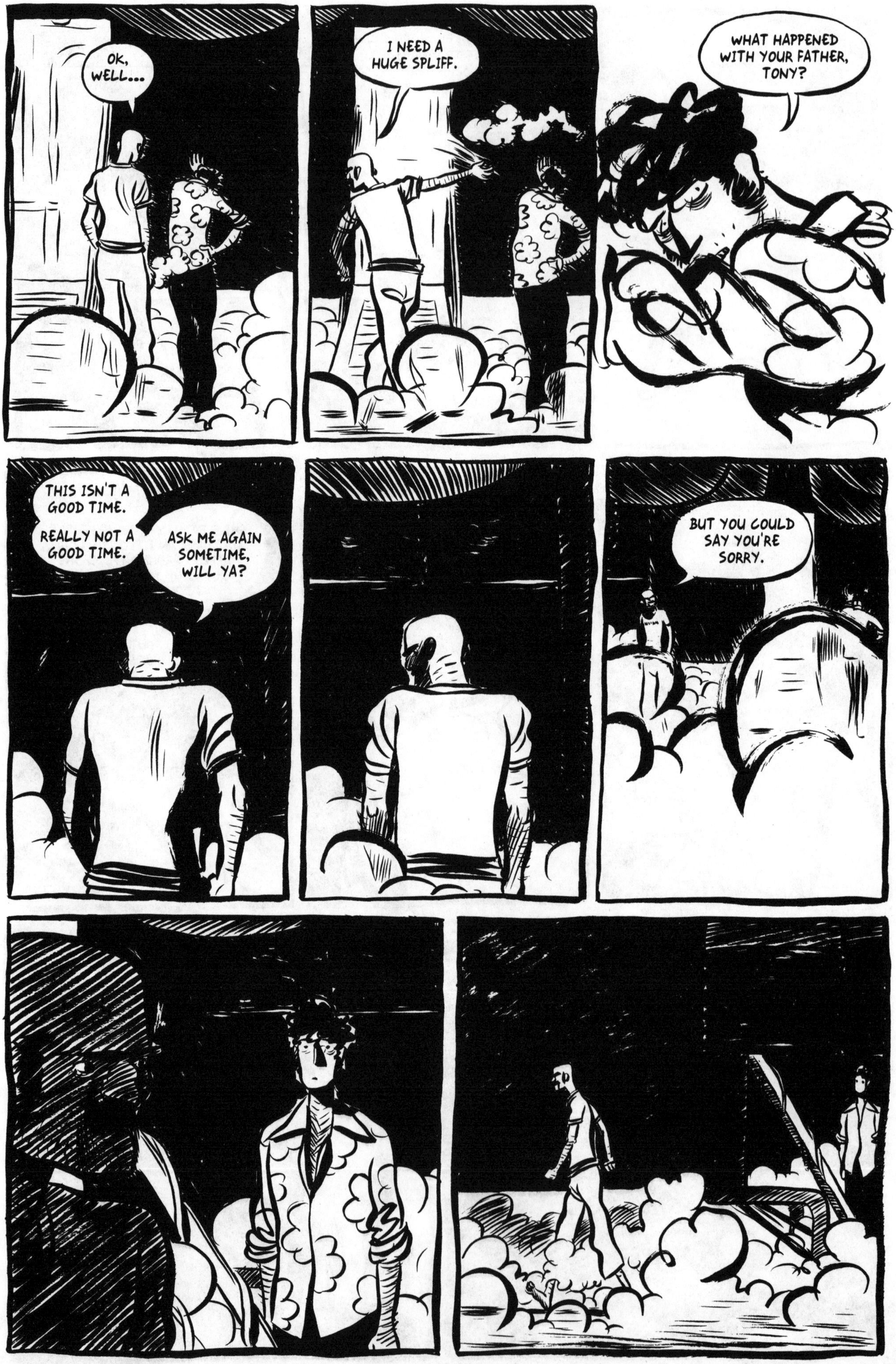
OK, WELL...
I NEED A HUGE SPLIFF.
WHAT HAPPENED WITH YOUR FATHER, TONY?
THIS ISN'T A GOOD TIME.
REALLY NOT A GOOD TIME.
ASK ME AGAIN SOMETIME, WILL YA?
BUT YOU COULD SAY YOU'RE SORRY.

GRAT GRAT
GRAT GRAT GRAT
HHSSSSSSS

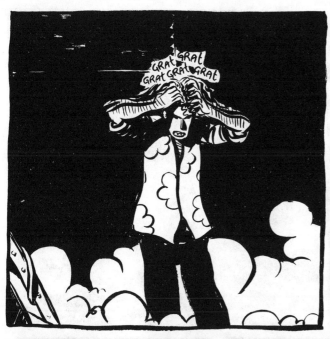

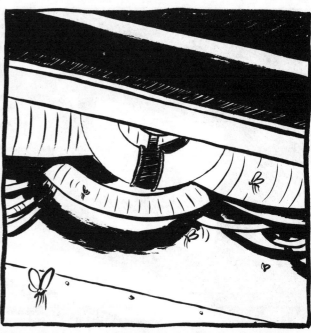

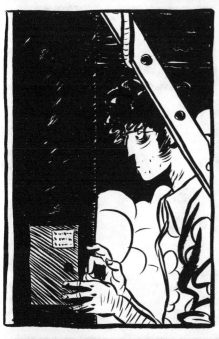

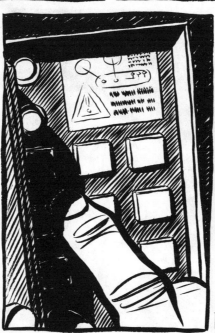

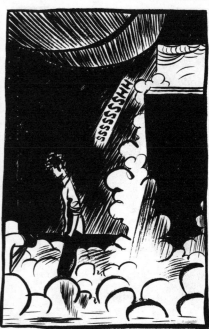

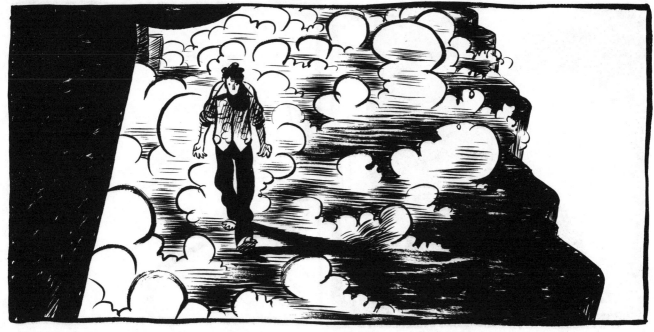

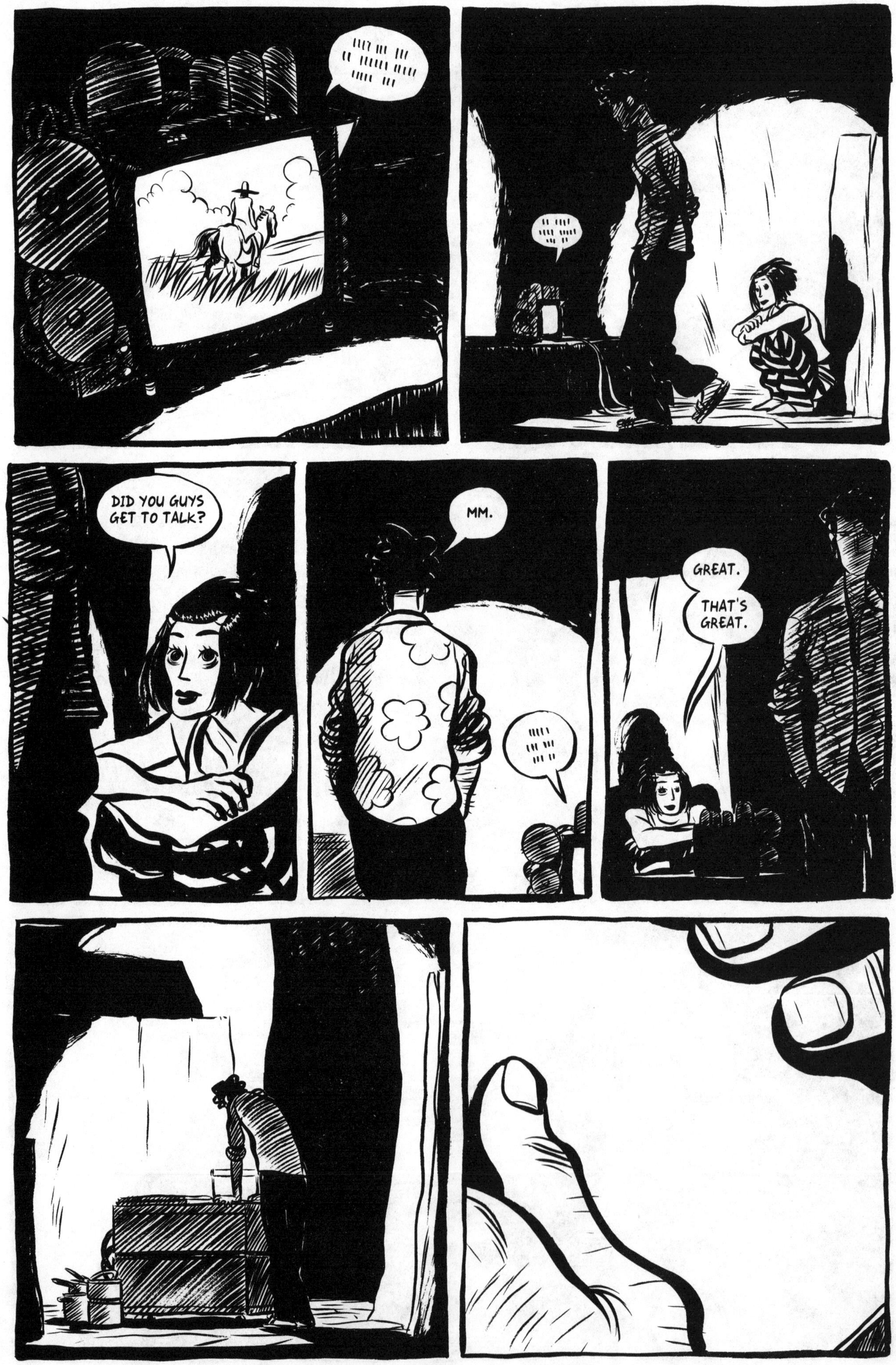
DID YOU GUYS GET TO TALK?
MM.
GREAT.
THAT'S GREAT.

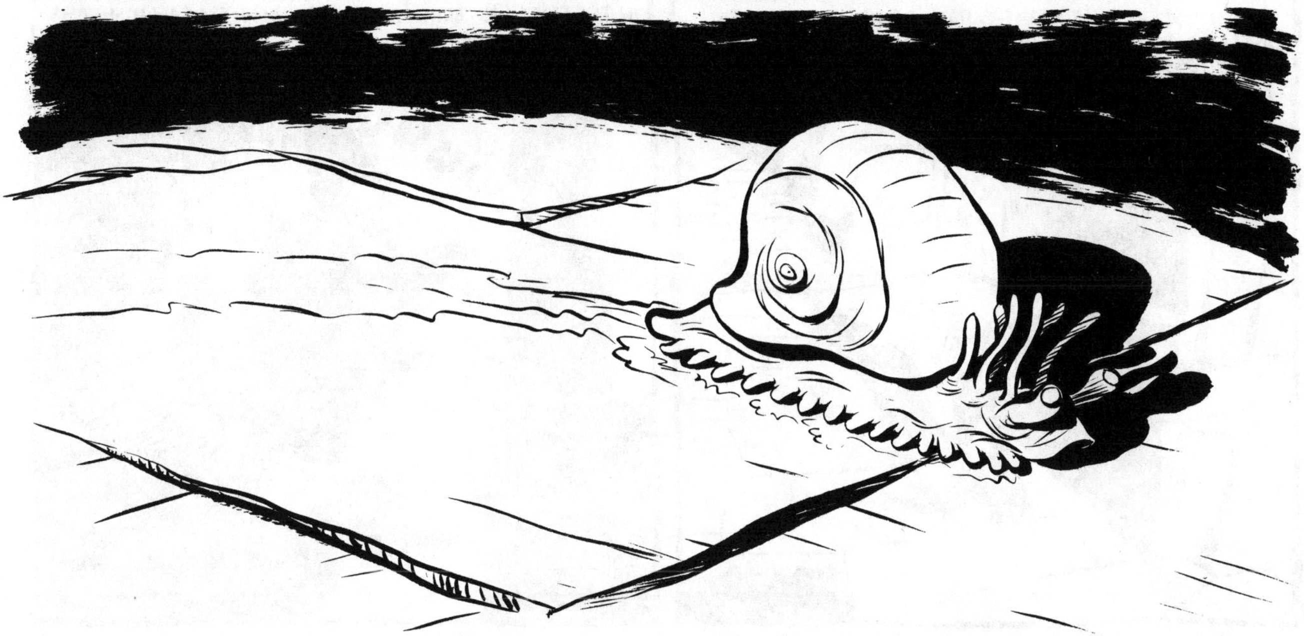

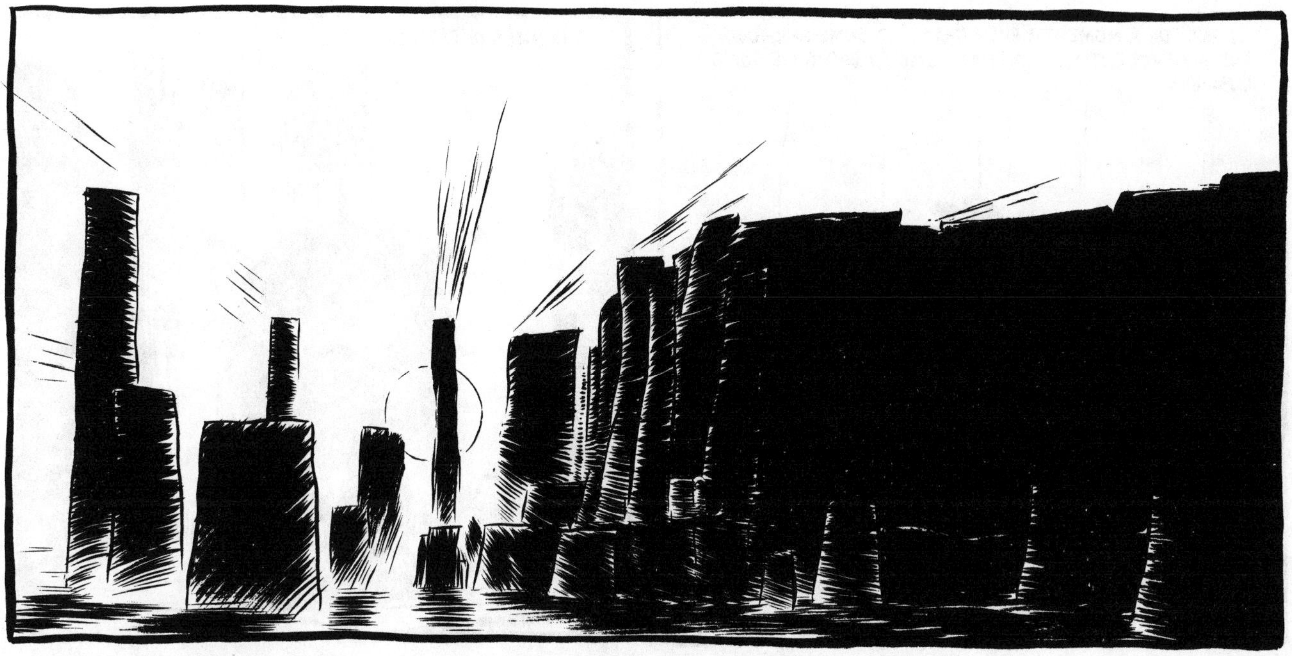

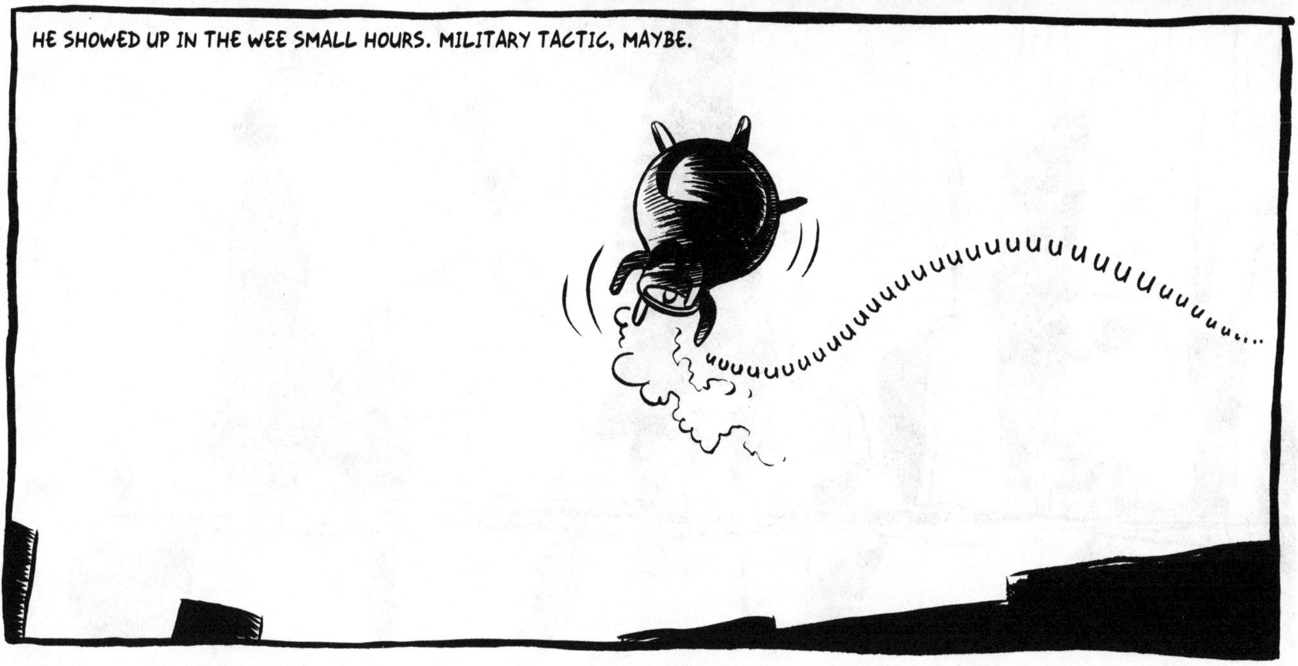
HE SHOWED UP IN THE WEE SMALL HOURS. MILITARY TACTIC, MAYBE.
uuuuuuuuuuuuuuuuuuuuuuuuuuuuuuuuuuuuuuuuu...

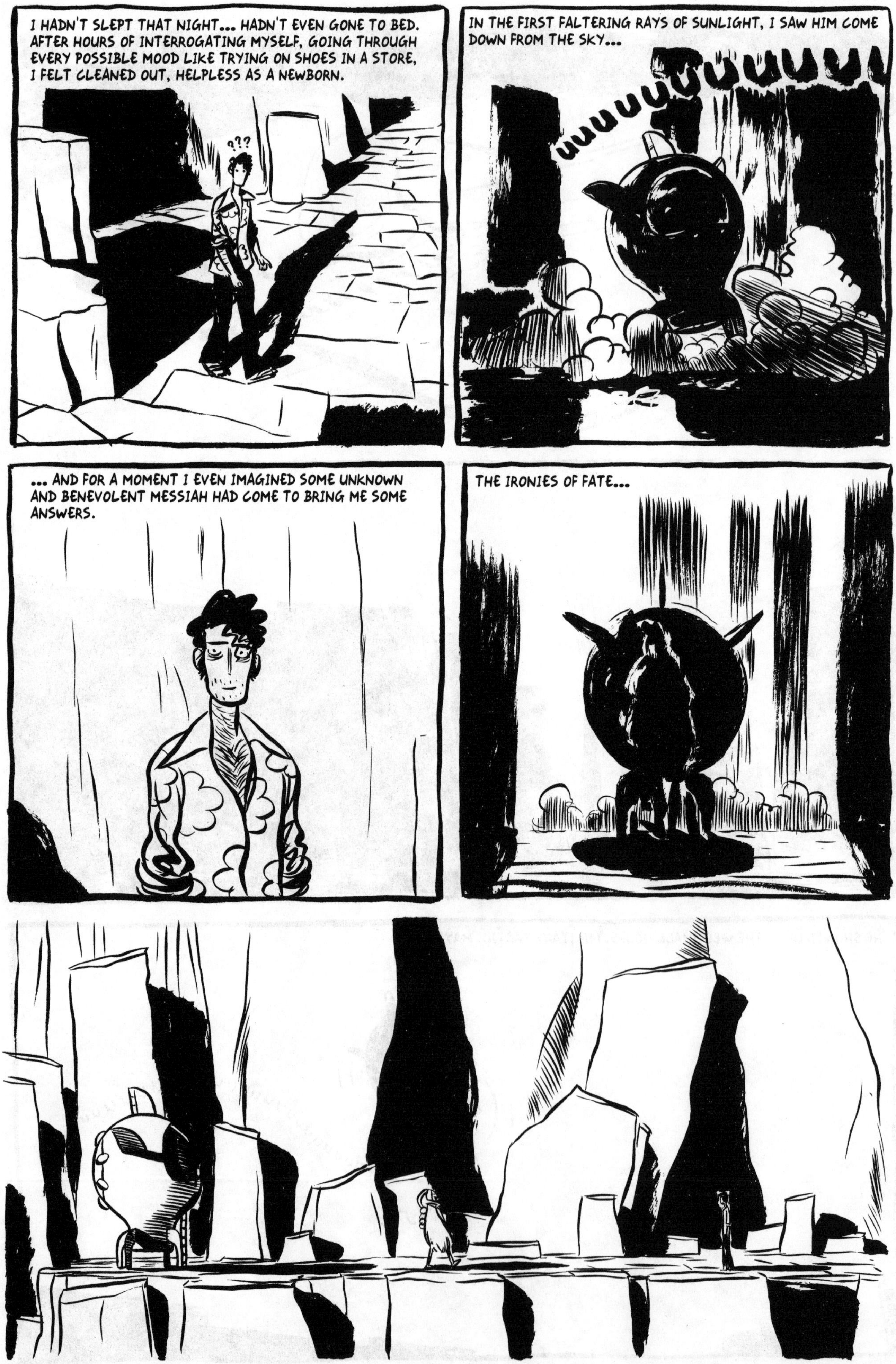
I HADN'T SLEPT THAT NIGHT... HADN'T EVEN GONE TO BED. AFTER HOURS OF INTERROGATING MYSELF, GOING THROUGH EVERY POSSIBLE MOOD LIKE TRYING ON SHOES IN A STORE, I FELT CLEANED OUT, HELPLESS AS A NEWBORN.
???
??
IN THE FIRST FALTERING RAYS OF SUNLIGHT, I SAW HIM COME DOWN FROM THE SKY...
UUUUUUUUUUUUUU
... AND FOR A MOMENT I EVEN IMAGINED SOME UNKNOWN AND BENEVOLENT MESSIAH HAD COME TO BRING ME SOME ANSWERS.
THE IRONIES OF FATE...

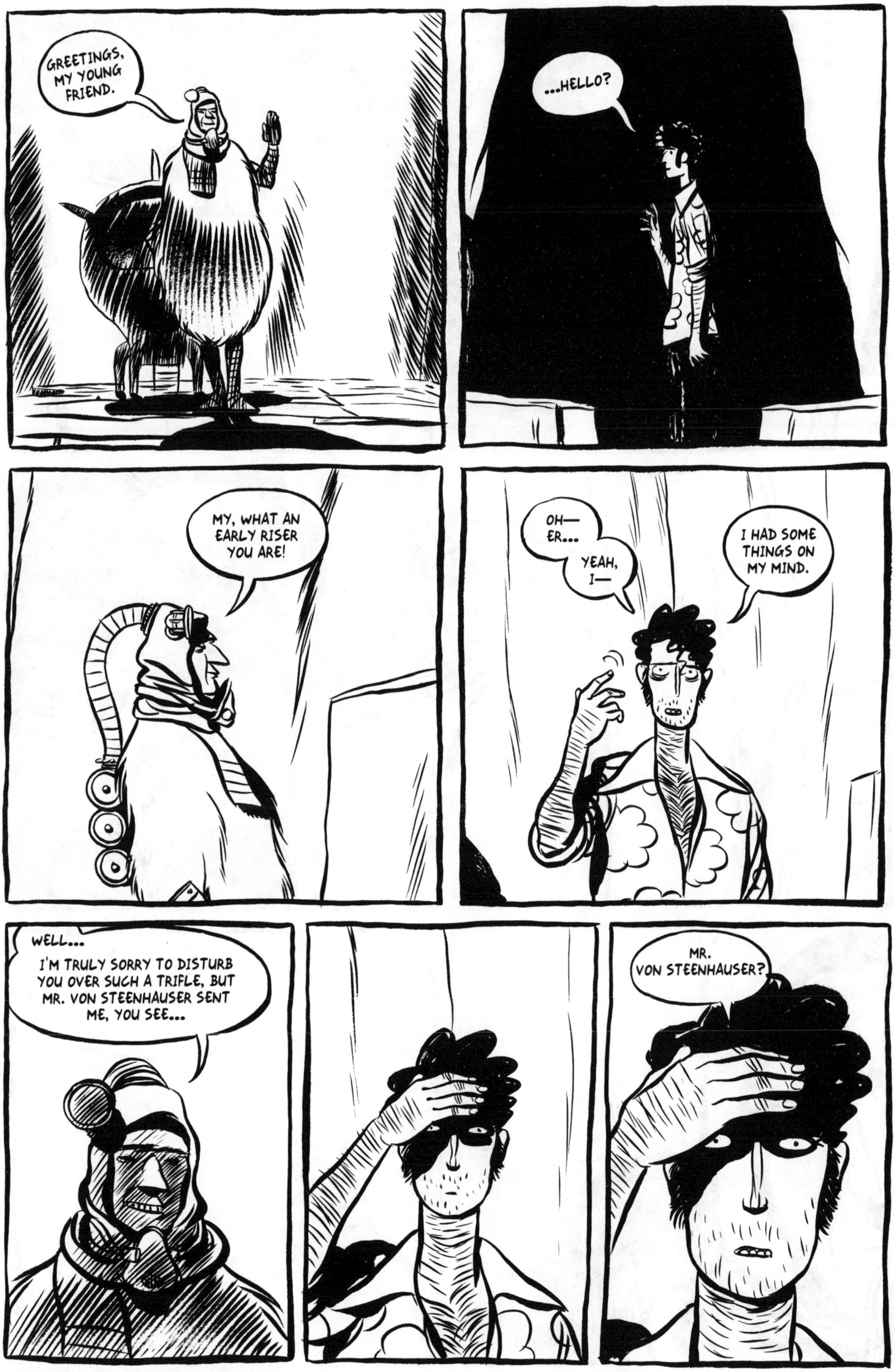
GREETINGS, MY YOUNG FRIEND.
...HELLO?
MY, WHAT AN EARLY RISER YOU ARE!
OH— ER...
YEAH, I—
I HAD SOME THINGS ON MY MIND.
WELL...
I'M TRULY SORRY TO DISTURB YOU OVER SUCH A TRIFLE, BUT MR. VON STEENHAUSER SENT ME, YOU SEE...
MR. VON STEENHAUSER?

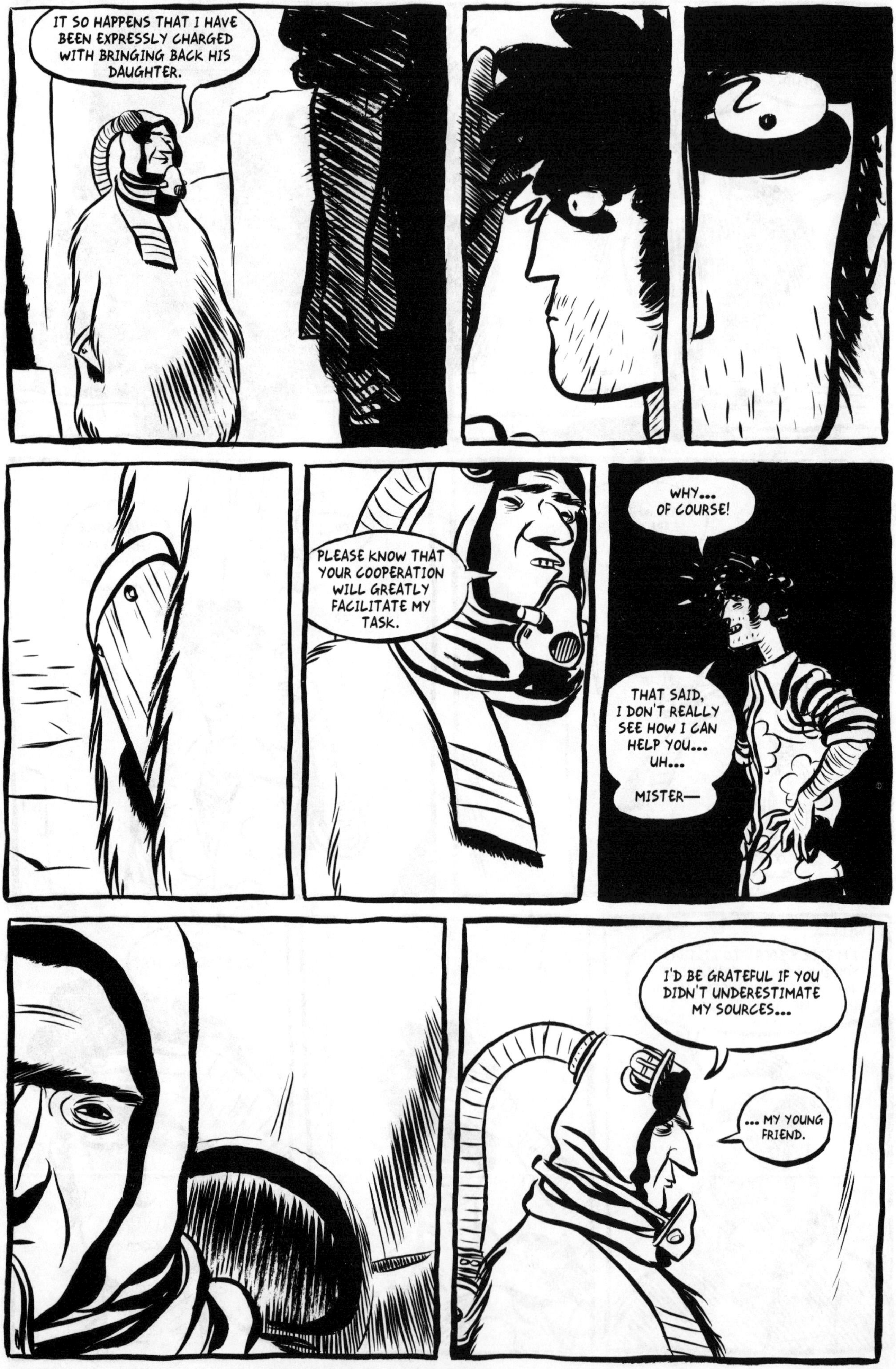
IT SO HAPPENS THAT I HAVE BEEN EXPRESSLY CHARGED WITH BRINGING BACK HIS DAUGHTER.
PLEASE KNOW THAT YOUR COOPERATION WILL GREATLY FACILITATE MY TASK.
WHY... OF COURSE!
THAT SAID, I DON'T REALLY SEE HOW I CAN HELP YOU... UH...
MISTER—
I'D BE GRATEFUL IF YOU DIDN'T UNDERESTIMATE MY SOURCES...
... MY YOUNG FRIEND.

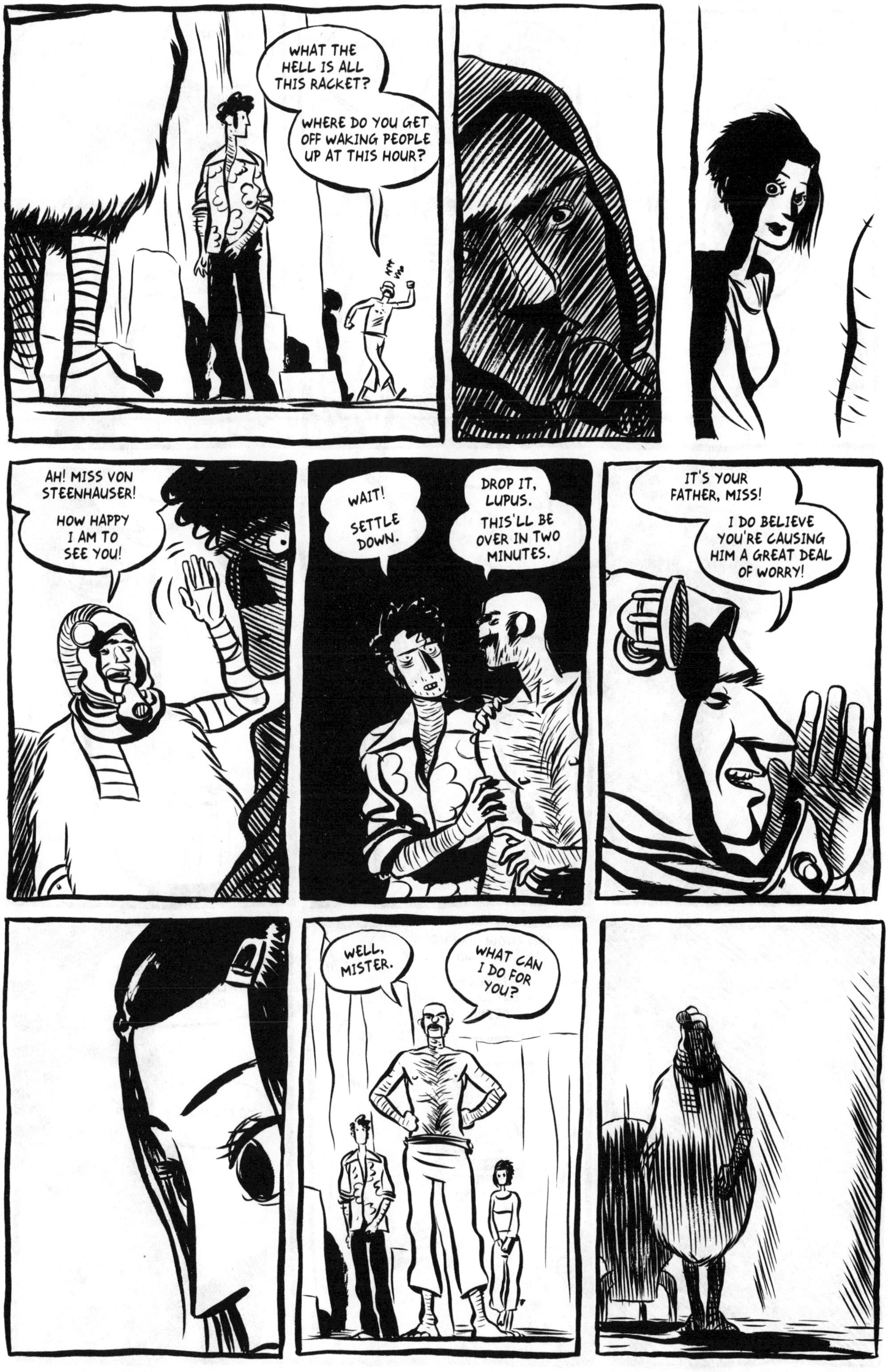
WHAT THE HELL IS ALL THIS RACKET?
WHERE DO YOU GET OFF WAKING PEOPLE UP AT THIS HOUR?
AH! MISS VON STEENHAUSER!
HOW HAPPY I AM TO SEE YOU!
WAIT! SETTLE DOWN.
DROP IT, LUPUS.
THIS'LL BE OVER IN TWO MINUTES.
IT'S YOUR FATHER, MISS!
I DO BELIEVE YOU'RE CAUSING HIM A GREAT DEAL OF WORRY!
WELL, MISTER.
WHAT CAN I DO FOR YOU?

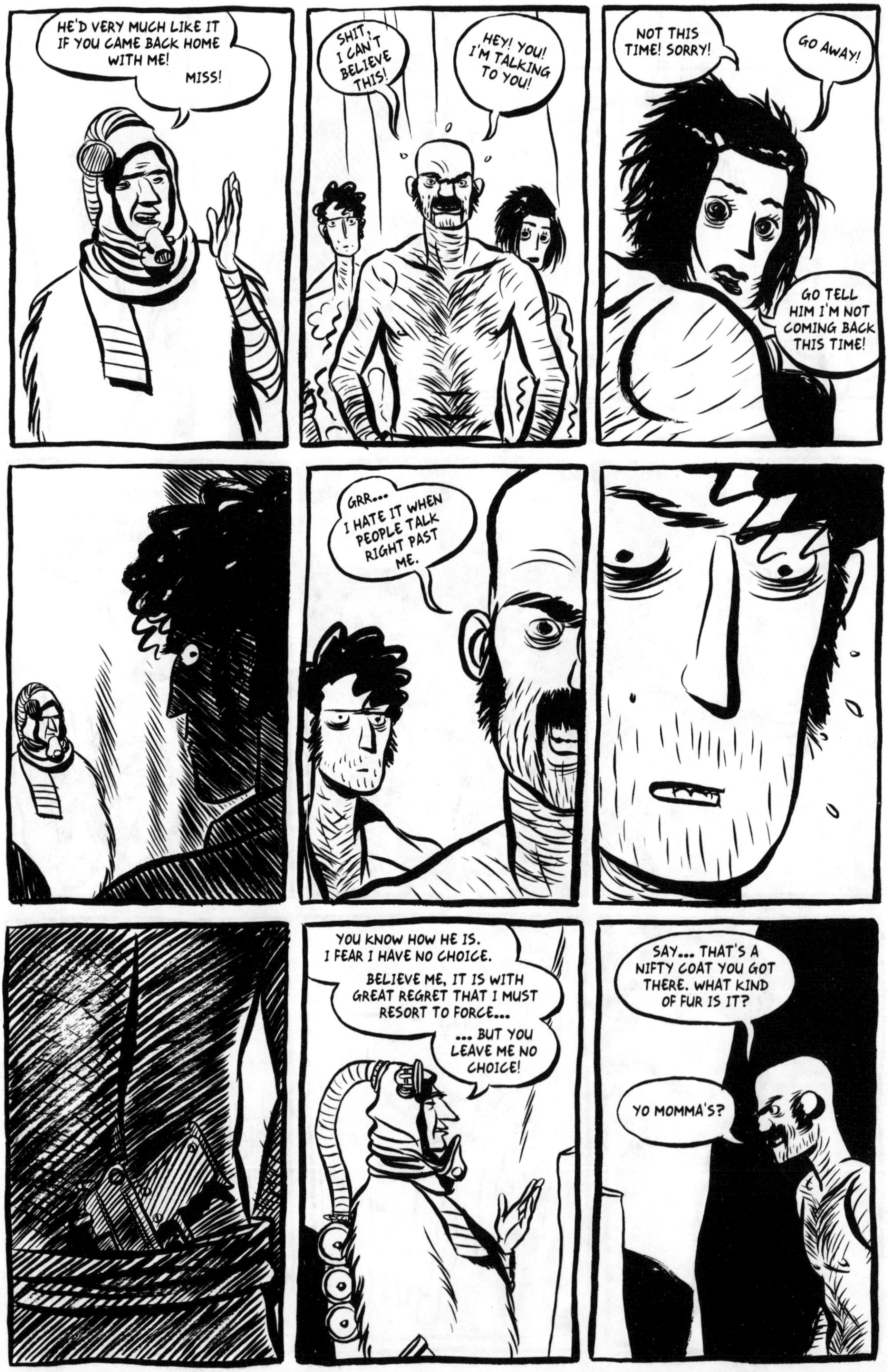

HE'D VERY MUCH LIKE IT IF YOU CAME BACK HOME WITH ME!
MISS!
SHIT, I CAN'T BELIEVE THIS!
HEY! YOU! I'M TALKING TO YOU!
NOT THIS TIME! SORRY!
GO AWAY!
GO TELL HIM I'M NOT COMING BACK THIS TIME!
GRR... I HATE IT WHEN PEOPLE TALK RIGHT PAST ME.
YOU KNOW HOW HE IS. I FEAR I HAVE NO CHOICE.
BELIEVE ME, IT IS WITH GREAT REGRET THAT I MUST RESORT TO FORCE...
... BUT YOU LEAVE ME NO CHOICE!
SAY... THAT'S A NIFTY COAT YOU GOT THERE. WHAT KIND OF FUR IS IT?
YO MOMMA'S?

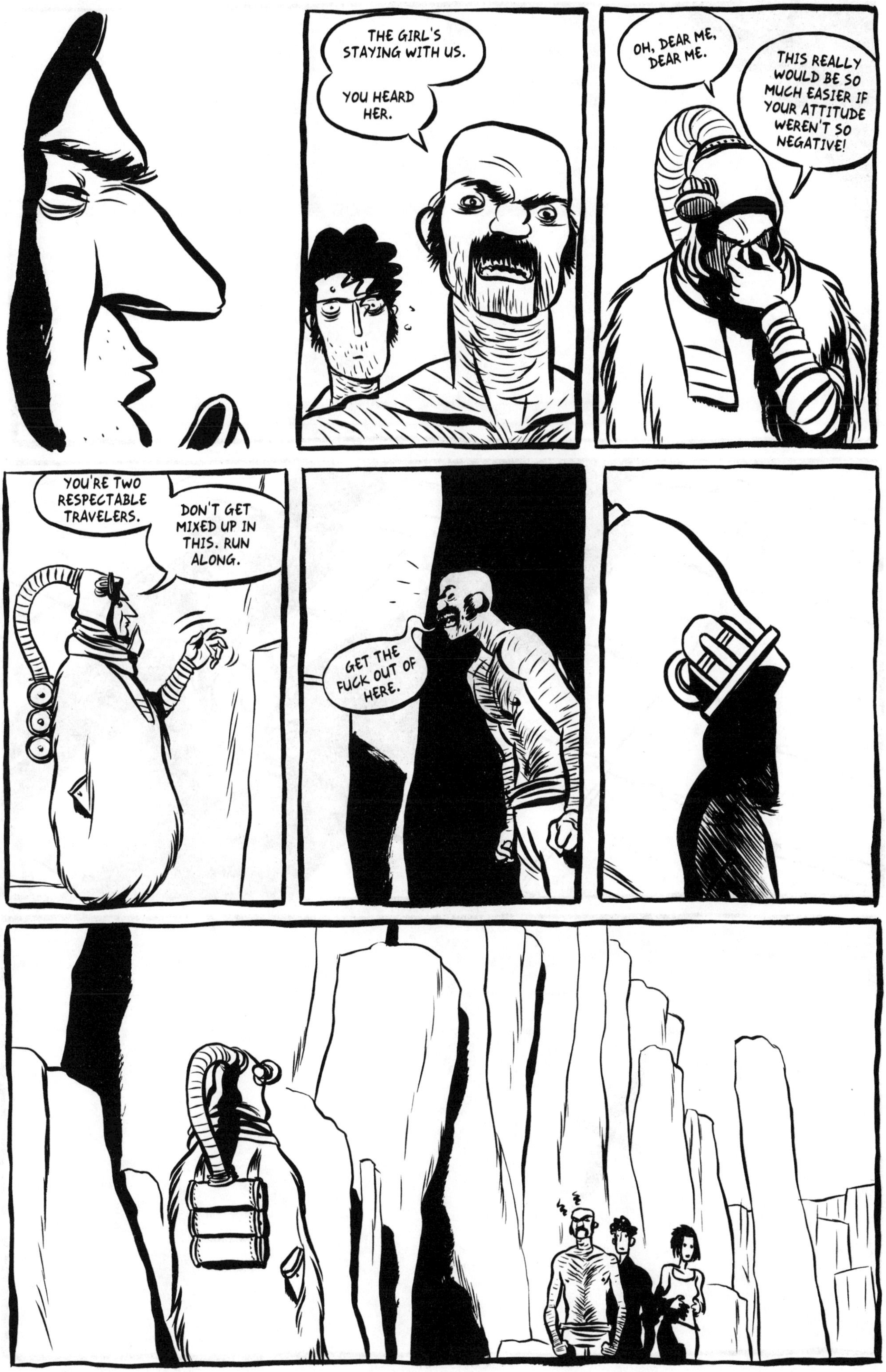
THE GIRL'S STAYING WITH US.
YOU HEARD HER.
OH, DEAR ME, DEAR ME.
THIS REALLY WOULD BE SO MUCH EASIER IF YOUR ATTITUDE WEREN'T SO NEGATIVE!
YOU'RE TWO RESPECTABLE TRAVELERS.
DON'T GET MIXED UP IN THIS. RUN ALONG.
GET THE FUCK OUT OF HERE.

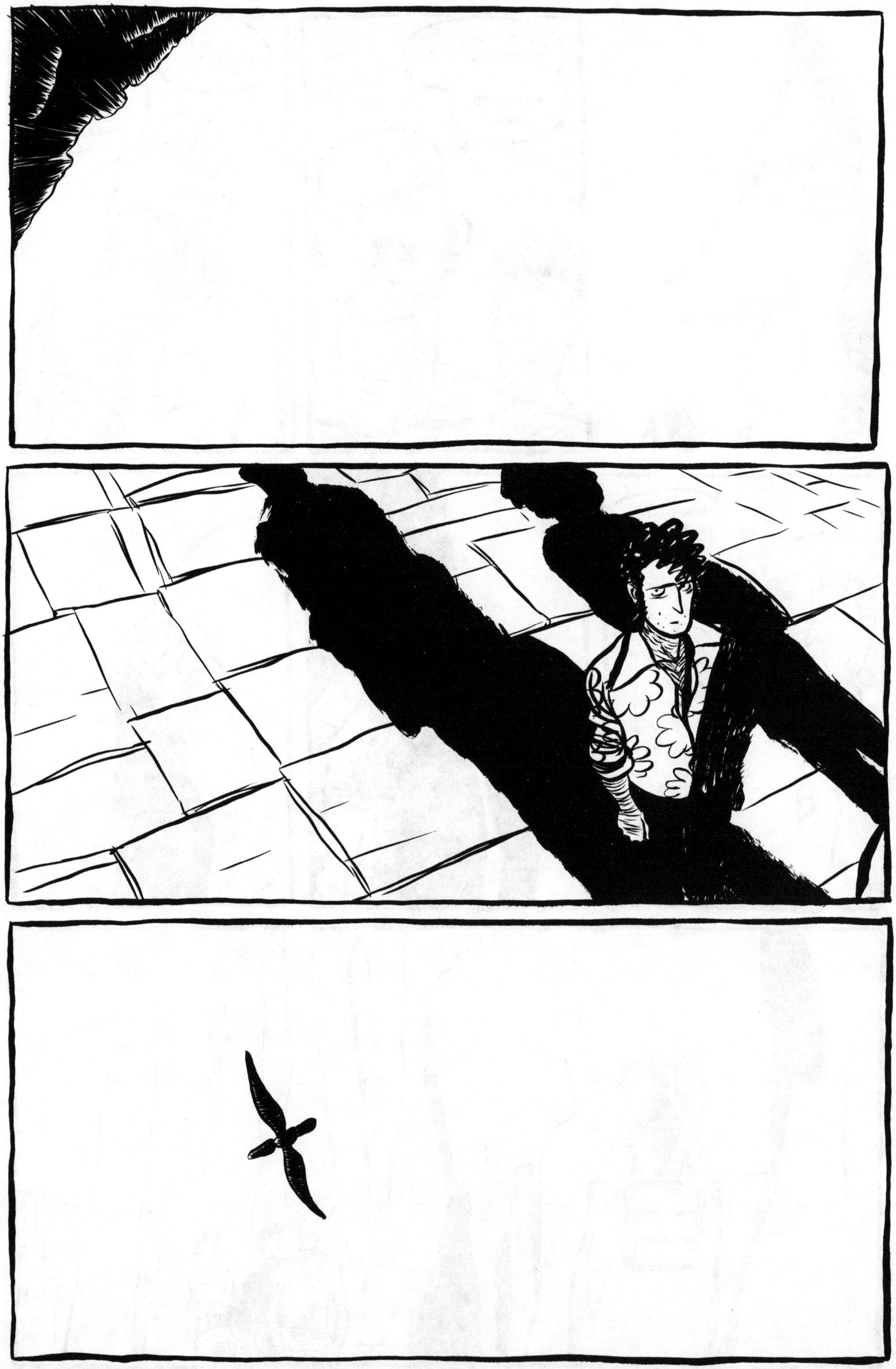

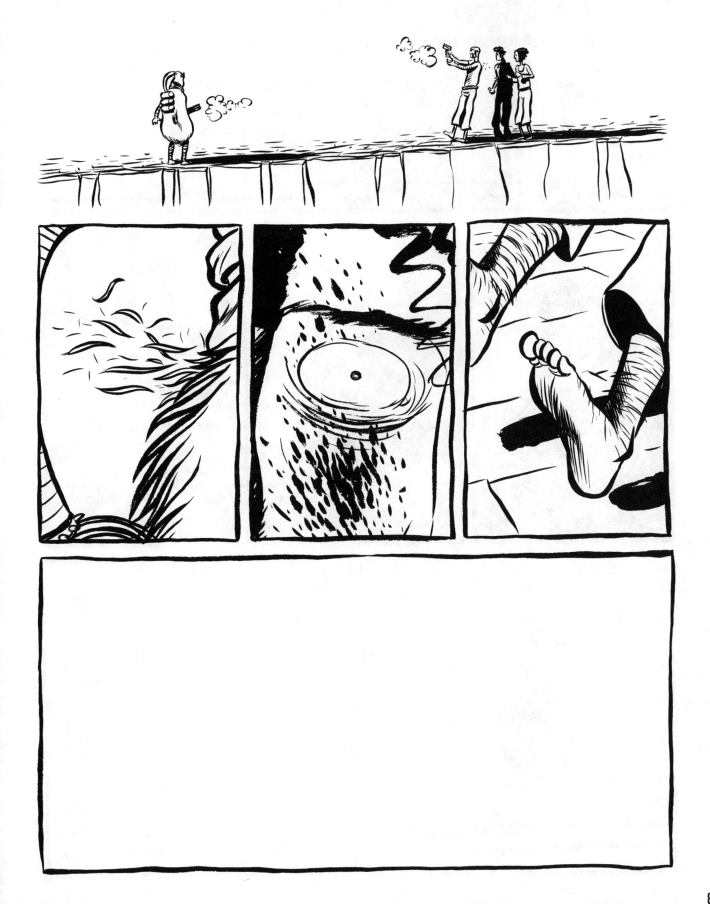

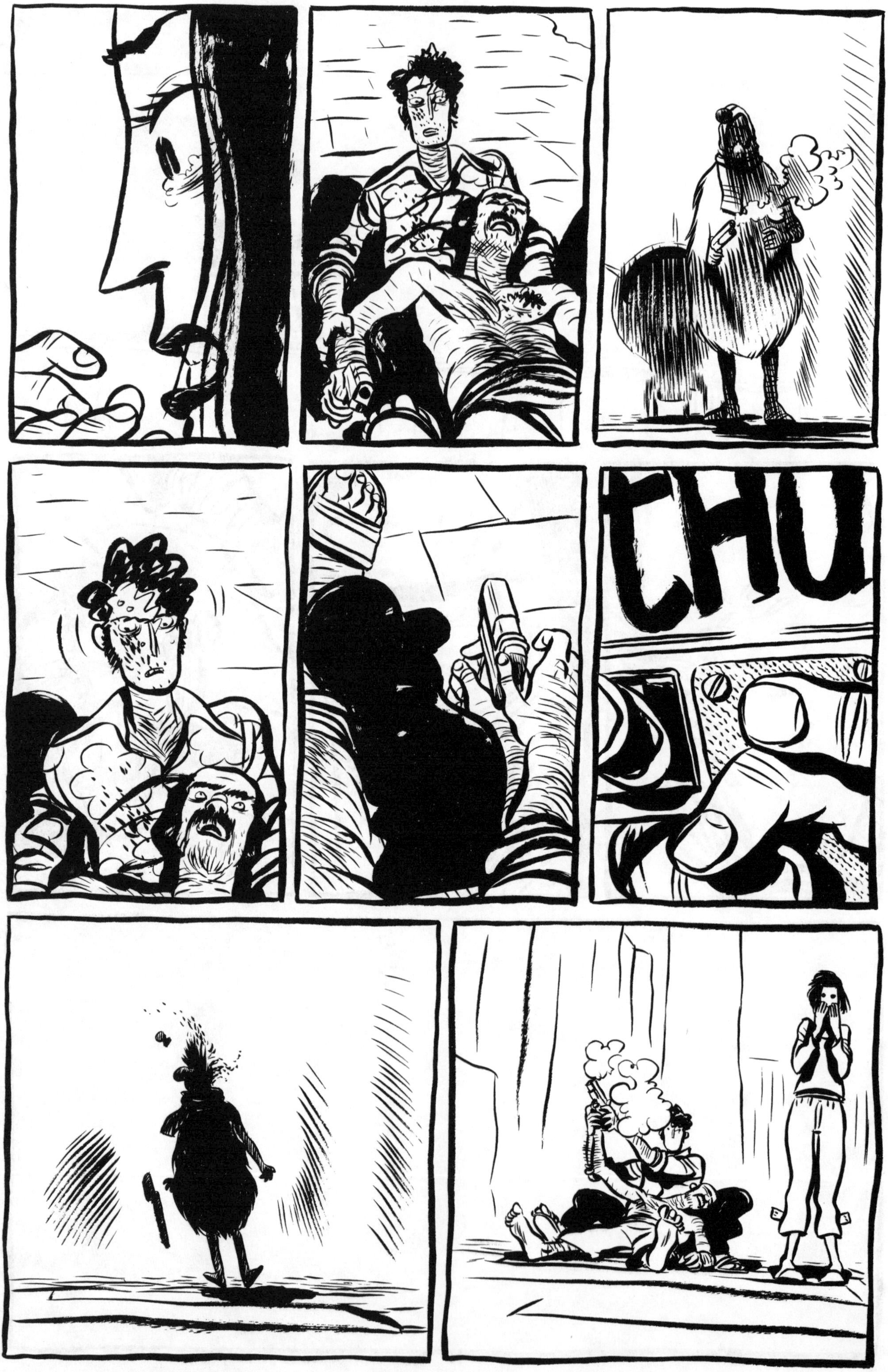
THU

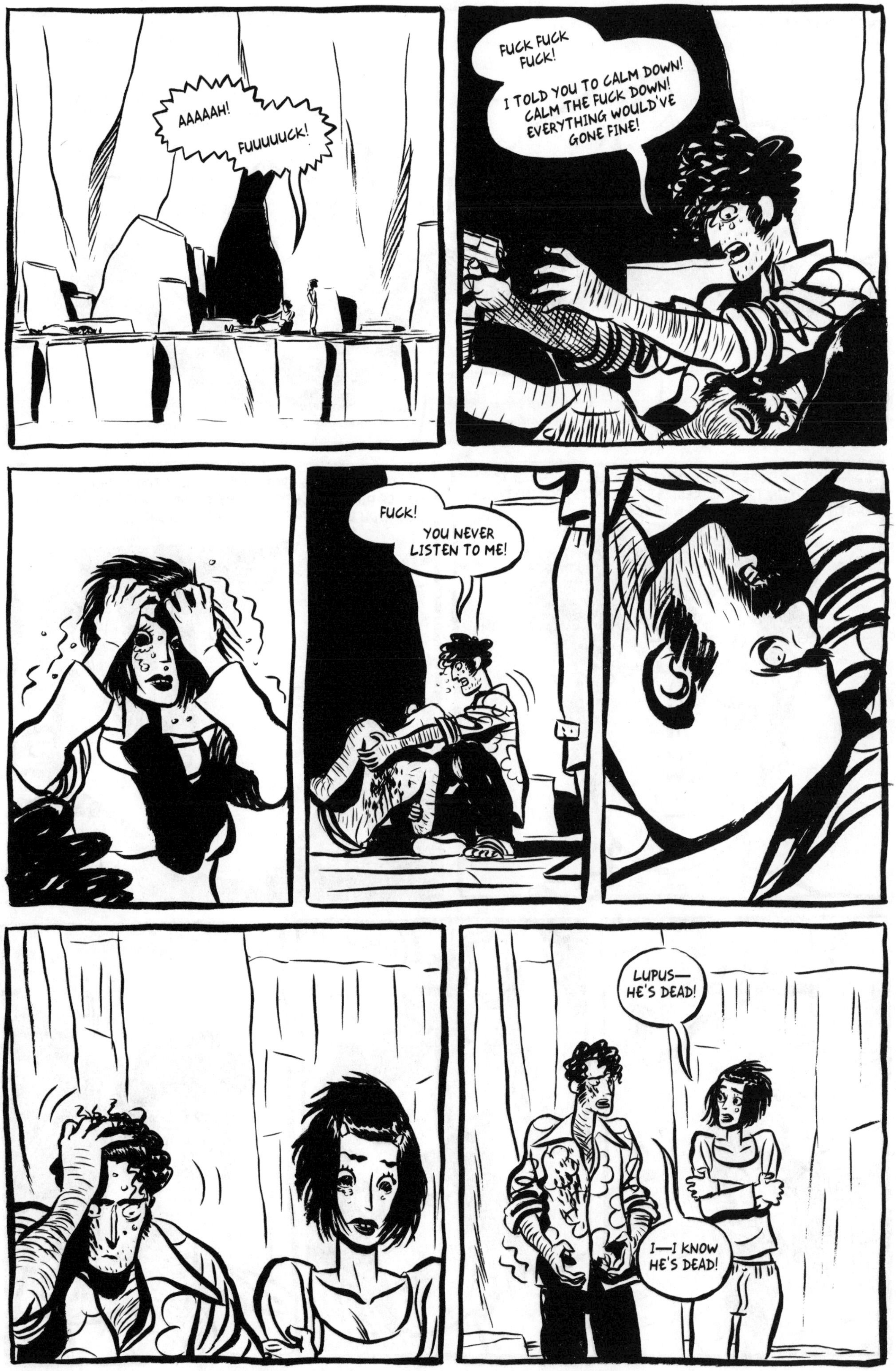
AAAAAH!
FUUUUUCK!
FUCK FUCK FUCK!
I TOLD YOU TO CALM DOWN! CALM THE FUCK DOWN! EVERYTHING WOULD'VE GONE FINE!
FUCK!
YOU NEVER LISTEN TO ME!
LUPUS— HE'S DEAD!
I—I KNOW HE'S DEAD!

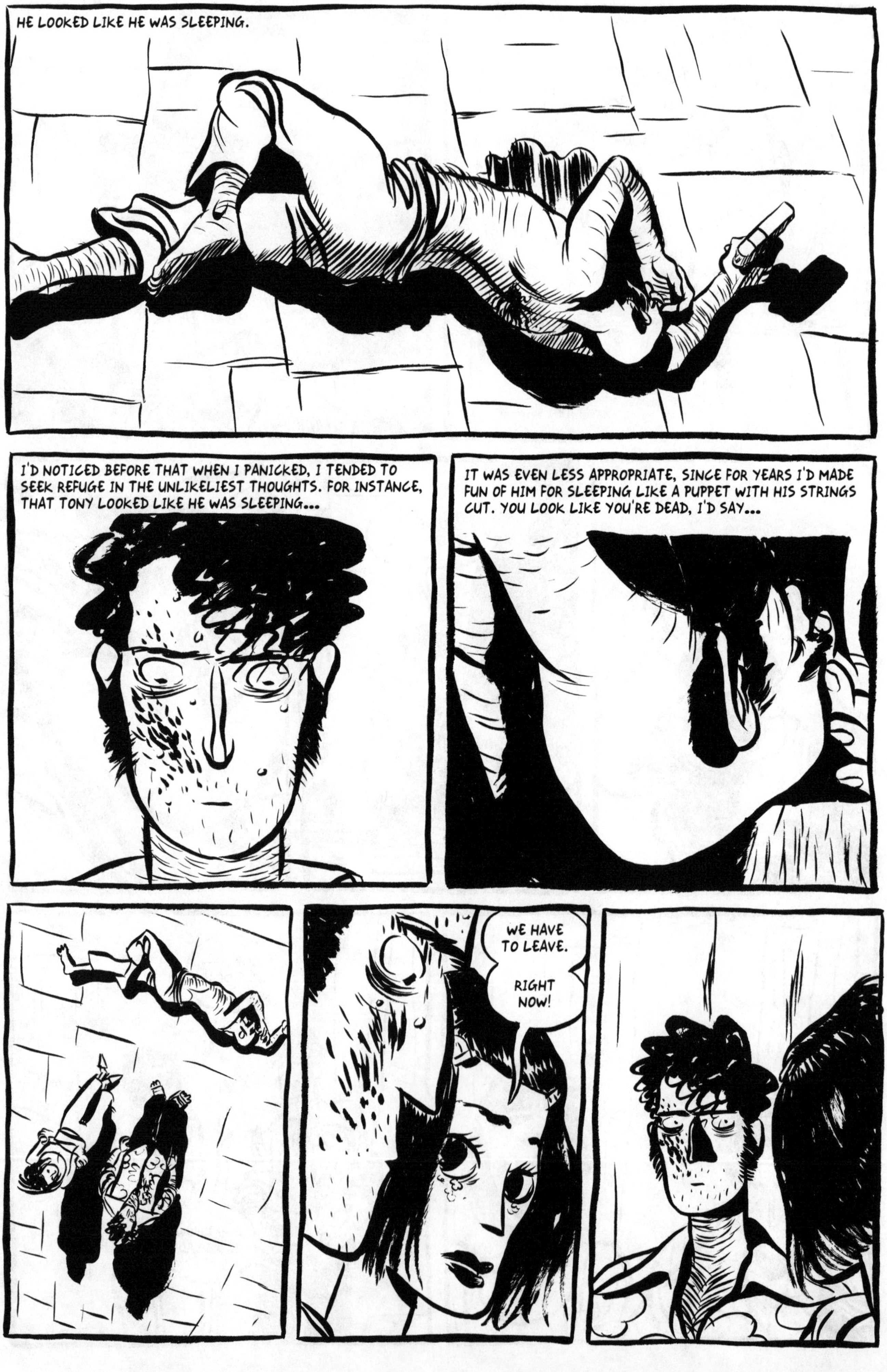
HE LOOKED LIKE HE WAS SLEEPING.
I'D NOTICED BEFORE THAT WHEN I PANICKED, I TENDED TO SEEK REFUGE IN THE UNLIKELIEST THOUGHTS. FOR INSTANCE, THAT TONY LOOKED LIKE HE WAS SLEEPING...
IT WAS EVEN LESS APPROPRIATE, SINCE FOR YEARS I'D MADE FUN OF HIM FOR SLEEPING LIKE A PUPPET WITH HIS STRINGS CUT. YOU LOOK LIKE YOU'RE DEAD, I'D SAY...
WE HAVE TO LEAVE.
RIGHT NOW!

AND MY HEAD SNAPPED INTO FUNCTIONAL MODE. A TOTAL REBOOT.

LUPUS?!

A PICK-ME-UP...

SOMETHING TO KEEP ME ON MY FEET...

KEEP ME LUCID...

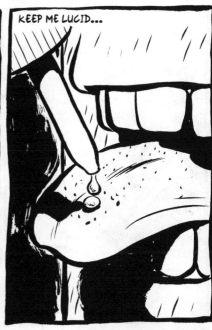

CHUCK THE DRUGS. CUSTOMS CHECK.

GET RID OF THE GUN.

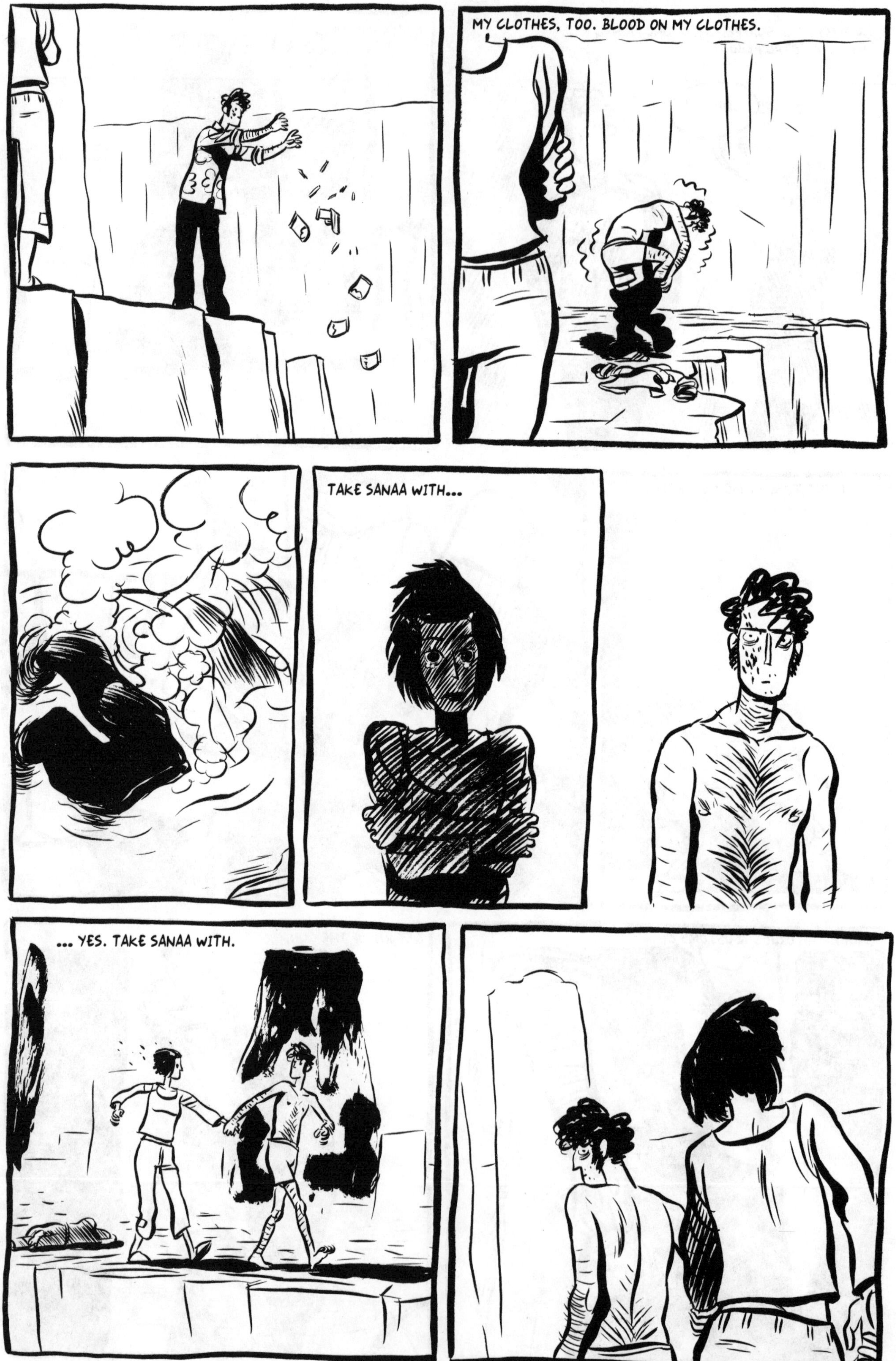

MY CLOTHES, TOO. BLOOD ON MY CLOTHES.
TAKE SANAA WITH...
... YES. TAKE SANAA WITH.

THE BODY! TOSS THE BODY?

NO. GET AWAY. NOW. I PROBABLY COULDN'T HAVE DONE IT ANYWAY.

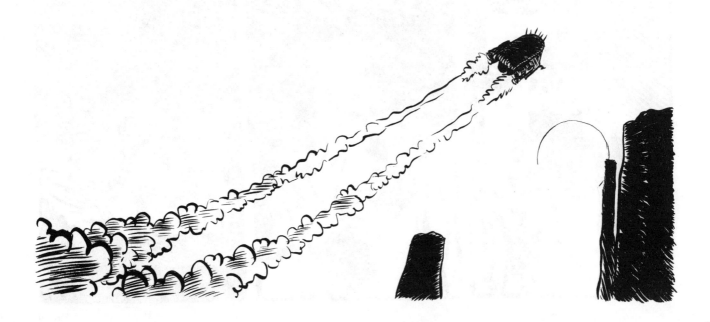

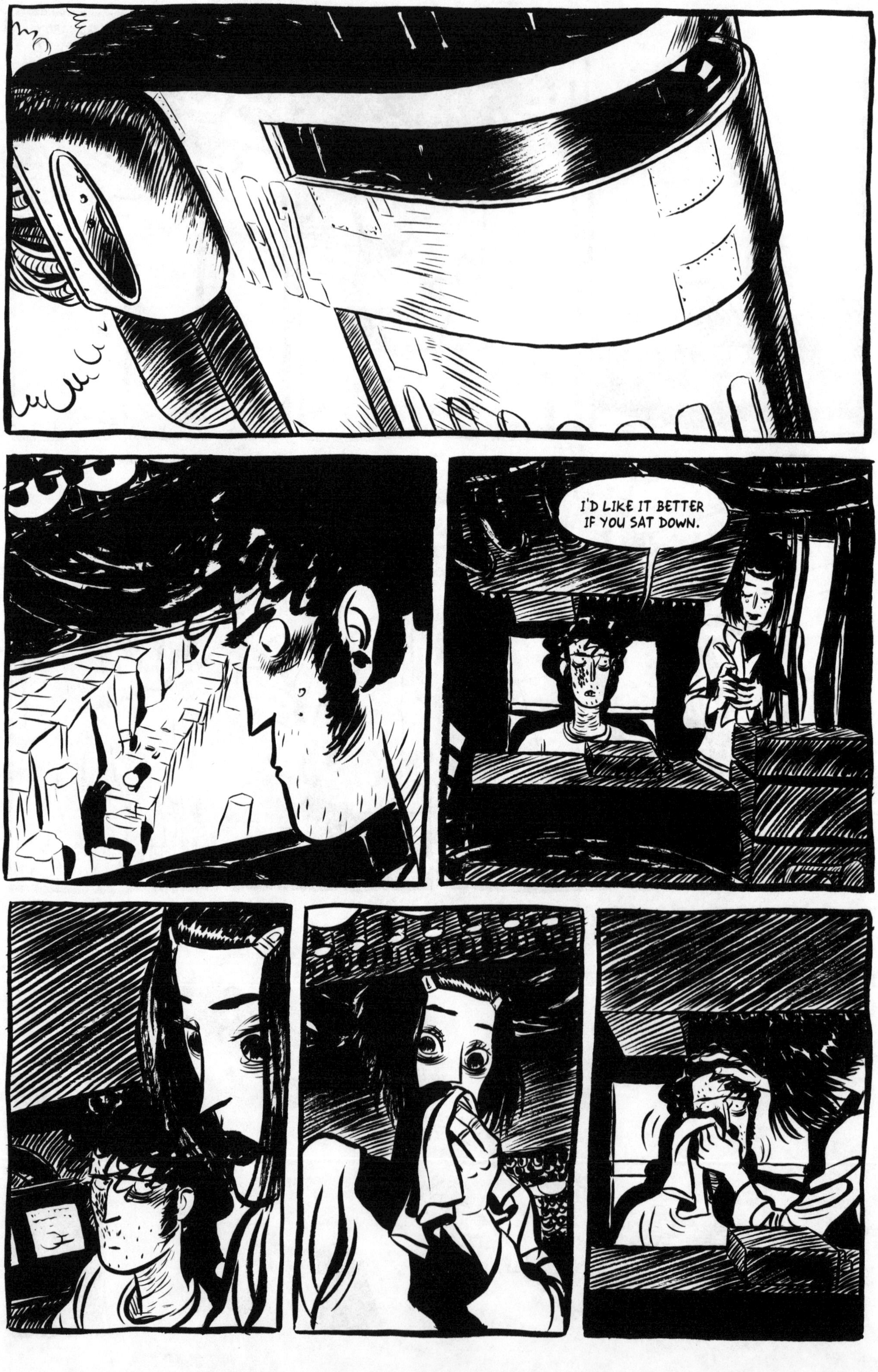
I'D LIKE IT BETTER IF YOU SAT DOWN.

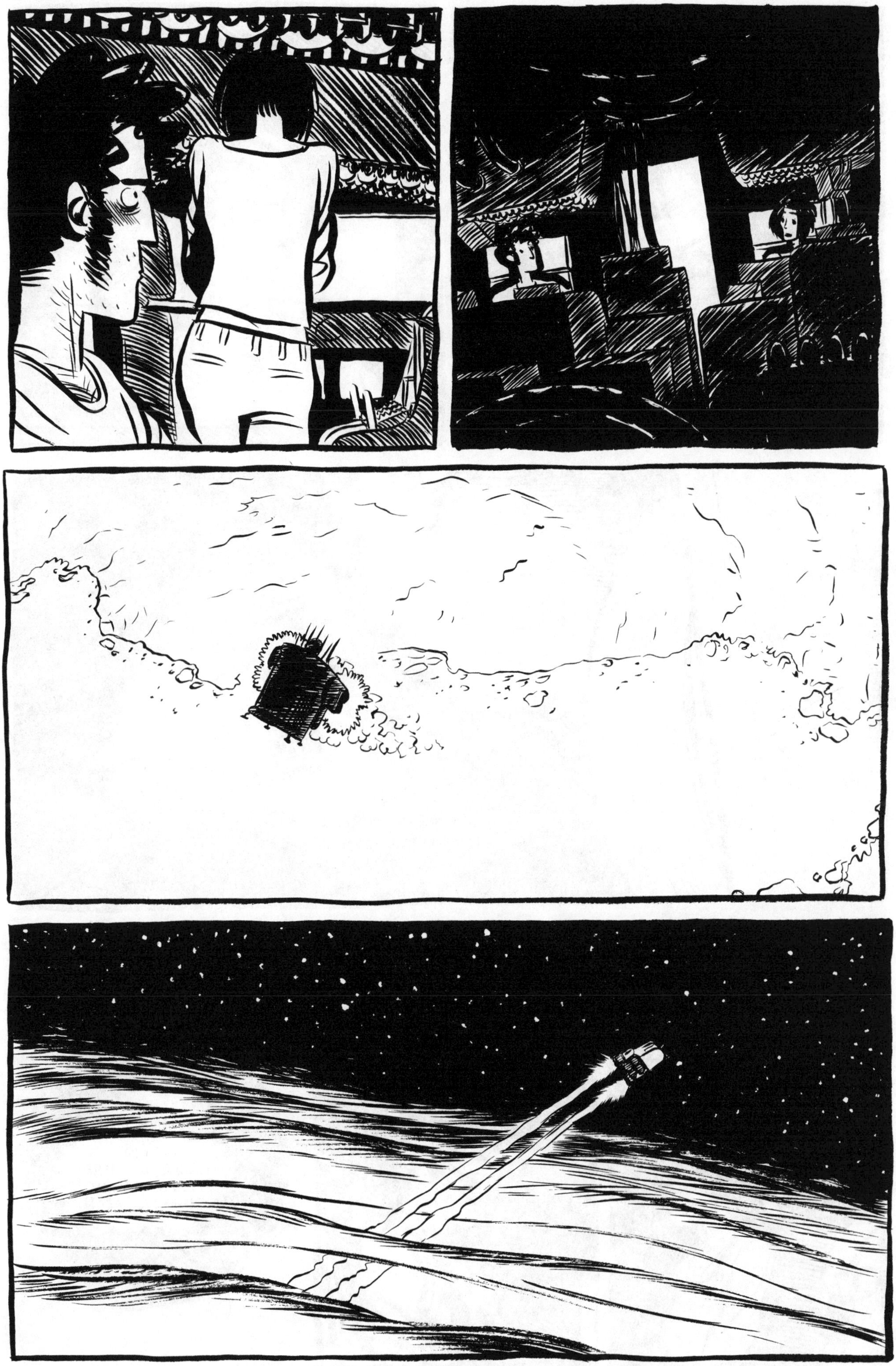

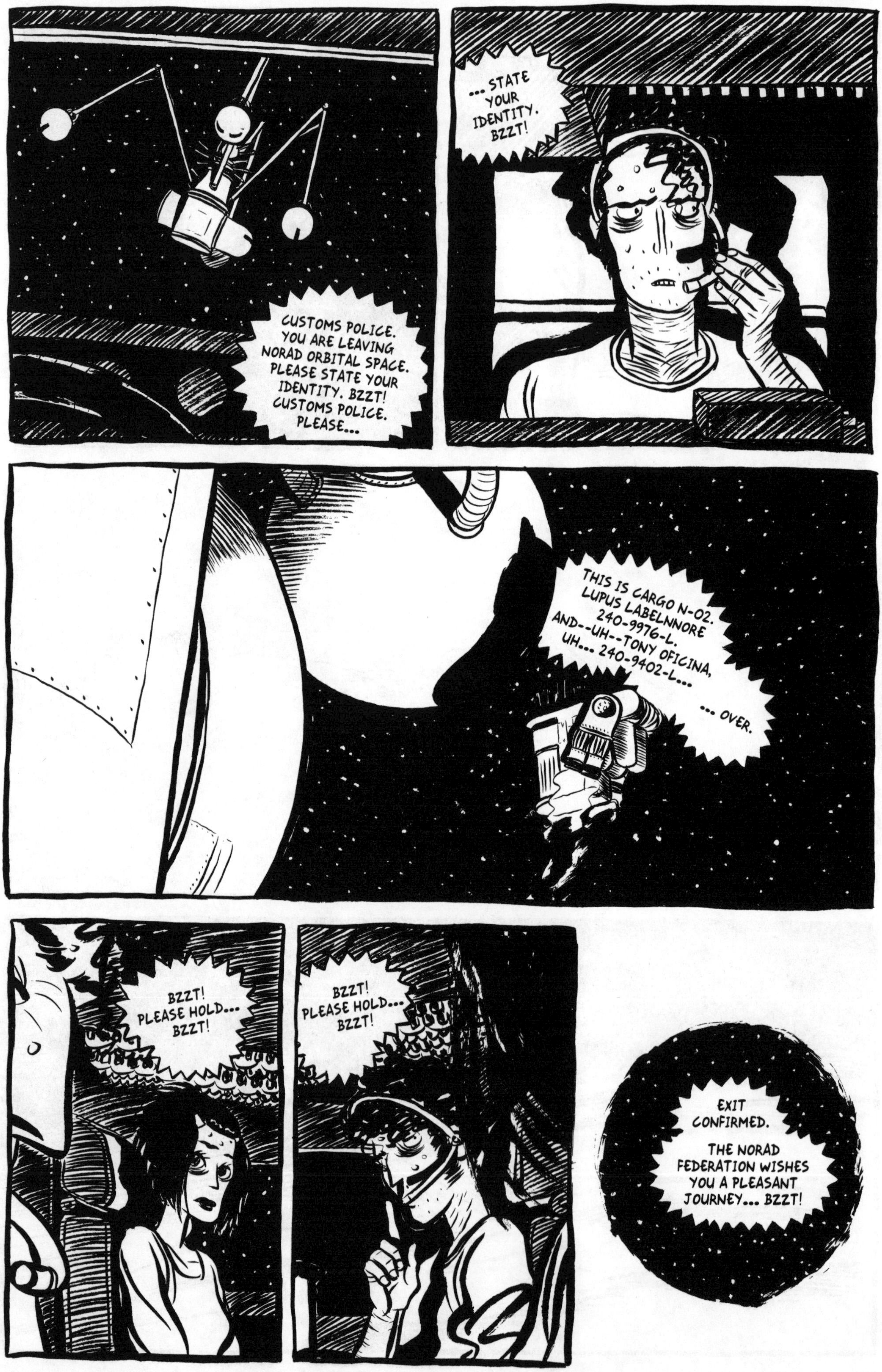
CUSTOMS POLICE. YOU ARE LEAVING NORAD ORBITAL SPACE. PLEASE STATE YOUR IDENTITY. BZZT! CUSTOMS POLICE. PLEASE...
... STATE YOUR IDENTITY. BZZT!
THIS IS CARGO N-02. LUPUS LABELNNORE 240-9976-L. AND--UH--TONY OFICINA, UH... 240-9402-L...
... OVER.
BZZT! PLEASE HOLD... BZZT!
BZZT! PLEASE HOLD... BZZT!
EXIT CONFIRMED.
THE NORAD FEDERATION WISHES YOU A PLEASANT JOURNEY... BZZT!

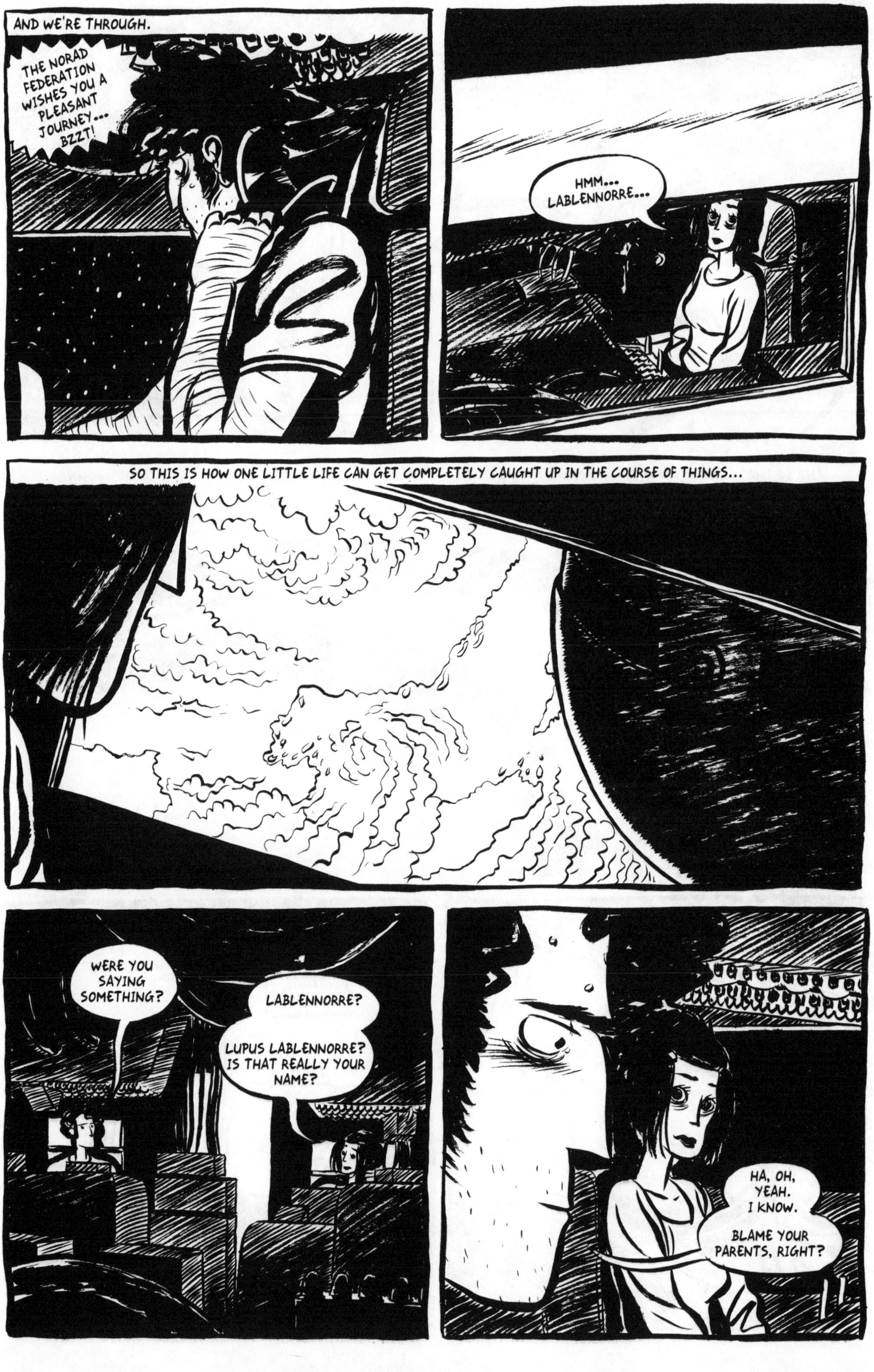

AND WE'RE THROUGH.
THE NORAD FEDERATION WISHES YOU A PLEASANT JOURNEY... BZZT!
HMM... LABLENNORRE...
SO THIS IS HOW ONE LITTLE LIFE CAN GET COMPLETELY CAUGHT UP IN THE COURSE OF THINGS...
WERE YOU SAYING SOMETHING?
LABLENNORRE?
LUPUS LABLENNORRE? IS THAT REALLY YOUR NAME?
HA, OH, YEAH. I KNOW.
BLAME YOUR PARENTS, RIGHT?

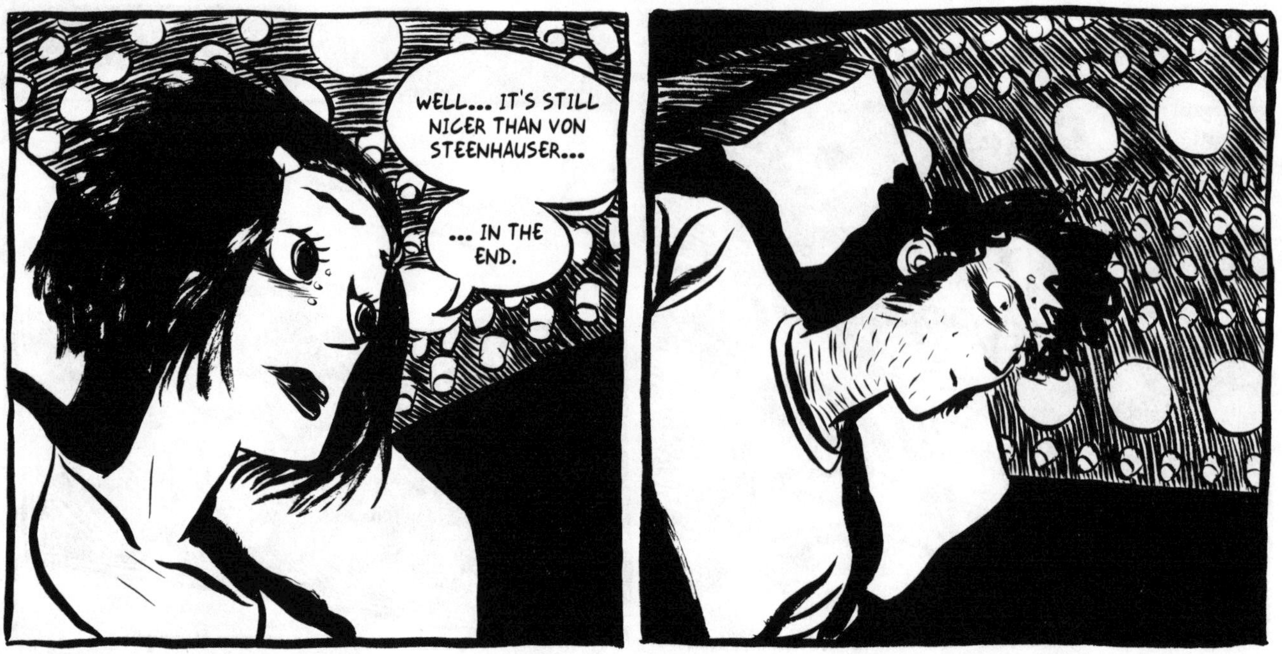
WELL... IT'S STILL NICER THAN VON STEENHAUSER...
... IN THE END.

AND SO THAT'S HOW A GIRL FROM NOWHERE MANAGED, IN A HANDFUL OF DAYS, TO TURN MY WHOLE LIFE UPSIDE DOWN, MAKING IT AN INCONCEIVABLE MESS.

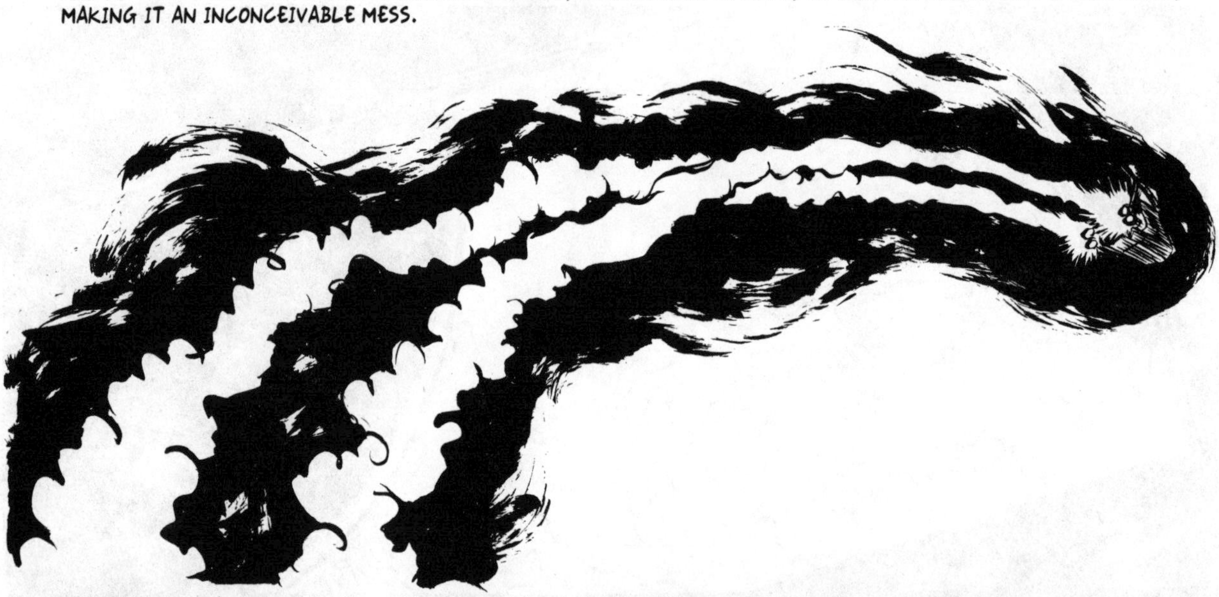

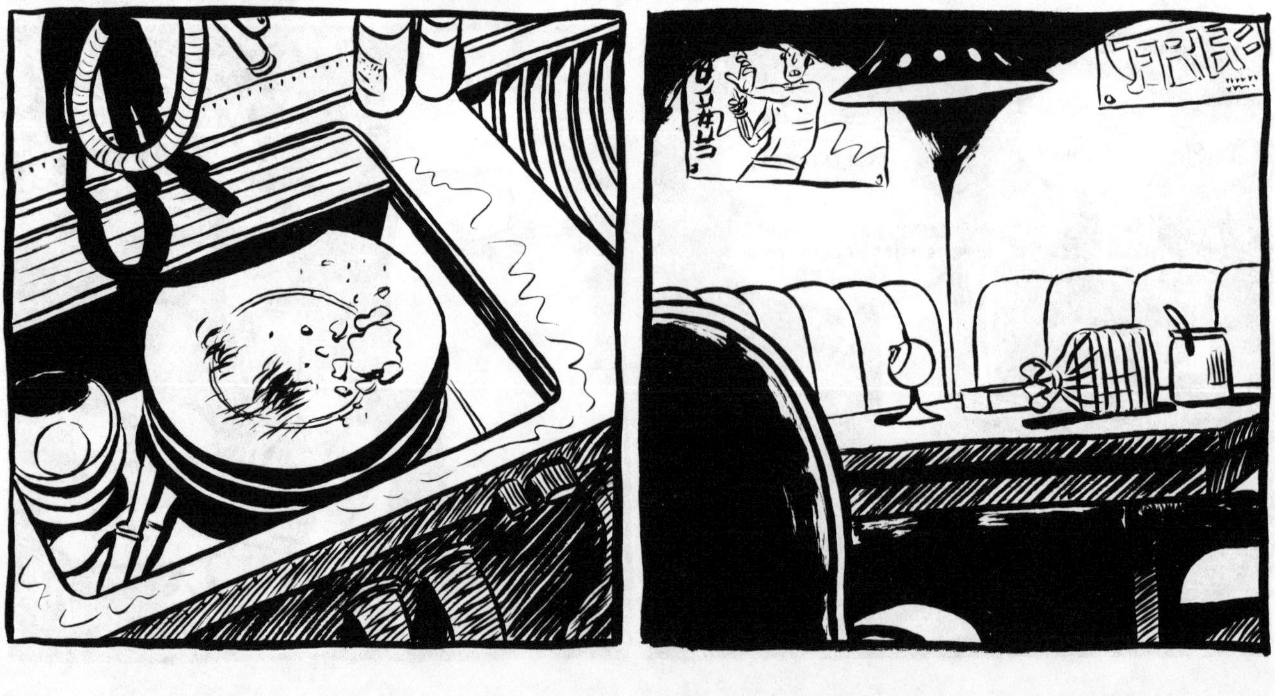

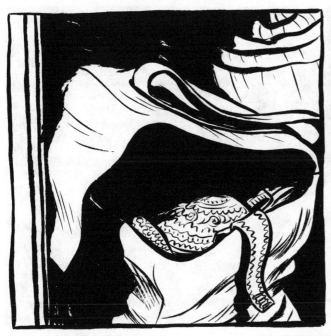

AND THAT'S HOW I WOUND UP WITH THIS ONE GIRL, OUT OF ALL THE GIRLS OUT THERE...

FLEEING GOD KNOWS WHO...

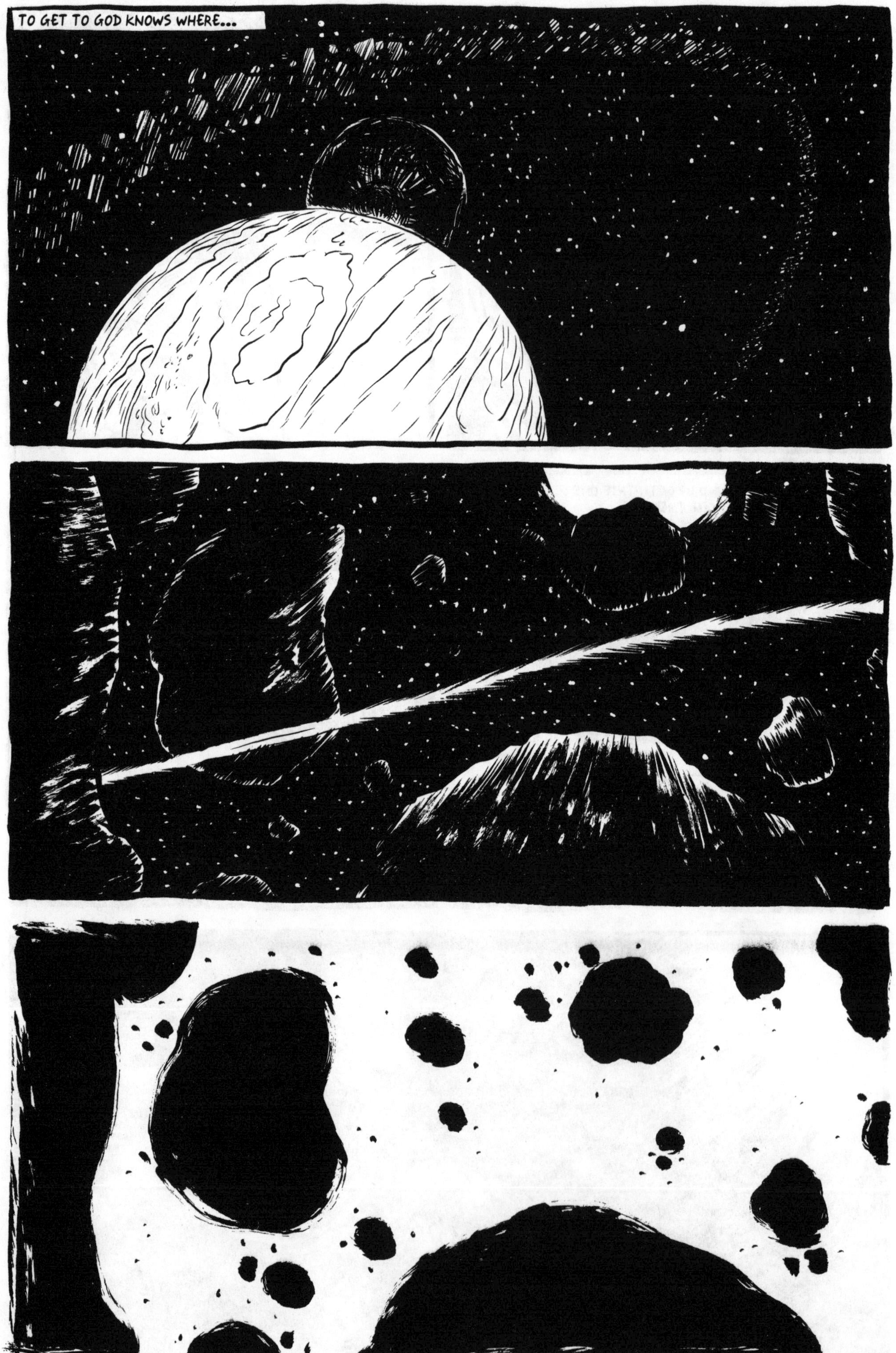
TO GET TO GOD KNOWS WHERE...

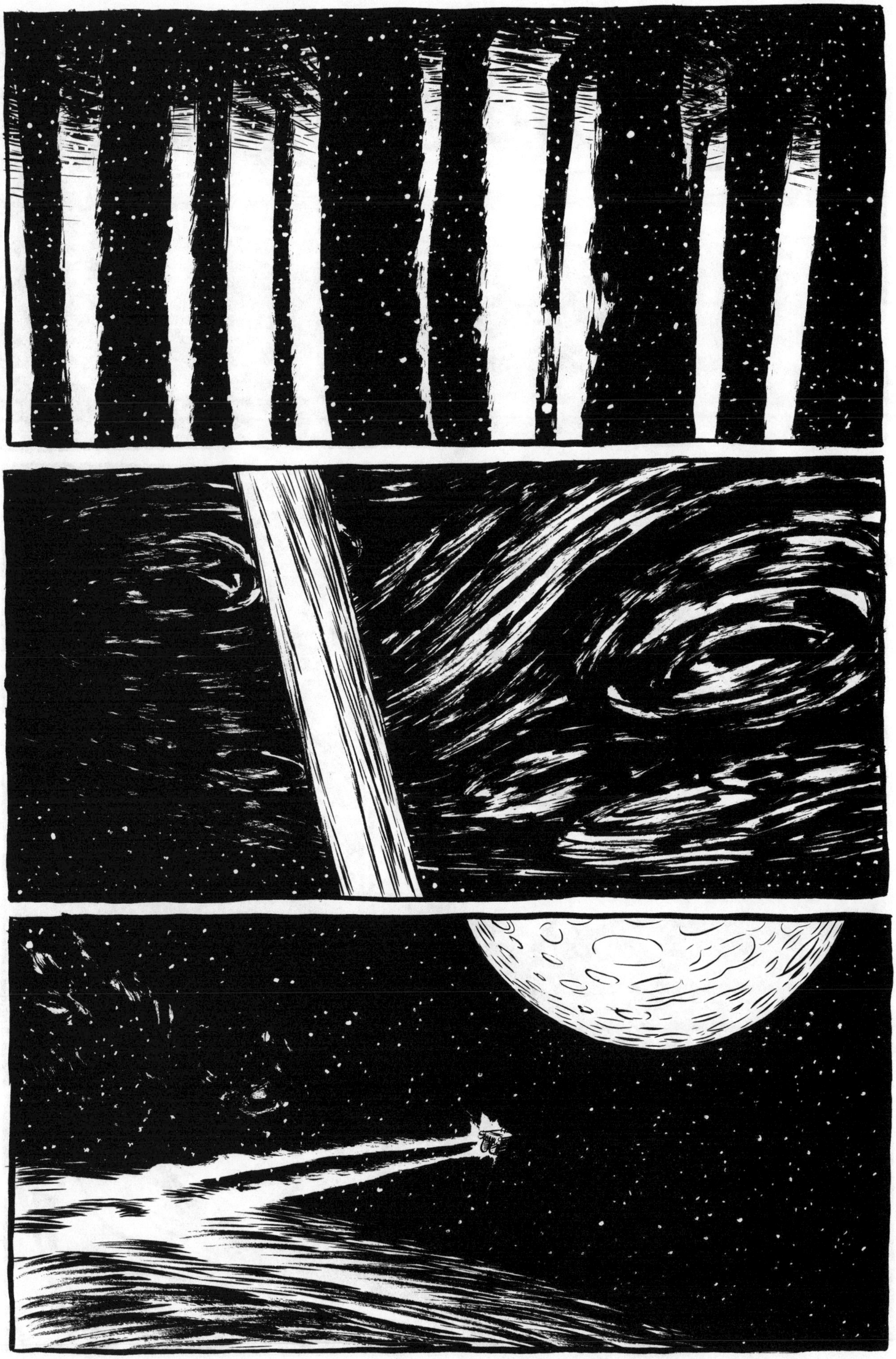

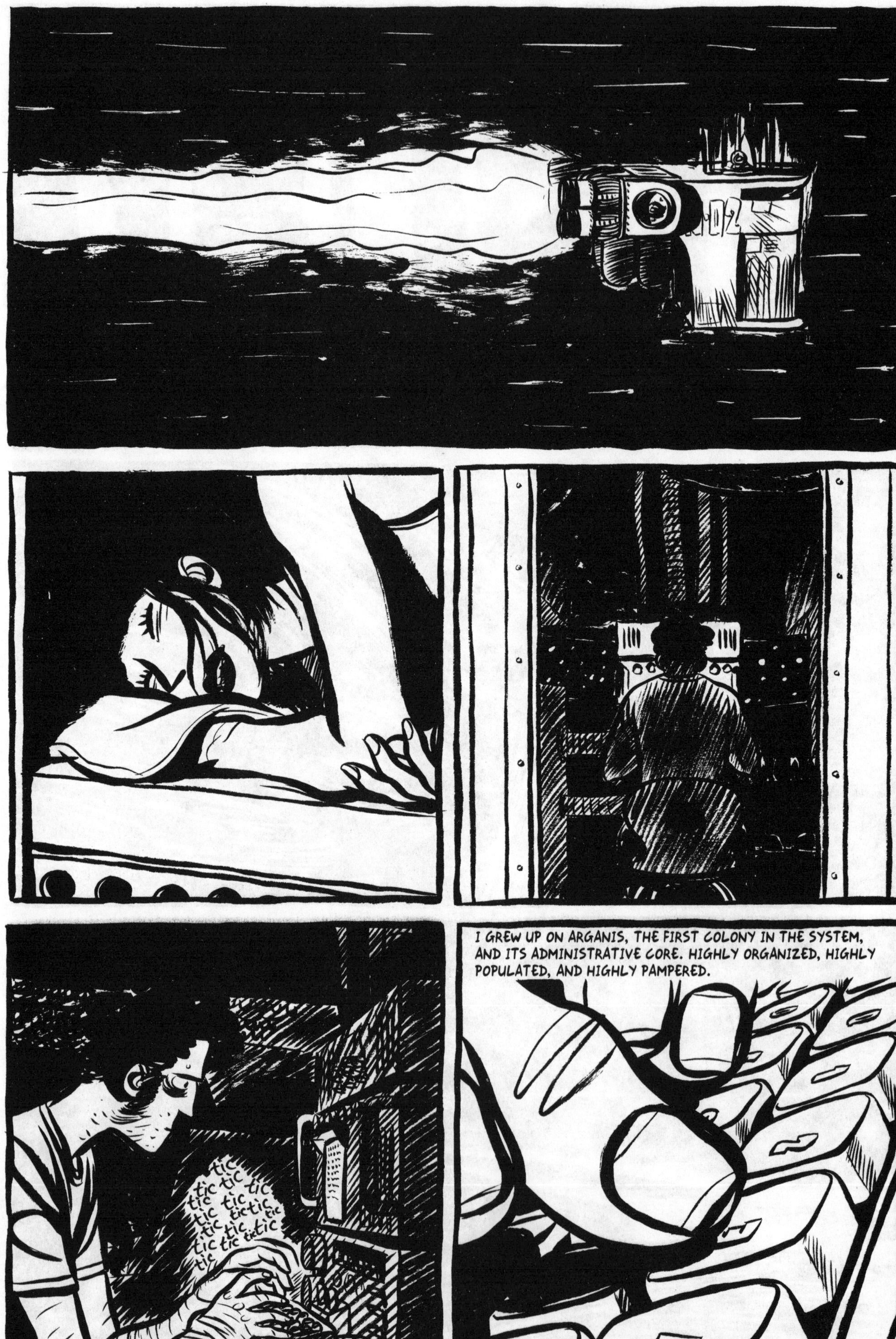

tic tic tic tic tic tic tic tic tic tic tic tic tic tic tic tic
I GREW UP ON ARGANIS, THE FIRST COLONY IN THE SYSTEM, AND ITS ADMINISTRATIVE CORE. HIGHLY ORGANIZED, HIGHLY POPULATED, AND HIGHLY PAMPERED.

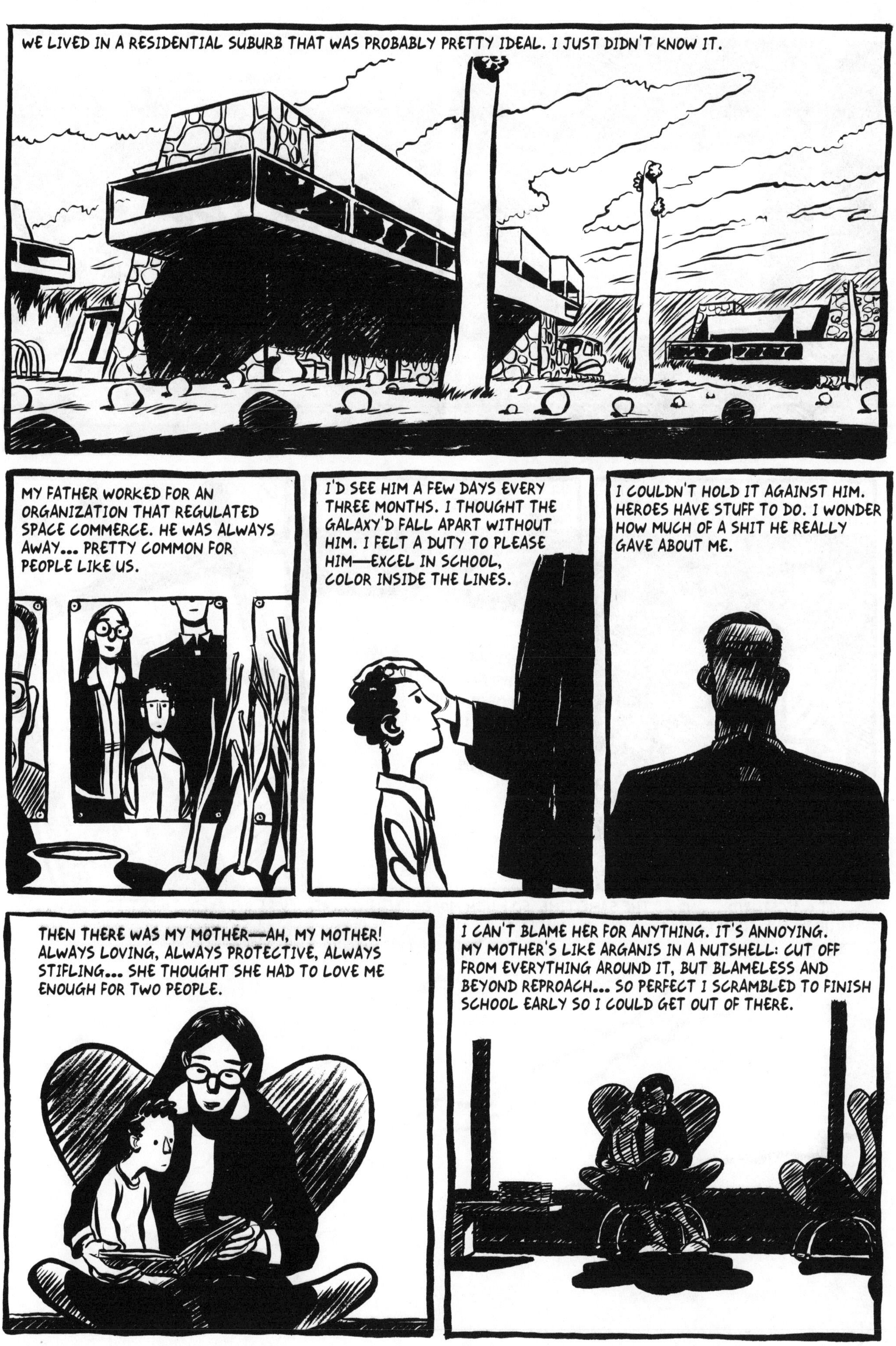

WE LIVED IN A RESIDENTIAL SUBURB THAT WAS PROBABLY PRETTY IDEAL. I JUST DIDN'T KNOW IT.
MY FATHER WORKED FOR AN ORGANIZATION THAT REGULATED SPACE COMMERCE. HE WAS ALWAYS AWAY... PRETTY COMMON FOR PEOPLE LIKE US.
I'D SEE HIM A FEW DAYS EVERY THREE MONTHS. I THOUGHT THE GALAXY'D FALL APART WITHOUT HIM. I FELT A DUTY TO PLEASE HIM—EXCEL IN SCHOOL, COLOR INSIDE THE LINES.
I COULDN'T HOLD IT AGAINST HIM. HEROES HAVE STUFF TO DO. I WONDER HOW MUCH OF A SHIT HE REALLY GAVE ABOUT ME.
THEN THERE WAS MY MOTHER—AH, MY MOTHER! ALWAYS LOVING, ALWAYS PROTECTIVE, ALWAYS STIFLING... SHE THOUGHT SHE HAD TO LOVE ME ENOUGH FOR TWO PEOPLE.
I CAN'T BLAME HER FOR ANYTHING. IT'S ANNOYING. MY MOTHER'S LIKE ARGANIS IN A NUTSHELL: CUT OFF FROM EVERYTHING AROUND IT, BUT BLAMELESS AND BEYOND REPROACH... SO PERFECT I SCRAMBLED TO FINISH SCHOOL EARLY SO I COULD GET OUT OF THERE.

BUT NOW I SUDDENLY NEEDED A DOSE OF MOTHERLY LOVE. JUST SOME BRIEF VIRTUAL CONTACT... TO REMIND ME WHERE I CAME FROM BEFORE I WENT ALONG ON MY WAY.

WE'D LEFT NORAD 15 HOURS AGO. I WROTE TO TELL HER EVERYTHING THAT HAPPENED, WITHOUT CANDY-COATING IT.

AND AT THE LAST MINUTE, RIGHT BEFORE SENDING IT, I ERASED IT ALL. I WROTE:

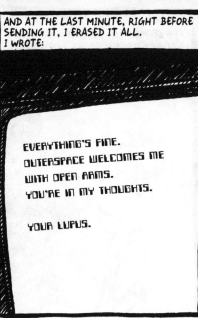

EVERYTHING'S FINE. OUTERSPACE WELCOMES ME WITH OPEN ARMS. YOU'RE IN MY THOUGHTS.

YOUR LUPUS.

IT WAS STUPID... AND AT THE SAME TIME, SO MUCH MORE. I FELT CALMER, MORE RELAXED. I WENT TO THROW UP IN THE TOILET.

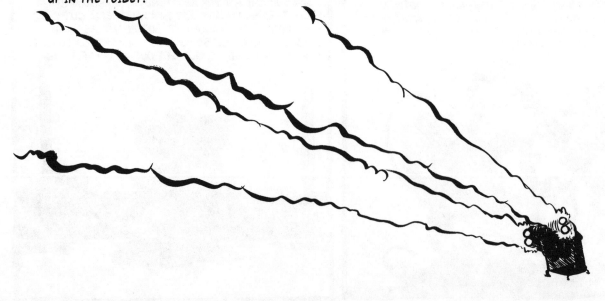

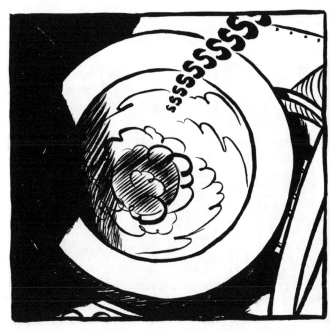

TONY'S DEATH HAD A SYMBOLIC DIMENSION THAT MADE IT STRANGELY BEARABLE.

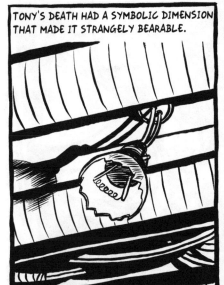

IF LIFE WAS A LADDER, LET'S JUST SAY I'D JUMPED THREE RUNGS ALL AT ONCE JUST NOW. BESIDES, IT WAS TOO SOON TO MISS HIM. NO... THAT WASN'T THE HARDEST PART.

I JUST KEPT THINKING: "THIS IS HORRIBLE... THE BIGGEST THING I'VE DONE IN MY WHOLE LIFE IS BLOW UP SOMEONE'S HEAD FROM SIXTY FEET, WITH MY FIRST SHOT."

I EVEN PUT MYSELF IN THAT GUY'S PLACE. IT SET OFF LITTLE PRICKLES AT THE BASE OF MY SKULL AND THE NAPE OF MY NECK.

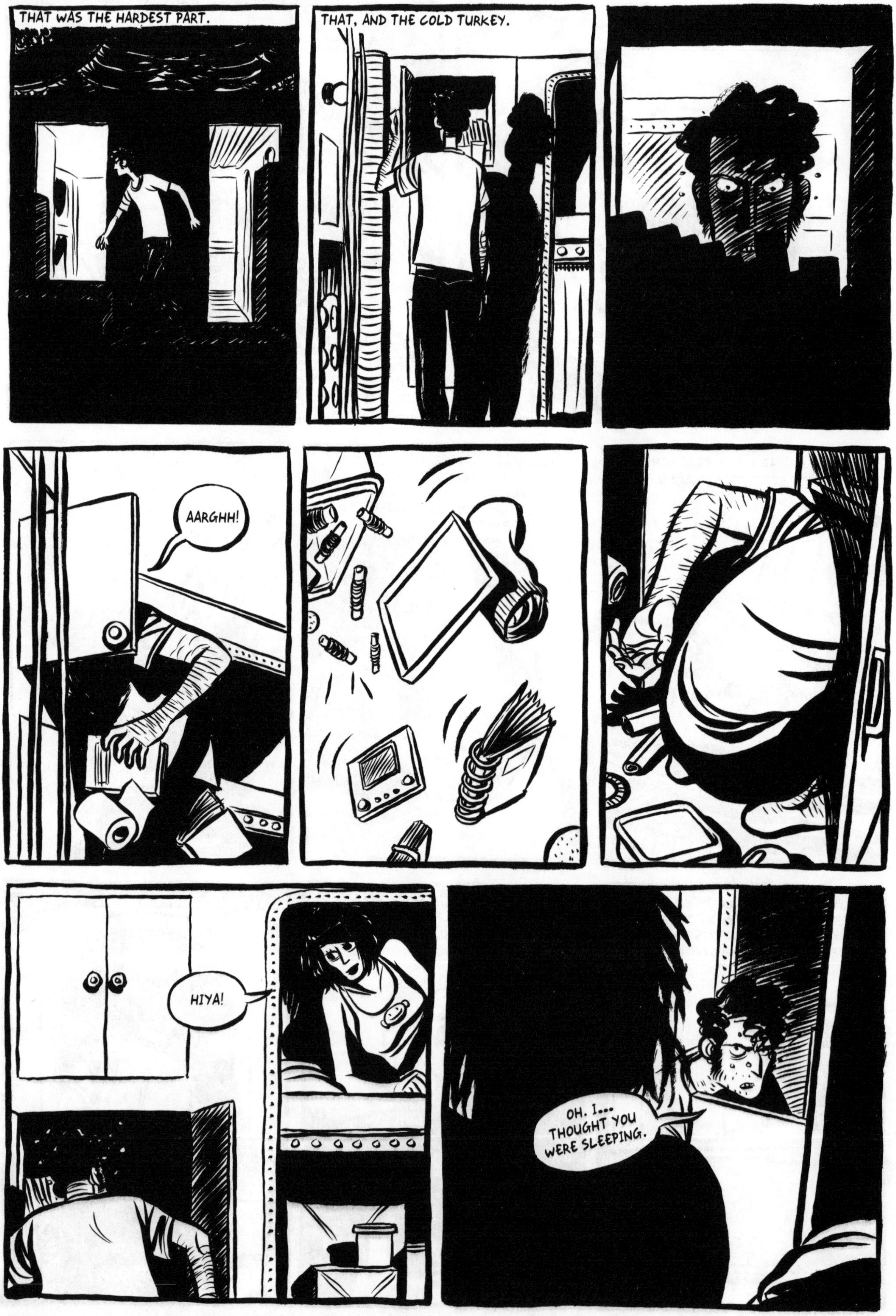
THAT WAS THE HARDEST PART.
THAT, AND THE COLD TURKEY.
AARGHH!
HIYA!
OH. I... THOUGHT YOU WERE SLEEPING.

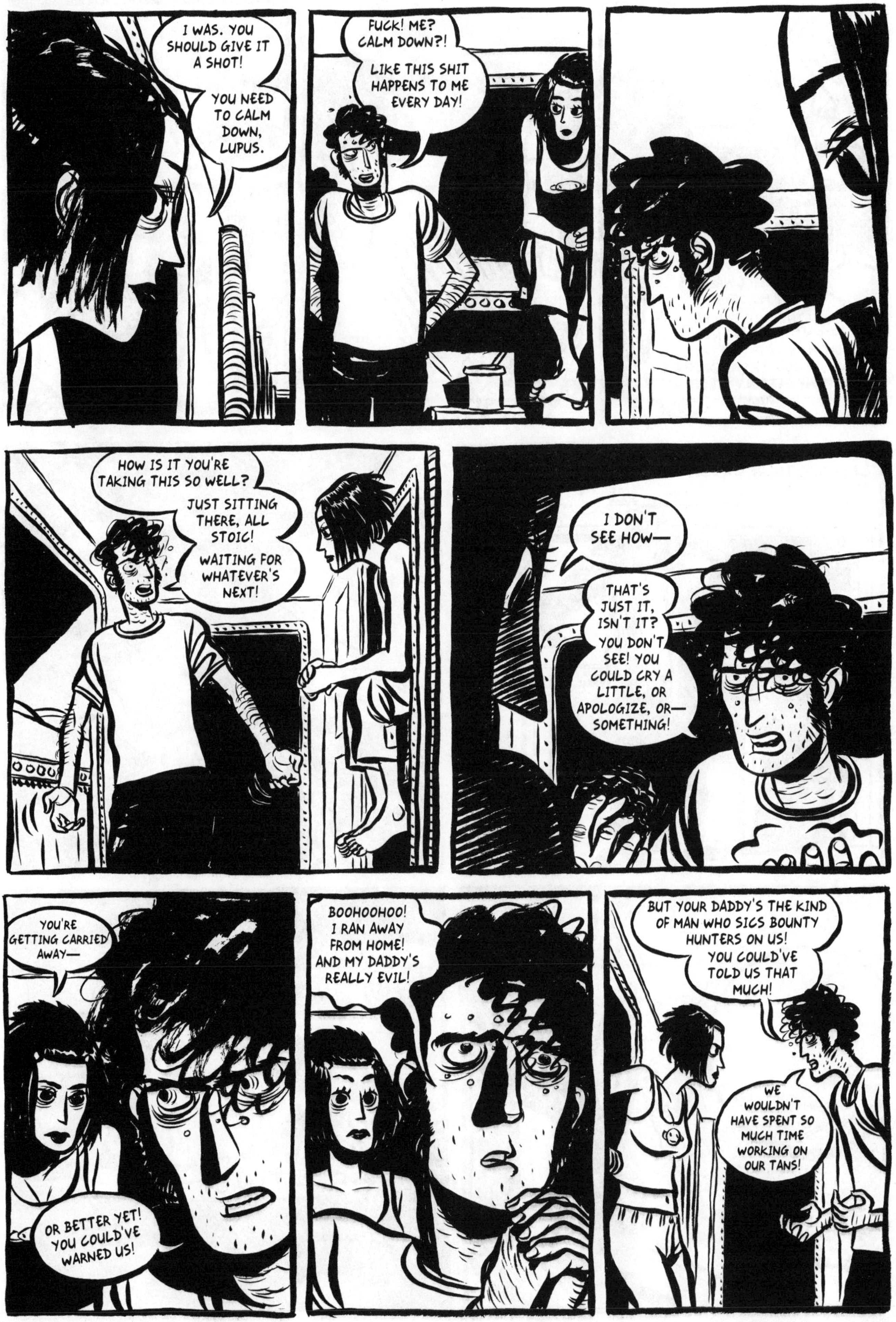
I WAS. YOU SHOULD GIVE IT A SHOT!
YOU NEED TO CALM DOWN, LUPUS.
FUCK! ME? CALM DOWN?!
LIKE THIS SHIT HAPPENS TO ME EVERY DAY!
HOW IS IT YOU'RE TAKING THIS SO WELL?
JUST SITTING THERE, ALL STOIC!
WAITING FOR WHATEVER'S NEXT!
I DON'T SEE HOW—
THAT'S JUST IT, ISN'T IT? YOU DON'T SEE! YOU COULD CRY A LITTLE, OR APOLOGIZE, OR— SOMETHING!
YOU'RE GETTING CARRIED AWAY—
OR BETTER YET! YOU COULD'VE WARNED US!
BOOHOOHOO! I RAN AWAY FROM HOME! AND MY DADDY'S REALLY EVIL!
BUT YOUR DADDY'S THE KIND OF MAN WHO SICS BOUNTY HUNTERS ON US!
YOU COULD'VE TOLD US THAT MUCH!
WE WOULDN'T HAVE SPENT SO MUCH TIME WORKING ON OUR TANS!

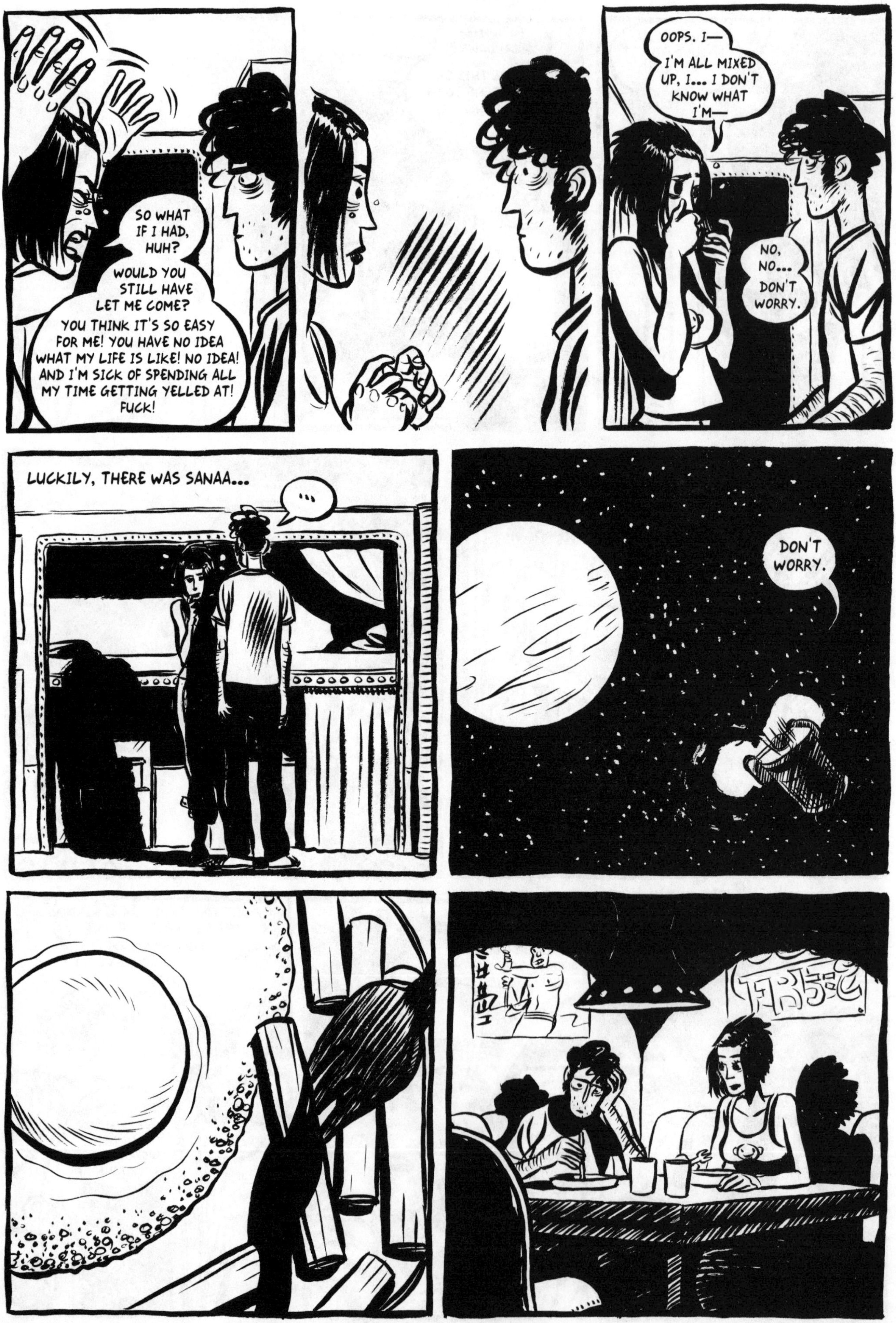

SO WHAT IF I HAD, HUH?
WOULD YOU STILL HAVE LET ME COME?
YOU THINK IT'S SO EASY FOR ME! YOU HAVE NO IDEA WHAT MY LIFE IS LIKE! NO IDEA! AND I'M SICK OF SPENDING ALL MY TIME GETTING YELLED AT! FUCK!
OOPS. I—
I'M ALL MIXED UP, I... I DON'T KNOW WHAT I'M—
NO, NO... DON'T WORRY.
LUCKILY, THERE WAS SANAA...
...
DON'T WORRY.

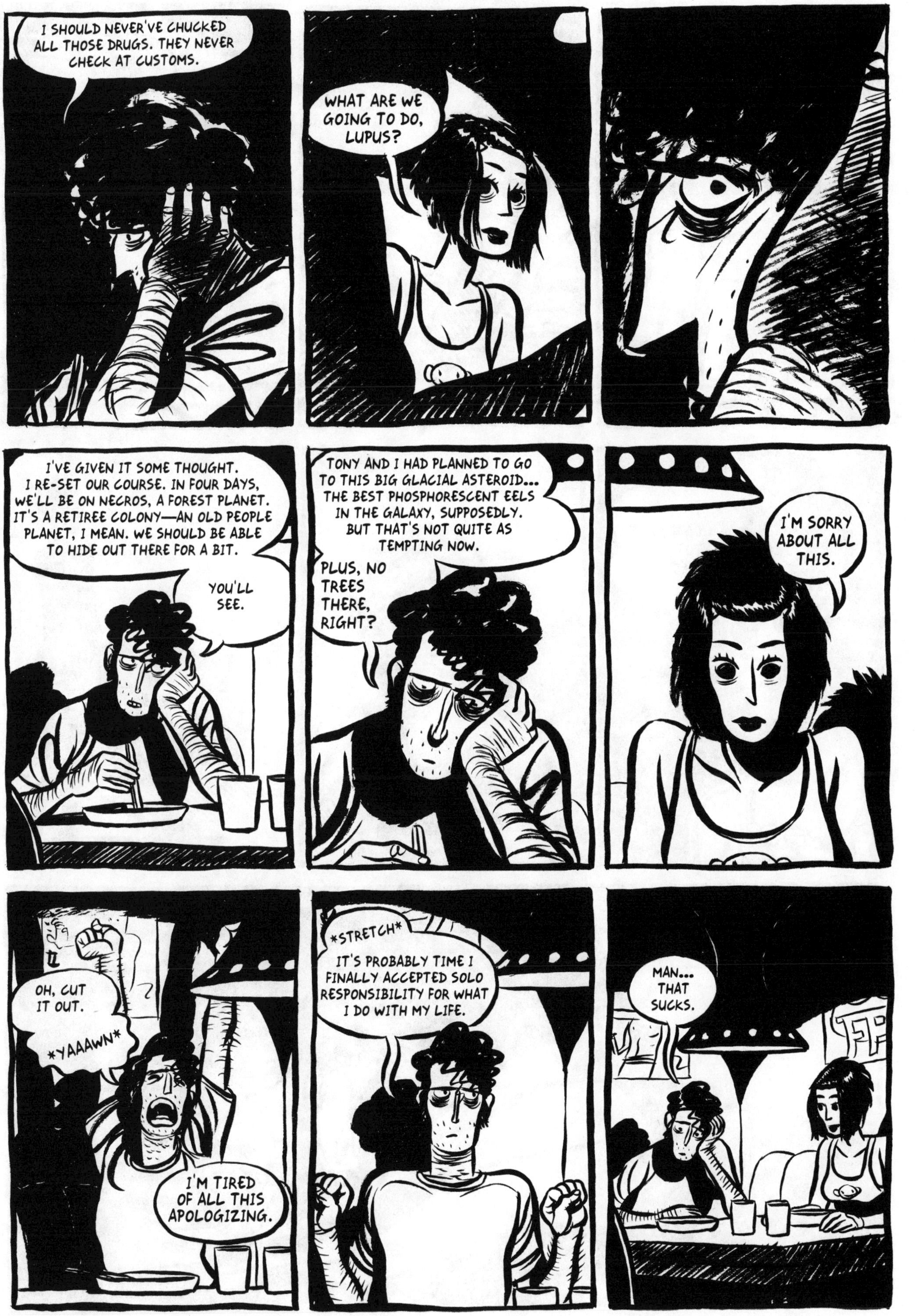
I SHOULD NEVER'VE CHUCKED ALL THOSE DRUGS. THEY NEVER CHECK AT CUSTOMS.
WHAT ARE WE GOING TO DO, LUPUS?
I'VE GIVEN IT SOME THOUGHT. I RE-SET OUR COURSE. IN FOUR DAYS, WE'LL BE ON NECROS, A FOREST PLANET. IT'S A RETIREE COLONY—AN OLD PEOPLE PLANET, I MEAN. WE SHOULD BE ABLE TO HIDE OUT THERE FOR A BIT.
YOU'LL SEE.
TONY AND I HAD PLANNED TO GO TO THIS BIG GLACIAL ASTEROID... THE BEST PHOSPHORESCENT EELS IN THE GALAXY, SUPPOSEDLY. BUT THAT'S NOT QUITE AS TEMPTING NOW.
PLUS, NO TREES THERE, RIGHT?
I'M SORRY ABOUT ALL THIS.
OH, CUT IT OUT.
YAAAWN
I'M TIRED OF ALL THIS APOLOGIZING.
STRETCH
IT'S PROBABLY TIME I FINALLY ACCEPTED SOLO RESPONSIBILITY FOR WHAT I DO WITH MY LIFE.
MAN... THAT SUCKS.

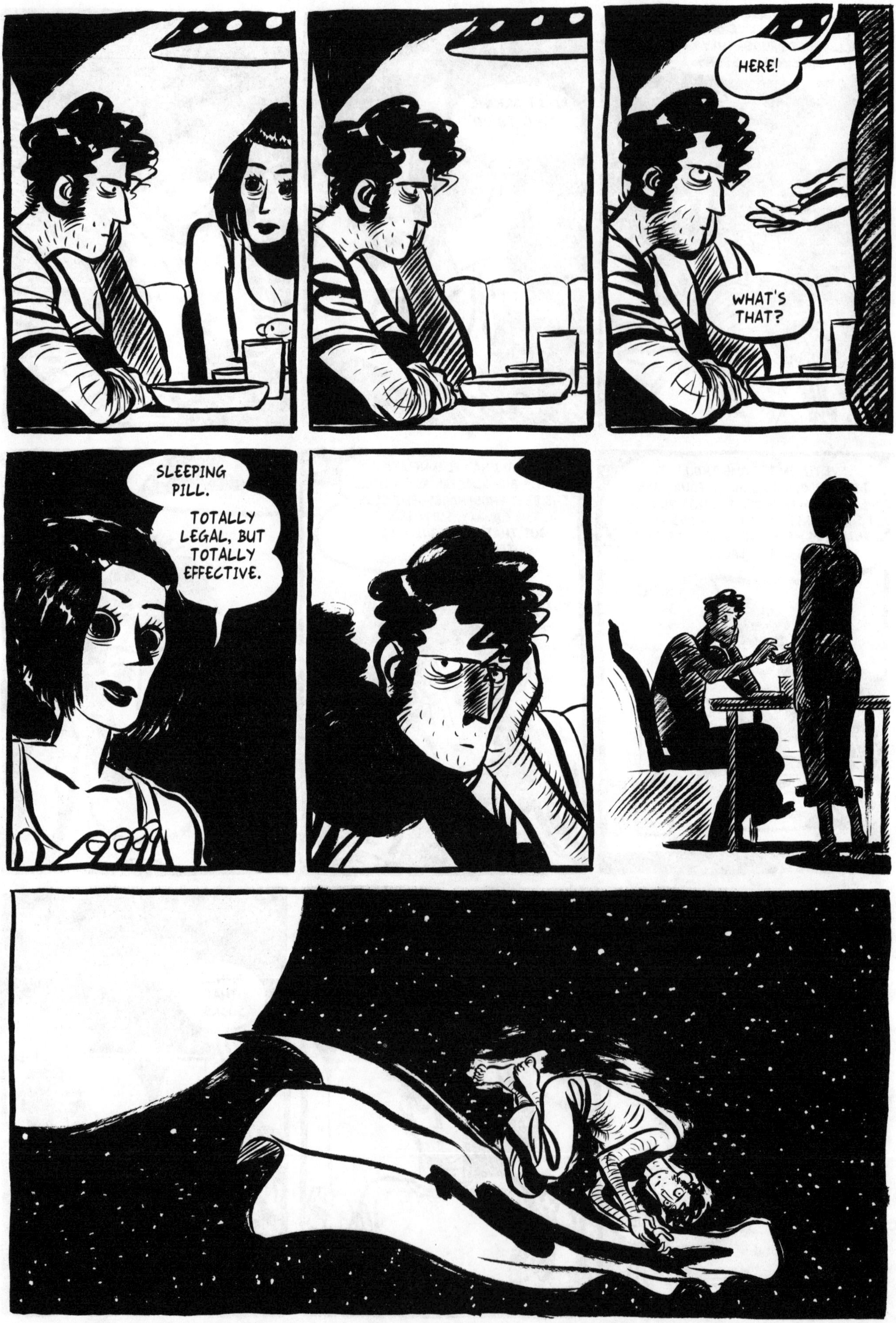
HERE!
WHAT'S THAT?
SLEEPING PILL.
TOTALLY LEGAL, BUT TOTALLY EFFECTIVE.

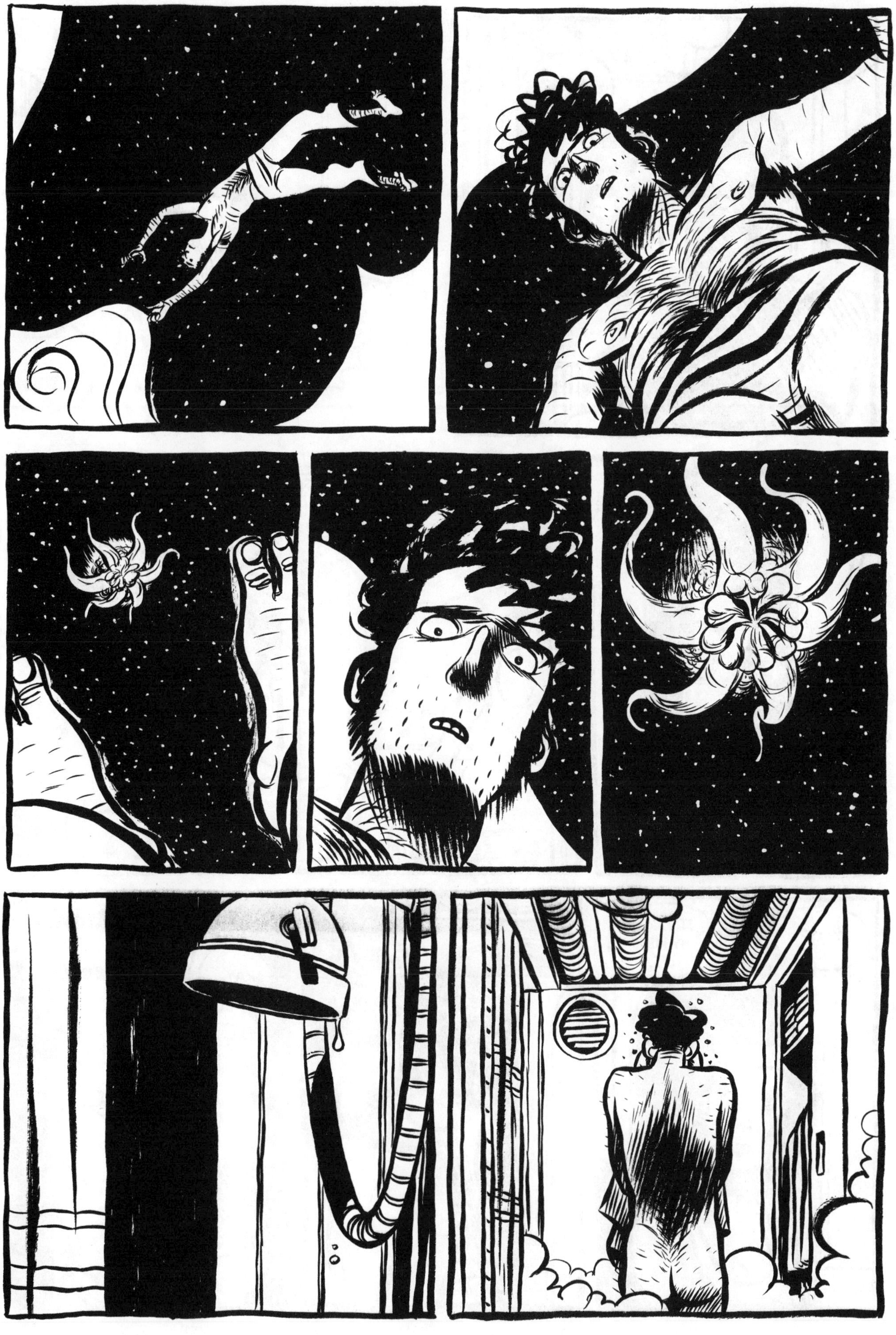

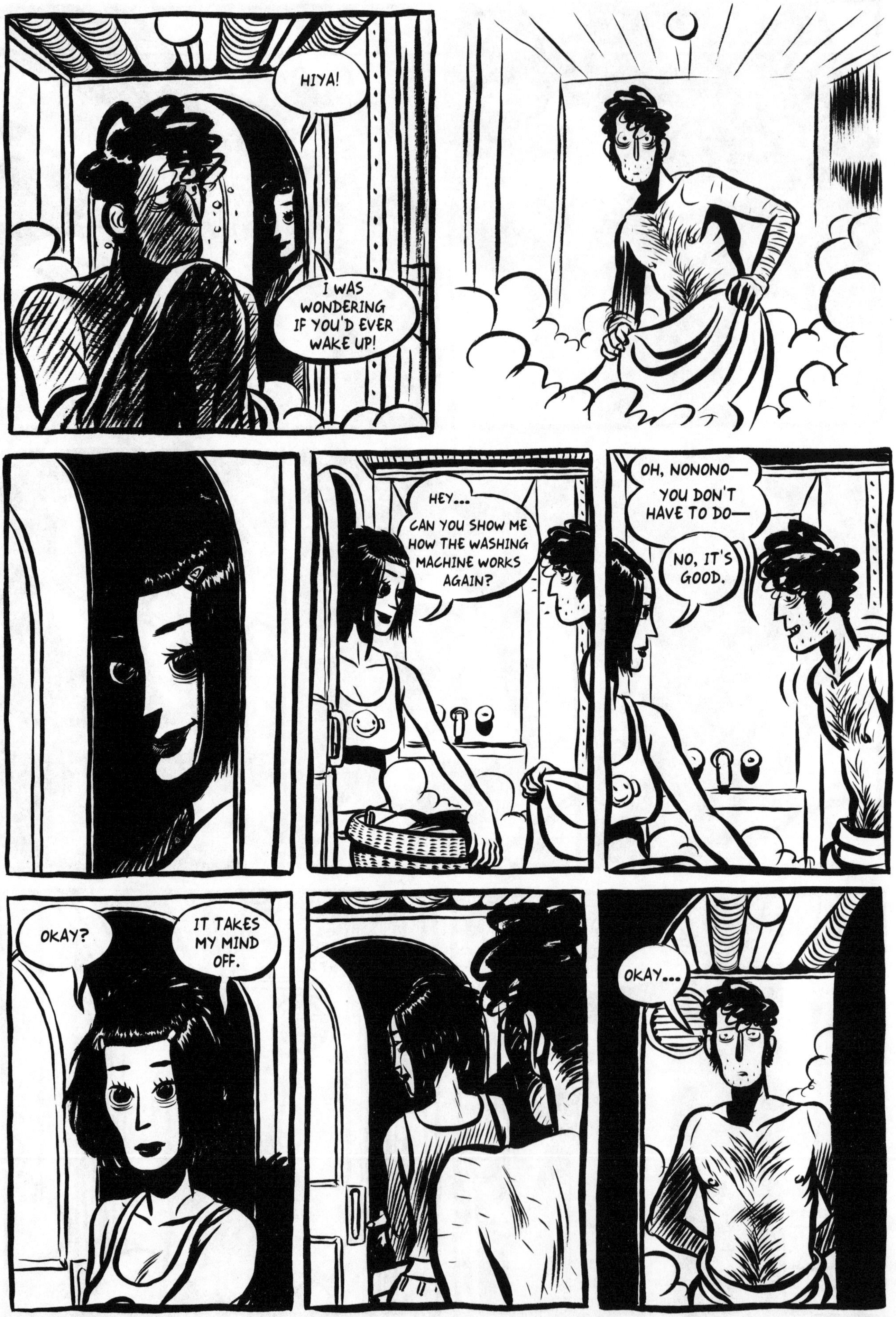
HIYA!
I WAS WONDERING IF YOU'D EVER WAKE UP!
HEY...
CAN YOU SHOW ME HOW THE WASHING MACHINE WORKS AGAIN?
OH, NONONO—
YOU DON'T HAVE TO DO—
NO, IT'S GOOD.
OKAY?
IT TAKES MY MIND OFF.
OKAY...

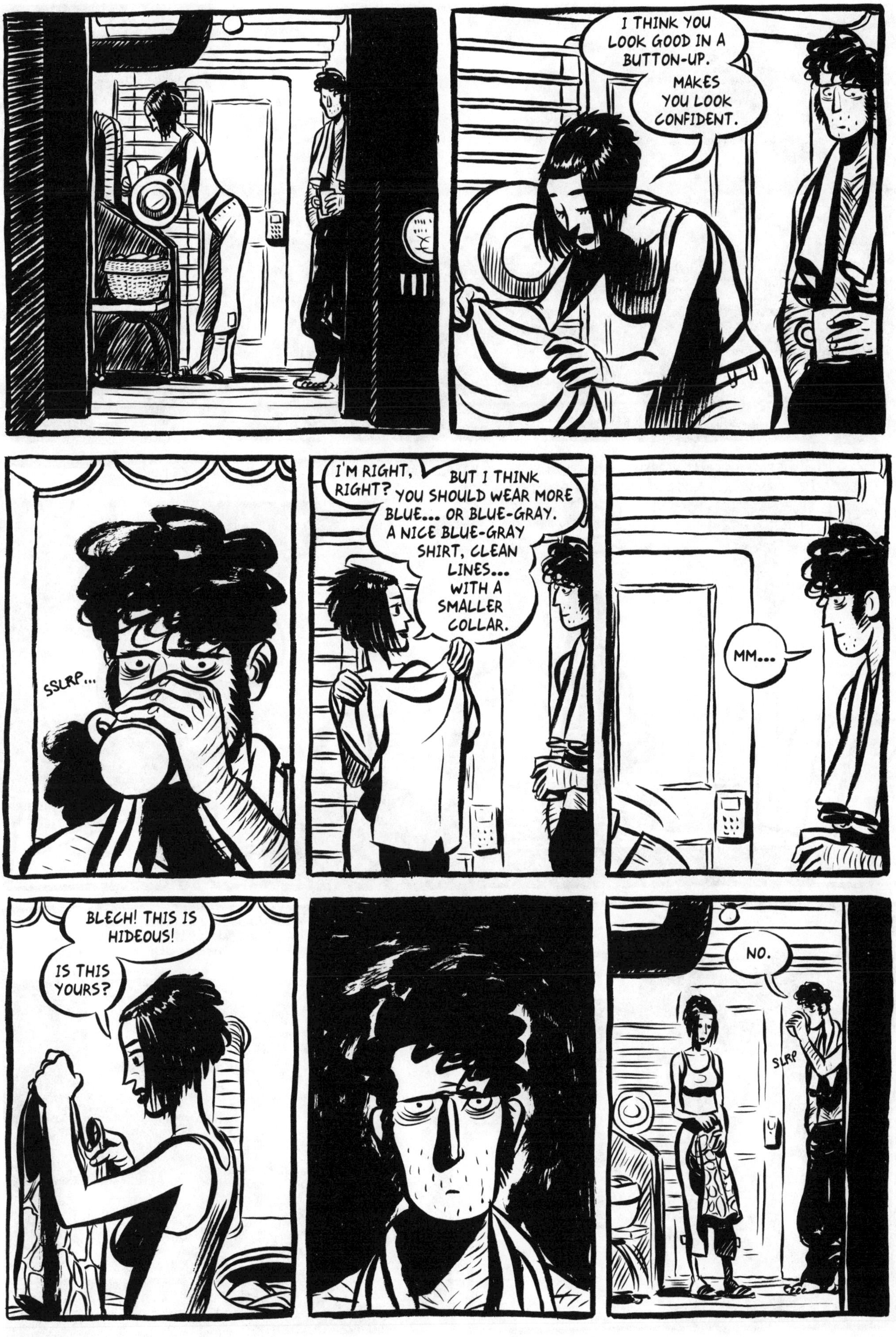
I THINK YOU LOOK GOOD IN A BUTTON-UP.
MAKES YOU LOOK CONFIDENT.
SSLRP...
I'M RIGHT, RIGHT?
BUT I THINK YOU SHOULD WEAR MORE BLUE... OR BLUE-GRAY. A NICE BLUE-GRAY SHIRT, CLEAN LINES... WITH A SMALLER COLLAR.
MM...
BLECH! THIS IS HIDEOUS!
IS THIS YOURS?
NO.
SLRP

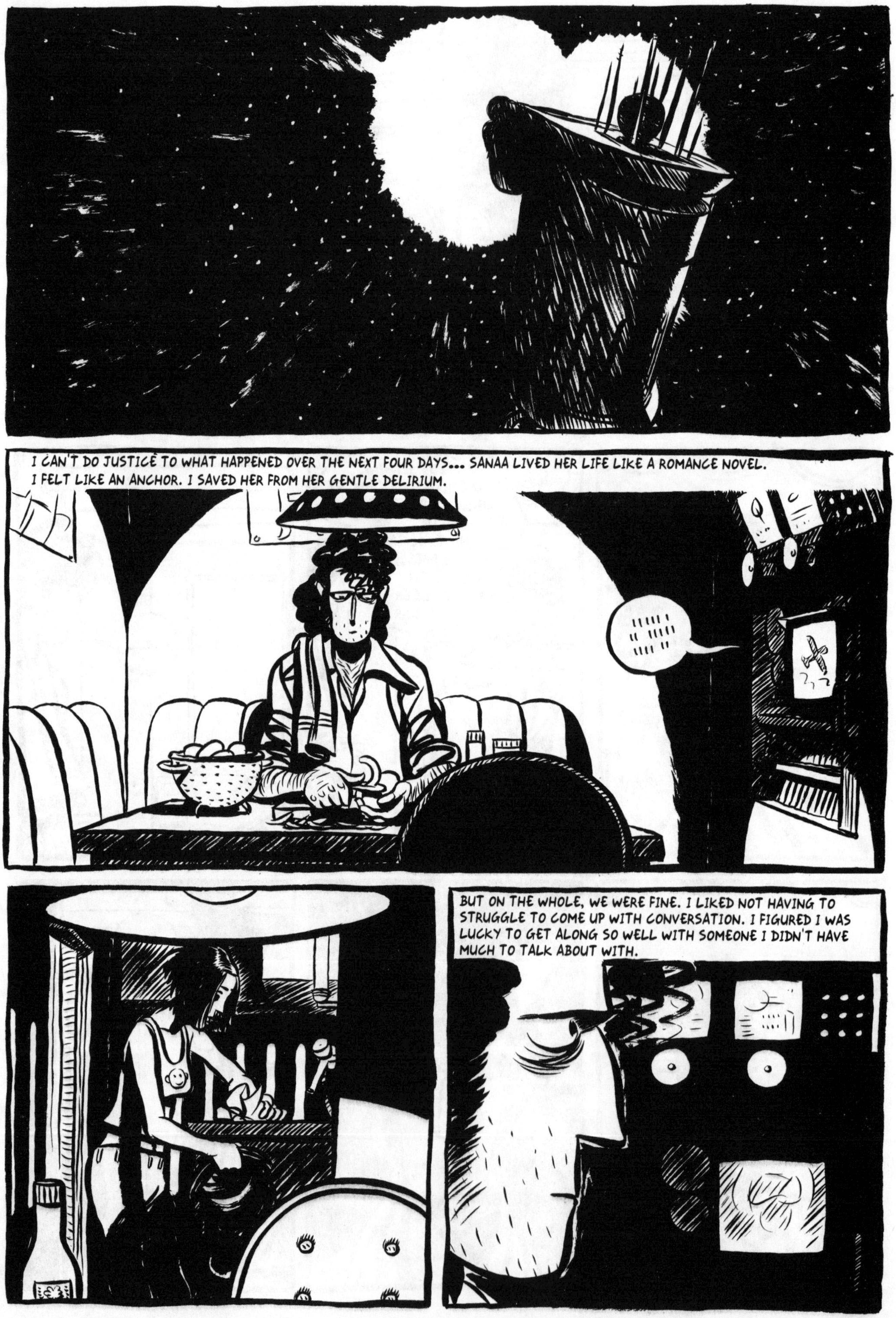
I CAN'T DO JUSTICE TO WHAT HAPPENED OVER THE NEXT FOUR DAYS... SANAA LIVED HER LIFE LIKE A ROMANCE NOVEL. I FELT LIKE AN ANCHOR. I SAVED HER FROM HER GENTLE DELIRIUM.
BUT ON THE WHOLE, WE WERE FINE. I LIKED NOT HAVING TO STRUGGLE TO COME UP WITH CONVERSATION. I FIGURED I WAS LUCKY TO GET ALONG SO WELL WITH SOMEONE I DIDN'T HAVE MUCH TO TALK ABOUT WITH.

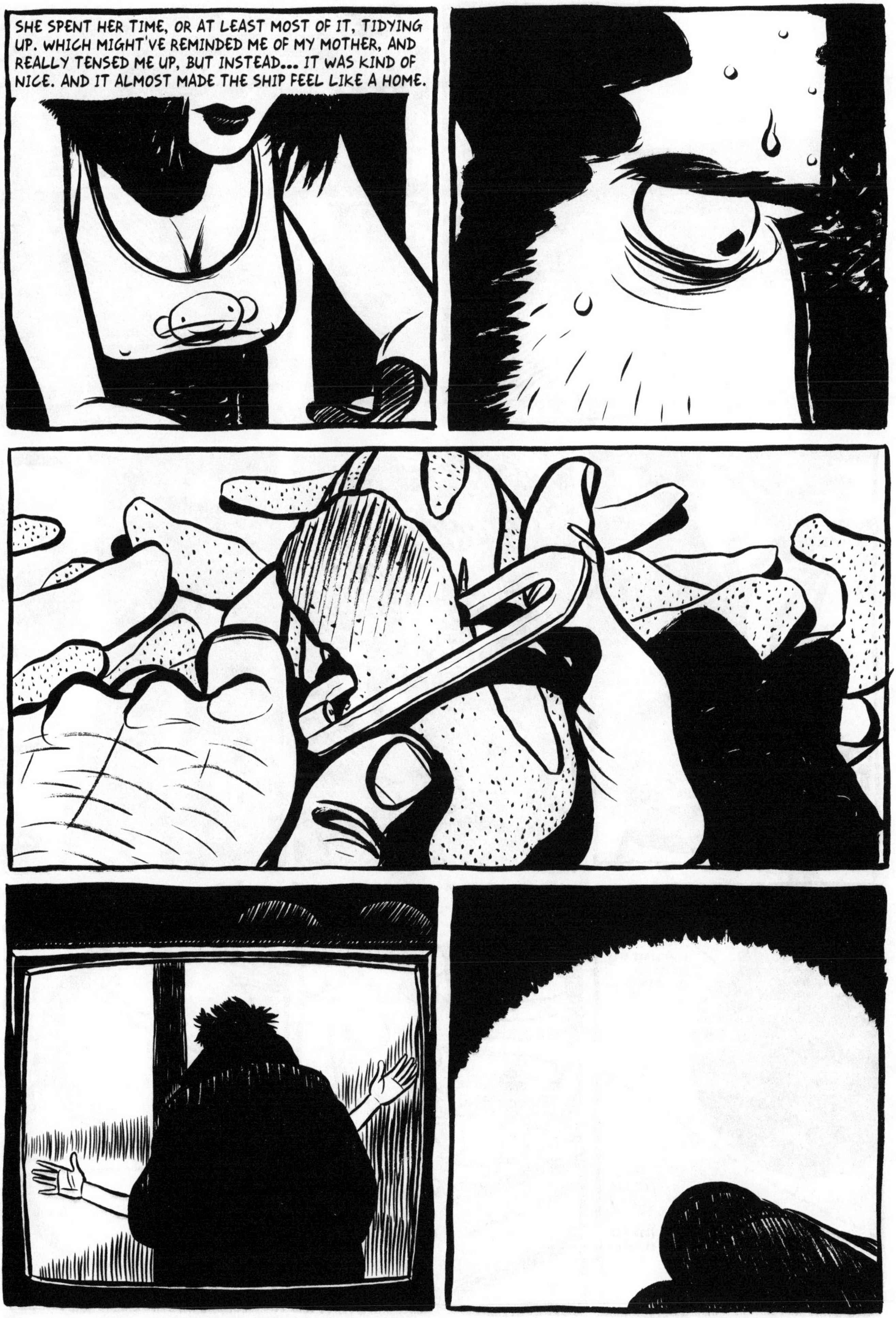
SHE SPENT HER TIME, OR AT LEAST MOST OF IT, TIDYING UP. WHICH MIGHT'VE REMINDED ME OF MY MOTHER, AND REALLY TENSED ME UP, BUT INSTEAD... IT WAS KIND OF NICE. AND IT ALMOST MADE THE SHIP FEEL LIKE A HOME.

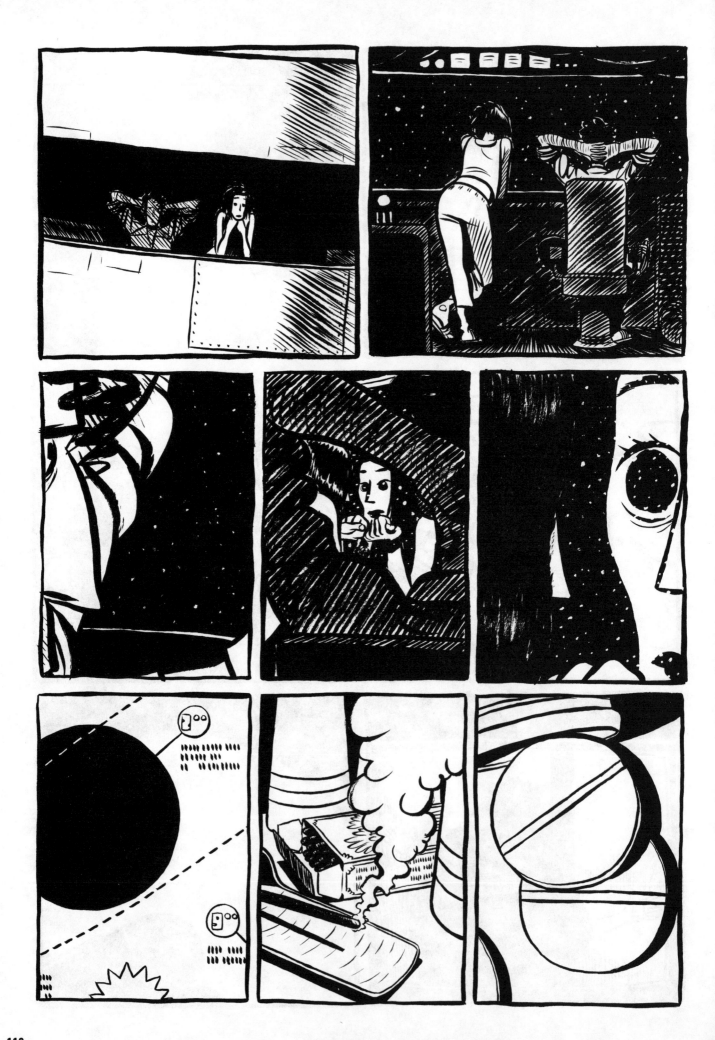

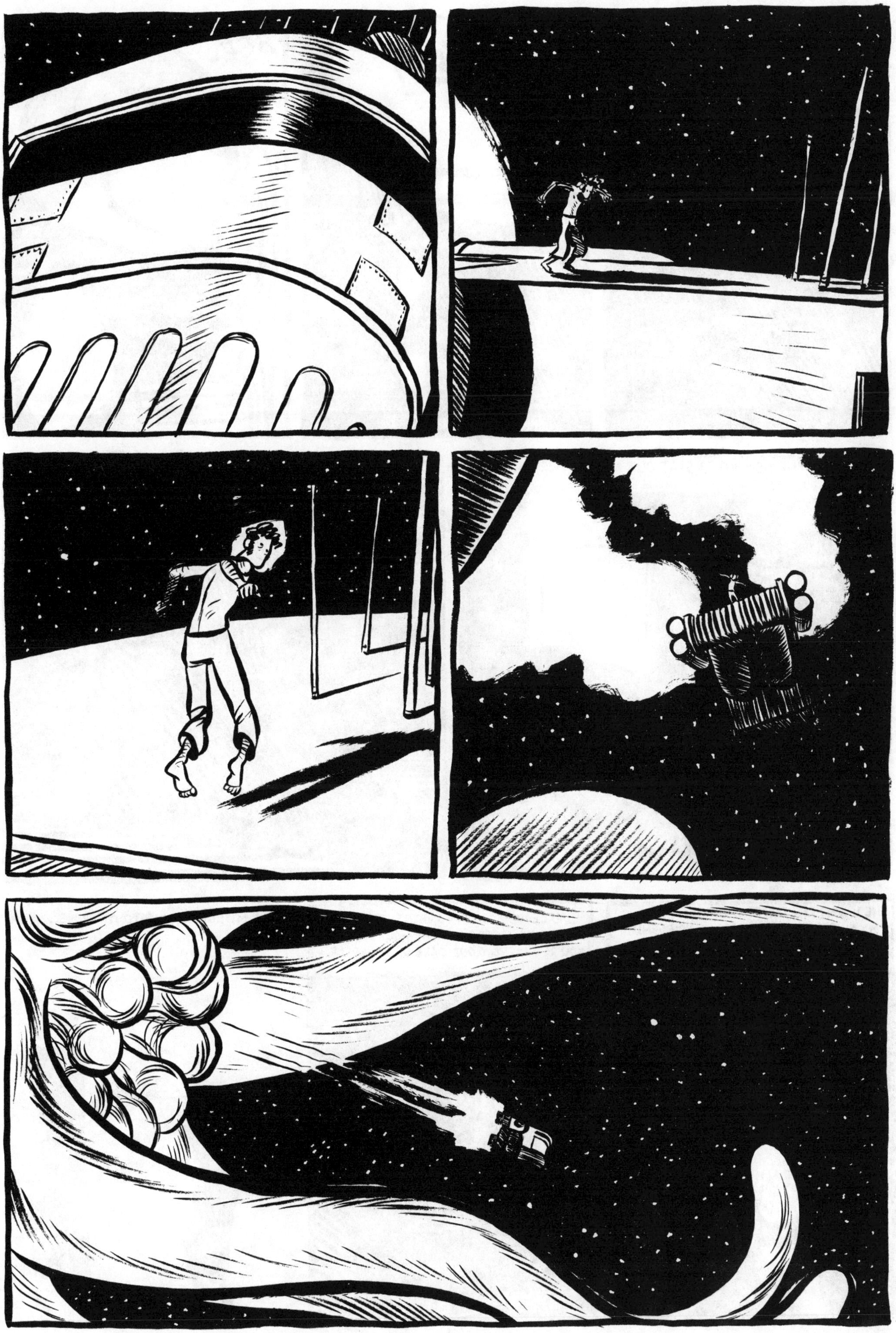

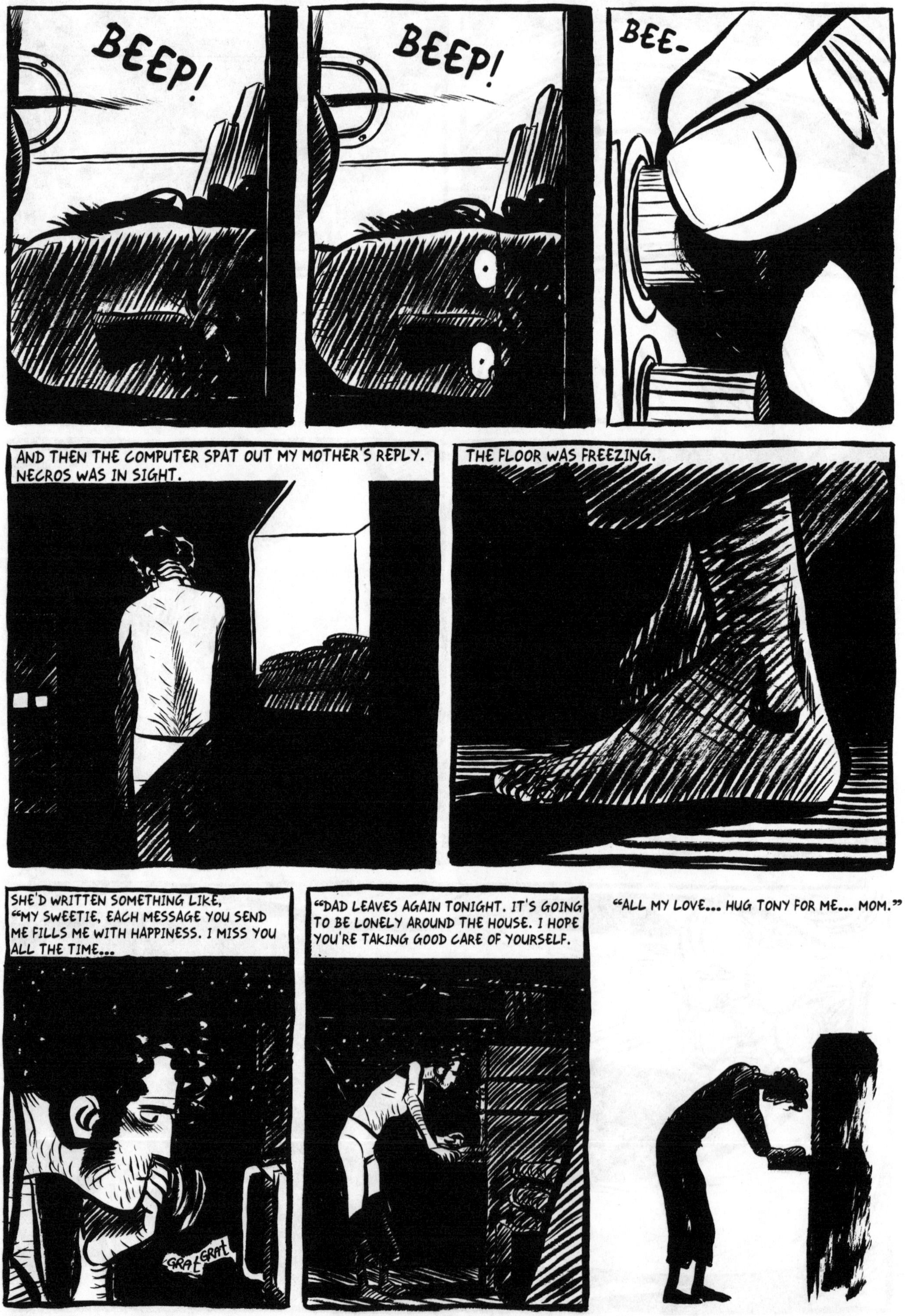
BEEP!
BEEP!
BEE-
AND THEN THE COMPUTER SPAT OUT MY MOTHER'S REPLY. NECROS WAS IN SIGHT.
THE FLOOR WAS FREEZING.
SHE'D WRITTEN SOMETHING LIKE, "MY SWEETIE, EACH MESSAGE YOU SEND ME FILLS ME WITH HAPPINESS. I MISS YOU ALL THE TIME...
GRAT GRAT
"DAD LEAVES AGAIN TONIGHT. IT'S GOING TO BE LONELY AROUND THE HOUSE. I HOPE YOU'RE TAKING GOOD CARE OF YOURSELF.
"ALL MY LOVE... HUG TONY FOR ME... MOM."

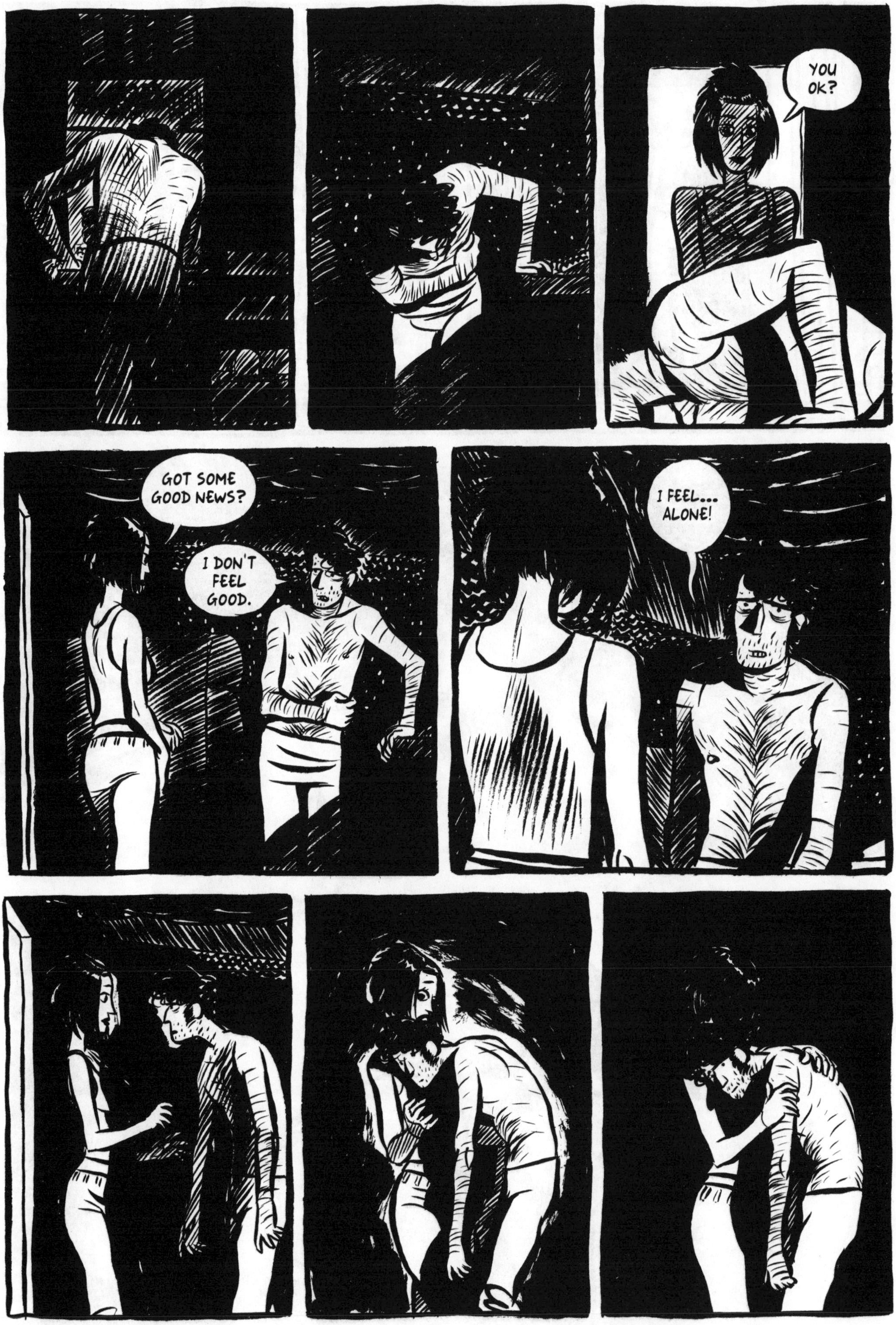
YOU OK?
GOT SOME GOOD NEWS?
I DON'T FEEL GOOD.
I FEEL... ALONE!

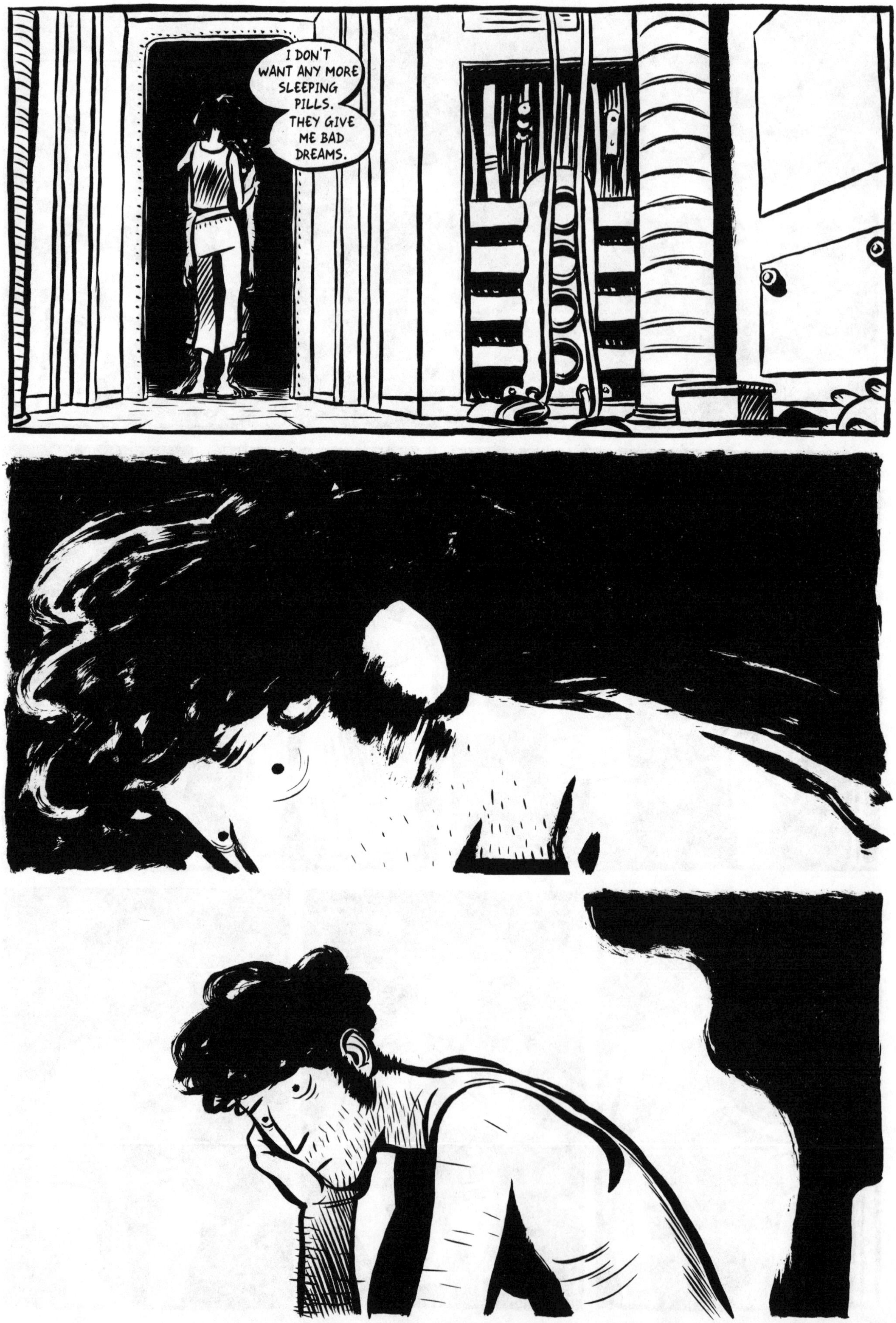
I DON'T WANT ANY MORE SLEEPING PILLS. THEY GIVE ME BAD DREAMS.

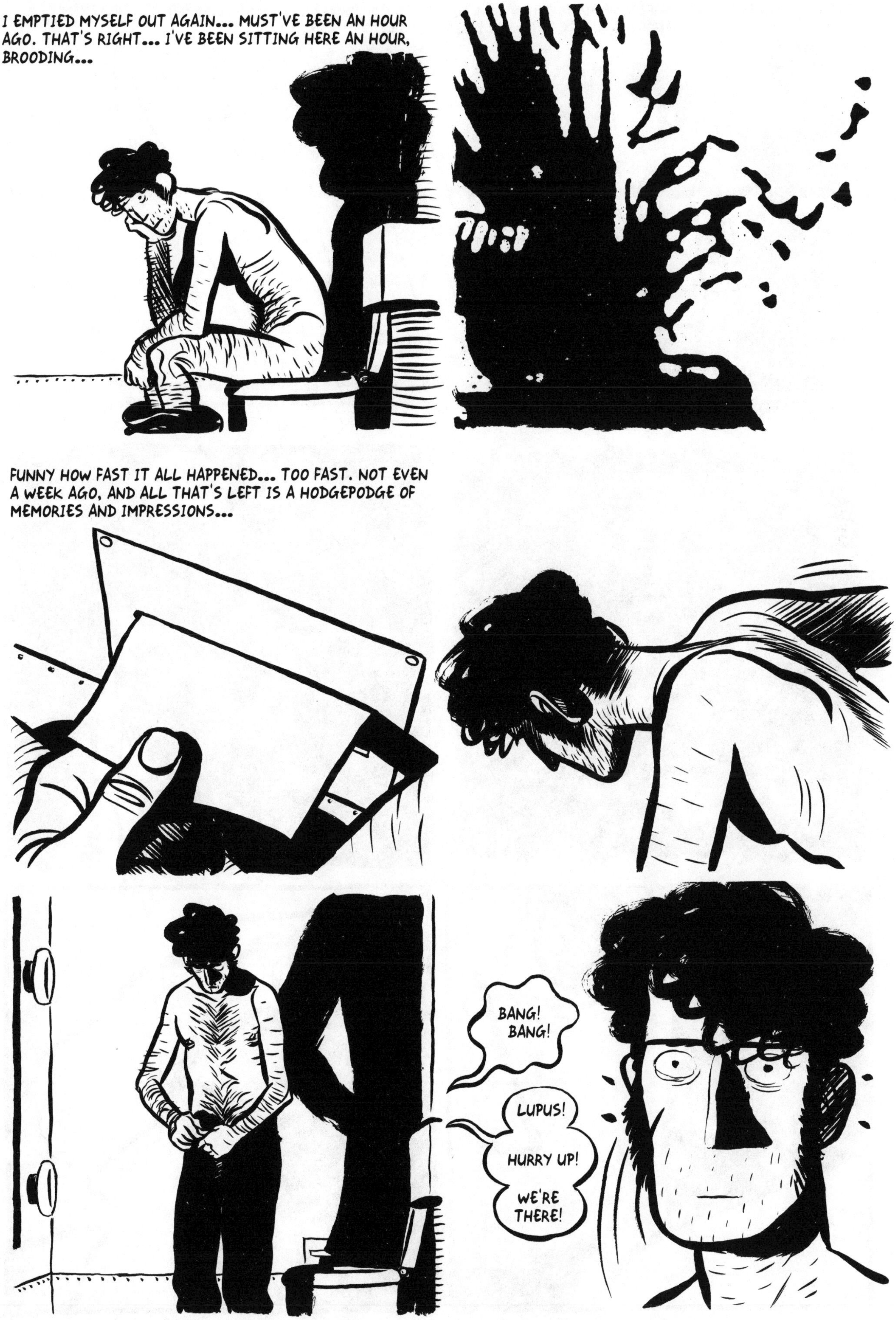
I EMPTIED MYSELF OUT AGAIN... MUST'VE BEEN AN HOUR AGO. THAT'S RIGHT... I'VE BEEN SITTING HERE AN HOUR, BROODING...
FUNNY HOW FAST IT ALL HAPPENED... TOO FAST. NOT EVEN A WEEK AGO, AND ALL THAT'S LEFT IS A HODGEPODGE OF MEMORIES AND IMPRESSIONS...
BANG! BANG!
LUPUS!
HURRY UP!
WE'RE THERE!

HER HUG HAD DONE ME A WORLD OF GOOD. SHE SMELLED LIGHTLY OF SWEAT... A GENTLE SCENT OF REALITY. A MERE SMELL HAD BEEN ENOUGH TO SET THE WORLD RIGHT, STEADY THE PRESENT.

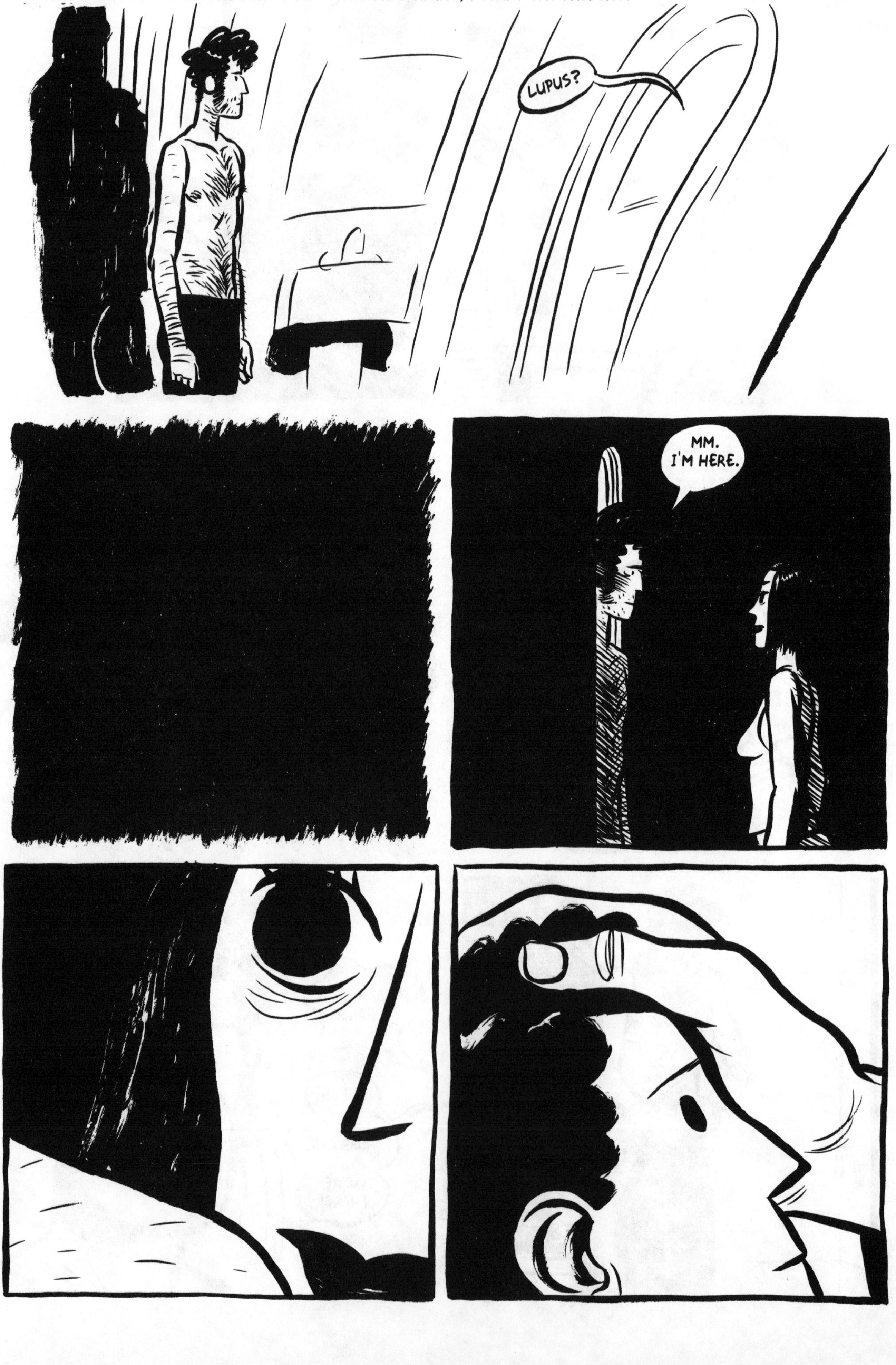
LUPUS?
MM. I'M HERE.

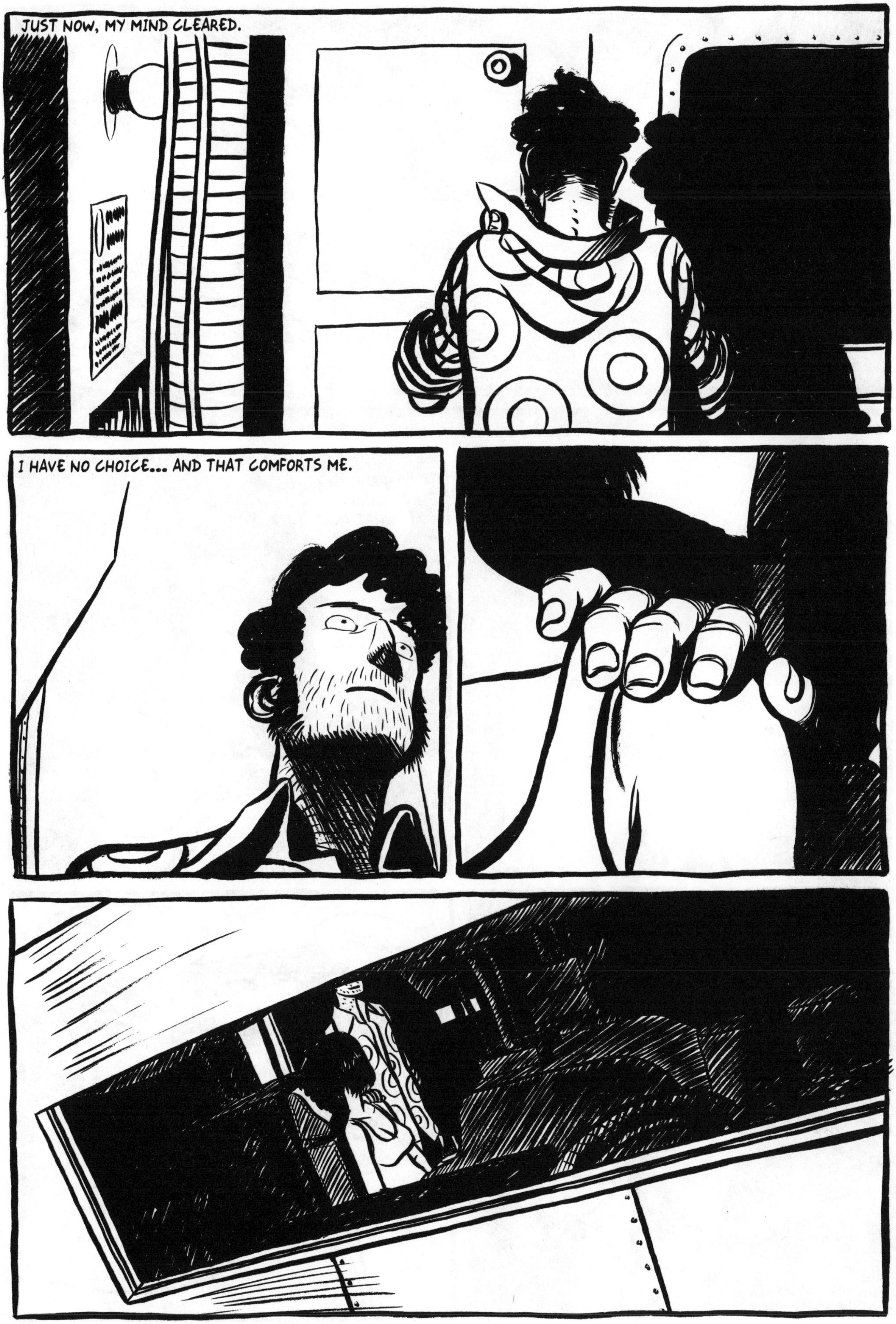
JUST NOW, MY MIND CLEARED.
I HAVE NO CHOICE... AND THAT COMFORTS ME.

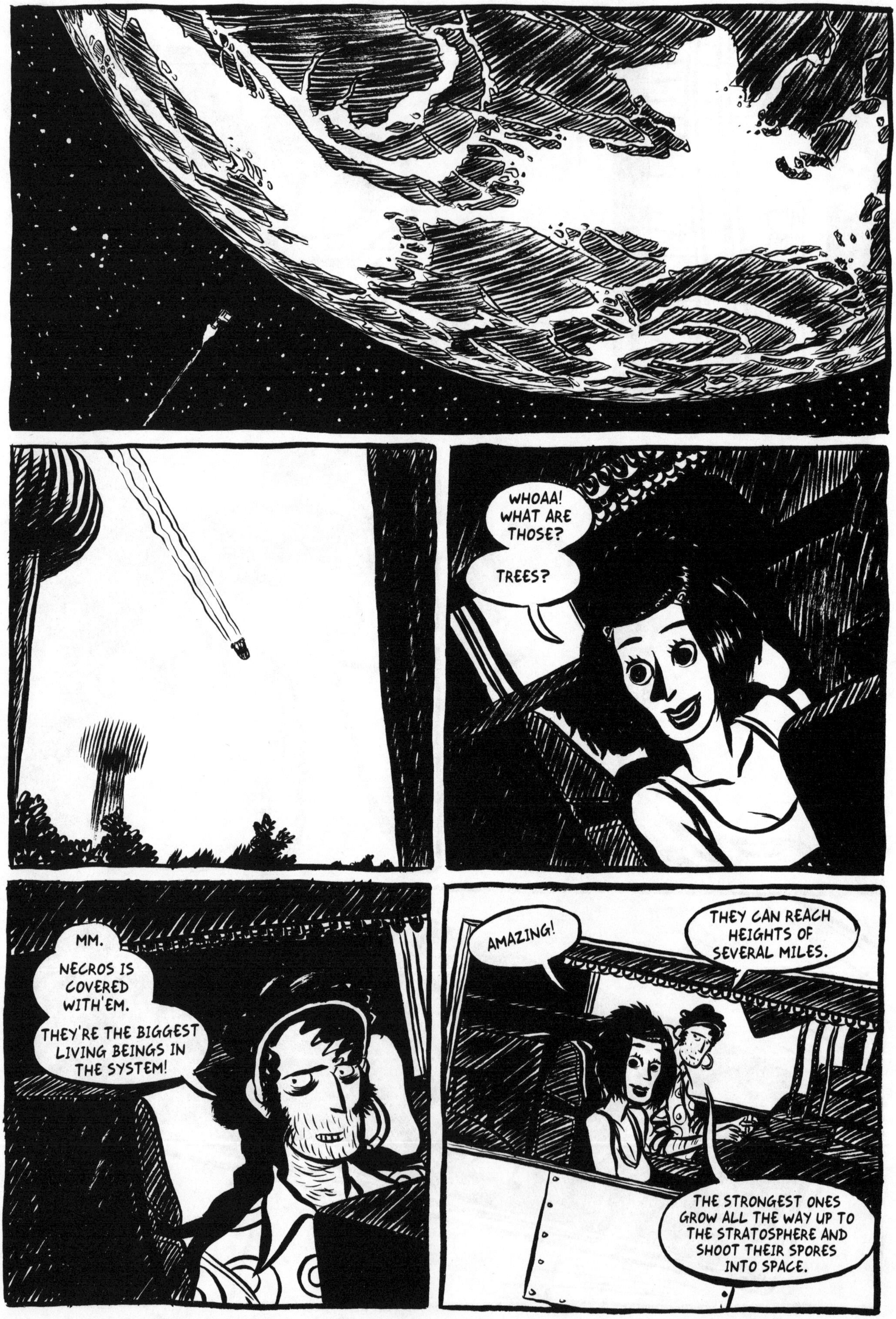
WHOAA! WHAT ARE THOSE?
TREES?
MM.
NECROS IS COVERED WITH'EM.
THEY'RE THE BIGGEST LIVING BEINGS IN THE SYSTEM!
AMAZING!
THEY CAN REACH HEIGHTS OF SEVERAL MILES.
THE STRONGEST ONES GROW ALL THE WAY UP TO THE STRATOSPHERE AND SHOOT THEIR SPORES INTO SPACE.

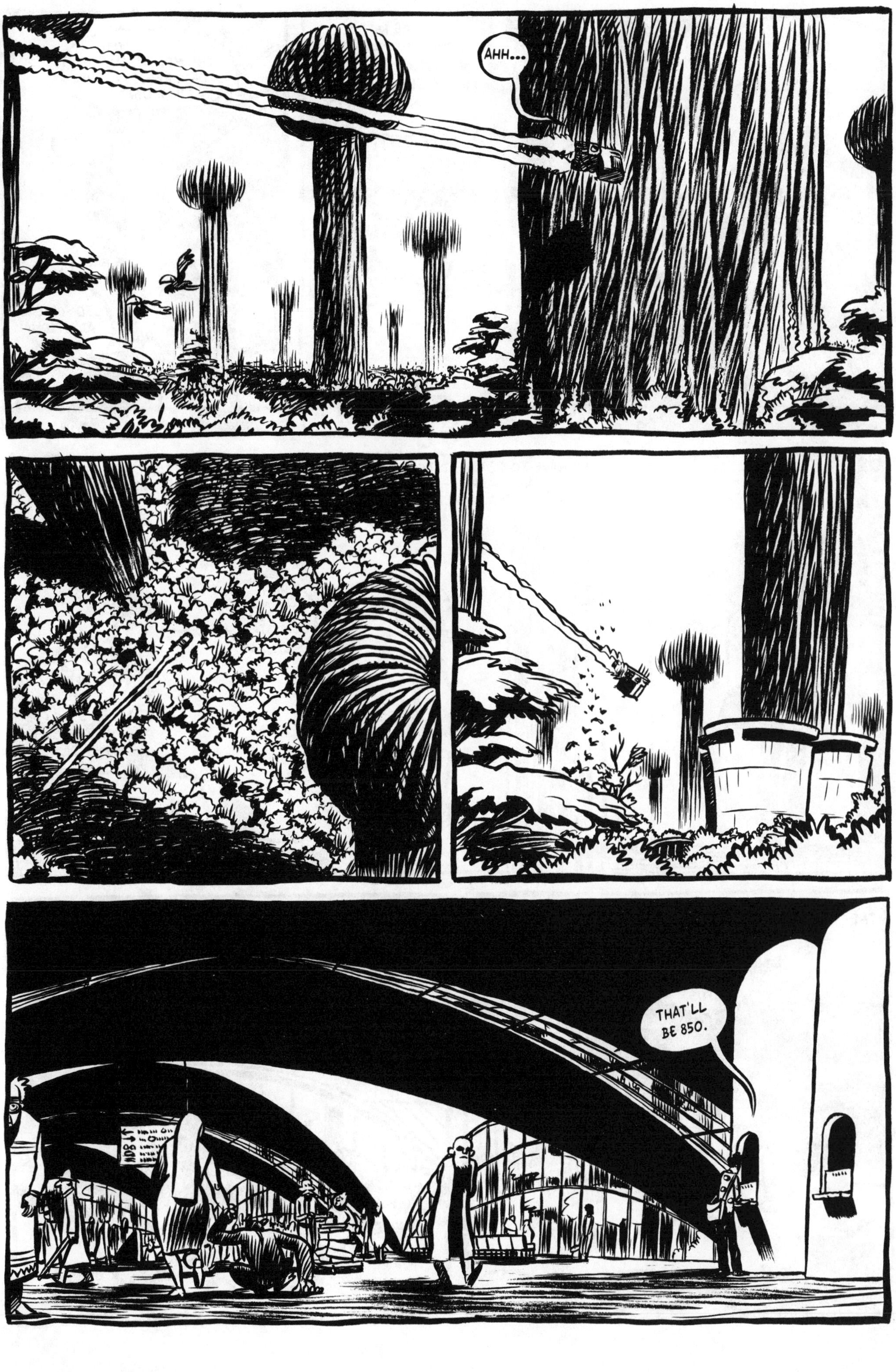
AHH...
THAT'LL BE 850.

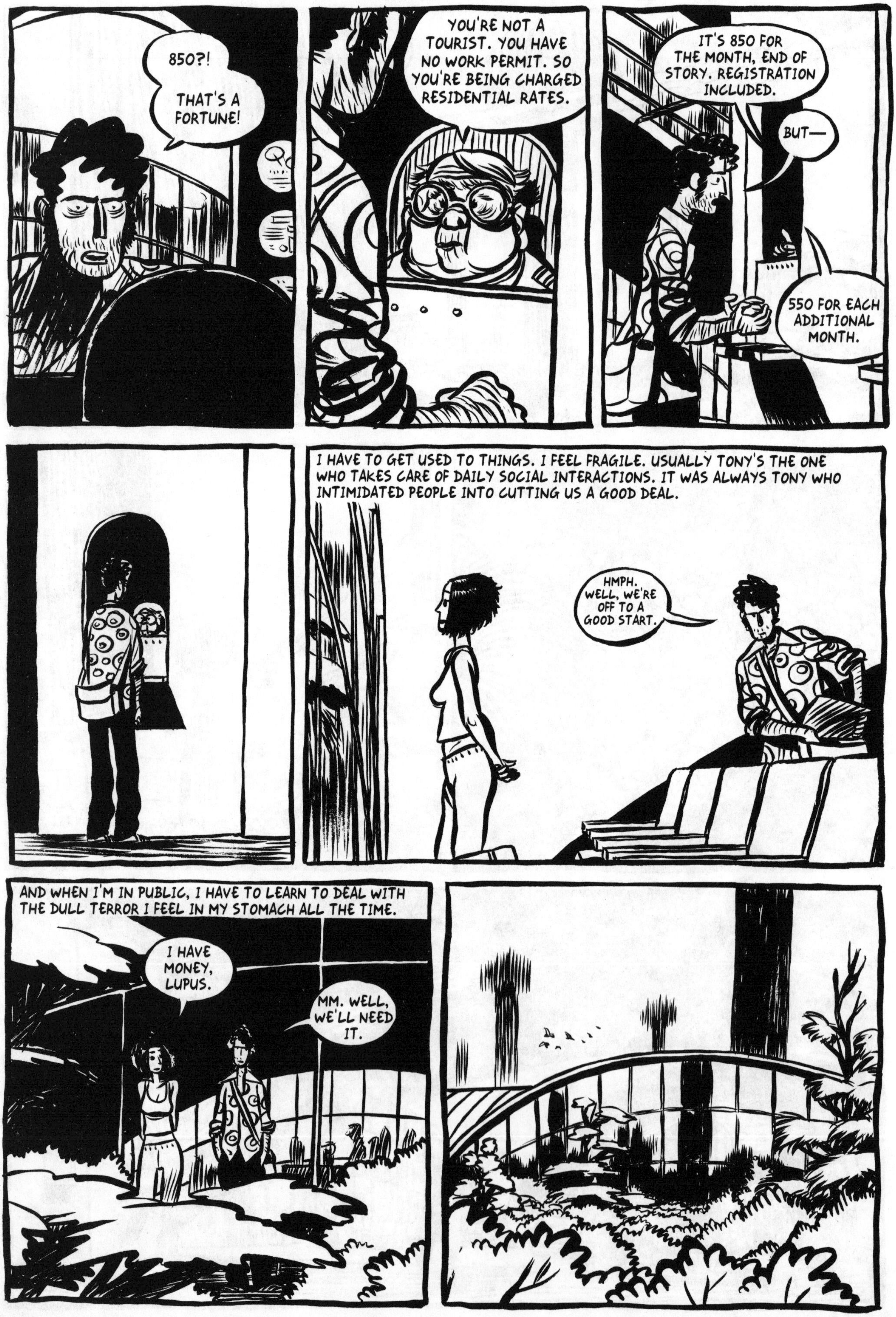
850?!
THAT'S A FORTUNE!
YOU'RE NOT A TOURIST. YOU HAVE NO WORK PERMIT. SO YOU'RE BEING CHARGED RESIDENTIAL RATES.
IT'S 850 FOR THE MONTH, END OF STORY. REGISTRATION INCLUDED.
BUT—
550 FOR EACH ADDITIONAL MONTH.
I HAVE TO GET USED TO THINGS. I FEEL FRAGILE. USUALLY TONY'S THE ONE WHO TAKES CARE OF DAILY SOCIAL INTERACTIONS. IT WAS ALWAYS TONY WHO INTIMIDATED PEOPLE INTO CUTTING US A GOOD DEAL.
HMPH. WELL, WE'RE OFF TO A GOOD START.
AND WHEN I'M IN PUBLIC, I HAVE TO LEARN TO DEAL WITH THE DULL TERROR I FEEL IN MY STOMACH ALL THE TIME.
I HAVE MONEY, LUPUS.
MM. WELL, WE'LL NEED IT.

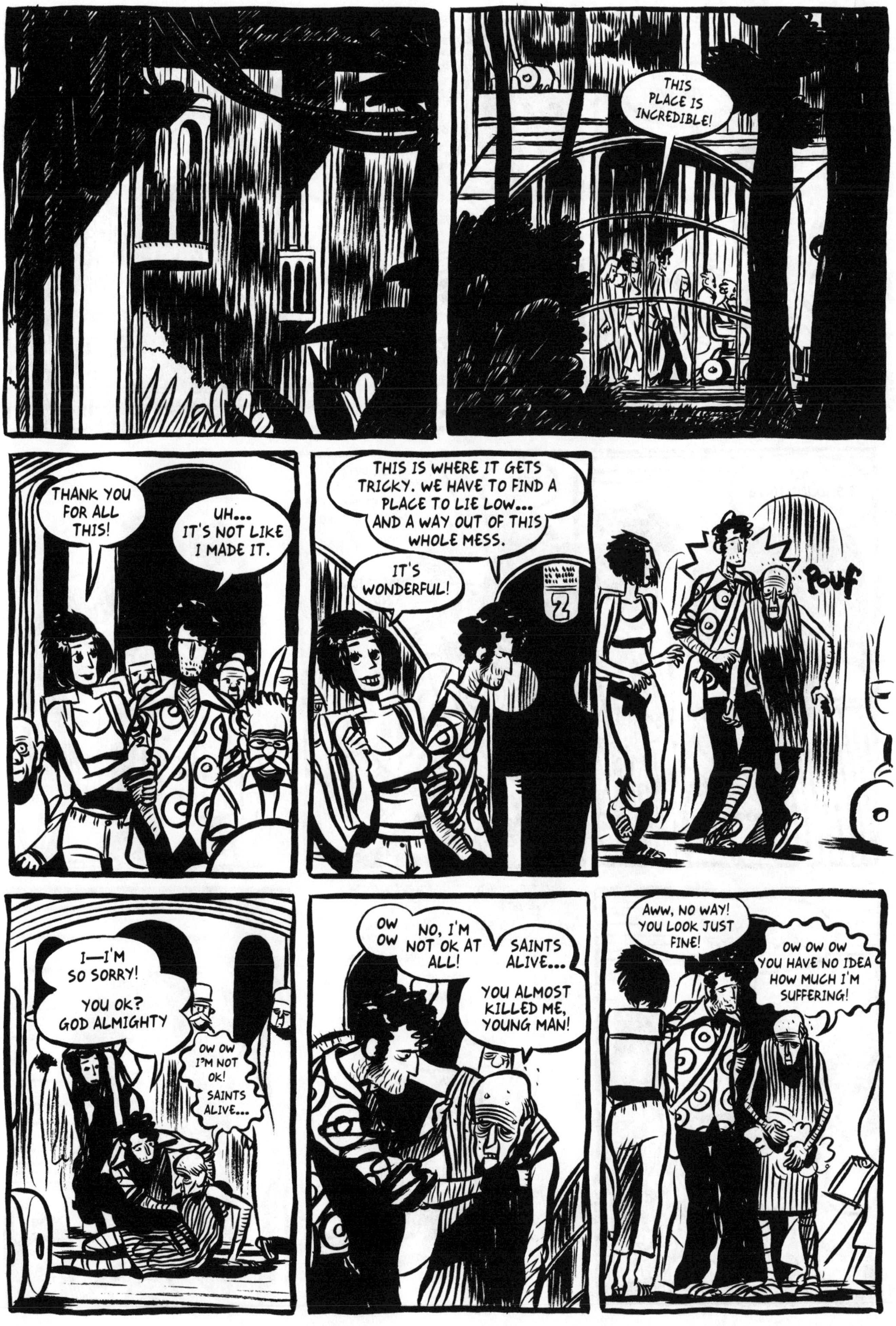
THIS PLACE IS INCREDIBLE!
THANK YOU FOR ALL THIS!
UH... IT'S NOT LIKE I MADE IT.
THIS IS WHERE IT GETS TRICKY. WE HAVE TO FIND A PLACE TO LIE LOW... AND A WAY OUT OF THIS WHOLE MESS.
IT'S WONDERFUL!
POUF
I—I'M SO SORRY!
YOU OK? GOD ALMIGHTY
OW OW I'M NOT OK! SAINTS ALIVE...
OW OW
NO, I'M NOT OK AT ALL!
SAINTS ALIVE...
YOU ALMOST KILLED ME, YOUNG MAN!
AWW, NO WAY! YOU LOOK JUST FINE!
OW OW OW YOU HAVE NO IDEA HOW MUCH I'M SUFFERING!

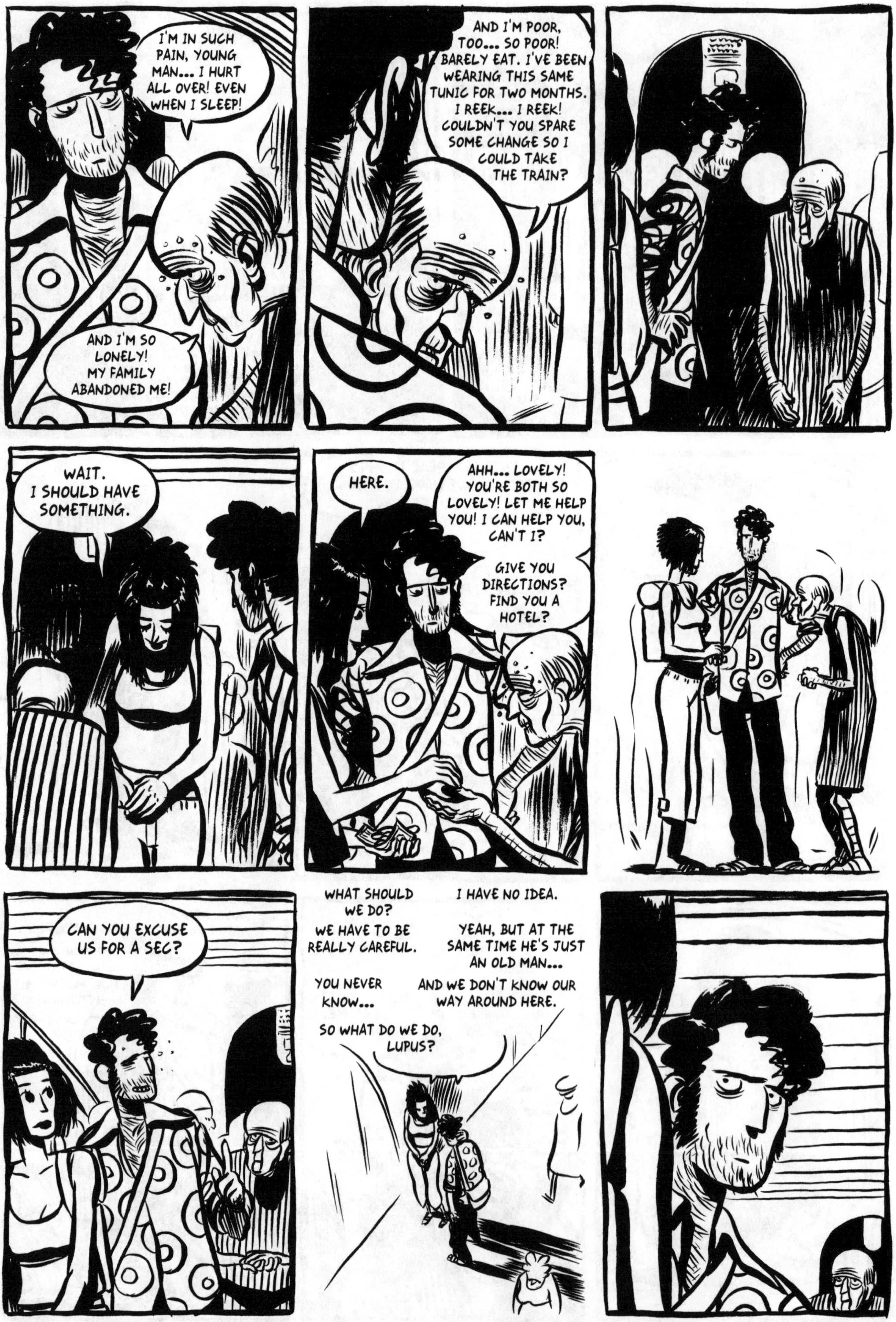

I'M IN SUCH PAIN, YOUNG MAN... I HURT ALL OVER! EVEN WHEN I SLEEP!
AND I'M SO LONELY! MY FAMILY ABANDONED ME!
AND I'M POOR, TOO... SO POOR! I BARELY EAT. I'VE BEEN WEARING THIS SAME TUNIC FOR TWO MONTHS. I REEK... I REEK! COULDN'T YOU SPARE SOME CHANGE SO I COULD TAKE THE TRAIN?
WAIT. I SHOULD HAVE SOMETHING.
HERE.
AHH... LOVELY! YOU'RE BOTH SO LOVELY! LET ME HELP YOU! I CAN HELP YOU, CAN'T I?
GIVE YOU DIRECTIONS? FIND YOU A HOTEL?
CAN YOU EXCUSE US FOR A SEC?
WHAT SHOULD WE DO?
I HAVE NO IDEA.
WE HAVE TO BE REALLY CAREFUL.
YEAH, BUT AT THE SAME TIME HE'S JUST AN OLD MAN...
YOU NEVER KNOW...
AND WE DON'T KNOW OUR WAY AROUND HERE.
SO WHAT DO WE DO, LUPUS?

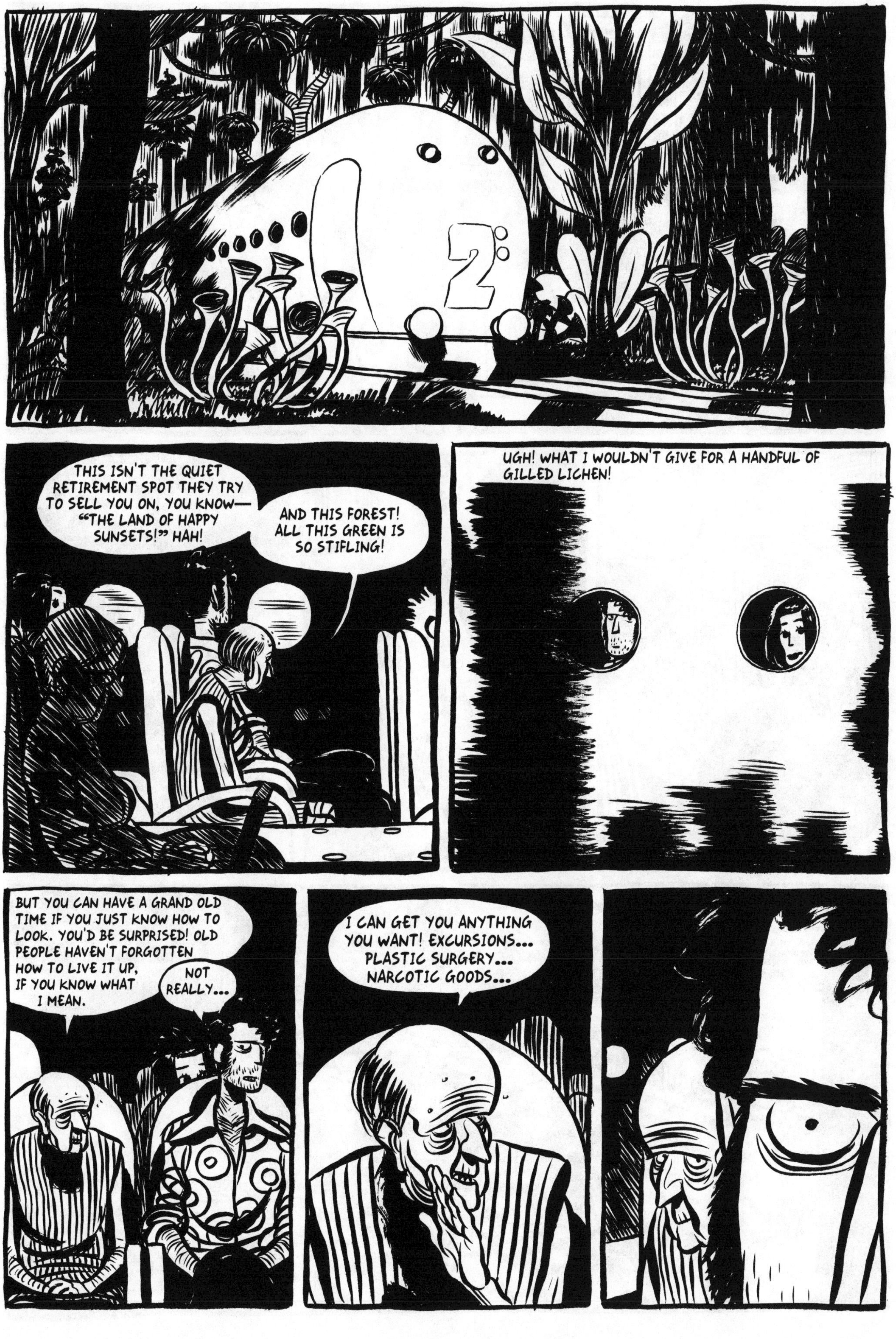
THIS ISN'T THE QUIET RETIREMENT SPOT THEY TRY TO SELL YOU ON, YOU KNOW—"THE LAND OF HAPPY SUNSETS!" HAH!
AND THIS FOREST! ALL THIS GREEN IS SO STIFLING!
UGH! WHAT I WOULDN'T GIVE FOR A HANDFUL OF GILLED LICHEN!
BUT YOU CAN HAVE A GRAND OLD TIME IF YOU JUST KNOW HOW TO LOOK. YOU'D BE SURPRISED! OLD PEOPLE HAVEN'T FORGOTTEN HOW TO LIVE IT UP, IF YOU KNOW WHAT I MEAN.
NOT REALLY...
I CAN GET YOU ANYTHING YOU WANT! EXCURSIONS... PLASTIC SURGERY... NARCOTIC GOODS...

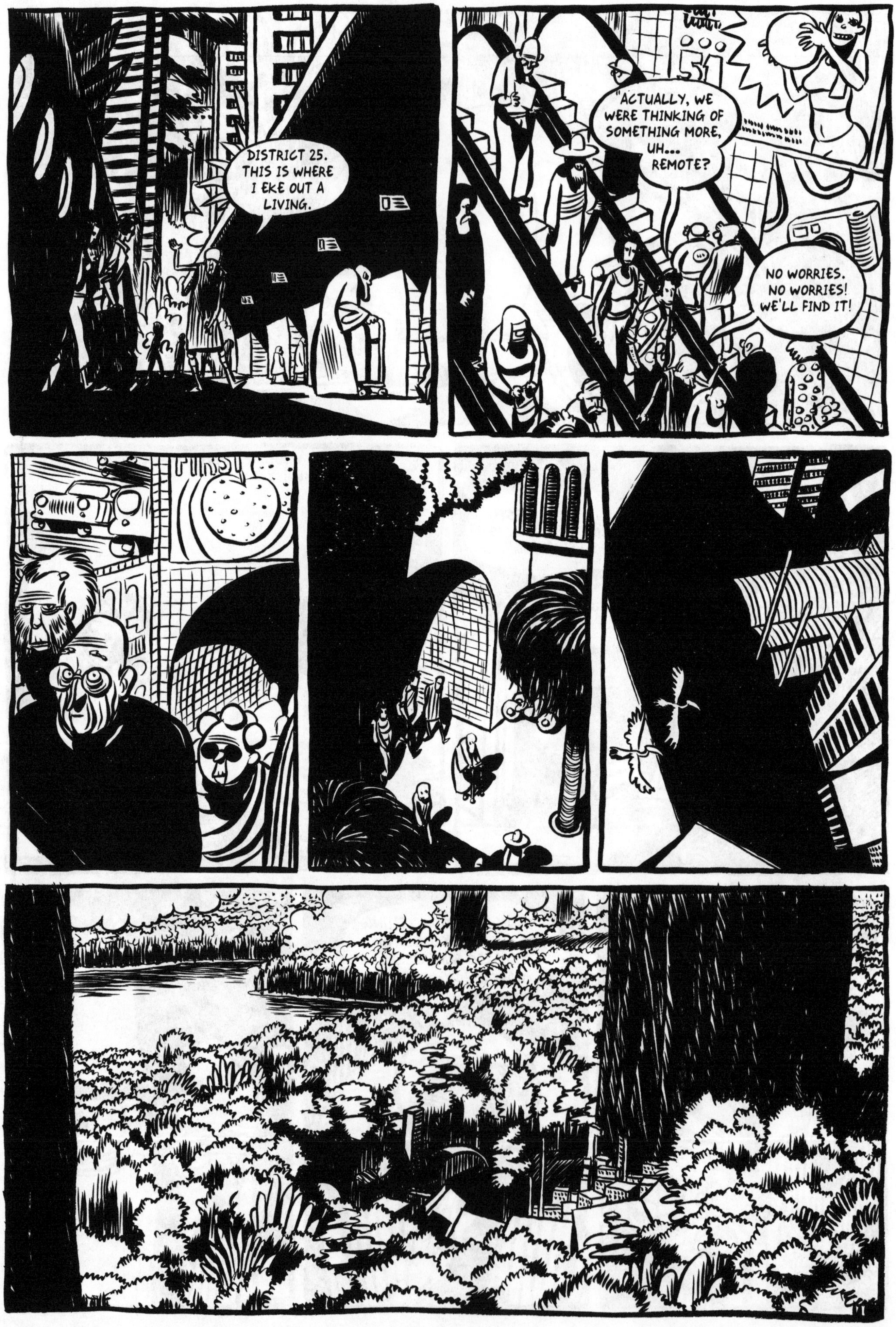
DISTRICT 25. THIS IS WHERE I EKE OUT A LIVING.
"ACTUALLY, WE WERE THINKING OF SOMETHING MORE, UH... REMOTE?
NO WORRIES. NO WORRIES! WE'LL FIND IT!

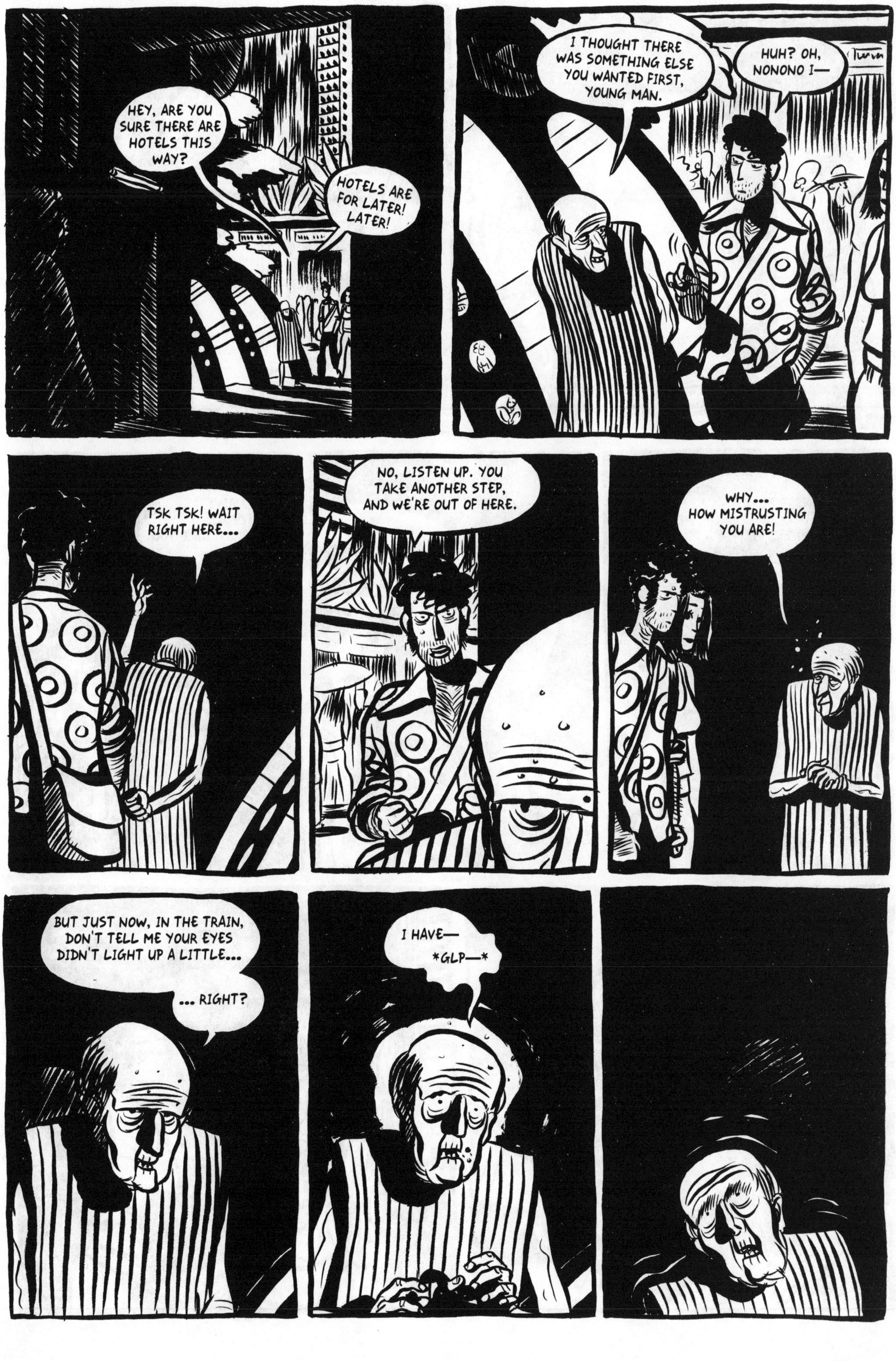
HEY, ARE YOU SURE THERE ARE HOTELS THIS WAY?
HOTELS ARE FOR LATER! LATER!
I THOUGHT THERE WAS SOMETHING ELSE YOU WANTED FIRST, YOUNG MAN.
HUH? OH, NONONO I—
TSK TSK! WAIT RIGHT HERE...
NO, LISTEN UP. YOU TAKE ANOTHER STEP, AND WE'RE OUT OF HERE.
WHY... HOW MISTRUSTING YOU ARE!
BUT JUST NOW, IN THE TRAIN, DON'T TELL ME YOUR EYES DIDN'T LIGHT UP A LITTLE...
... RIGHT?
I HAVE—
GLP—

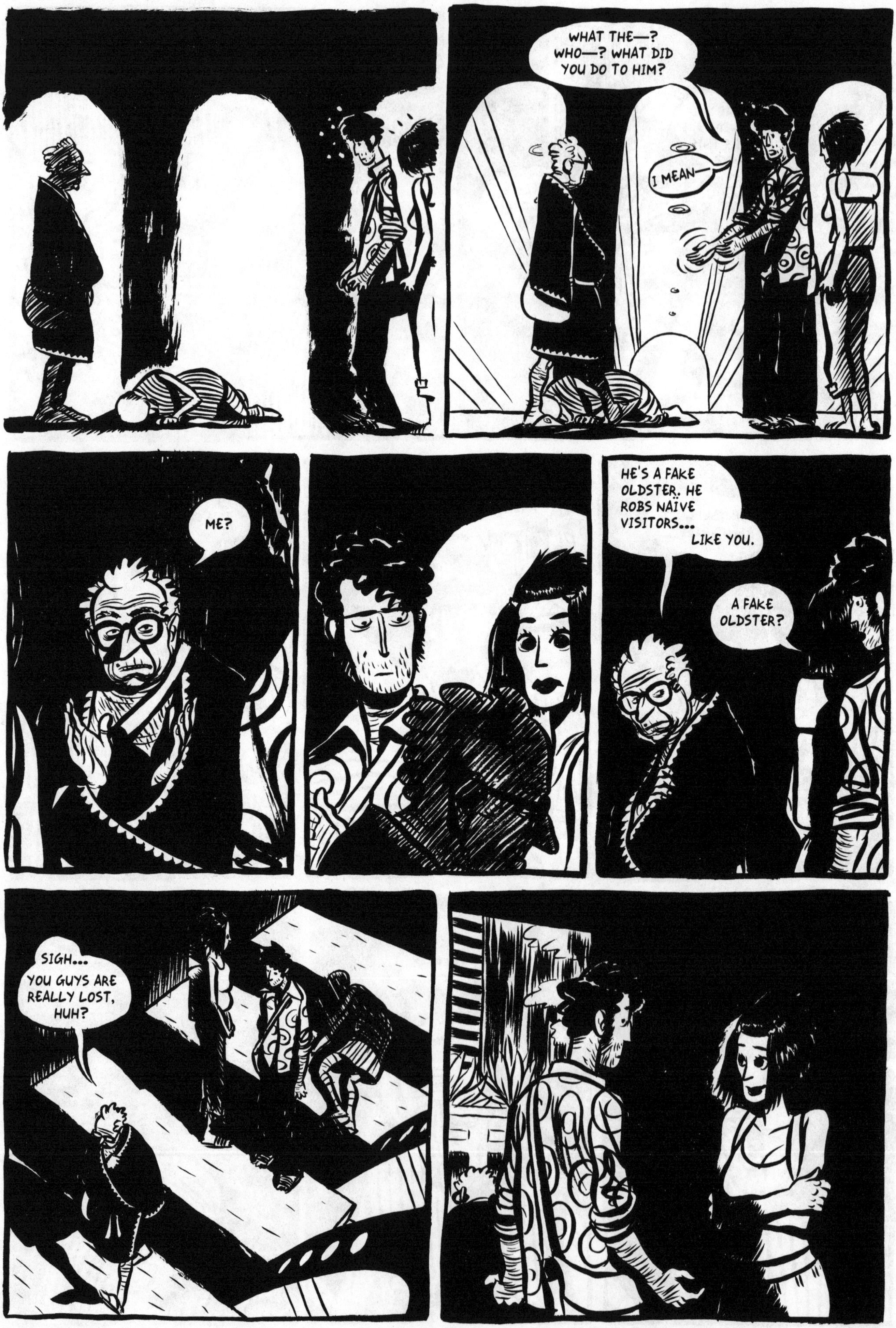
WHAT THE—? WHO—? WHAT DID YOU DO TO HIM?
I MEAN—
ME?
HE'S A FAKE OLDSTER. HE ROBS NAÏVE VISITORS... LIKE YOU.
A FAKE OLDSTER?
SIGH... YOU GUYS ARE REALLY LOST, HUH?

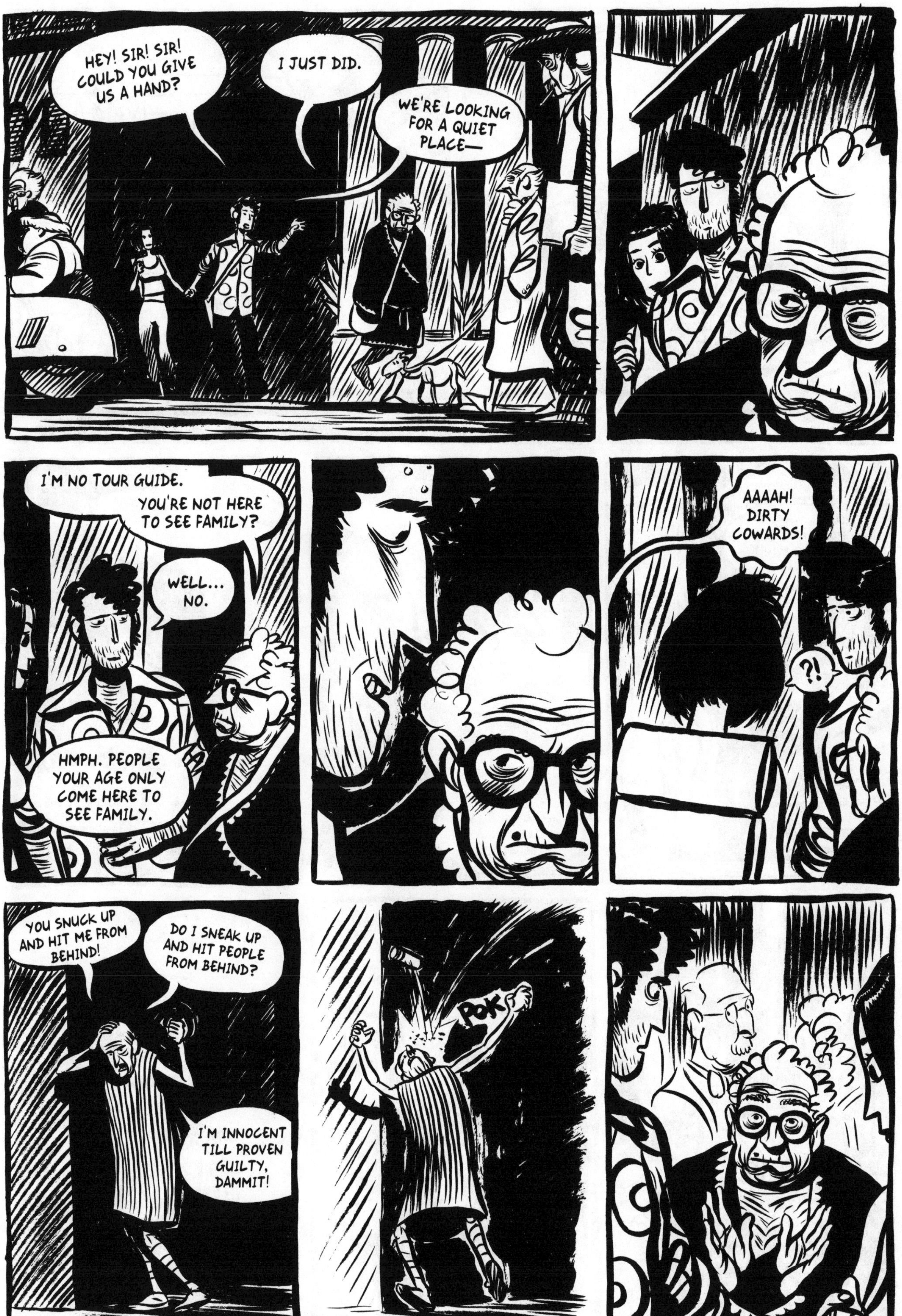
HEY! SIR! SIR! COULD YOU GIVE US A HAND?
I JUST DID.
WE'RE LOOKING FOR A QUIET PLACE—
I'M NO TOUR GUIDE.
YOU'RE NOT HERE TO SEE FAMILY?
WELL... NO.
HMPH. PEOPLE YOUR AGE ONLY COME HERE TO SEE FAMILY.
AAAAH! DIRTY COWARDS!
?!
YOU SNUCK UP AND HIT ME FROM BEHIND!
DO I SNEAK UP AND HIT PEOPLE FROM BEHIND?
I'M INNOCENT TILL PROVEN GUILTY, DAMMIT!
POK

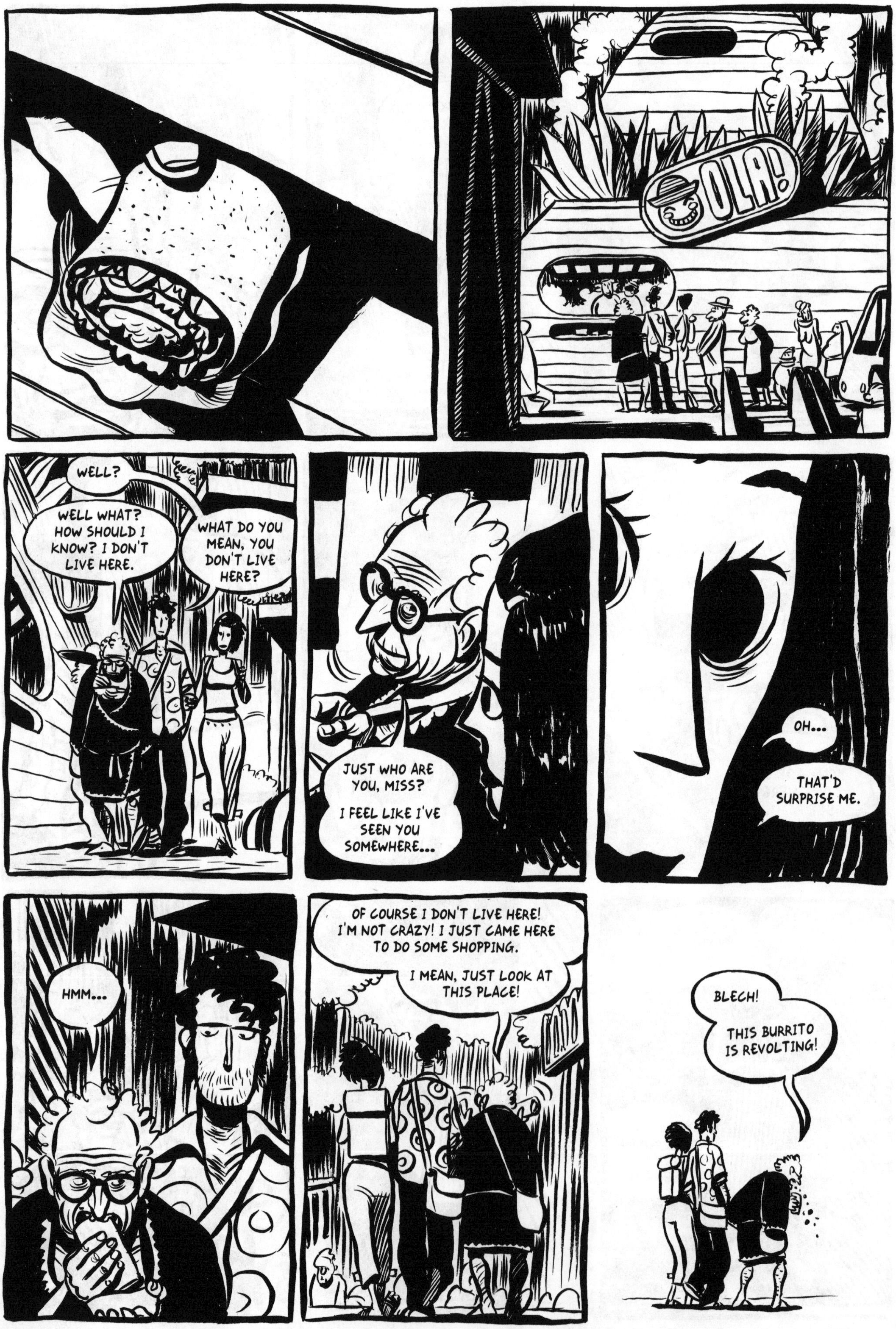
OLA!
WELL?
WELL WHAT? HOW SHOULD I KNOW? I DON'T LIVE HERE.
WHAT DO YOU MEAN, YOU DON'T LIVE HERE?
JUST WHO ARE YOU, MISS?
I FEEL LIKE I'VE SEEN YOU SOMEWHERE...
OH...
THAT'D SURPRISE ME.
HMM...
OF COURSE I DON'T LIVE HERE! I'M NOT CRAZY! I JUST CAME HERE TO DO SOME SHOPPING.
I MEAN, JUST LOOK AT THIS PLACE!
BLECH!
THIS BURRITO IS REVOLTING!

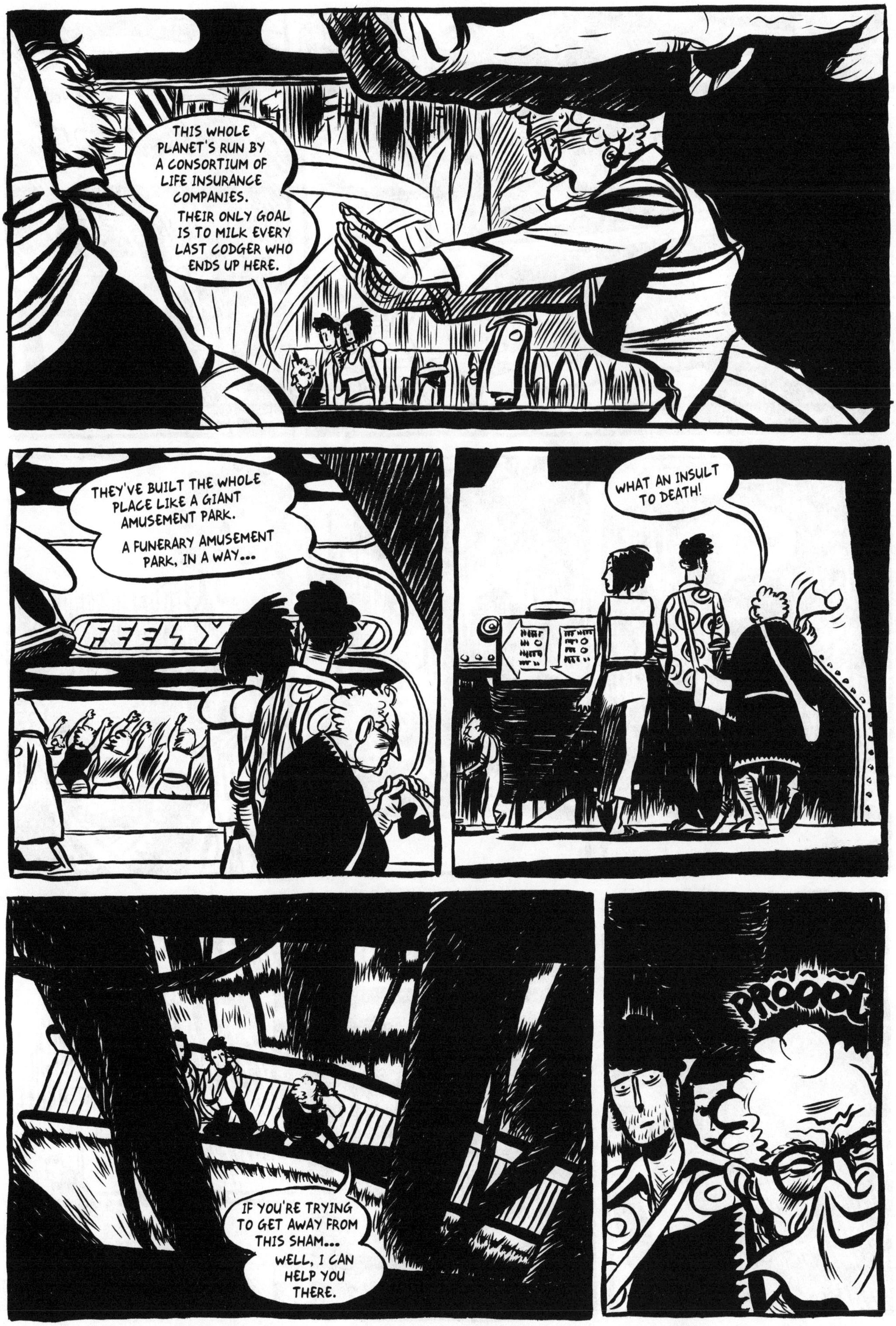
THIS WHOLE PLANET'S RUN BY A CONSORTIUM OF LIFE INSURANCE COMPANIES.
THEIR ONLY GOAL IS TO MILK EVERY LAST CODGER WHO ENDS UP HERE.
THEY'VE BUILT THE WHOLE PLACE LIKE A GIANT AMUSEMENT PARK.
A FUNERARY AMUSEMENT PARK, IN A WAY...
WHAT AN INSULT TO DEATH!
IF YOU'RE TRYING TO GET AWAY FROM THIS SHAM...
WELL, I CAN HELP YOU THERE.
PROOOT

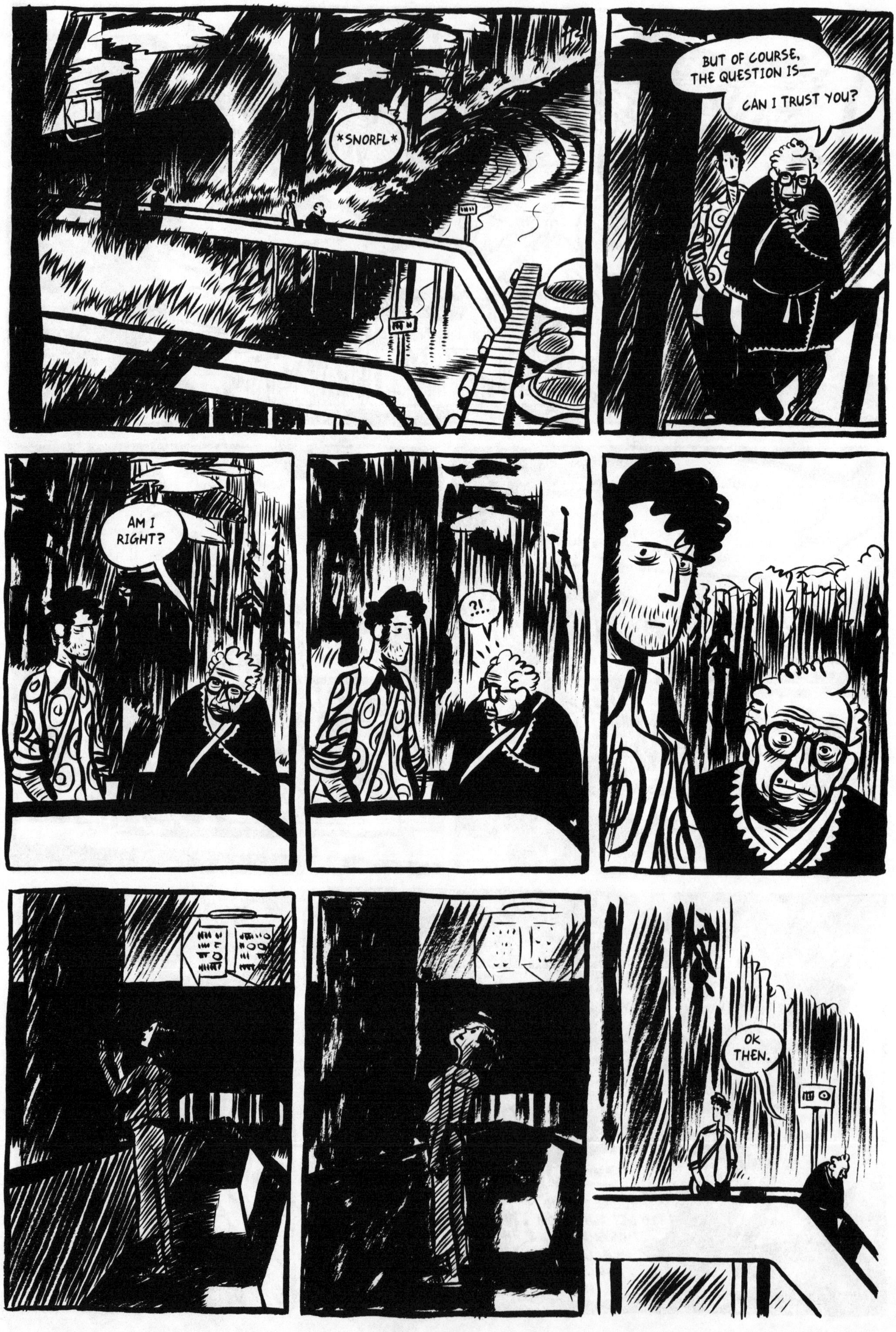
SNORFL
BUT OF COURSE, THE QUESTION IS—
CAN I TRUST YOU?
AM I RIGHT?
?!.
OK THEN.

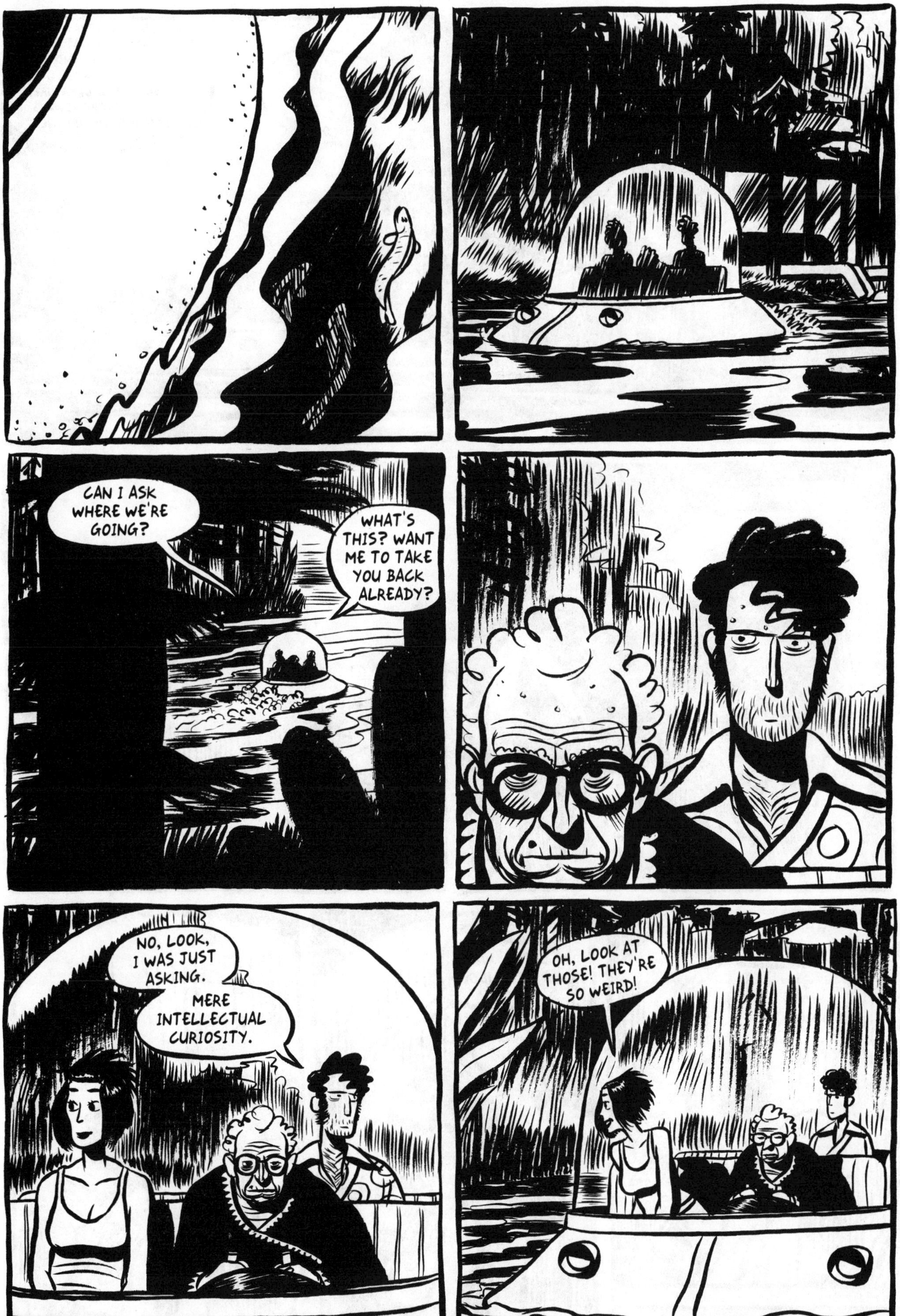
CAN I ASK WHERE WE'RE GOING?
WHAT'S THIS? WANT ME TO TAKE YOU BACK ALREADY?
NO, LOOK, I WAS JUST ASKING.
MERE INTELLECTUAL CURIOSITY.
OH, LOOK AT THOSE! THEY'RE SO WEIRD!

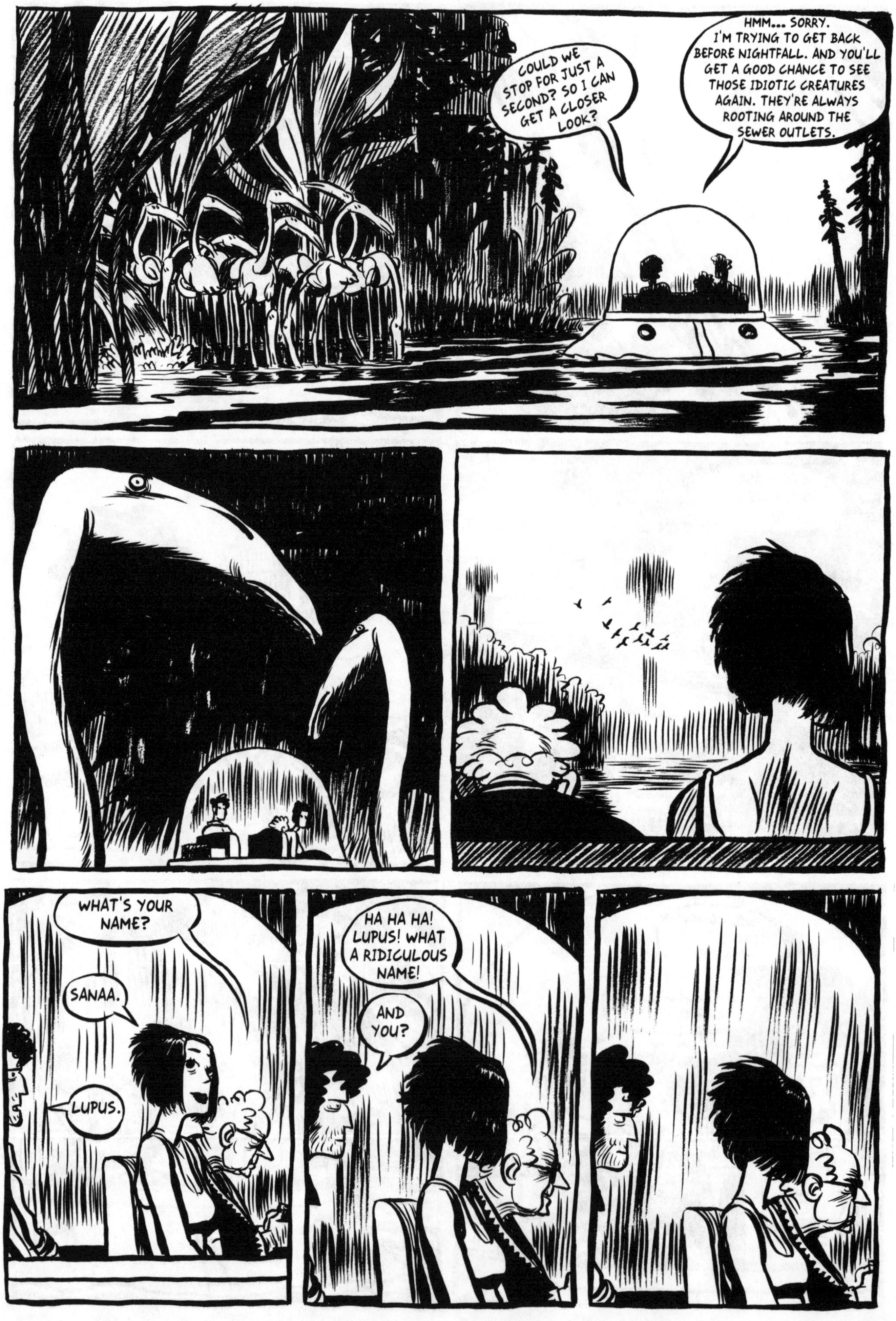
COULD WE STOP FOR JUST A SECOND? SO I CAN GET A CLOSER LOOK?
HMM... SORRY. I'M TRYING TO GET BACK BEFORE NIGHTFALL. AND YOU'LL GET A GOOD CHANCE TO SEE THOSE IDIOTIC CREATURES AGAIN. THEY'RE ALWAYS ROOTING AROUND THE SEWER OUTLETS.
WHAT'S YOUR NAME?
SANAA.
LUPUS.
HA HA HA! LUPUS! WHAT A RIDICULOUS NAME!
AND YOU?

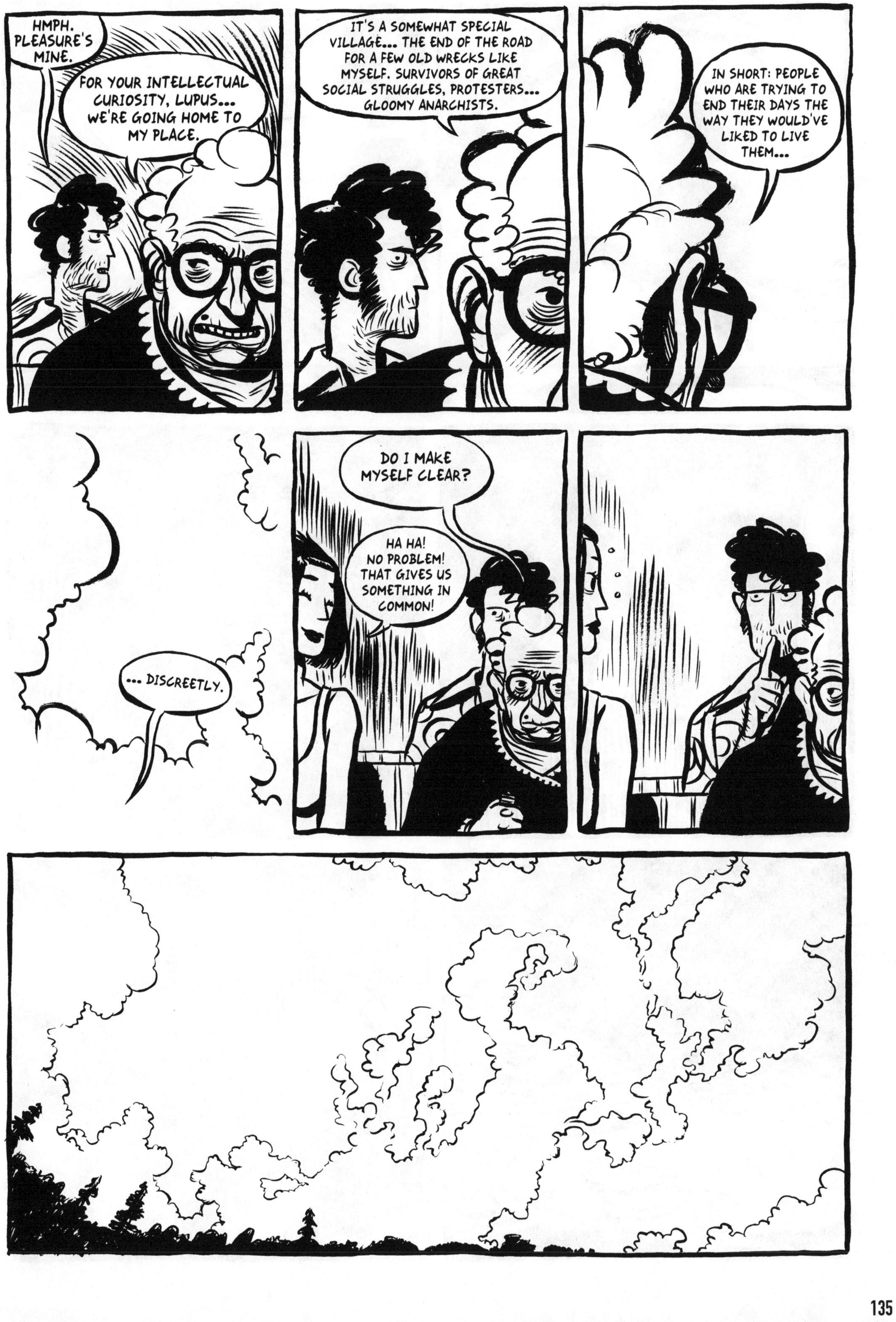
HMPH. PLEASURE'S MINE.
FOR YOUR INTELLECTUAL CURIOSITY, LUPUS... WE'RE GOING HOME TO MY PLACE.
IT'S A SOMEWHAT SPECIAL VILLAGE... THE END OF THE ROAD FOR A FEW OLD WRECKS LIKE MYSELF. SURVIVORS OF GREAT SOCIAL STRUGGLES, PROTESTERS... GLOOMY ANARCHISTS.
IN SHORT: PEOPLE WHO ARE TRYING TO END THEIR DAYS THE WAY THEY WOULD'VE LIKED TO LIVE THEM...
... DISCREETLY.
DO I MAKE MYSELF CLEAR?
HA HA! NO PROBLEM! THAT GIVES US SOMETHING IN COMMON!

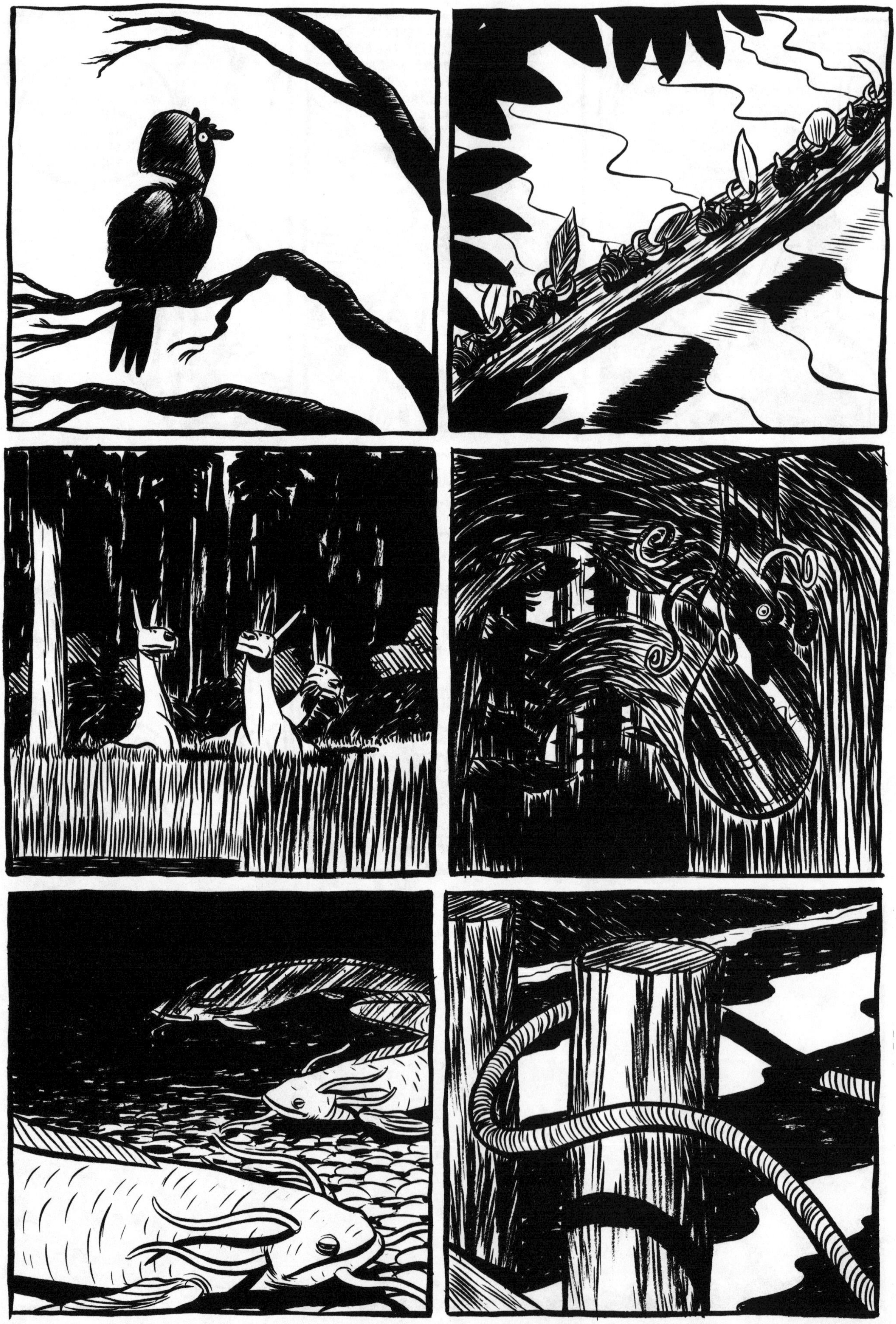

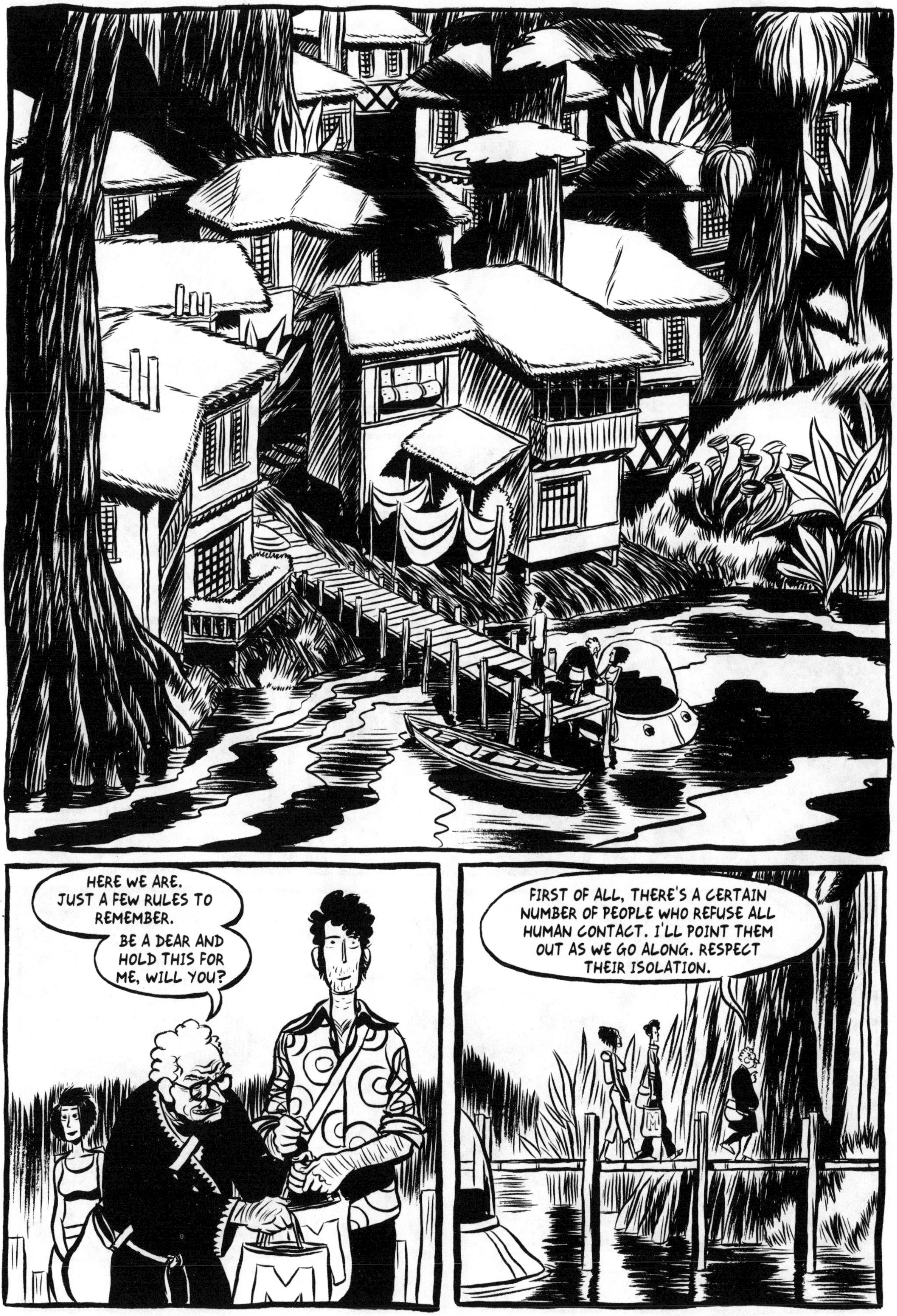
HERE WE ARE. JUST A FEW RULES TO REMEMBER.
BE A DEAR AND HOLD THIS FOR ME, WILL YOU?
FIRST OF ALL, THERE'S A CERTAIN NUMBER OF PEOPLE WHO REFUSE ALL HUMAN CONTACT. I'LL POINT THEM OUT AS WE GO ALONG. RESPECT THEIR ISOLATION.

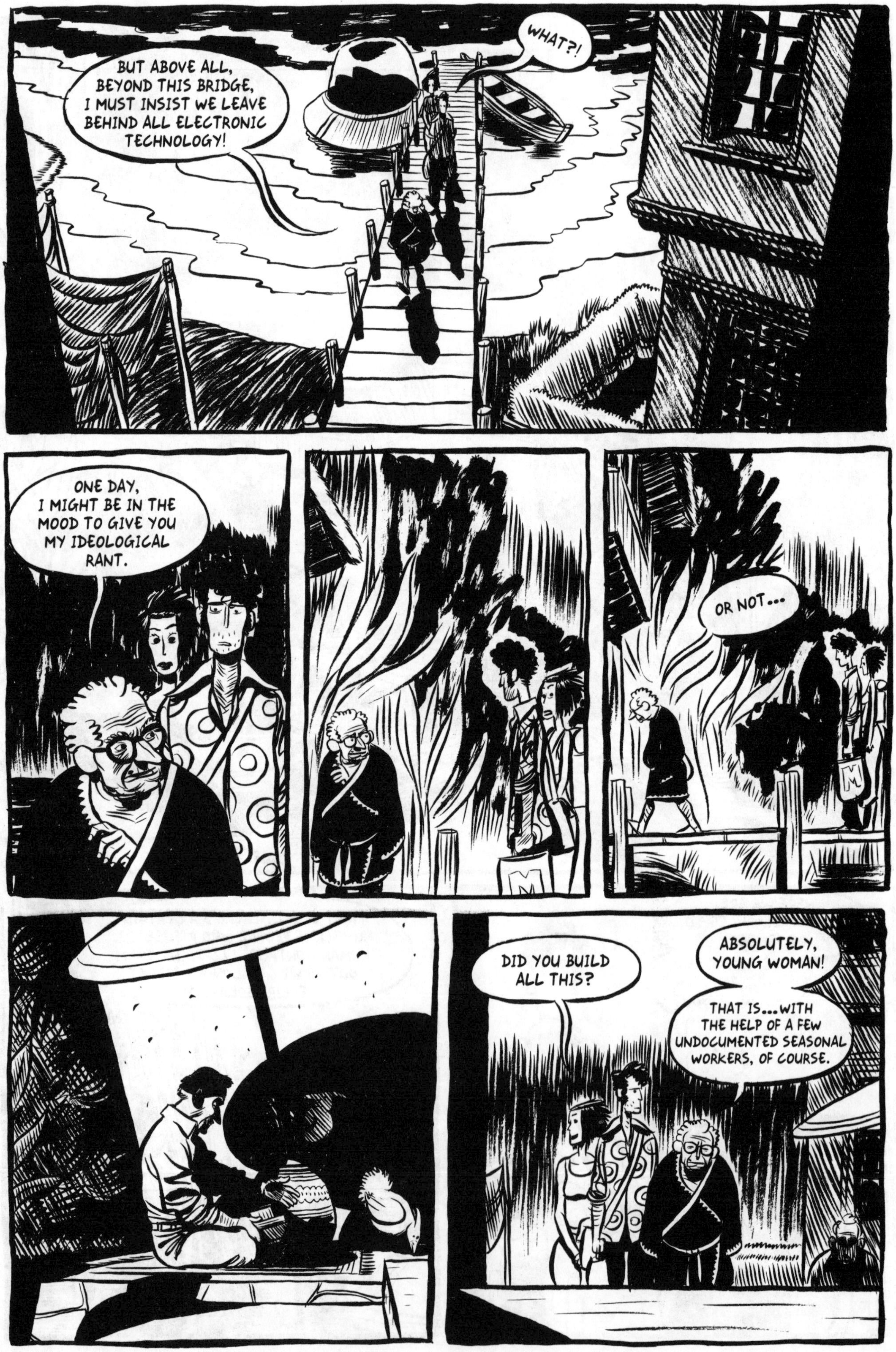
BUT ABOVE ALL, BEYOND THIS BRIDGE, I MUST INSIST WE LEAVE BEHIND ALL ELECTRONIC TECHNOLOGY!
WHAT?!
ONE DAY, I MIGHT BE IN THE MOOD TO GIVE YOU MY IDEOLOGICAL RANT.
OR NOT...
DID YOU BUILD ALL THIS?
ABSOLUTELY, YOUNG WOMAN!
THAT IS...WITH THE HELP OF A FEW UNDOCUMENTED SEASONAL WORKERS, OF COURSE.

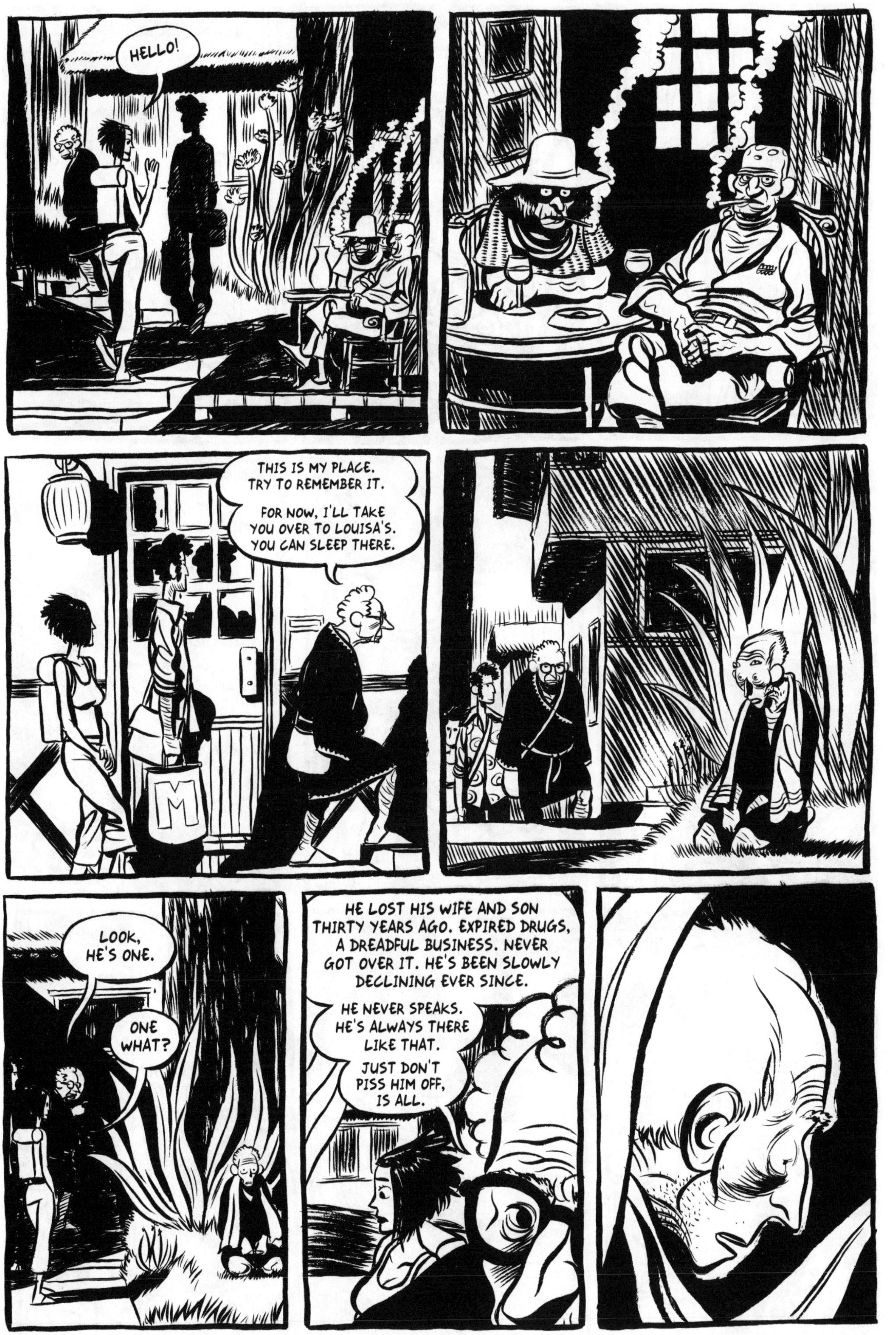
HELLO!
THIS IS MY PLACE. TRY TO REMEMBER IT.
FOR NOW, I'LL TAKE YOU OVER TO LOUISA'S. YOU CAN SLEEP THERE.
M
LOOK, HE'S ONE.
ONE WHAT?
HE LOST HIS WIFE AND SON THIRTY YEARS AGO. EXPIRED DRUGS, A DREADFUL BUSINESS. NEVER GOT OVER IT. HE'S BEEN SLOWLY DECLINING EVER SINCE.
HE NEVER SPEAKS. HE'S ALWAYS THERE LIKE THAT.
JUST DON'T PISS HIM OFF, IS ALL.

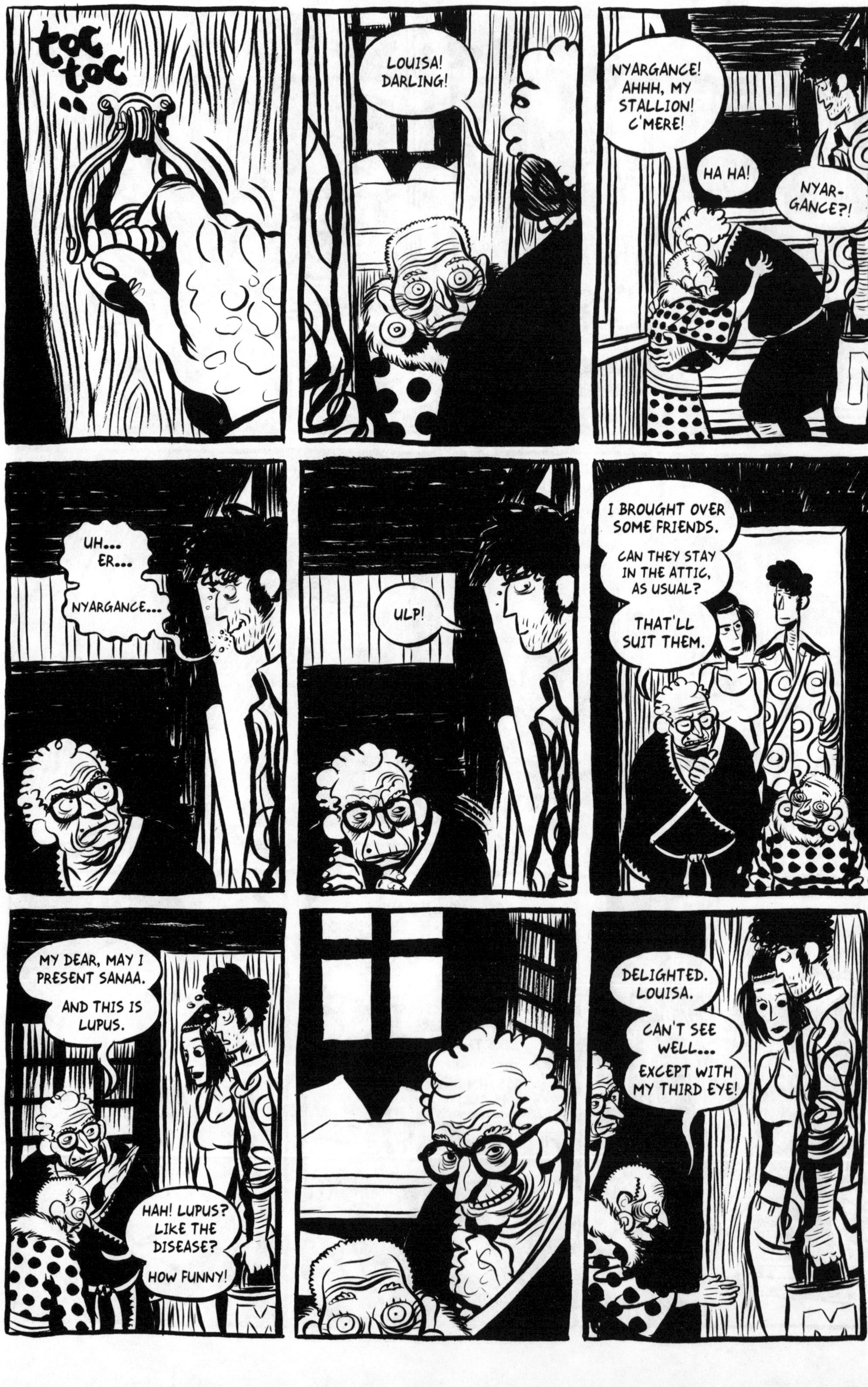
toc toc
LOUISA! DARLING!
NYARGANCE! AHHH, MY STALLION! C'MERE!
HA HA!
NYAR-GANCE?!
UH... ER... NYARGANCE...
ULP!
I BROUGHT OVER SOME FRIENDS.
CAN THEY STAY IN THE ATTIC, AS USUAL?
THAT'LL SUIT THEM.
MY DEAR, MAY I PRESENT SANAA.
AND THIS IS LUPUS.
HAH! LUPUS? LIKE THE DISEASE?
HOW FUNNY!
DELIGHTED. LOUISA.
CAN'T SEE WELL...
EXCEPT WITH MY THIRD EYE!

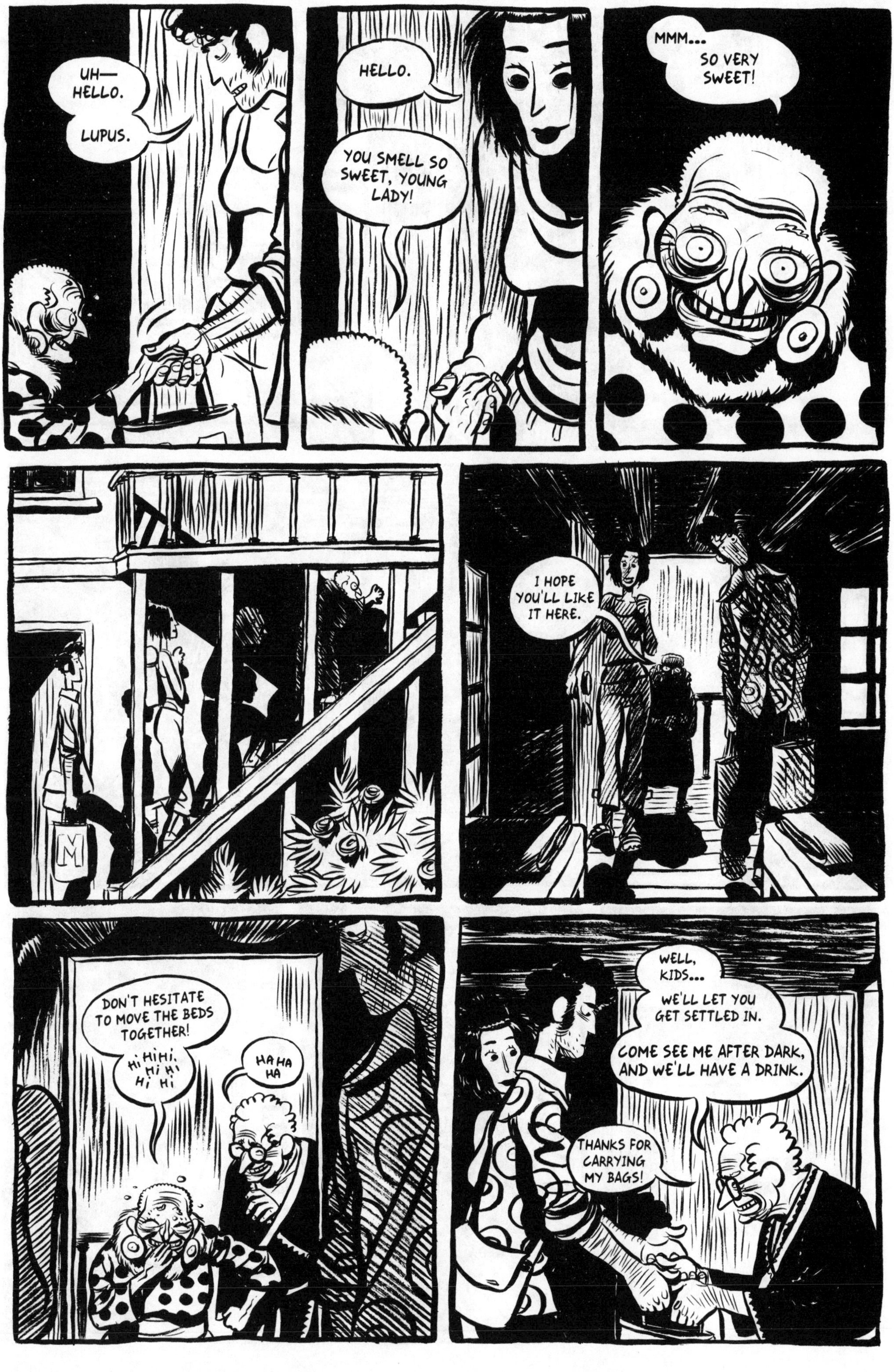
UH—
HELLO.
LUPUS.
HELLO.
YOU SMELL SO SWEET, YOUNG LADY!
MMM...
SO VERY SWEET!
I HOPE YOU'LL LIKE IT HERE.
DON'T HESITATE TO MOVE THE BEDS TOGETHER!
HI HI HI HI HI HI HI
HA HA HA
WELL, KIDS...
WE'LL LET YOU GET SETTLED IN.
COME SEE ME AFTER DARK, AND WE'LL HAVE A DRINK.
THANKS FOR CARRYING MY BAGS!

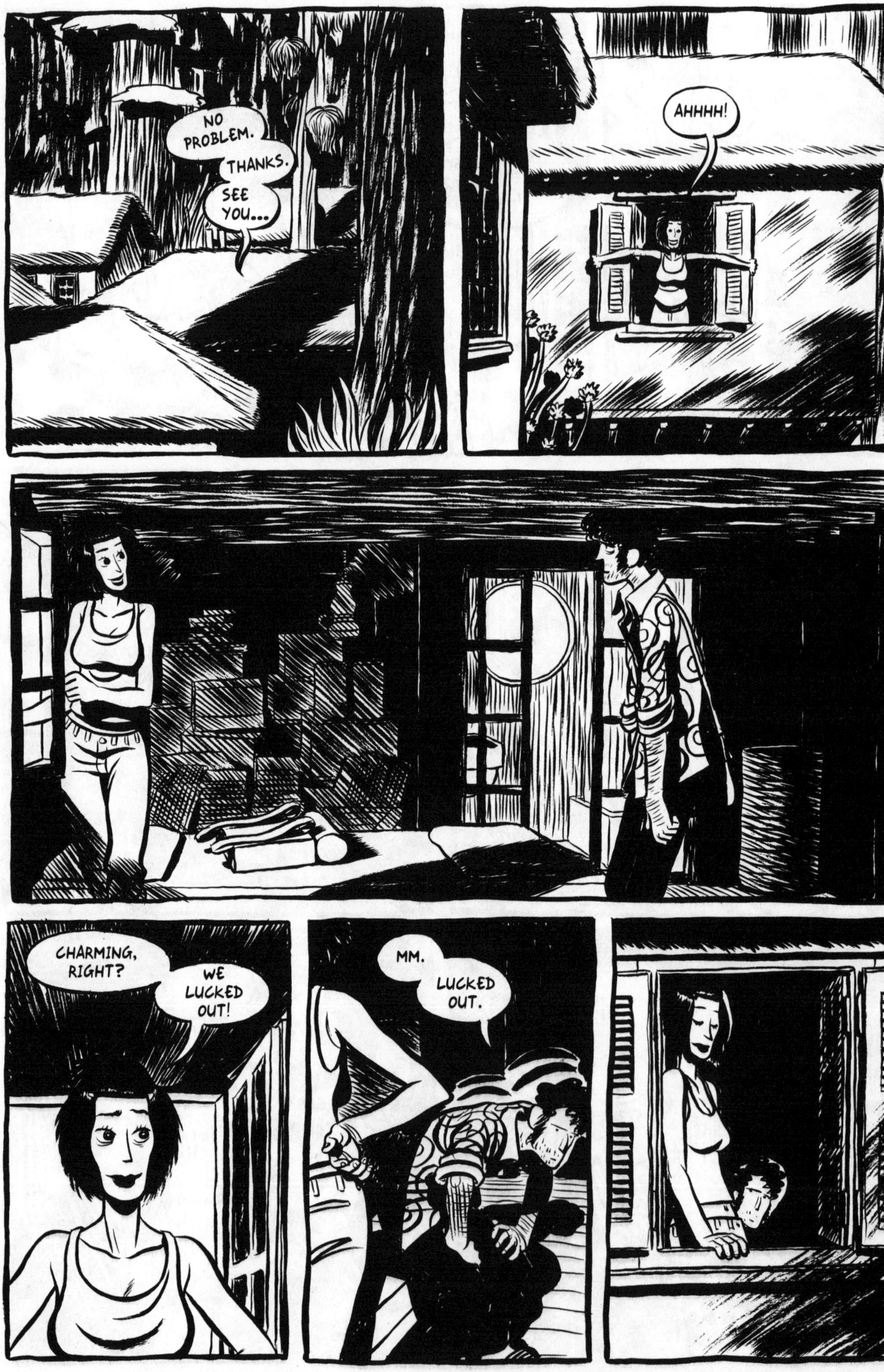
NO PROBLEM.
THANKS.
SEE YOU...
AHHHH!
CHARMING, RIGHT?
WE LUCKED OUT!
MM.
LUCKED OUT.

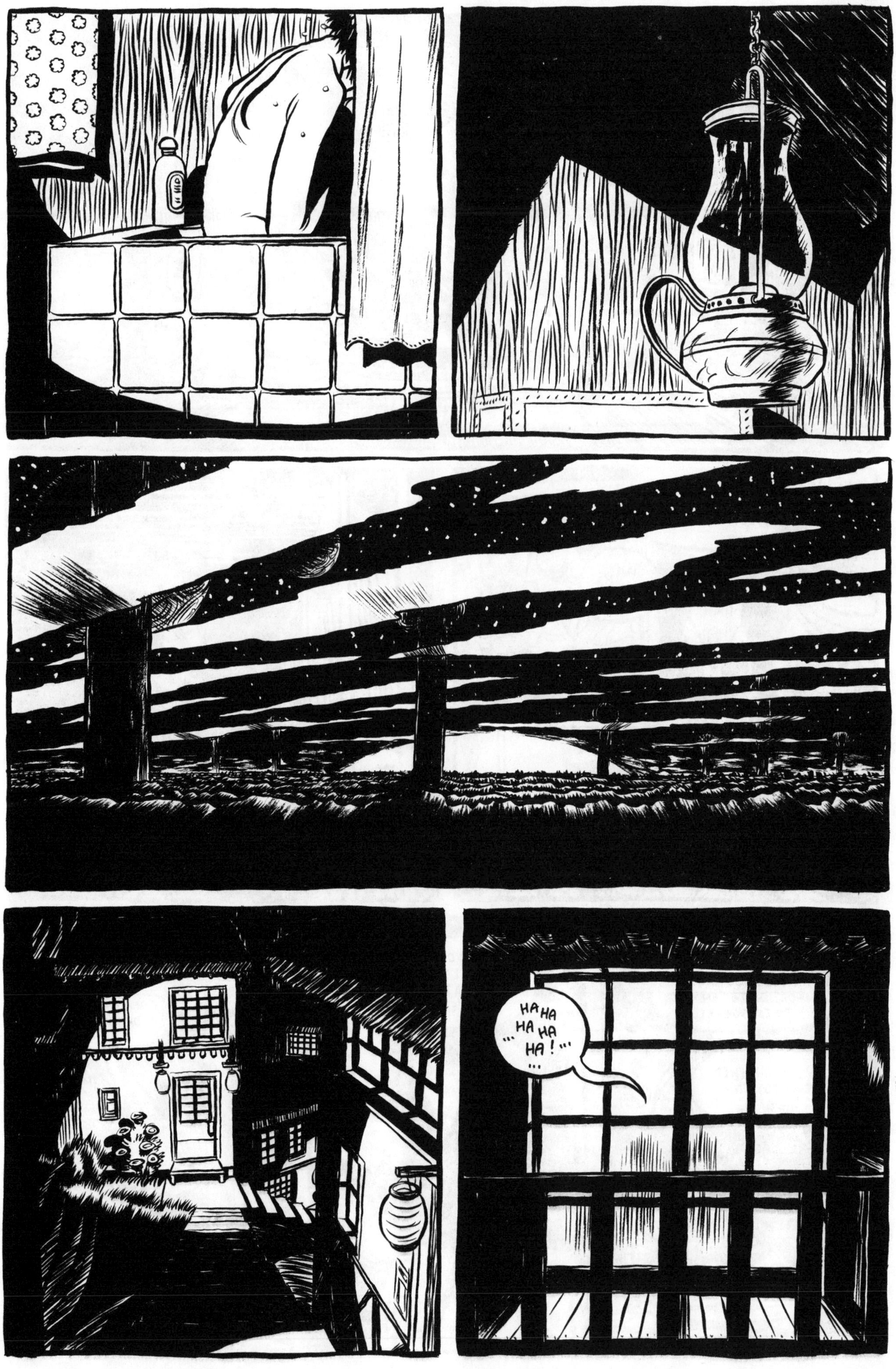
HA HA HA HA ... HA! ... ...

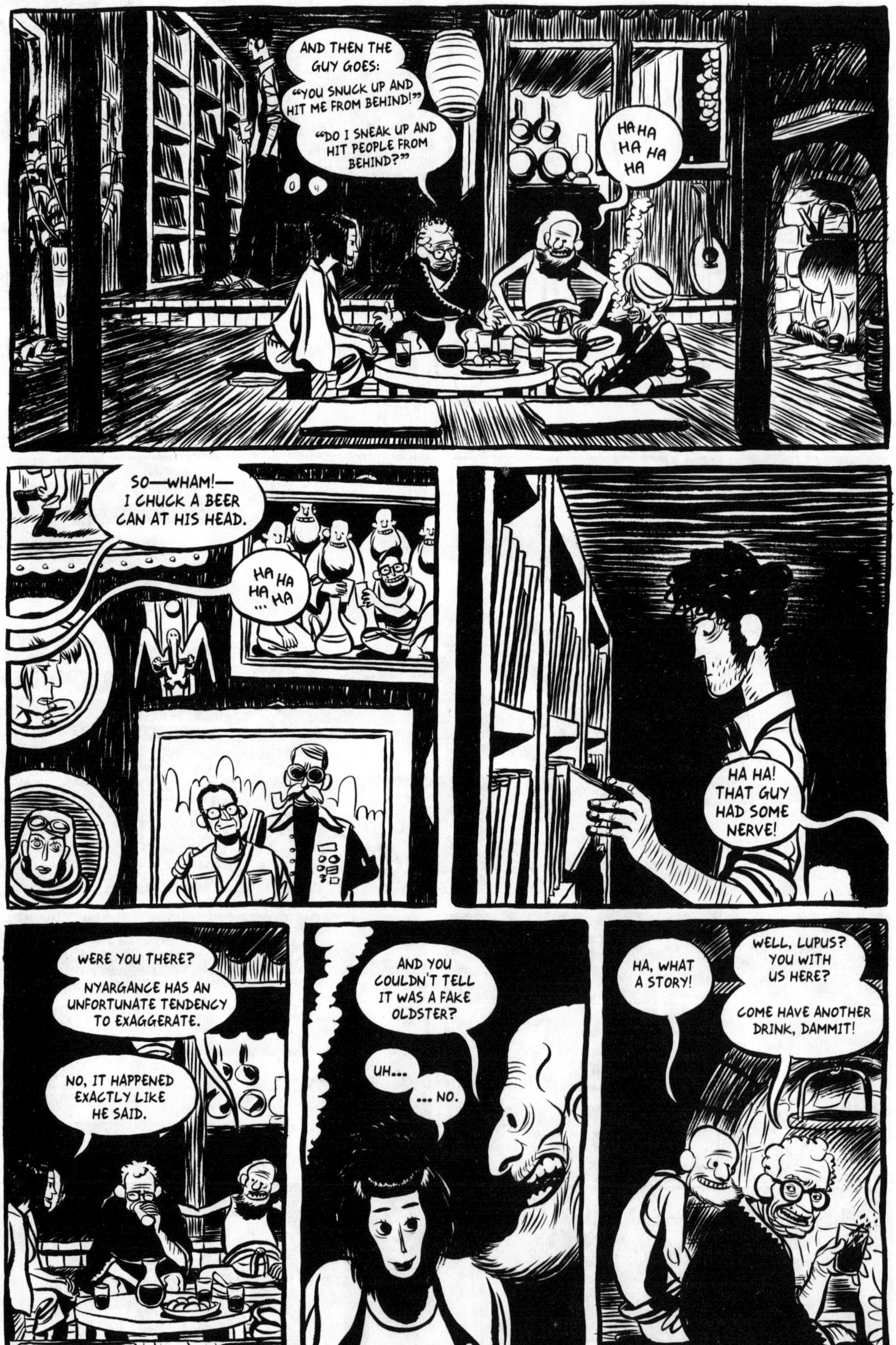

AND THEN THE GUY GOES:
"YOU SNUCK UP AND HIT ME FROM BEHIND!"
"DO I SNEAK UP AND HIT PEOPLE FROM BEHIND?"
HA HA HA HA HA
SO—WHAM!— I CHUCK A BEER CAN AT HIS HEAD.
HA HA HA ... HA
HA HA! THAT GUY HAD SOME NERVE!
WERE YOU THERE?
NYARGANCE HAS AN UNFORTUNATE TENDENCY TO EXAGGERATE.
NO, IT HAPPENED EXACTLY LIKE HE SAID.
AND YOU COULDN'T TELL IT WAS A FAKE OLDSTER?
UH...
... NO.
HA, WHAT A STORY!
WELL, LUPUS? YOU WITH US HERE?
COME HAVE ANOTHER DRINK, DAMMIT!

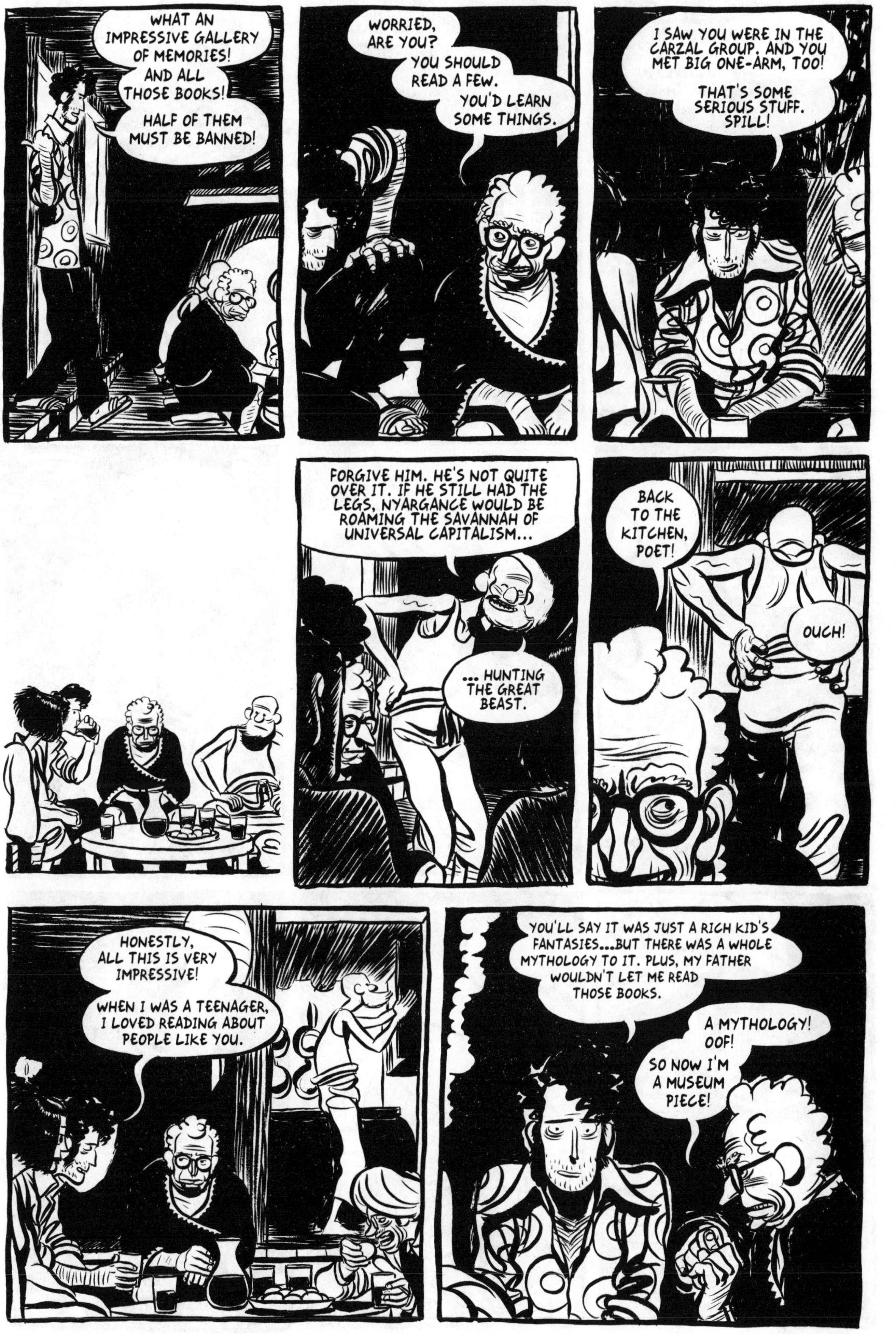
WHAT AN IMPRESSIVE GALLERY OF MEMORIES!
AND ALL THOSE BOOKS!
HALF OF THEM MUST BE BANNED!
WORRIED, ARE YOU?
YOU SHOULD READ A FEW.
YOU'D LEARN SOME THINGS.
I SAW YOU WERE IN THE CARZAL GROUP. AND YOU MET BIG ONE-ARM, TOO!
THAT'S SOME SERIOUS STUFF. SPILL!
FORGIVE HIM. HE'S NOT QUITE OVER IT. IF HE STILL HAD THE LEGS, NYARGANCE WOULD BE ROAMING THE SAVANNAH OF UNIVERSAL CAPITALISM...
... HUNTING THE GREAT BEAST.
BACK TO THE KITCHEN, POET!
OUCH!
HONESTLY, ALL THIS IS VERY IMPRESSIVE!
WHEN I WAS A TEENAGER, I LOVED READING ABOUT PEOPLE LIKE YOU.
YOU'LL SAY IT WAS JUST A RICH KID'S FANTASIES...BUT THERE WAS A WHOLE MYTHOLOGY TO IT. PLUS, MY FATHER WOULDN'T LET ME READ THOSE BOOKS.
A MYTHOLOGY! OOF!
SO NOW I'M A MUSEUM PIECE!

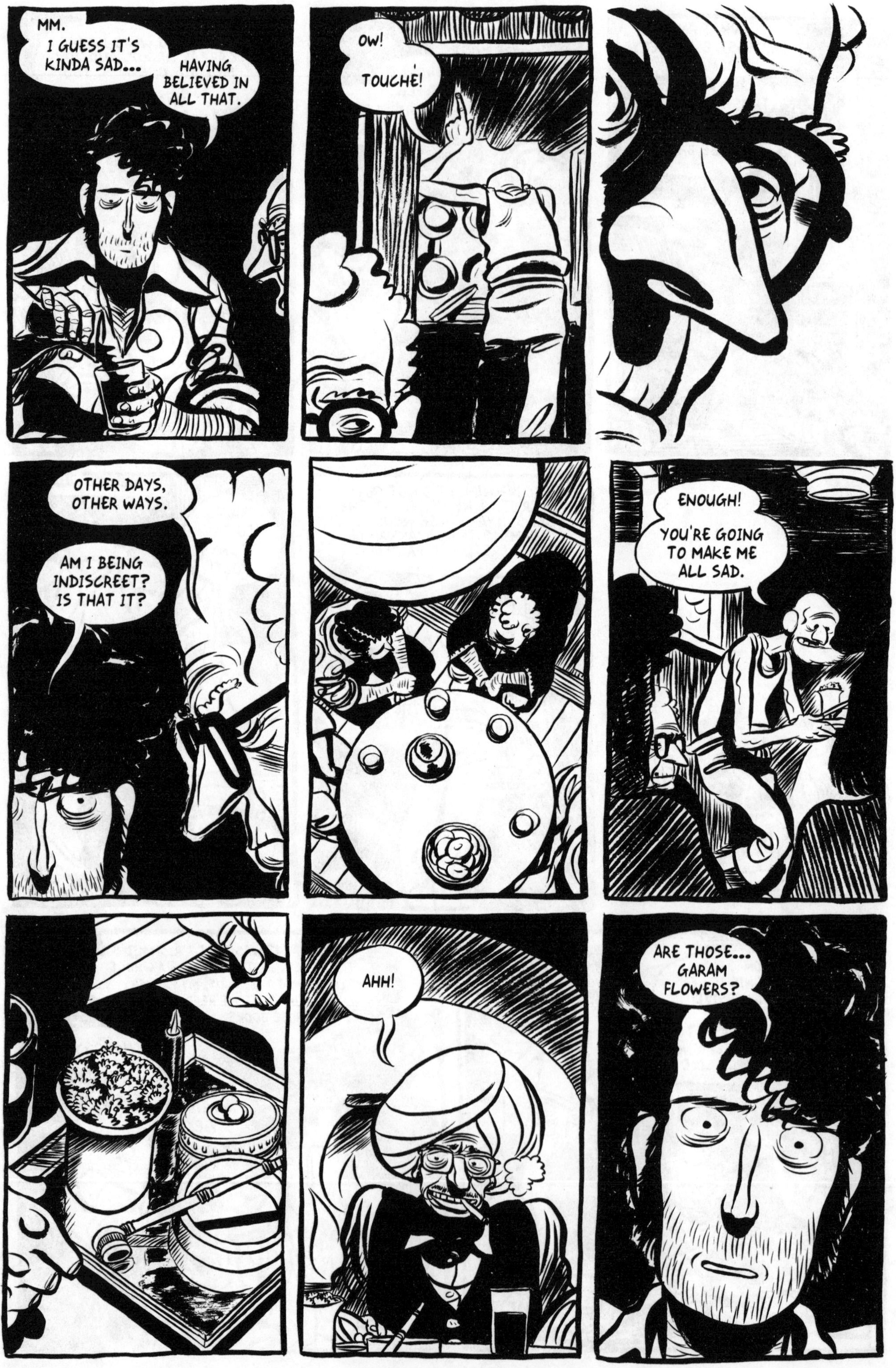
MM.
I GUESS IT'S KINDA SAD...
HAVING BELIEVED IN ALL THAT.
OW!
TOUCHÉ!
OTHER DAYS, OTHER WAYS.
AM I BEING INDISCREET? IS THAT IT?
ENOUGH!
YOU'RE GOING TO MAKE ME ALL SAD.
AHH!
ARE THOSE... GARAM FLOWERS?

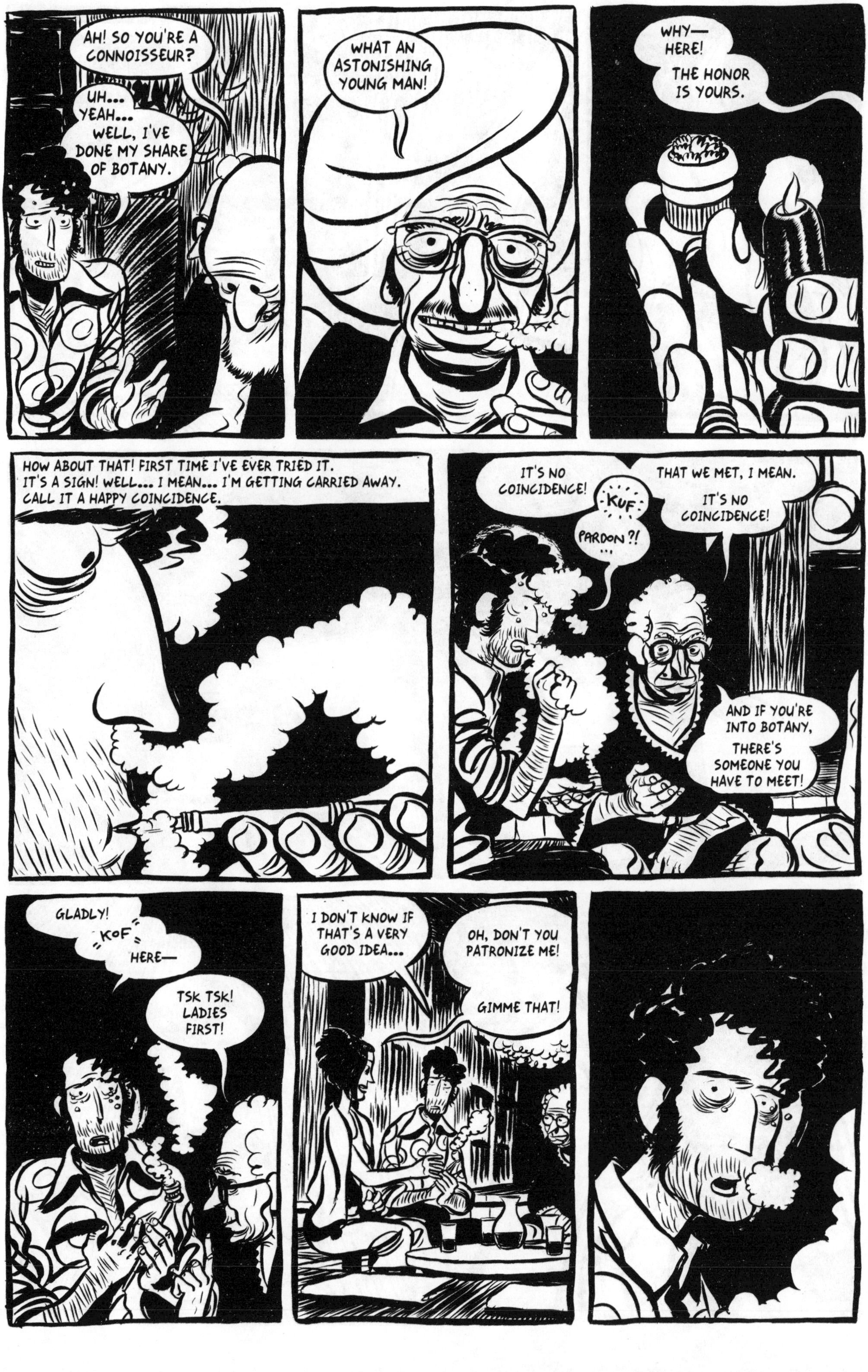
AH! SO YOU'RE A CONNOISSEUR?
UH... YEAH... WELL, I'VE DONE MY SHARE OF BOTANY.
WHAT AN ASTONISHING YOUNG MAN!
WHY— HERE!
THE HONOR IS YOURS.
HOW ABOUT THAT! FIRST TIME I'VE EVER TRIED IT. IT'S A SIGN! WELL... I MEAN... I'M GETTING CARRIED AWAY. CALL IT A HAPPY COINCIDENCE.
IT'S NO COINCIDENCE!
KUF
PARDON?! ...
THAT WE MET, I MEAN.
IT'S NO COINCIDENCE!
AND IF YOU'RE INTO BOTANY,
THERE'S SOMEONE YOU HAVE TO MEET!
GLADLY!
KOF
HERE—
TSK TSK! LADIES FIRST!
I DON'T KNOW IF THAT'S A VERY GOOD IDEA...
OH, DON'T YOU PATRONIZE ME!
GIMME THAT!

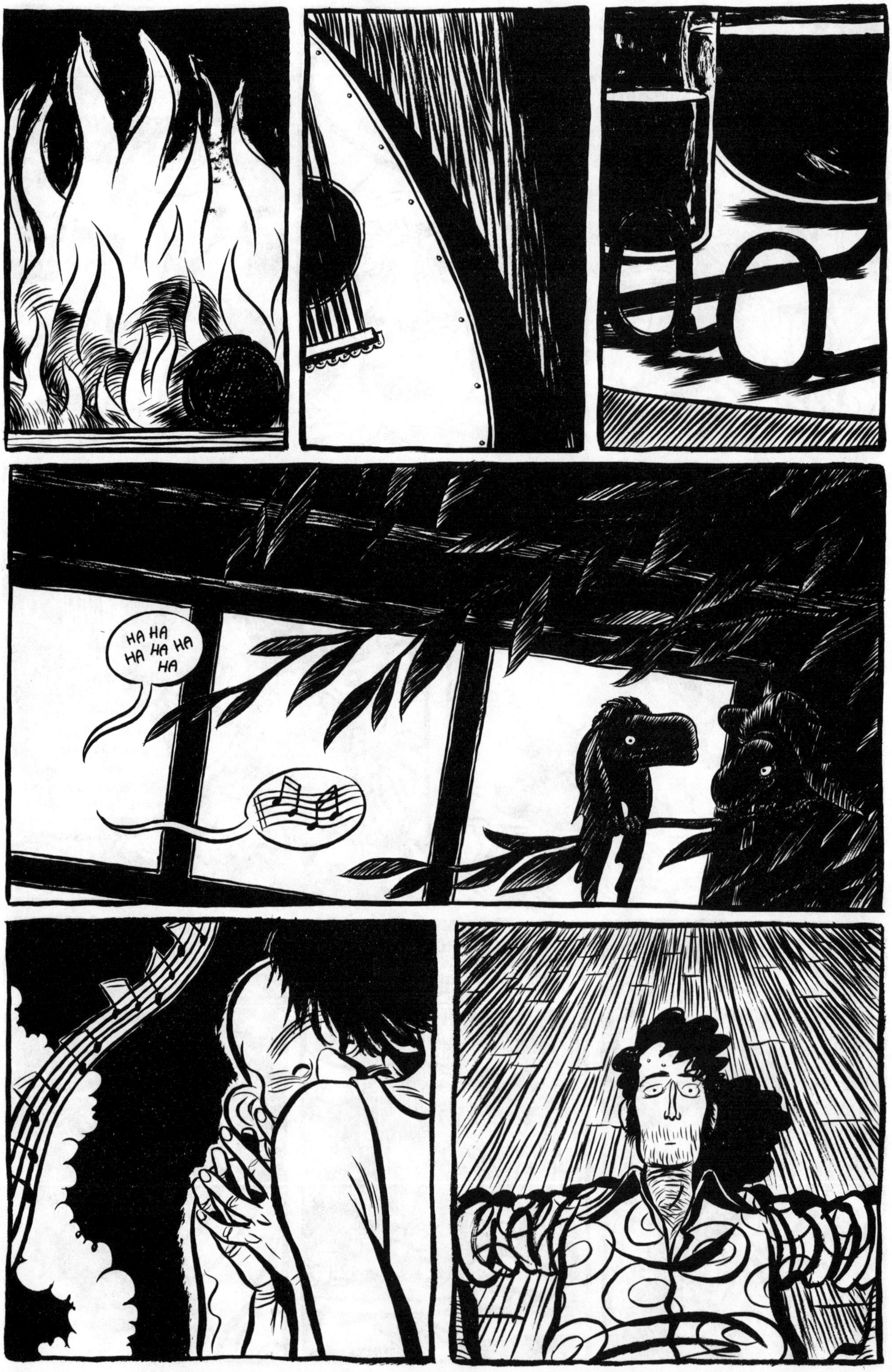
HA HA HA HA HA HA

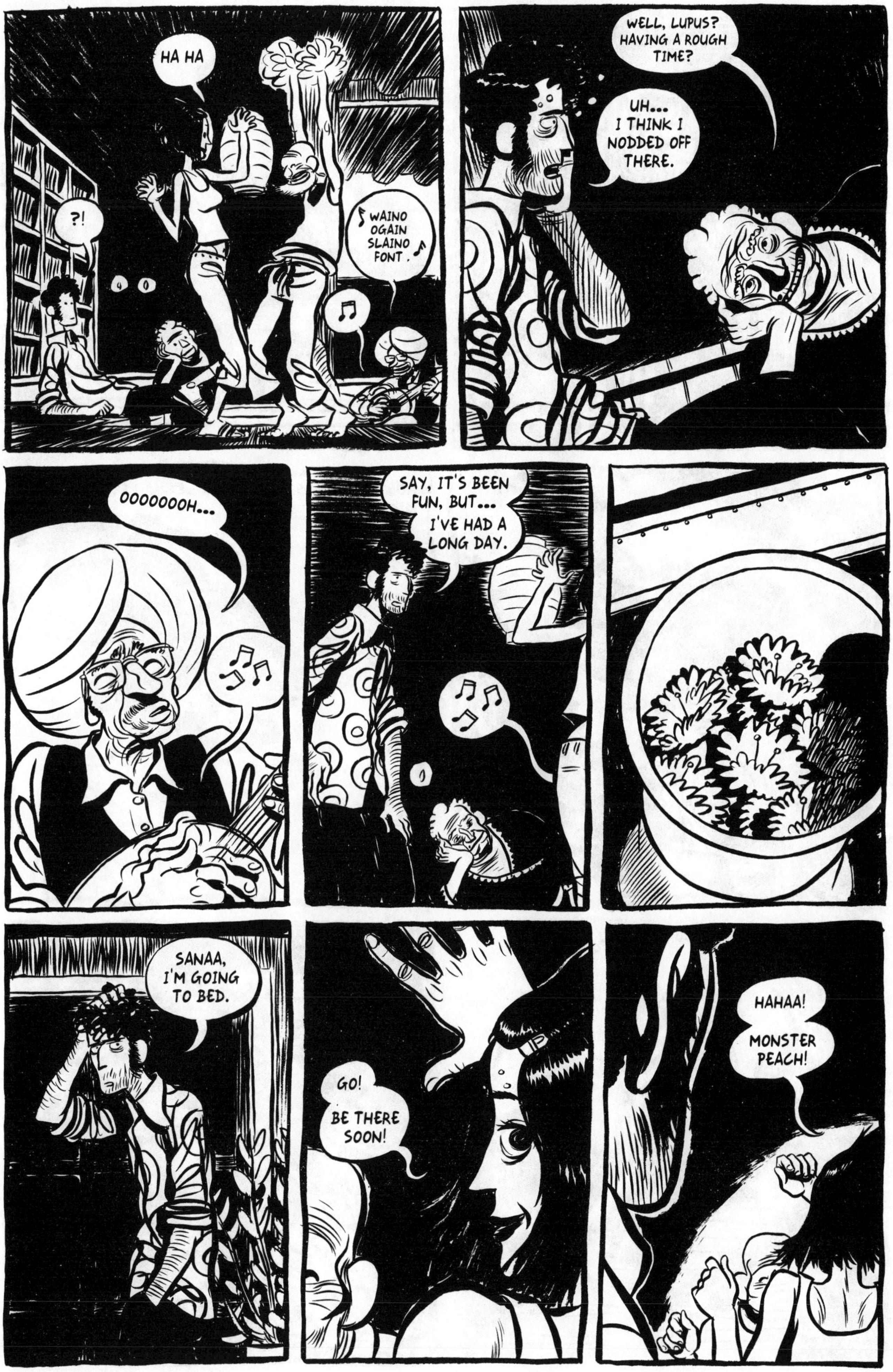
HA HA
?!
WAINO OGAIN SLAINO FONT.
WELL, LUPUS? HAVING A ROUGH TIME?
UH... I THINK I NODDED OFF THERE.
OOOOOOOH...
SAY, IT'S BEEN FUN, BUT...
I'VE HAD A LONG DAY.
SANAA, I'M GOING TO BED.
GO!
BE THERE SOON!
HAHAA!
MONSTER PEACH!

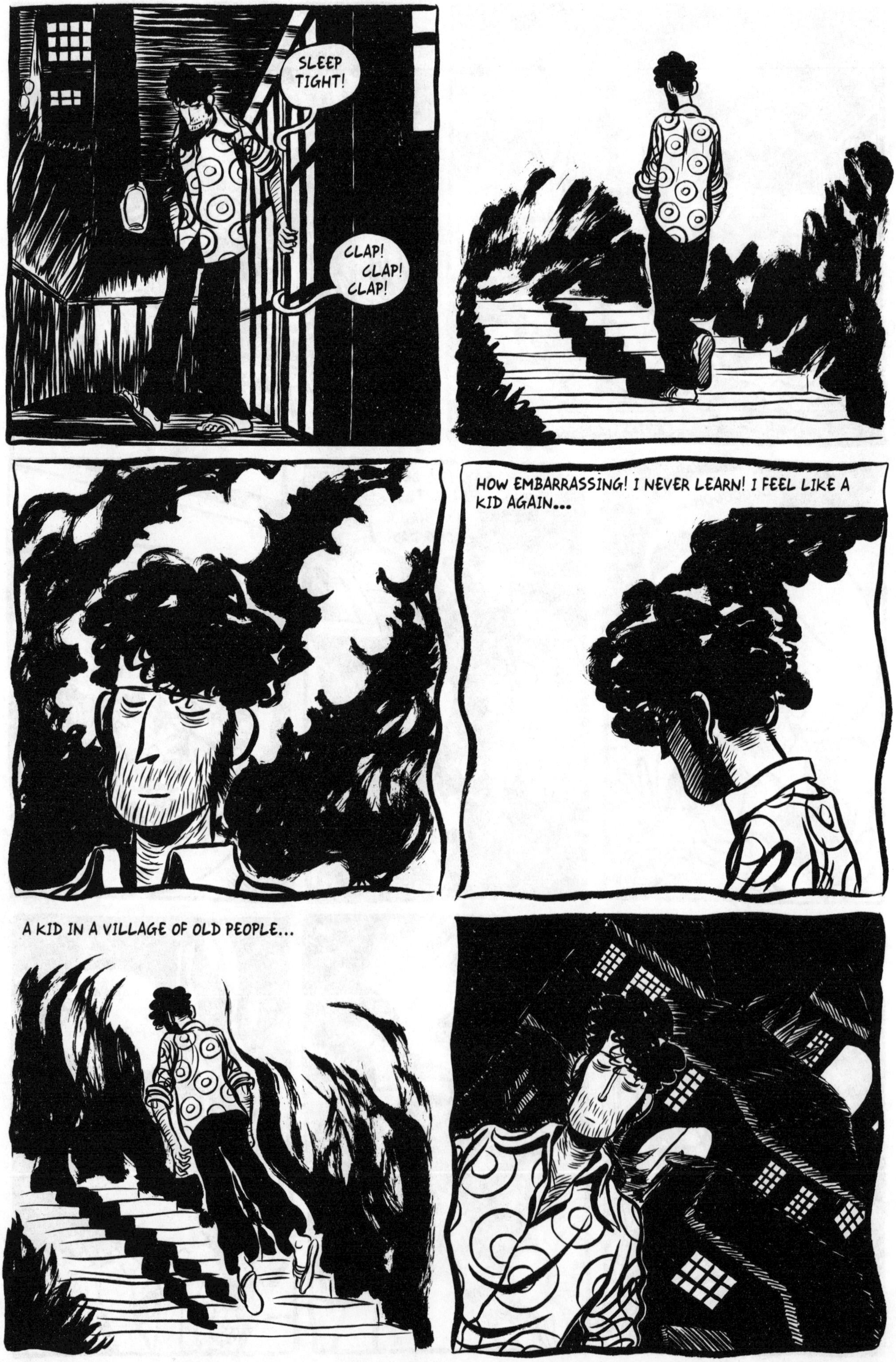
SLEEP TIGHT!
CLAP! CLAP! CLAP!
HOW EMBARRASSING! I NEVER LEARN! I FEEL LIKE A KID AGAIN...
A KID IN A VILLAGE OF OLD PEOPLE...

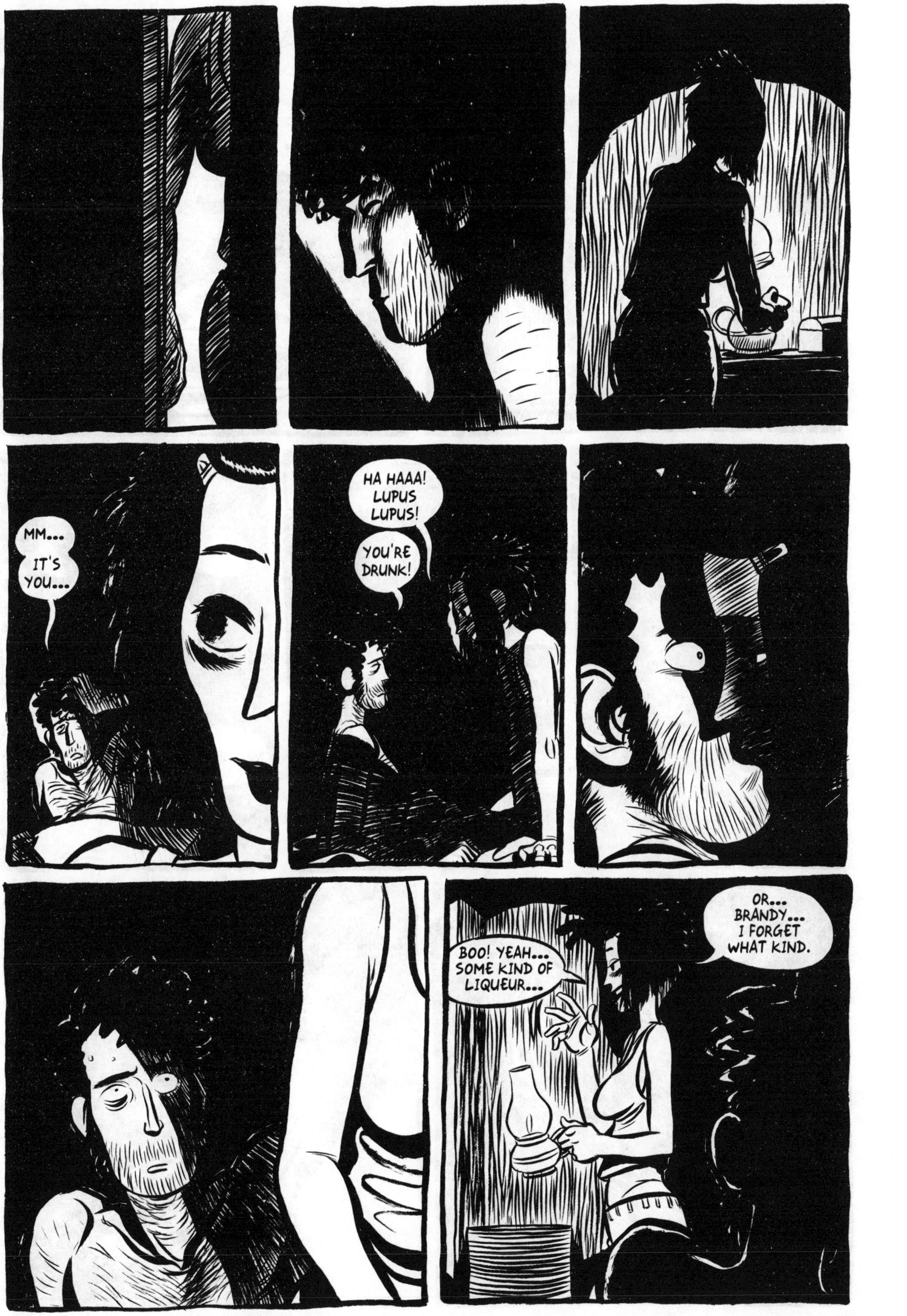
MM...
IT'S YOU...
HA HAAA! LUPUS LUPUS!
YOU'RE DRUNK!
BOO! YEAH... SOME KIND OF LIQUEUR...
OR... BRANDY... I FORGET WHAT KIND.

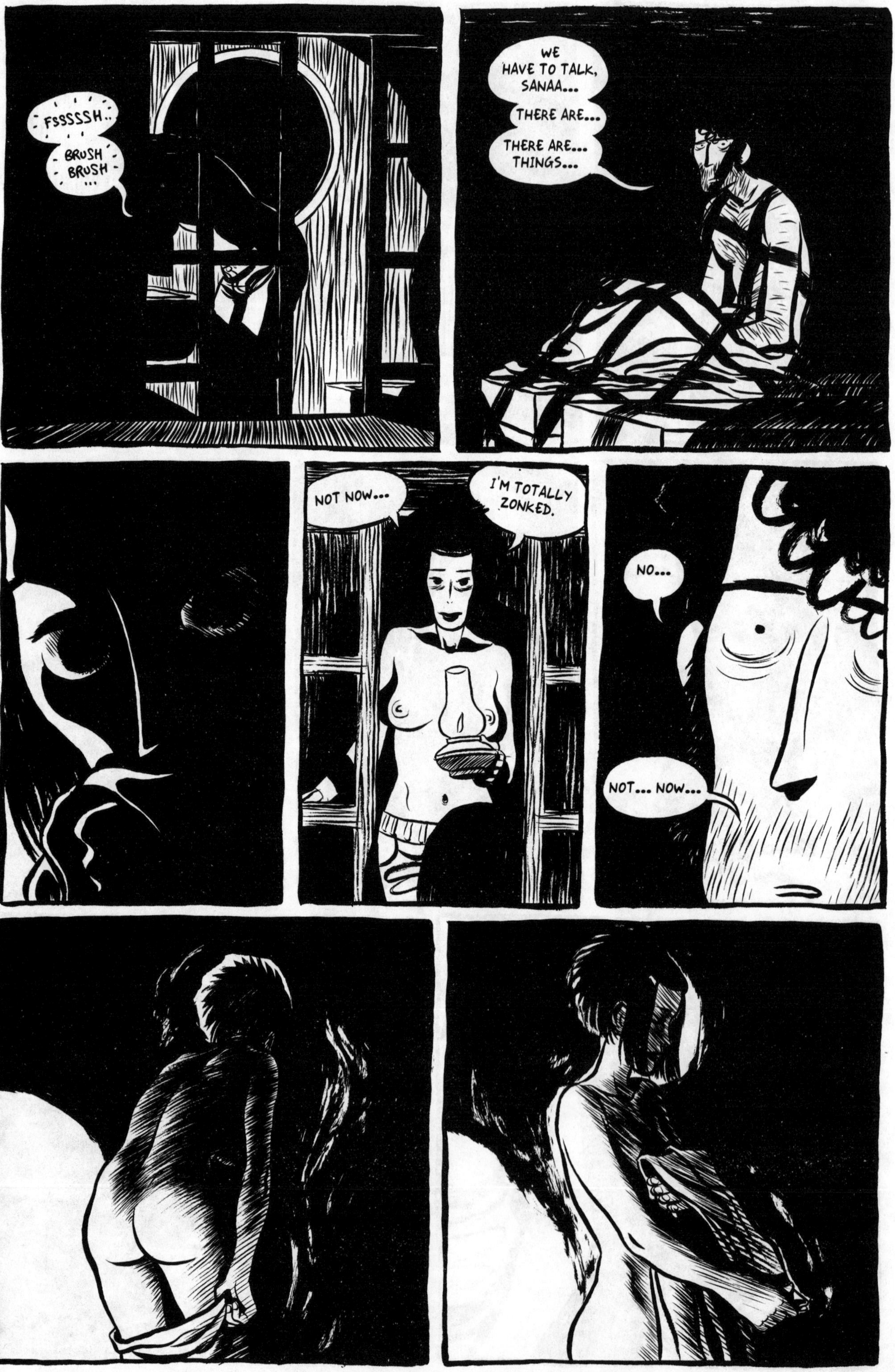
FSSSSSH..
BRUSH BRUSH ...
WE HAVE TO TALK, SANAA...
THERE ARE...
THERE ARE... THINGS...
NOT NOW...
I'M TOTALLY ZONKED.
NO...
NOT... NOW...

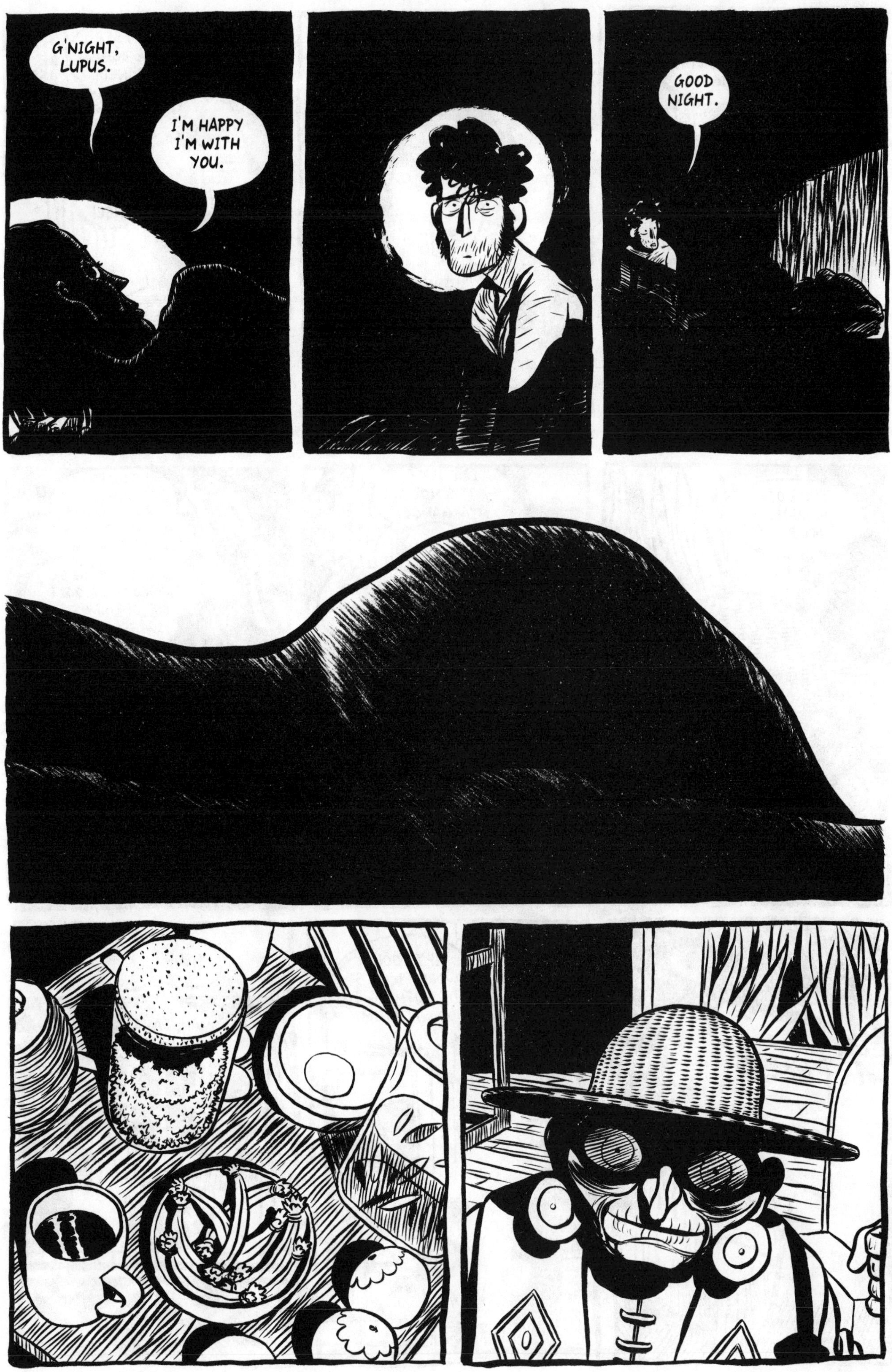
G'NIGHT, LUPUS.
I'M HAPPY I'M WITH YOU.
GOOD NIGHT.

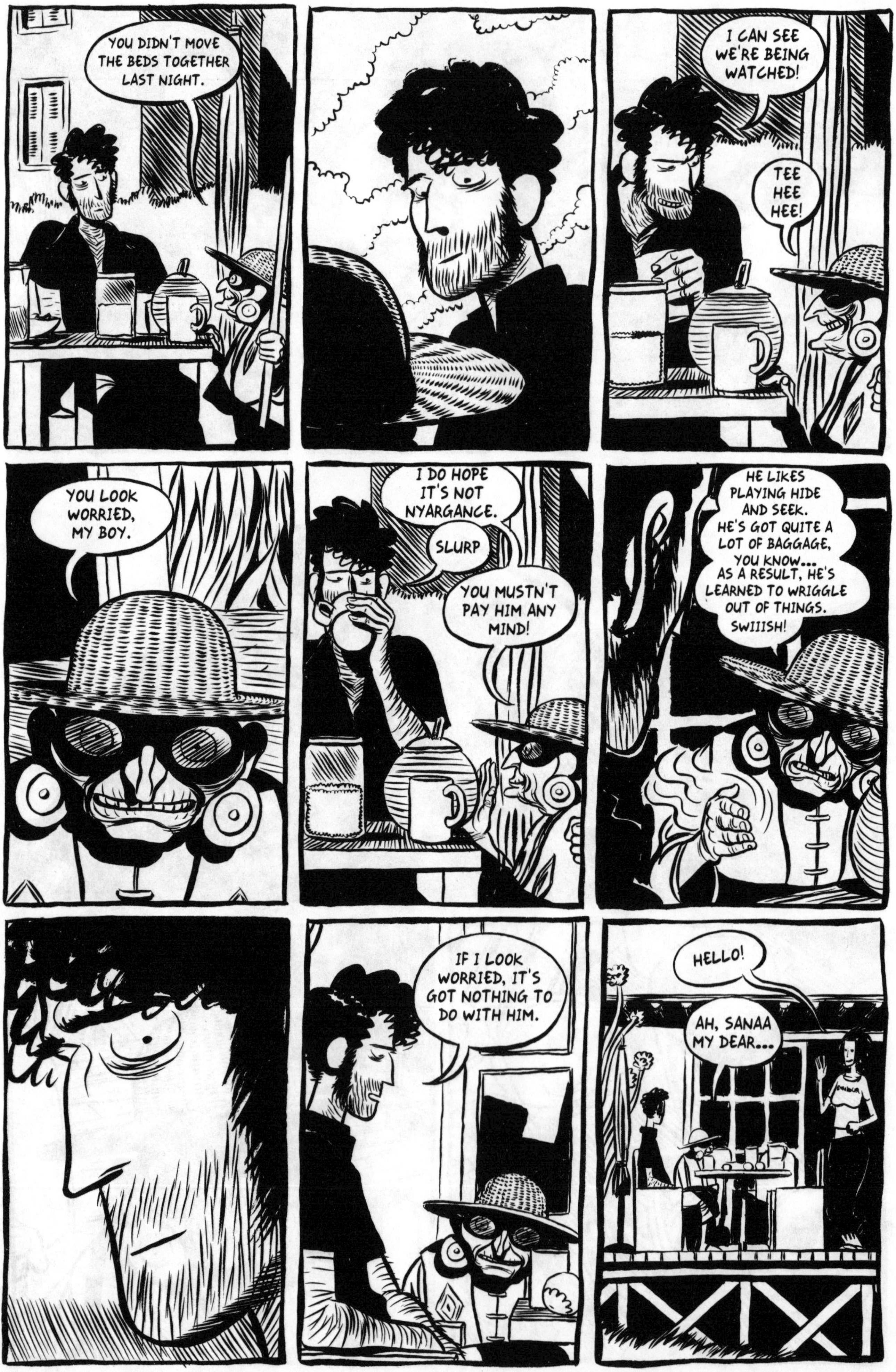
YOU DIDN'T MOVE THE BEDS TOGETHER LAST NIGHT.
I CAN SEE WE'RE BEING WATCHED!
TEE HEE HEE!
YOU LOOK WORRIED, MY BOY.
I DO HOPE IT'S NOT NYARGANCE.
SLURP
YOU MUSTN'T PAY HIM ANY MIND!
HE LIKES PLAYING HIDE AND SEEK. HE'S GOT QUITE A LOT OF BAGGAGE, YOU KNOW... AS A RESULT, HE'S LEARNED TO WRIGGLE OUT OF THINGS. SWIIISH!
IF I LOOK WORRIED, IT'S GOT NOTHING TO DO WITH HIM.
HELLO!
AH, SANAA MY DEAR...

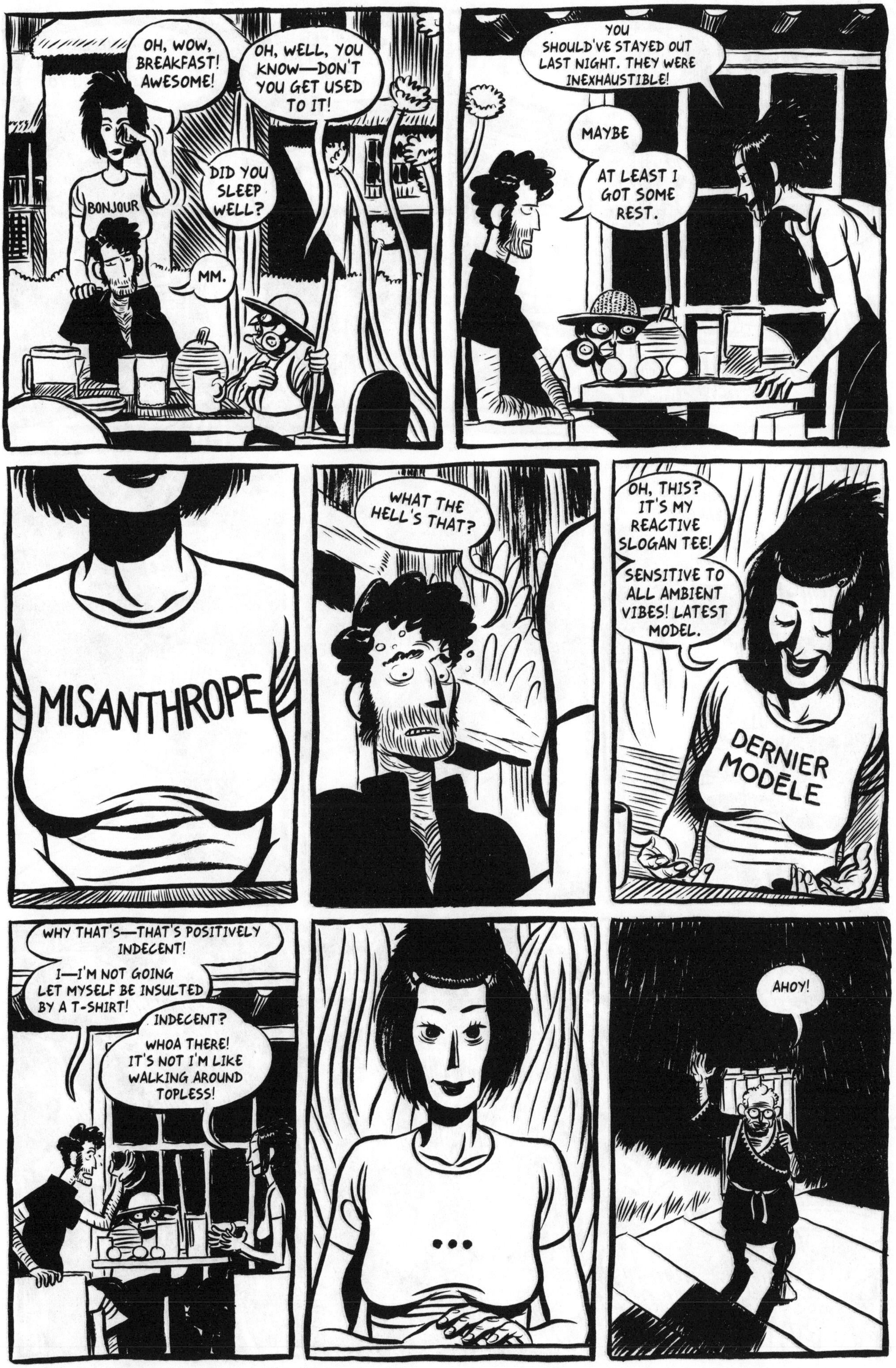
OH, WOW, BREAKFAST! AWESOME!
OH, WELL, YOU KNOW—DON'T YOU GET USED TO IT!
BONJOUR
DID YOU SLEEP WELL?
MM.
YOU SHOULD'VE STAYED OUT LAST NIGHT. THEY WERE INEXHAUSTIBLE!
MAYBE
AT LEAST I GOT SOME REST.
MISANTHROPE
WHAT THE HELL'S THAT?
OH, THIS? IT'S MY REACTIVE SLOGAN TEE!
SENSITIVE TO ALL AMBIENT VIBES! LATEST MODEL.
DERNIER MODÈLE
WHY THAT'S—THAT'S POSITIVELY INDECENT!
I—I'M NOT GOING LET MYSELF BE INSULTED BY A T-SHIRT!
INDECENT?
WHOA THERE! IT'S NOT I'M LIKE WALKING AROUND TOPLESS!
...
AHOY!

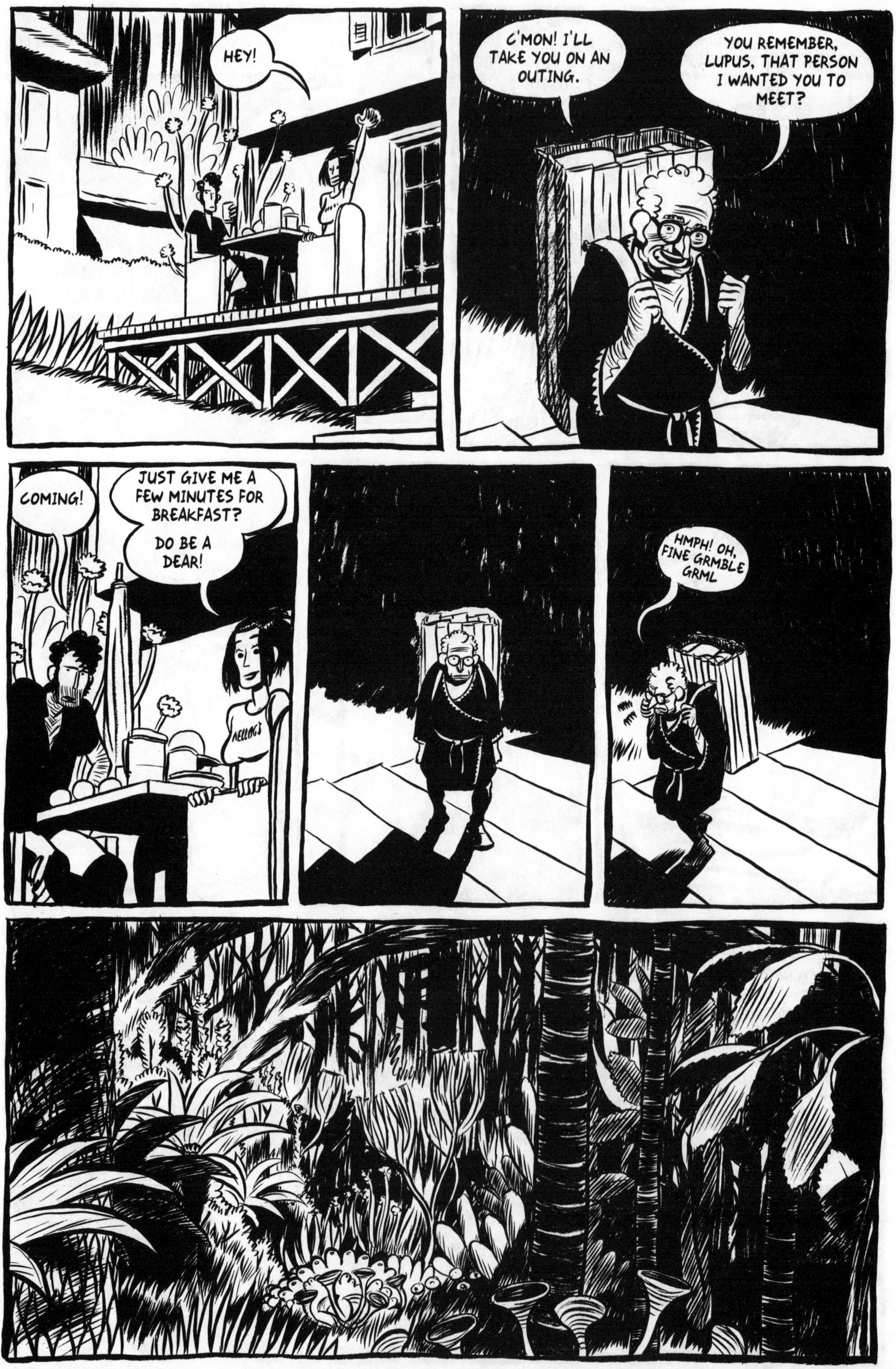
HEY!
C'MON! I'LL TAKE YOU ON AN OUTING.
YOU REMEMBER, LUPUS, THAT PERSON I WANTED YOU TO MEET?
COMING!
JUST GIVE ME A FEW MINUTES FOR BREAKFAST?
DO BE A DEAR!
KELLOG'S
HMPH! OH, FINE GRMBLE GRML

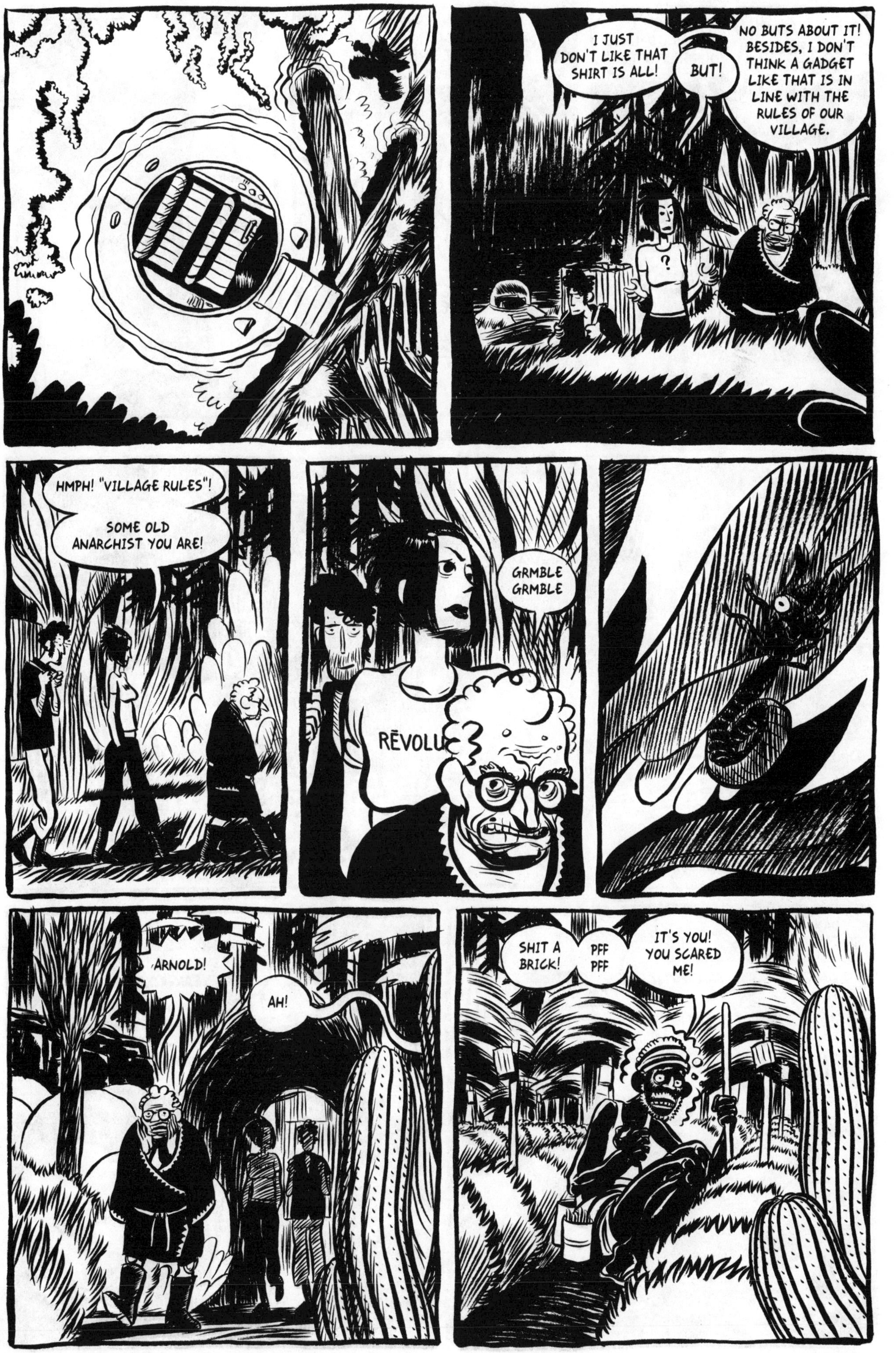
I JUST DON'T LIKE THAT SHIRT IS ALL!
BUT!
NO BUTS ABOUT IT! BESIDES, I DON'T THINK A GADGET LIKE THAT IS IN LINE WITH THE RULES OF OUR VILLAGE.
?
HMPH! "VILLAGE RULES"!
SOME OLD ANARCHIST YOU ARE!
GRMBLE GRMBLE
RĒVOLU
ARNOLD!
AH!
SHIT A BRICK!
PFF PFF
IT'S YOU! YOU SCARED ME!

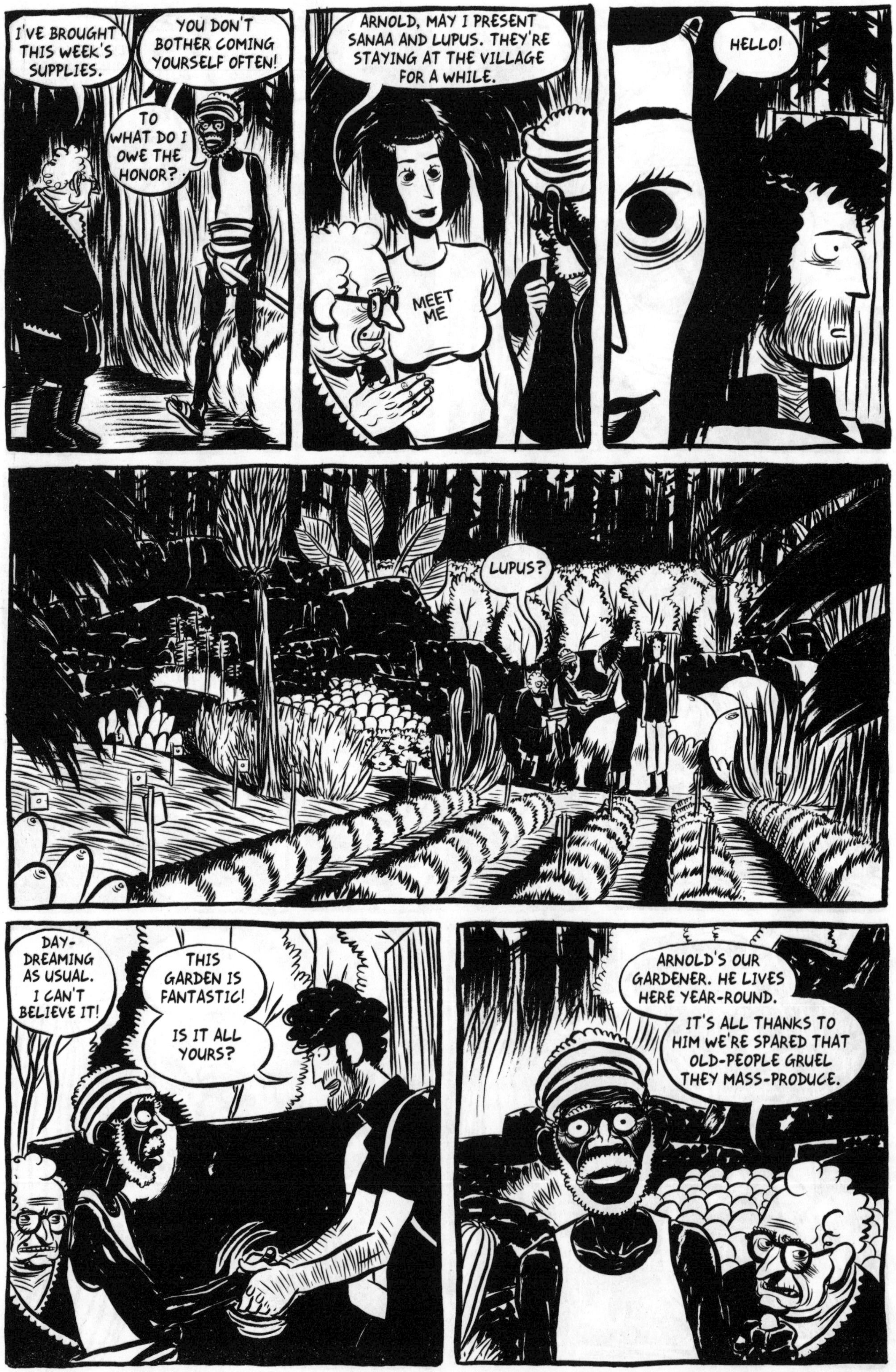
I'VE BROUGHT THIS WEEK'S SUPPLIES.
YOU DON'T BOTHER COMING YOURSELF OFTEN!
TO WHAT DO I OWE THE HONOR?
ARNOLD, MAY I PRESENT SANAA AND LUPUS. THEY'RE STAYING AT THE VILLAGE FOR A WHILE.
MEET ME
HELLO!
LUPUS?
DAY-DREAMING AS USUAL. I CAN'T BELIEVE IT!
THIS GARDEN IS FANTASTIC!
IS IT ALL YOURS?
ARNOLD'S OUR GARDENER. HE LIVES HERE YEAR-ROUND.
IT'S ALL THANKS TO HIM WE'RE SPARED THAT OLD-PEOPLE GRUEL THEY MASS-PRODUCE.

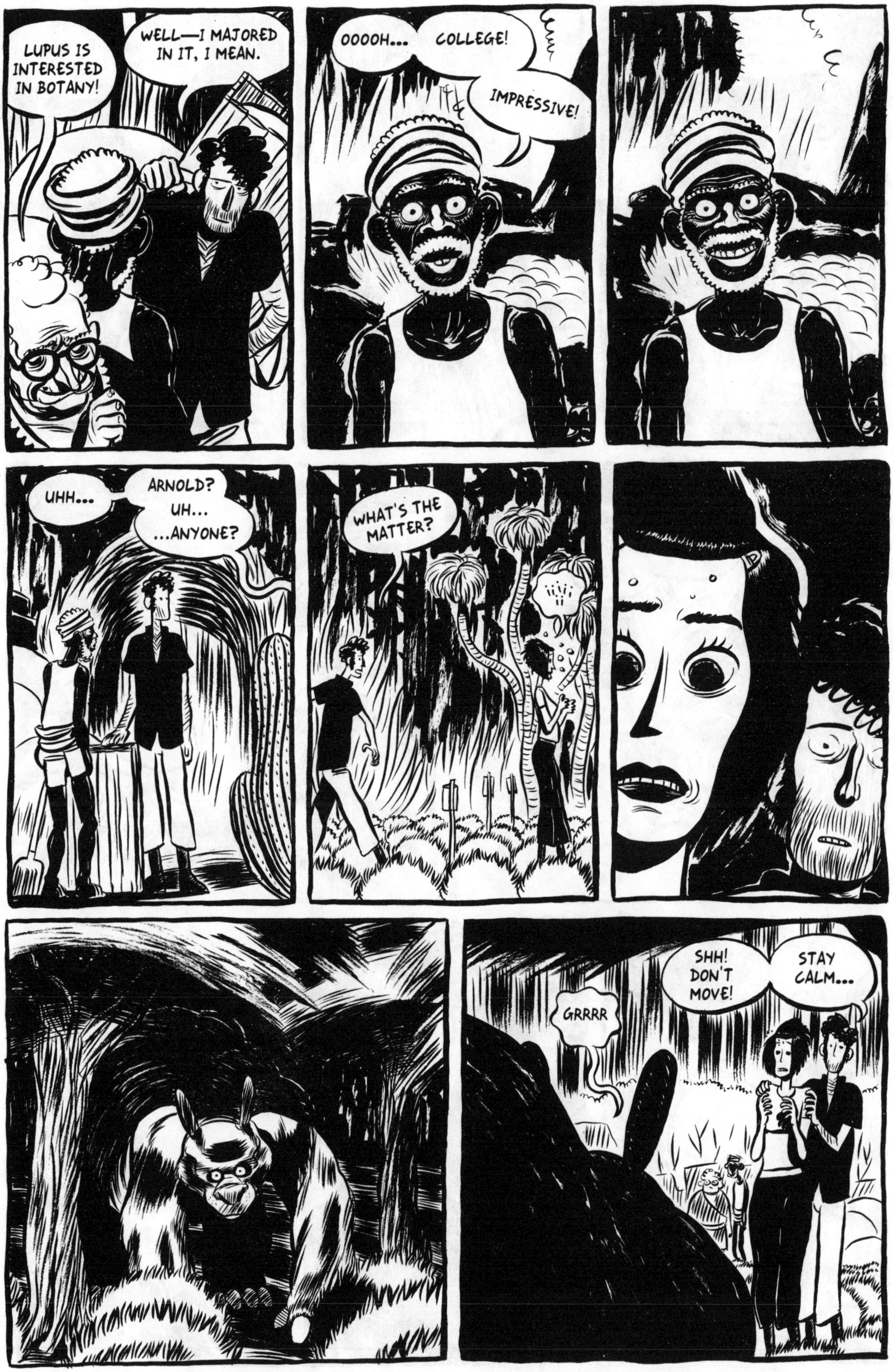

LUPUS IS INTERESTED IN BOTANY!
WELL—I MAJORED IN IT, I MEAN.
OOOOH... COLLEGE!
IMPRESSIVE!
UHH...
ARNOLD? UH... ...ANYONE?
WHAT'S THE MATTER?
GRRRR
SHH! DON'T MOVE!
STAY CALM...

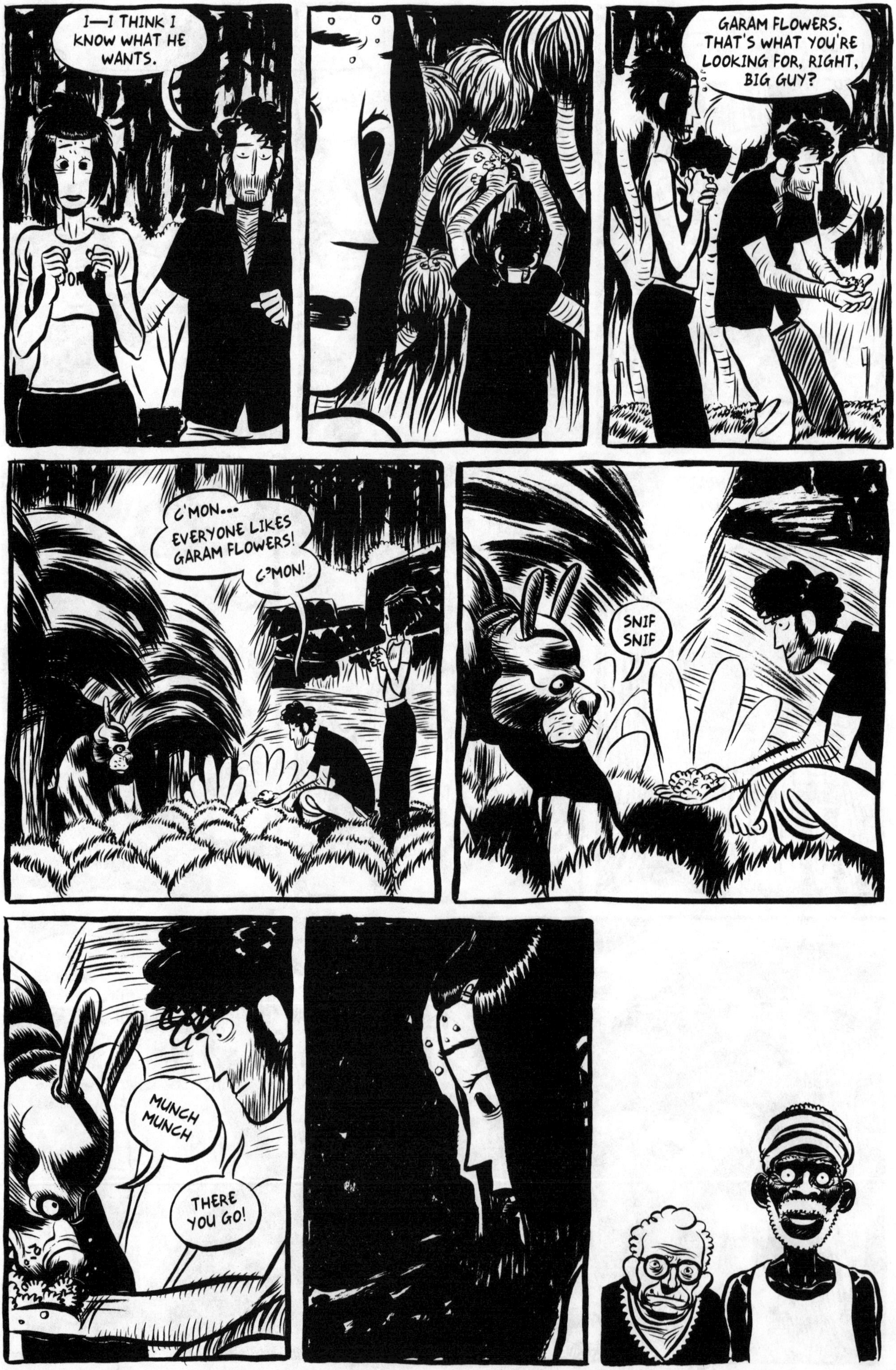
I—I THINK I KNOW WHAT HE WANTS.
GARAM FLOWERS. THAT'S WHAT YOU'RE LOOKING FOR, RIGHT, BIG GUY?
C'MON... EVERYONE LIKES GARAM FLOWERS!
C'MON!
SNIF SNIF
MUNCH MUNCH
THERE YOU GO!

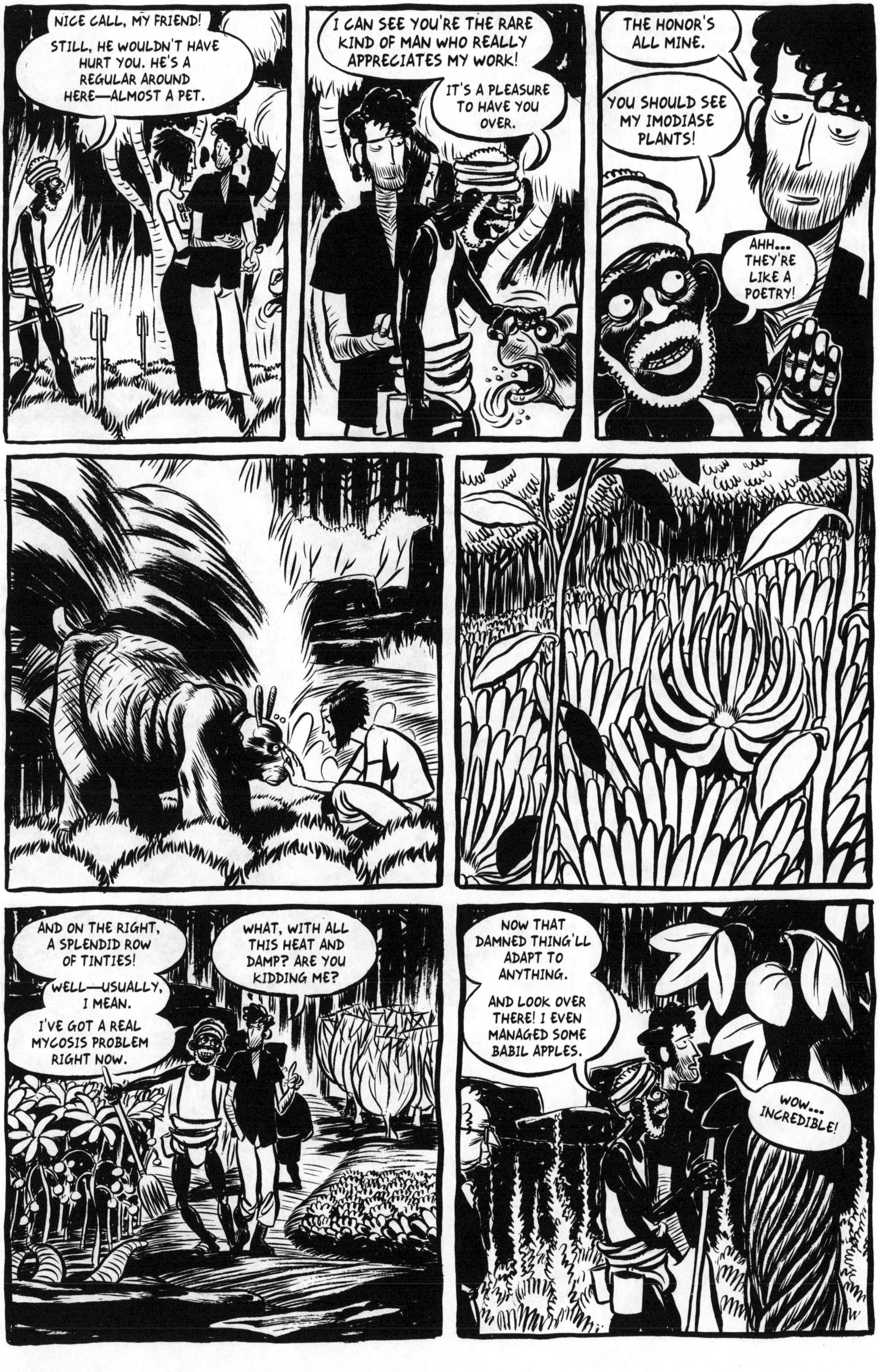
NICE CALL, MY FRIEND!
STILL, HE WOULDN'T HAVE HURT YOU. HE'S A REGULAR AROUND HERE—ALMOST A PET.
I CAN SEE YOU'RE THE RARE KIND OF MAN WHO REALLY APPRECIATES MY WORK!
IT'S A PLEASURE TO HAVE YOU OVER.
THE HONOR'S ALL MINE.
YOU SHOULD SEE MY IMODIASE PLANTS!
AHH... THEY'RE LIKE A POETRY!
AND ON THE RIGHT, A SPLENDID ROW OF TINTIES!
WHAT, WITH ALL THIS HEAT AND DAMP? ARE YOU KIDDING ME?
WELL—USUALLY, I MEAN.
I'VE GOT A REAL MYCOSIS PROBLEM RIGHT NOW.
NOW THAT DAMNED THING'LL ADAPT TO ANYTHING.
AND LOOK OVER THERE! I EVEN MANAGED SOME BABIL APPLES.
WOW... INCREDIBLE!

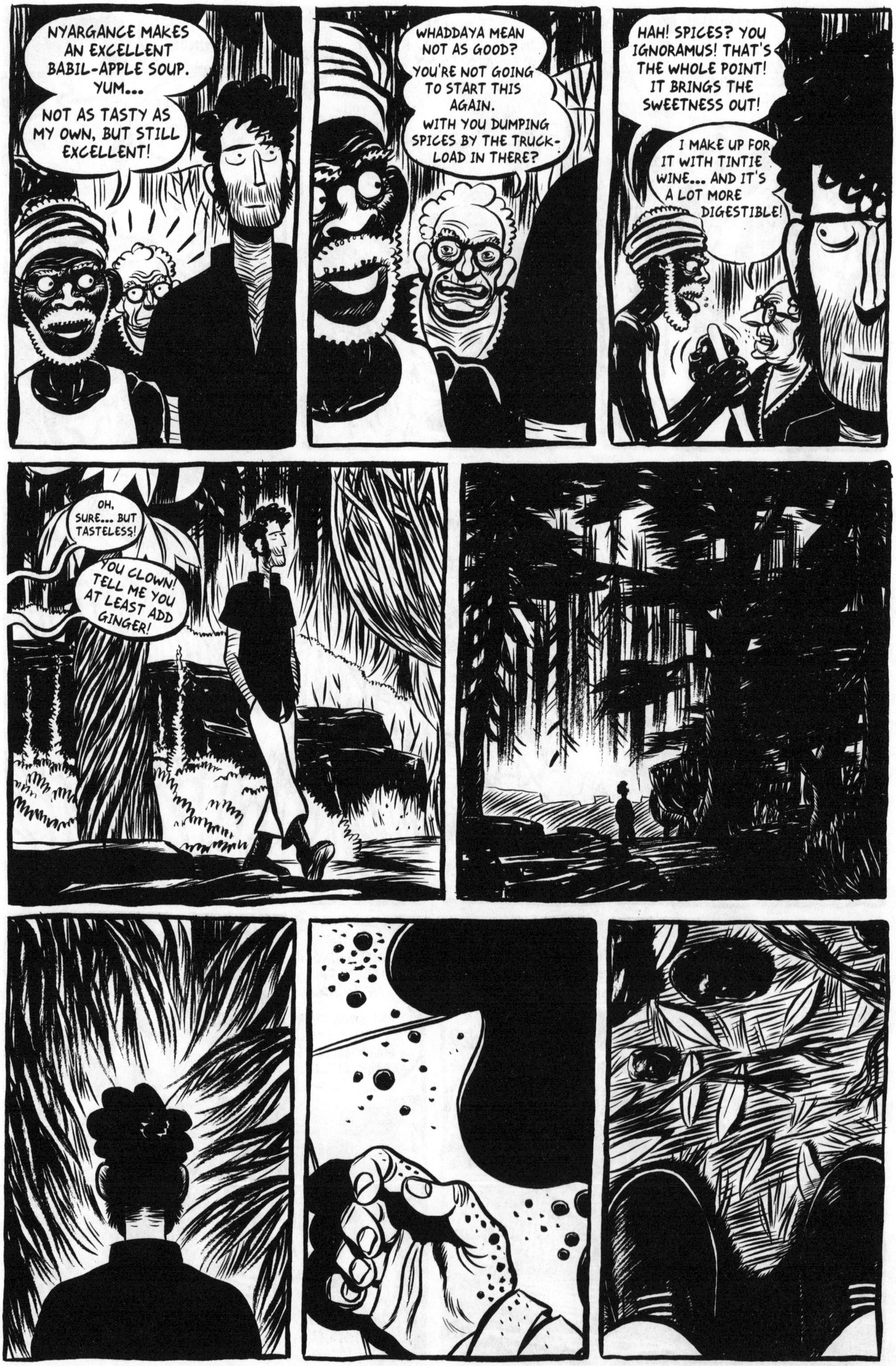
NYARGANCE MAKES AN EXCELLENT BABIL-APPLE SOUP. YUM...
NOT AS TASTY AS MY OWN, BUT STILL EXCELLENT!
WHADDAYA MEAN NOT AS GOOD?
YOU'RE NOT GOING TO START THIS AGAIN. WITH YOU DUMPING SPICES BY THE TRUCK-LOAD IN THERE?
HAH! SPICES? YOU IGNORAMUS! THAT'S THE WHOLE POINT! IT BRINGS THE SWEETNESS OUT!
I MAKE UP FOR IT WITH TINTIE WINE... AND IT'S A LOT MORE DIGESTIBLE!
OH, SURE... BUT TASTELESS!
YOU CLOWN! TELL ME YOU AT LEAST ADD GINGER!

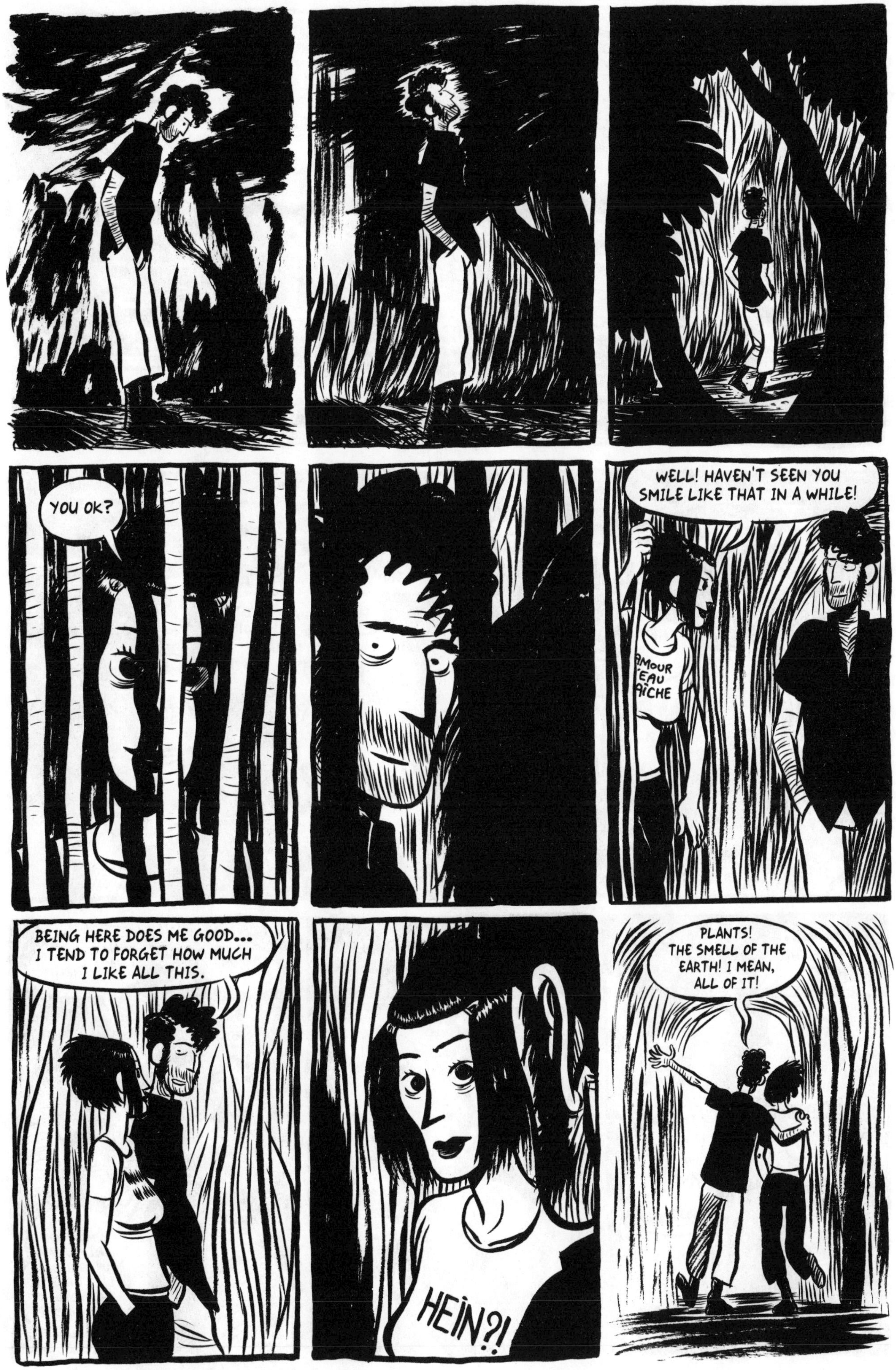
YOU OK?
WELL! HAVEN'T SEEN YOU SMILE LIKE THAT IN A WHILE!
BEING HERE DOES ME GOOD... I TEND TO FORGET HOW MUCH I LIKE ALL THIS.
HEIN?!
PLANTS! THE SMELL OF THE EARTH! I MEAN, ALL OF IT!

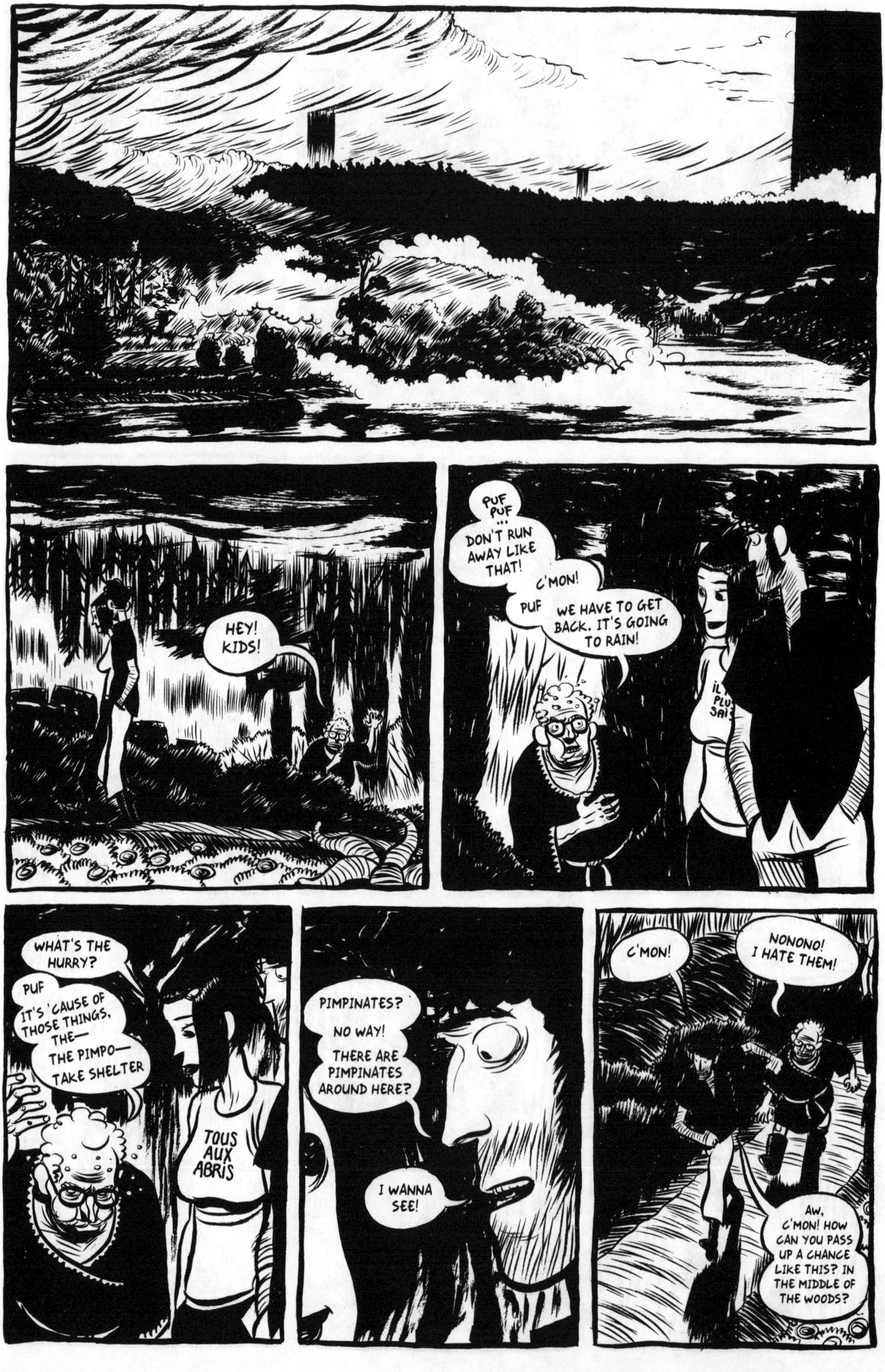

HEY! KIDS!
PUF PUF ... DON'T RUN AWAY LIKE THAT!
C'MON!
PUF
WE HAVE TO GET BACK. IT'S GOING TO RAIN!
WHAT'S THE HURRY?
PUF
IT'S 'CAUSE OF THOSE THINGS, THE—
THE PIMPO—
TAKE SHELTER
TOUS AUX ABRIS
PIMPINATES?
NO WAY!
THERE ARE PIMPINATES AROUND HERE?
I WANNA SEE!
C'MON!
NONONO! I HATE THEM!
AW, C'MON! HOW CAN YOU PASS UP A CHANCE LIKE THIS? IN THE MIDDLE OF THE WOODS?

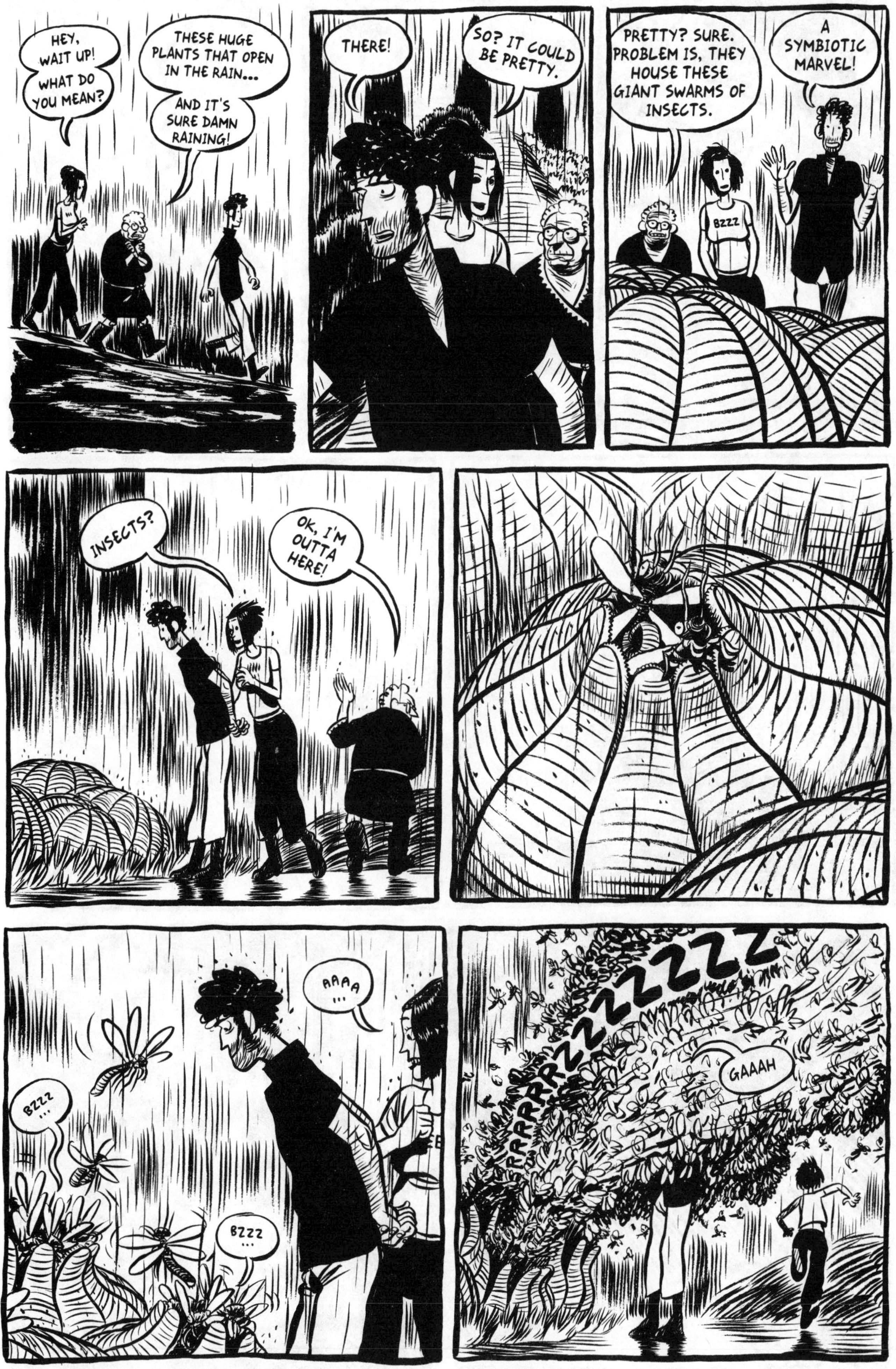
HEY, WAIT UP! WHAT DO YOU MEAN?
THESE HUGE PLANTS THAT OPEN IN THE RAIN...
AND IT'S SURE DAMN RAINING!
THERE!
SO? IT COULD BE PRETTY.
PRETTY? SURE. PROBLEM IS, THEY HOUSE THESE GIANT SWARMS OF INSECTS.
A SYMBIOTIC MARVEL!
BZZZ
INSECTS?
OK, I'M OUTTA HERE!
AAAA ...
BZZZ ...
BZZZ ...
RRRRRRRZZZZZZZZZZ
GAAAH

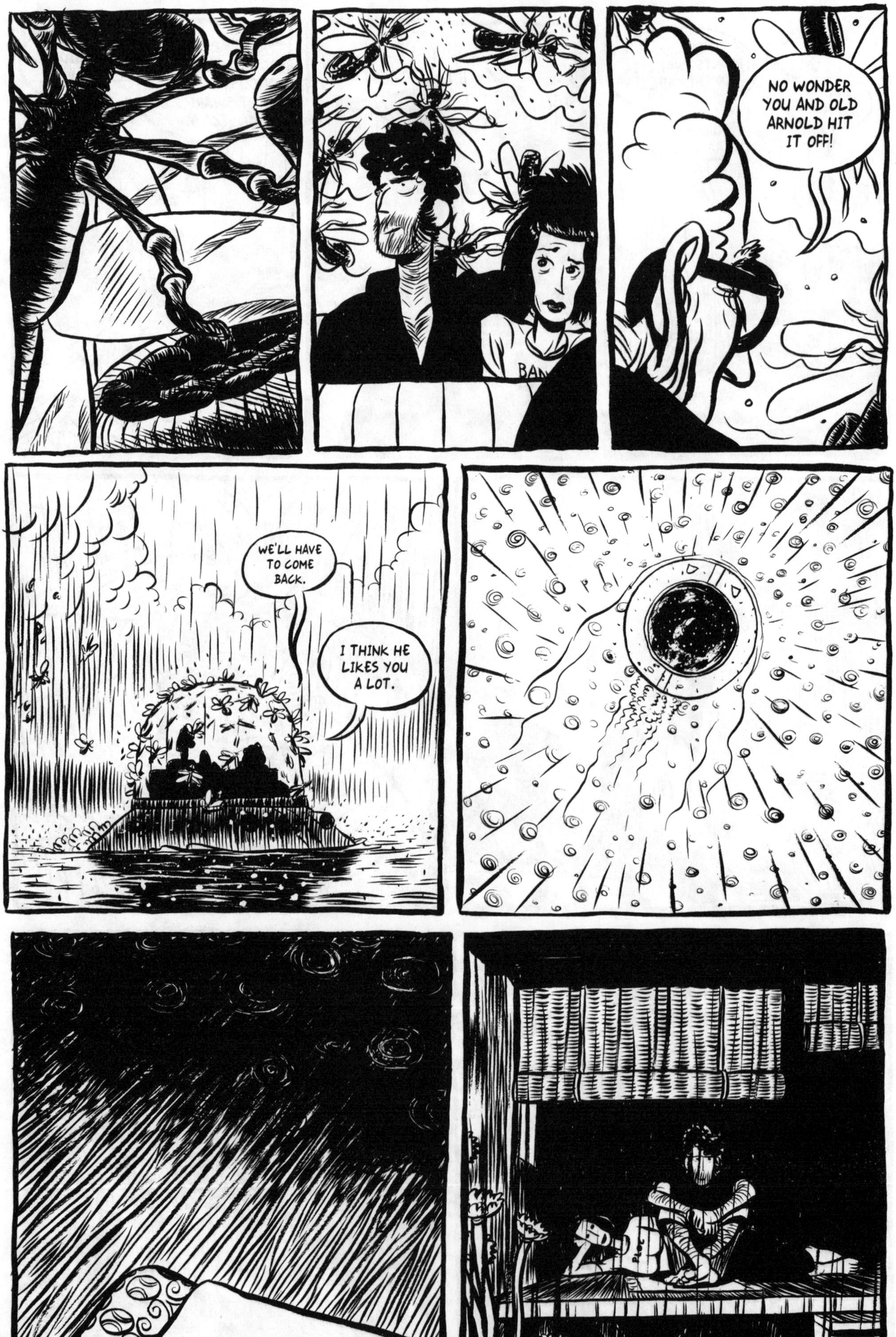
NO WONDER YOU AND OLD ARNOLD HIT IT OFF!
WE'LL HAVE TO COME BACK.
I THINK HE LIKES YOU A LOT.

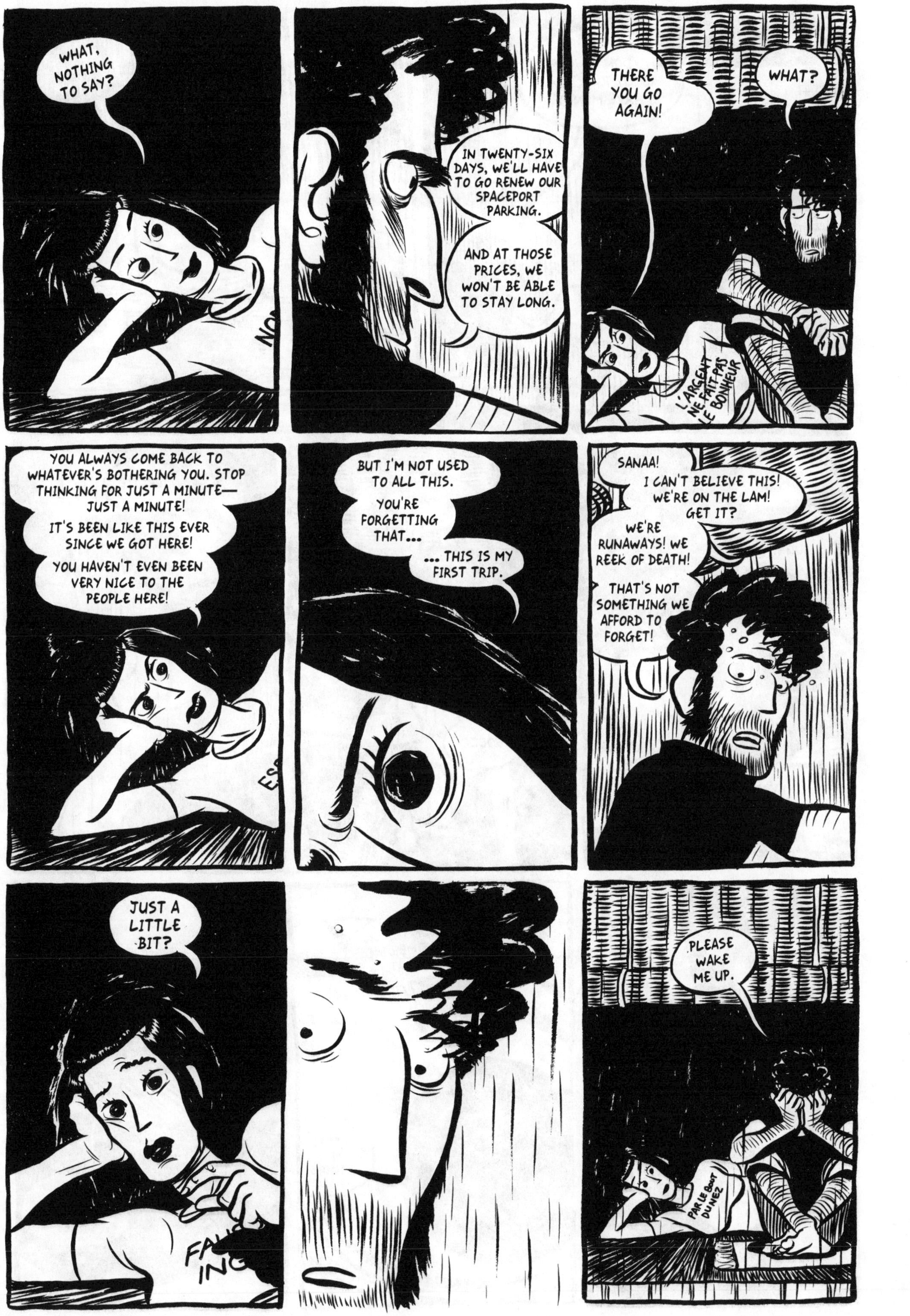
WHAT, NOTHING TO SAY?
IN TWENTY-SIX DAYS, WE'LL HAVE TO GO RENEW OUR SPACEPORT PARKING.
AND AT THOSE PRICES, WE WON'T BE ABLE TO STAY LONG.
THERE YOU GO AGAIN!
WHAT?
L'ARGENT NE FAIT PAS LE BONHEUR
YOU ALWAYS COME BACK TO WHATEVER'S BOTHERING YOU. STOP THINKING FOR JUST A MINUTE—JUST A MINUTE!
IT'S BEEN LIKE THIS EVER SINCE WE GOT HERE!
YOU HAVEN'T EVEN BEEN VERY NICE TO THE PEOPLE HERE!
BUT I'M NOT USED TO ALL THIS.
YOU'RE FORGETTING THAT...
... THIS IS MY FIRST TRIP.
SANAA!
I CAN'T BELIEVE THIS! WE'RE ON THE LAM! GET IT?
WE'RE RUNAWAYS! WE REEK OF DEATH!
THAT'S NOT SOMETHING WE AFFORD TO FORGET!
JUST A LITTLE BIT?
PLEASE WAKE ME UP.
PAR LE BOUT DU NEZ

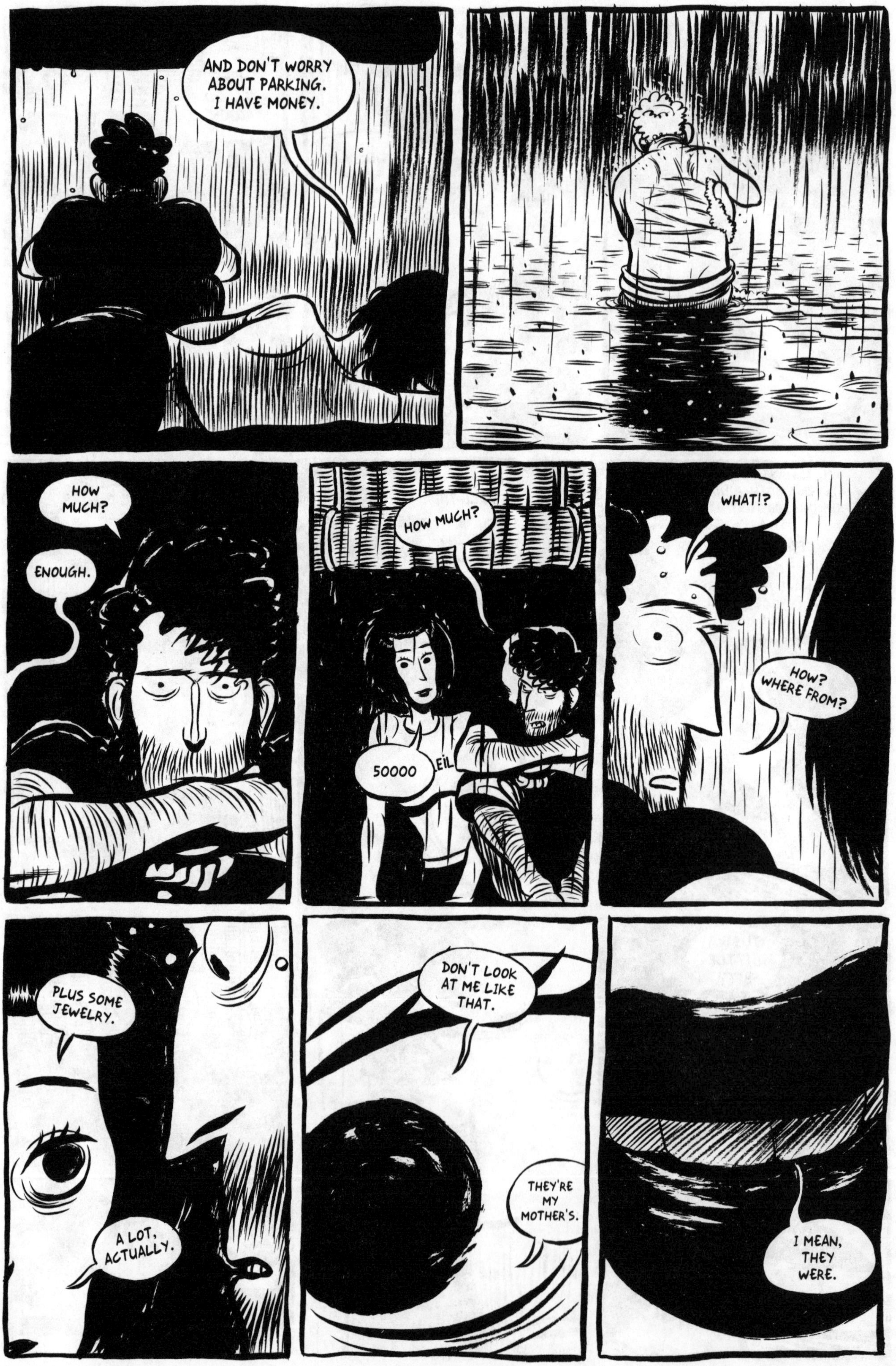
AND DON'T WORRY ABOUT PARKING. I HAVE MONEY.
HOW MUCH?
ENOUGH.
HOW MUCH?
50000
EIL
WHAT!?
HOW? WHERE FROM?
PLUS SOME JEWELRY.
A LOT, ACTUALLY.
DON'T LOOK AT ME LIKE THAT.
THEY'RE MY MOTHER'S.
I MEAN, THEY WERE.

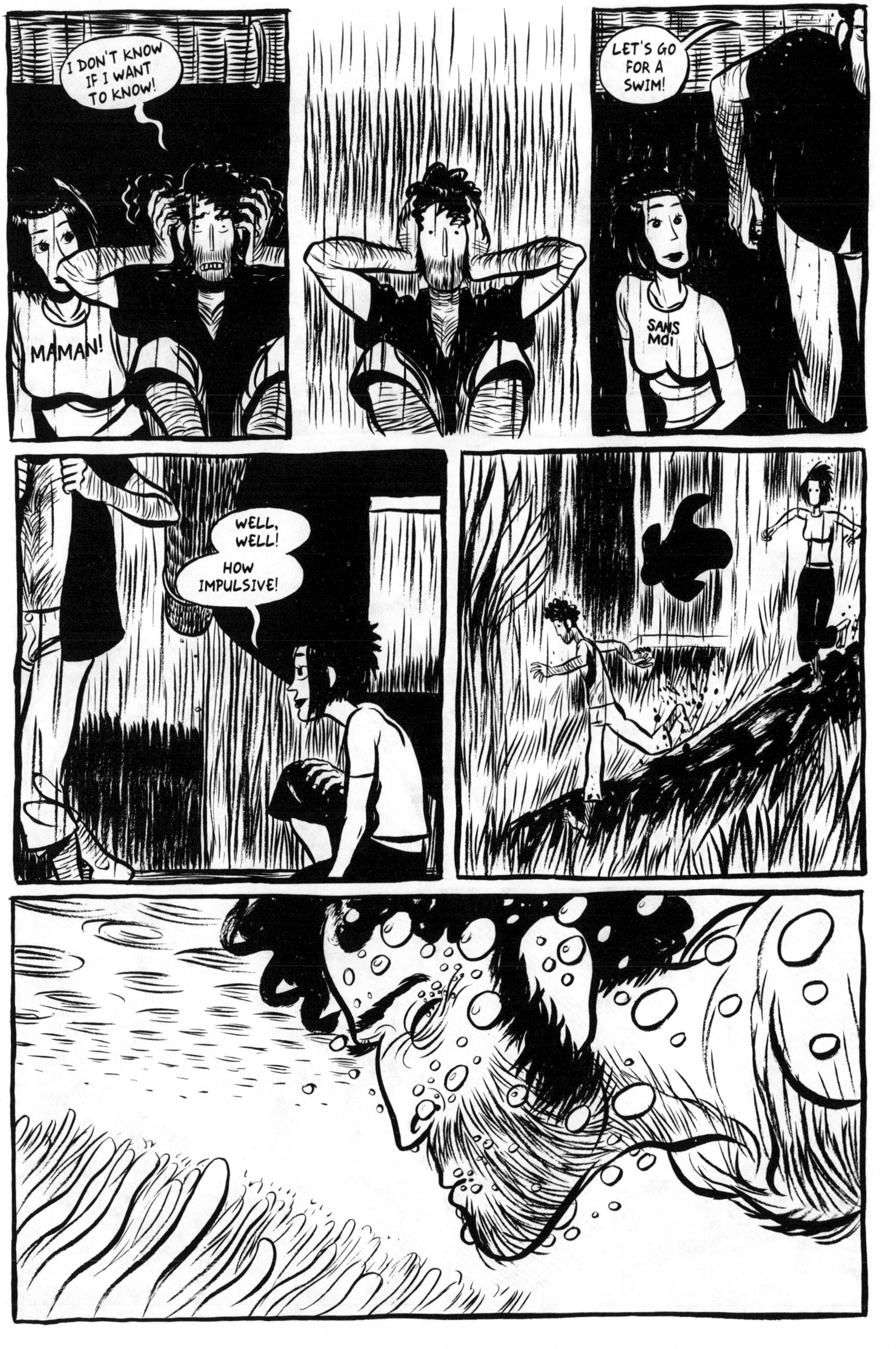
I DON'T KNOW IF I WANT TO KNOW!
MAMAN!
LET'S GO FOR A SWIM!
SANS MOI
WELL, WELL!
HOW IMPULSIVE!

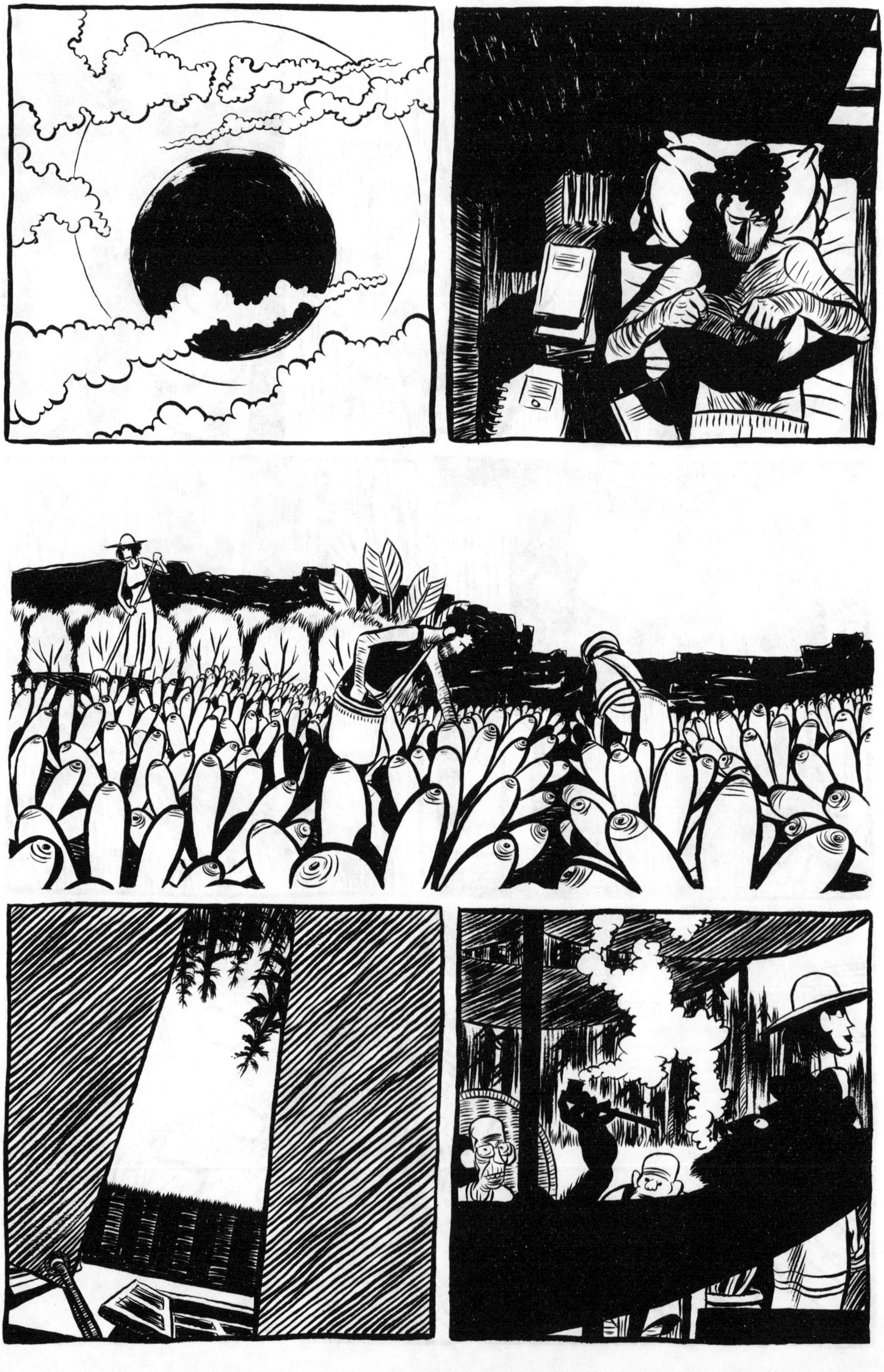

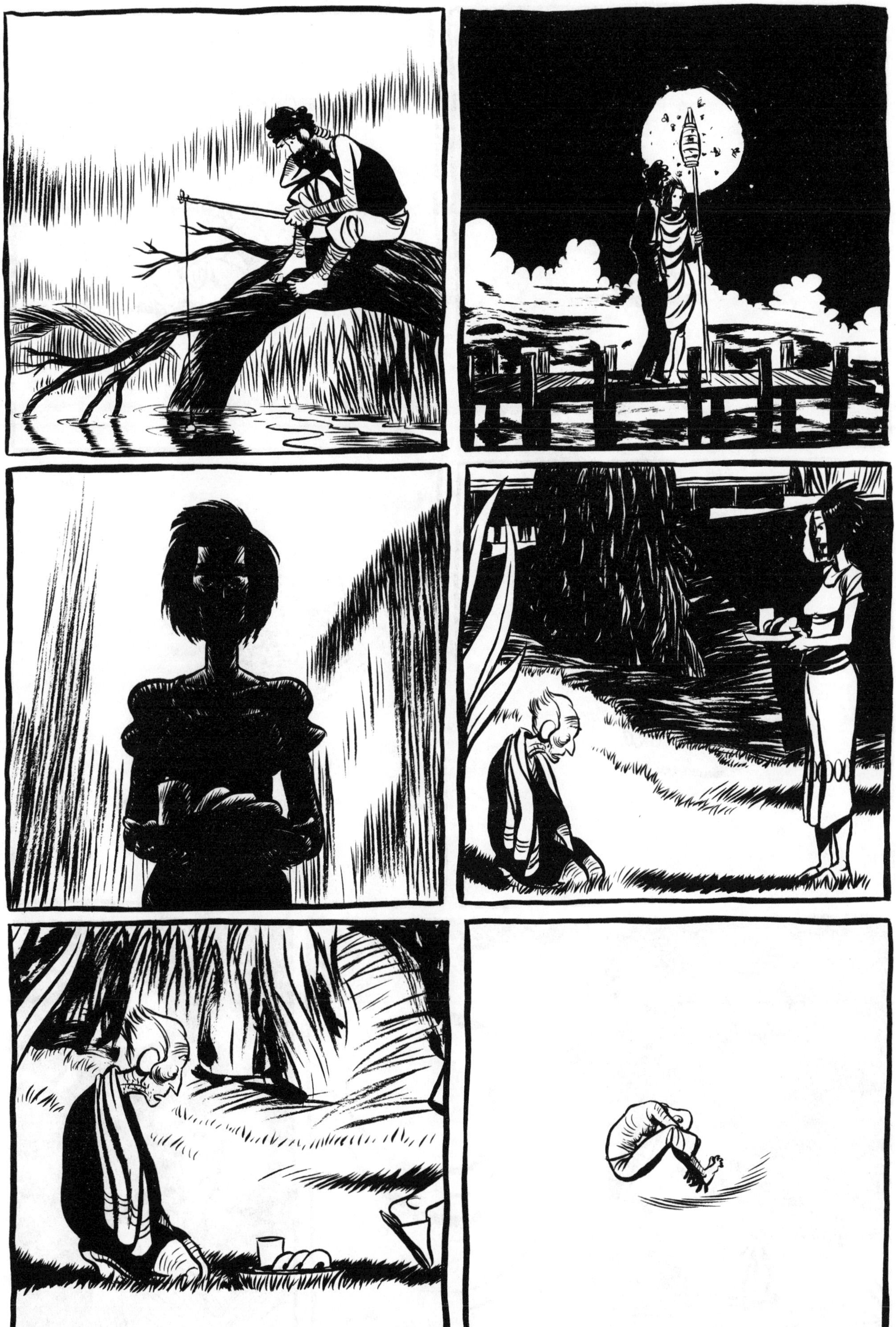

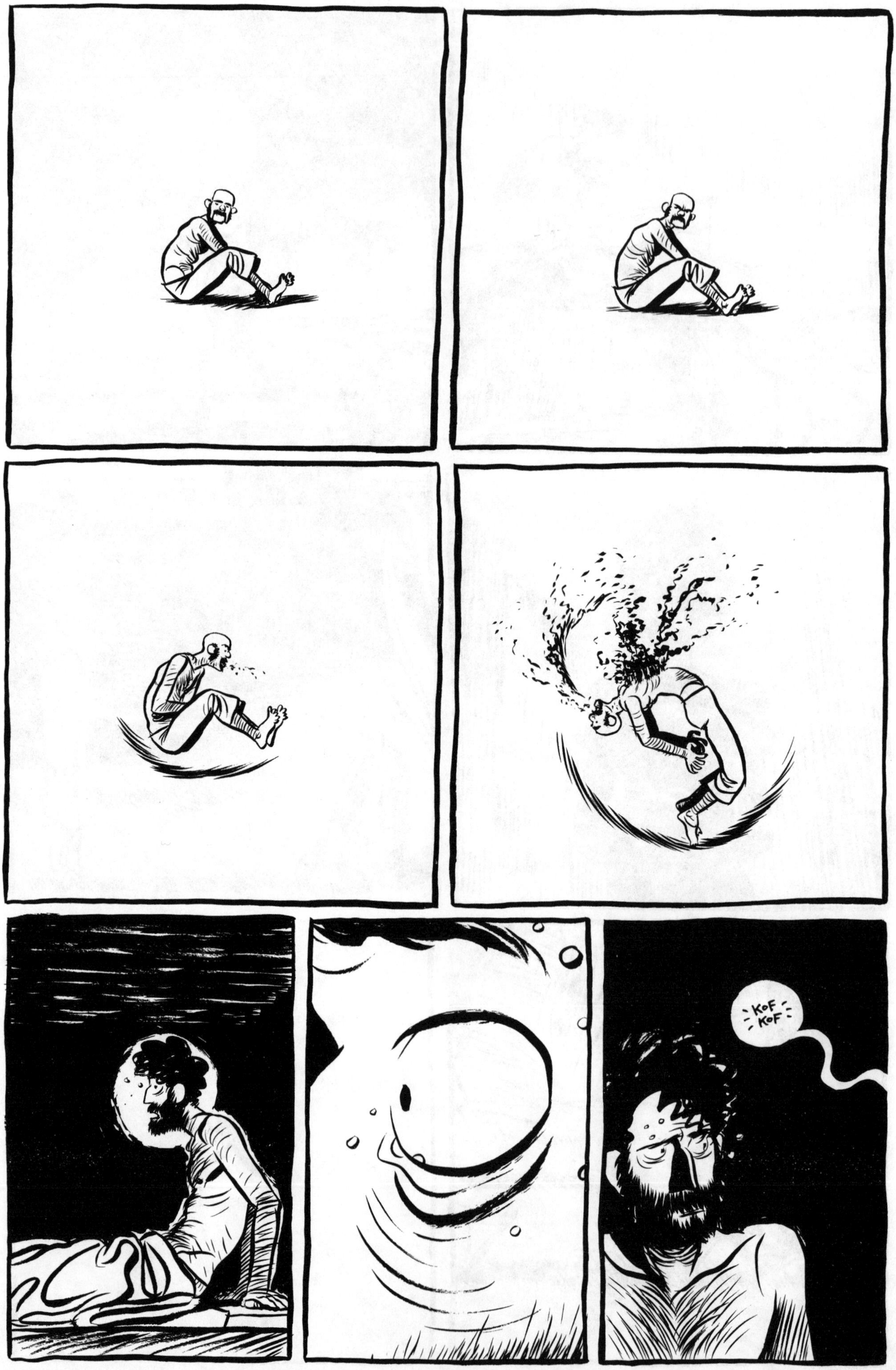
KOF KOF

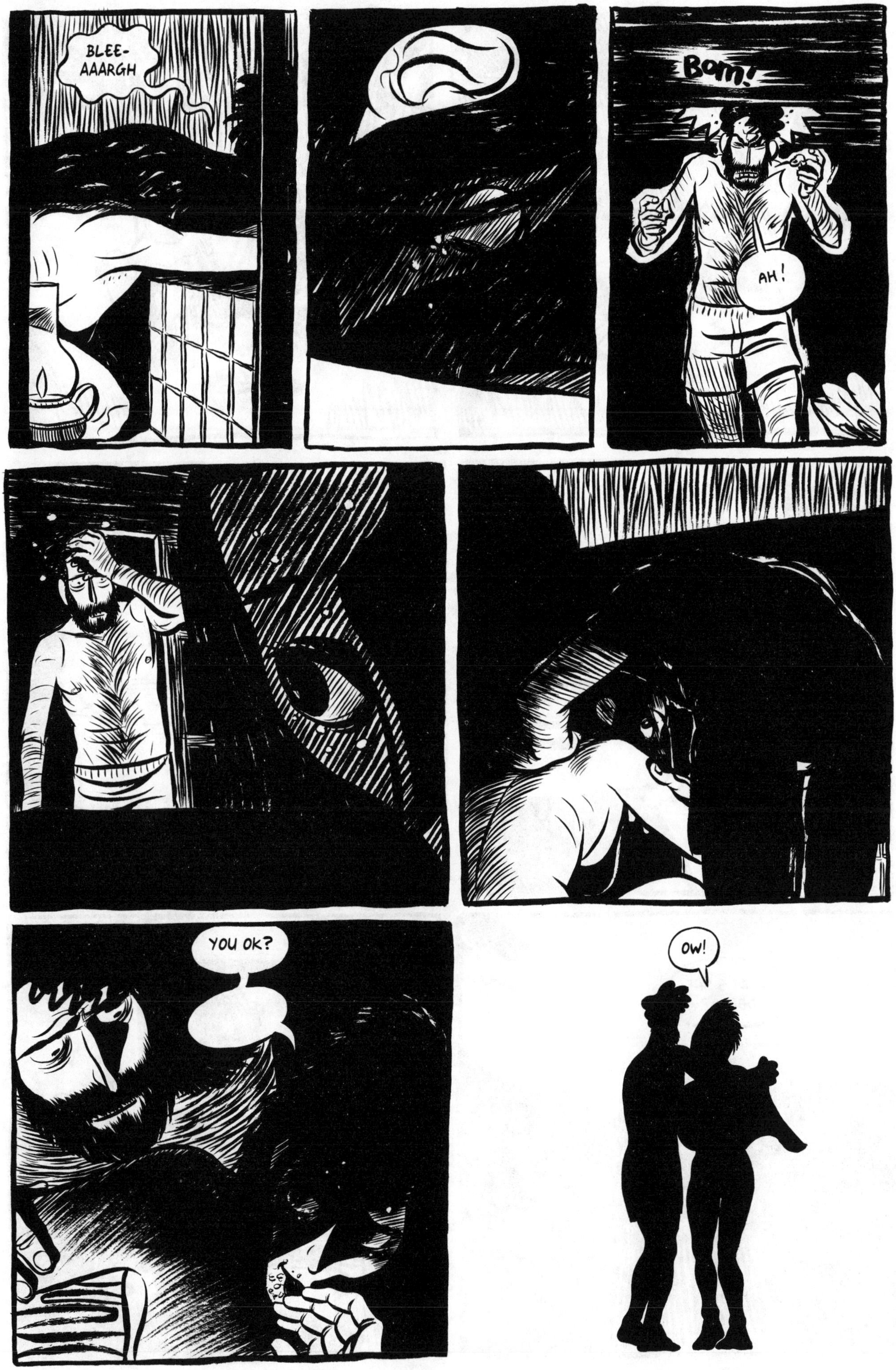
BLEE-
AAARGH
Bom!
AH!
YOU OK?
OW!

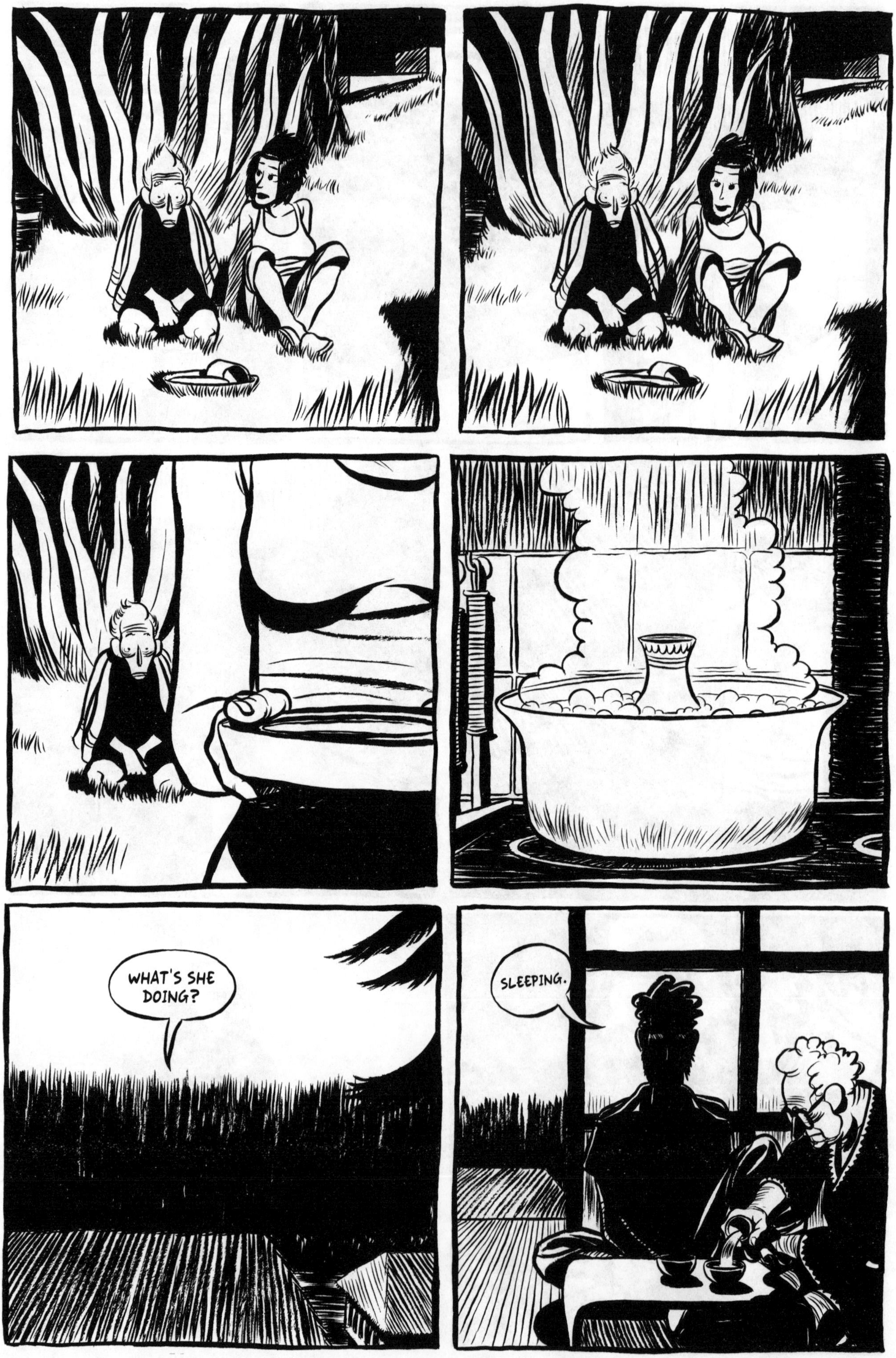
WHAT'S SHE DOING?
SLEEPING.

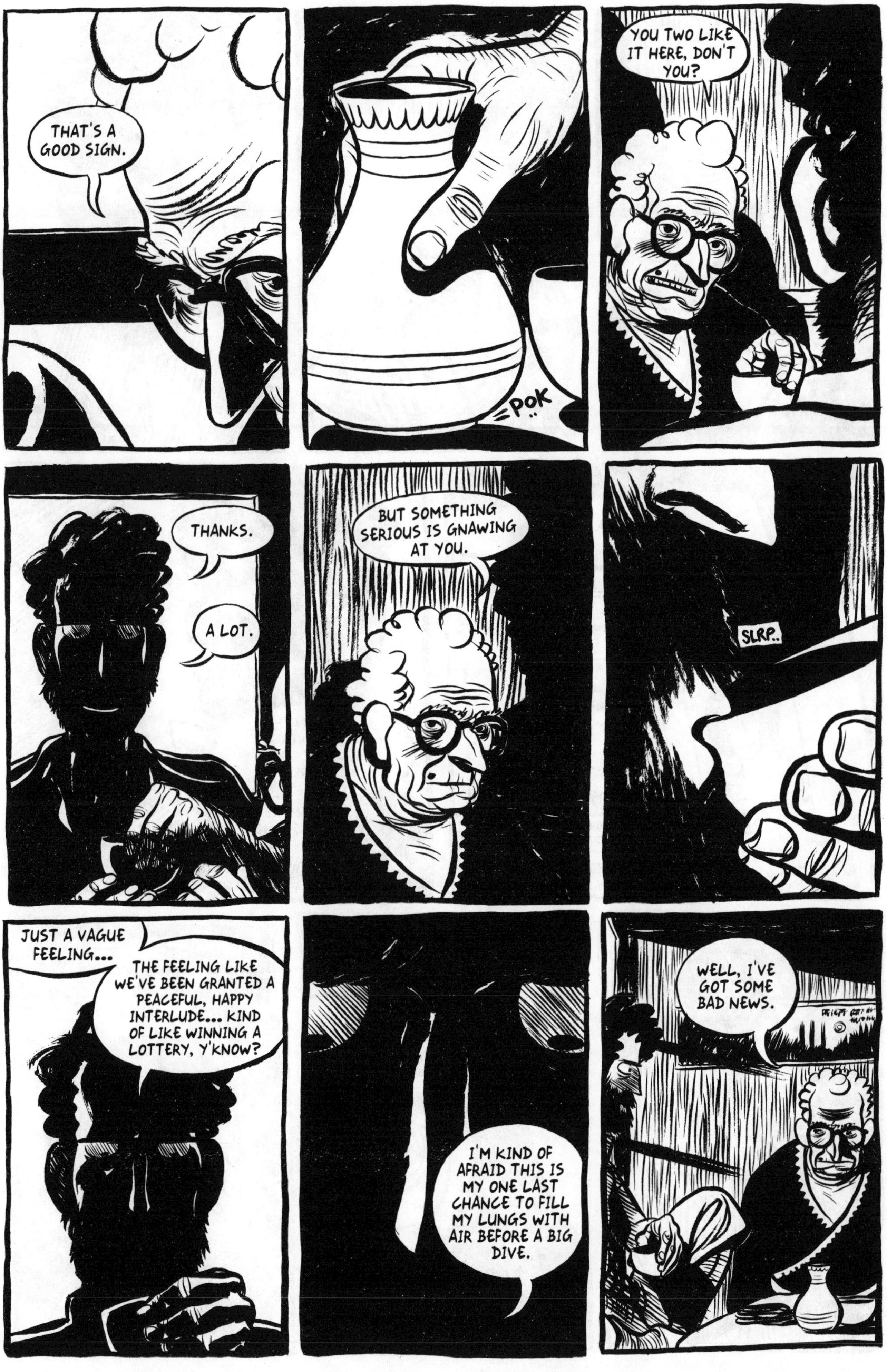
THAT'S A GOOD SIGN.
POK
YOU TWO LIKE IT HERE, DON'T YOU?
THANKS.
A LOT.
BUT SOMETHING SERIOUS IS GNAWING AT YOU.
SLRP..
JUST A VAGUE FEELING...
THE FEELING LIKE WE'VE BEEN GRANTED A PEACEFUL, HAPPY INTERLUDE... KIND OF LIKE WINNING A LOTTERY, Y'KNOW?
I'M KIND OF AFRAID THIS IS MY ONE LAST CHANCE TO FILL MY LUNGS WITH AIR BEFORE A BIG DIVE.
WELL, I'VE GOT SOME BAD NEWS.

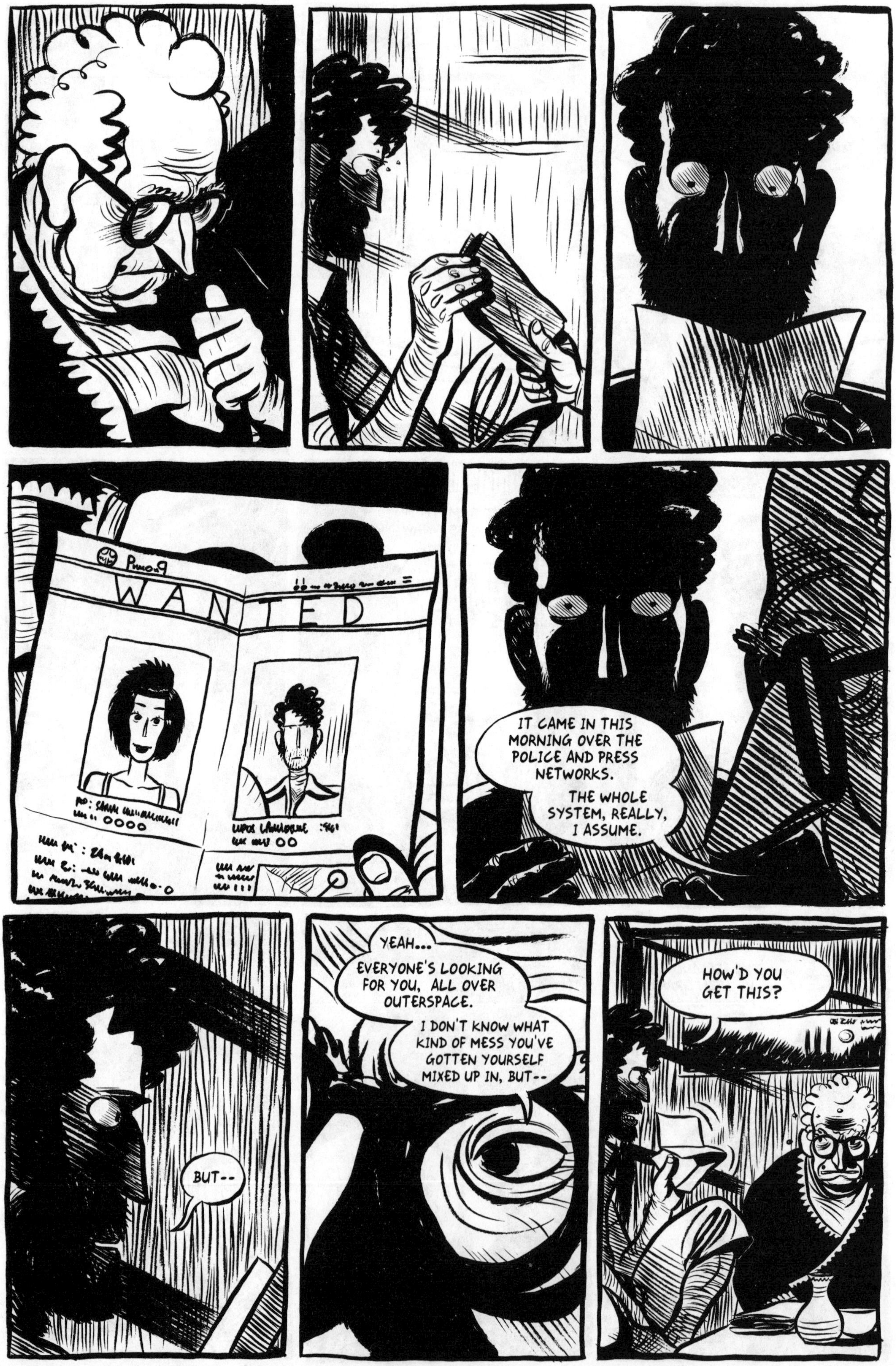
WANTED
IT CAME IN THIS MORNING OVER THE POLICE AND PRESS NETWORKS.
THE WHOLE SYSTEM, REALLY, I ASSUME.
BUT--
YEAH...
EVERYONE'S LOOKING FOR YOU, ALL OVER OUTERSPACE.
I DON'T KNOW WHAT KIND OF MESS YOU'VE GOTTEN YOURSELF MIXED UP IN, BUT--
HOW'D YOU GET THIS?

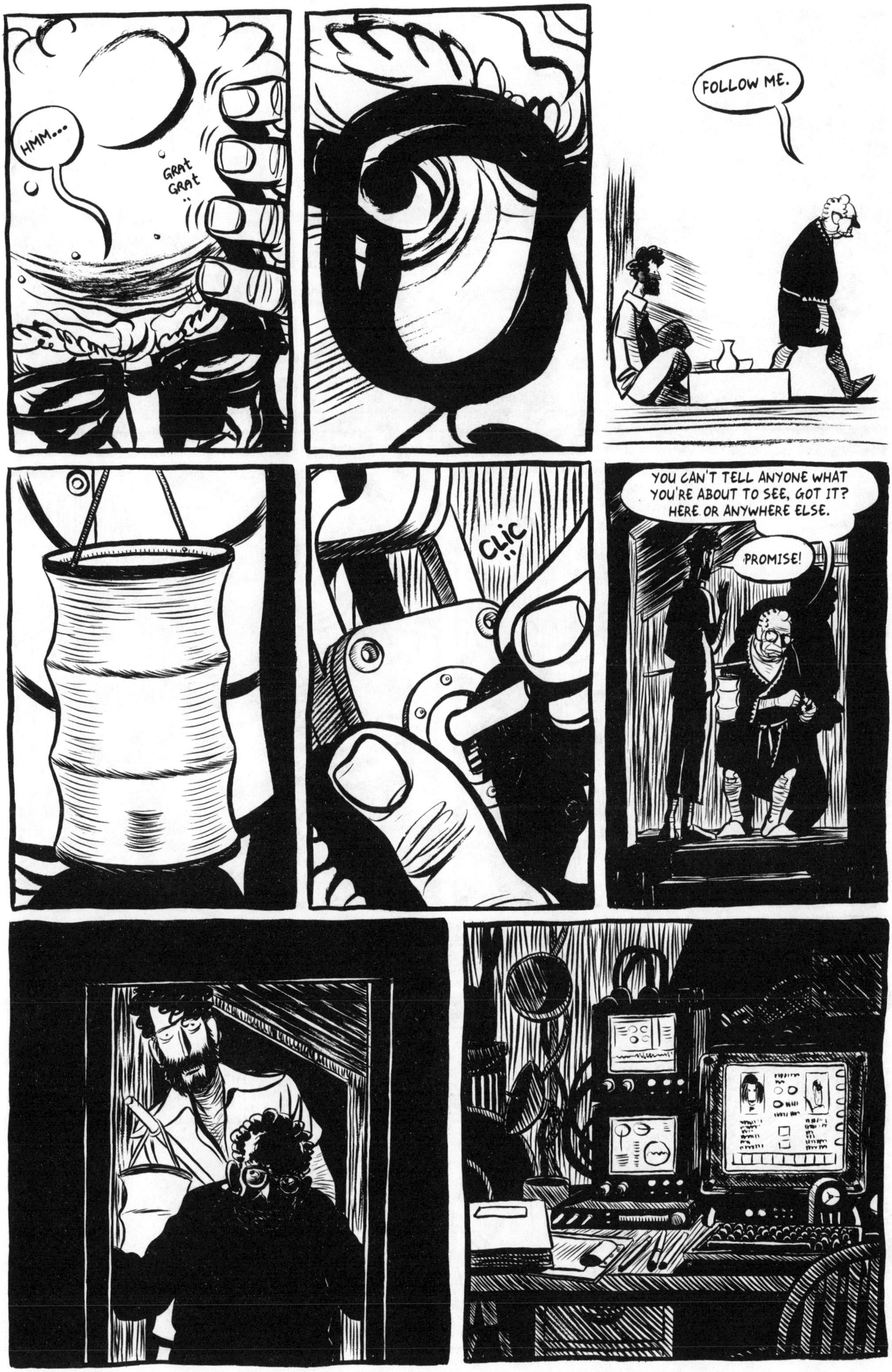
HMM...
GRAT GRAT
FOLLOW ME.
CLIC
YOU CAN'T TELL ANYONE WHAT YOU'RE ABOUT TO SEE, GOT IT? HERE OR ANYWHERE ELSE.
PROMISE!

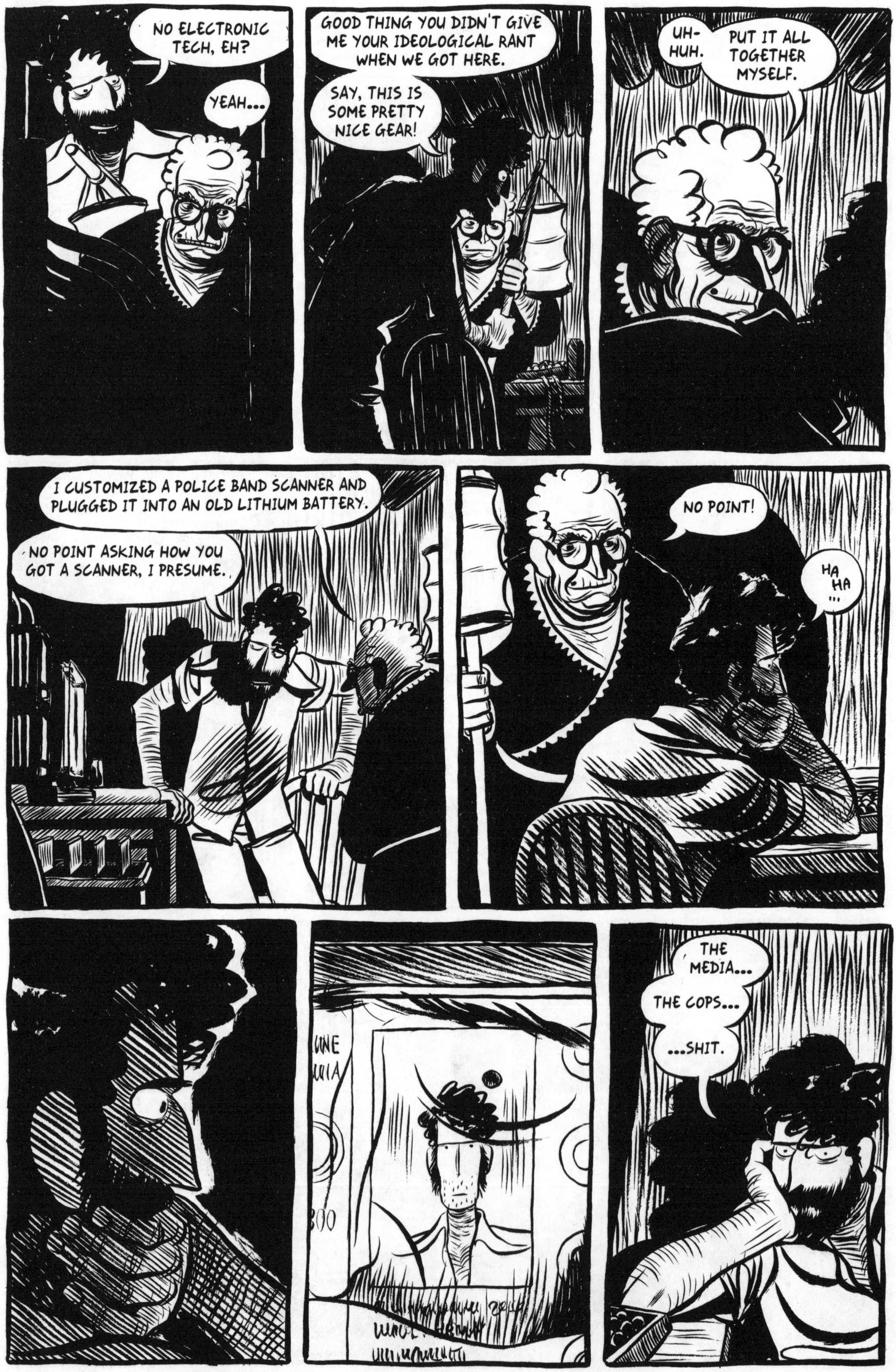
NO ELECTRONIC TECH, EH?
YEAH...
GOOD THING YOU DIDN'T GIVE ME YOUR IDEOLOGICAL RANT WHEN WE GOT HERE.
SAY, THIS IS SOME PRETTY NICE GEAR!
UH-HUH.
PUT IT ALL TOGETHER MYSELF.
I CUSTOMIZED A POLICE BAND SCANNER AND PLUGGED IT INTO AN OLD LITHIUM BATTERY.
NO POINT ASKING HOW YOU GOT A SCANNER, I PRESUME.
NO POINT!
HA HA ...
THE MEDIA...
THE COPS...
...SHIT.

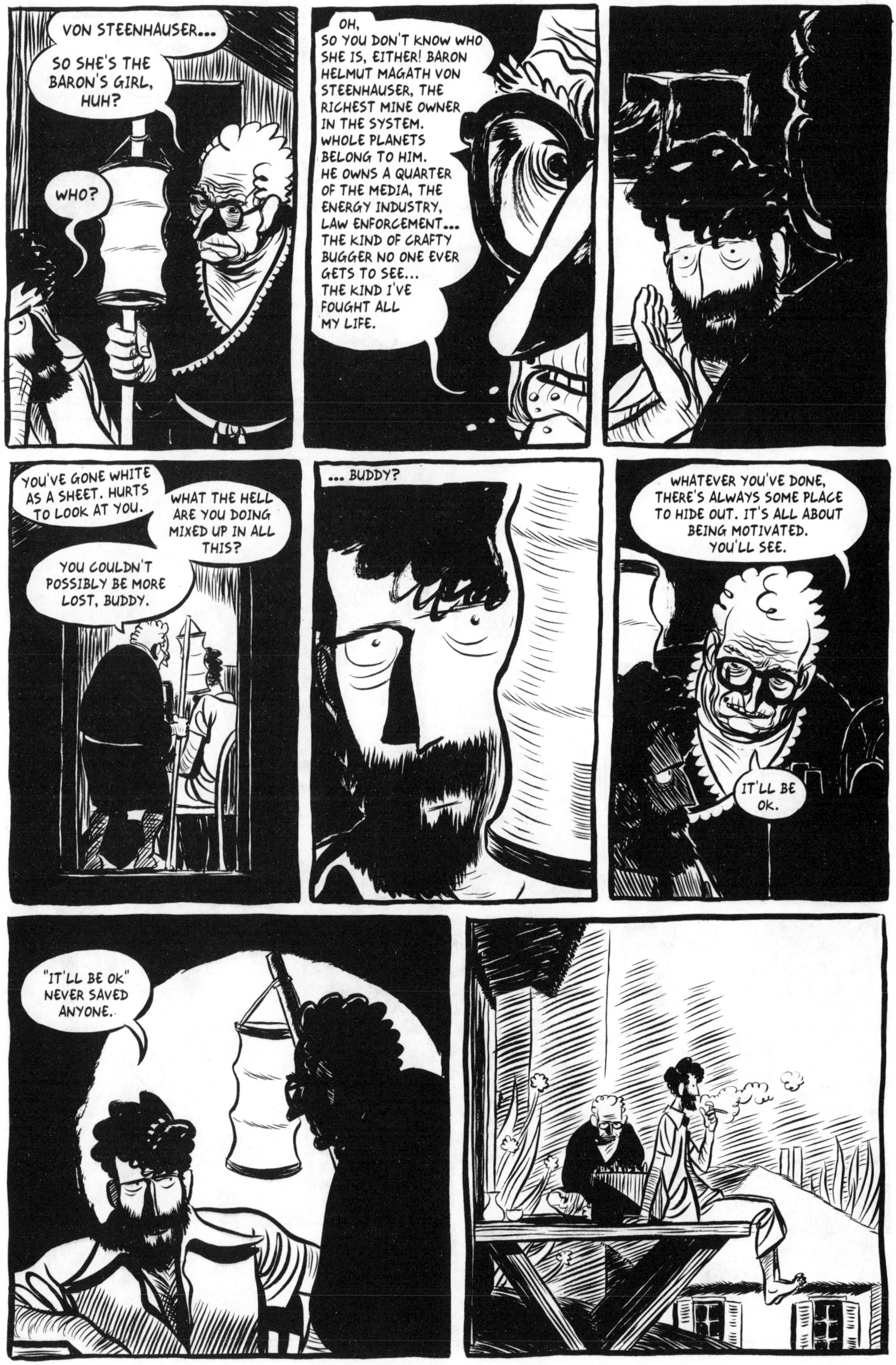
VON STEENHAUSER...
SO SHE'S THE BARON'S GIRL, HUH?
WHO?
OH, SO YOU DON'T KNOW WHO SHE IS, EITHER! BARON HELMUT MAGATH VON STEENHAUSER, THE RICHEST MINE OWNER IN THE SYSTEM. WHOLE PLANETS BELONG TO HIM. HE OWNS A QUARTER OF THE MEDIA, THE ENERGY INDUSTRY, LAW ENFORCEMENT... THE KIND OF CRAFTY BUGGER NO ONE EVER GETS TO SEE... THE KIND I'VE FOUGHT ALL MY LIFE.
YOU'VE GONE WHITE AS A SHEET. HURTS TO LOOK AT YOU.
WHAT THE HELL ARE YOU DOING MIXED UP IN ALL THIS?
YOU COULDN'T POSSIBLY BE MORE LOST, BUDDY.
... BUDDY?
WHATEVER YOU'VE DONE, THERE'S ALWAYS SOME PLACE TO HIDE OUT. IT'S ALL ABOUT BEING MOTIVATED. YOU'LL SEE.
IT'LL BE OK.
"IT'LL BE OK" NEVER SAVED ANYONE.

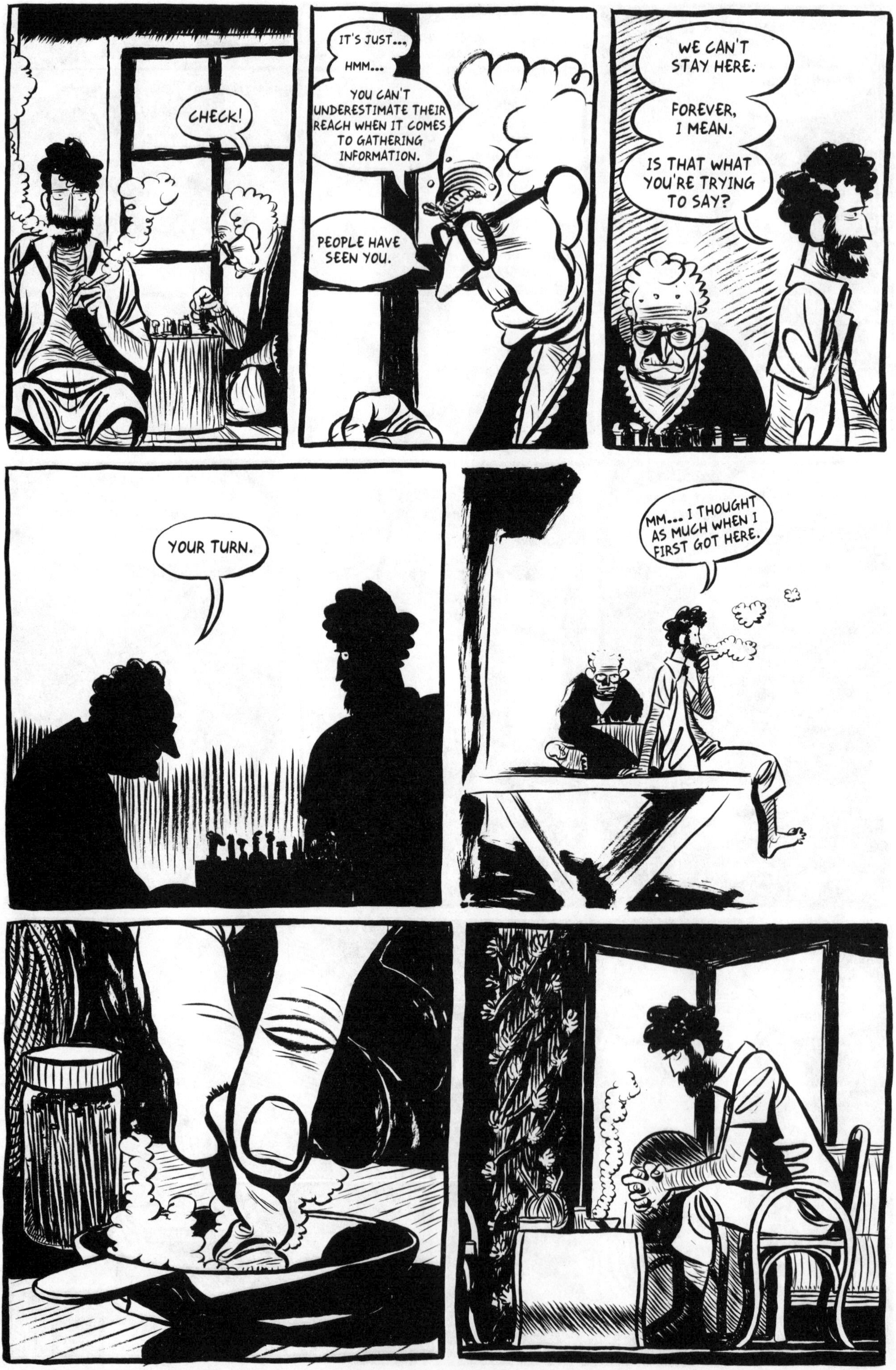
CHECK!
IT'S JUST...
HMM...
YOU CAN'T UNDERESTIMATE THEIR REACH WHEN IT COMES TO GATHERING INFORMATION.
PEOPLE HAVE SEEN YOU.
WE CAN'T STAY HERE.
FOREVER, I MEAN.
IS THAT WHAT YOU'RE TRYING TO SAY?
YOUR TURN.
MM... I THOUGHT AS MUCH WHEN I FIRST GOT HERE.

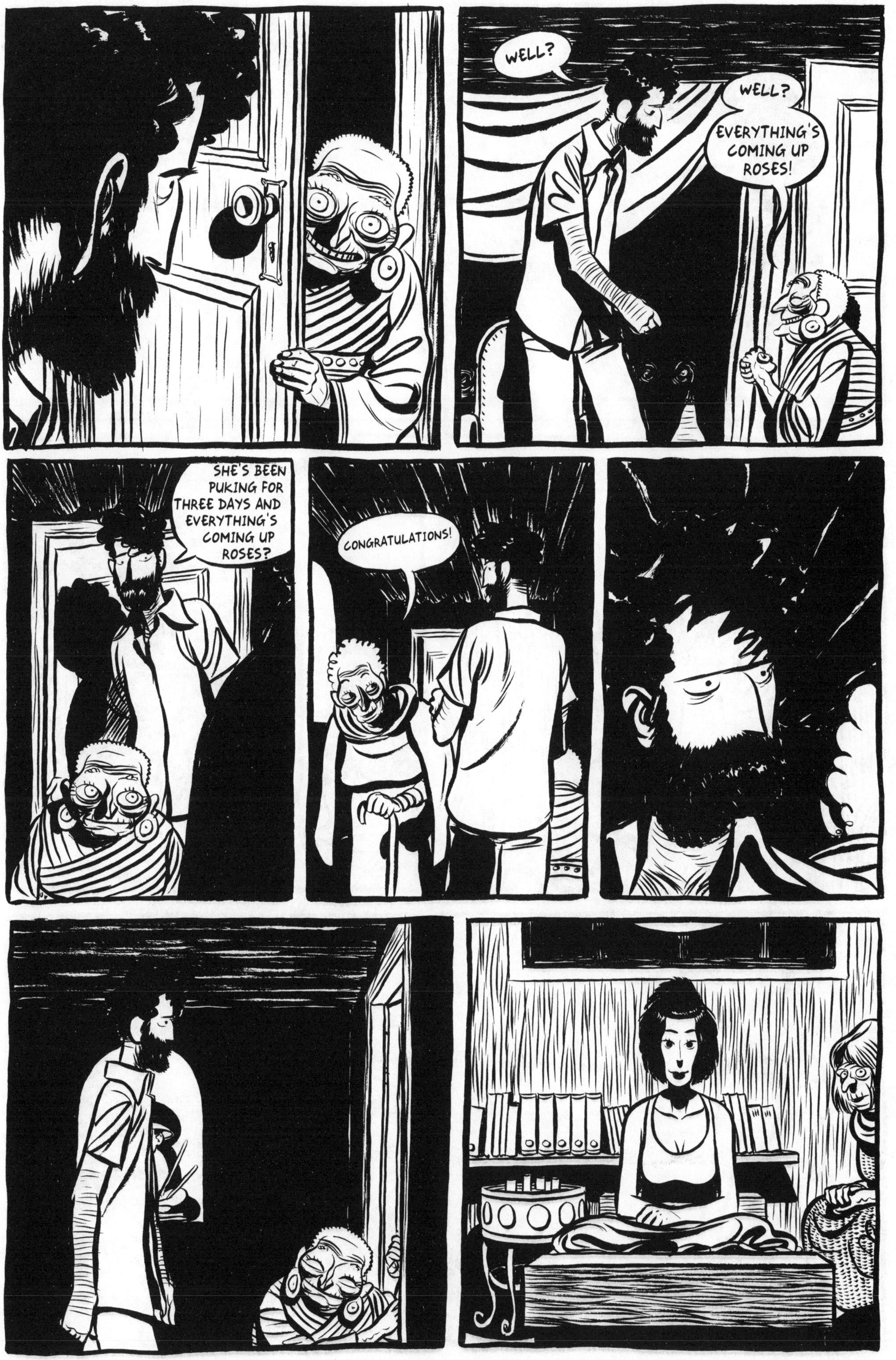
WELL?
WELL?
EVERYTHING'S COMING UP ROSES!
SHE'S BEEN PUKING FOR THREE DAYS AND EVERYTHING'S COMING UP ROSES?
CONGRATULATIONS!

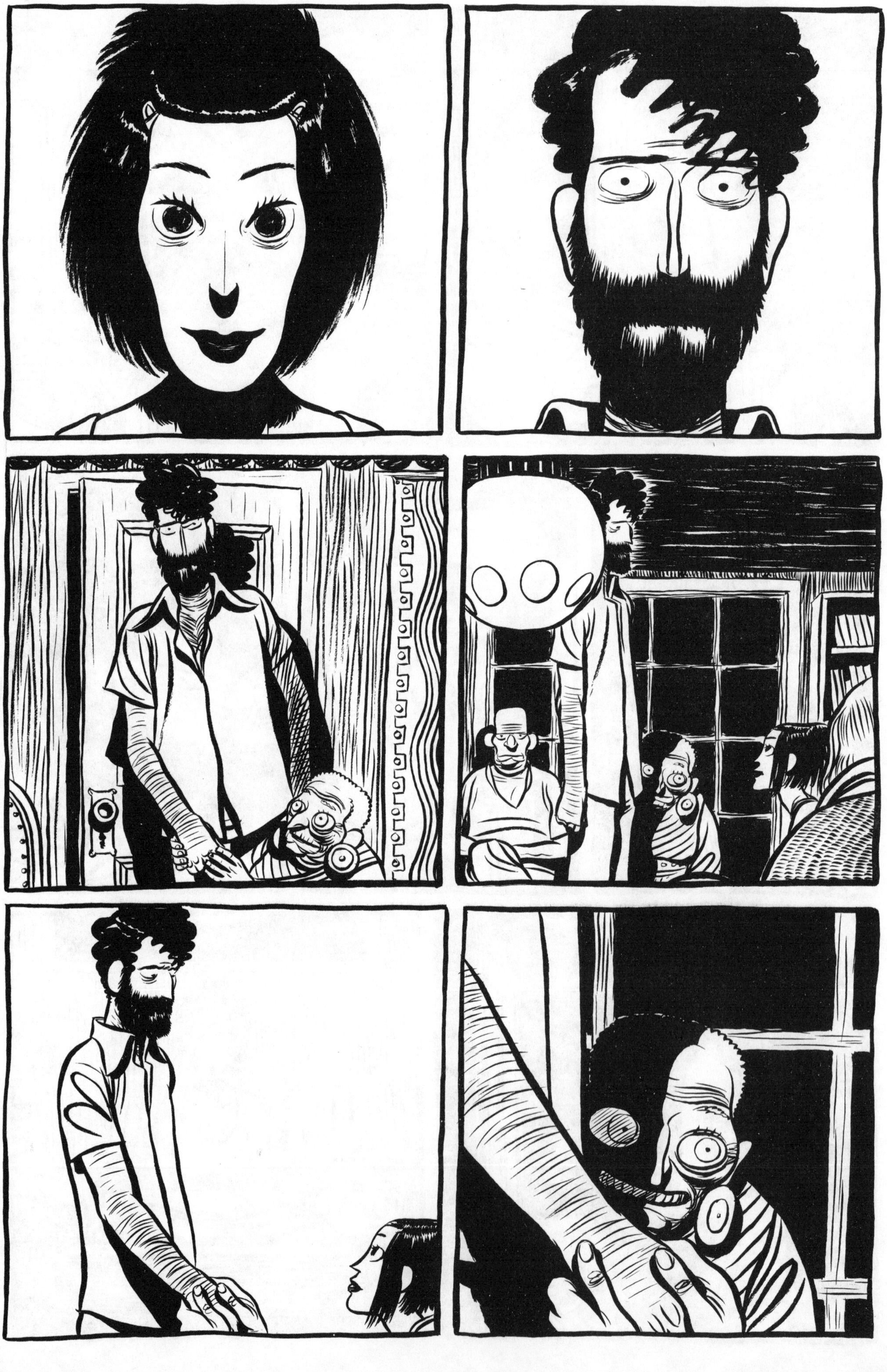

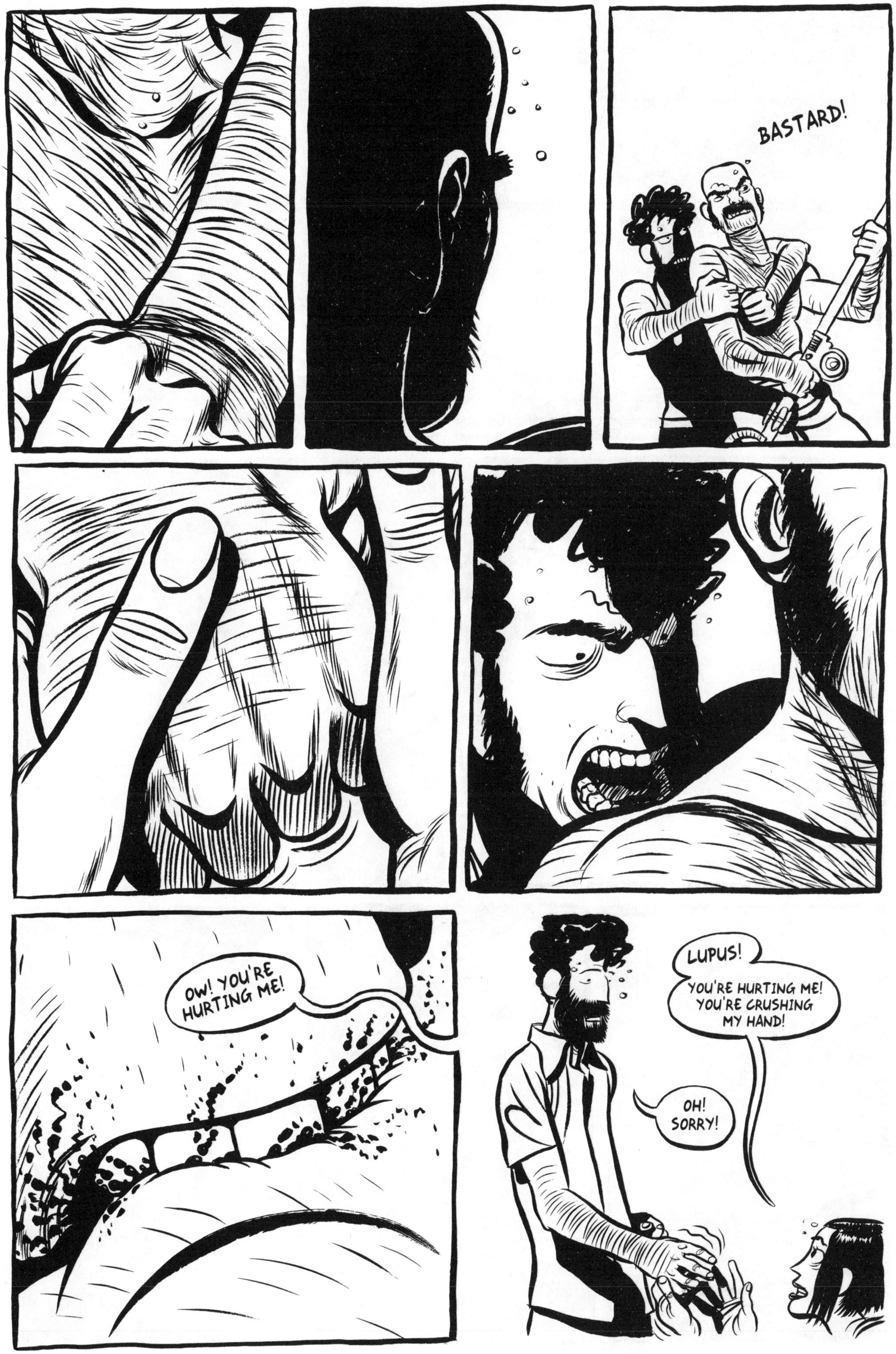
BASTARD!
OW! YOU'RE HURTING ME!
LUPUS!
YOU'RE HURTING ME! YOU'RE CRUSHING MY HAND!
OH! SORRY!

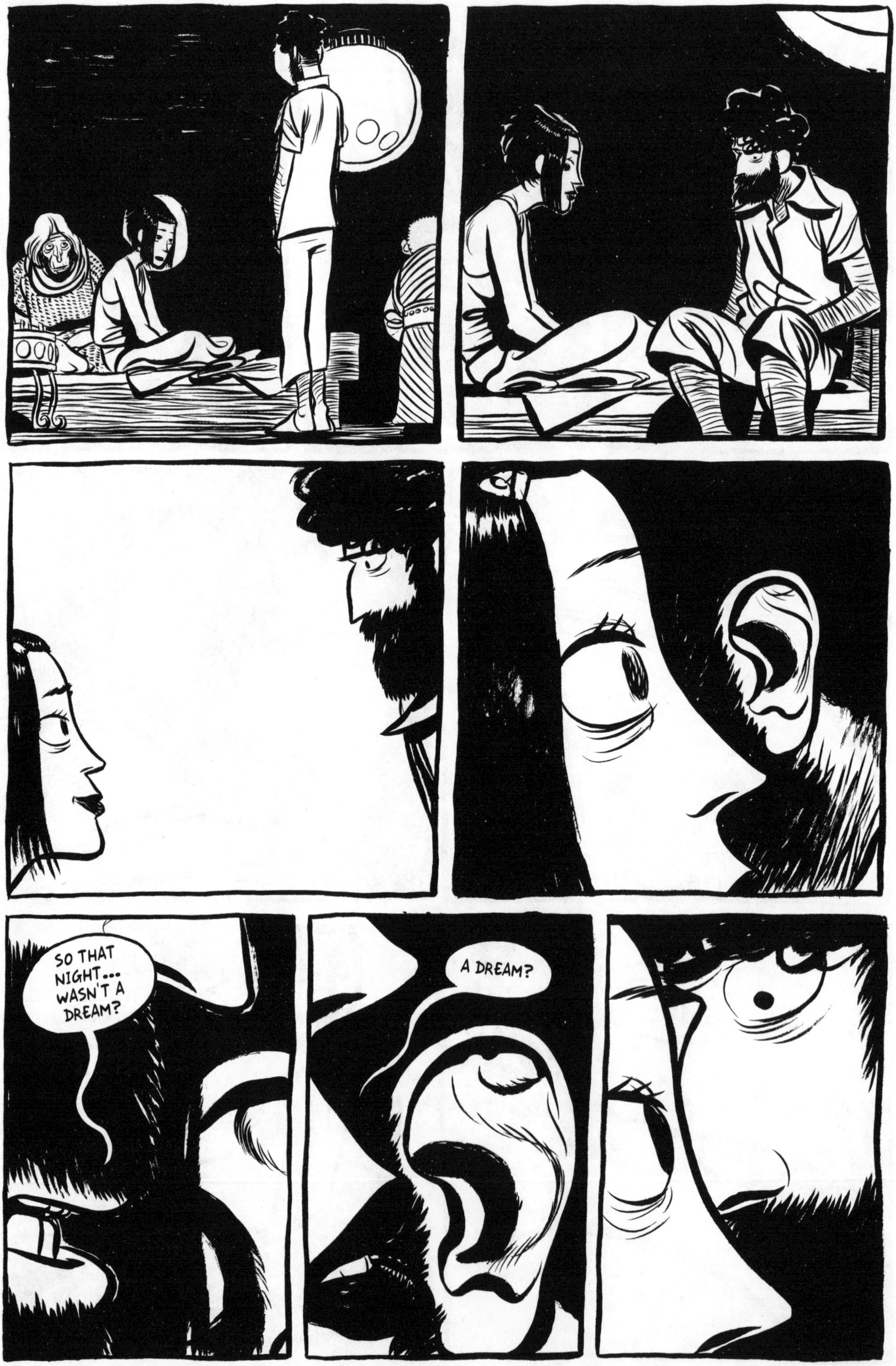
SO THAT NIGHT... WASN'T A DREAM?
A DREAM?

YOU KNOW WHAT I MEAN.

.... SORRY ....

WE SAID WE'D STOP SAYING SORRY.

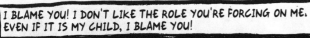

I BLAME YOU! I DON'T LIKE THE ROLE YOU'RE FORCING ON ME. EVEN IF IT IS MY CHILD, I BLAME YOU!

IT'LL BE OK.

I'LL BE BACK RIGHT AWAY. I NEED SOME PEACE AND QUIET. MY EARS ARE BUZZING A LITTLE.

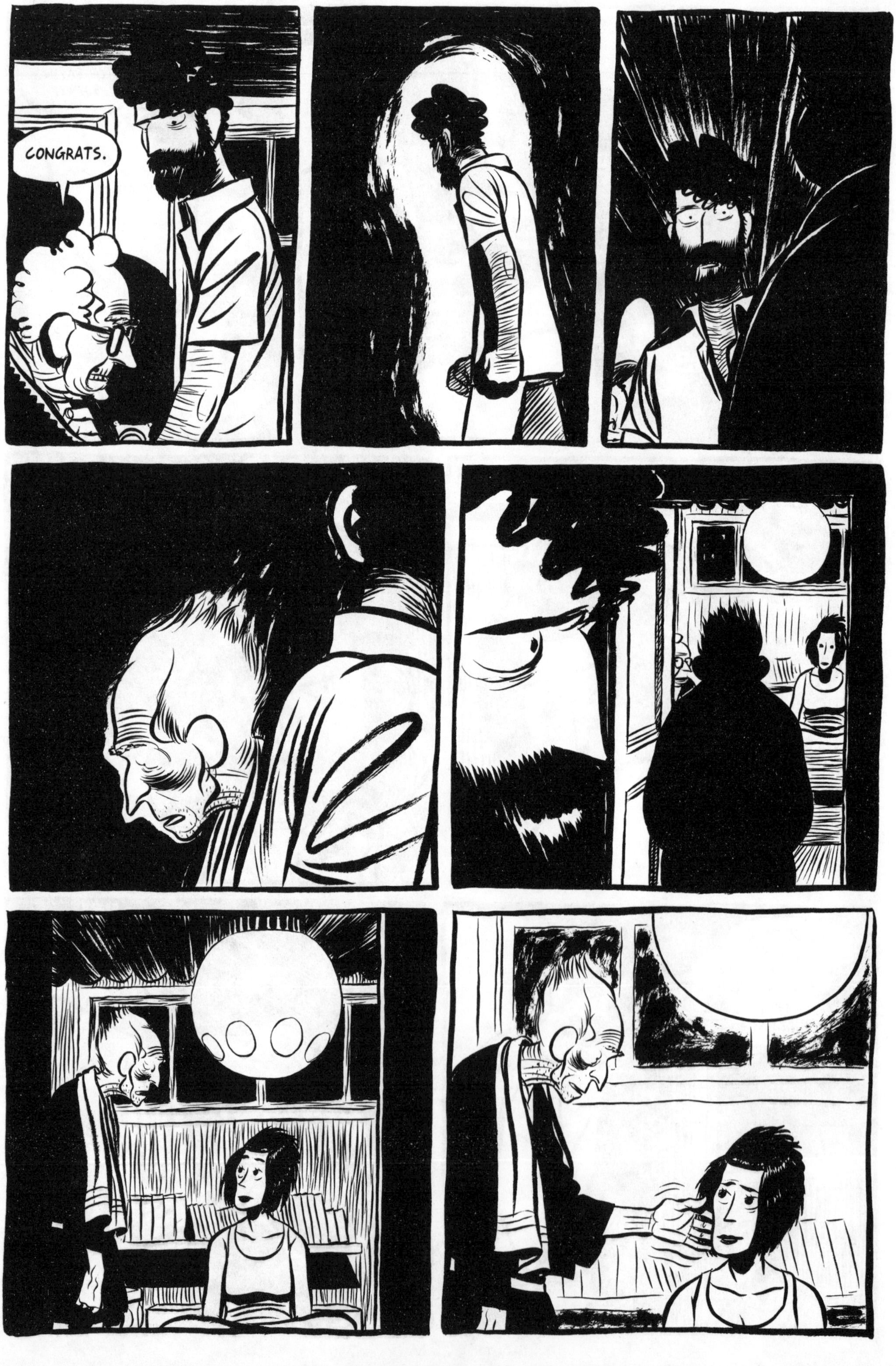
CONGRATS.

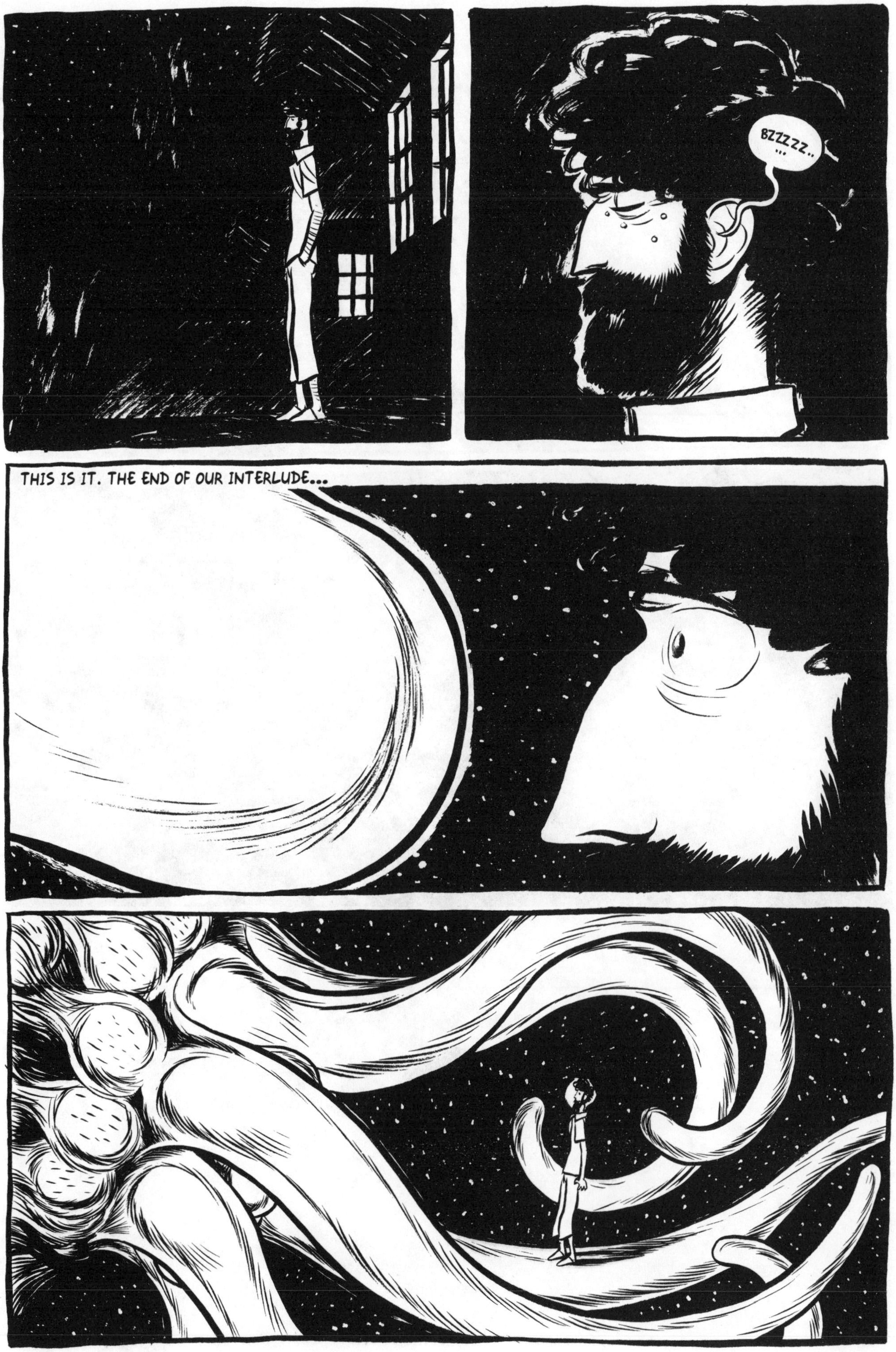
BZZZZZ.. ...
THIS IS IT. THE END OF OUR INTERLUDE...

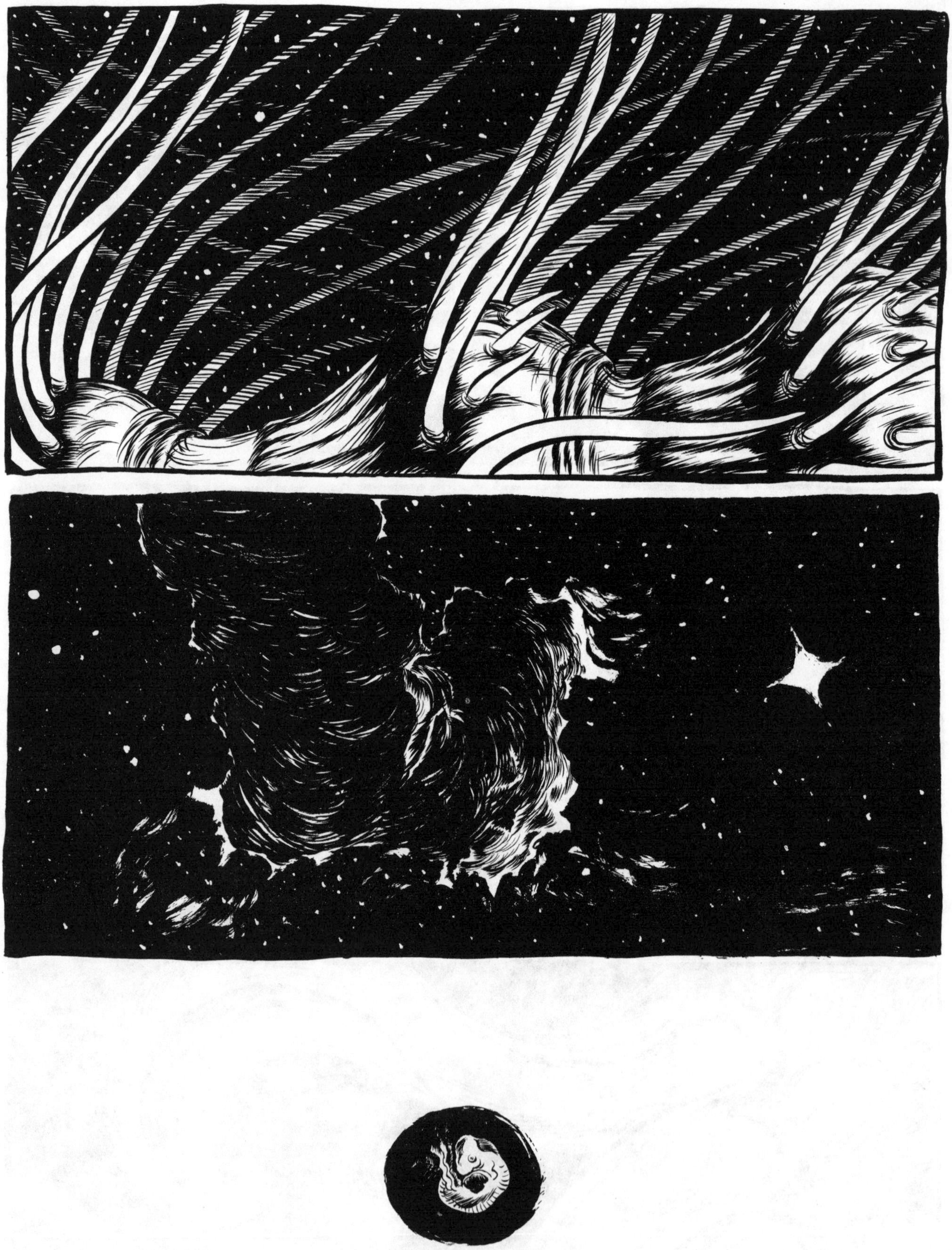

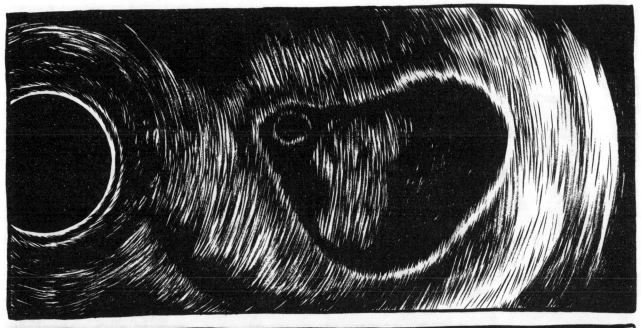

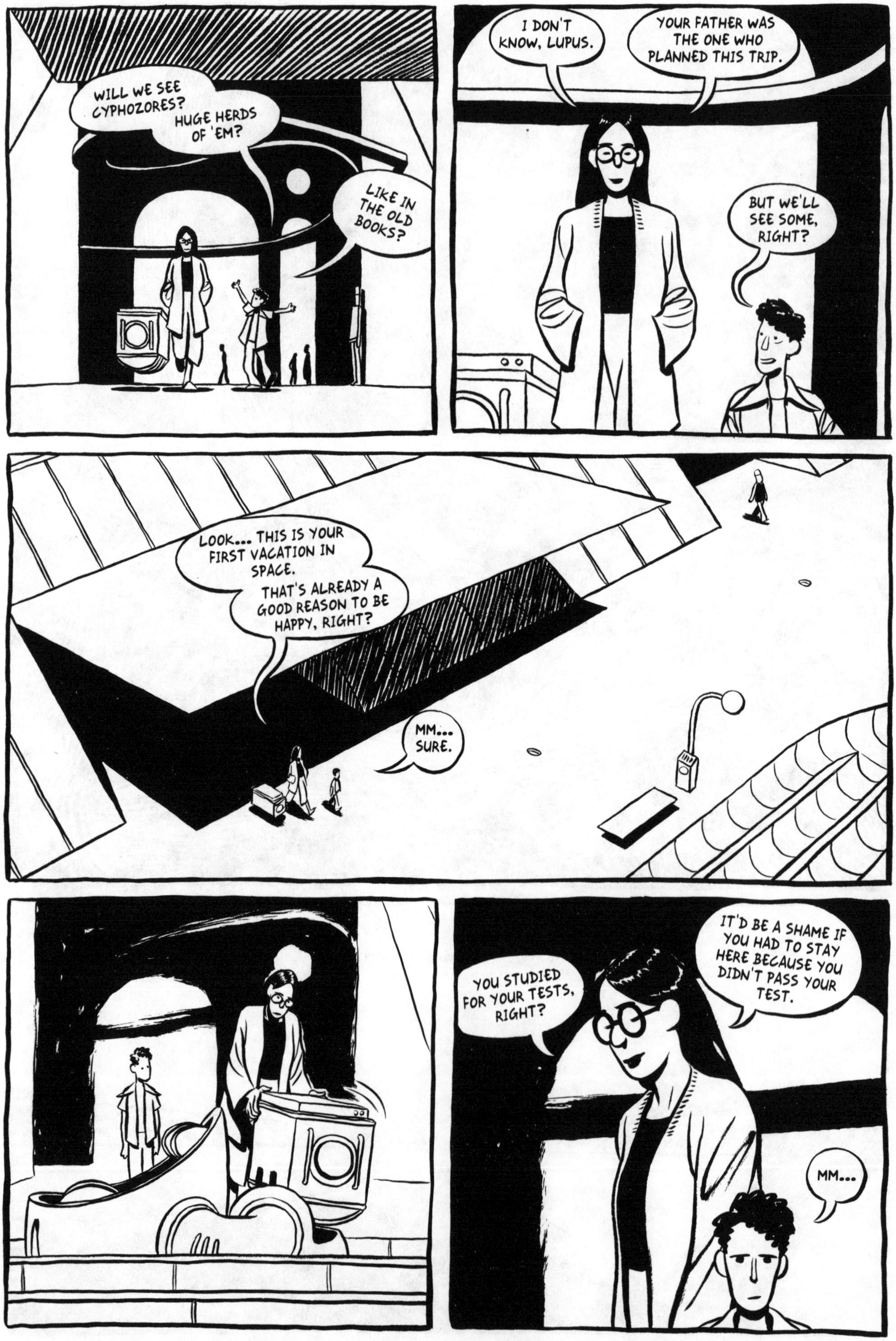
WILL WE SEE CYPHOZORES?
HUGE HERDS OF 'EM?
LIKE IN THE OLD BOOKS?
I DON'T KNOW, LUPUS.
YOUR FATHER WAS THE ONE WHO PLANNED THIS TRIP.
BUT WE'LL SEE SOME, RIGHT?
LOOK... THIS IS YOUR FIRST VACATION IN SPACE.
THAT'S ALREADY A GOOD REASON TO BE HAPPY, RIGHT?
MM... SURE.
YOU STUDIED FOR YOUR TESTS, RIGHT?
IT'D BE A SHAME IF YOU HAD TO STAY HERE BECAUSE YOU DIDN'T PASS YOUR TEST.
MM...

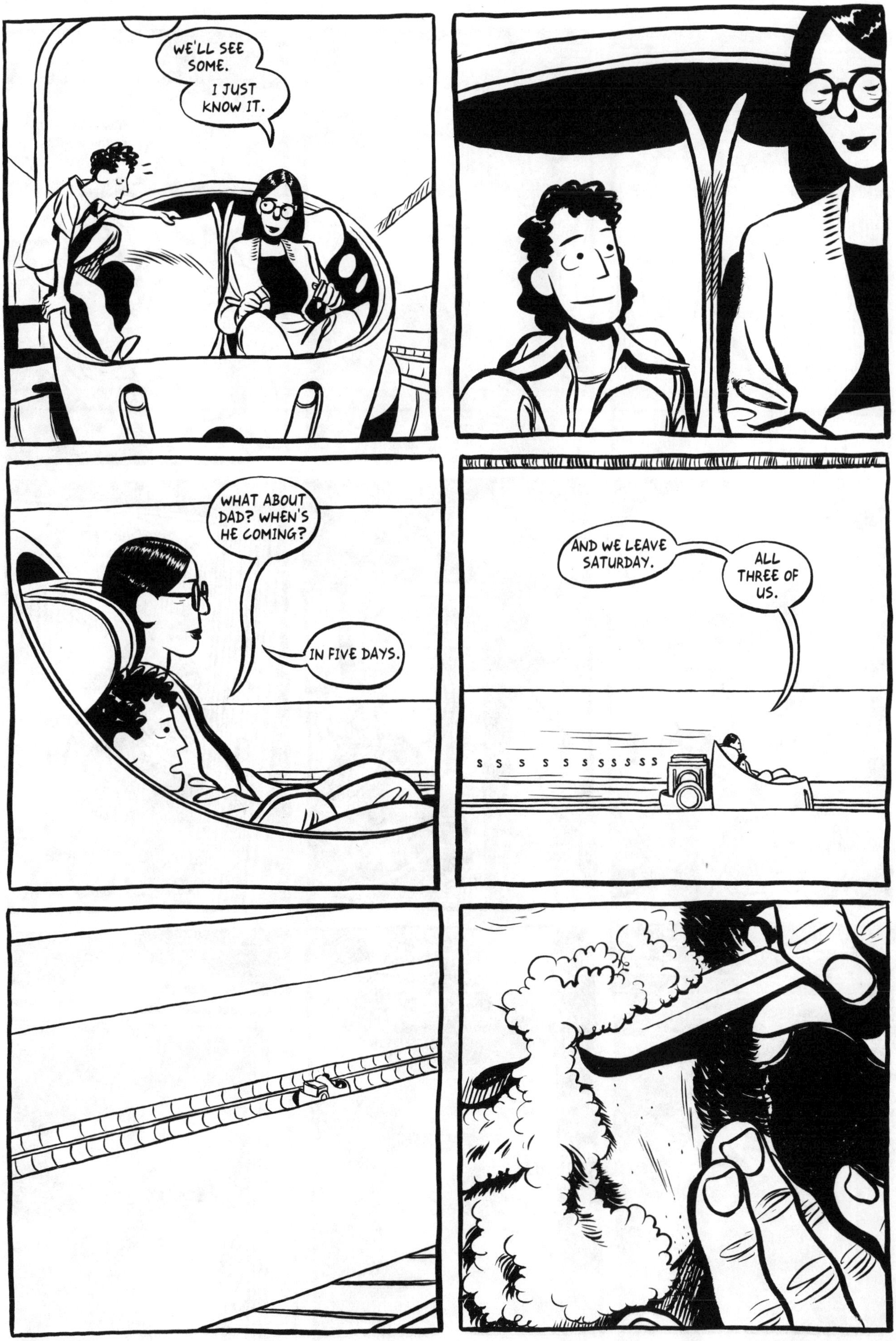
WE'LL SEE SOME.
I JUST KNOW IT.
WHAT ABOUT DAD? WHEN'S HE COMING?
IN FIVE DAYS.
AND WE LEAVE SATURDAY.
ALL THREE OF US.
S S S S S S S S S S S S

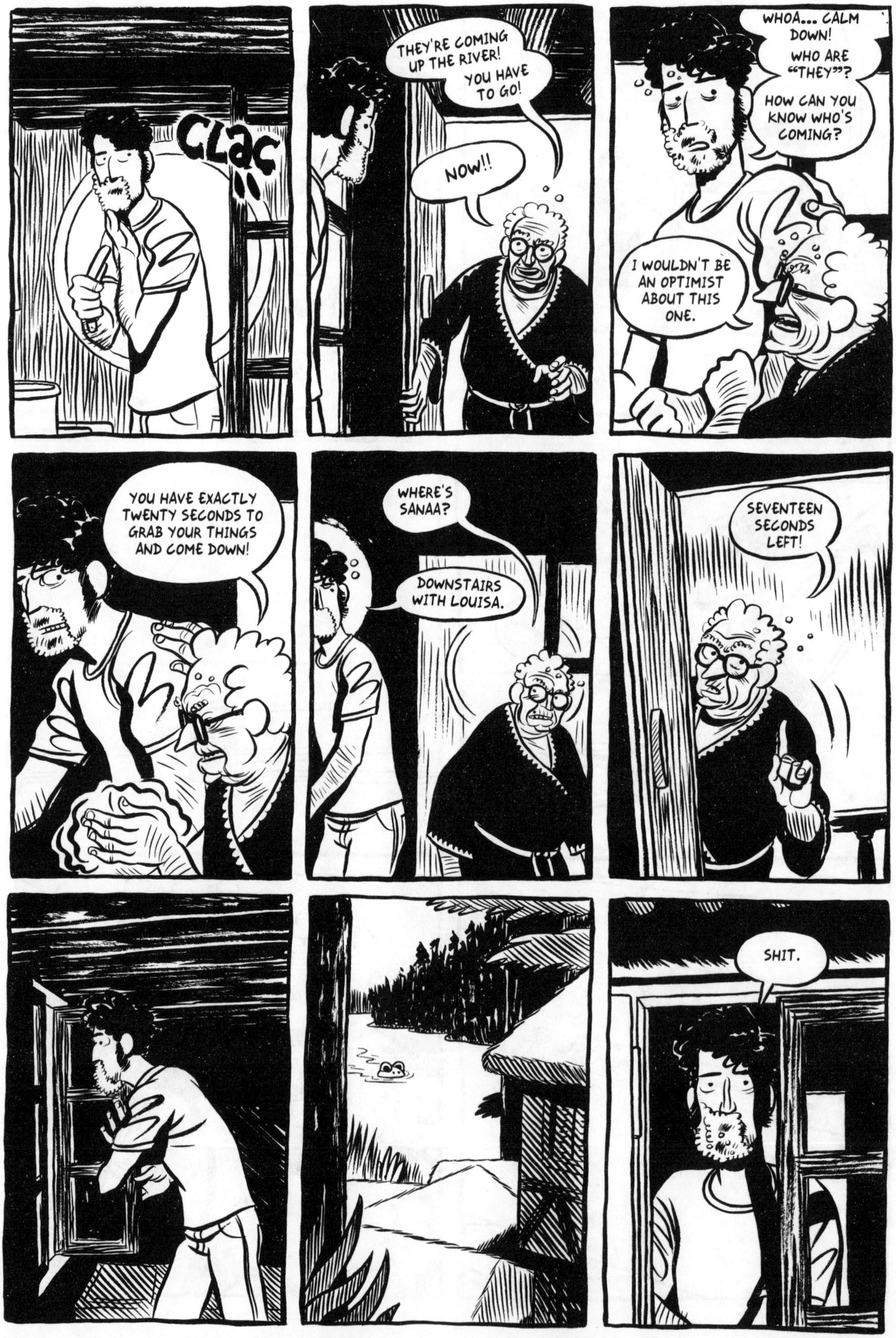
CLAC
THEY'RE COMING UP THE RIVER!
YOU HAVE TO GO!
NOW!!
WHOA... CALM DOWN!
WHO ARE "THEY"?
HOW CAN YOU KNOW WHO'S COMING?
I WOULDN'T BE AN OPTIMIST ABOUT THIS ONE.
YOU HAVE EXACTLY TWENTY SECONDS TO GRAB YOUR THINGS AND COME DOWN!
WHERE'S SANAA?
DOWNSTAIRS WITH LOUISA.
SEVENTEEN SECONDS LEFT!
SHIT.

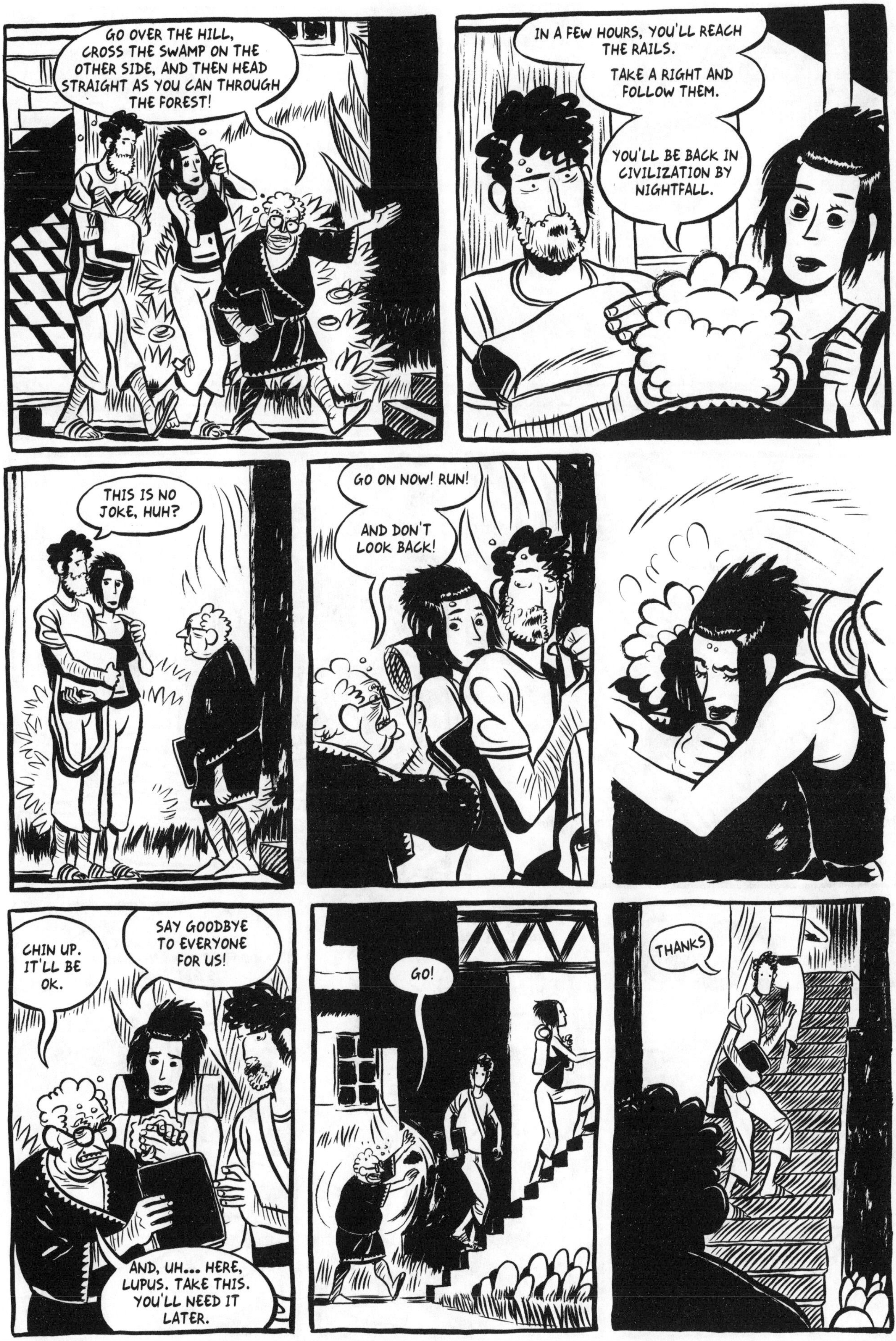
GO OVER THE HILL, CROSS THE SWAMP ON THE OTHER SIDE, AND THEN HEAD STRAIGHT AS YOU CAN THROUGH THE FOREST!
IN A FEW HOURS, YOU'LL REACH THE RAILS.
TAKE A RIGHT AND FOLLOW THEM.
YOU'LL BE BACK IN CIVILIZATION BY NIGHTFALL.
THIS IS NO JOKE, HUH?
GO ON NOW! RUN!
AND DON'T LOOK BACK!
CHIN UP. IT'LL BE OK.
SAY GOODBYE TO EVERYONE FOR US!
AND, UH... HERE, LUPUS. TAKE THIS. YOU'LL NEED IT LATER.
GO!
THANKS

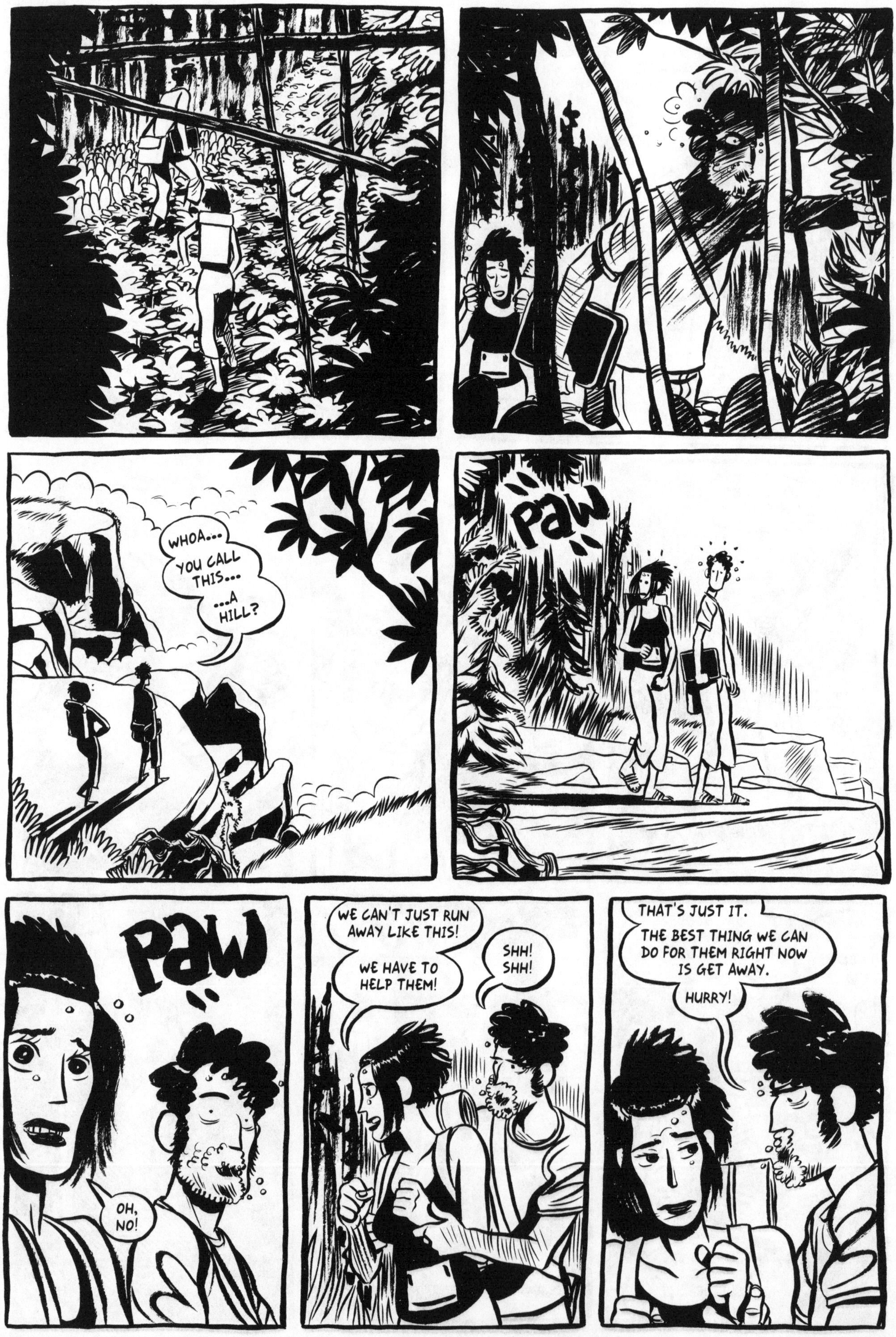
WHOA... YOU CALL THIS... ...A HILL?
PAW
PAW
OH, NO!
WE CAN'T JUST RUN AWAY LIKE THIS!
WE HAVE TO HELP THEM!
SHH! SHH!
THAT'S JUST IT.
THE BEST THING WE CAN DO FOR THEM RIGHT NOW IS GET AWAY.
HURRY!

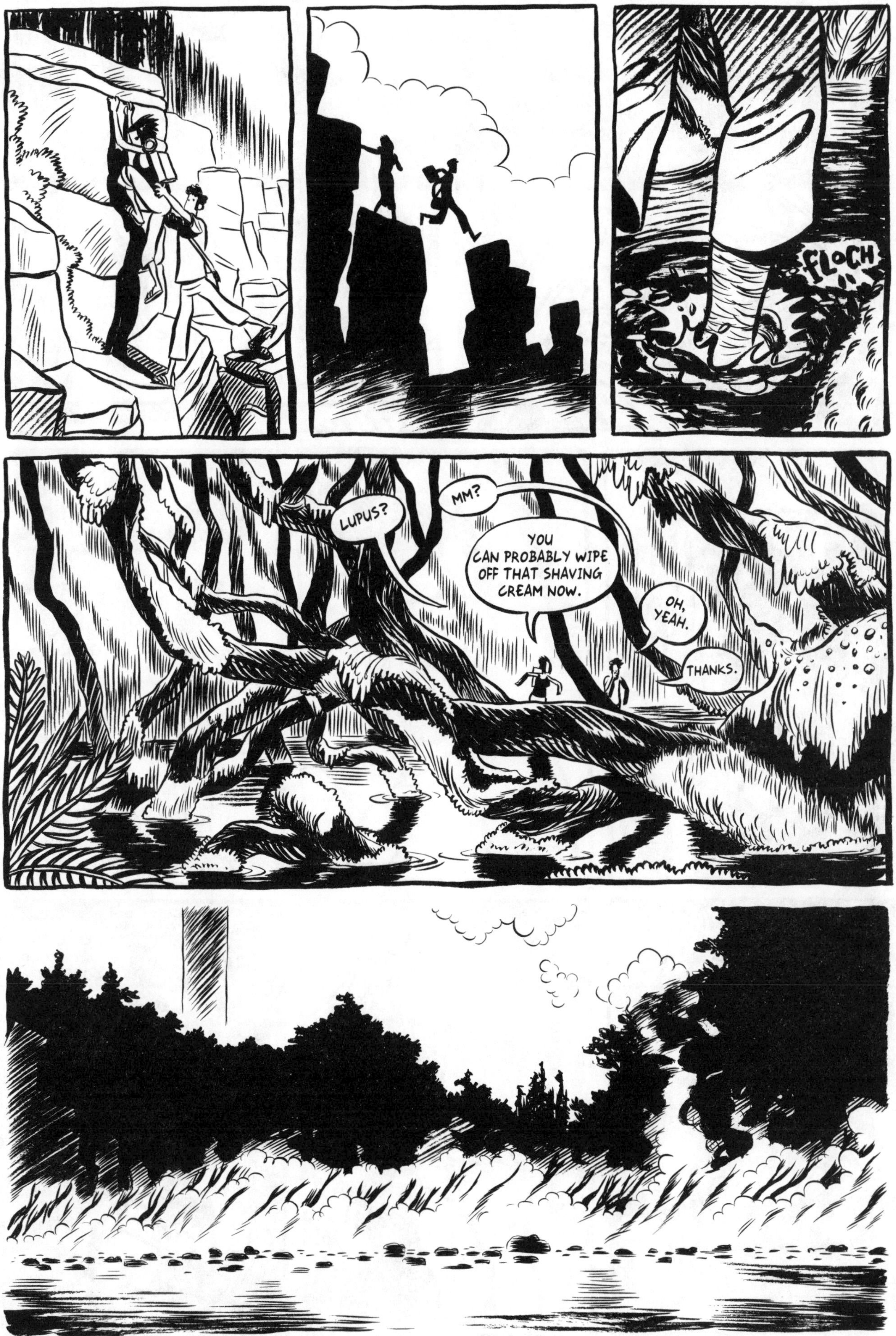
FLOCH
LUPUS?
MM?
YOU CAN PROBABLY WIPE OFF THAT SHAVING CREAM NOW.
OH, YEAH.
THANKS.

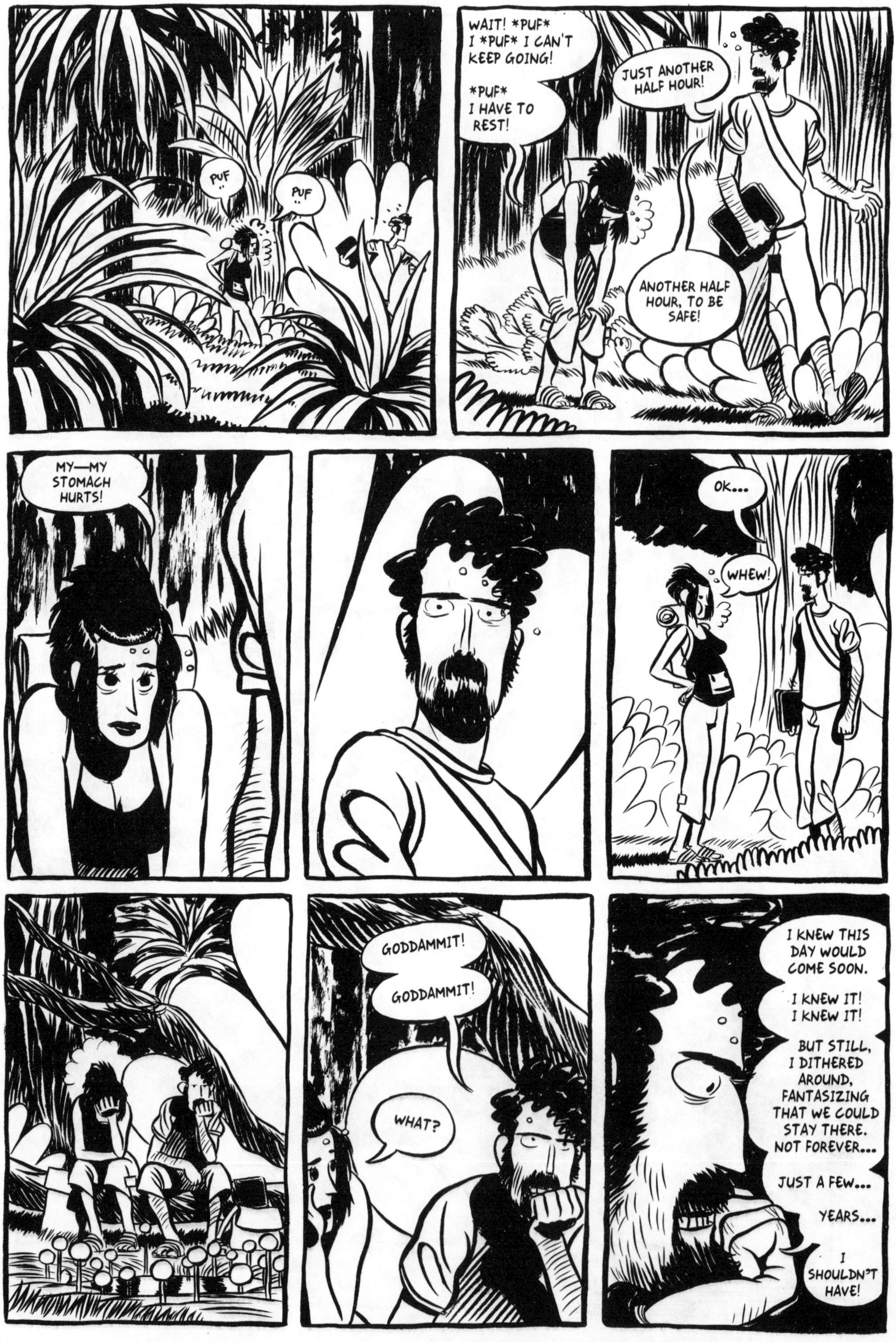
PUF
PUF
WAIT! *PUF* I *PUF* I CAN'T KEEP GOING!
PUF I HAVE TO REST!
JUST ANOTHER HALF HOUR!
ANOTHER HALF HOUR, TO BE SAFE!
MY—MY STOMACH HURTS!
OK...
WHEW!
GODDAMMIT!
GODDAMMIT!
WHAT?
I KNEW THIS DAY WOULD COME SOON.
I KNEW IT! I KNEW IT!
BUT STILL, I DITHERED AROUND, FANTASIZING THAT WE COULD STAY THERE. NOT FOREVER...
JUST A FEW...
YEARS...
I SHOULDN'T HAVE!

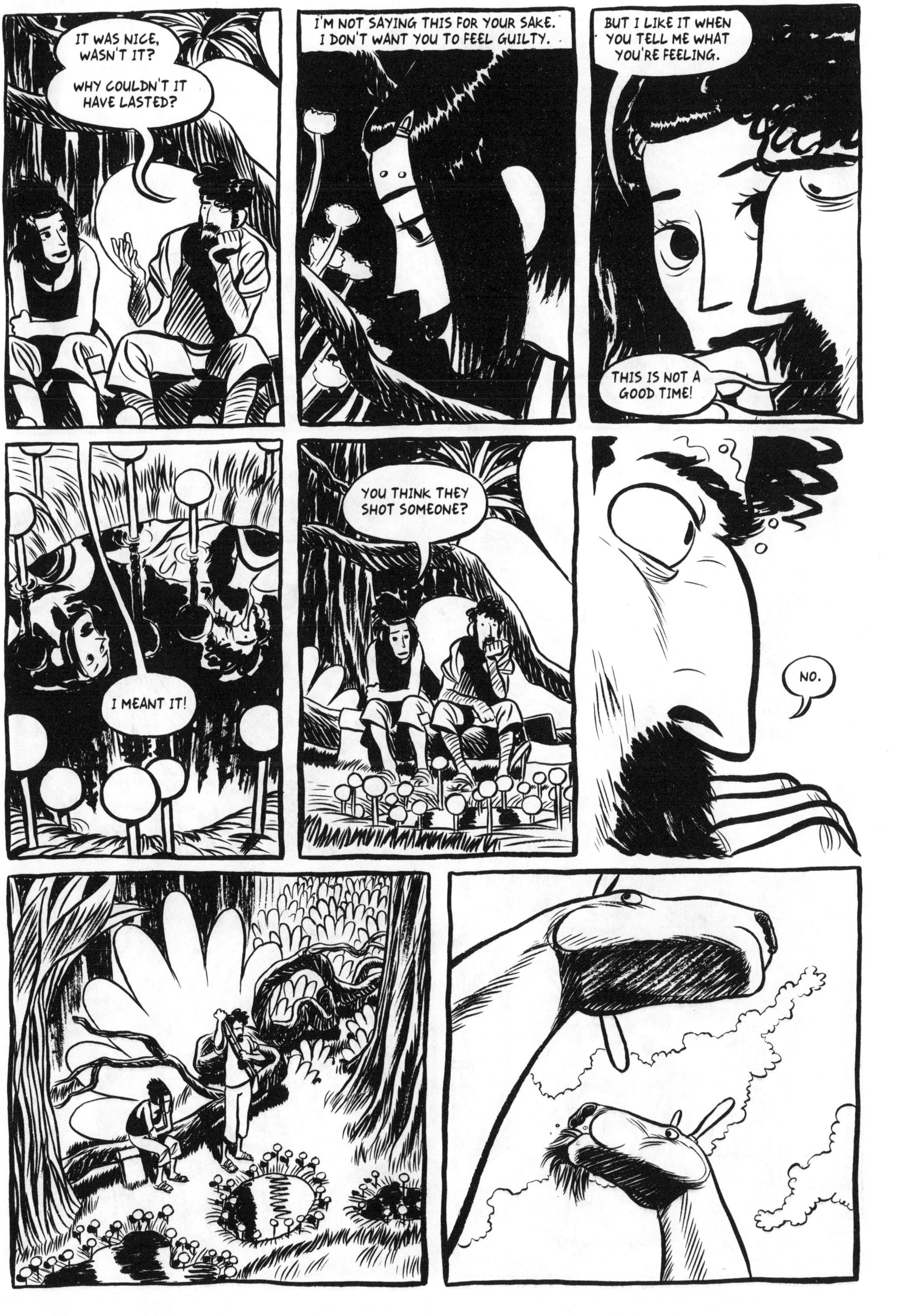
IT WAS NICE, WASN'T IT?
WHY COULDN'T IT HAVE LASTED?
I'M NOT SAYING THIS FOR YOUR SAKE. I DON'T WANT YOU TO FEEL GUILTY.
BUT I LIKE IT WHEN YOU TELL ME WHAT YOU'RE FEELING.
THIS IS NOT A GOOD TIME!
I MEANT IT!
YOU THINK THEY SHOT SOMEONE?
NO.

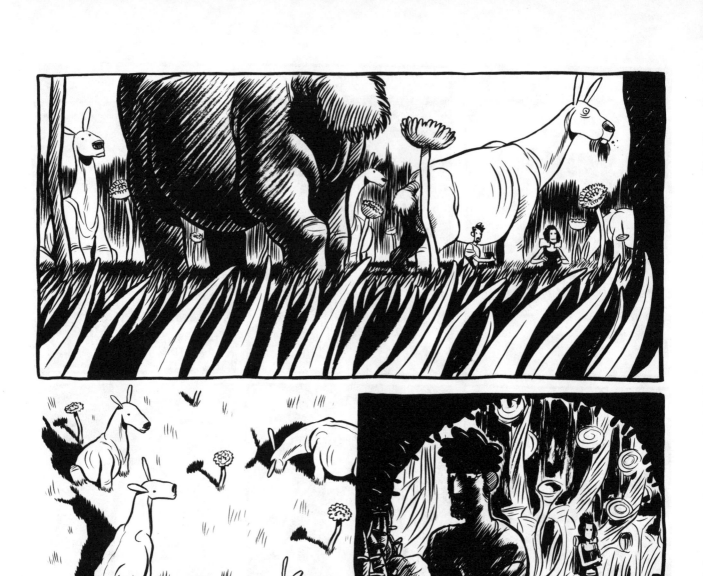

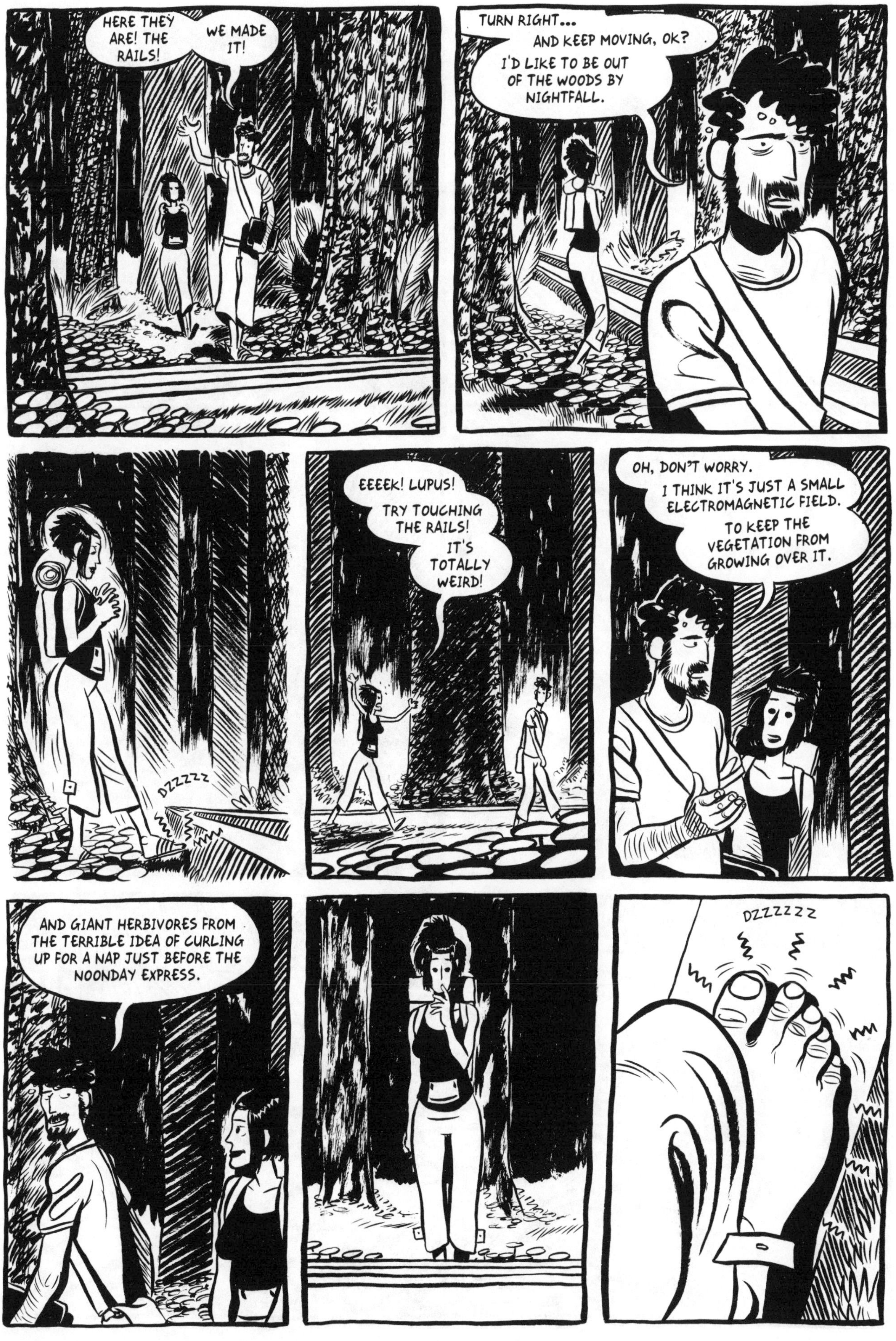
HERE THEY ARE! THE RAILS!
WE MADE IT!
TURN RIGHT...
AND KEEP MOVING, OK?
I'D LIKE TO BE OUT OF THE WOODS BY NIGHTFALL.
DZZZZZ
EEEEK! LUPUS!
TRY TOUCHING THE RAILS!
IT'S TOTALLY WEIRD!
OH, DON'T WORRY.
I THINK IT'S JUST A SMALL ELECTROMAGNETIC FIELD.
TO KEEP THE VEGETATION FROM GROWING OVER IT.
AND GIANT HERBIVORES FROM THE TERRIBLE IDEA OF CURLING UP FOR A NAP JUST BEFORE THE NOONDAY EXPRESS.
DZZZZZZ

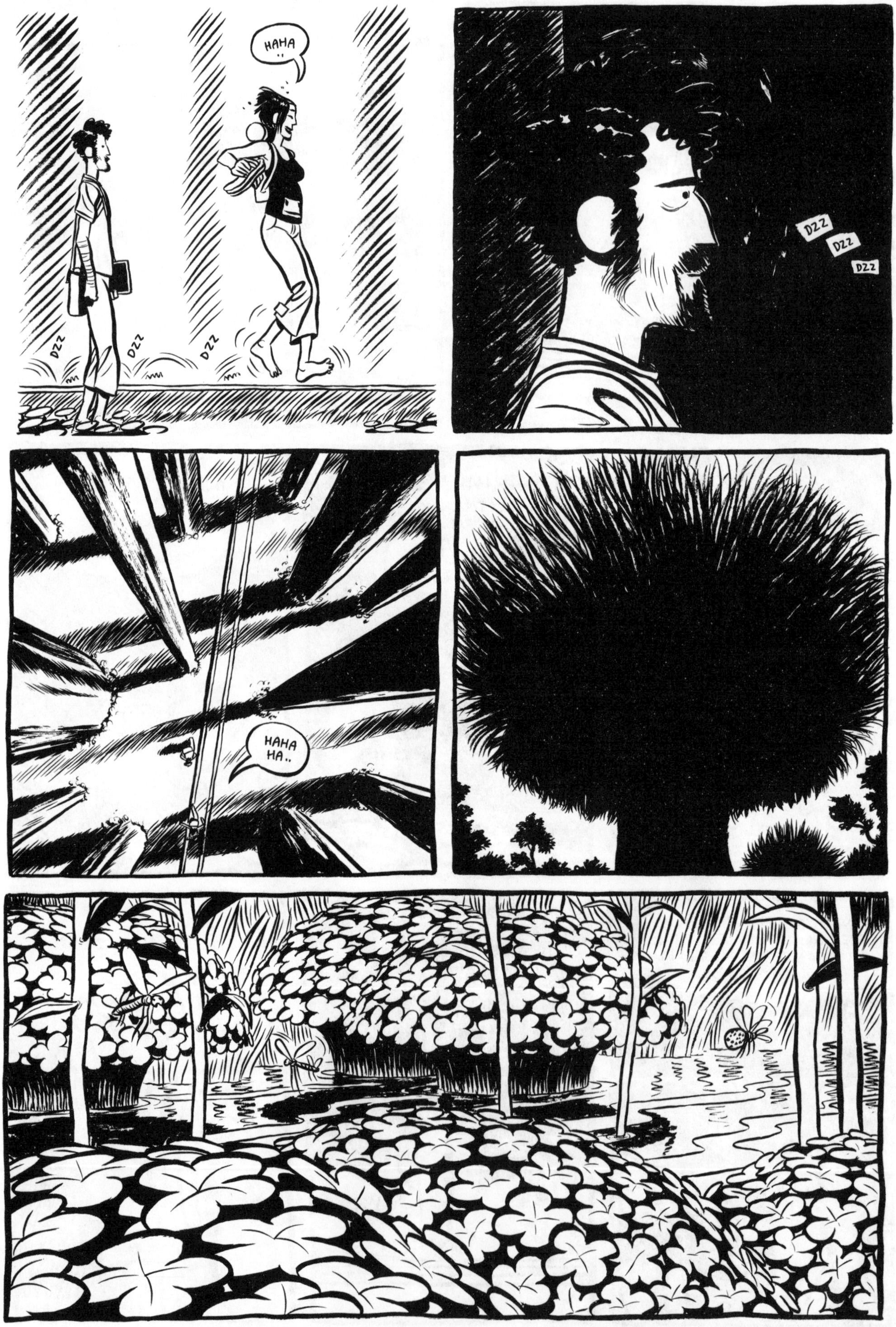
HAHA
..
DZZ
DZZ
DZZ
DZZ
DZZ
DZZ
HAHA
HA..

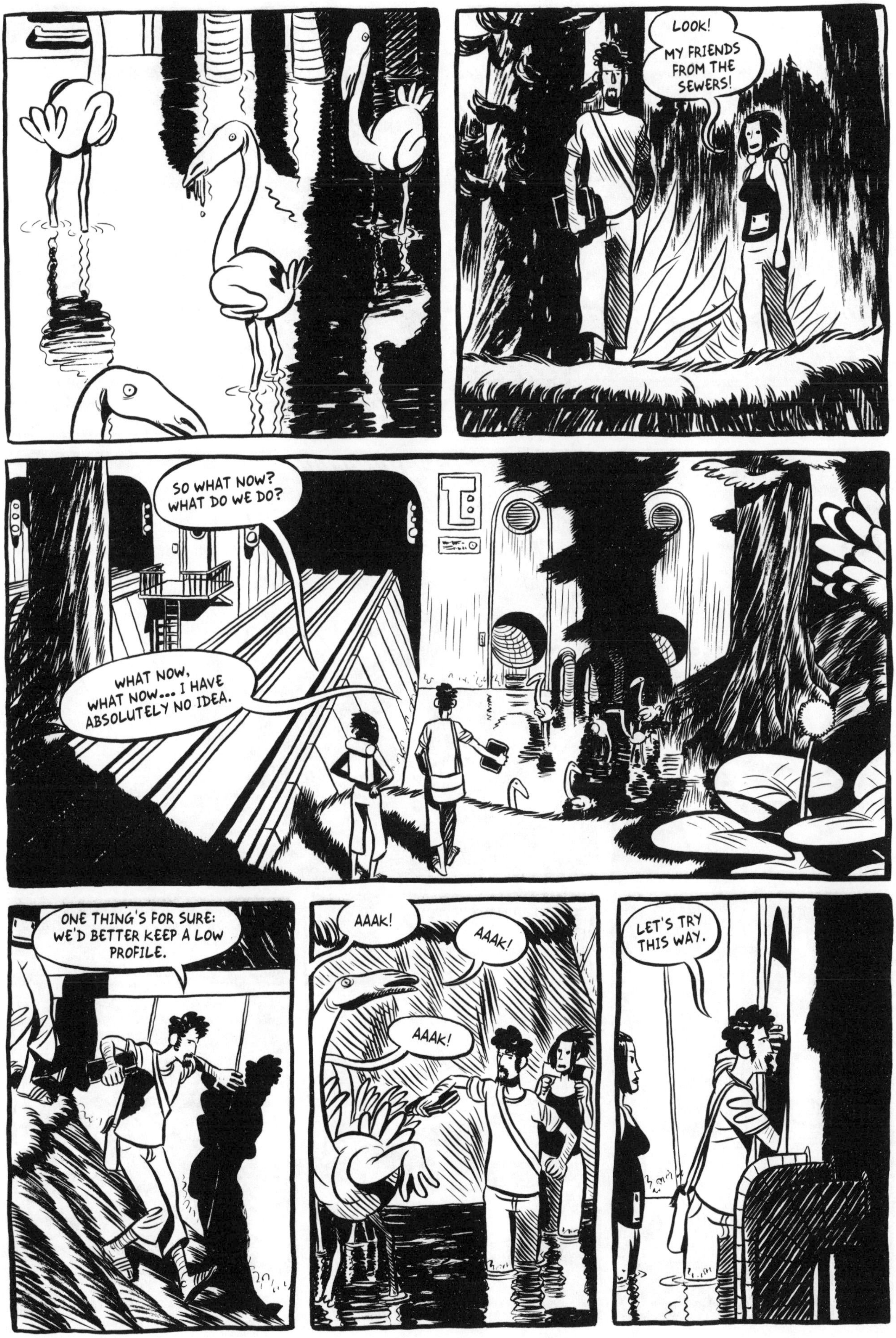
LOOK!
MY FRIENDS FROM THE SEWERS!
SO WHAT NOW? WHAT DO WE DO?
WHAT NOW, WHAT NOW... I HAVE ABSOLUTELY NO IDEA.
ONE THING'S FOR SURE: WE'D BETTER KEEP A LOW PROFILE.
AAAK!
AAAK!
AAAK!
LET'S TRY THIS WAY.

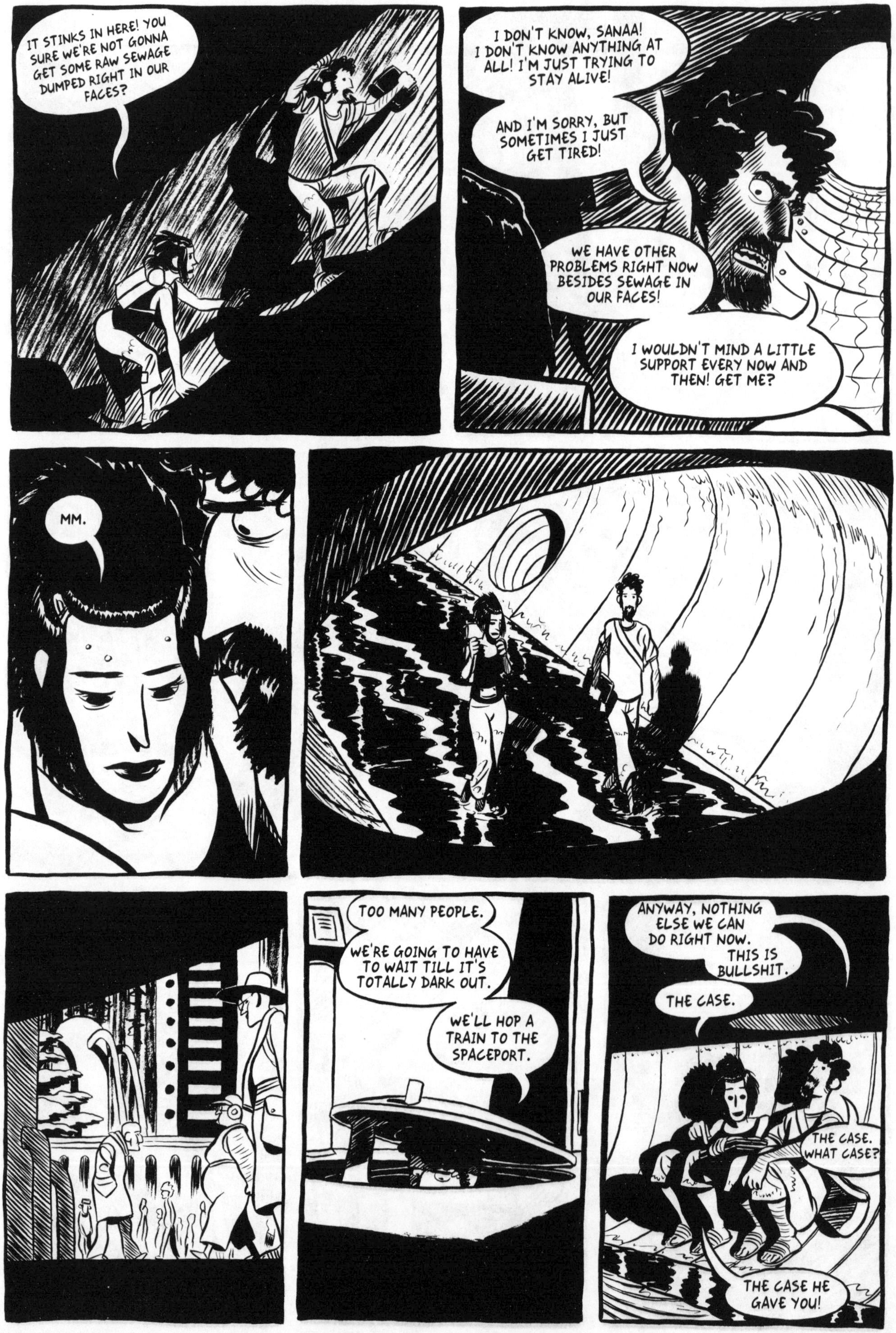
IT STINKS IN HERE! YOU SURE WE'RE NOT GONNA GET SOME RAW SEWAGE DUMPED RIGHT IN OUR FACES?
I DON'T KNOW, SANAA! I DON'T KNOW ANYTHING AT ALL! I'M JUST TRYING TO STAY ALIVE!
AND I'M SORRY, BUT SOMETIMES I JUST GET TIRED!
WE HAVE OTHER PROBLEMS RIGHT NOW BESIDES SEWAGE IN OUR FACES!
I WOULDN'T MIND A LITTLE SUPPORT EVERY NOW AND THEN! GET ME?
MM.
TOO MANY PEOPLE.
WE'RE GOING TO HAVE TO WAIT TILL IT'S TOTALLY DARK OUT.
WE'LL HOP A TRAIN TO THE SPACEPORT.
ANYWAY, NOTHING ELSE WE CAN DO RIGHT NOW.
THIS IS BULLSHIT.
THE CASE.
THE CASE. WHAT CASE?
THE CASE HE GAVE YOU!

OH, RIGHT! THANKS!

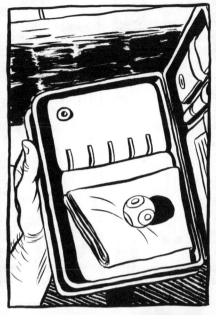

WHAT'S THAT THING?

BZZT

HELLO? HELLO? LUPUS?

NYARGANCE?!

AWESOME!

ARE YOU OK? WE HEARD TWO SHOTS!

NO, NO, EVERYONE'S FINE.

JUST SOME OLD INTIMIDATION TACTICS.

EVERYONE HERE'S PRETTY THICK-SKINNED.

YOU GUYS FOCUS ON YOURSELVES. WHERE ARE YOU?

WE'RE HIDING OUT IN THE SEWERS.

IT'S NOT VERY GLAMOROUS.

I THOUGHT I'D WAIT TILL LATE NIGHT, TO BE LESS CONSPICUOUS.

GOOD. THE SEWER WAS A GOOD IDEA.

IT'LL HELP COVER YOUR TRACKS. THOSE GUYS HAVE SNIFFERS.

BUT DON'T HANG AROUND TOO LONG.

WHAT CHOICE DO WE HAVE? IT'S NOT LIKE WE'RE IN DISGUISE!

HAH! I SEE YOU HAVEN'T OPENED YOUR GIFT YET!

WHAT DO YOU—

HAH! CALL ME BACK LATER!

CLIC

?!?

205

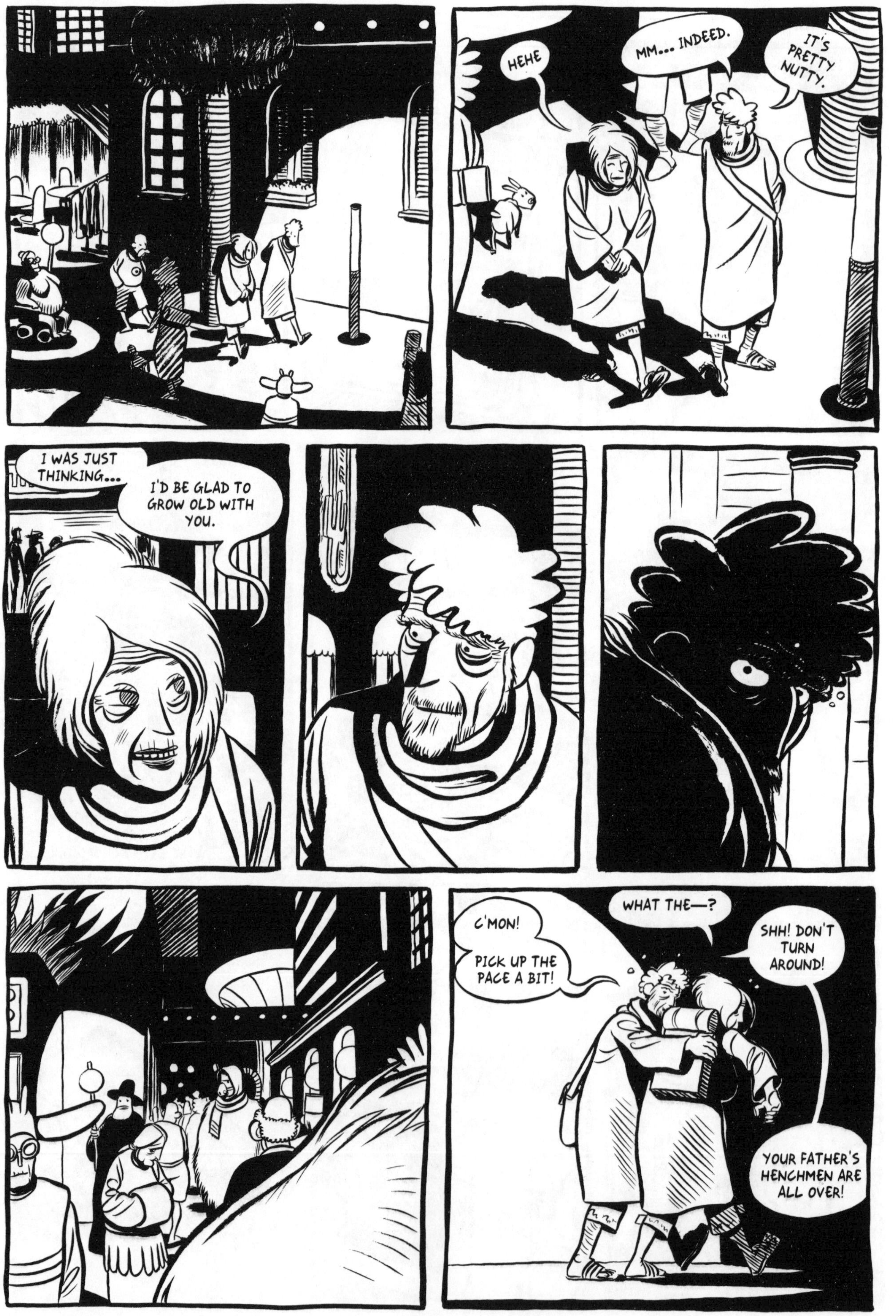
HEHE
MM... INDEED.
IT'S PRETTY NUTTY.
I WAS JUST THINKING...
I'D BE GLAD TO GROW OLD WITH YOU.
C'MON!
PICK UP THE PACE A BIT!
WHAT THE—?
SHH! DON'T TURN AROUND!
YOUR FATHER'S HENCHMEN ARE ALL OVER!

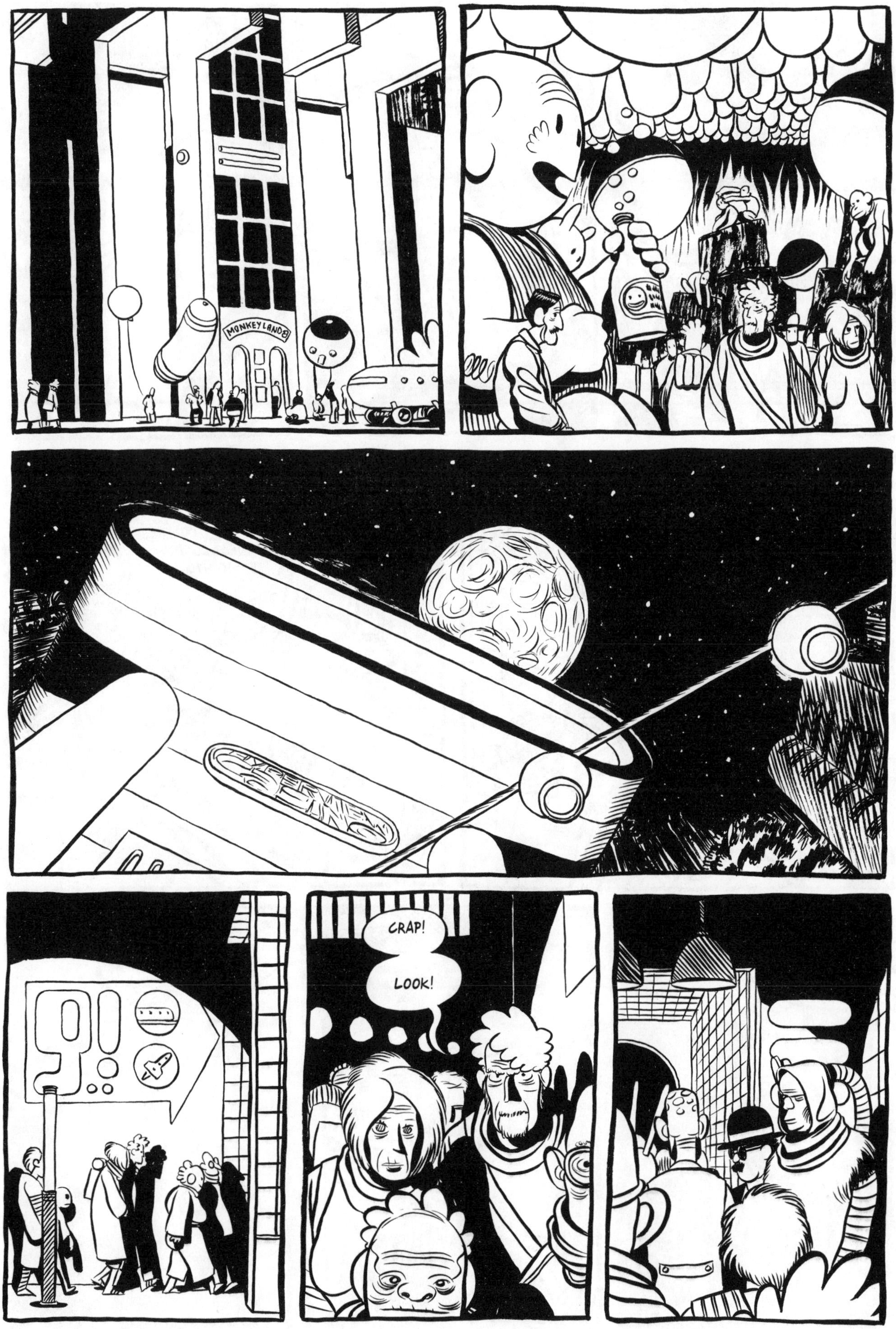
MONKEYLAND
CRAP!
LOOK!

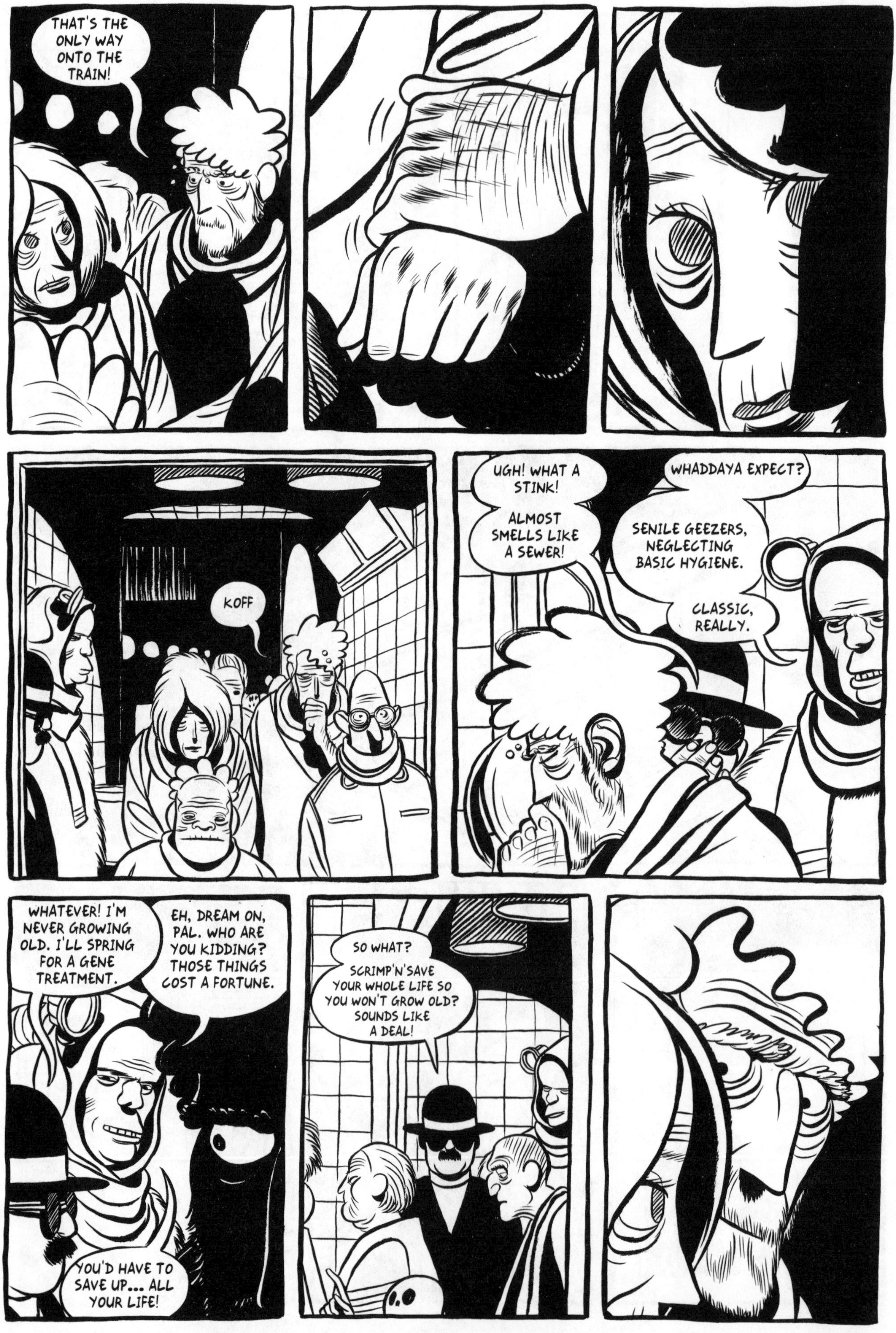
THAT'S THE ONLY WAY ONTO THE TRAIN!
KOFF
UGH! WHAT A STINK!
ALMOST SMELLS LIKE A SEWER!
WHADDAYA EXPECT?
SENILE GEEZERS, NEGLECTING BASIC HYGIENE.
CLASSIC, REALLY.
WHATEVER! I'M NEVER GROWING OLD. I'LL SPRING FOR A GENE TREATMENT.
EH, DREAM ON, PAL. WHO ARE YOU KIDDING? THOSE THINGS COST A FORTUNE.
YOU'D HAVE TO SAVE UP... ALL YOUR LIFE!
SO WHAT?
SCRIMP'N'SAVE YOUR WHOLE LIFE SO YOU WON'T GROW OLD? SOUNDS LIKE A DEAL!

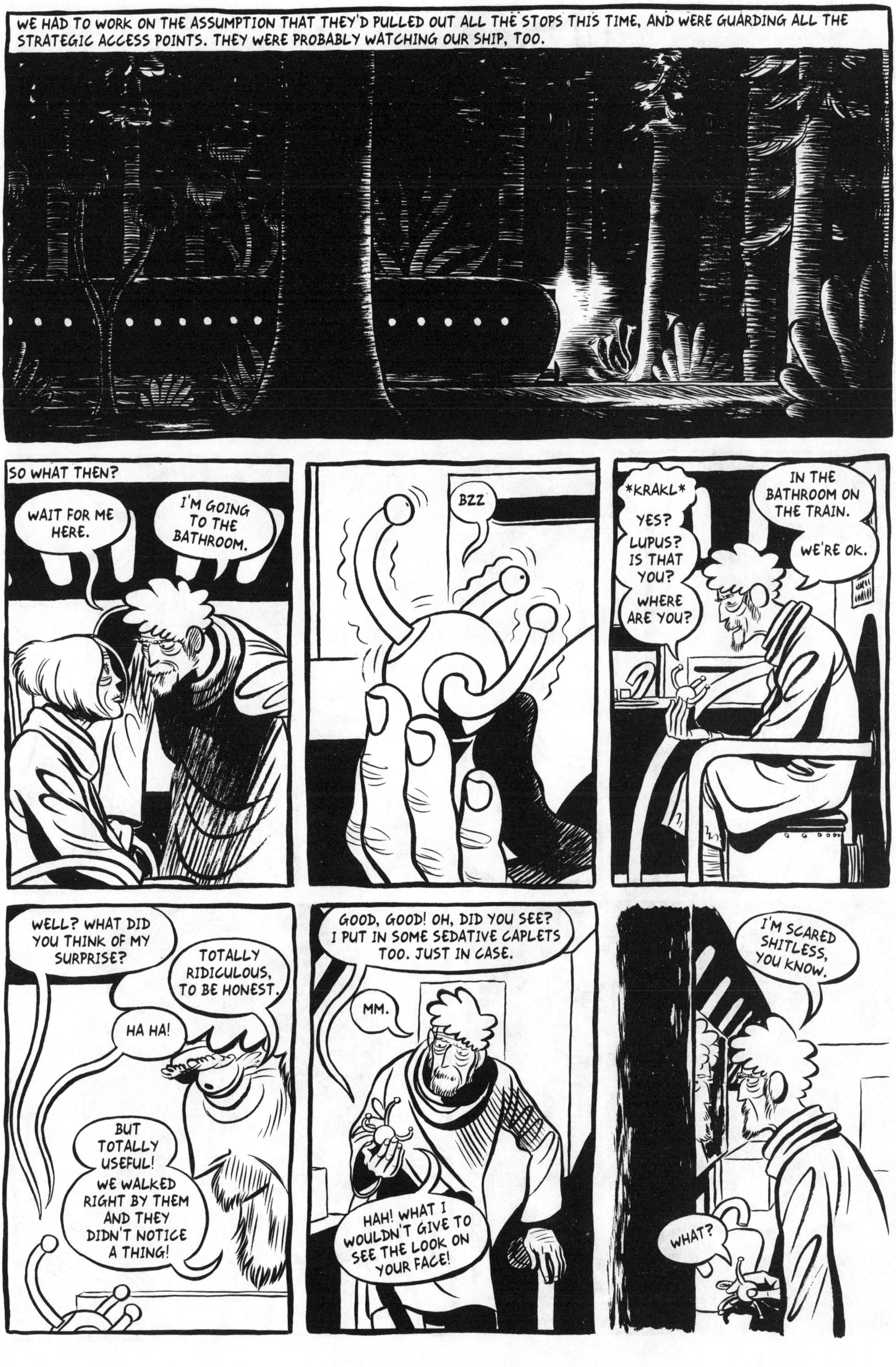
WE HAD TO WORK ON THE ASSUMPTION THAT THEY'D PULLED OUT ALL THE STOPS THIS TIME, AND WERE GUARDING ALL THE STRATEGIC ACCESS POINTS. THEY WERE PROBABLY WATCHING OUR SHIP, TOO.
SO WHAT THEN?
I'M GOING TO THE BATHROOM.
WAIT FOR ME HERE.
BZZ
KRAKL
YES?
LUPUS? IS THAT YOU?
WHERE ARE YOU?
IN THE BATHROOM ON THE TRAIN.
WE'RE OK.
WELL? WHAT DID YOU THINK OF MY SURPRISE?
TOTALLY RIDICULOUS, TO BE HONEST.
HA HA!
BUT TOTALLY USEFUL!
WE WALKED RIGHT BY THEM AND THEY DIDN'T NOTICE A THING!
GOOD, GOOD! OH, DID YOU SEE? I PUT IN SOME SEDATIVE CAPLETS TOO. JUST IN CASE.
MM.
HAH! WHAT I WOULDN'T GIVE TO SEE THE LOOK ON YOUR FACE!
I'M SCARED SHITLESS, YOU KNOW.
WHAT?

I'M REALLY SCARED. I...
I HAVE NO IDEA AT ALL WHAT I'M DOING.
NOW'S NOT THE TIME! YOU ALONE IN THERE?
OR WHY I'M DOING IT...
LEAVE NECROS AS SOON AS YOU CAN! YOU CAN THINK ABOUT ALL THAT LATER!
AND WHATEVER YOU DO, TAKE CARE OF HER.
TAKE CARE OF HER...
LUPUS?
YES.
YOU'LL PULL THROUGH.
I'M GONNA MISS YOU.
HERE.
JUST IN CASE...
5

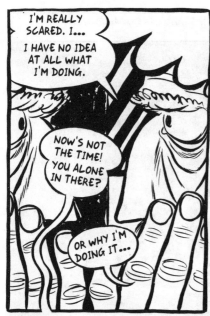

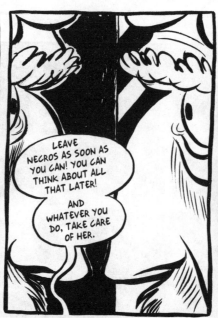

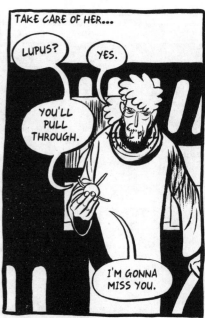

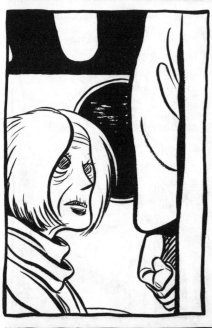

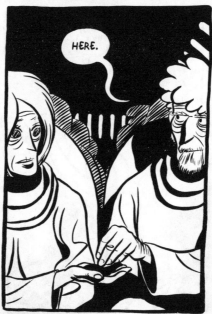

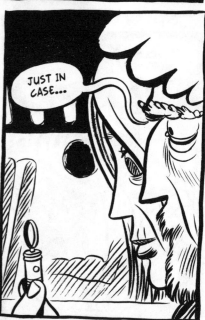

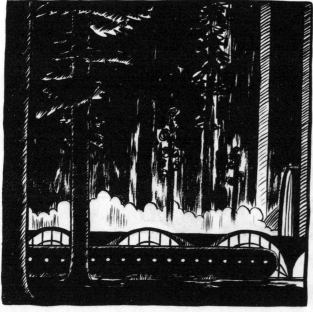

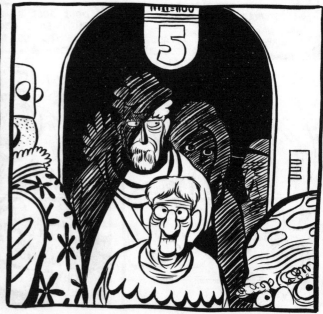

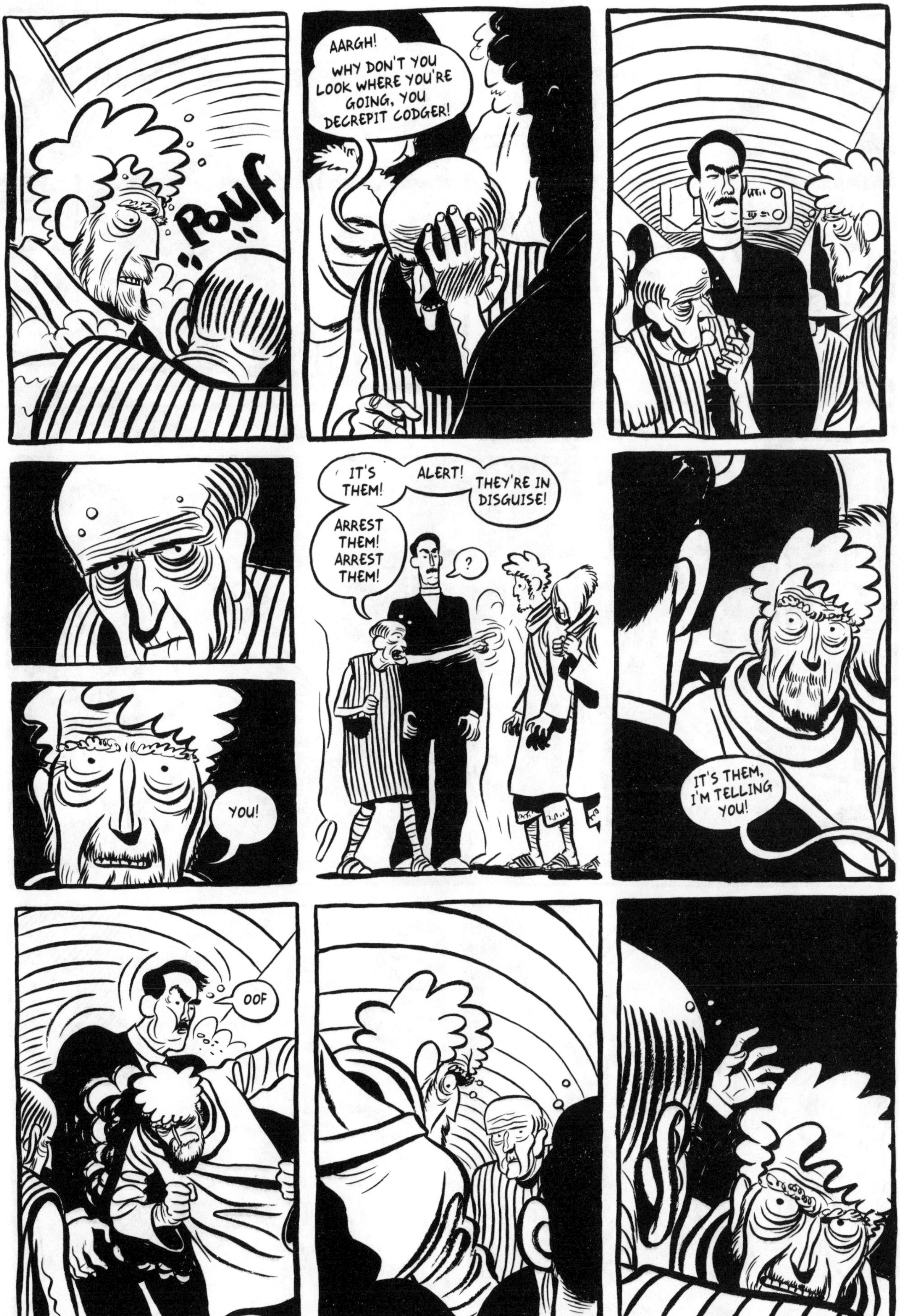
POUF
AARGH!
WHY DON'T YOU LOOK WHERE YOU'RE GOING, YOU DECREPIT CODGER!
YOU!
IT'S THEM!
ALERT!
THEY'RE IN DISGUISE!
ARREST THEM! ARREST THEM!
?
IT'S THEM, I'M TELLING YOU!
OOF

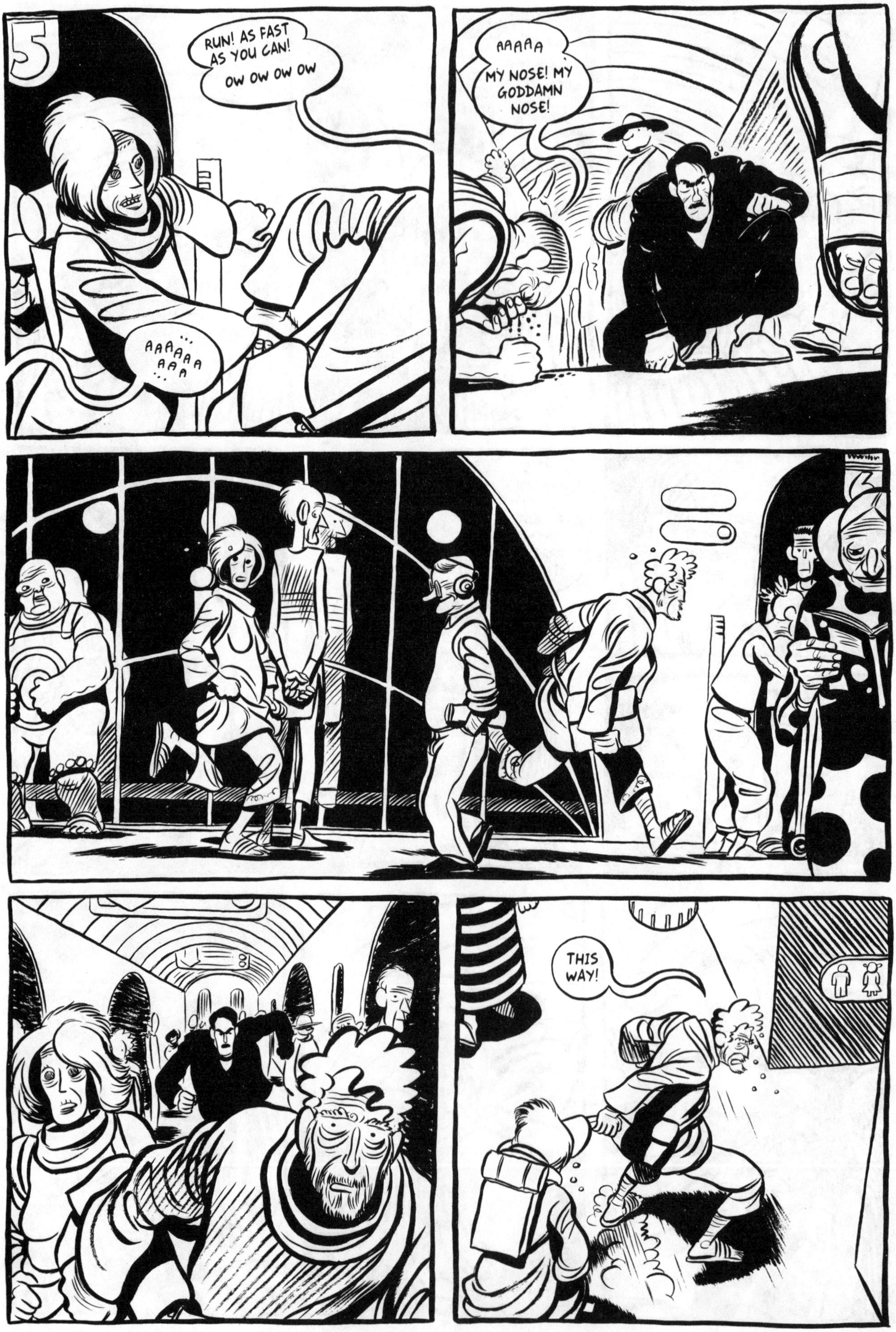
5
RUN! AS FAST AS YOU CAN!
OW OW OW OW
... AAAAAA AAA ...
AAAAA
MY NOSE! MY GODDAMN NOSE!
THIS WAY!

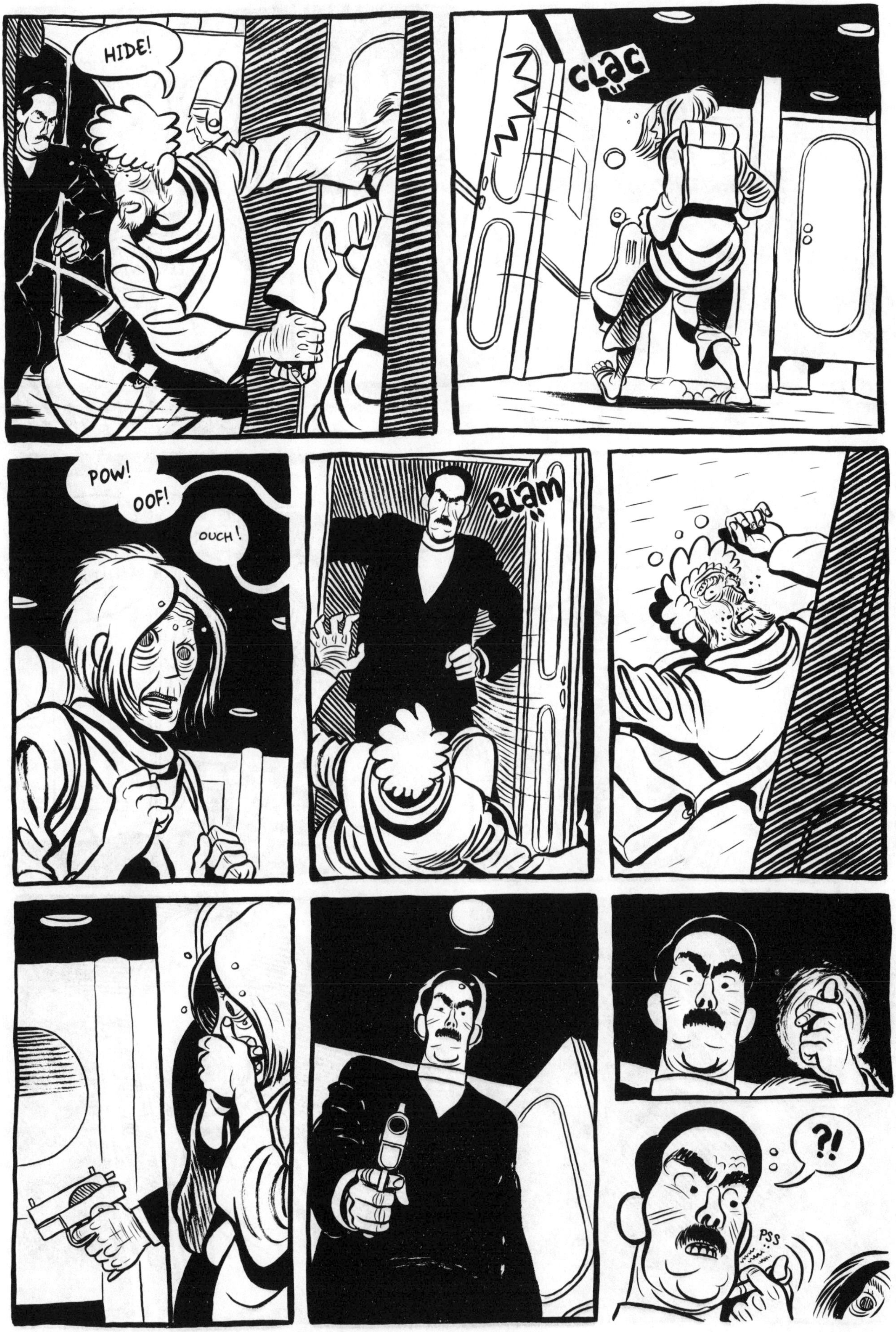
HIDE!
CLAC
WHAM
POW!
OOF!
OUCH!
BLAM
?!
PSS

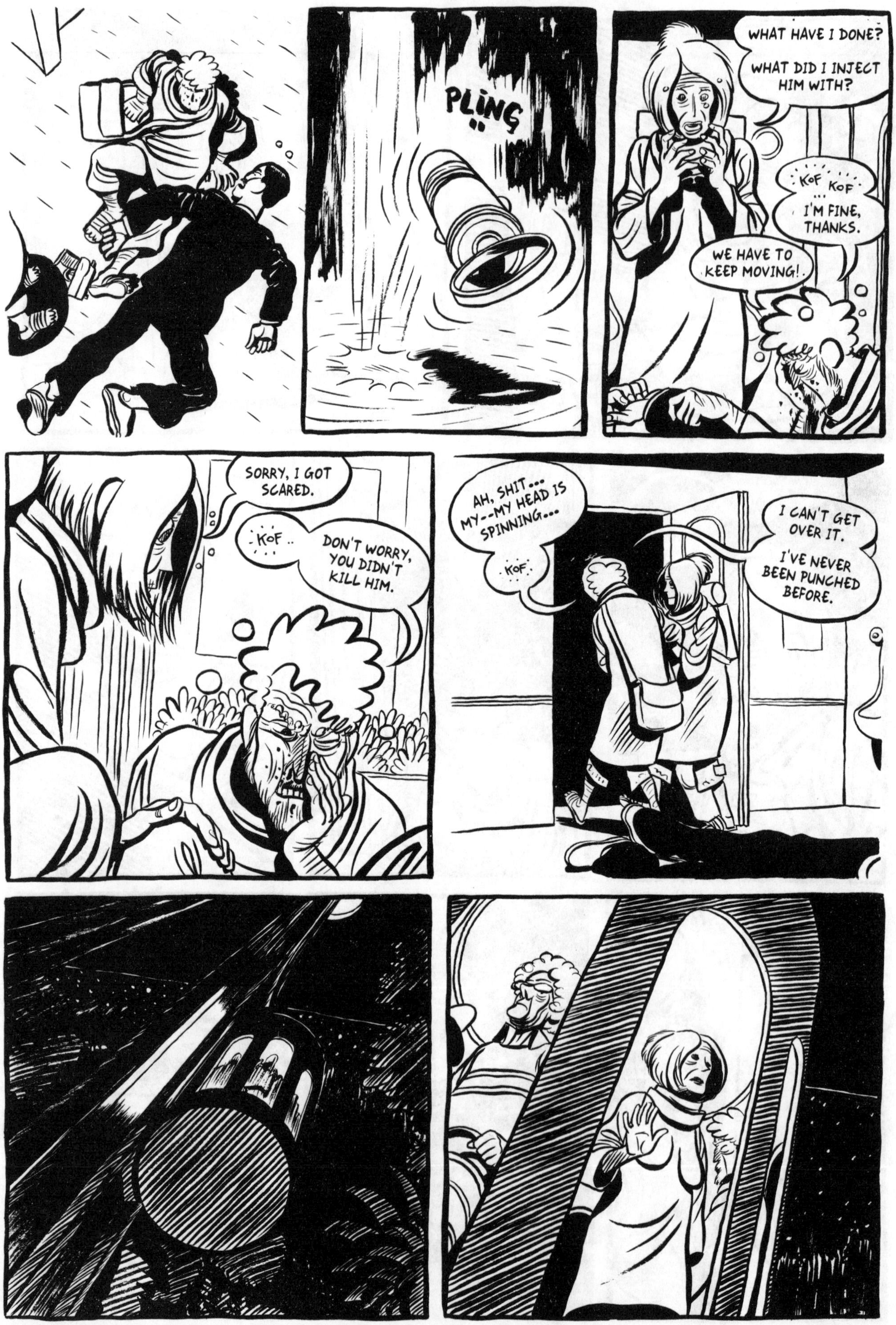
PLING
WHAT HAVE I DONE?
WHAT DID I INJECT HIM WITH?
KOF ... KOF
I'M FINE, THANKS.
WE HAVE TO KEEP MOVING!
SORRY, I GOT SCARED.
KOF
DON'T WORRY, YOU DIDN'T KILL HIM.
AH, SHIT... MY--MY HEAD IS SPINNING...
KOF
I CAN'T GET OVER IT.
I'VE NEVER BEEN PUNCHED BEFORE.

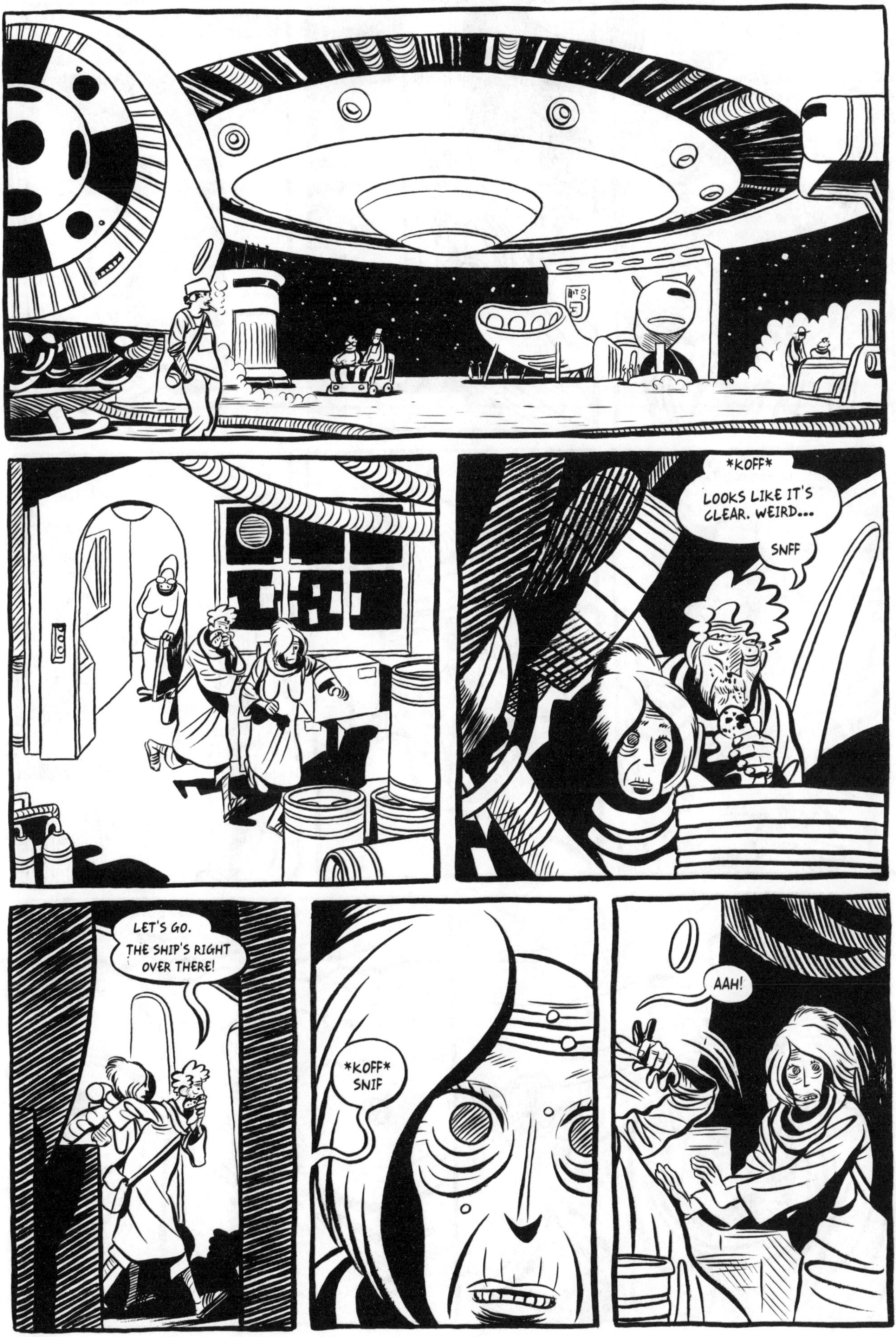
KOFF
LOOKS LIKE IT'S CLEAR. WEIRD...
SNFF
LET'S GO. THE SHIP'S RIGHT OVER THERE!
KOFF SNIF
AAH!

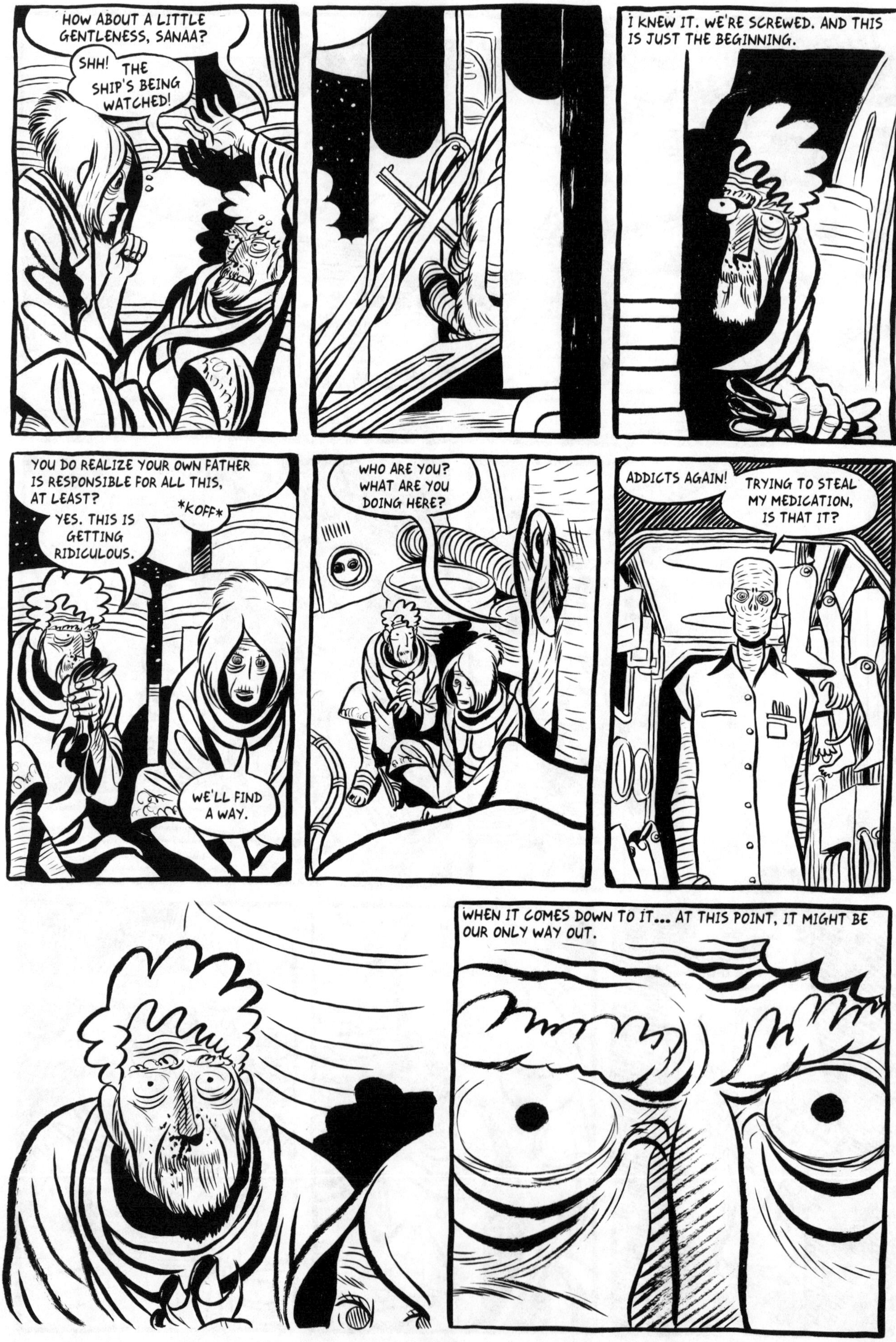

HOW ABOUT A LITTLE GENTLENESS, SANAA?
SHH!
THE SHIP'S BEING WATCHED!
I KNEW IT. WE'RE SCREWED. AND THIS IS JUST THE BEGINNING.
YOU DO REALIZE YOUR OWN FATHER IS RESPONSIBLE FOR ALL THIS, AT LEAST?
YES. THIS IS GETTING RIDICULOUS.
KOFF
WE'LL FIND A WAY.
WHO ARE YOU? WHAT ARE YOU DOING HERE?
ADDICTS AGAIN!
TRYING TO STEAL MY MEDICATION, IS THAT IT?
WHEN IT COMES DOWN TO IT... AT THIS POINT, IT MIGHT BE OUR ONLY WAY OUT.

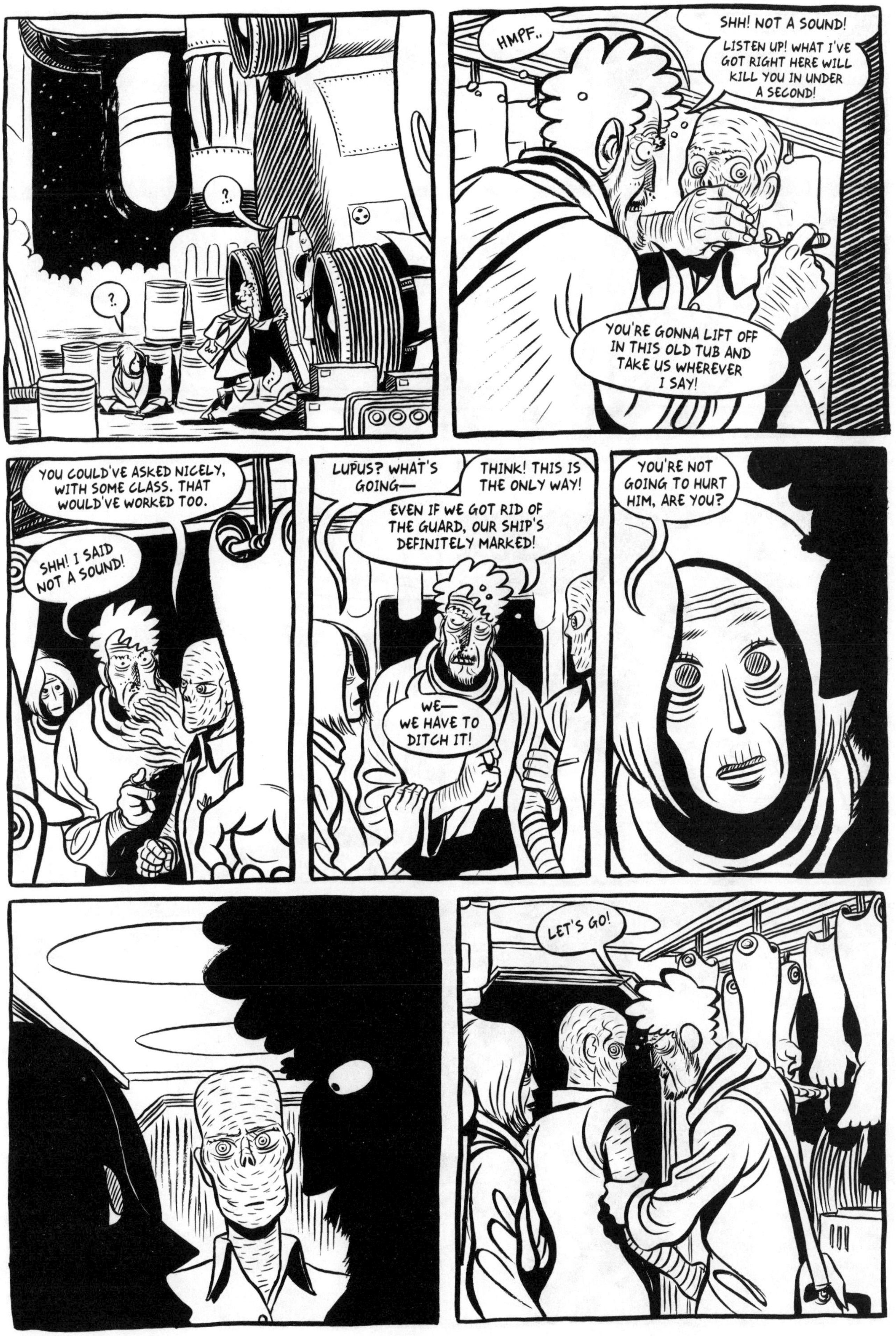
?
?
HMPF..
SHH! NOT A SOUND!
LISTEN UP! WHAT I'VE GOT RIGHT HERE WILL KILL YOU IN UNDER A SECOND!
YOU'RE GONNA LIFT OFF IN THIS OLD TUB AND TAKE US WHEREVER I SAY!
YOU COULD'VE ASKED NICELY, WITH SOME CLASS. THAT WOULD'VE WORKED TOO.
SHH! I SAID NOT A SOUND!
LUPUS? WHAT'S GOING—
THINK! THIS IS THE ONLY WAY!
EVEN IF WE GOT RID OF THE GUARD, OUR SHIP'S DEFINITELY MARKED!
WE— WE HAVE TO DITCH IT!
YOU'RE NOT GOING TO HURT HIM, ARE YOU?
LET'S GO!

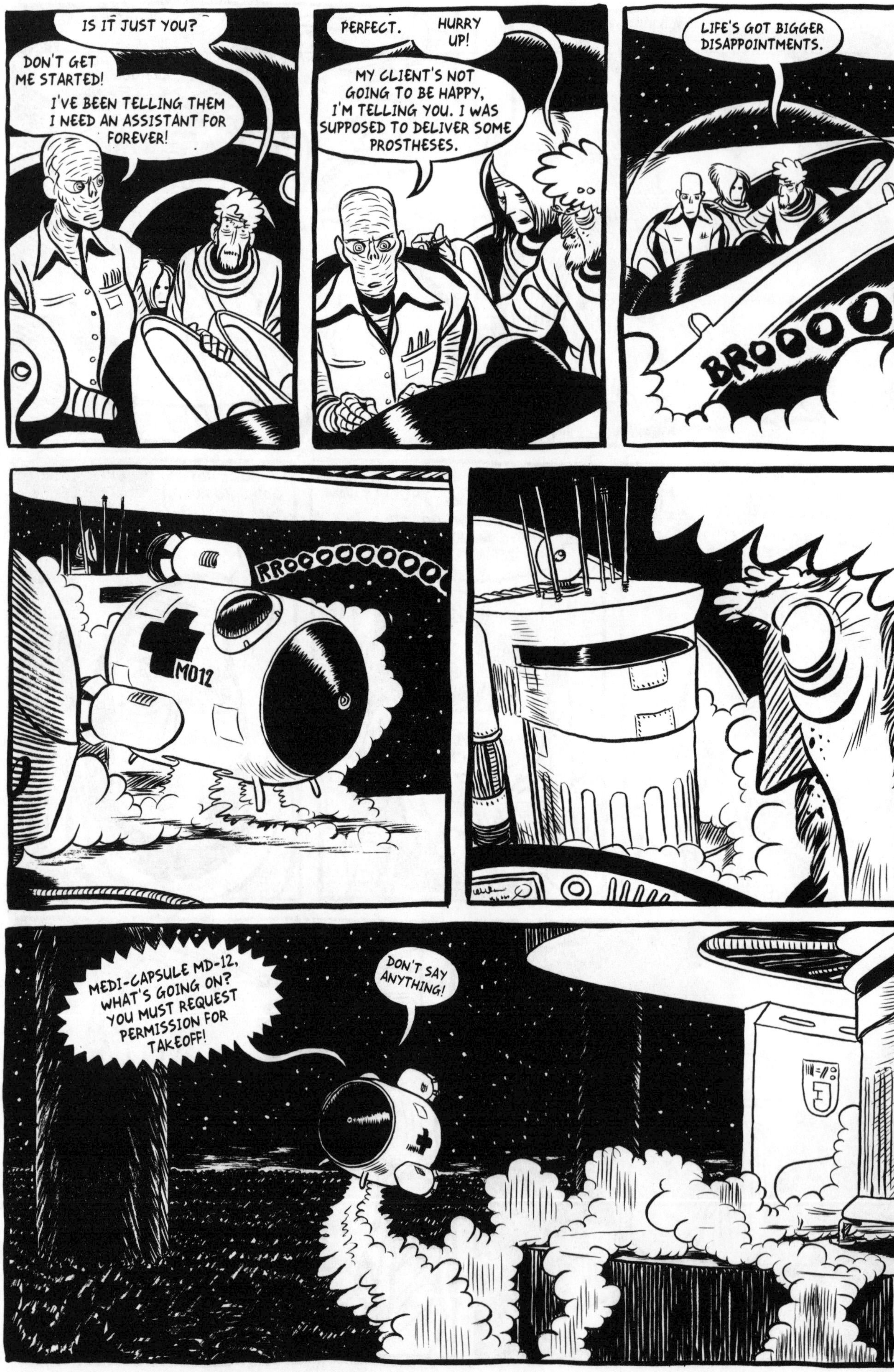

IS IT JUST YOU?
DON'T GET ME STARTED!
I'VE BEEN TELLING THEM I NEED AN ASSISTANT FOR FOREVER!
PERFECT.
HURRY UP!
MY CLIENT'S NOT GOING TO BE HAPPY, I'M TELLING YOU. I WAS SUPPOSED TO DELIVER SOME PROSTHESES.
LIFE'S GOT BIGGER DISAPPOINTMENTS.
BROOOOO
RROOOOOOOOOO
MD12
MEDI-CAPSULE MD-12, WHAT'S GOING ON? YOU MUST REQUEST PERMISSION FOR TAKEOFF!
DON'T SAY ANYTHING!

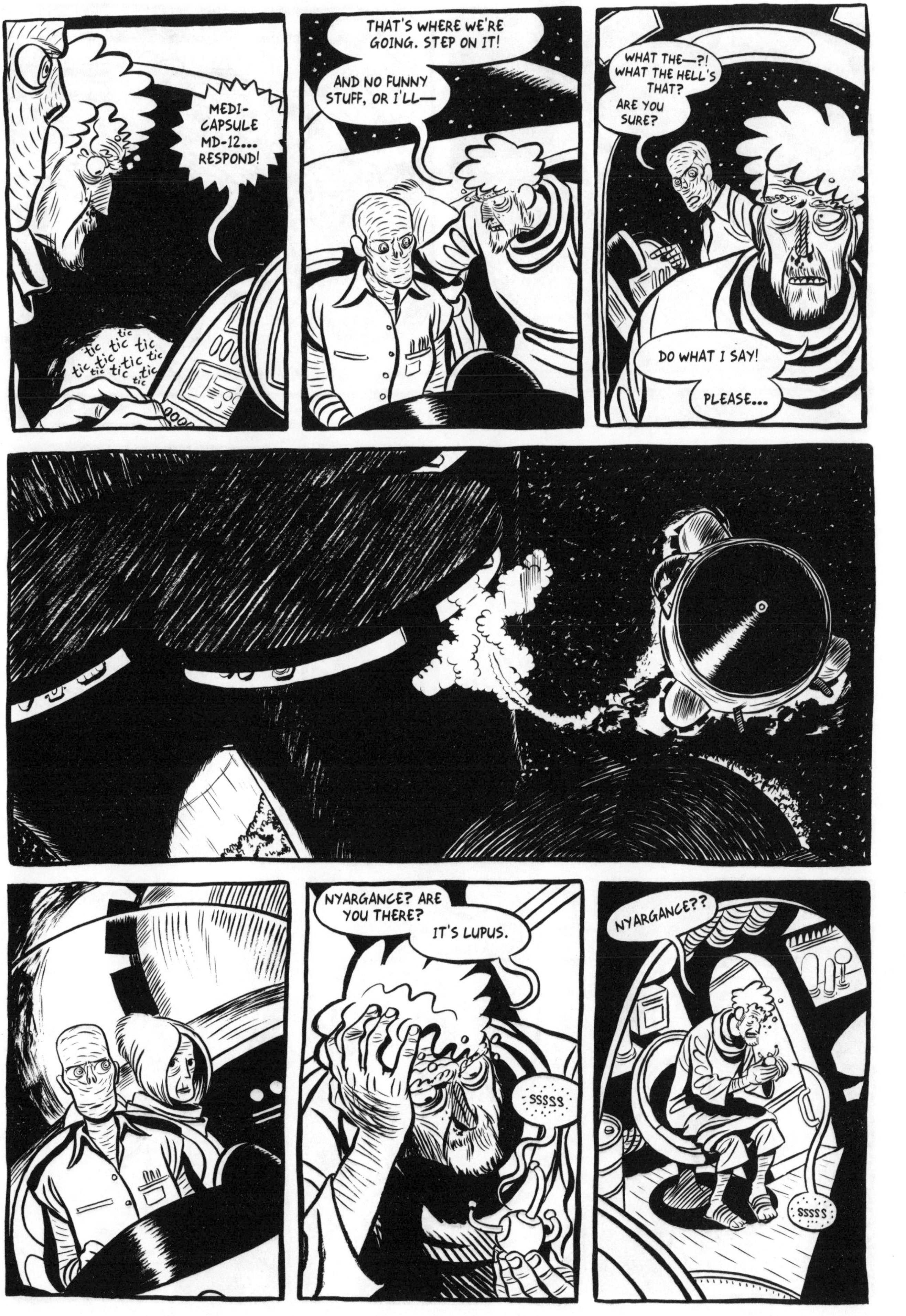
MEDI-CAPSULE MD-12... RESPOND!
tic tic tic tic tic tic tic tic tic tic tic
THAT'S WHERE WE'RE GOING. STEP ON IT!
AND NO FUNNY STUFF, OR I'LL—
WHAT THE—?! WHAT THE HELL'S THAT?
ARE YOU SURE?
DO WHAT I SAY!
PLEASE...
NYARGANCE? ARE YOU THERE?
IT'S LUPUS.
SSSSS
NYARGANCE??
SSSSS

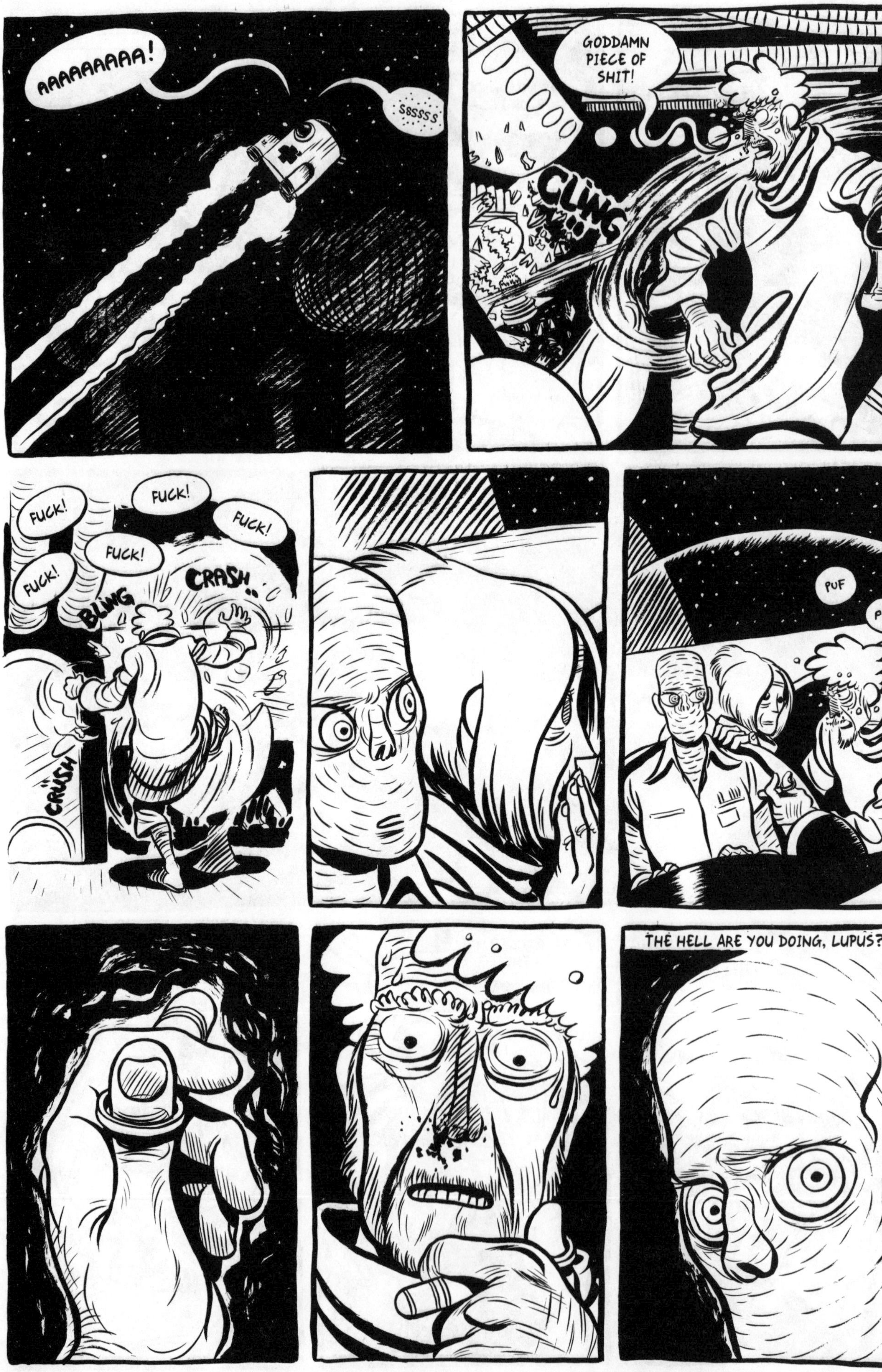
AAAAAAAAA!
SSSSSS
GODDAMN PIECE OF SHIT!
CLING
FUCK!
FUCK!
FUCK!
FUCK!
FUCK!
BLING
CRASH
CRUSH
PUF
PUF
THE HELL ARE YOU DOING, LUPUS?

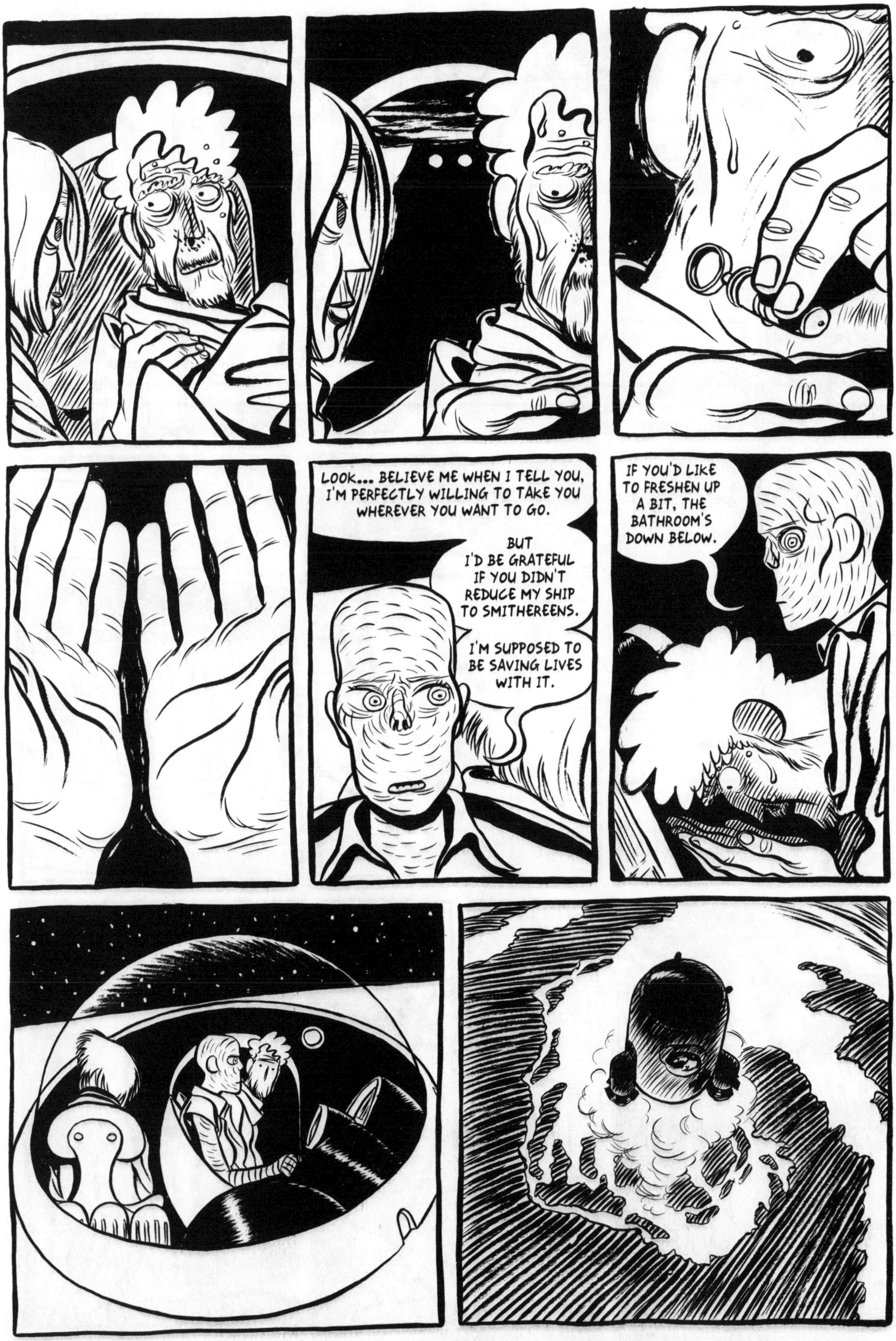
LOOK... BELIEVE ME WHEN I TELL YOU, I'M PERFECTLY WILLING TO TAKE YOU WHEREVER YOU WANT TO GO.
BUT I'D BE GRATEFUL IF YOU DIDN'T REDUCE MY SHIP TO SMITHEREENS.
I'M SUPPOSED TO BE SAVING LIVES WITH IT.
IF YOU'D LIKE TO FRESHEN UP A BIT, THE BATHROOM'S DOWN BELOW.

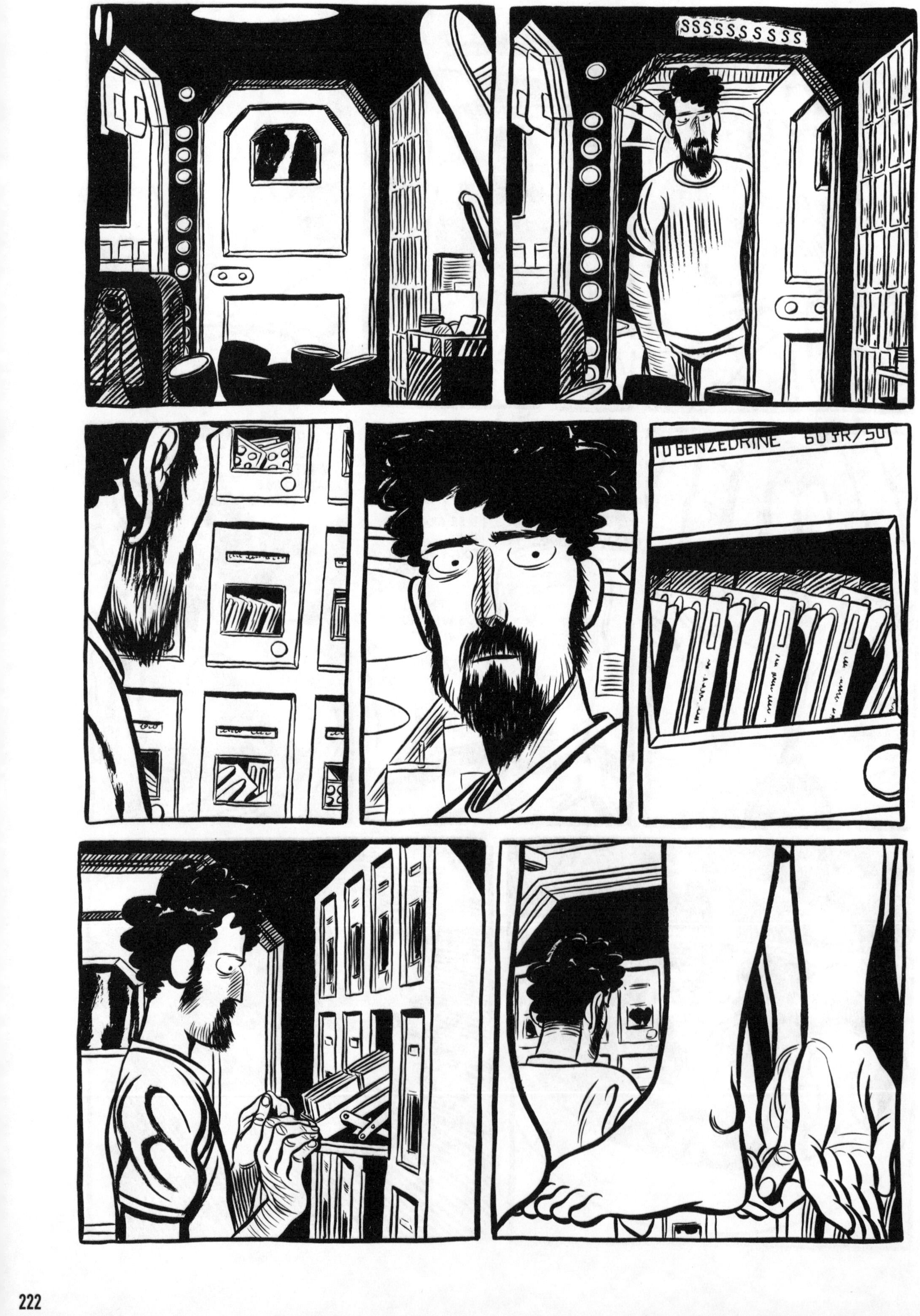
SSSSSSSSSS
BENZEDRINE

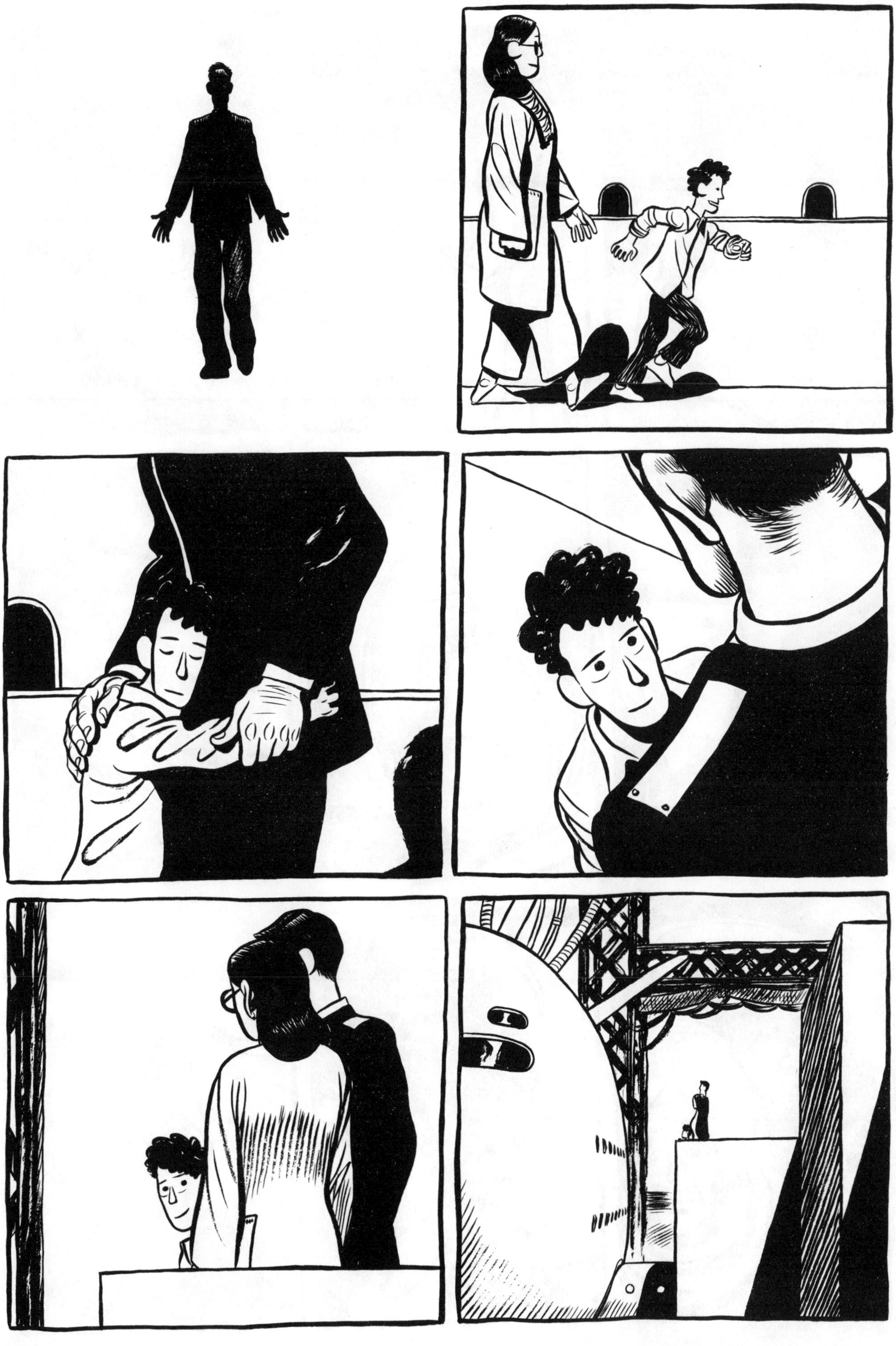

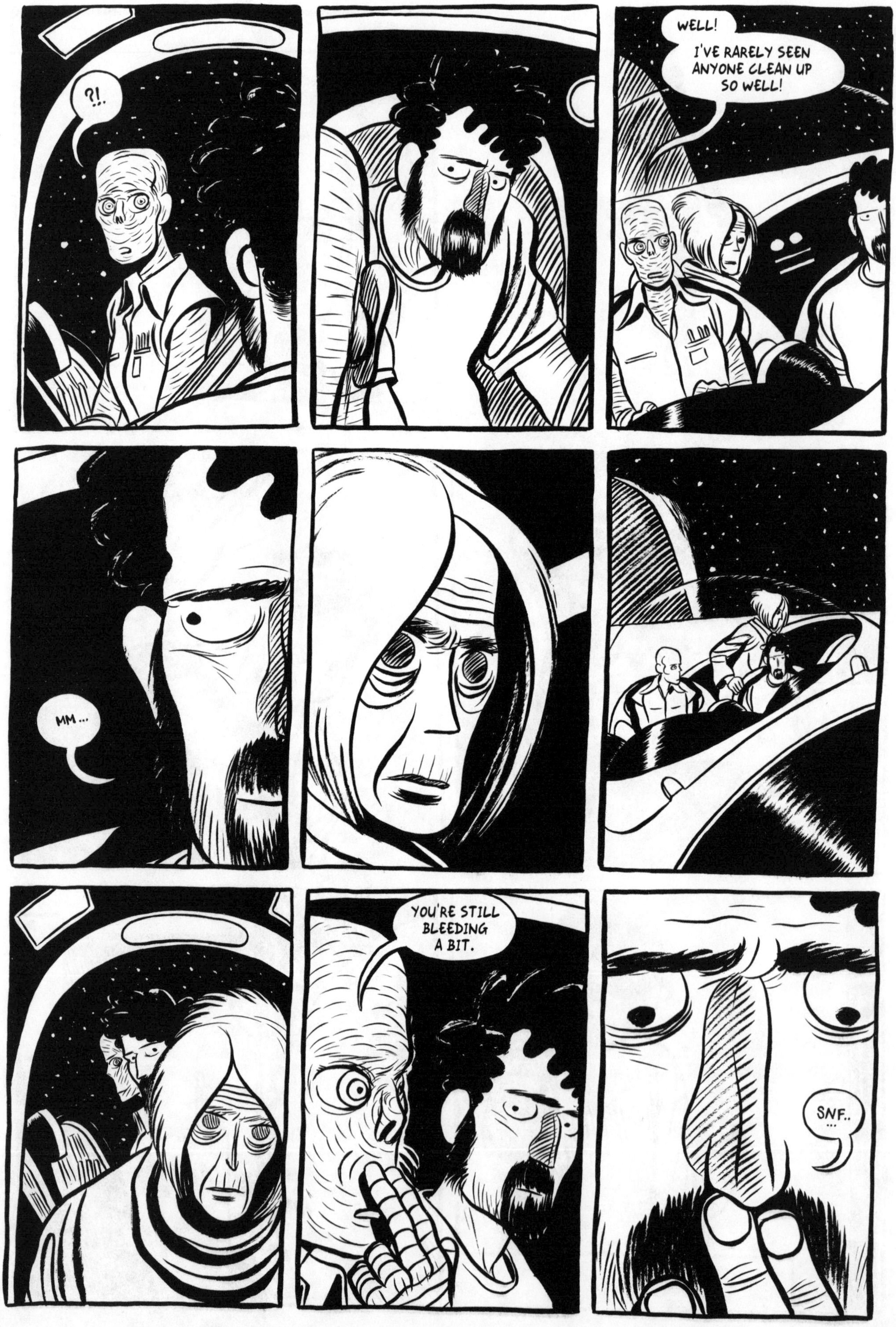
?!.
WELL!
I'VE RARELY SEEN ANYONE CLEAN UP SO WELL!
MM...
YOU'RE STILL BLEEDING A BIT.
SNF.. ...

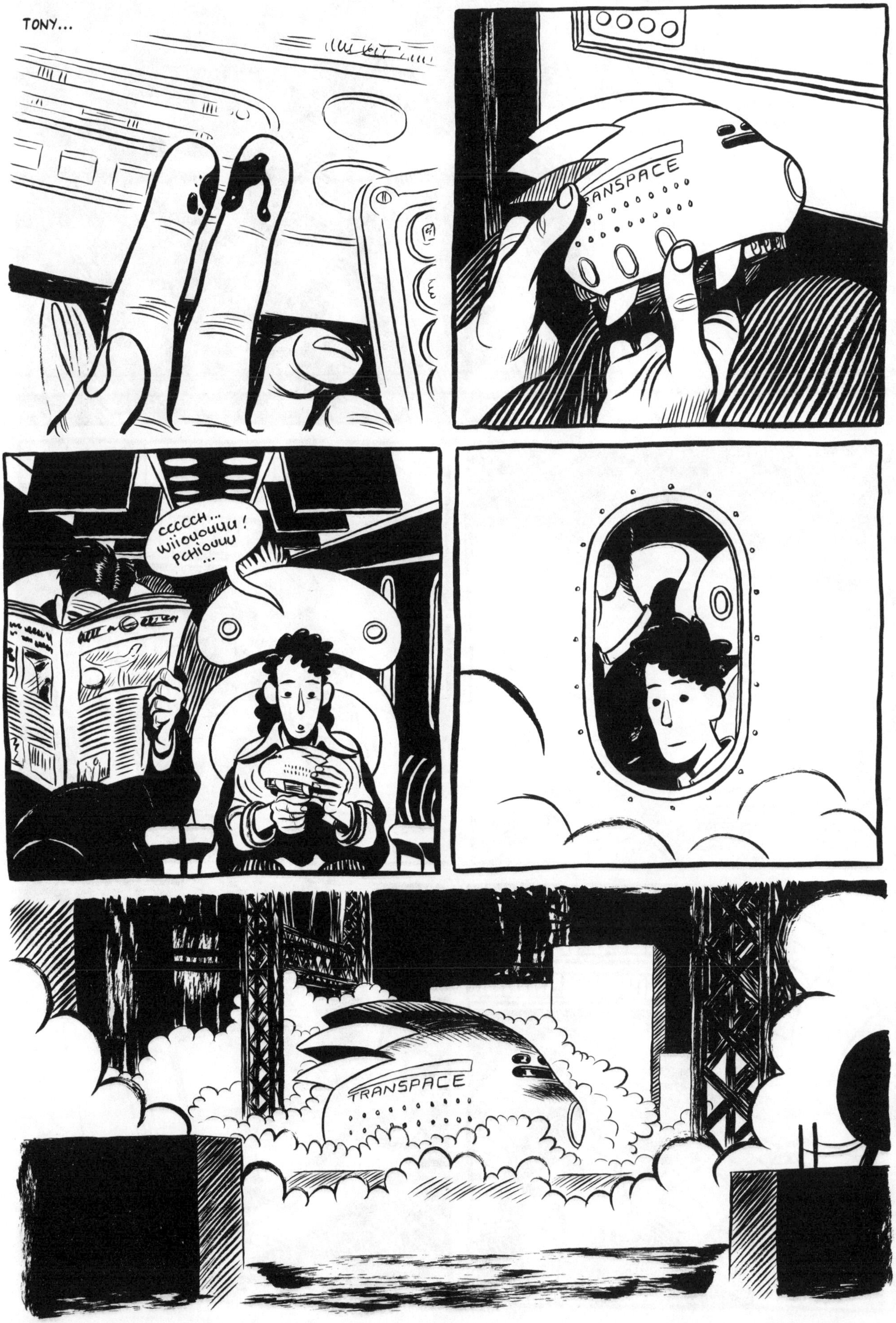
TONY...
TRANSPACE
CCCCCH... WIIOUOUUU! PCHIOUUU ...
TRANSPACE

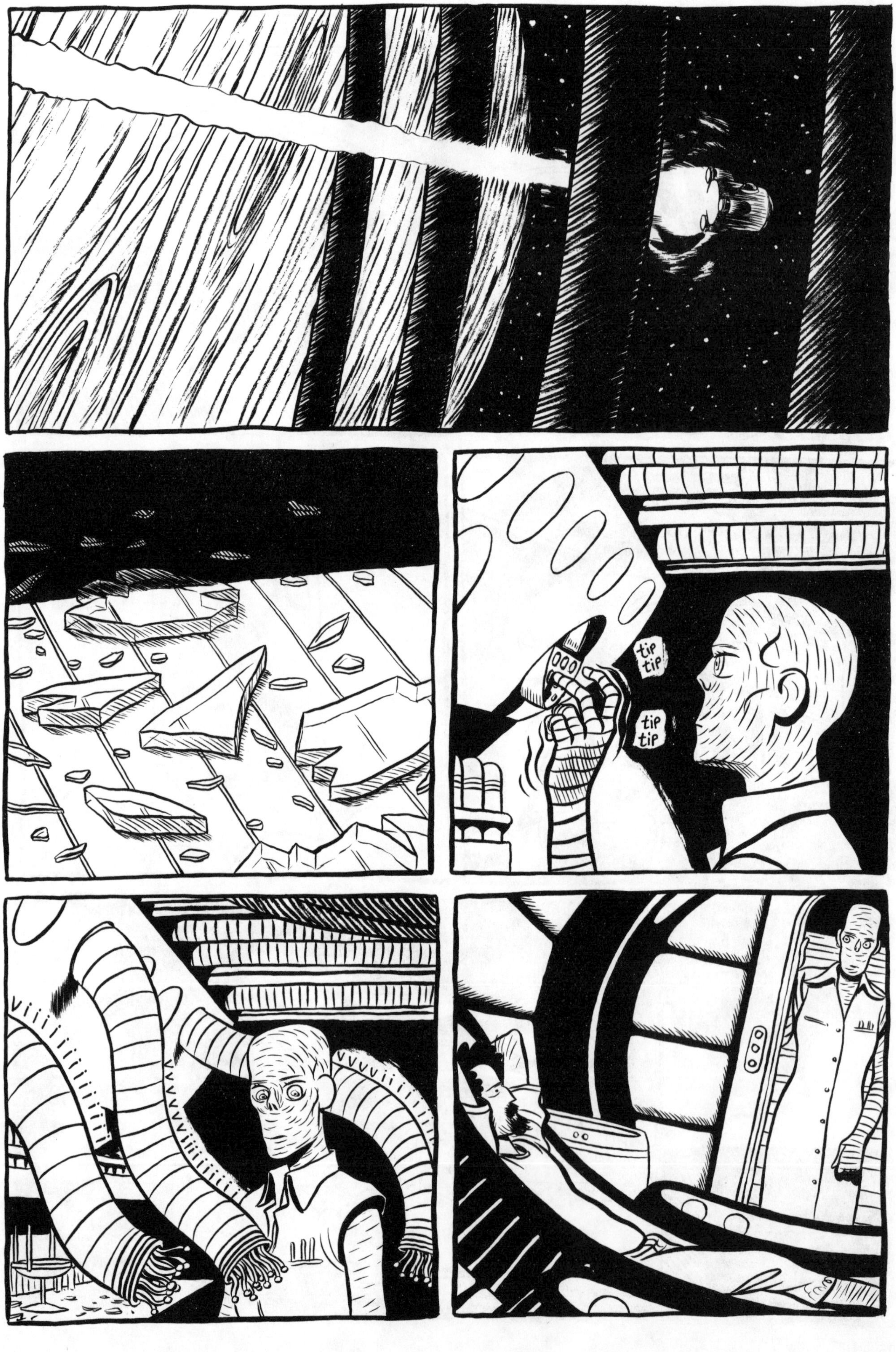
tip tip
tip tip

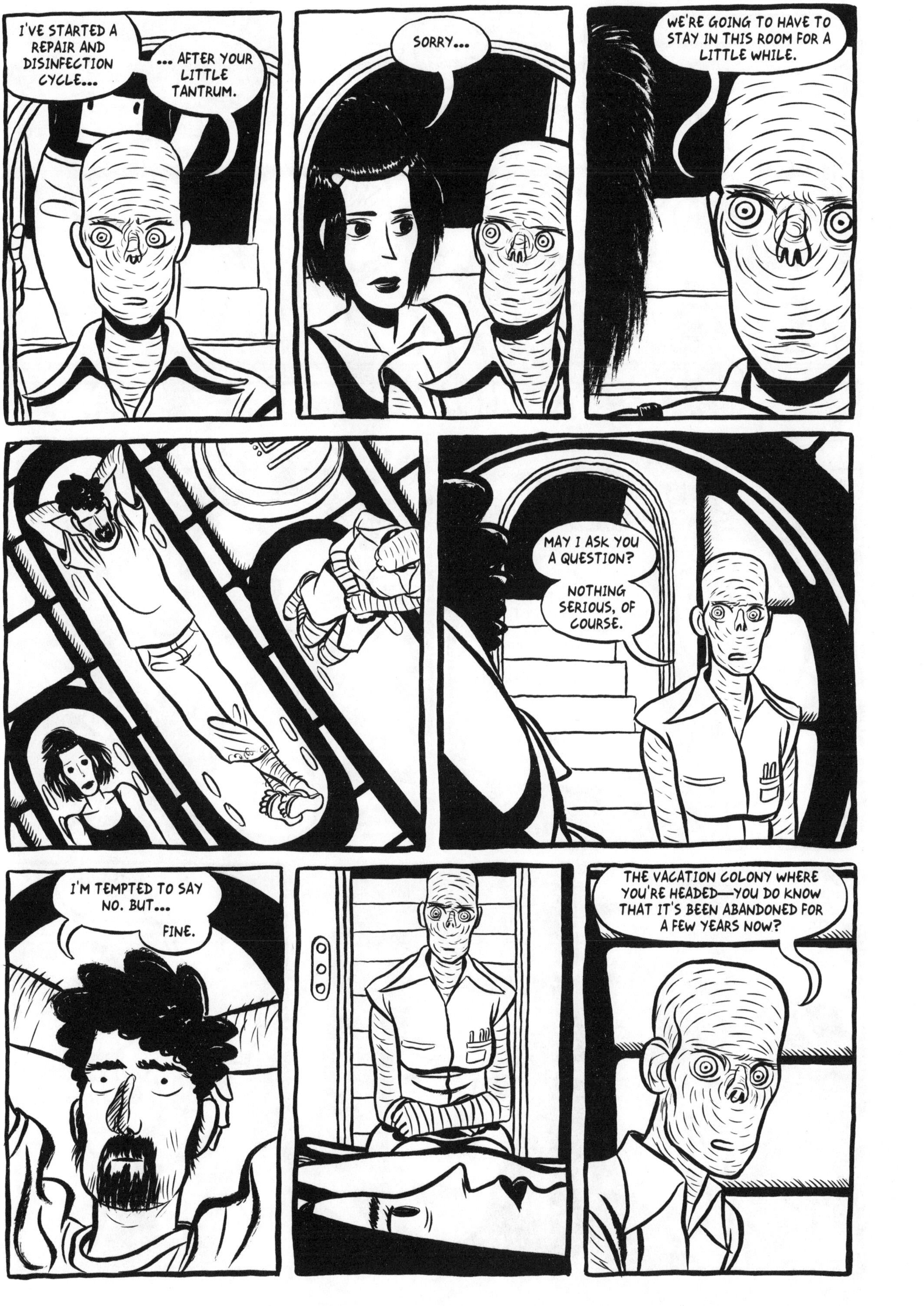
I'VE STARTED A REPAIR AND DISINFECTION CYCLE...
... AFTER YOUR LITTLE TANTRUM.
SORRY...
WE'RE GOING TO HAVE TO STAY IN THIS ROOM FOR A LITTLE WHILE.
MAY I ASK YOU A QUESTION?
NOTHING SERIOUS, OF COURSE.
I'M TEMPTED TO SAY NO. BUT...
FINE.
THE VACATION COLONY WHERE YOU'RE HEADED—YOU DO KNOW THAT IT'S BEEN ABANDONED FOR A FEW YEARS NOW?

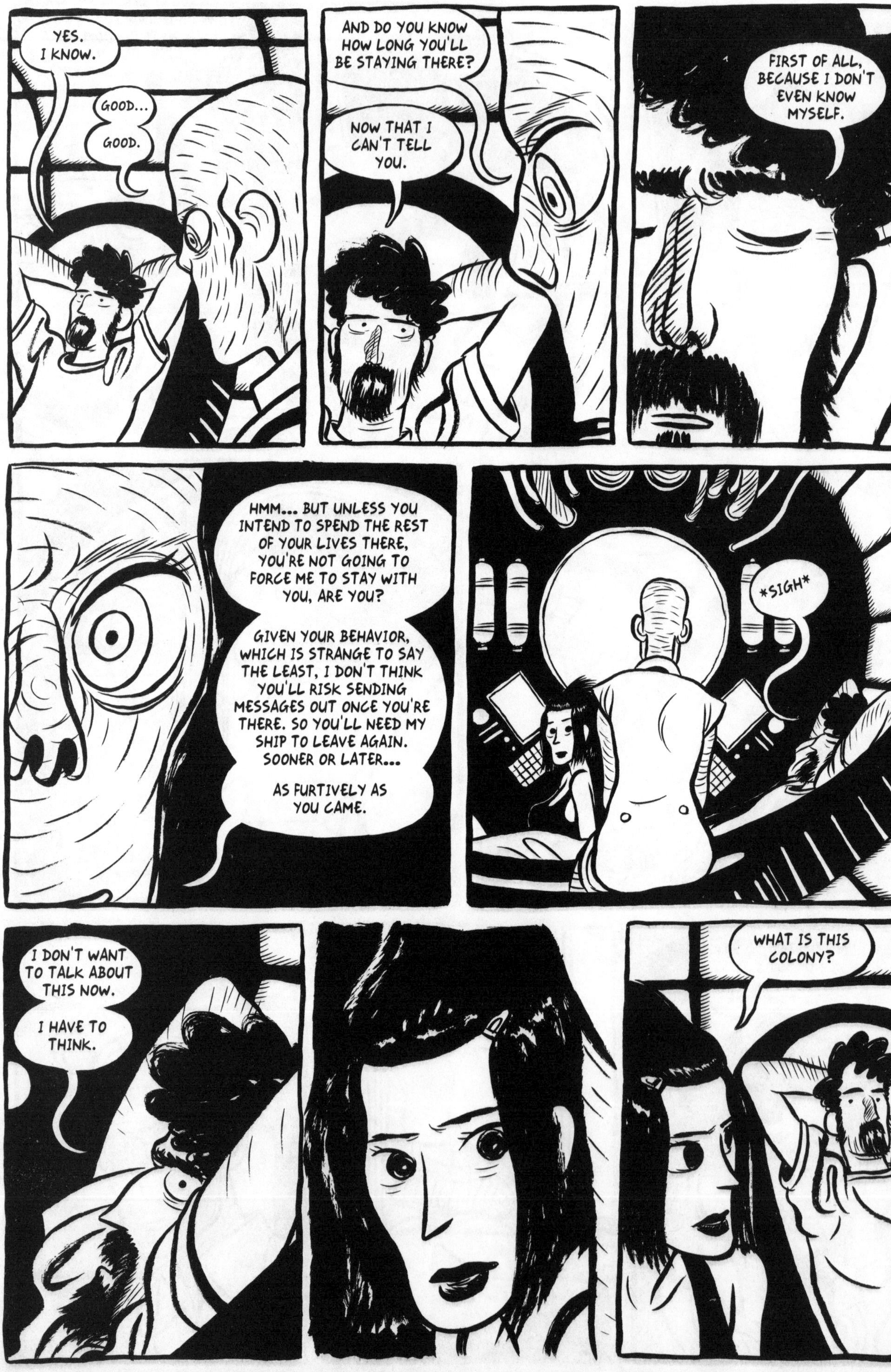
YES. I KNOW.
GOOD...
GOOD.
AND DO YOU KNOW HOW LONG YOU'LL BE STAYING THERE?
NOW THAT I CAN'T TELL YOU.
FIRST OF ALL, BECAUSE I DON'T EVEN KNOW MYSELF.
HMM... BUT UNLESS YOU INTEND TO SPEND THE REST OF YOUR LIVES THERE, YOU'RE NOT GOING TO FORCE ME TO STAY WITH YOU, ARE YOU?
GIVEN YOUR BEHAVIOR, WHICH IS STRANGE TO SAY THE LEAST, I DON'T THINK YOU'LL RISK SENDING MESSAGES OUT ONCE YOU'RE THERE. SO YOU'LL NEED MY SHIP TO LEAVE AGAIN. SOONER OR LATER...
AS FURTIVELY AS YOU CAME.
SIGH
I DON'T WANT TO TALK ABOUT THIS NOW.
I HAVE TO THINK.
WHAT IS THIS COLONY?

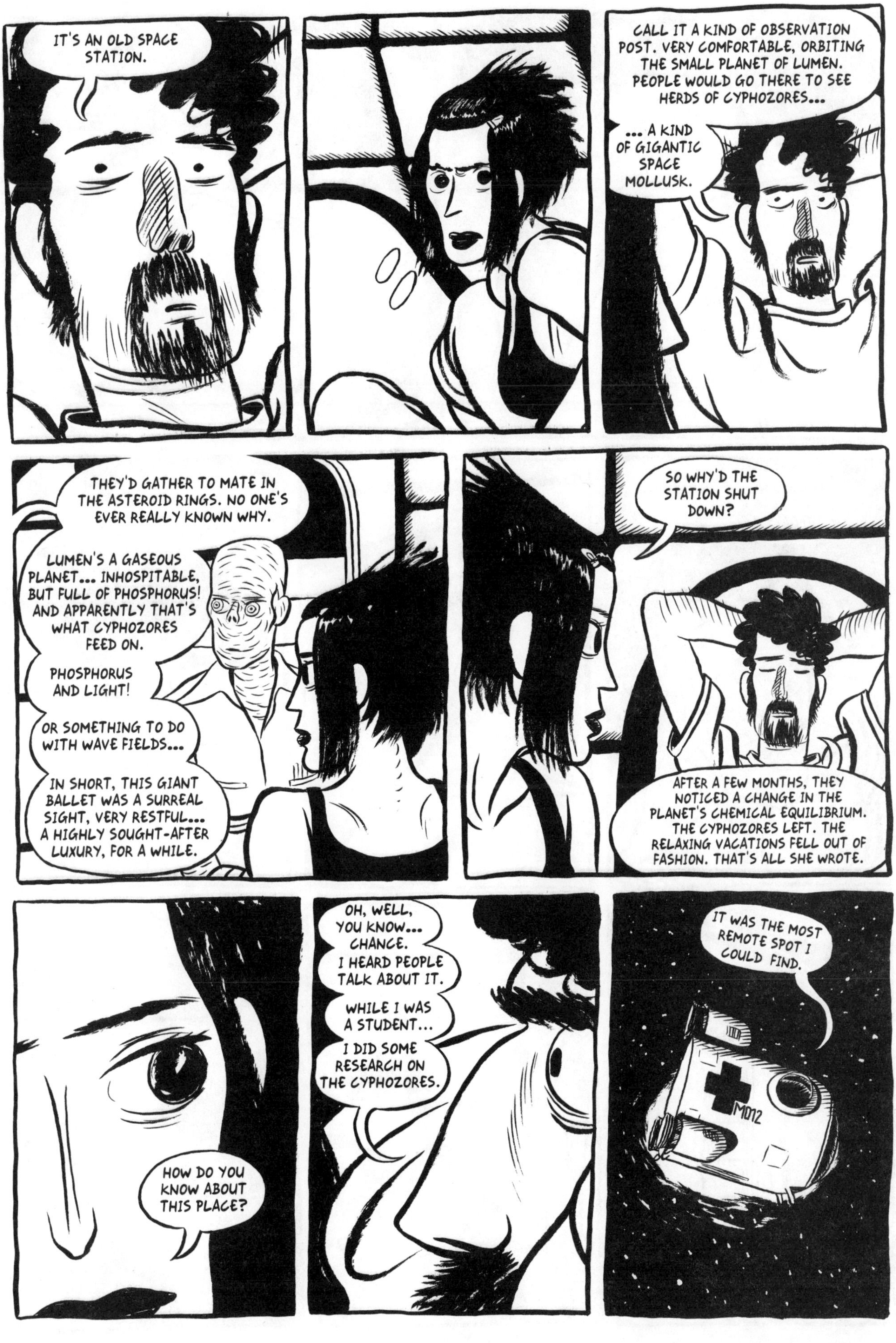
IT'S AN OLD SPACE STATION.
CALL IT A KIND OF OBSERVATION POST. VERY COMFORTABLE, ORBITING THE SMALL PLANET OF LUMEN. PEOPLE WOULD GO THERE TO SEE HERDS OF CYPHOZORES...
... A KIND OF GIGANTIC SPACE MOLLUSK.
THEY'D GATHER TO MATE IN THE ASTEROID RINGS. NO ONE'S EVER REALLY KNOWN WHY.
LUMEN'S A GASEOUS PLANET... INHOSPITABLE, BUT FULL OF PHOSPHORUS! AND APPARENTLY THAT'S WHAT CYPHOZORES FEED ON.
PHOSPHORUS AND LIGHT!
OR SOMETHING TO DO WITH WAVE FIELDS...
IN SHORT, THIS GIANT BALLET WAS A SURREAL SIGHT, VERY RESTFUL... A HIGHLY SOUGHT-AFTER LUXURY, FOR A WHILE.
SO WHY'D THE STATION SHUT DOWN?
AFTER A FEW MONTHS, THEY NOTICED A CHANGE IN THE PLANET'S CHEMICAL EQUILIBRIUM. THE CYPHOZORES LEFT. THE RELAXING VACATIONS FELL OUT OF FASHION. THAT'S ALL SHE WROTE.
HOW DO YOU KNOW ABOUT THIS PLACE?
OH, WELL, YOU KNOW... CHANCE.
I HEARD PEOPLE TALK ABOUT IT.
WHILE I WAS A STUDENT...
I DID SOME RESEARCH ON THE CYPHOZORES.
IT WAS THE MOST REMOTE SPOT I COULD FIND.
M012

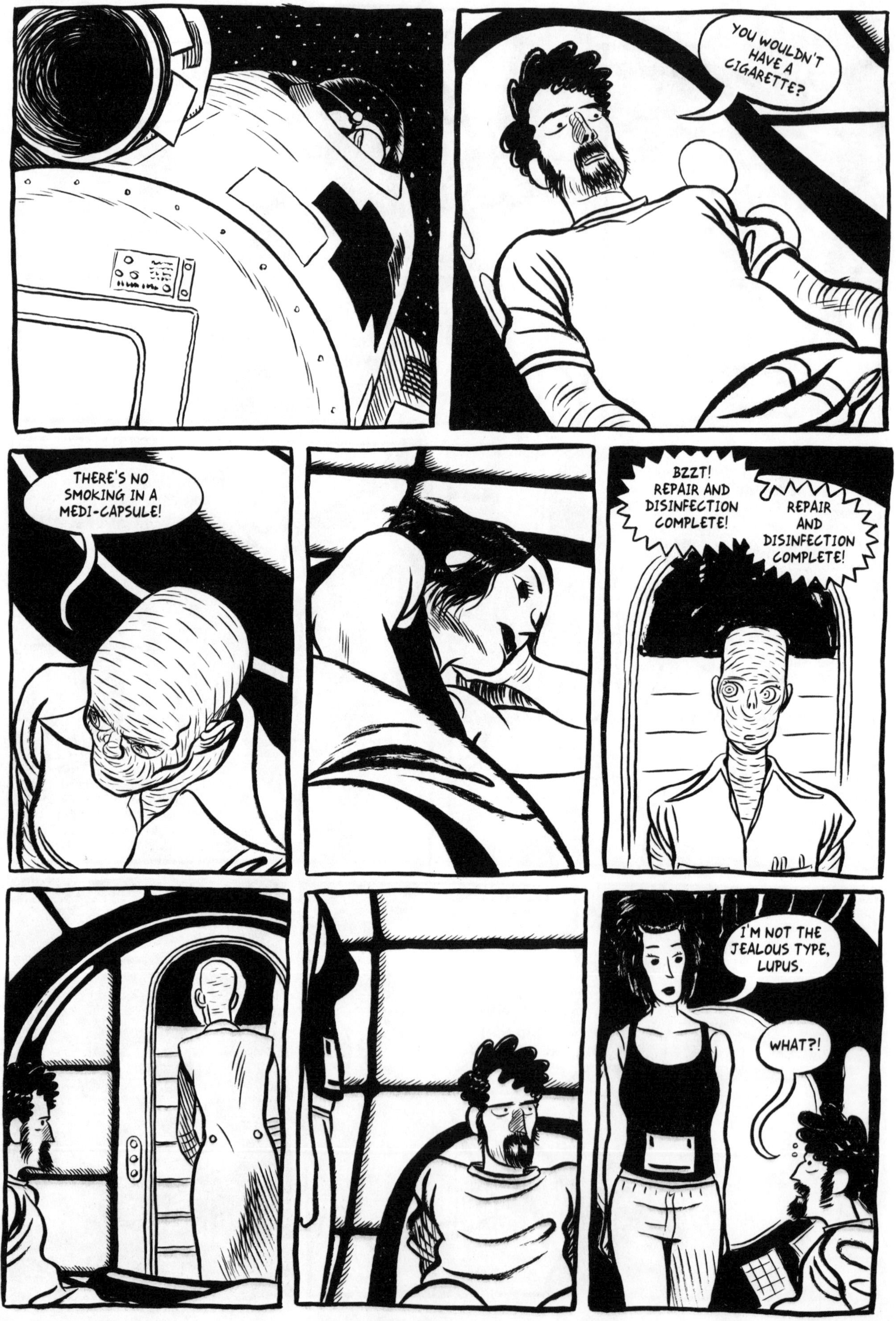
YOU WOULDN'T HAVE A CIGARETTE?
THERE'S NO SMOKING IN A MEDI-CAPSULE!
BZZT! REPAIR AND DISINFECTION COMPLETE!
REPAIR AND DISINFECTION COMPLETE!
I'M NOT THE JEALOUS TYPE, LUPUS.
WHAT?!

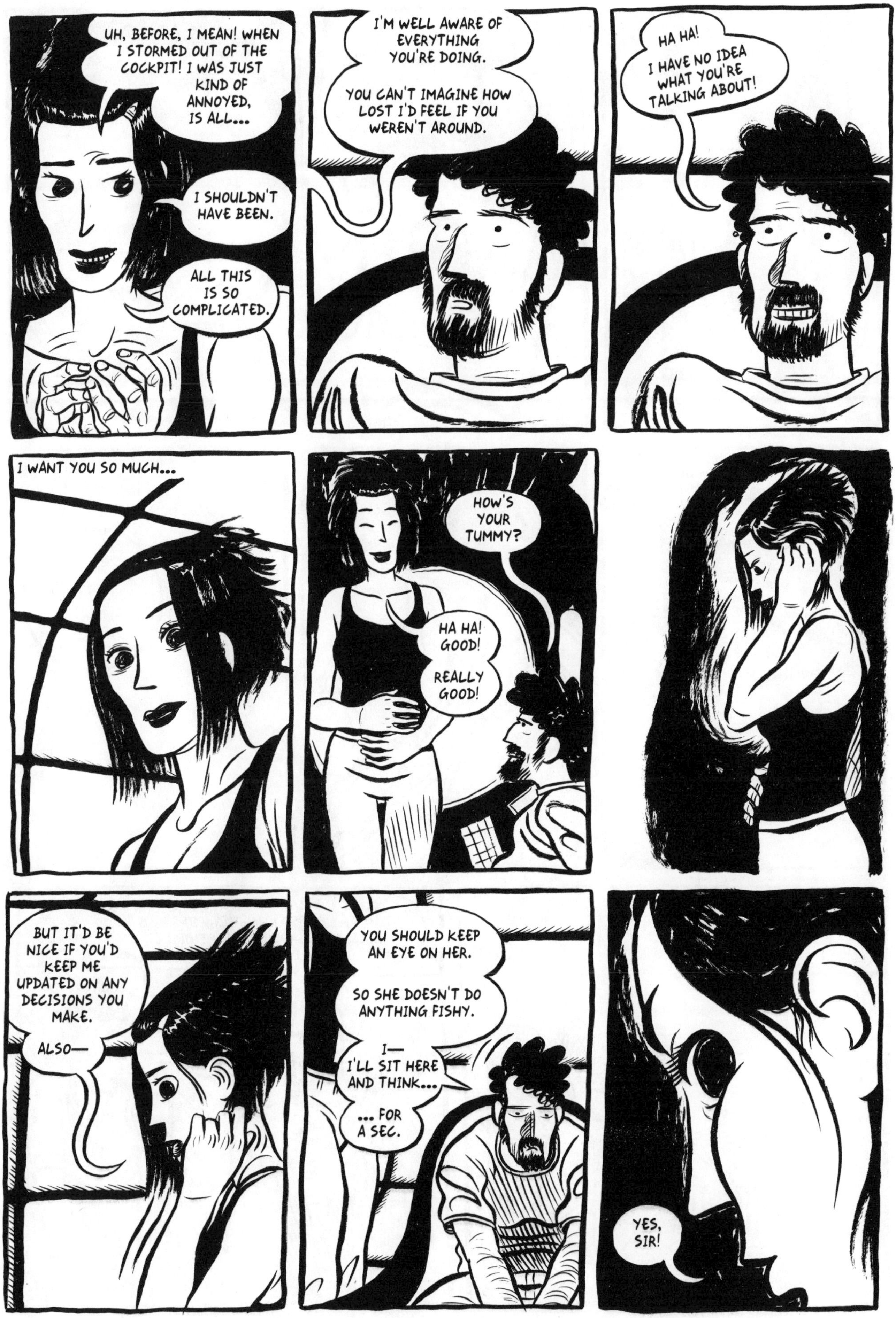
UH, BEFORE, I MEAN! WHEN I STORMED OUT OF THE COCKPIT! I WAS JUST KIND OF ANNOYED, IS ALL...
I SHOULDN'T HAVE BEEN.
ALL THIS IS SO COMPLICATED.
I'M WELL AWARE OF EVERYTHING YOU'RE DOING.
YOU CAN'T IMAGINE HOW LOST I'D FEEL IF YOU WEREN'T AROUND.
HA HA!
I HAVE NO IDEA WHAT YOU'RE TALKING ABOUT!
I WANT YOU SO MUCH...
HOW'S YOUR TUMMY?
HA HA! GOOD!
REALLY GOOD!
BUT IT'D BE NICE IF YOU'D KEEP ME UPDATED ON ANY DECISIONS YOU MAKE.
ALSO—
YOU SHOULD KEEP AN EYE ON HER.
SO SHE DOESN'T DO ANYTHING FISHY.
I— I'LL SIT HERE AND THINK...
... FOR A SEC.
YES, SIR!

I'M WELL WITHIN MY RIGHTS. IT'S PAIN MEDICINE, AFTER ALL. AND MY NOSE HURTS.

SNF
··

CRAK

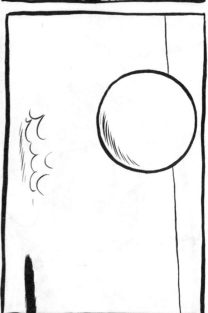

HONESTLY, I JUST DON'T GET YOU! YOUR DAD'S A NCO, SO KNOWING WHAT HE'S LIKE, HOW CAN YOU EVEN THINK OF JOINING THE ARMY? YOU'RE GONNA HATE EVERY SECOND OF IT!

YOU! OF ALL PEOPLE!

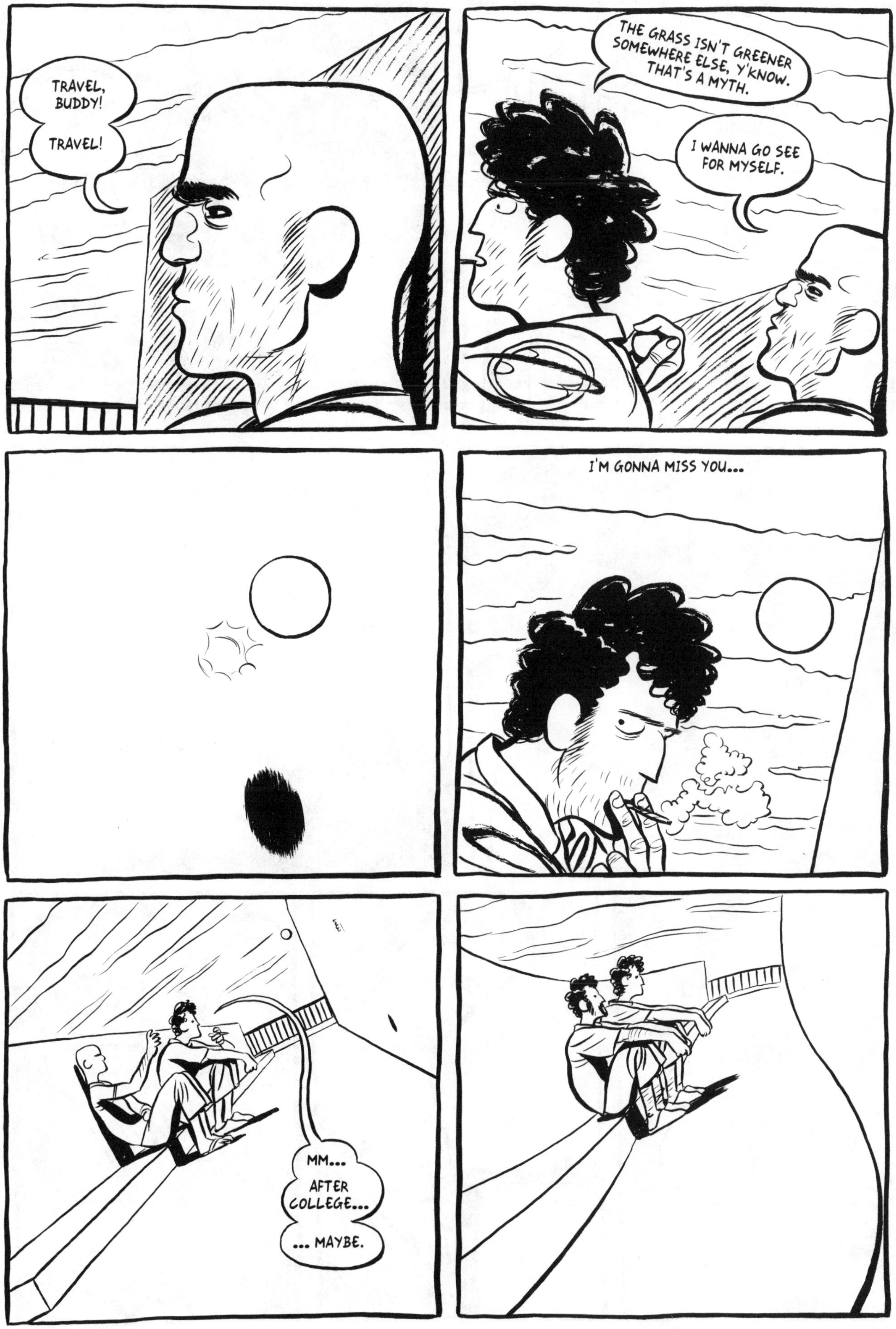
TRAVEL, BUDDY!
TRAVEL!
THE GRASS ISN'T GREENER SOMEWHERE ELSE, Y'KNOW. THAT'S A MYTH.
I WANNA GO SEE FOR MYSELF.
I'M GONNA MISS YOU...
MM... AFTER COLLEGE...
... MAYBE.

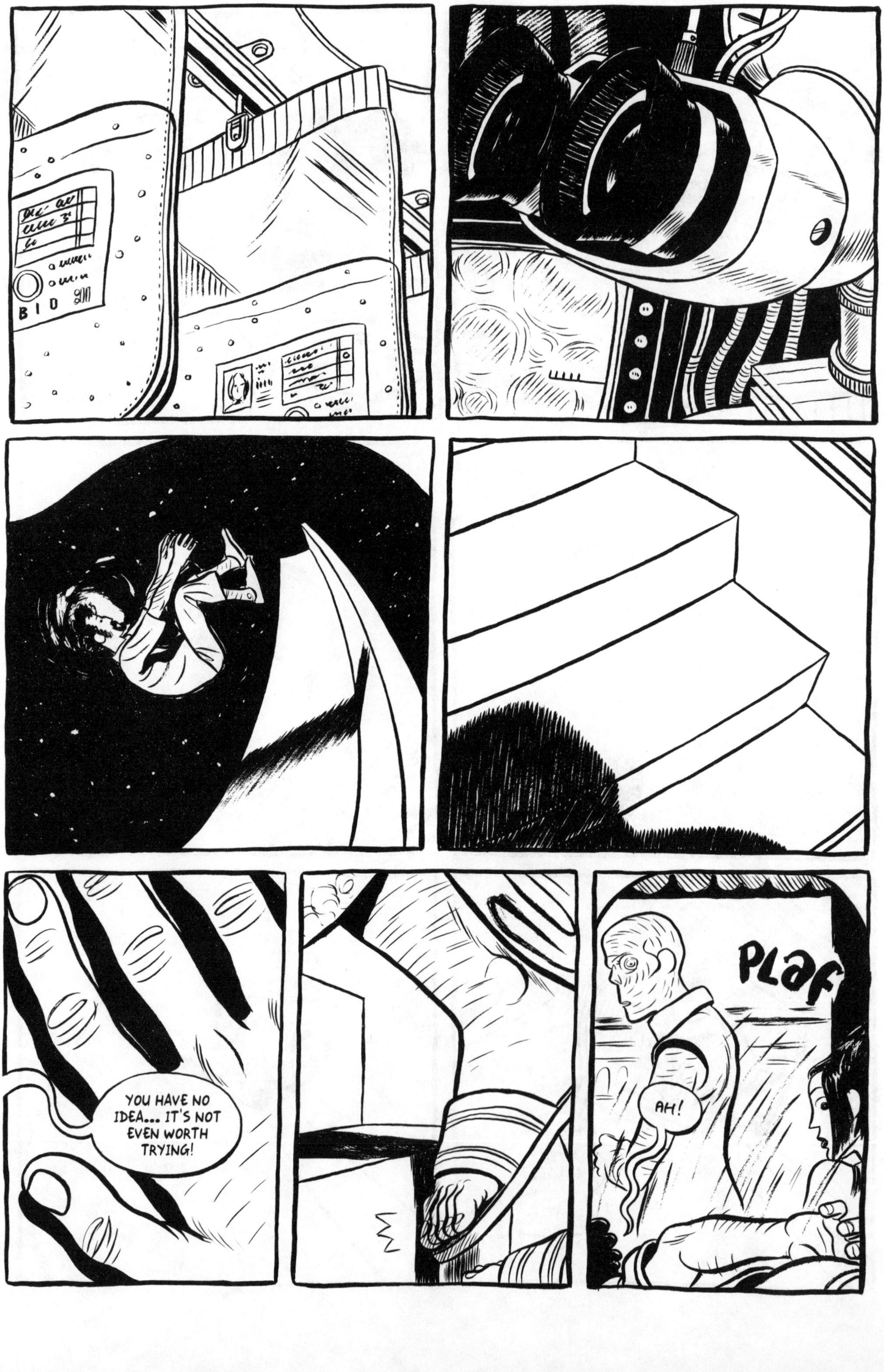
YOU HAVE NO IDEA... IT'S NOT EVEN WORTH TRYING!
PLAF
AH!

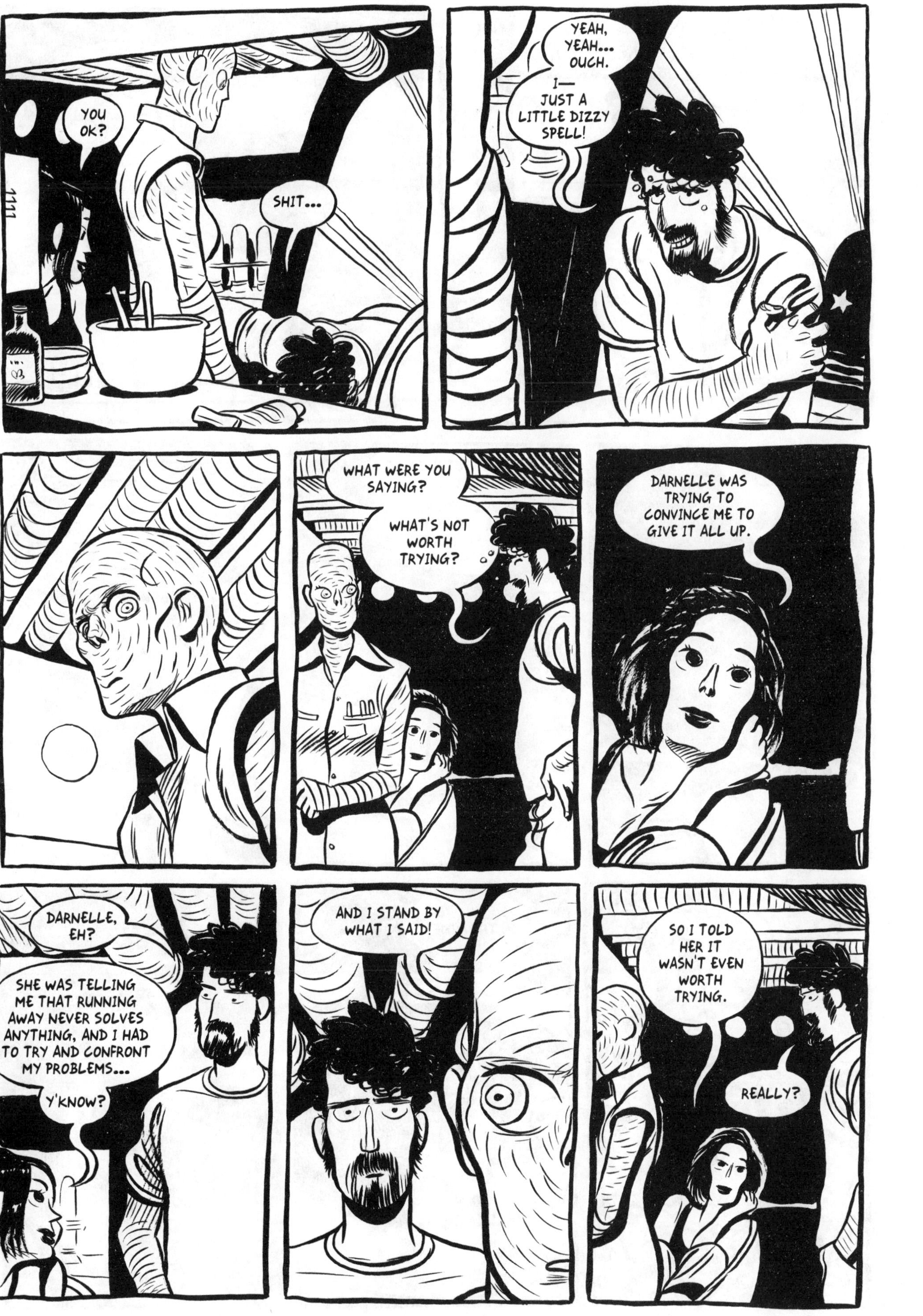
YOU OK?
SHIT...
YEAH, YEAH... OUCH.
I— JUST A LITTLE DIZZY SPELL!
WHAT WERE YOU SAYING?
WHAT'S NOT WORTH TRYING?
DARNELLE WAS TRYING TO CONVINCE ME TO GIVE IT ALL UP.
DARNELLE, EH?
SHE WAS TELLING ME THAT RUNNING AWAY NEVER SOLVES ANYTHING, AND I HAD TO TRY AND CONFRONT MY PROBLEMS...
Y'KNOW?
AND I STAND BY WHAT I SAID!
SO I TOLD HER IT WASN'T EVEN WORTH TRYING.
REALLY?

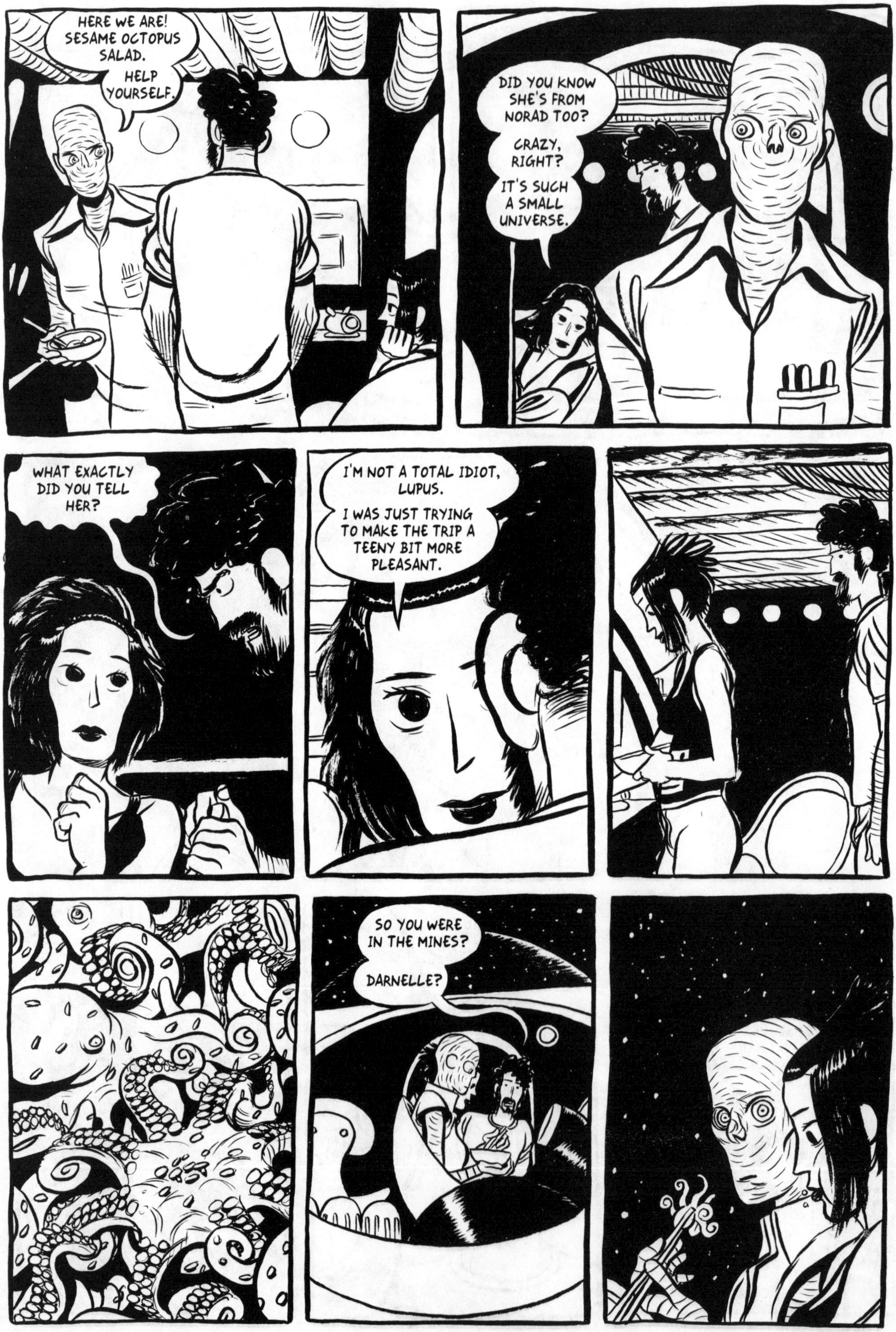
HERE WE ARE! SESAME OCTOPUS SALAD.
HELP YOURSELF.
DID YOU KNOW SHE'S FROM NORAD TOO?
CRAZY, RIGHT?
IT'S SUCH A SMALL UNIVERSE.
WHAT EXACTLY DID YOU TELL HER?
I'M NOT A TOTAL IDIOT, LUPUS.
I WAS JUST TRYING TO MAKE THE TRIP A TEENY BIT MORE PLEASANT.
SO YOU WERE IN THE MINES?
DARNELLE?

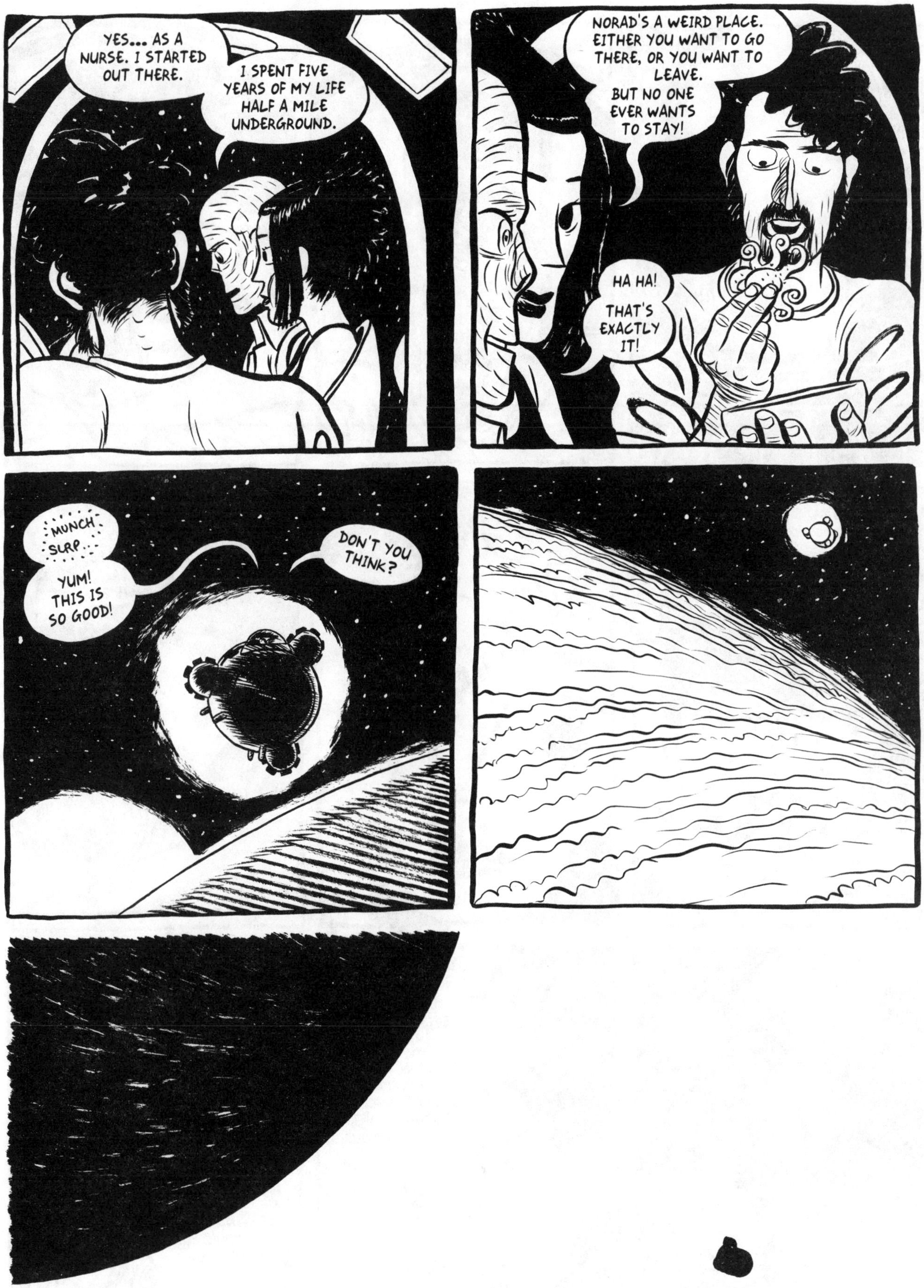
YES... AS A NURSE. I STARTED OUT THERE.
I SPENT FIVE YEARS OF MY LIFE HALF A MILE UNDERGROUND.
NORAD'S A WEIRD PLACE. EITHER YOU WANT TO GO THERE, OR YOU WANT TO LEAVE.
BUT NO ONE EVER WANTS TO STAY!
HA HA!
THAT'S EXACTLY IT!
MUNCH SLRP...
YUM! THIS IS SO GOOD!
DON'T YOU THINK?

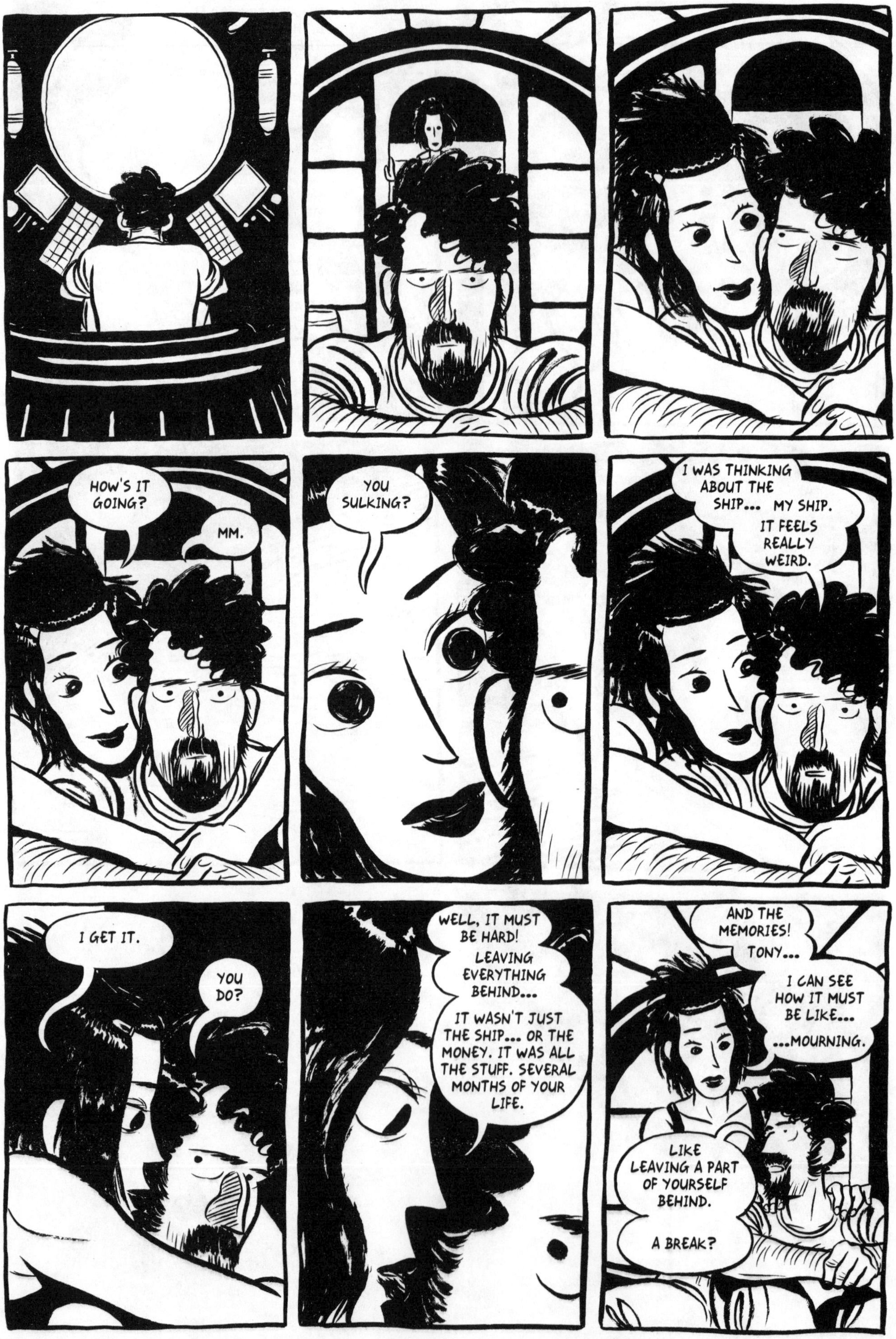
HOW'S IT GOING?
MM.
YOU SULKING?
I WAS THINKING ABOUT THE SHIP... MY SHIP.
IT FEELS REALLY WEIRD.
I GET IT.
YOU DO?
WELL, IT MUST BE HARD!
LEAVING EVERYTHING BEHIND...
IT WASN'T JUST THE SHIP... OR THE MONEY. IT WAS ALL THE STUFF. SEVERAL MONTHS OF YOUR LIFE.
AND THE MEMORIES!
TONY...
I CAN SEE HOW IT MUST BE LIKE...
...MOURNING.
LIKE LEAVING A PART OF YOURSELF BEHIND.
A BREAK?

YEAH...

YEAH... THAT'S JUST IT!

WHAT?

IT'S NOT A BREAK.

AT ALL.

I COULDN'T CARE LESS.

THAT'S THE WEIRD PART.

OH.

BZZT! MD-12, THIS IS PCIM! MD-12! RESPOND! BZZT!

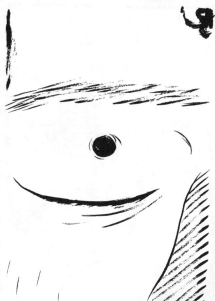

BZZT... DARNELLE! DO YOU COPY? BZZT... YOU MUST BE THERE! BZZ...

BZZT! SEND US A SIGNAL! ANYTHING AT ALL! BZZT!

239

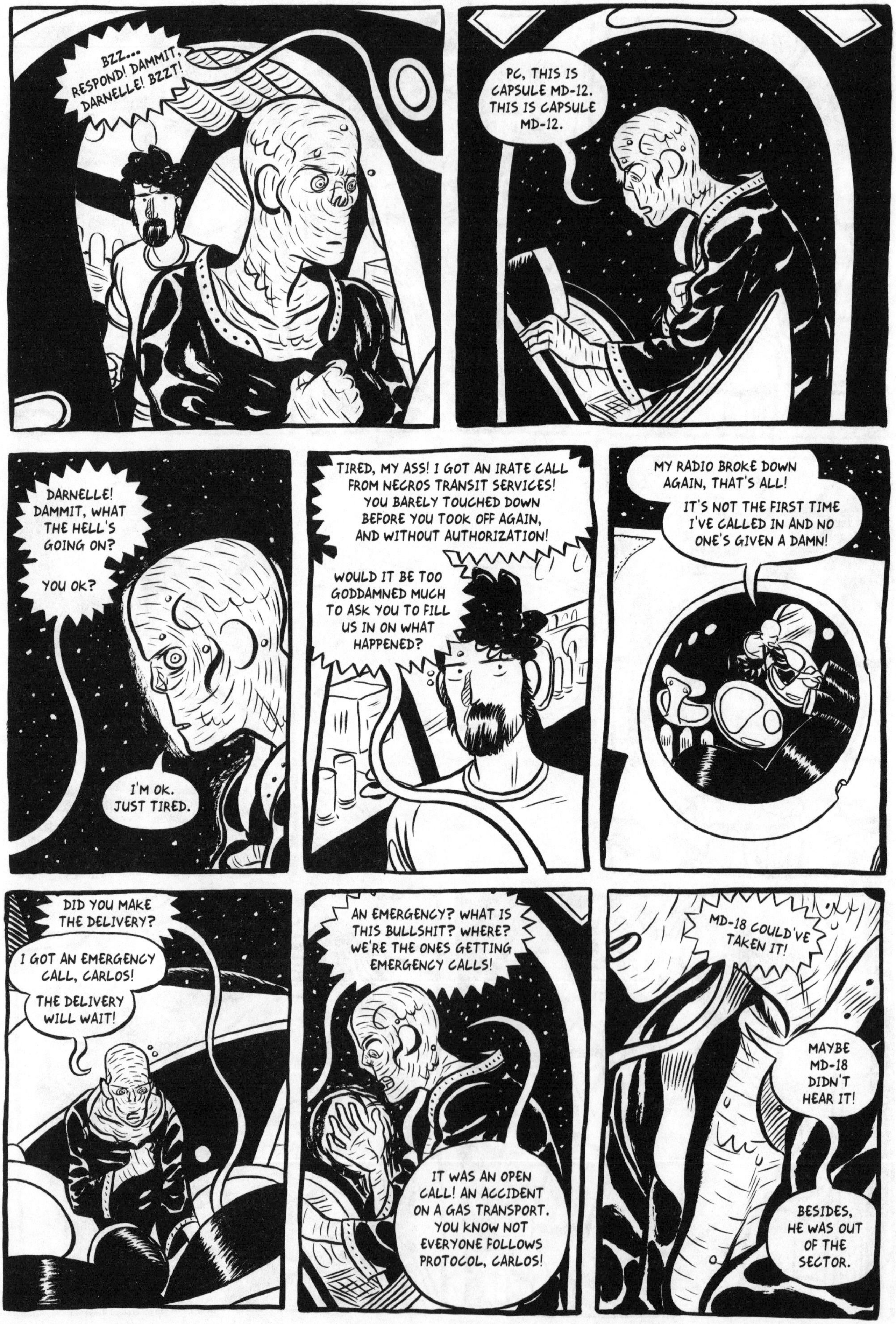
BZZ... RESPOND! DAMMIT, DARNELLE! BZZT!
PC, THIS IS CAPSULE MD-12. THIS IS CAPSULE MD-12.
DARNELLE! DAMMIT, WHAT THE HELL'S GOING ON?
YOU OK?
I'M OK. JUST TIRED.
TIRED, MY ASS! I GOT AN IRATE CALL FROM NECROS TRANSIT SERVICES! YOU BARELY TOUCHED DOWN BEFORE YOU TOOK OFF AGAIN, AND WITHOUT AUTHORIZATION!
WOULD IT BE TOO GODDAMNED MUCH TO ASK YOU TO FILL US IN ON WHAT HAPPENED?
MY RADIO BROKE DOWN AGAIN, THAT'S ALL!
IT'S NOT THE FIRST TIME I'VE CALLED IN AND NO ONE'S GIVEN A DAMN!
DID YOU MAKE THE DELIVERY?
I GOT AN EMERGENCY CALL, CARLOS!
THE DELIVERY WILL WAIT!
AN EMERGENCY? WHAT IS THIS BULLSHIT? WHERE? WE'RE THE ONES GETTING EMERGENCY CALLS!
IT WAS AN OPEN CALL! AN ACCIDENT ON A GAS TRANSPORT. YOU KNOW NOT EVERYONE FOLLOWS PROTOCOL, CARLOS!
MD-18 COULD'VE TAKEN IT!
MAYBE MD-18 DIDN'T HEAR IT!
BESIDES, HE WAS OUT OF THE SECTOR.

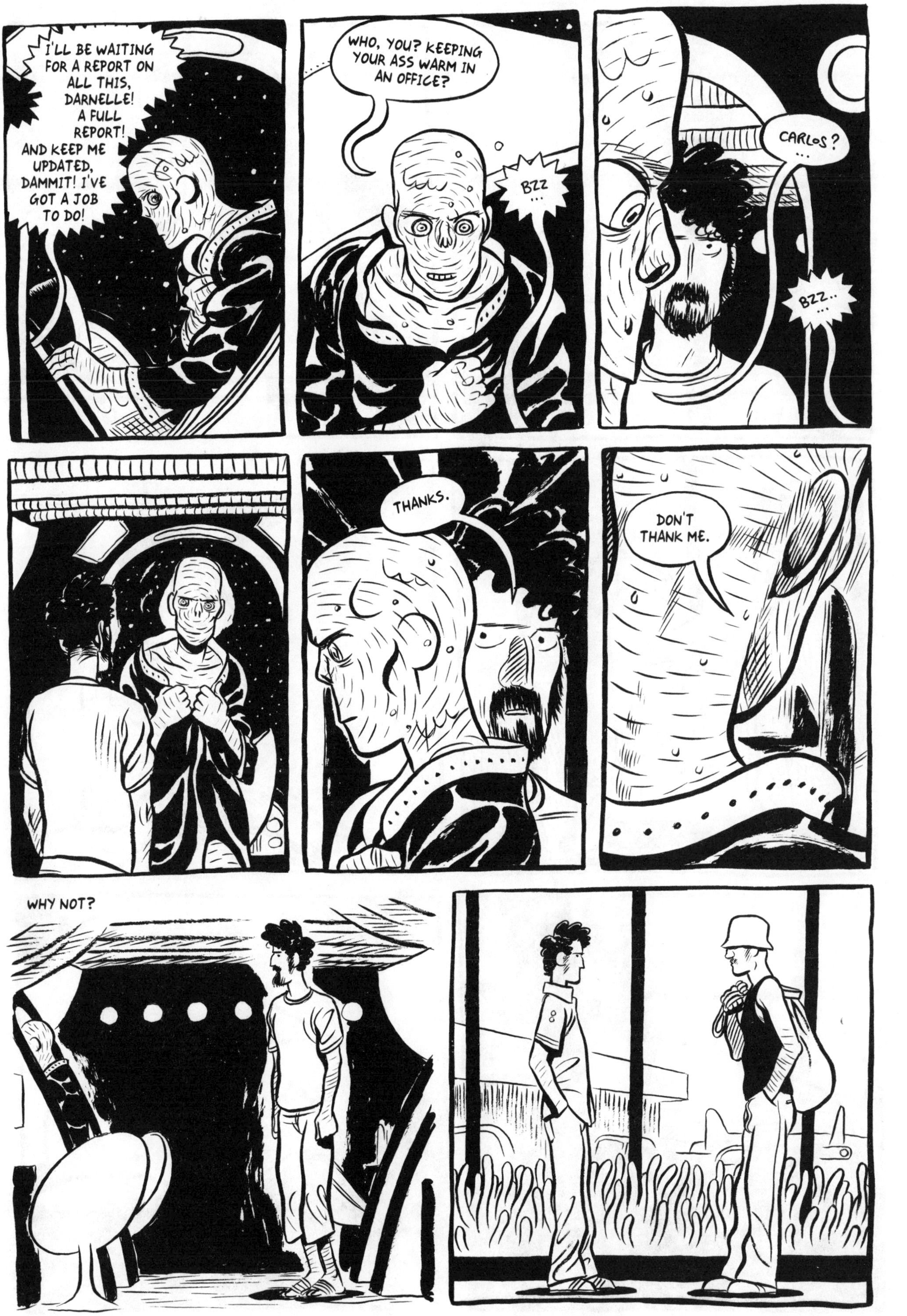
I'LL BE WAITING FOR A REPORT ON ALL THIS, DARNELLE! A FULL REPORT!
AND KEEP ME UPDATED, DAMMIT! I'VE GOT A JOB TO DO!
WHO, YOU? KEEPING YOUR ASS WARM IN AN OFFICE?
BZZ ...
CARLOS? ...
BZZ.. ...
THANKS.
DON'T THANK ME.
WHY NOT?

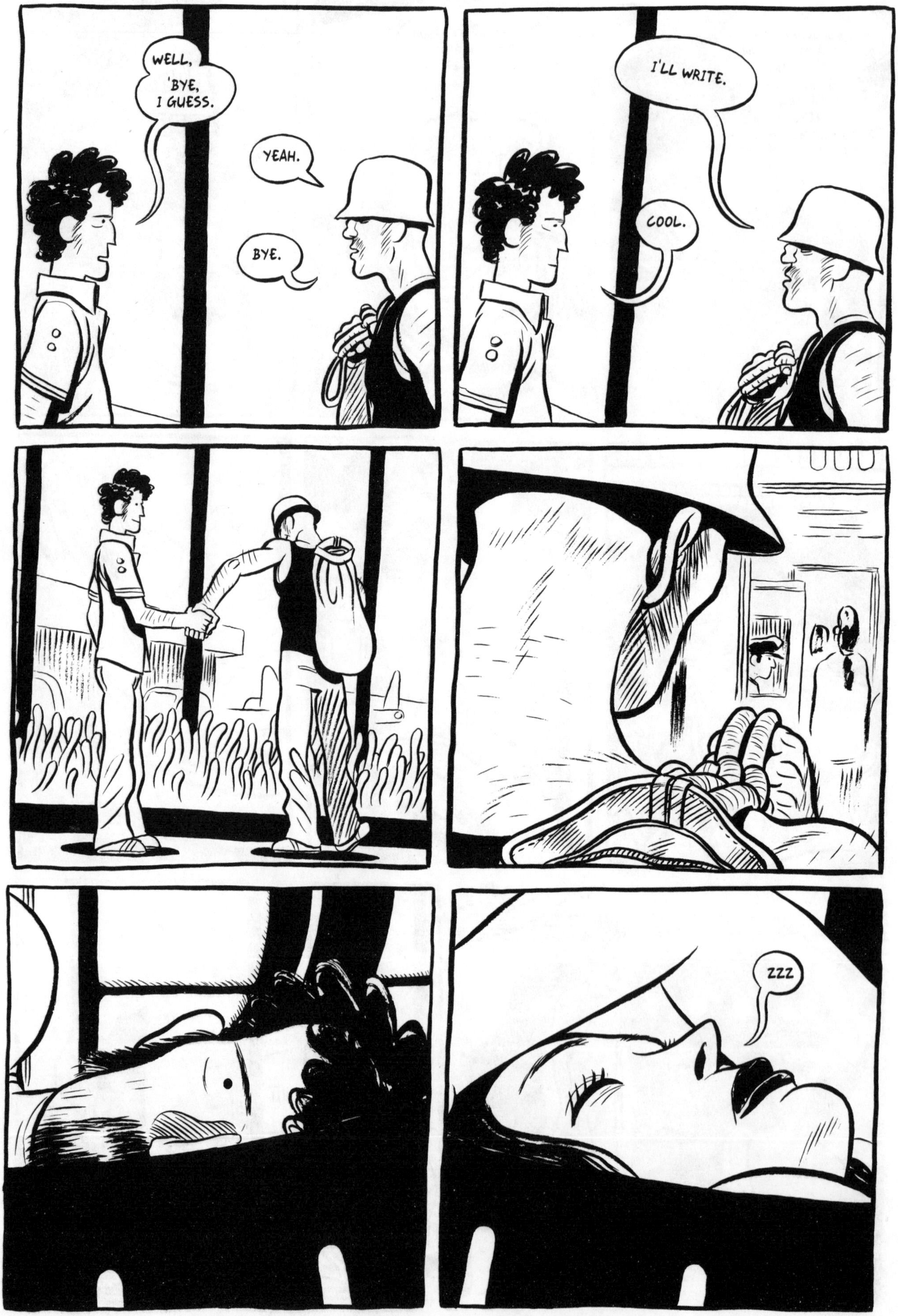
WELL, 'BYE, I GUESS.
YEAH.
BYE.
I'LL WRITE.
COOL.
ZZZ

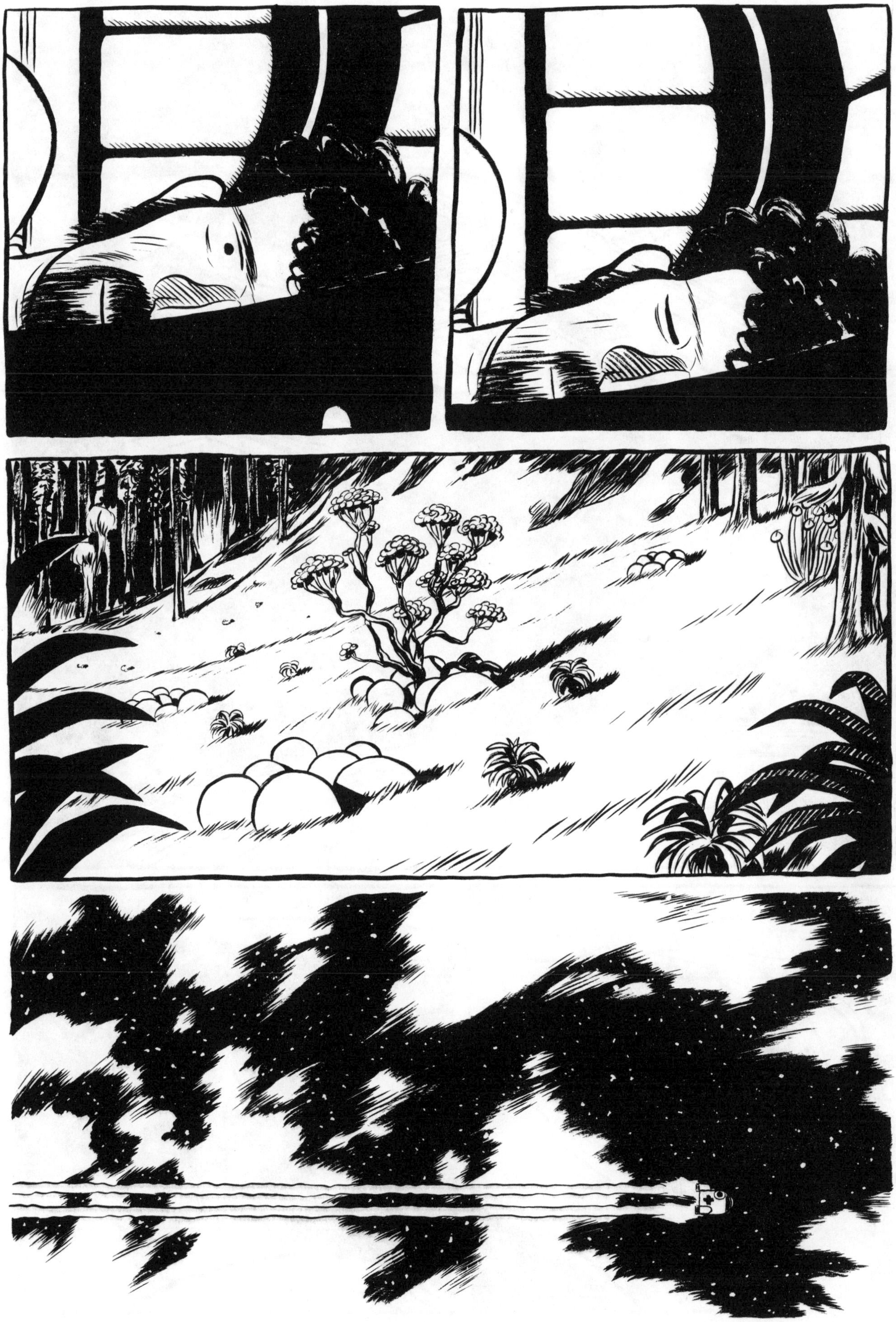

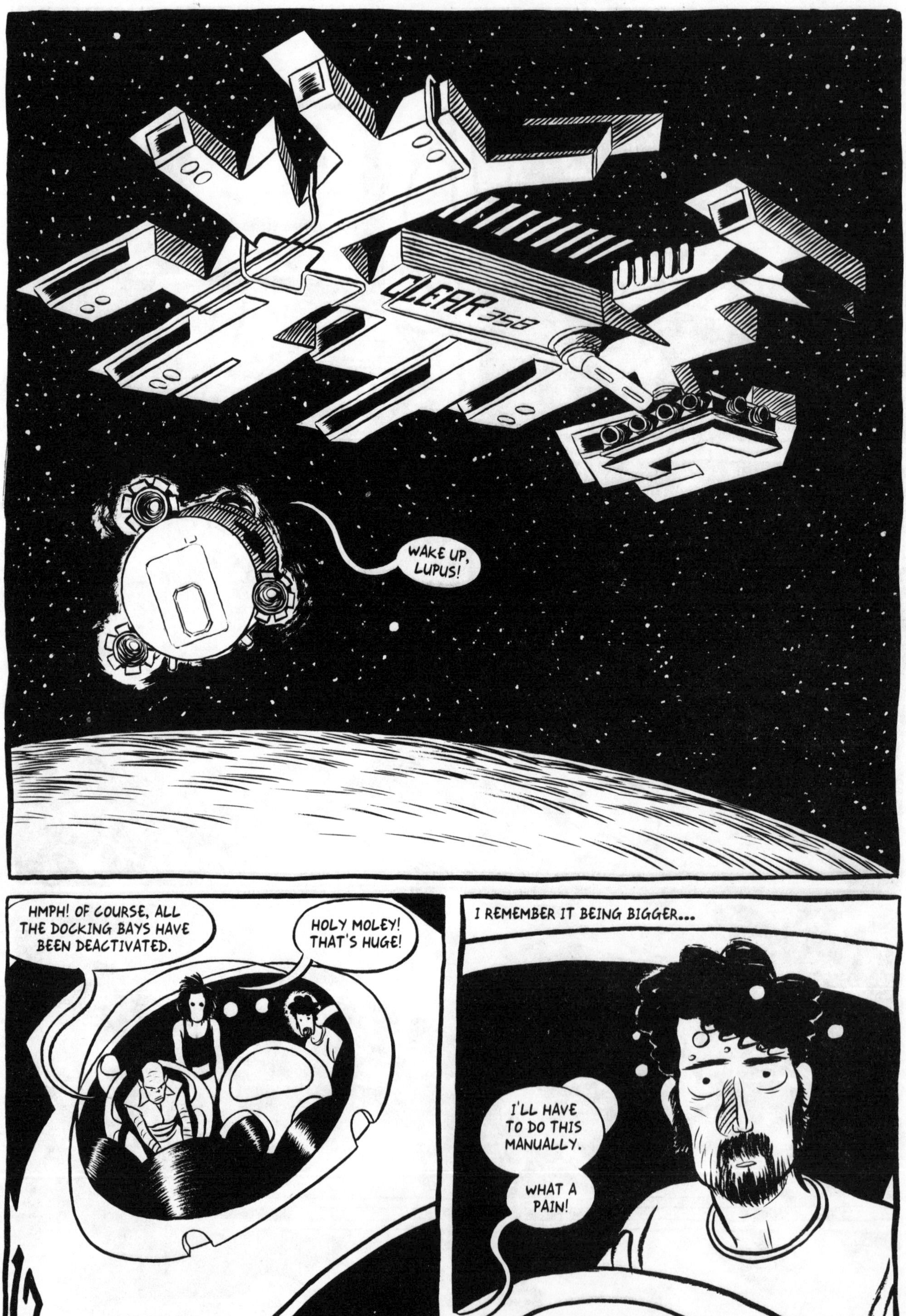
CLEAR 358
WAKE UP, LUPUS!
HMPH! OF COURSE, ALL THE DOCKING BAYS HAVE BEEN DEACTIVATED.
HOLY MOLEY! THAT'S HUGE!
I REMEMBER IT BEING BIGGER...
I'LL HAVE TO DO THIS MANUALLY.
WHAT A PAIN!

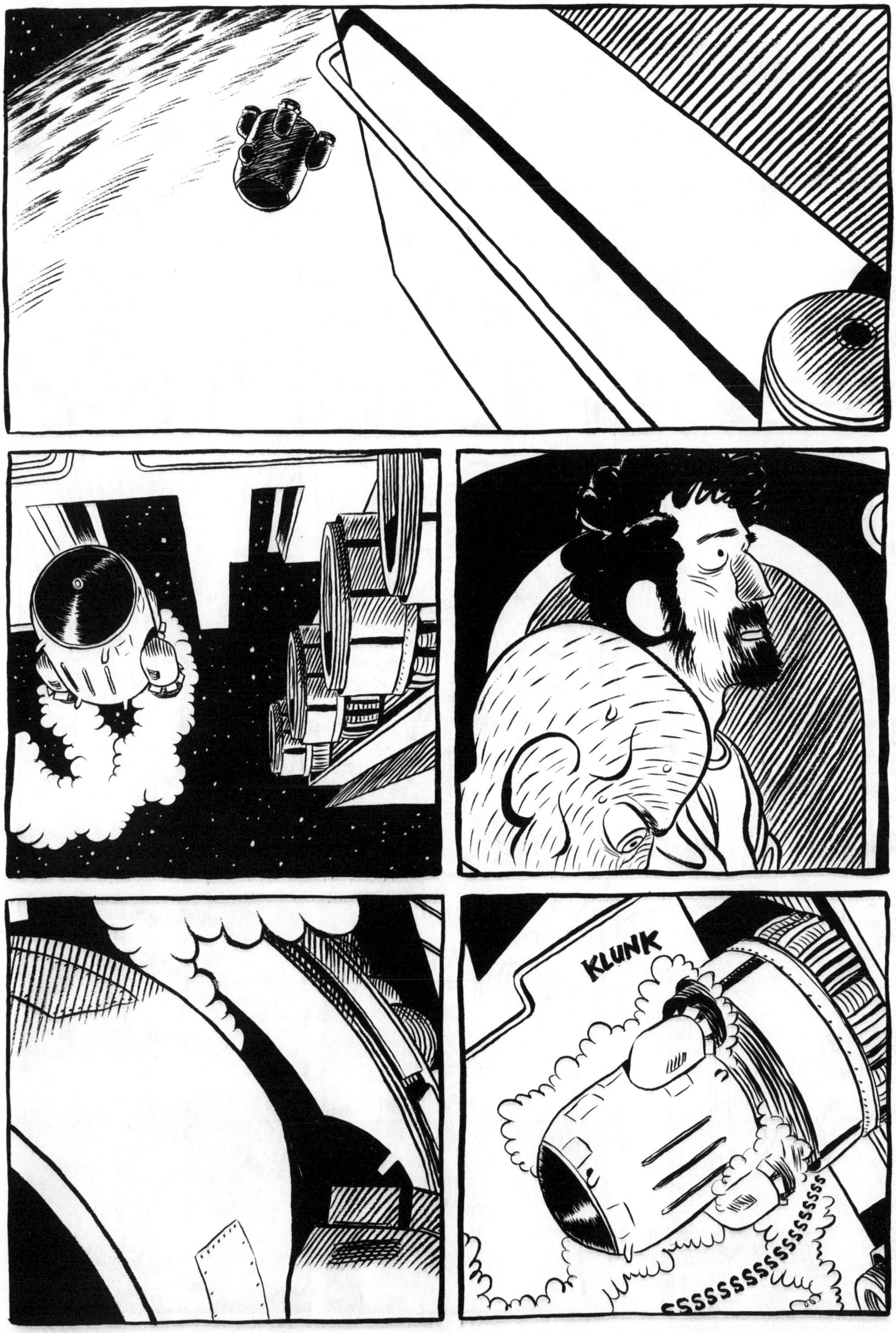
KLUNK
SSSSSSSSSSSSSSSSSSSSSS

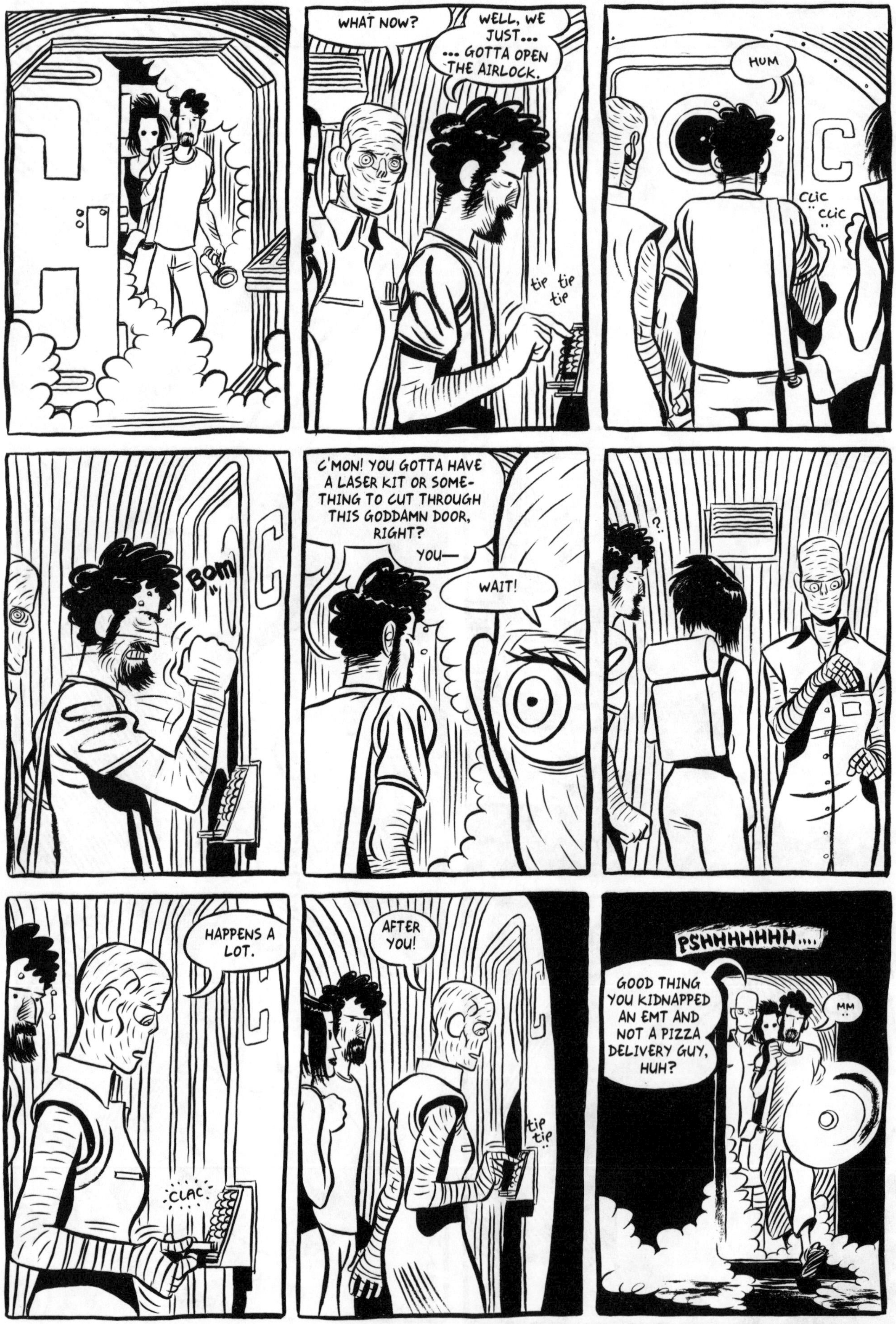
WHAT NOW?
WELL, WE JUST... ...GOTTA OPEN THE AIRLOCK.
tip tip tip
HUM
CLIC CLIC
BOM
C'MON! YOU GOTTA HAVE A LASER KIT OR SOMETHING TO CUT THROUGH THIS GODDAMN DOOR, RIGHT?
YOU—
WAIT!
?
HAPPENS A LOT.
CLAC
AFTER YOU!
tip tip
PSHHHHHHH....
GOOD THING YOU KIDNAPPED AN EMT AND NOT A PIZZA DELIVERY GUY, HUH?
MM

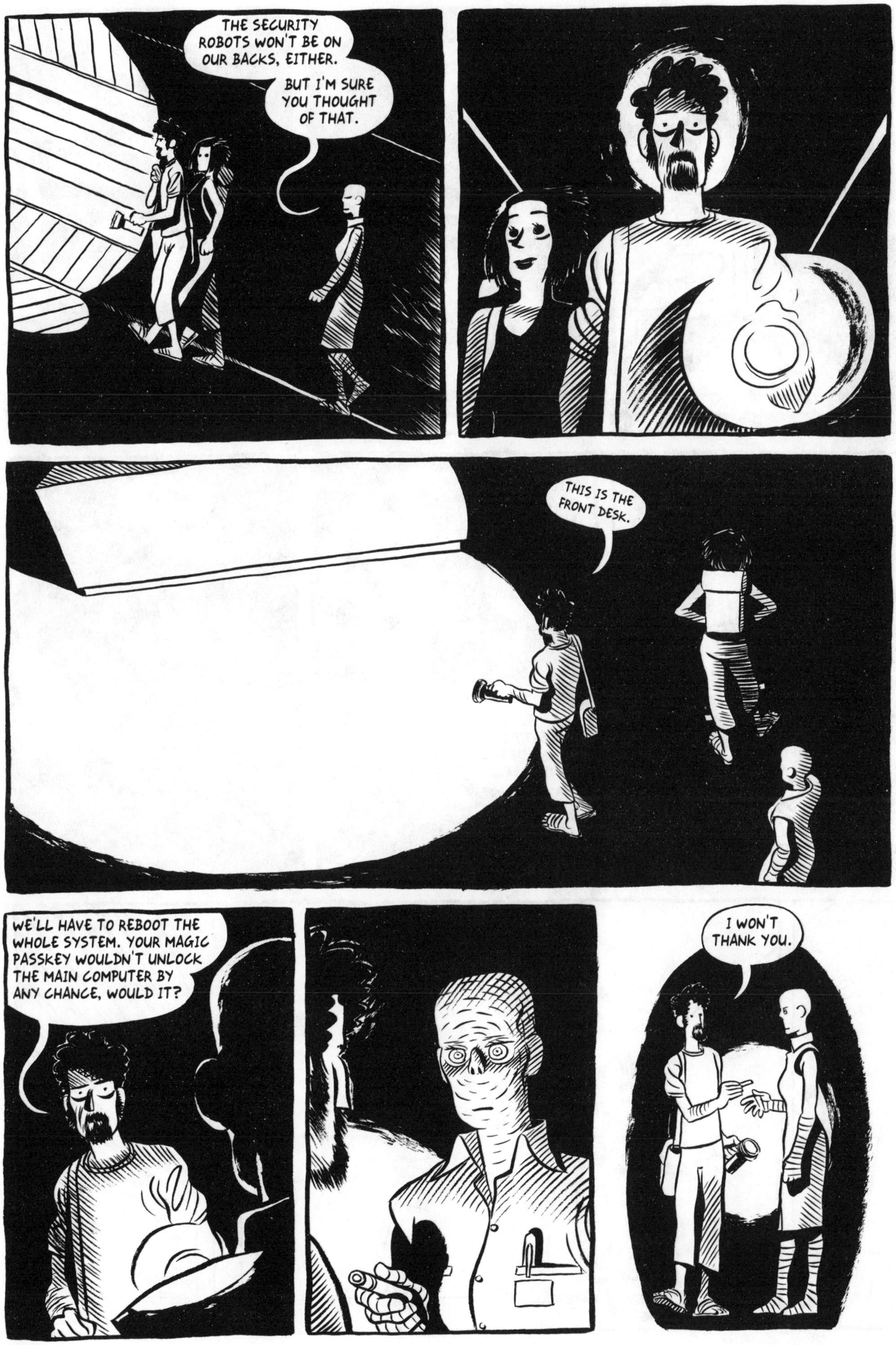
THE SECURITY ROBOTS WON'T BE ON OUR BACKS, EITHER.
BUT I'M SURE YOU THOUGHT OF THAT.
THIS IS THE FRONT DESK.
WE'LL HAVE TO REBOOT THE WHOLE SYSTEM. YOUR MAGIC PASSKEY WOULDN'T UNLOCK THE MAIN COMPUTER BY ANY CHANCE, WOULD IT?
I WON'T THANK YOU.

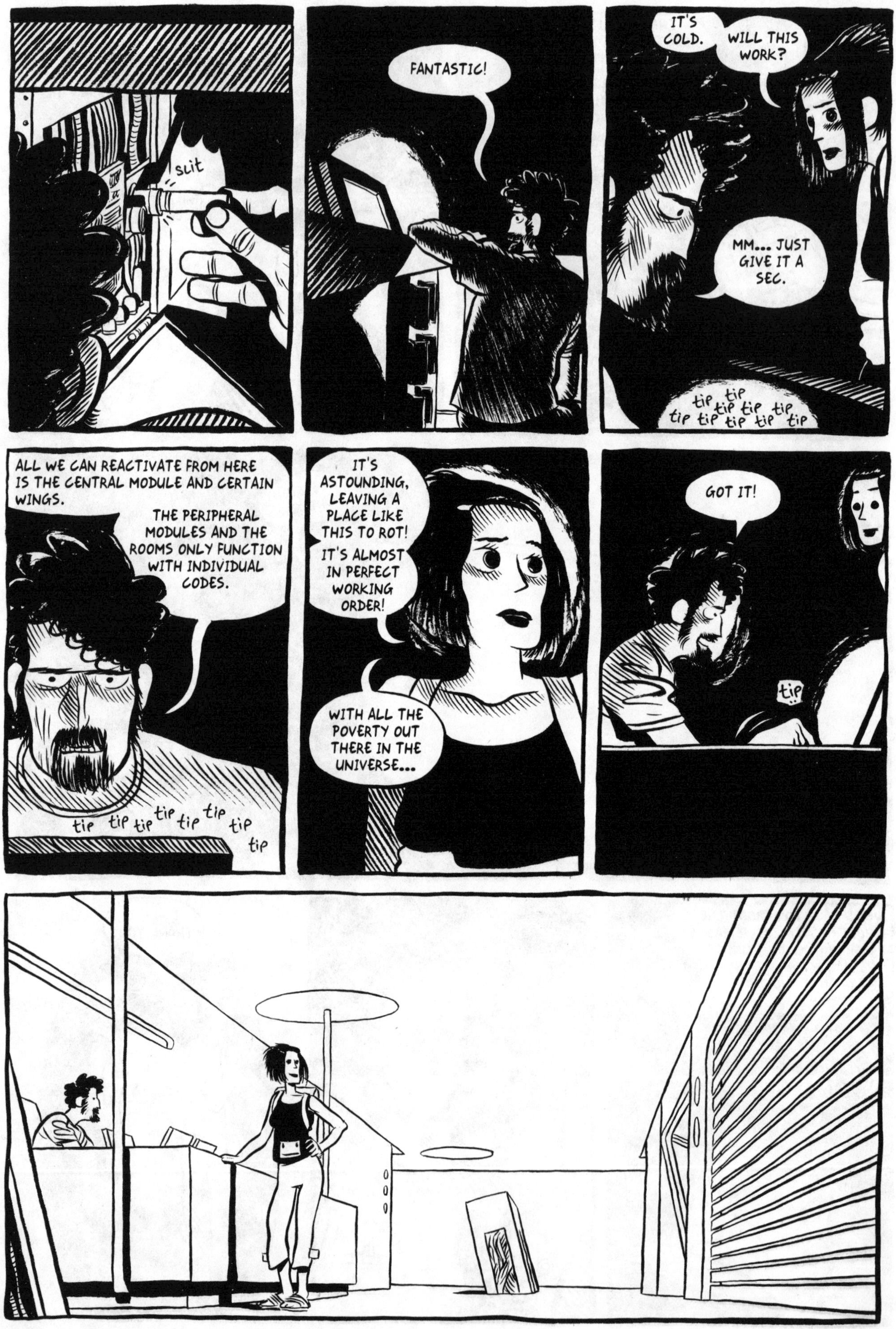
SLIT
FANTASTIC!
IT'S COLD.
WILL THIS WORK?
MM... JUST GIVE IT A SEC.
tip tip tip tip tip tip tip tip tip tip tip
ALL WE CAN REACTIVATE FROM HERE IS THE CENTRAL MODULE AND CERTAIN WINGS.
THE PERIPHERAL MODULES AND THE ROOMS ONLY FUNCTION WITH INDIVIDUAL CODES.
tip tip tip tip tip tip tip tip
IT'S ASTOUNDING, LEAVING A PLACE LIKE THIS TO ROT!
IT'S ALMOST IN PERFECT WORKING ORDER!
WITH ALL THE POVERTY OUT THERE IN THE UNIVERSE...
GOT IT!
tip

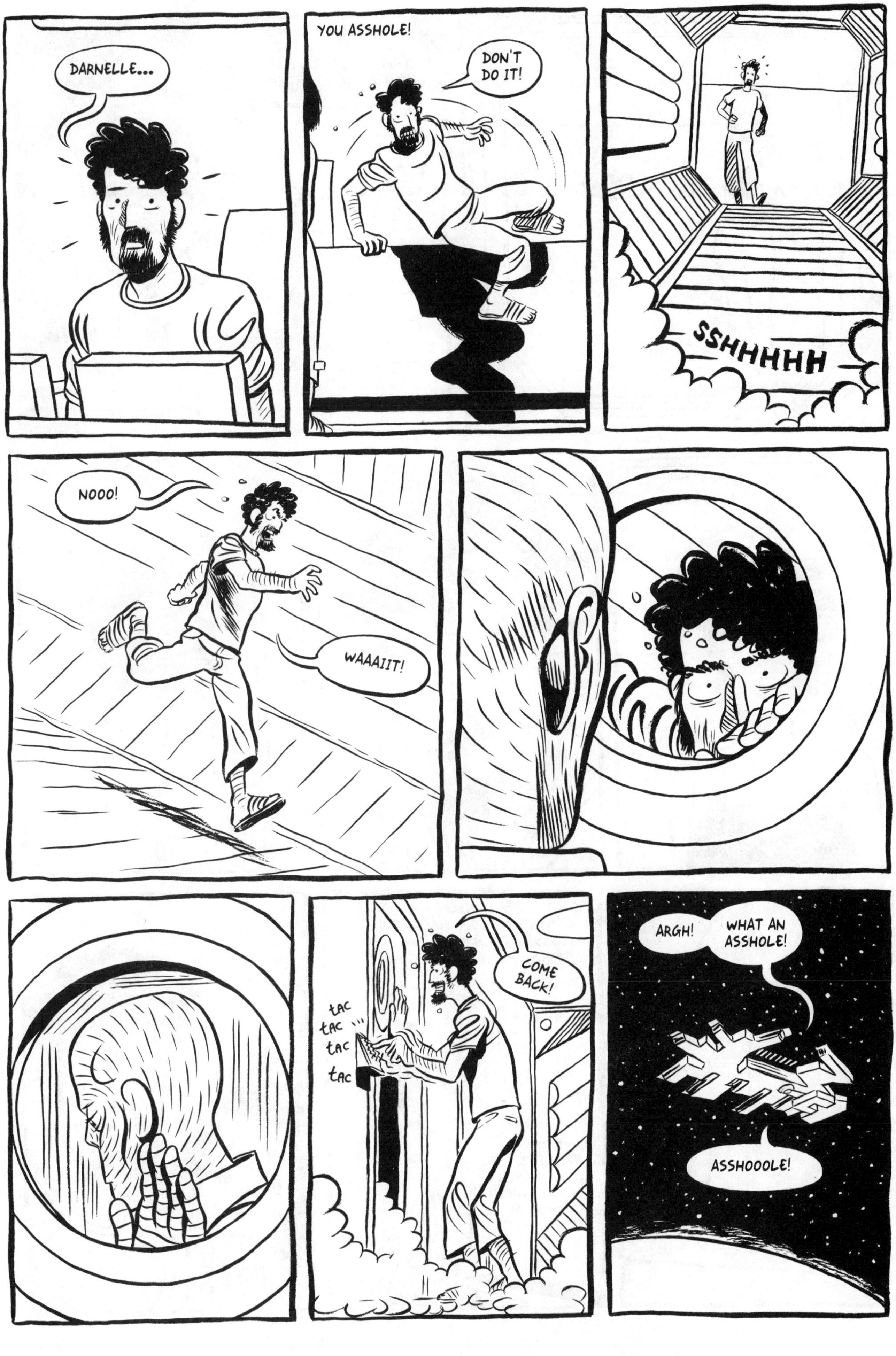
DARNELLE...
YOU ASSHOLE!
DON'T DO IT!
SSHHHHH
NOOO!
WAAAIIT!
COME BACK!
tac
tac
tac
tac
ARGH!
WHAT AN ASSHOLE!
ASSHOOOLE!

LUPUS?..

WE'RE FUCKED, SANAA. THIS TIME WE'RE THROUGH. SHE'S GOING TO TURN US RIGHT IN...

IN TWO DAYS, EVERY COP AND BOUNTY HUNTER IN THE SYSTEM'LL BE HERE CIRCLING US!

MAYBE NOT...

COME LOOK.

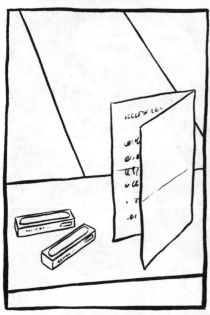

"I WON'T TELL ANYONE. TRUST ME, IT'S NOT MY JOB. YOU'LL TURN YOURSELVES IN WHEN THE TIME COMES. SORRY... GOOD LUCK."

"P.S. I LEFT YOU WHAT YOU COULD'VE STOLEN FROM ME."

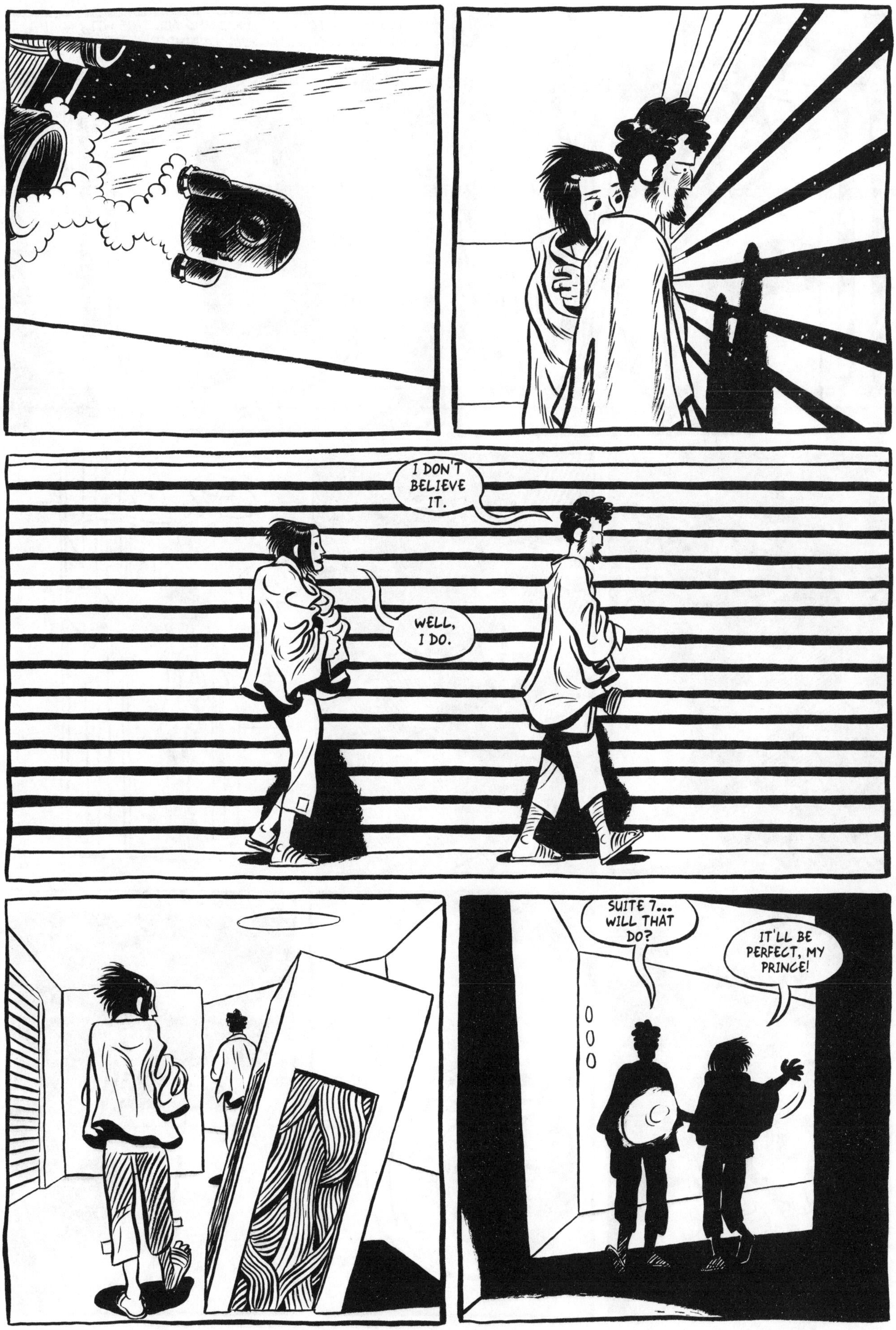
I DON'T BELIEVE IT.
WELL, I DO.
SUITE 7... WILL THAT DO?
IT'LL BE PERFECT, MY PRINCE!

IS THIS GOING TO WORK? I'M DOING ALL THIS WITH SUCH CONFIDENCE... OR TOTAL FOOLHARDINESS. WHAT IF IT DOESN'T WORK?

COME....

LUPUS?

IT'S OVER HERE.

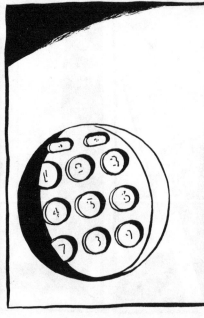

6247A... OR 6742A?

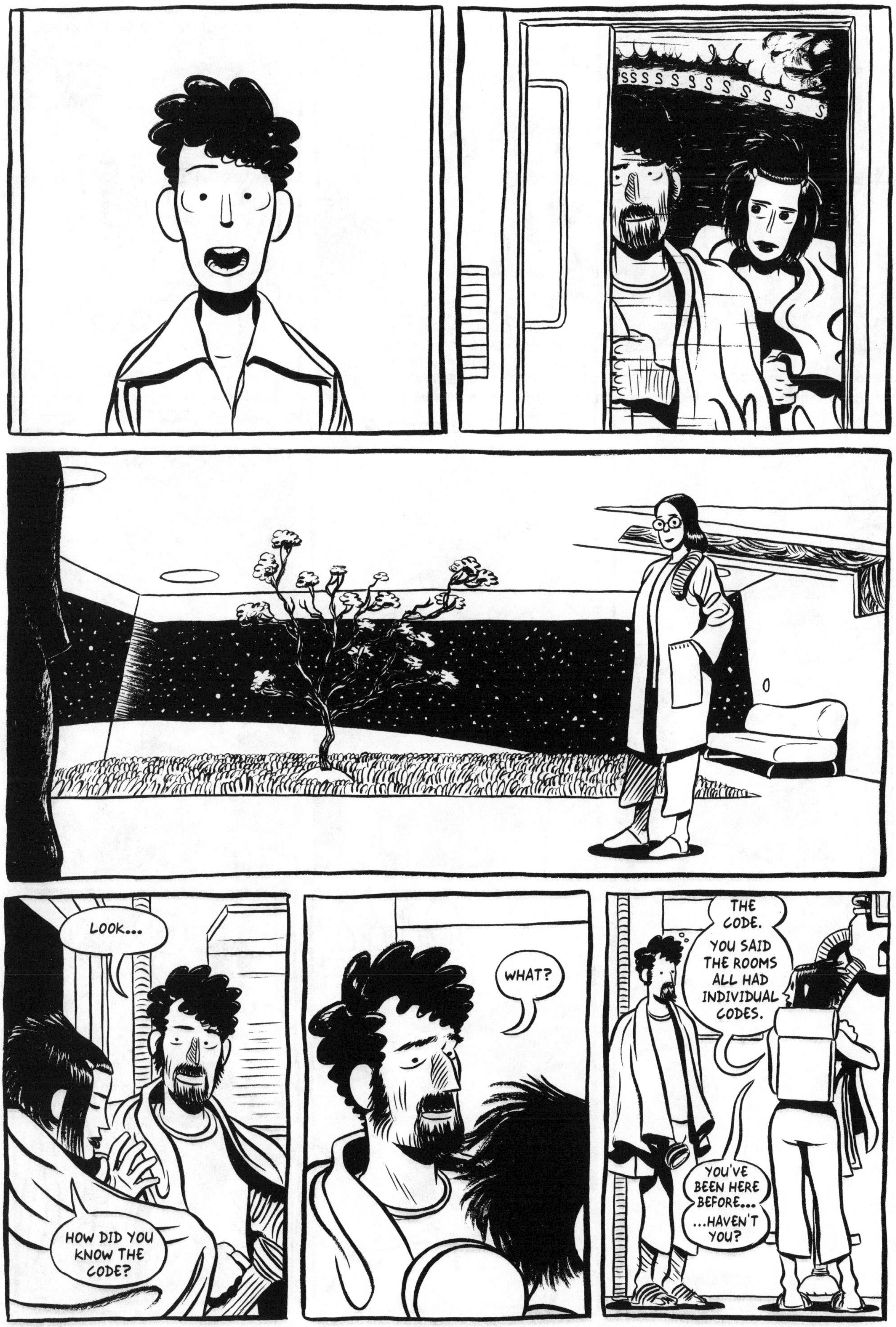
SSSSSSSSSSSS
LOOK...
HOW DID YOU KNOW THE CODE?
WHAT?
THE CODE.
YOU SAID THE ROOMS ALL HAD INDIVIDUAL CODES.
YOU'VE BEEN HERE BEFORE...
...HAVEN'T YOU?

OK, LOOK... YES. I'VE BEEN HERE BEFORE. IT WAS YEARS AGO, ON VACATION WITH MY PARENTS. THERE, I SAID IT. AND YES, I KEEP SECRETS.

I HAVE NO REAL EXPLANATION FOR WHY...

BUT IT'S NOT THAT SIMPLE! IT'S HARD FOR ME TO ADMIT THAT WITH THE ENTIRE UNIVERSE TO PICK FROM, I COULDN'T COME UP WITH ANY PLACE BETTER TO ESCAPE TO THAN SOMEWHERE FROM MY CHILDHOOD!

IT'S RIDICULOUS AND EXASPERATING, BUT IT'S THE BEST I CAN DO.

NOW STOP MAKING A BIG DEAL ABOUT IT, AND JUST LOOK WHERE WE ARE, WILL YA?

OH, MY—

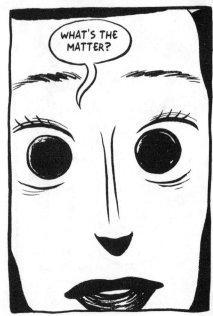

WHAT'S THE MATTER?

AH!

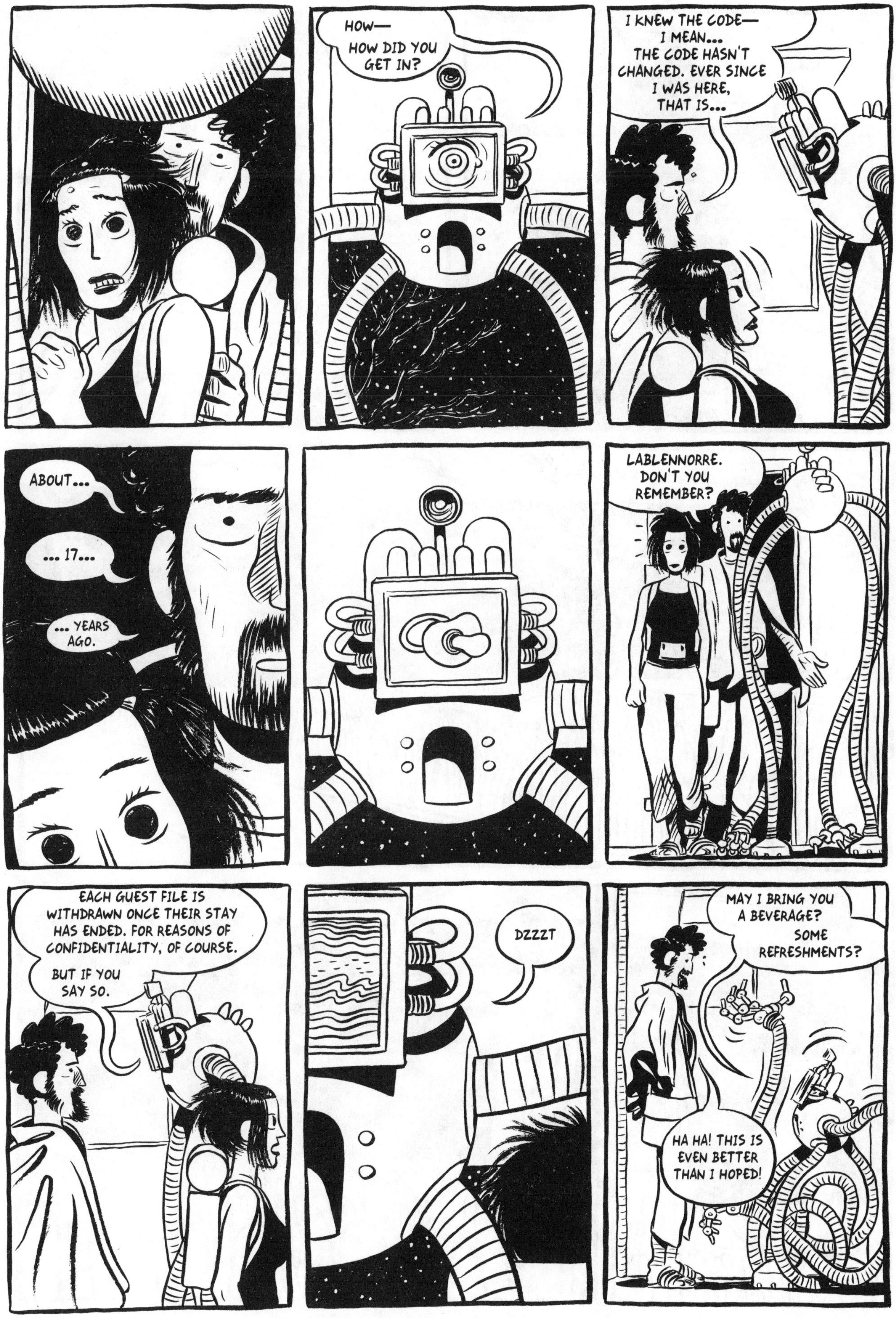
HOW—
HOW DID YOU GET IN?
I KNEW THE CODE— I MEAN... THE CODE HASN'T CHANGED. EVER SINCE I WAS HERE, THAT IS...
ABOUT...
... 17...
... YEARS AGO.
LABLENNORRE. DON'T YOU REMEMBER?
EACH GUEST FILE IS WITHDRAWN ONCE THEIR STAY HAS ENDED. FOR REASONS OF CONFIDENTIALITY, OF COURSE.
BUT IF YOU SAY SO.
DZZZT
MAY I BRING YOU A BEVERAGE?
SOME REFRESHMENTS?
HA HA! THIS IS EVEN BETTER THAN I HOPED!

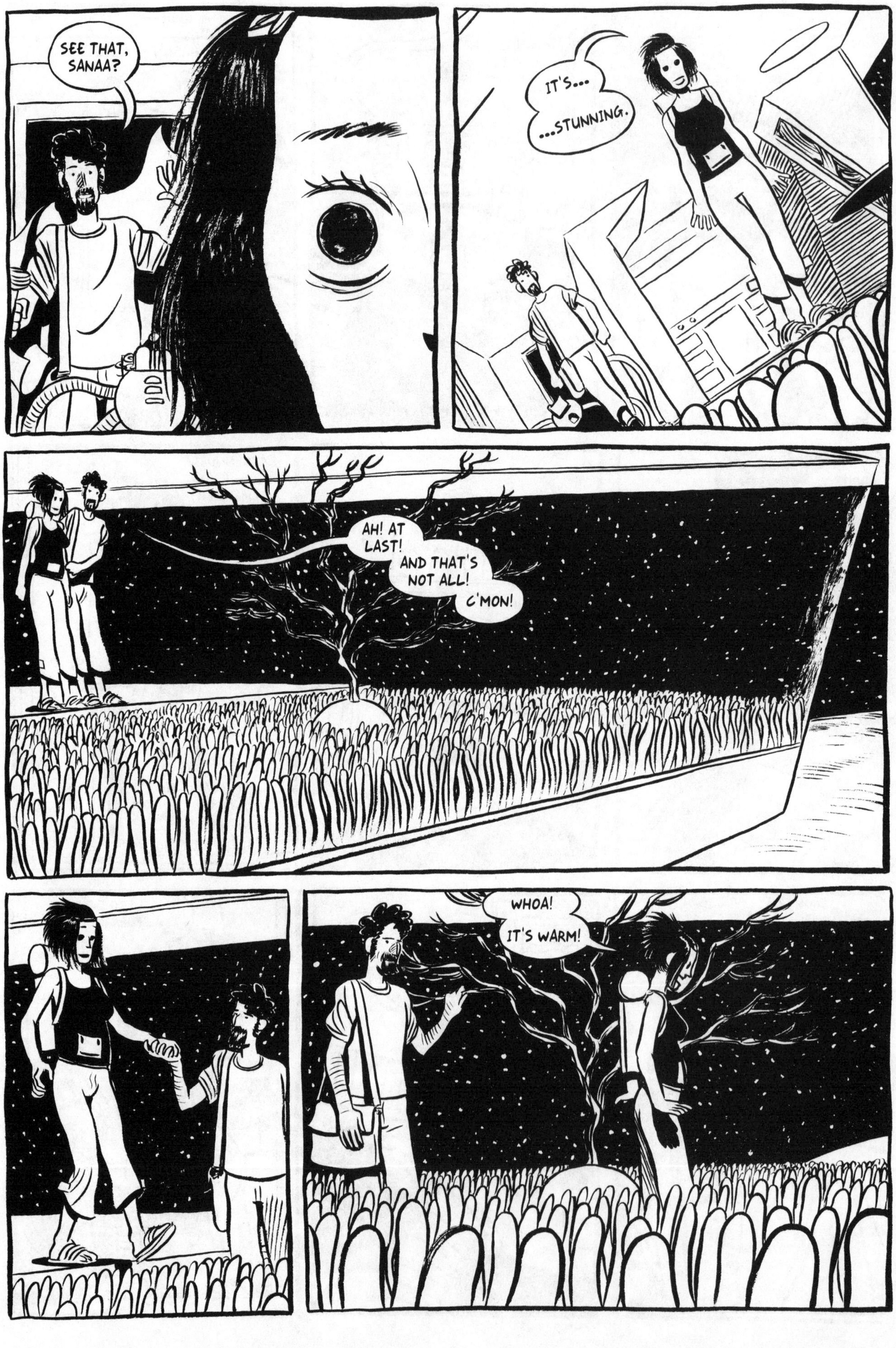
SEE THAT, SANAA?
IT'S...
...STUNNING.
AH! AT LAST!
AND THAT'S NOT ALL!
C'MON!
WHOA!
IT'S WARM!

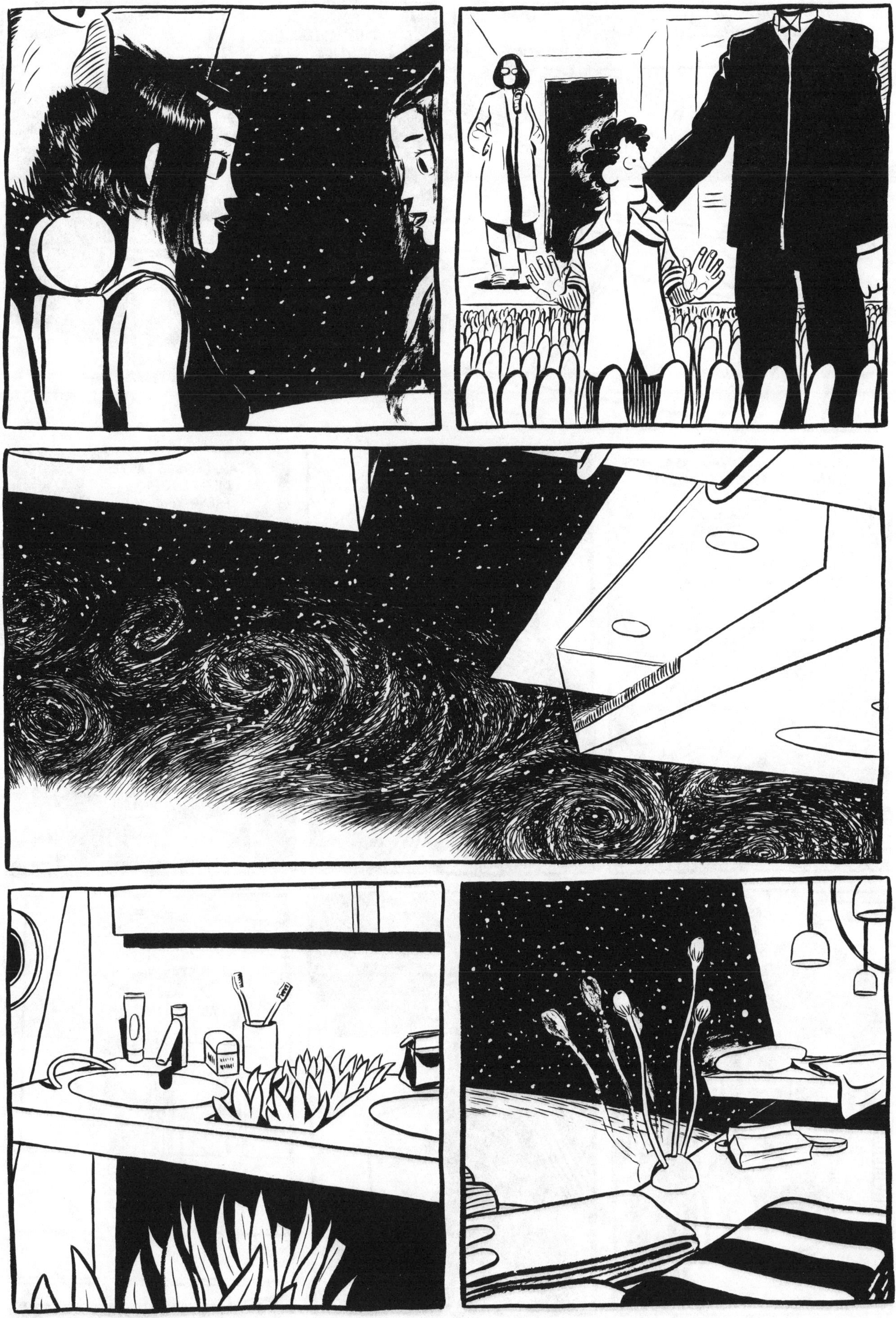

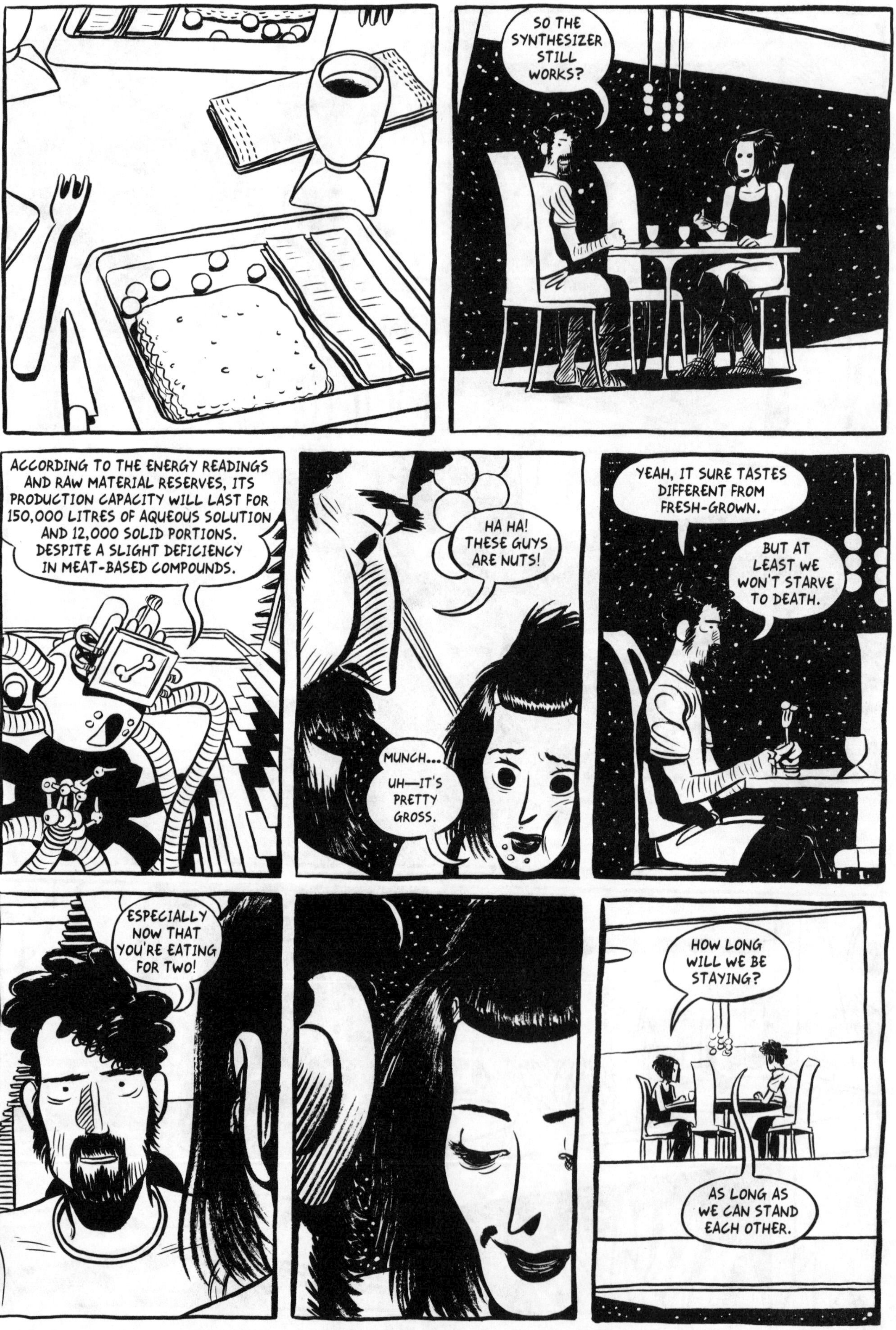
SO THE SYNTHESIZER STILL WORKS?
ACCORDING TO THE ENERGY READINGS AND RAW MATERIAL RESERVES, ITS PRODUCTION CAPACITY WILL LAST FOR 150,000 LITRES OF AQUEOUS SOLUTION AND 12,000 SOLID PORTIONS. DESPITE A SLIGHT DEFICIENCY IN MEAT-BASED COMPOUNDS.
HA HA! THESE GUYS ARE NUTS!
MUNCH...
UH—IT'S PRETTY GROSS.
YEAH, IT SURE TASTES DIFFERENT FROM FRESH-GROWN.
BUT AT LEAST WE WON'T STARVE TO DEATH.
ESPECIALLY NOW THAT YOU'RE EATING FOR TWO!
HOW LONG WILL WE BE STAYING?
AS LONG AS WE CAN STAND EACH OTHER.

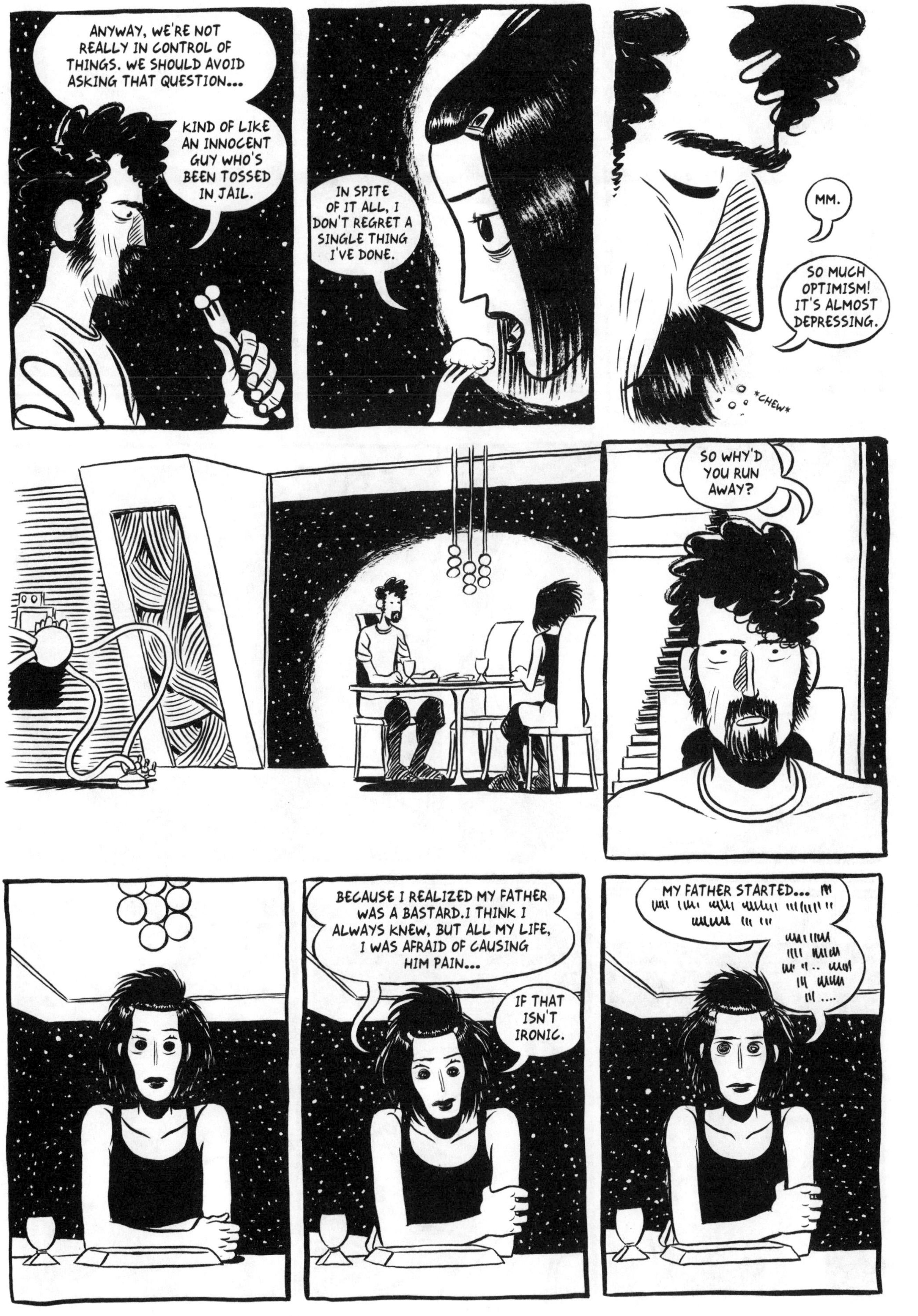

ANYWAY, WE'RE NOT REALLY IN CONTROL OF THINGS. WE SHOULD AVOID ASKING THAT QUESTION...
KIND OF LIKE AN INNOCENT GUY WHO'S BEEN TOSSED IN JAIL.
IN SPITE OF IT ALL, I DON'T REGRET A SINGLE THING I'VE DONE.
MM.
SO MUCH OPTIMISM! IT'S ALMOST DEPRESSING.
CHEW
SO WHY'D YOU RUN AWAY?
BECAUSE I REALIZED MY FATHER WAS A BASTARD. I THINK I ALWAYS KNEW, BUT ALL MY LIFE, I WAS AFRAID OF CAUSING HIM PAIN...
IF THAT ISN'T IRONIC.
MY FATHER STARTED...

LUPUS...
...

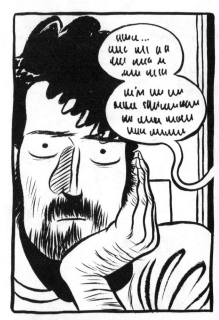

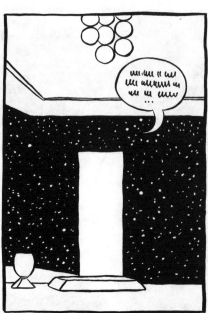

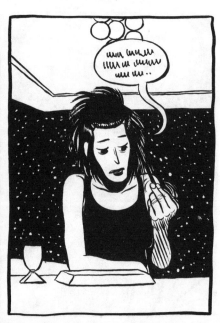

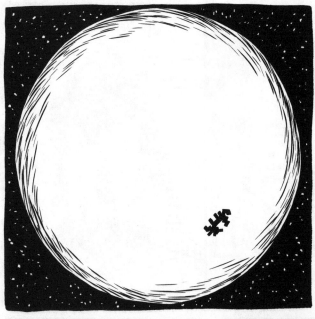

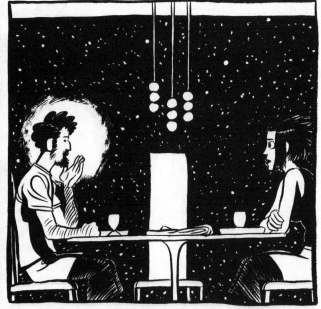

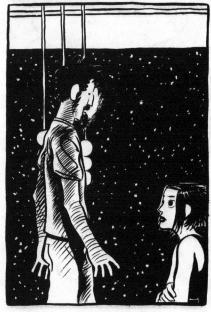

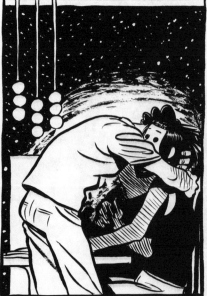

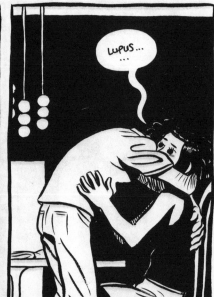

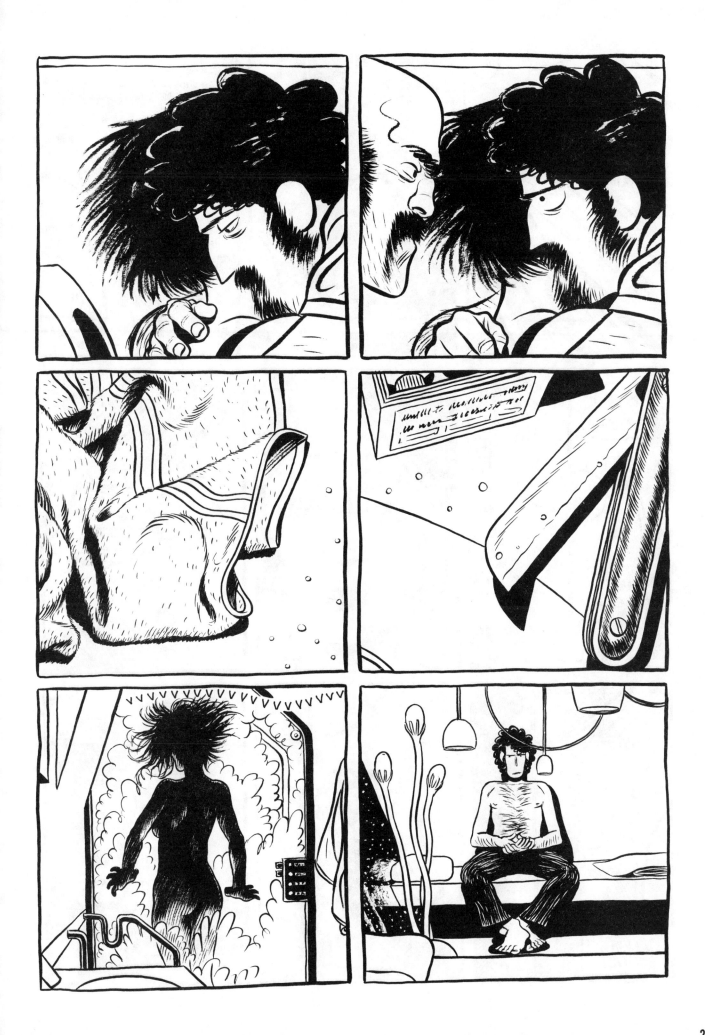

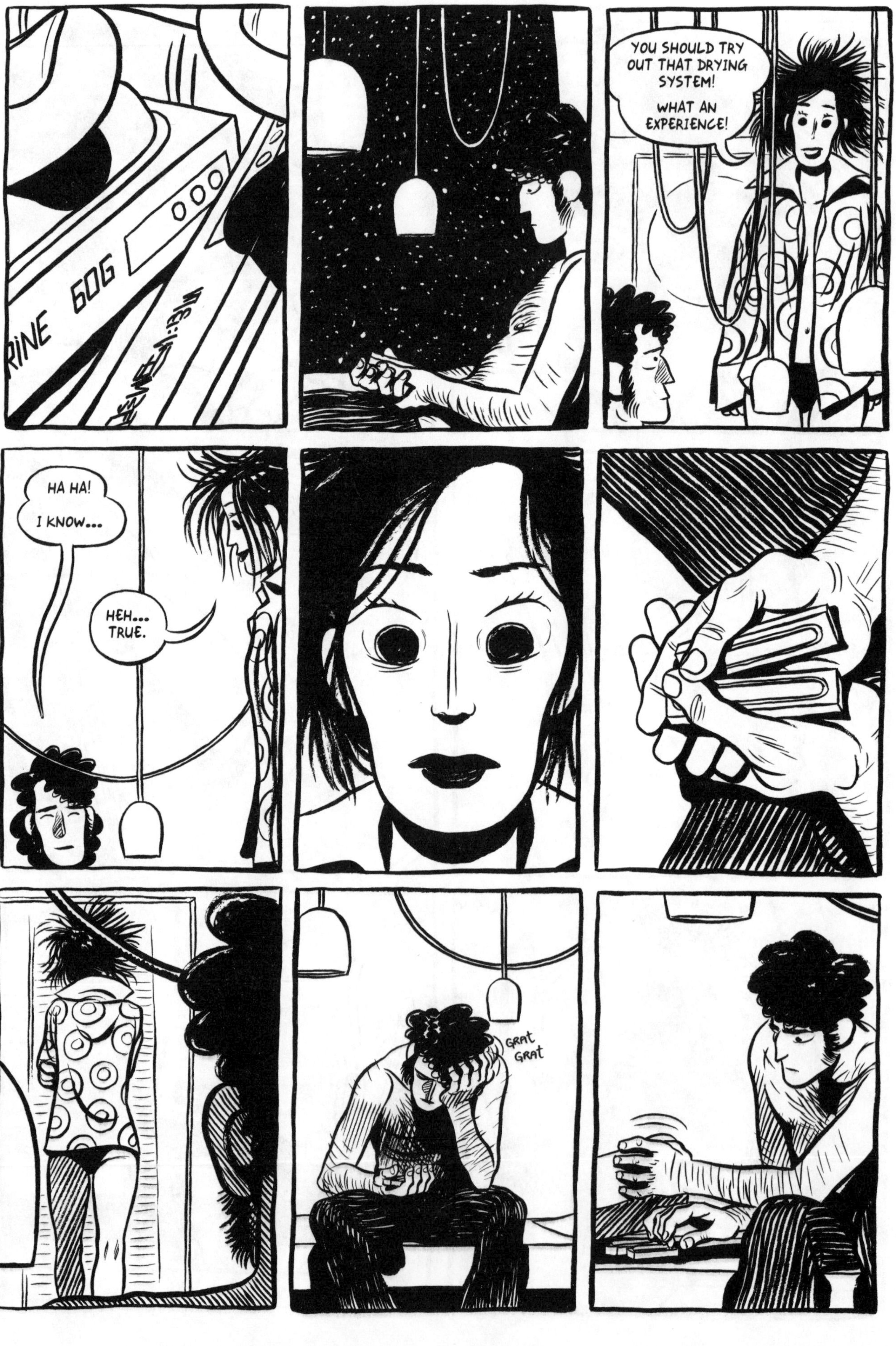
RINE 60G
YOU SHOULD TRY OUT THAT DRYING SYSTEM!
WHAT AN EXPERIENCE!
HA HA!
I KNOW...
HEH... TRUE.
GRAT GRAT

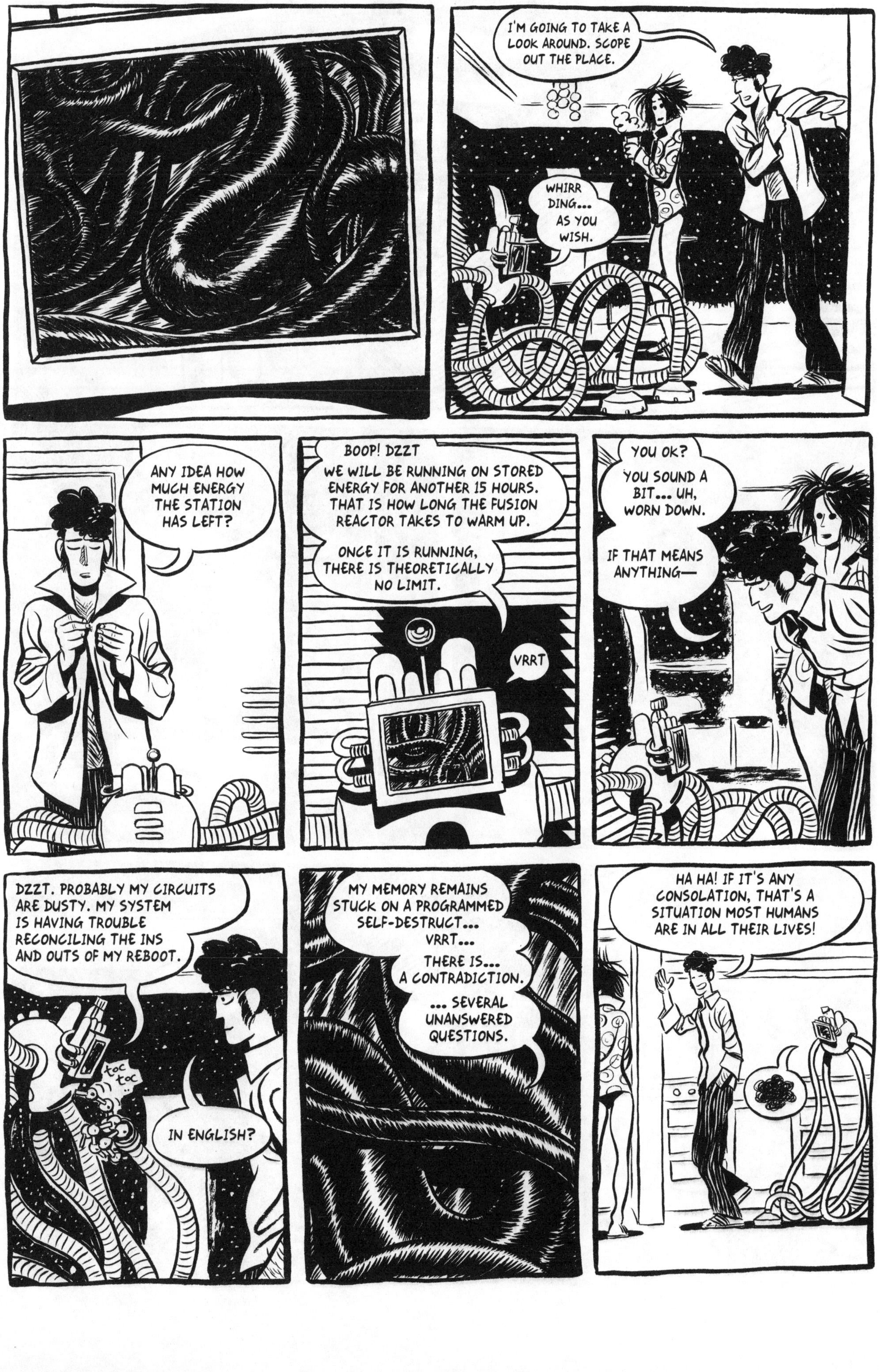

I'M GOING TO TAKE A LOOK AROUND. SCOPE OUT THE PLACE.
WHIRR DING... AS YOU WISH.
ANY IDEA HOW MUCH ENERGY THE STATION HAS LEFT?
BOOP! DZZT
WE WILL BE RUNNING ON STORED ENERGY FOR ANOTHER 15 HOURS. THAT IS HOW LONG THE FUSION REACTOR TAKES TO WARM UP.
ONCE IT IS RUNNING, THERE IS THEORETICALLY NO LIMIT.
VRRT
YOU OK?
YOU SOUND A BIT... UH, WORN DOWN.
IF THAT MEANS ANYTHING—
DZZT. PROBABLY MY CIRCUITS ARE DUSTY. MY SYSTEM IS HAVING TROUBLE RECONCILING THE INS AND OUTS OF MY REBOOT.
toc toc
IN ENGLISH?
MY MEMORY REMAINS STUCK ON A PROGRAMMED SELF-DESTRUCT...
VRRT...
THERE IS... A CONTRADICTION.
... SEVERAL UNANSWERED QUESTIONS.
HA HA! IF IT'S ANY CONSOLATION, THAT'S A SITUATION MOST HUMANS ARE IN ALL THEIR LIVES!

SO THAT'S THE LOUNGE...

AH!

THEY EVEN LEFT ALL THE ALCOHOL!

GOOD NEWS!

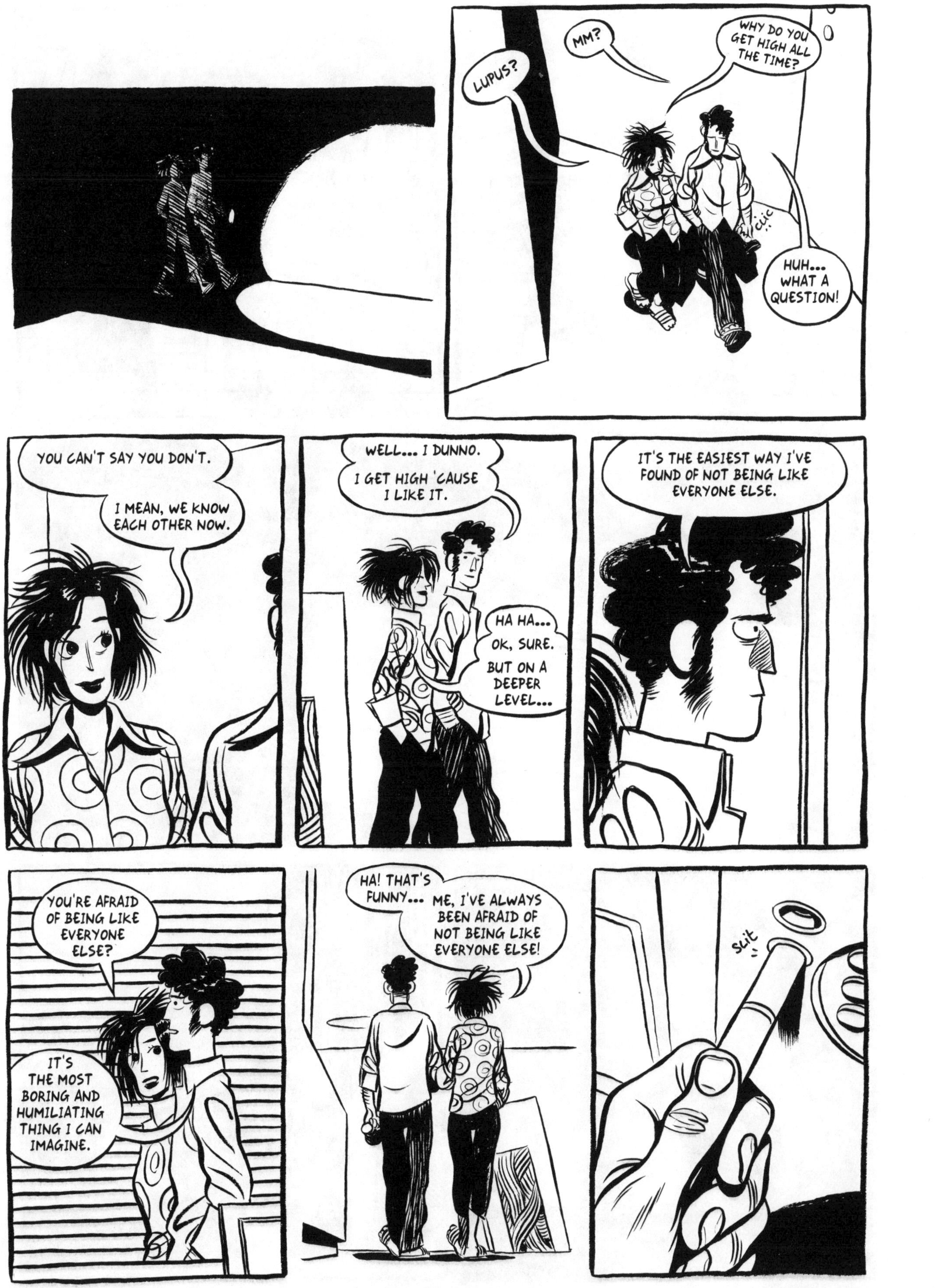
WHY DO YOU GET HIGH ALL THE TIME?
MM?
LUPUS?
CLIC
HUH... WHAT A QUESTION!
YOU CAN'T SAY YOU DON'T.
I MEAN, WE KNOW EACH OTHER NOW.
WELL... I DUNNO.
I GET HIGH 'CAUSE I LIKE IT.
HA HA...
OK, SURE.
BUT ON A DEEPER LEVEL...
IT'S THE EASIEST WAY I'VE FOUND OF NOT BEING LIKE EVERYONE ELSE.
YOU'RE AFRAID OF BEING LIKE EVERYONE ELSE?
IT'S THE MOST BORING AND HUMILIATING THING I CAN IMAGINE.
HA! THAT'S FUNNY...
ME, I'VE ALWAYS BEEN AFRAID OF NOT BEING LIKE EVERYONE ELSE!
SLIT

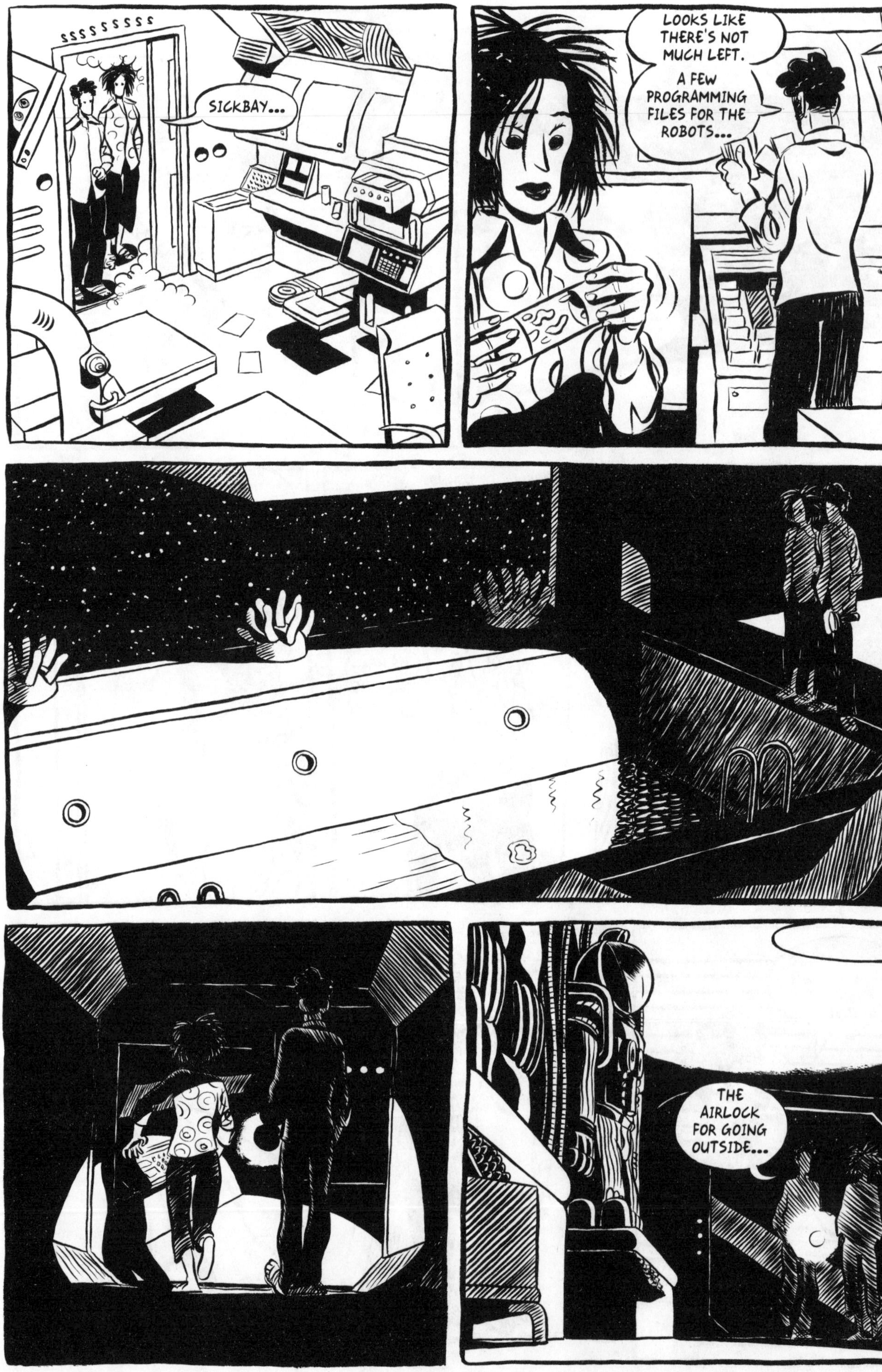
SSSSSSSSS
SICKBAY...
LOOKS LIKE THERE'S NOT MUCH LEFT.
A FEW PROGRAMMING FILES FOR THE ROBOTS...
THE AIRLOCK FOR GOING OUTSIDE...

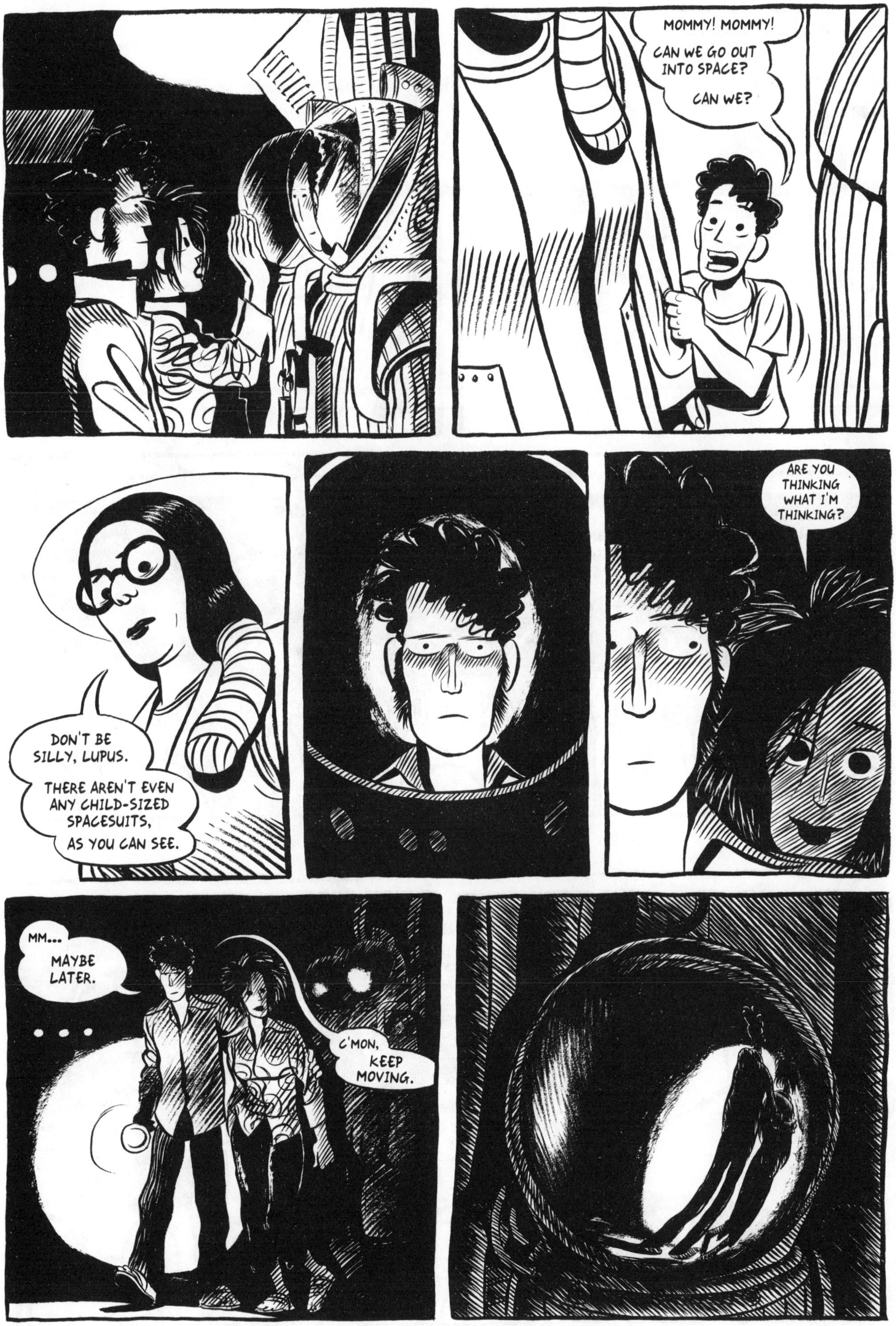
MOMMY! MOMMY!
CAN WE GO OUT INTO SPACE?
CAN WE?
DON'T BE SILLY, LUPUS.
THERE AREN'T EVEN ANY CHILD-SIZED SPACESUITS,
AS YOU CAN SEE.
ARE YOU THINKING WHAT I'M THINKING?
MM... MAYBE LATER.
...
C'MON, KEEP MOVING.

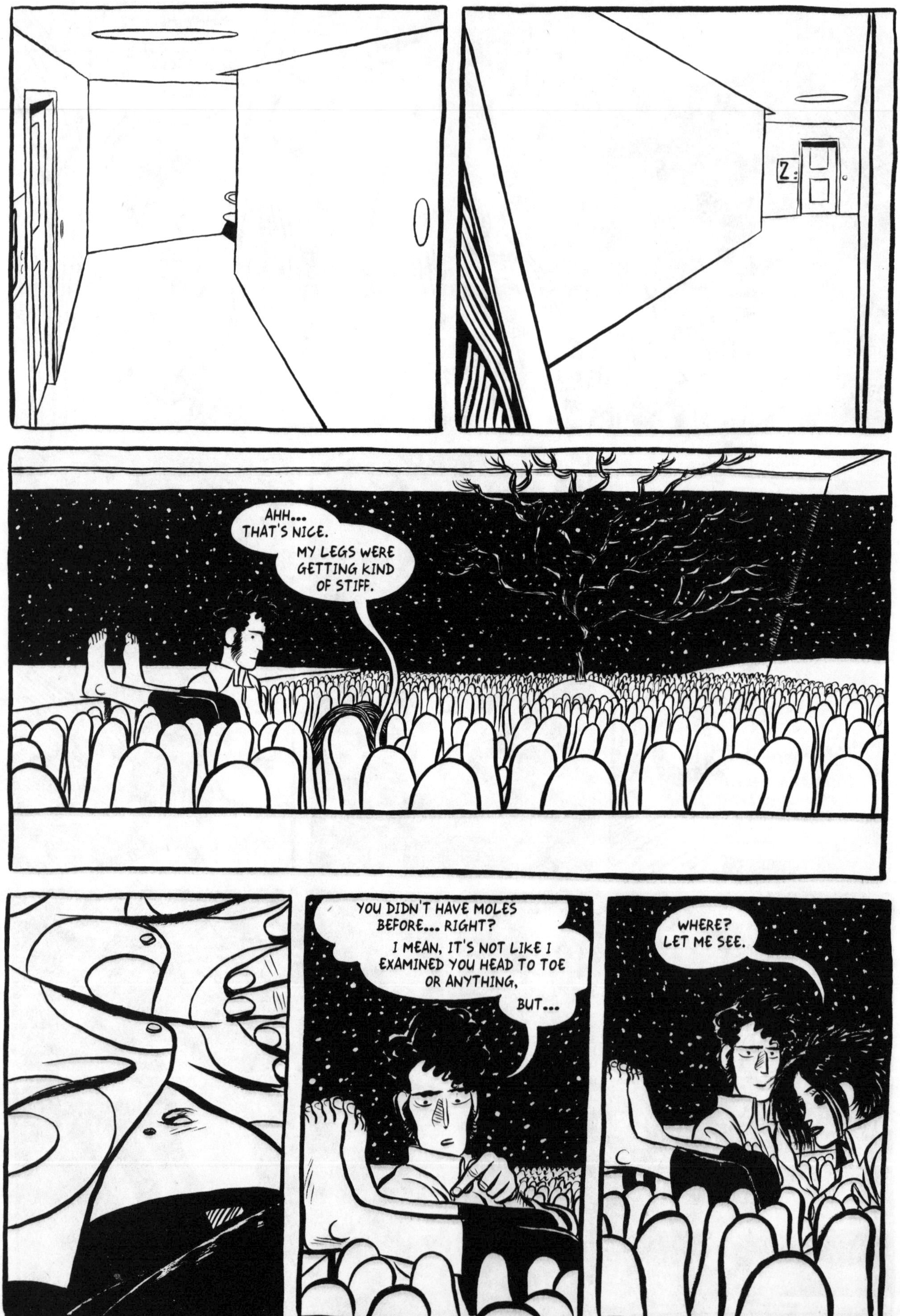
AHH... THAT'S NICE.
MY LEGS WERE GETTING KIND OF STIFF.
YOU DIDN'T HAVE MOLES BEFORE... RIGHT?
I MEAN, IT'S NOT LIKE I EXAMINED YOU HEAD TO TOE OR ANYTHING,
BUT...
WHERE? LET ME SEE.

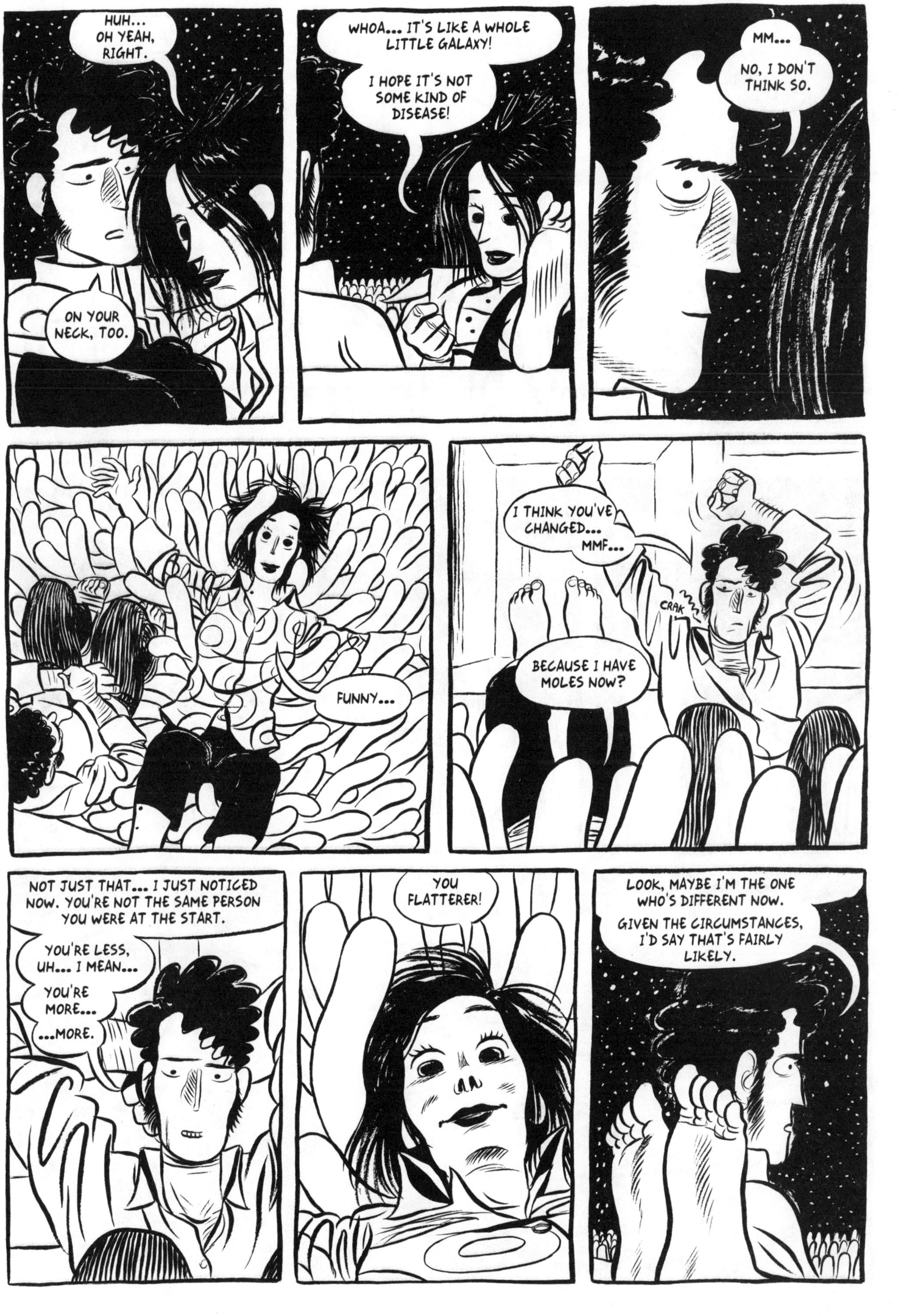
HUH... OH YEAH, RIGHT.
ON YOUR NECK, TOO.
WHOA... IT'S LIKE A WHOLE LITTLE GALAXY!
I HOPE IT'S NOT SOME KIND OF DISEASE!
MM...
NO, I DON'T THINK SO.
FUNNY...
I THINK YOU'VE CHANGED... MMF...
CRAK
BECAUSE I HAVE MOLES NOW?
NOT JUST THAT... I JUST NOTICED NOW. YOU'RE NOT THE SAME PERSON YOU WERE AT THE START.
YOU'RE LESS, UH... I MEAN...
YOU'RE MORE...
...MORE.
YOU FLATTERER!
LOOK, MAYBE I'M THE ONE WHO'S DIFFERENT NOW.
GIVEN THE CIRCUMSTANCES, I'D SAY THAT'S FAIRLY LIKELY.

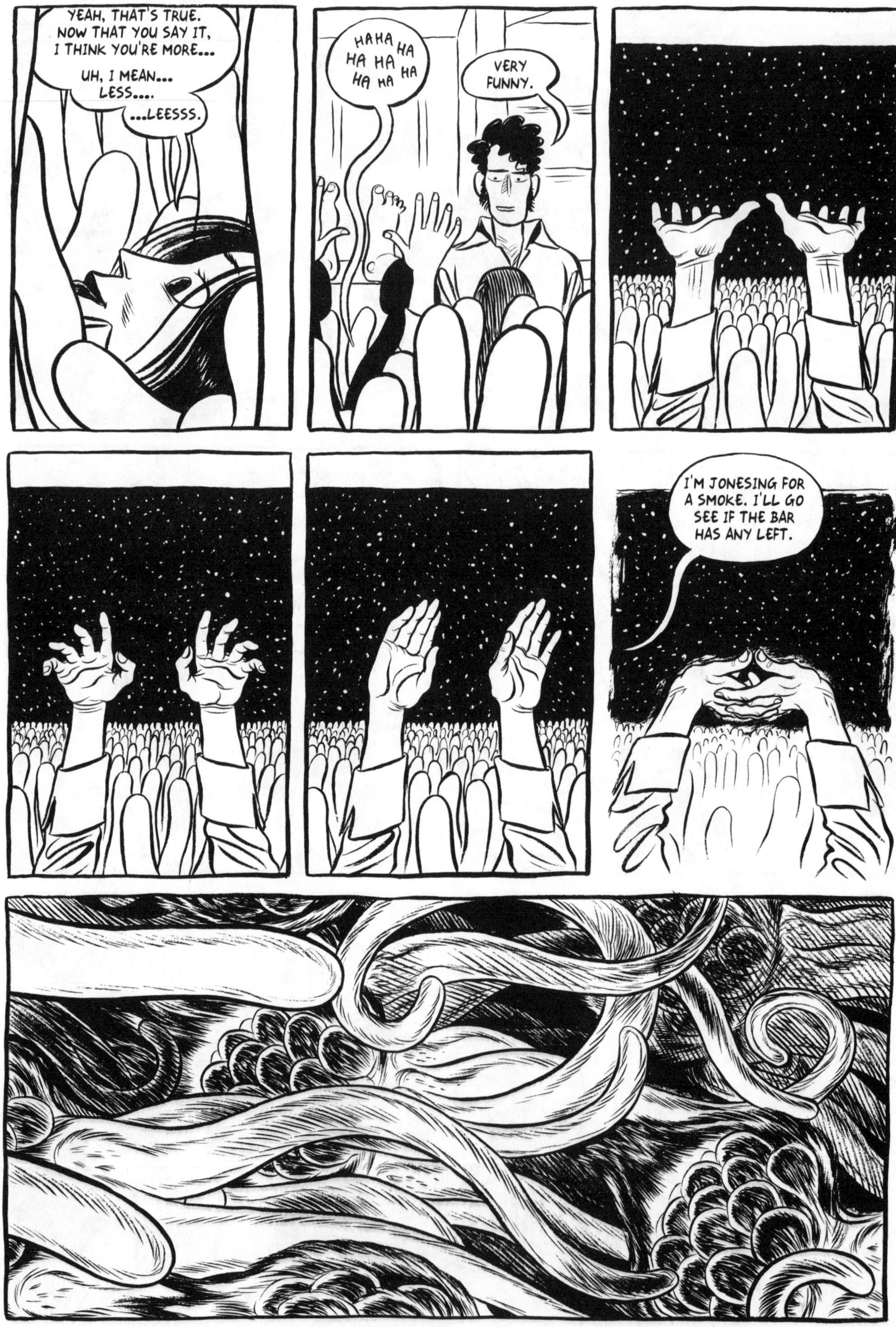
YEAH, THAT'S TRUE. NOW THAT YOU SAY IT, I THINK YOU'RE MORE...
UH, I MEAN... LESS....
...LEESSS.
HAHA HA HA HA HA HA HA HA
VERY FUNNY.
I'M JONESING FOR A SMOKE. I'LL GO SEE IF THE BAR HAS ANY LEFT.

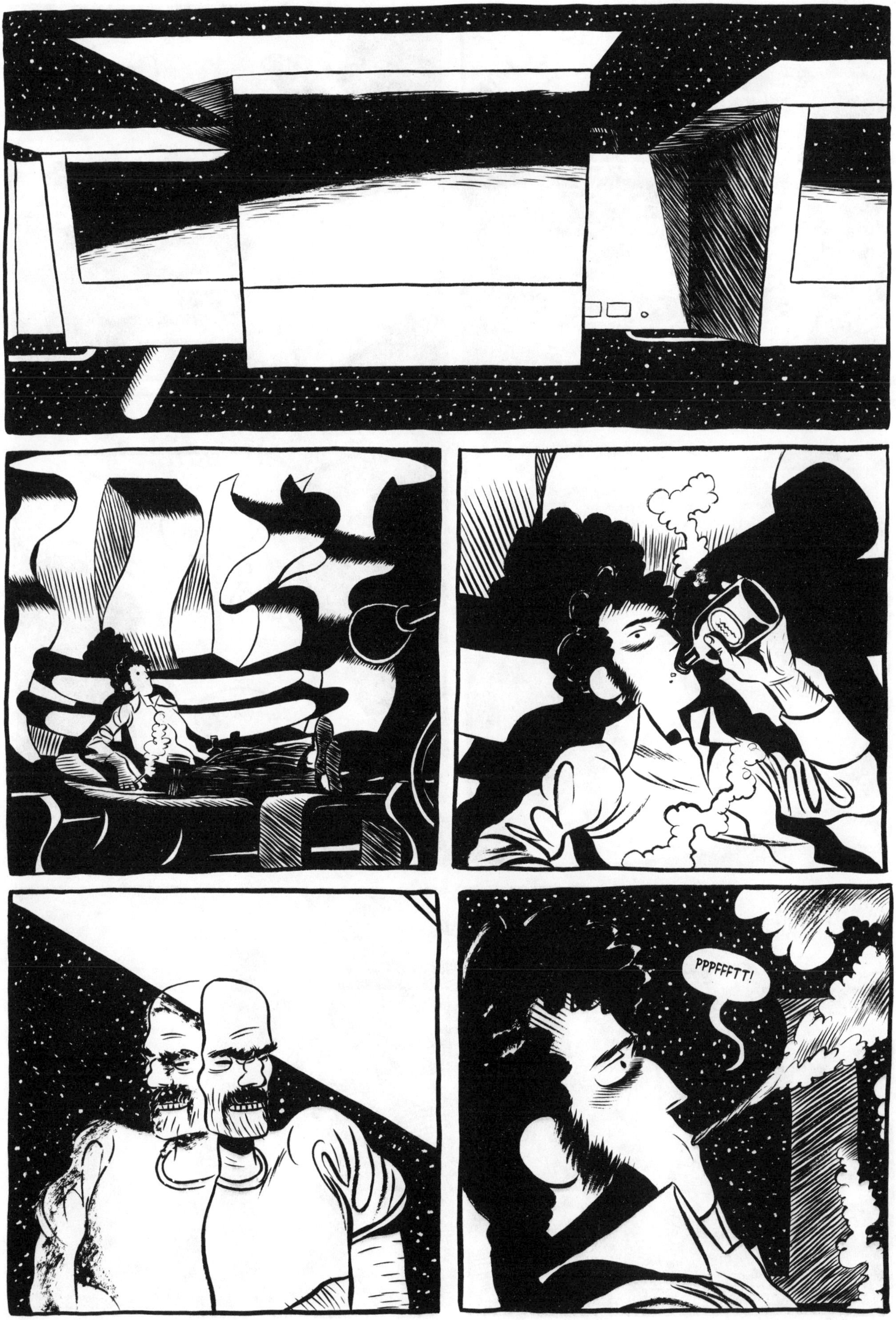
PPPFFFTT!

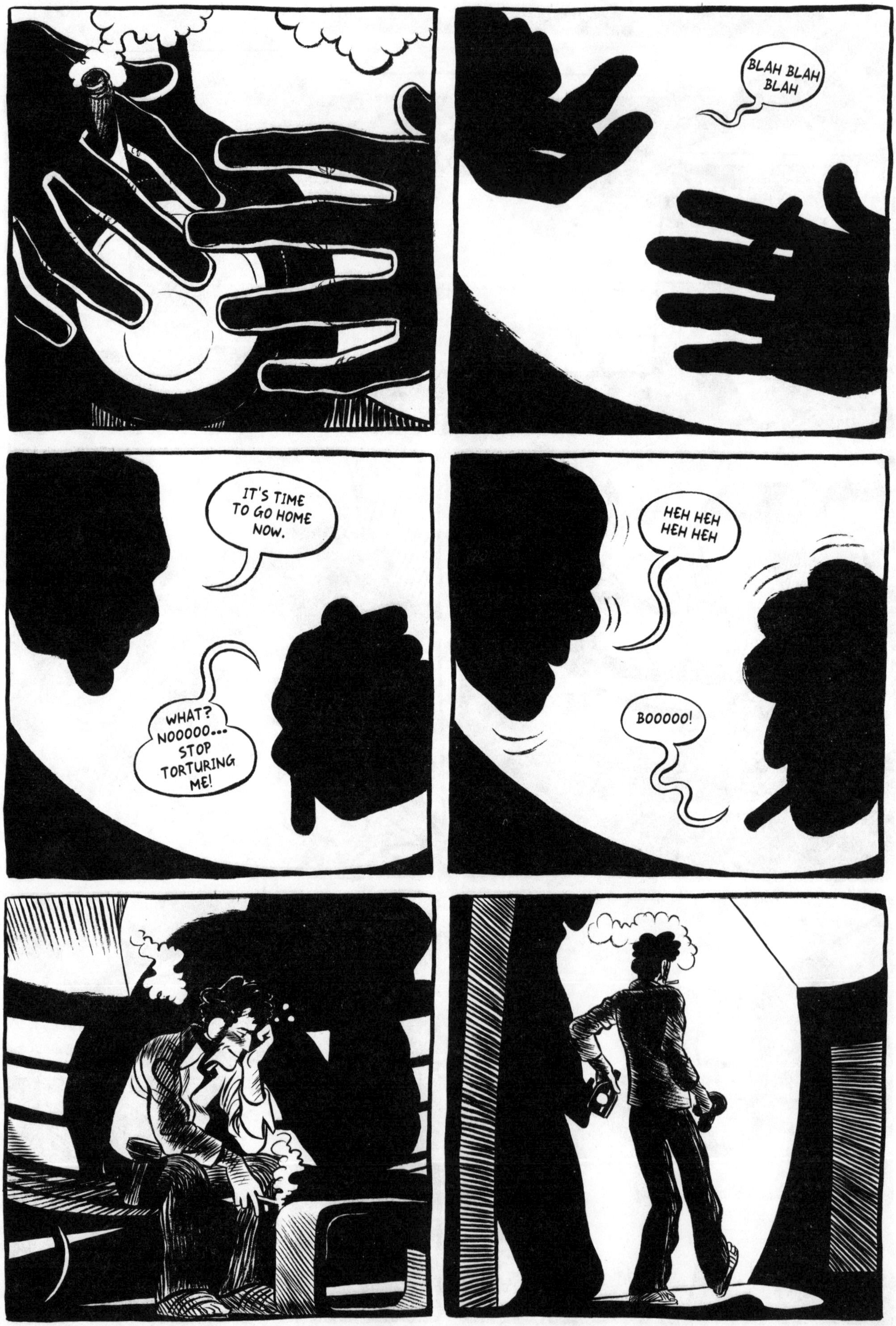
BLAH BLAH BLAH
IT'S TIME TO GO HOME NOW.
WHAT? NOOOOO... STOP TORTURING ME!
HEH HEH HEH HEH
BOOOOO!

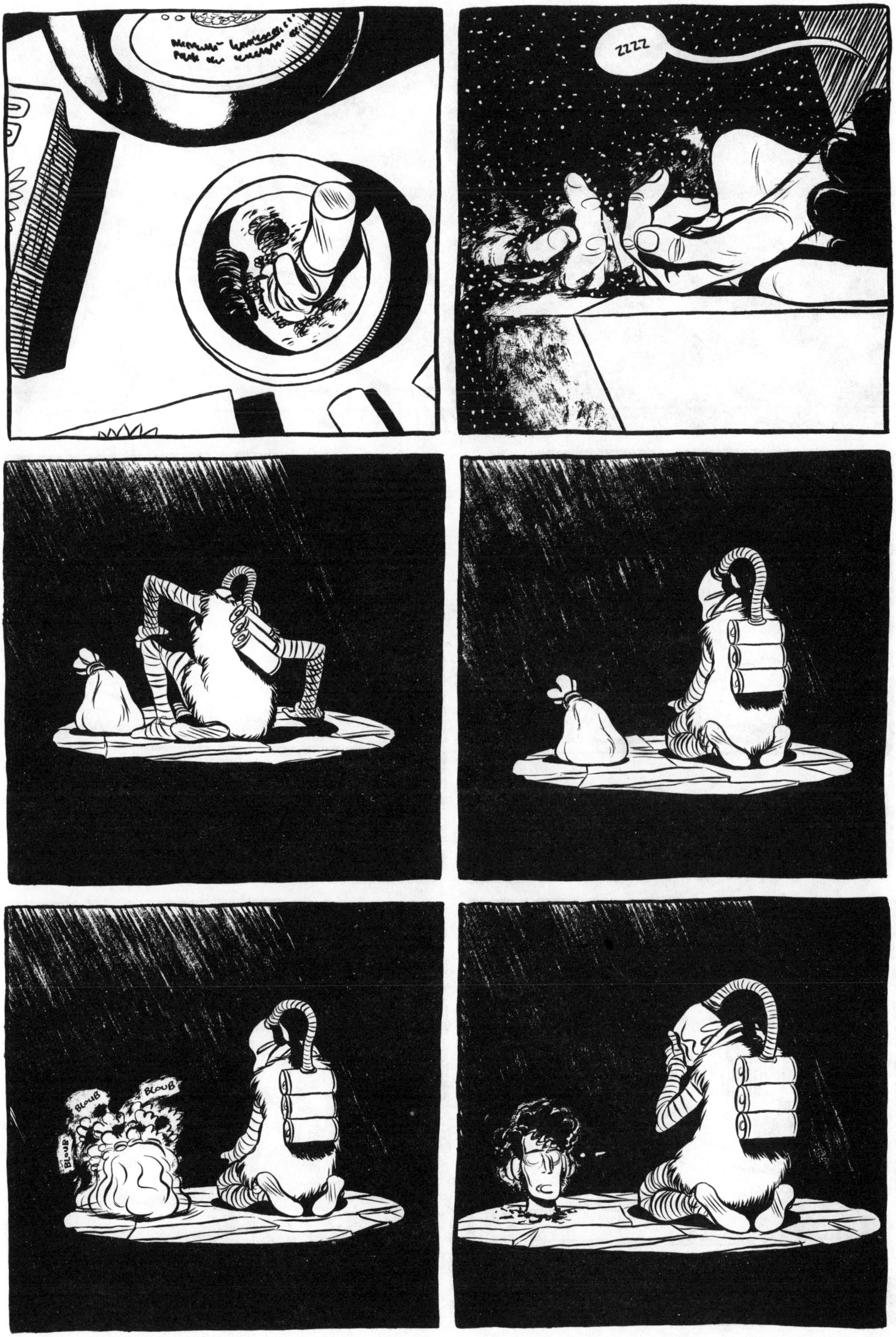
ZZZZ
BLOUB
BLOUB
BLOUB

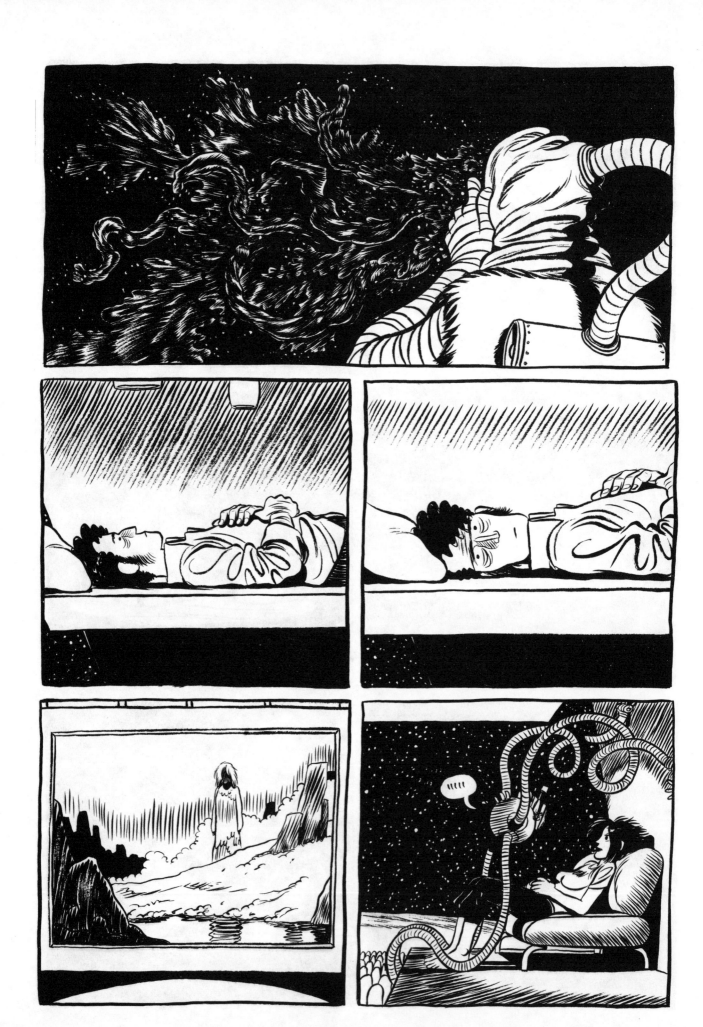

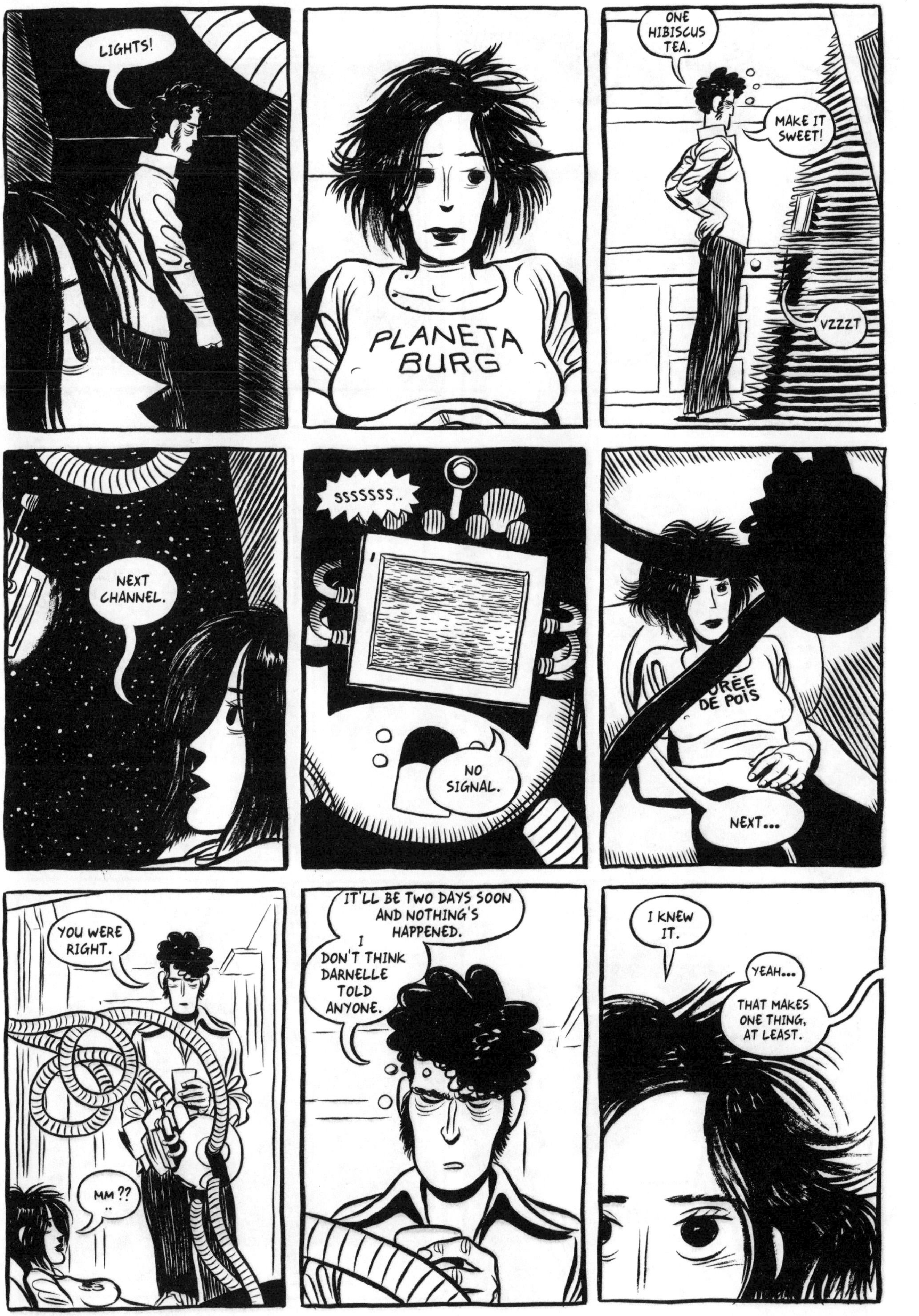

LIGHTS!
ONE HIBISCUS TEA.
MAKE IT SWEET!
VZZZT
NEXT CHANNEL.
SSSSSSS..
NO SIGNAL.
PURÉE DE POIS
NEXT...
YOU WERE RIGHT.
MM??
IT'LL BE TWO DAYS SOON AND NOTHING'S HAPPENED.
I DON'T THINK DARNELLE TOLD ANYONE.
I KNEW IT.
YEAH...
THAT MAKES ONE THING, AT LEAST.

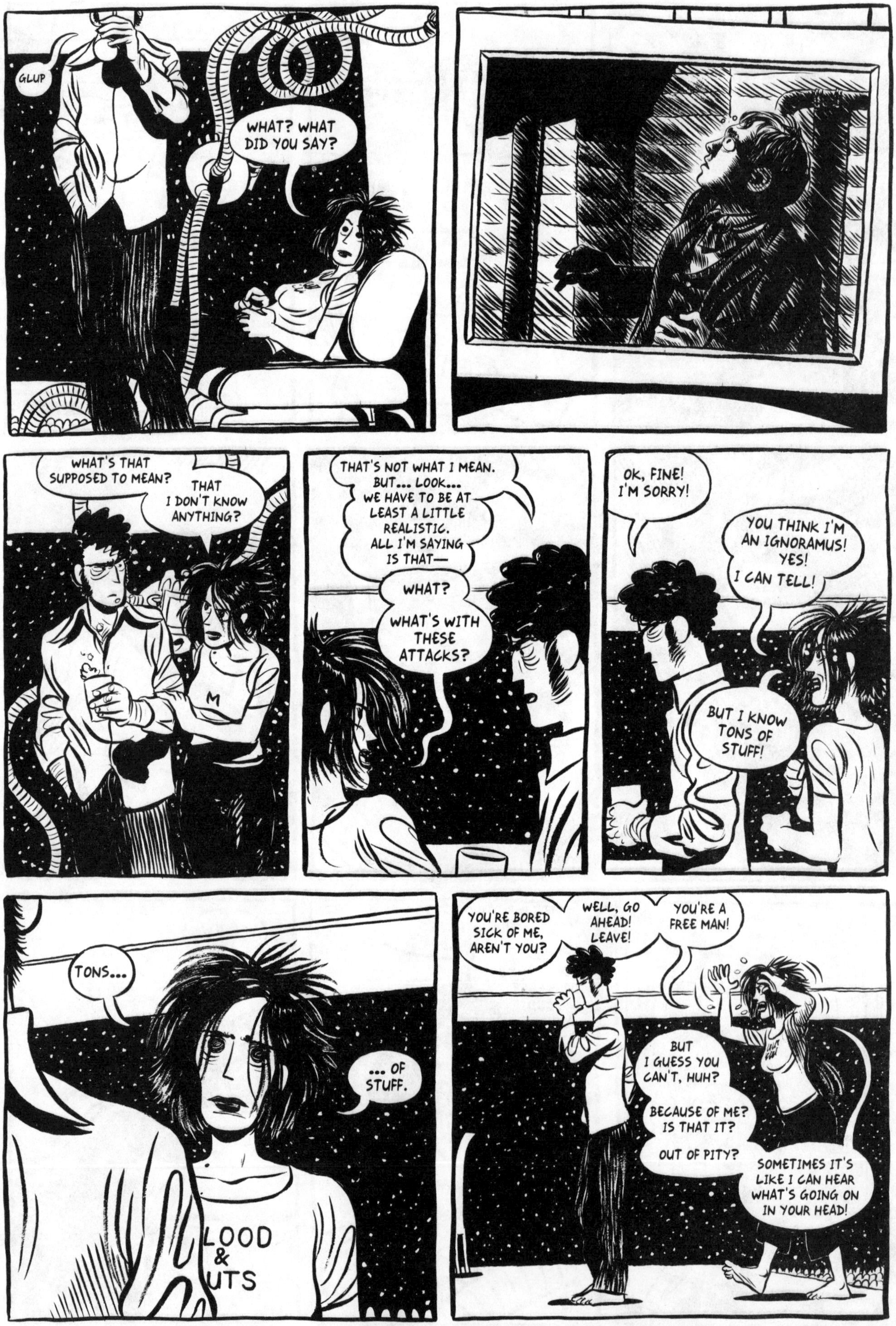
GLUP
WHAT? WHAT DID YOU SAY?
WHAT'S THAT SUPPOSED TO MEAN?
THAT I DON'T KNOW ANYTHING?
M
THAT'S NOT WHAT I MEAN. BUT... LOOK... WE HAVE TO BE AT LEAST A LITTLE REALISTIC. ALL I'M SAYING IS THAT—
WHAT?
WHAT'S WITH THESE ATTACKS?
OK, FINE! I'M SORRY!
YOU THINK I'M AN IGNORAMUS! YES! I CAN TELL!
BUT I KNOW TONS OF STUFF!
TONS...
... OF STUFF.
LOOD & UTS
YOU'RE BORED SICK OF ME, AREN'T YOU?
WELL, GO AHEAD! LEAVE!
YOU'RE A FREE MAN!
BUT I GUESS YOU CAN'T, HUH?
BECAUSE OF ME? IS THAT IT?
OUT OF PITY?
SOMETIMES IT'S LIKE I CAN HEAR WHAT'S GOING ON IN YOUR HEAD!

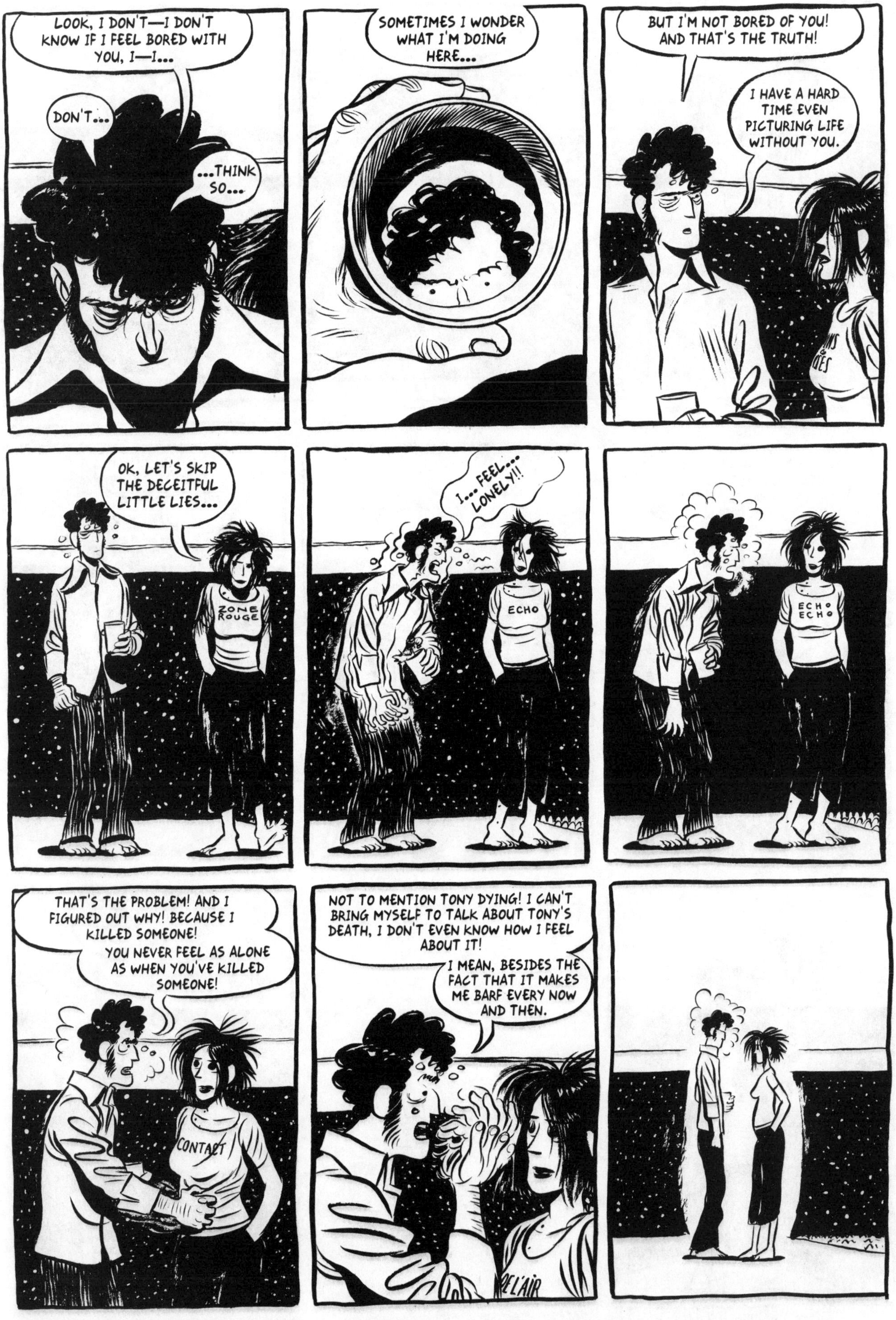
LOOK, I DON'T—I DON'T KNOW IF I FEEL BORED WITH YOU, I—I...
DON'T...
...THINK SO...
SOMETIMES I WONDER WHAT I'M DOING HERE...
BUT I'M NOT BORED OF YOU! AND THAT'S THE TRUTH!
I HAVE A HARD TIME EVEN PICTURING LIFE WITHOUT YOU.
OK, LET'S SKIP THE DECEITFUL LITTLE LIES...
ZONE ROUGE
I... FEEL... LONELY!!
ECHO
ECHO ECHO
THAT'S THE PROBLEM! AND I FIGURED OUT WHY! BECAUSE I KILLED SOMEONE!
YOU NEVER FEEL AS ALONE AS WHEN YOU'VE KILLED SOMEONE!
CONTACT
NOT TO MENTION TONY DYING! I CAN'T BRING MYSELF TO TALK ABOUT TONY'S DEATH, I DON'T EVEN KNOW HOW I FEEL ABOUT IT!
I MEAN, BESIDES THE FACT THAT IT MAKES ME BARF EVERY NOW AND THEN.
DE L'AIR

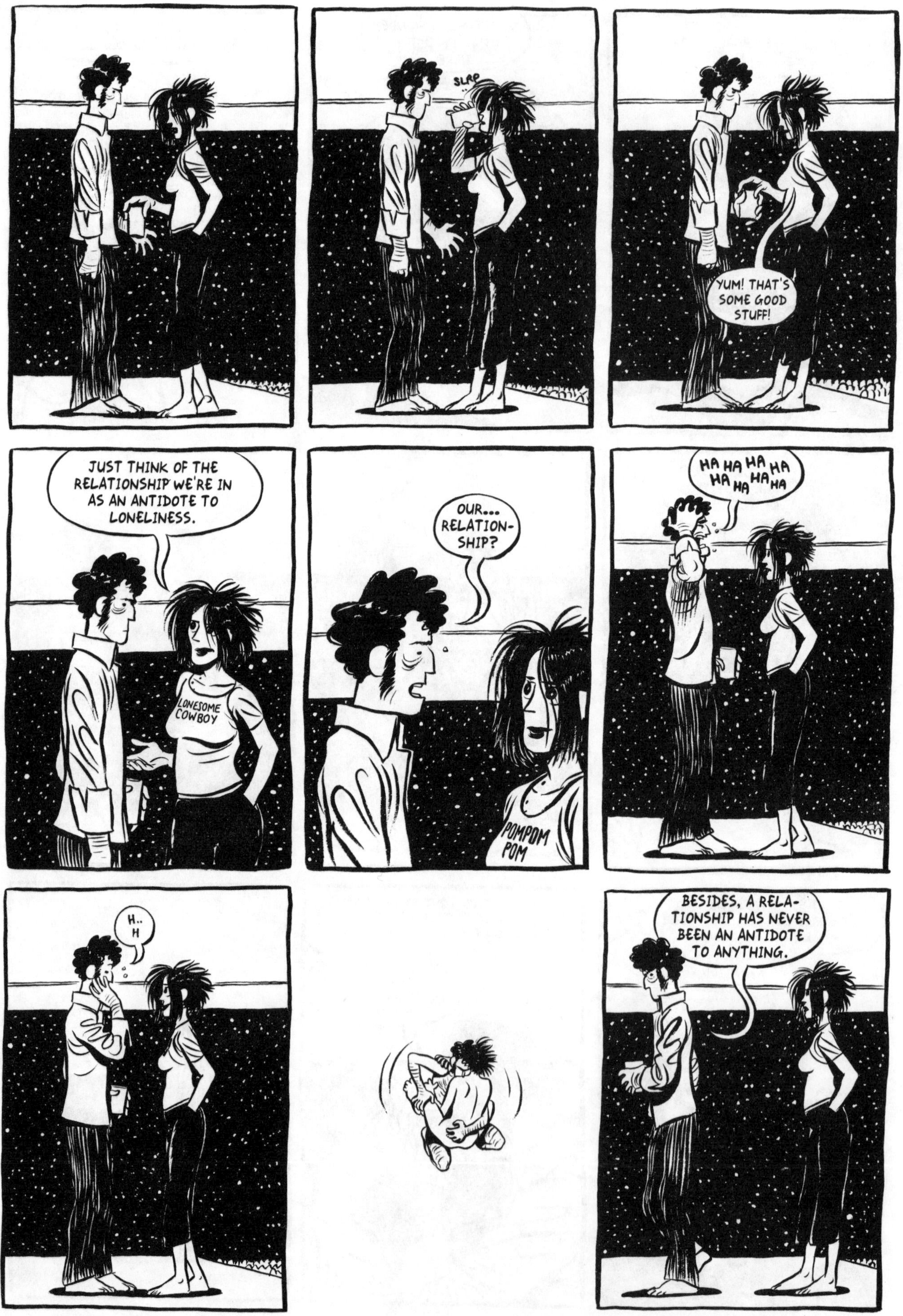
SLRP
YUM! THAT'S SOME GOOD STUFF!
JUST THINK OF THE RELATIONSHIP WE'RE IN AS AN ANTIDOTE TO LONELINESS.
LONESOME COWBOY
OUR... RELATIONSHIP?
POMPOM POM
HA HA HA HA HA HA HA HA HA
H.. H
BESIDES, A RELATIONSHIP HAS NEVER BEEN AN ANTIDOTE TO ANYTHING.

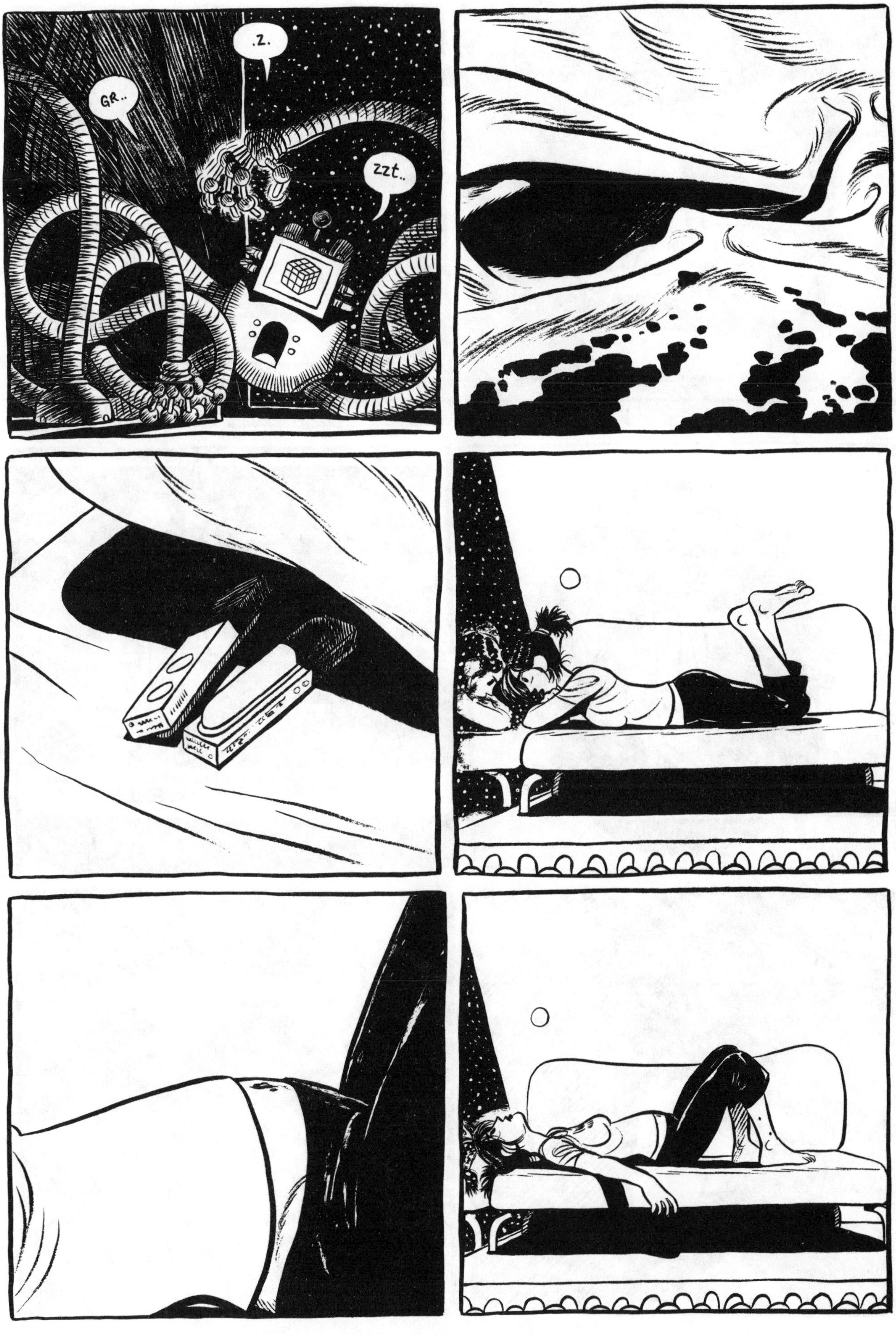

GR..
.Z.
zzt..

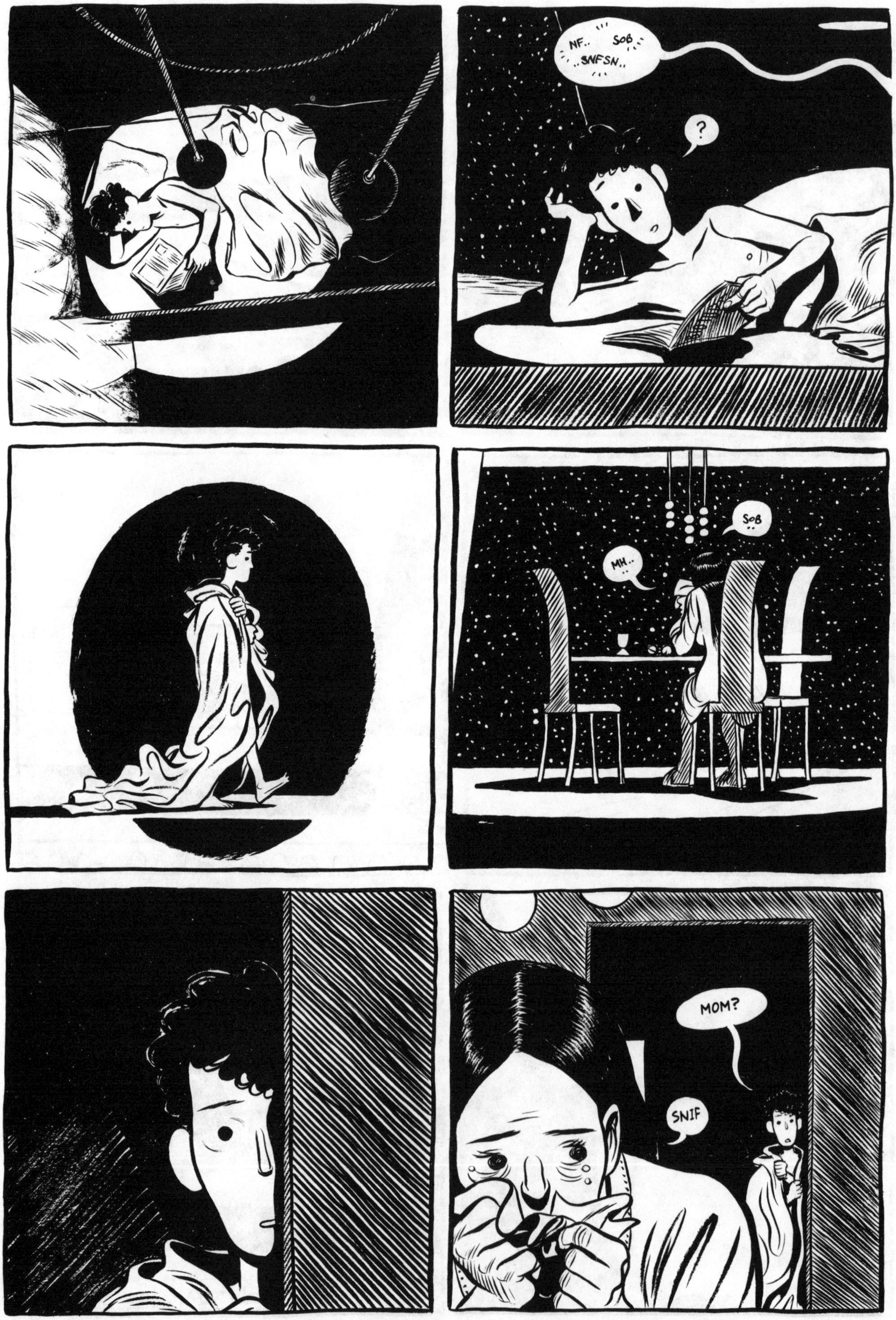
NF.. SOB ..SNFSN..
?
SOB
MH..
MOM?
SNIF

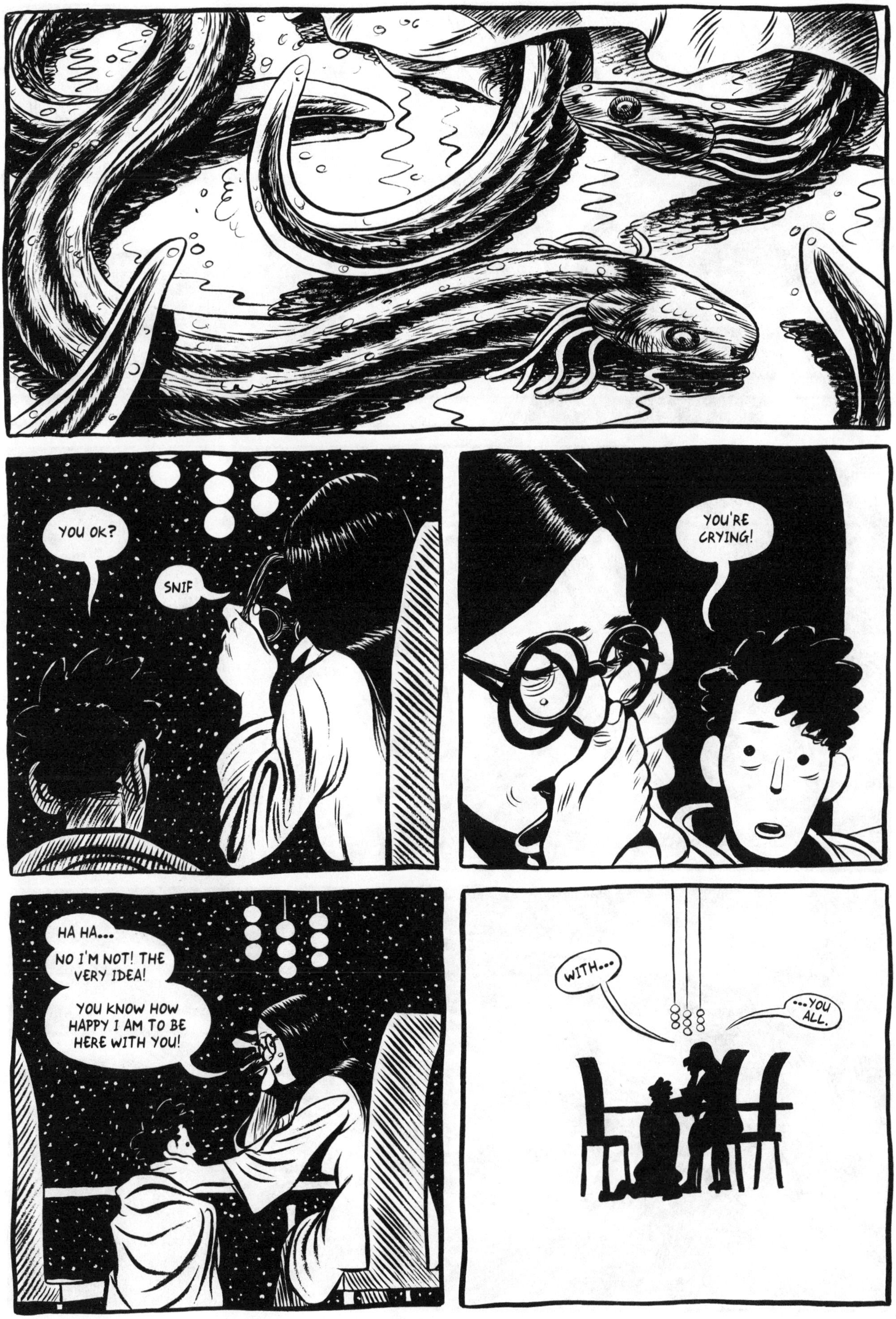
YOU OK?
SNIF
YOU'RE CRYING!
HA HA...
NO I'M NOT! THE VERY IDEA!
YOU KNOW HOW HAPPY I AM TO BE HERE WITH YOU!
WITH...
...YOU ALL.

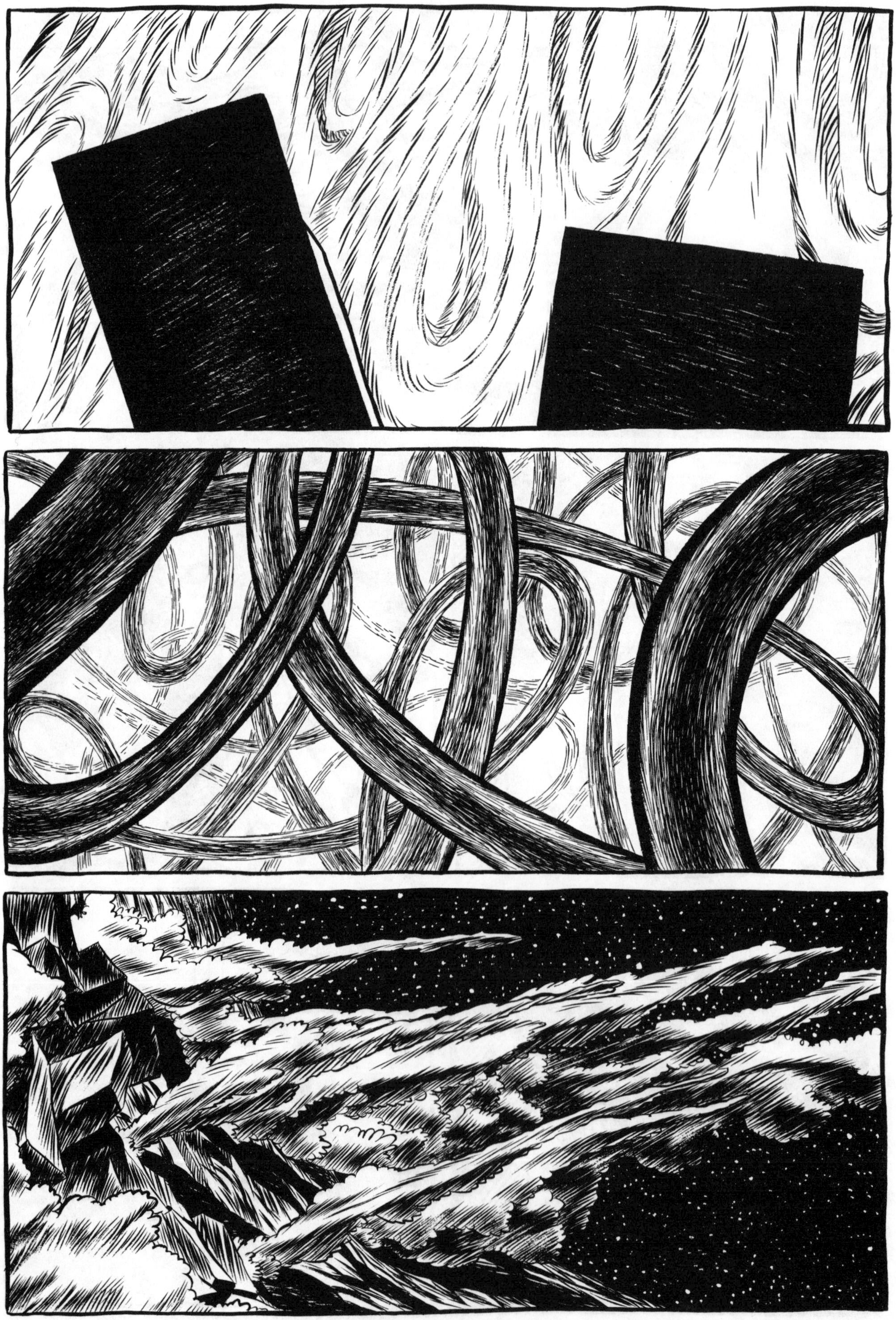

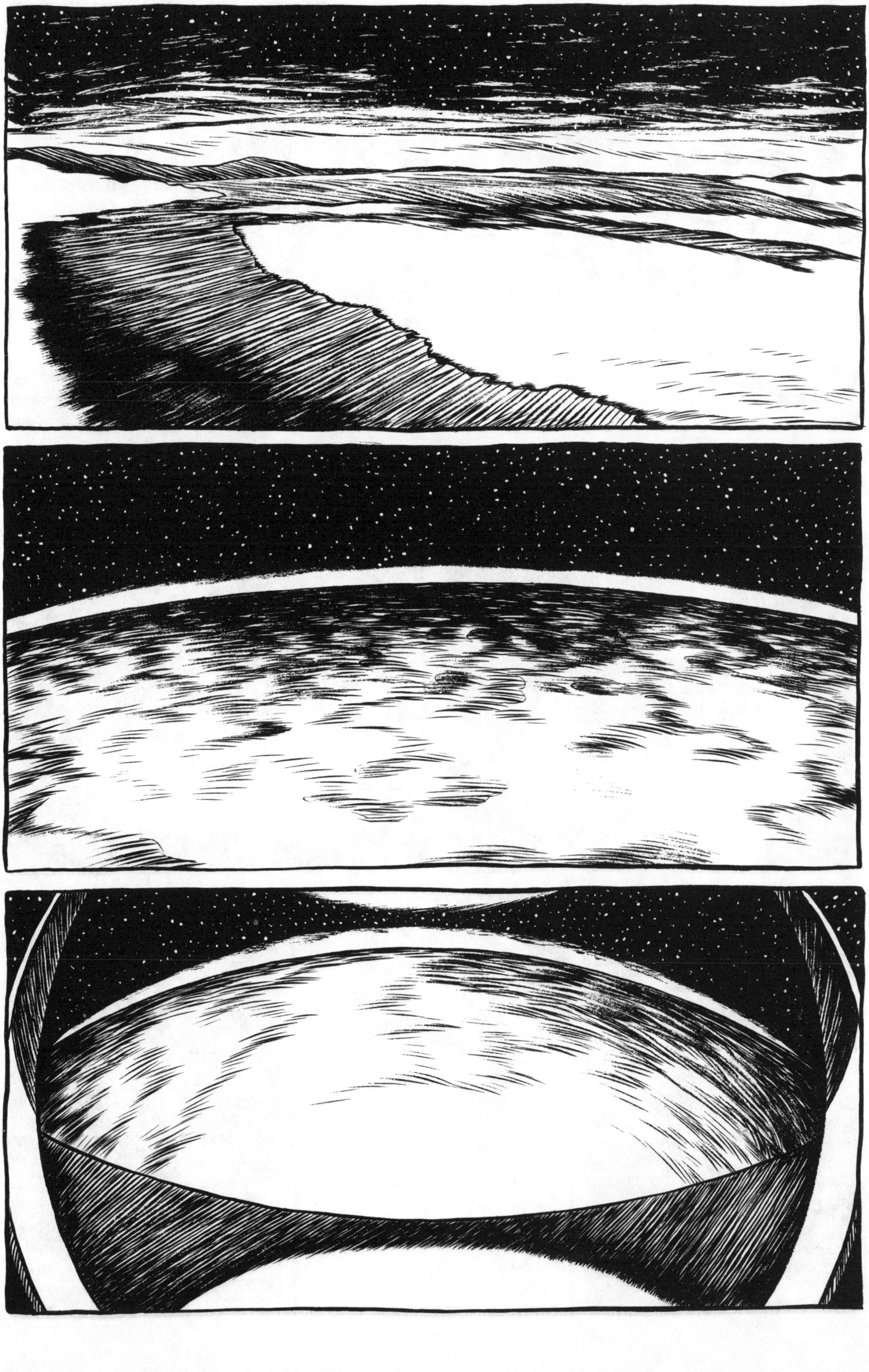

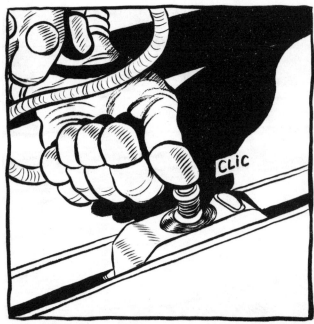

CLIC

HAHAHA.. ..

EVERY-THING GOING WELL?

IT'S AMAZING!

TOO BAD WE CAN'T BOTH BE OUT HERE AT ONCE!

JUST WAIT A LITTLE LONGER, YOU'LL LOVE IT!

HAHA .. HA..

WHAT AN INCREDIBLE SENSE OF FREEDOM!

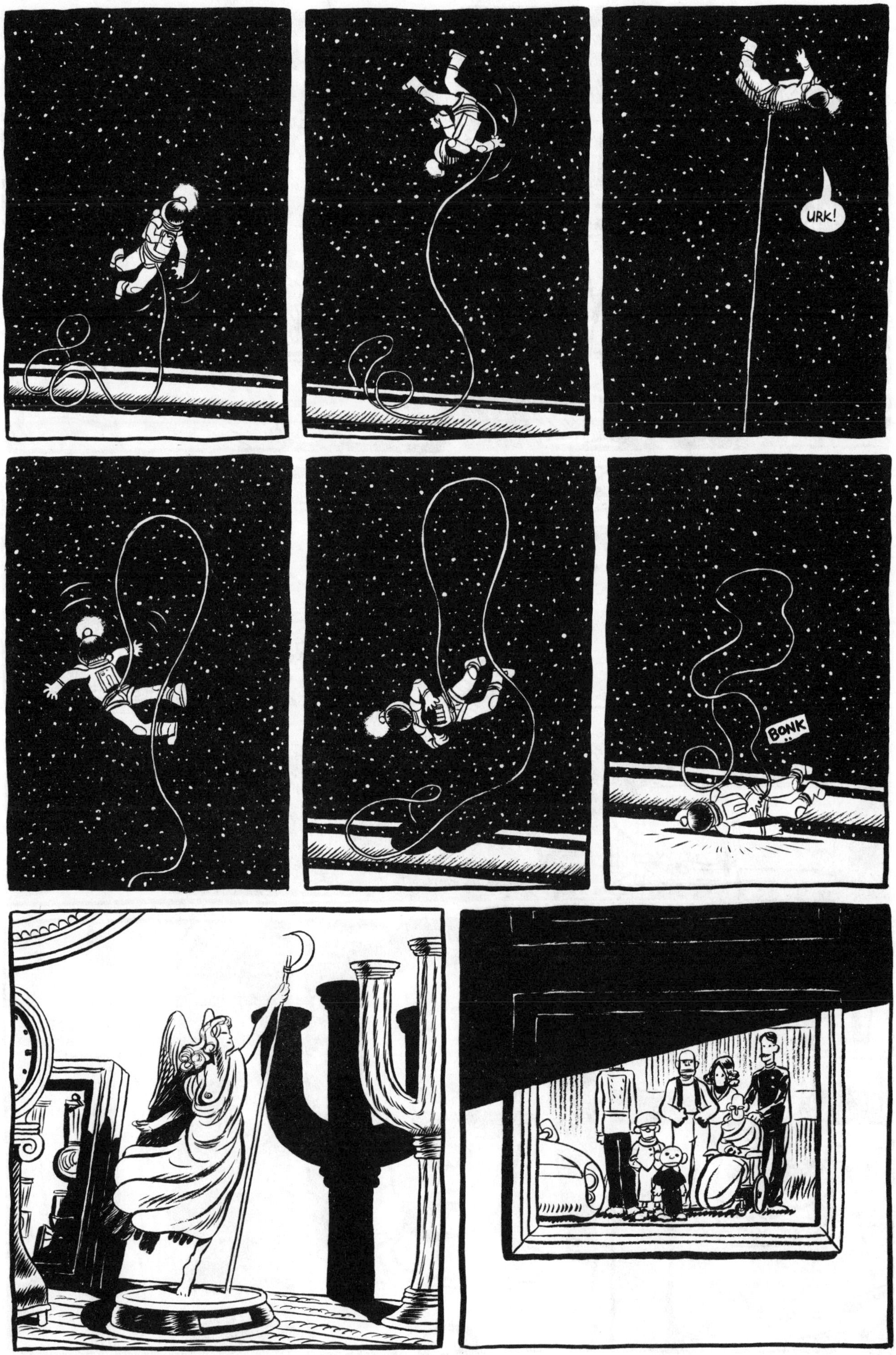
URK!
BONK

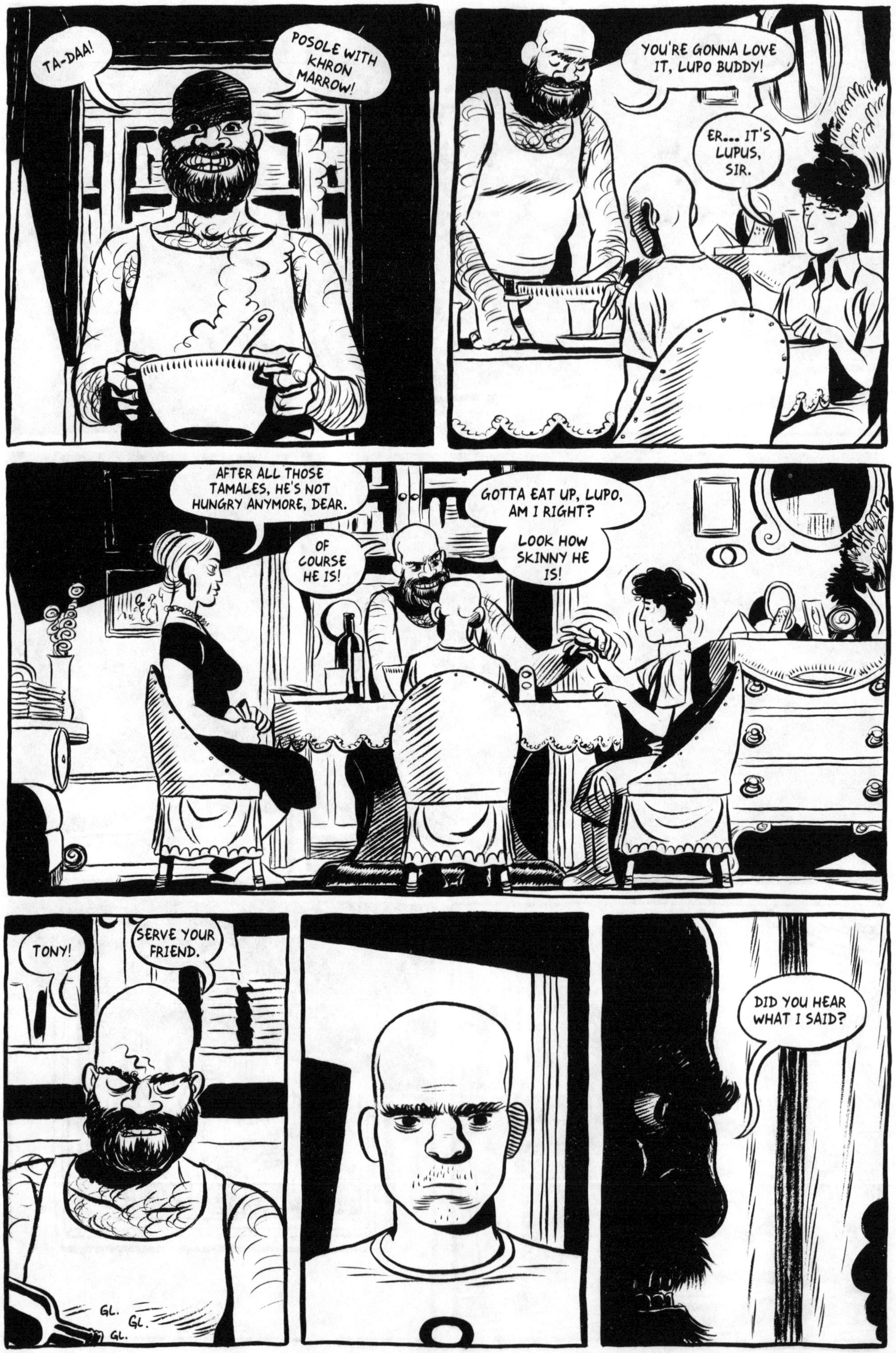
TA-DAA!
POSOLE WITH KHRON MARROW!
YOU'RE GONNA LOVE IT, LUPO BUDDY!
ER... IT'S LUPUS, SIR.
AFTER ALL THOSE TAMALES, HE'S NOT HUNGRY ANYMORE, DEAR.
OF COURSE HE IS!
GOTTA EAT UP, LUPO, AM I RIGHT?
LOOK HOW SKINNY HE IS!
TONY!
SERVE YOUR FRIEND.
GL. GL. GL.
DID YOU HEAR WHAT I SAID?

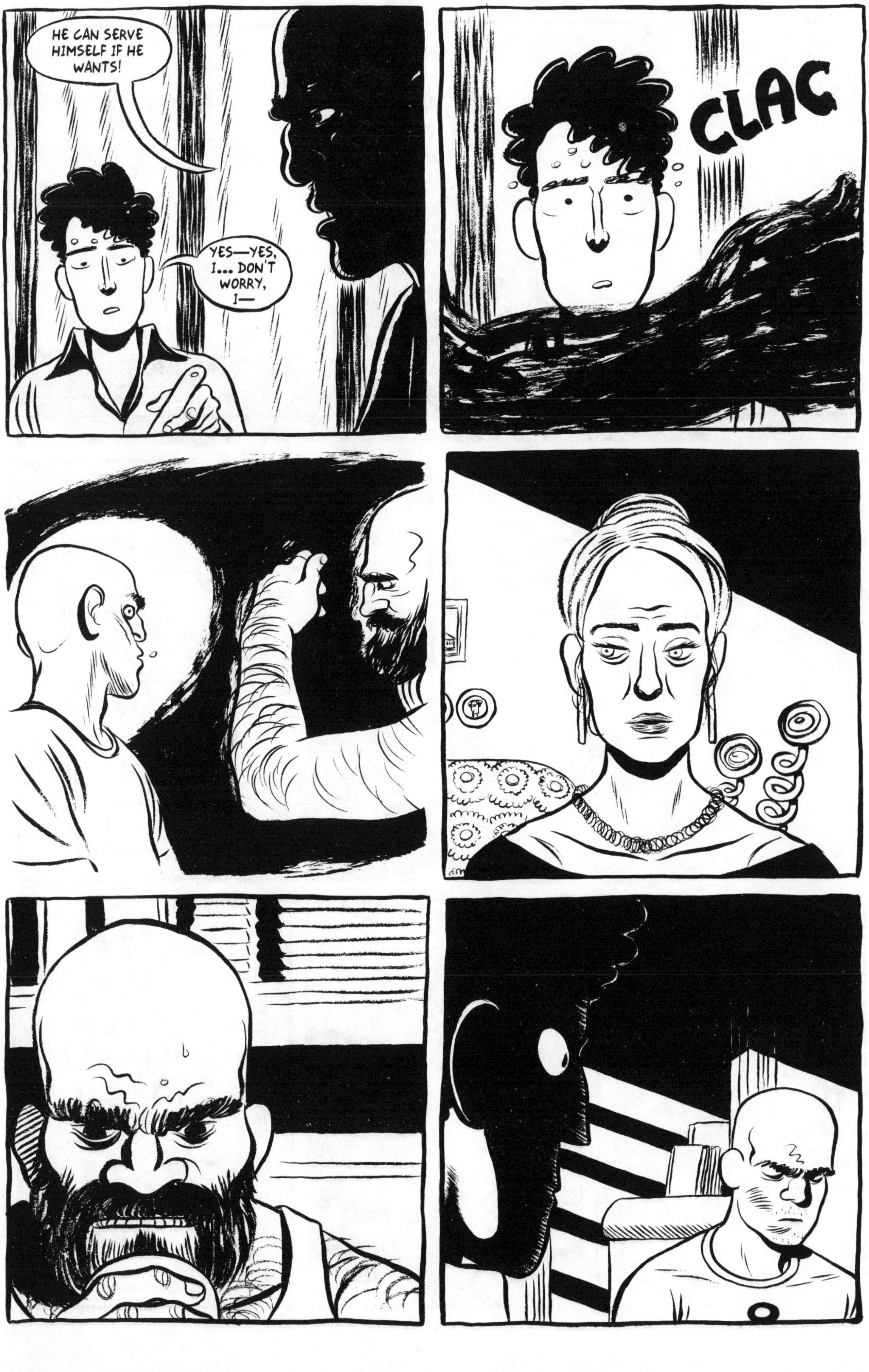
HE CAN SERVE HIMSELF IF HE WANTS!
YES—YES, I... DON'T WORRY, I—
CLAC

SANAA!
?
FROT FROT FROT FROT FROT
FROT
FROT
FROT
WHAT ARE YOU SCOURING AWAY AT?
CLEANING...
STAIN...
LARGE STAIN...
DZZ
FROT
FROT

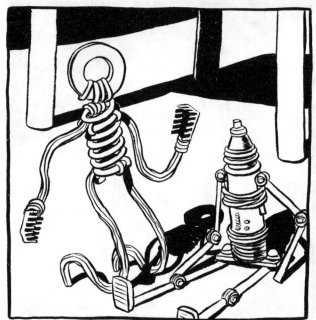

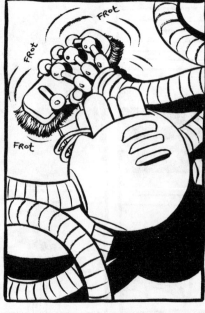

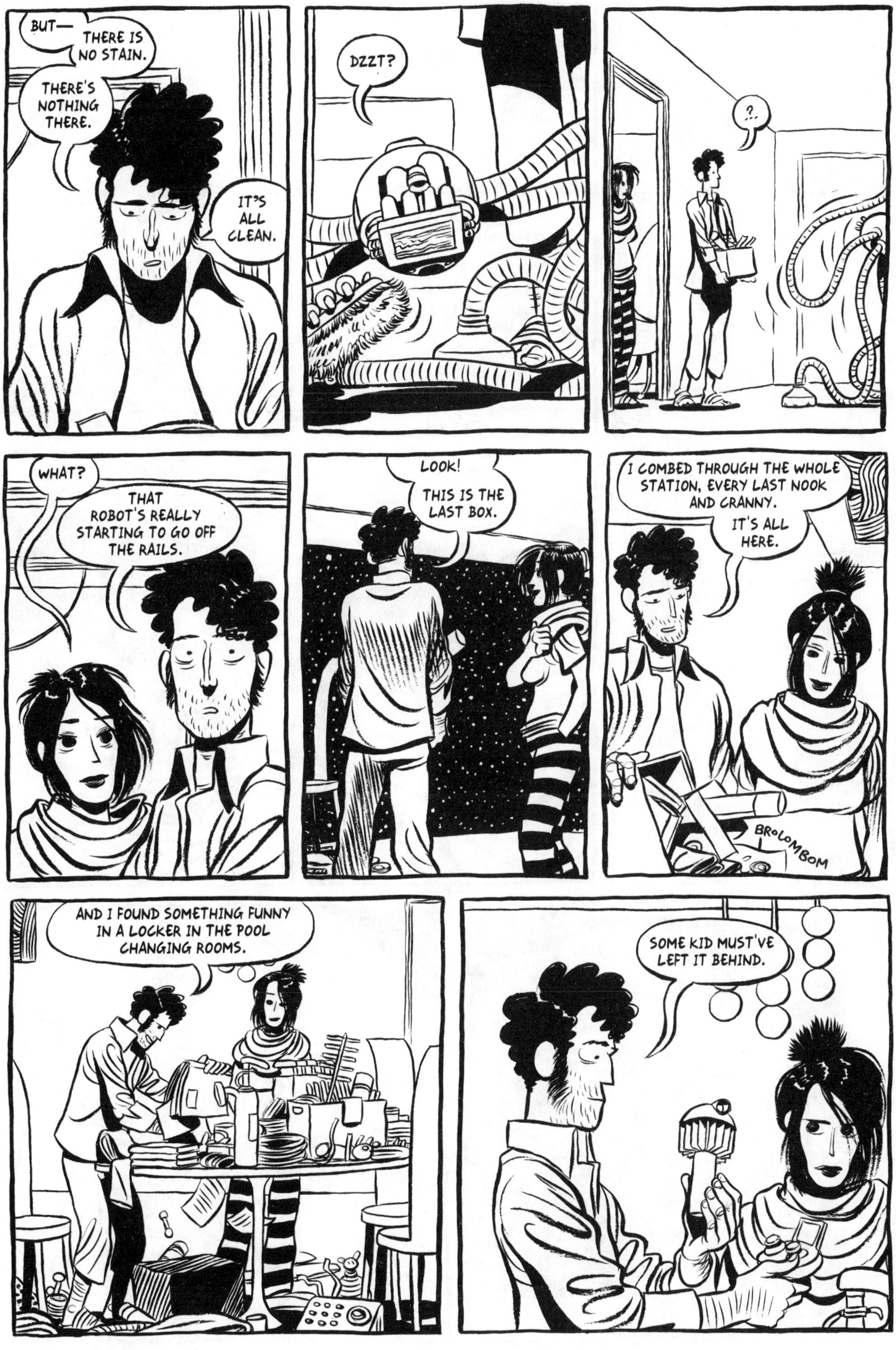
BUT—
THERE IS NO STAIN.
THERE'S NOTHING THERE.
IT'S ALL CLEAN.
DZZT?
?..
WHAT?
THAT ROBOT'S REALLY STARTING TO GO OFF THE RAILS.
LOOK!
THIS IS THE LAST BOX.
I COMBED THROUGH THE WHOLE STATION, EVERY LAST NOOK AND CRANNY.
IT'S ALL HERE.
BROLOMBOM
AND I FOUND SOMETHING FUNNY IN A LOCKER IN THE POOL CHANGING ROOMS.
SOME KID MUST'VE LEFT IT BEHIND.

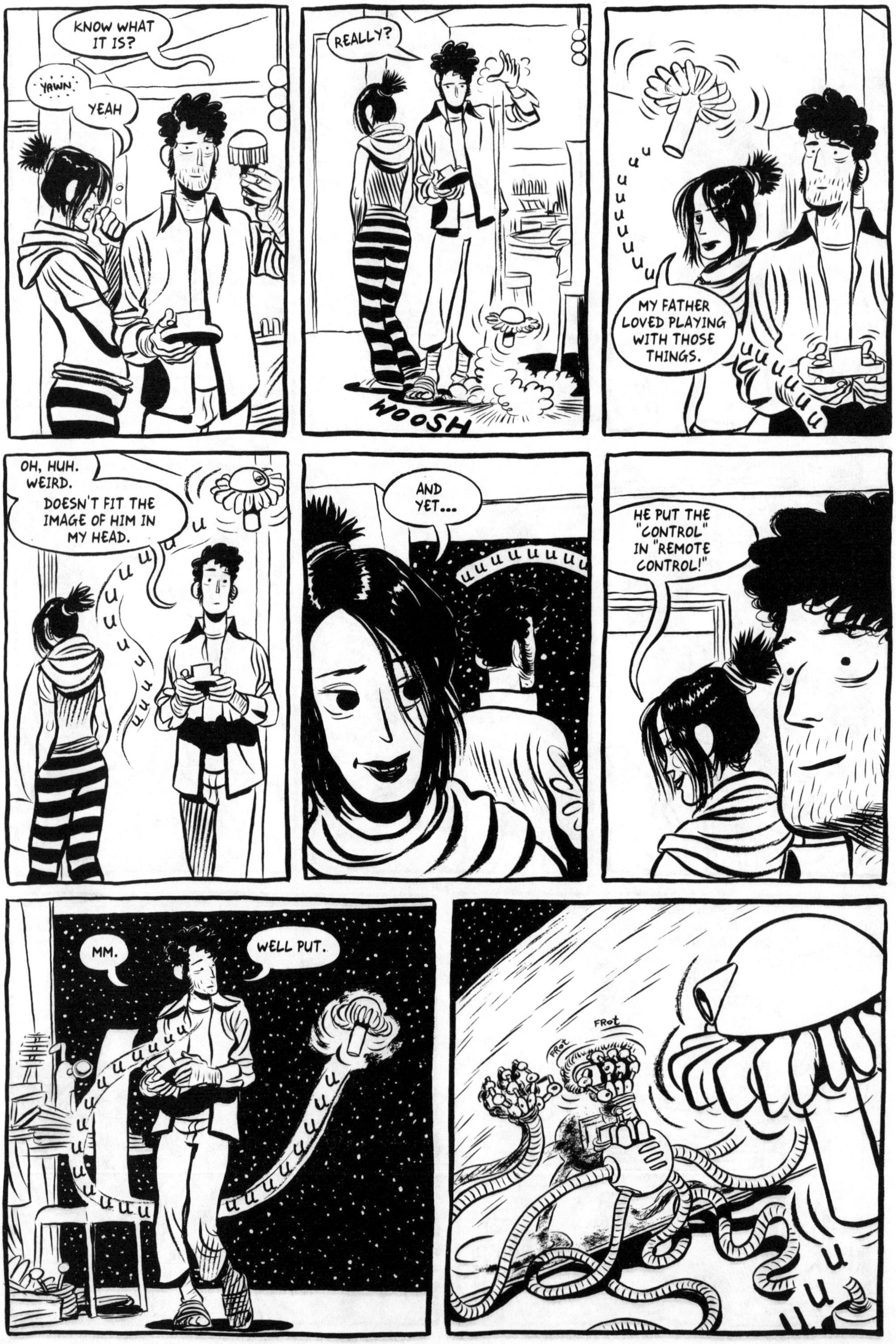
KNOW WHAT IT IS?
YAWN
YEAH
REALLY?
WOOSH
MY FATHER LOVED PLAYING WITH THOSE THINGS.
OH, HUH. WEIRD.
DOESN'T FIT THE IMAGE OF HIM IN MY HEAD.
AND YET...
HE PUT THE "CONTROL" IN "REMOTE CONTROL!"
MM.
WELL PUT.
FROT
FROT

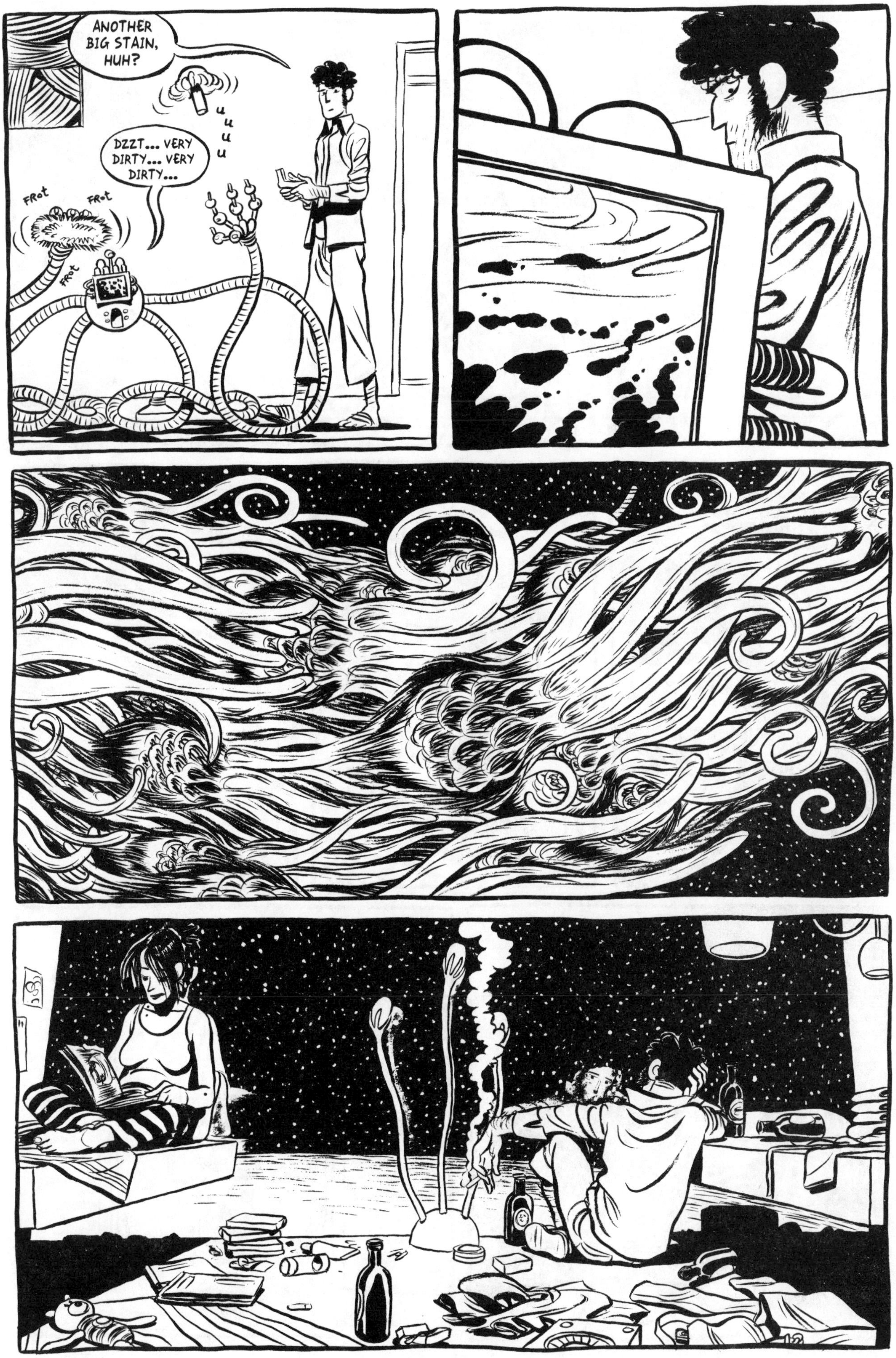
ANOTHER BIG STAIN, HUH?
DZZT... VERY DIRTY... VERY DIRTY...
FROT
FROT
FROT

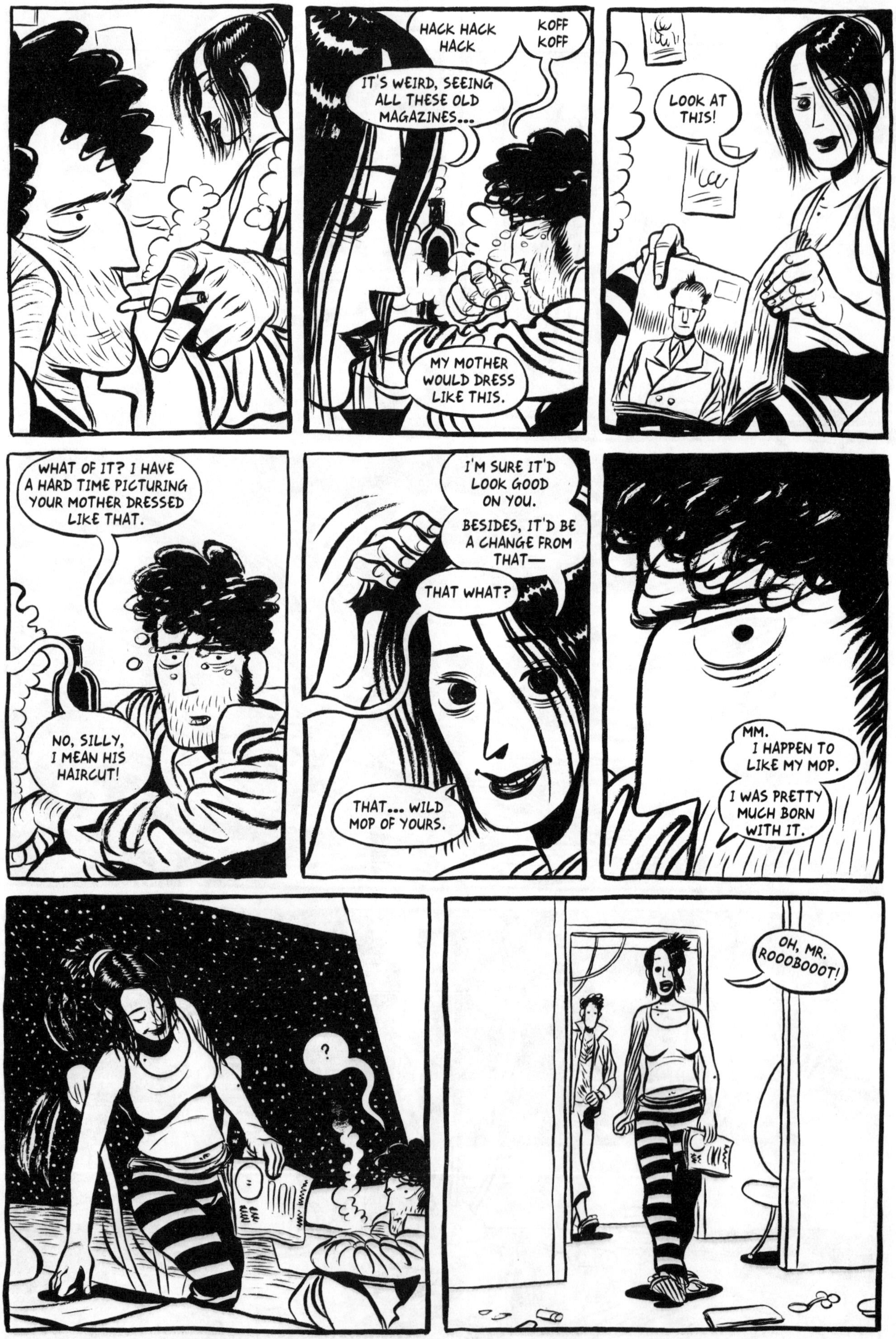
HACK HACK HACK
KOFF KOFF
IT'S WEIRD, SEEING ALL THESE OLD MAGAZINES...
MY MOTHER WOULD DRESS LIKE THIS.
LOOK AT THIS!
WHAT OF IT? I HAVE A HARD TIME PICTURING YOUR MOTHER DRESSED LIKE THAT.
NO, SILLY, I MEAN HIS HAIRCUT!
I'M SURE IT'D LOOK GOOD ON YOU.
BESIDES, IT'D BE A CHANGE FROM THAT—
THAT WHAT?
THAT... WILD MOP OF YOURS.
MM. I HAPPEN TO LIKE MY MOP.
I WAS PRETTY MUCH BORN WITH IT.
?
OH, MR. ROOOBOOOT!

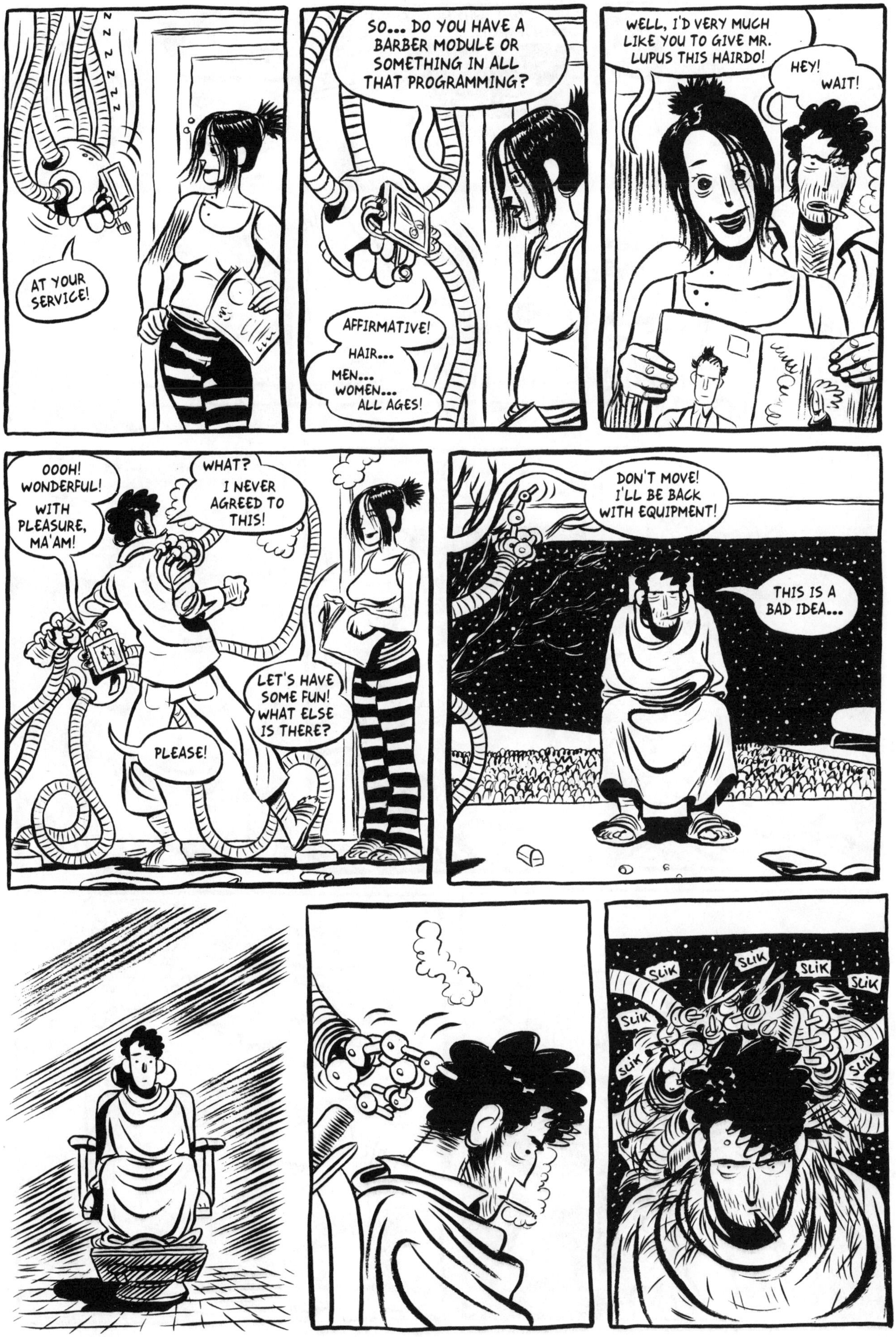
Z Z Z Z Z Z
AT YOUR SERVICE!
SO... DO YOU HAVE A BARBER MODULE OR SOMETHING IN ALL THAT PROGRAMMING?
AFFIRMATIVE!
HAIR...
MEN... WOMEN... ALL AGES!
WELL, I'D VERY MUCH LIKE YOU TO GIVE MR. LUPUS THIS HAIRDO!
HEY! WAIT!
OOOH! WONDERFUL! WITH PLEASURE, MA'AM!
WHAT? I NEVER AGREED TO THIS!
LET'S HAVE SOME FUN! WHAT ELSE IS THERE?
PLEASE!
DON'T MOVE! I'LL BE BACK WITH EQUIPMENT!
THIS IS A BAD IDEA...
SLIK
SLIK
SLIK
SLIK
SLIK
SLIK
SLIK

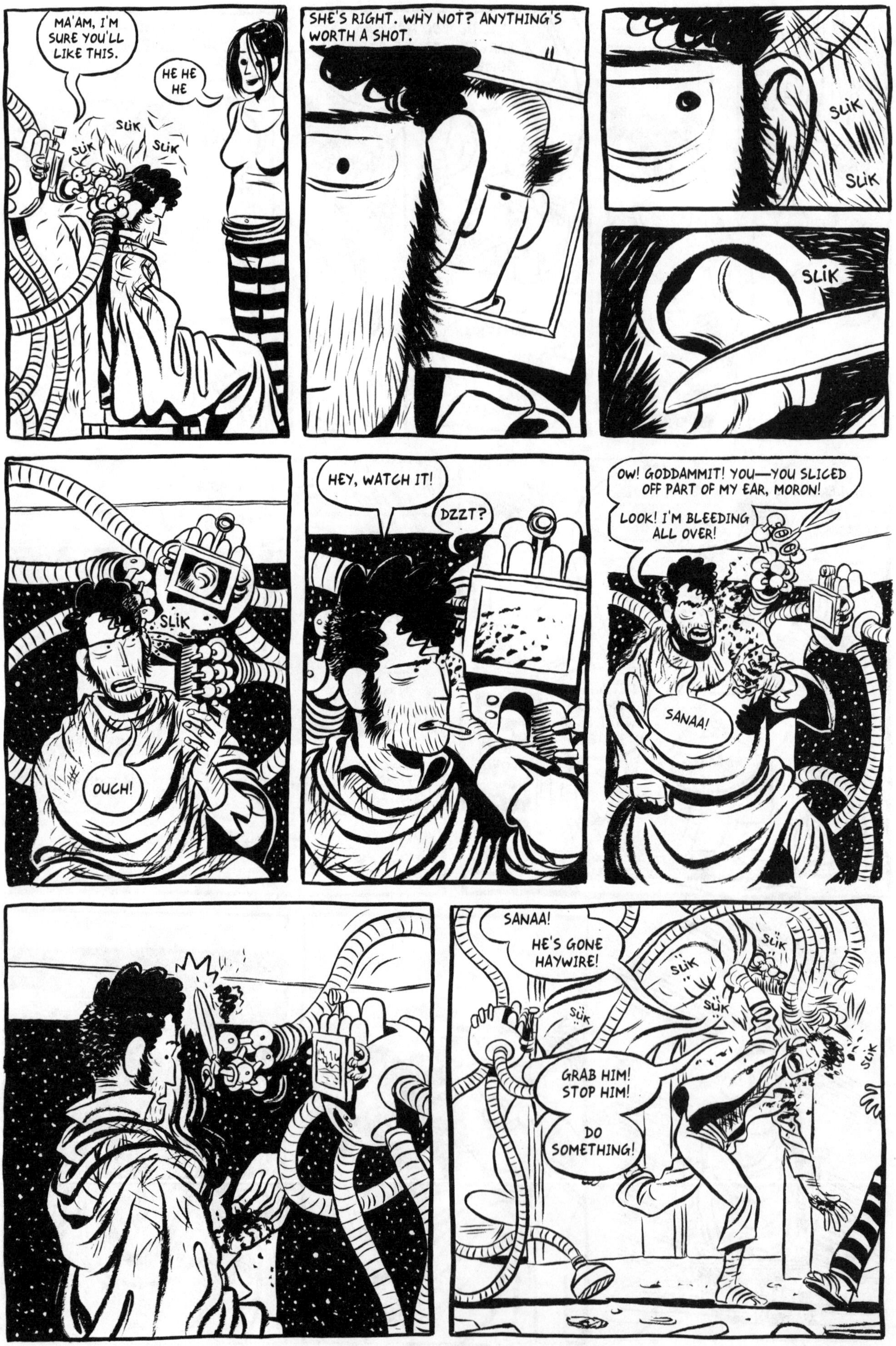
MA'AM, I'M SURE YOU'LL LIKE THIS.
HE HE HE
SLIK
SLIK
SLIK
SHE'S RIGHT. WHY NOT? ANYTHING'S WORTH A SHOT.
SLIK
SLIK
SLIK
SLIK
OUCH!
HEY, WATCH IT!
DZZT?
OW! GODDAMMIT! YOU—YOU SLICED OFF PART OF MY EAR, MORON!
LOOK! I'M BLEEDING ALL OVER!
SANAA!
SANAA!
HE'S GONE HAYWIRE!
SLIK
SLIK
SLIK
SLIK
SLIK
GRAB HIM! STOP HIM!
DO SOMETHING!

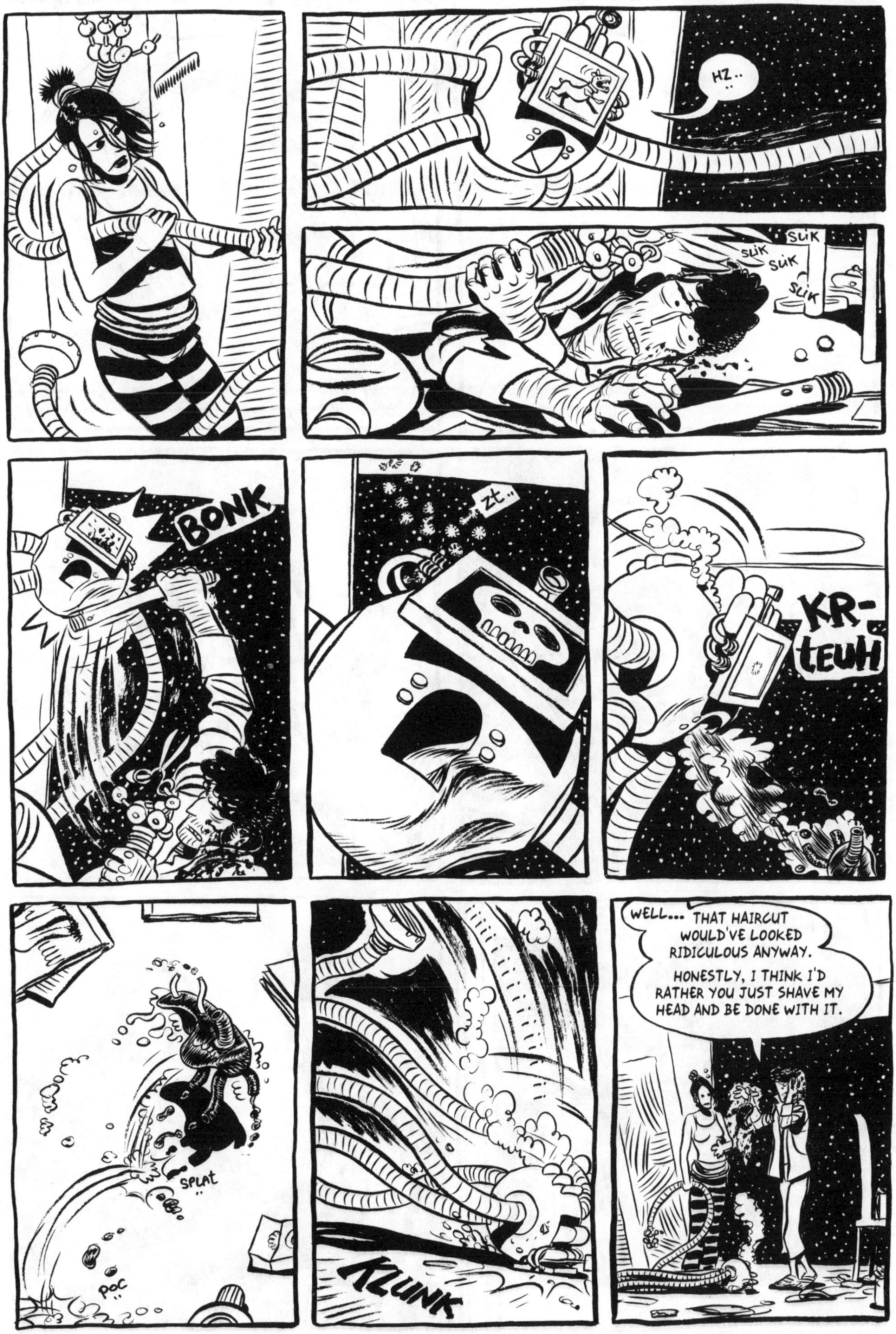
HZ..
SLIK
SLIK
SLIK
SLIK
BONK
zt..
KR-TEUH
SPLAT
POC
KLUNK
WELL... THAT HAIRCUT WOULD'VE LOOKED RIDICULOUS ANYWAY.
HONESTLY, I THINK I'D RATHER YOU JUST SHAVE MY HEAD AND BE DONE WITH IT.

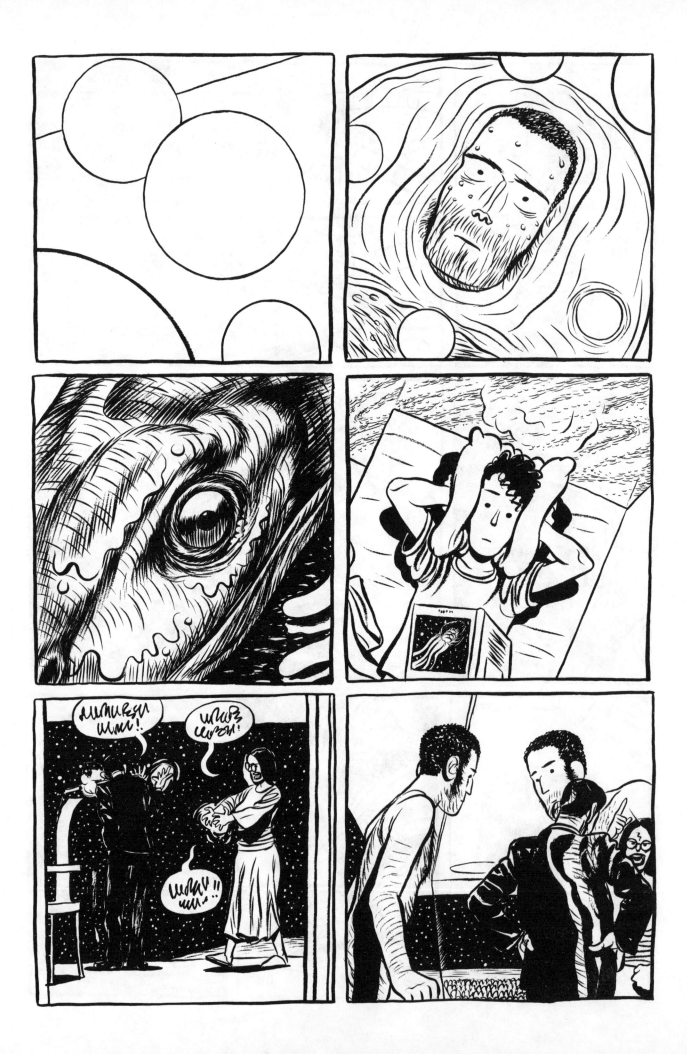

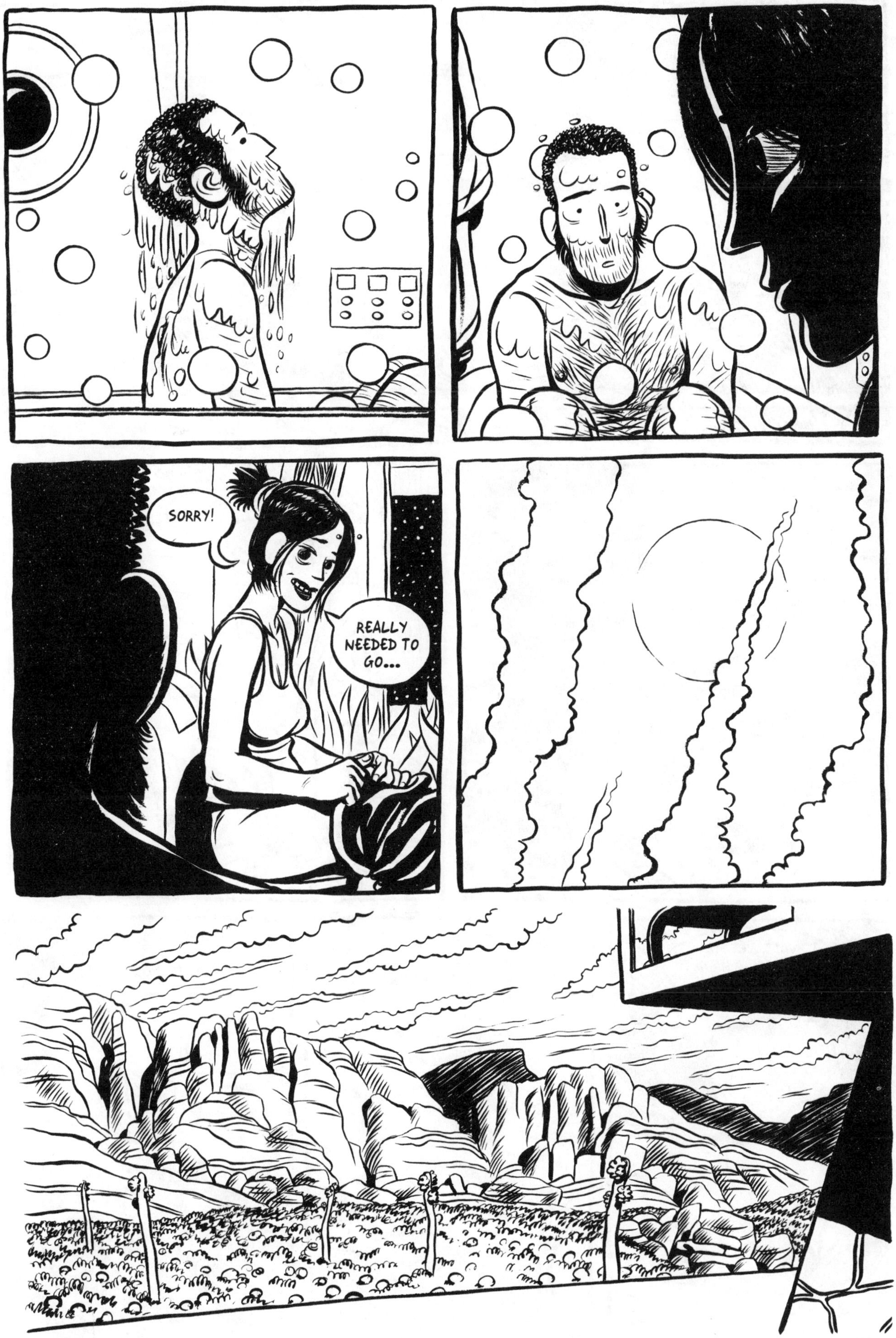
SORRY!
REALLY NEEDED TO GO...

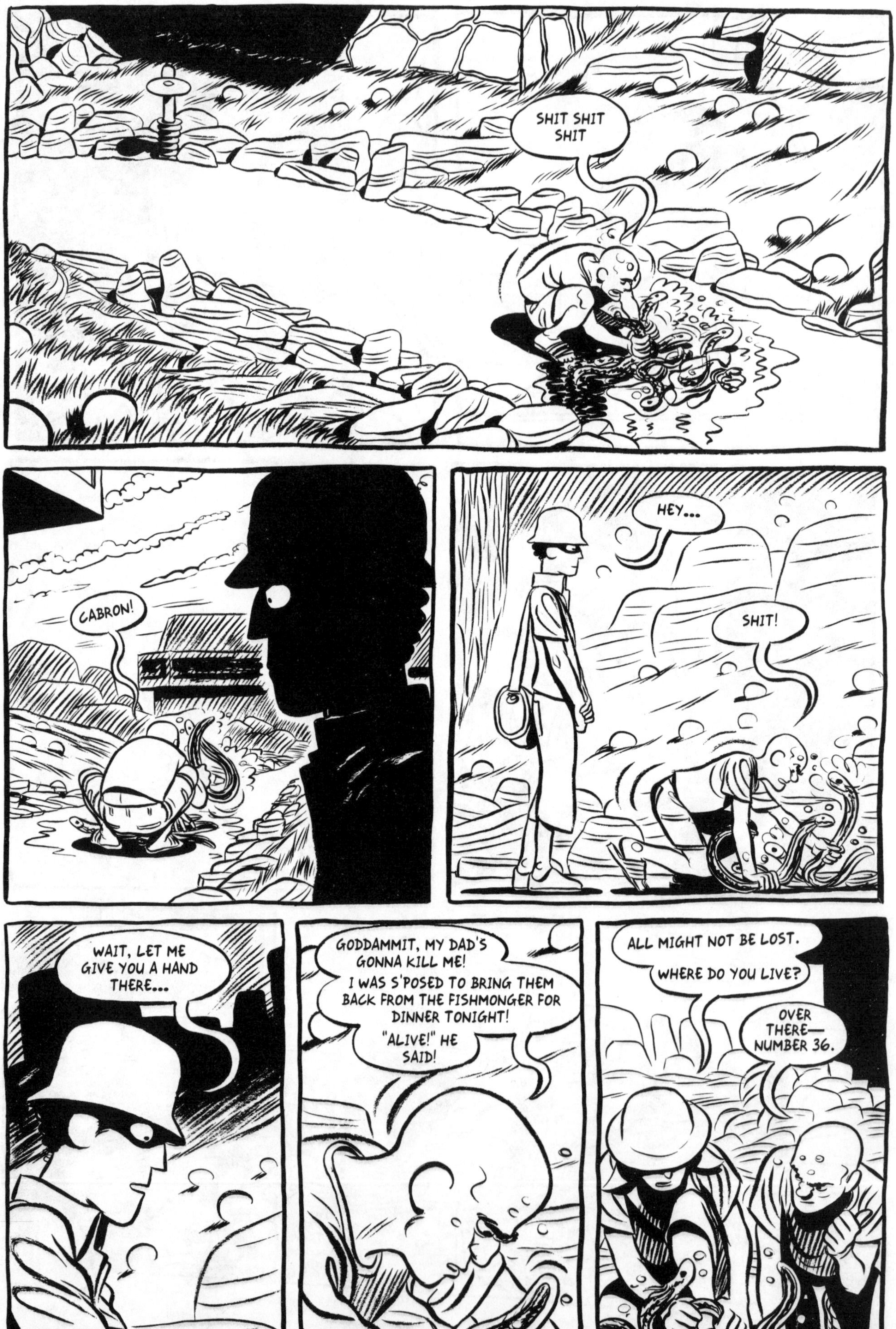
SHIT SHIT SHIT
CABRON!
HEY...
SHIT!
WAIT, LET ME GIVE YOU A HAND THERE...
GODDAMMIT, MY DAD'S GONNA KILL ME!
I WAS S'POSED TO BRING THEM BACK FROM THE FISHMONGER FOR DINNER TONIGHT!
"ALIVE!" HE SAID!
ALL MIGHT NOT BE LOST.
WHERE DO YOU LIVE?
OVER THERE— NUMBER 36.

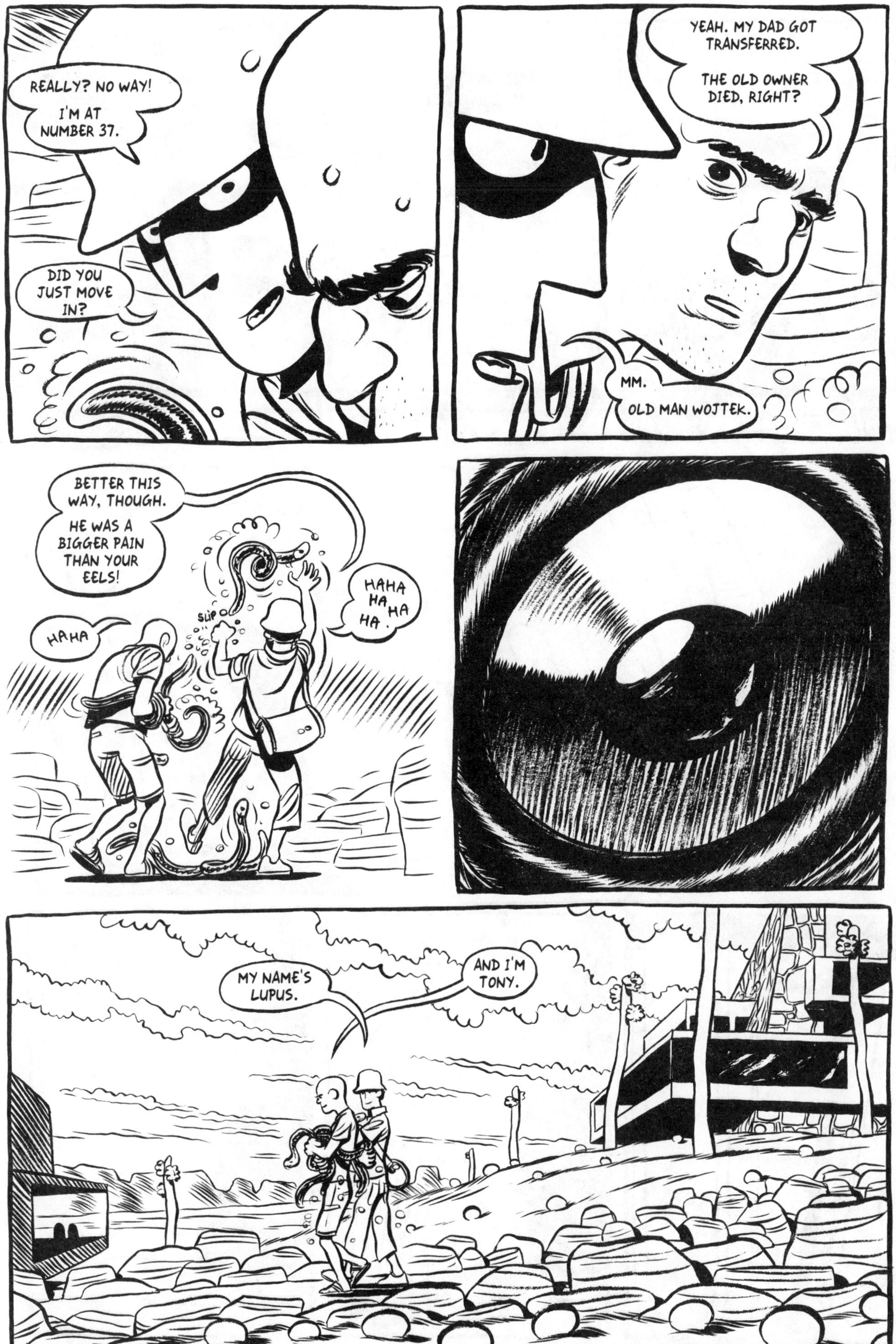
REALLY? NO WAY!
I'M AT NUMBER 37.
DID YOU JUST MOVE IN?
YEAH. MY DAD GOT TRANSFERRED.
THE OLD OWNER DIED, RIGHT?
MM.
OLD MAN WOJTEK.
BETTER THIS WAY, THOUGH.
HE WAS A BIGGER PAIN THAN YOUR EELS!
SLIP
HAHA
HAHA HA HA HA.
MY NAME'S LUPUS.
AND I'M TONY.

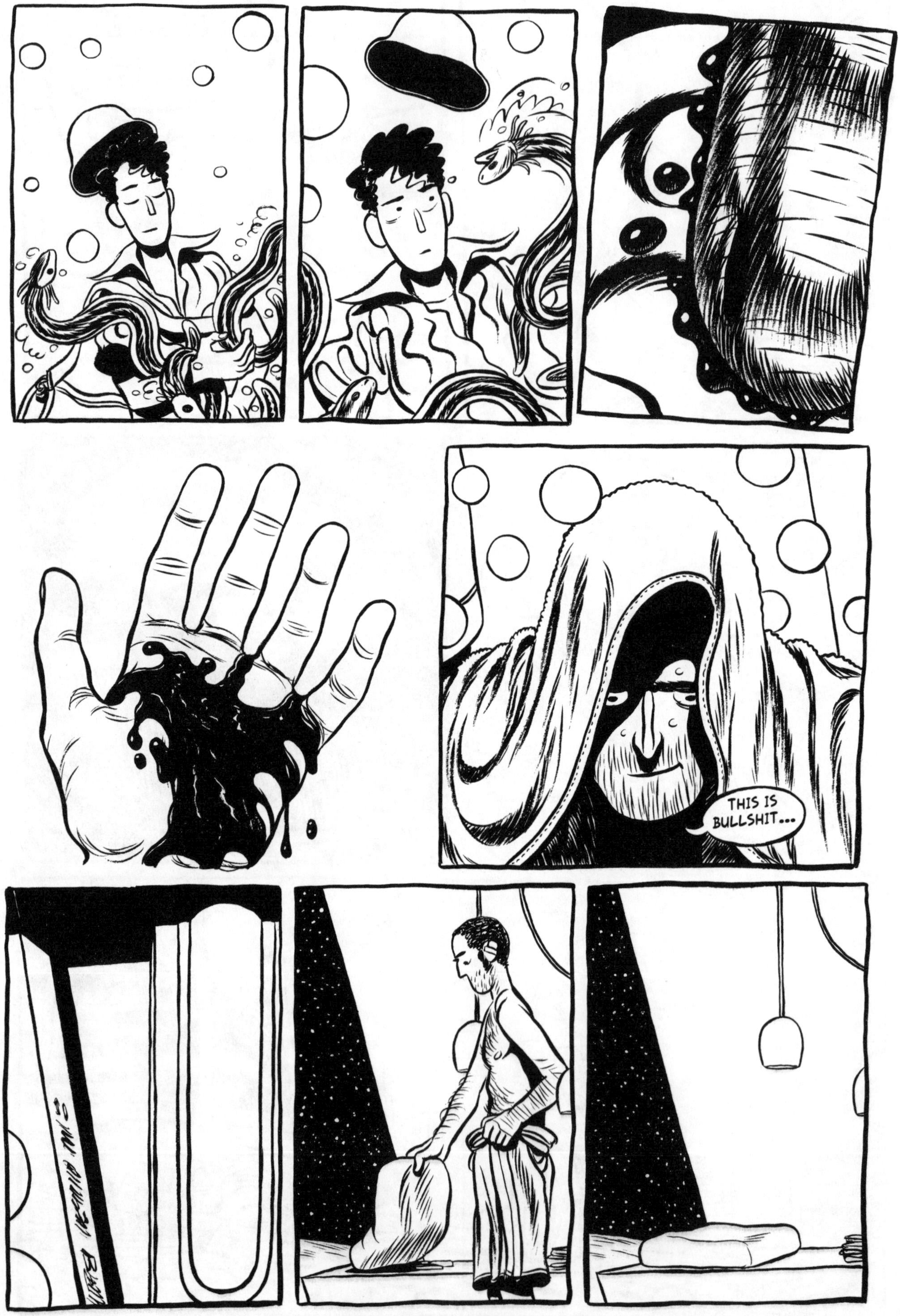
THIS IS BULLSHIT...

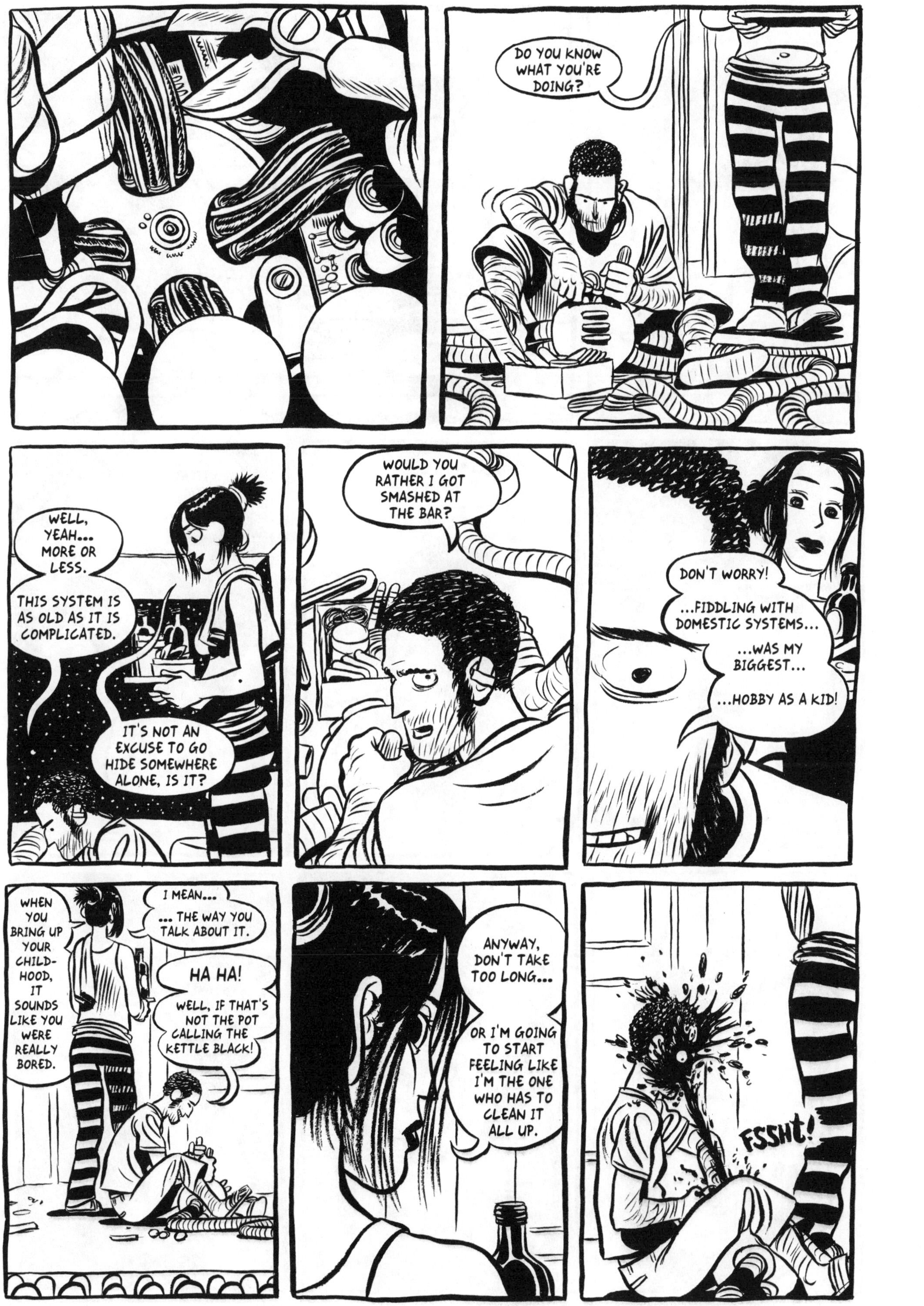
DO YOU KNOW WHAT YOU'RE DOING?
WELL, YEAH... MORE OR LESS.
THIS SYSTEM IS AS OLD AS IT IS COMPLICATED.
IT'S NOT AN EXCUSE TO GO HIDE SOMEWHERE ALONE, IS IT?
WOULD YOU RATHER I GOT SMASHED AT THE BAR?
DON'T WORRY!
...FIDDLING WITH DOMESTIC SYSTEMS...
...WAS MY BIGGEST...
...HOBBY AS A KID!
WHEN YOU BRING UP YOUR CHILD-HOOD, IT SOUNDS LIKE YOU WERE REALLY BORED.
I MEAN...
... THE WAY YOU TALK ABOUT IT.
HA HA!
WELL, IF THAT'S NOT THE POT CALLING THE KETTLE BLACK!
ANYWAY, DON'T TAKE TOO LONG...
OR I'M GOING TO START FEELING LIKE I'M THE ONE WHO HAS TO CLEAN IT ALL UP.
FSSHt!

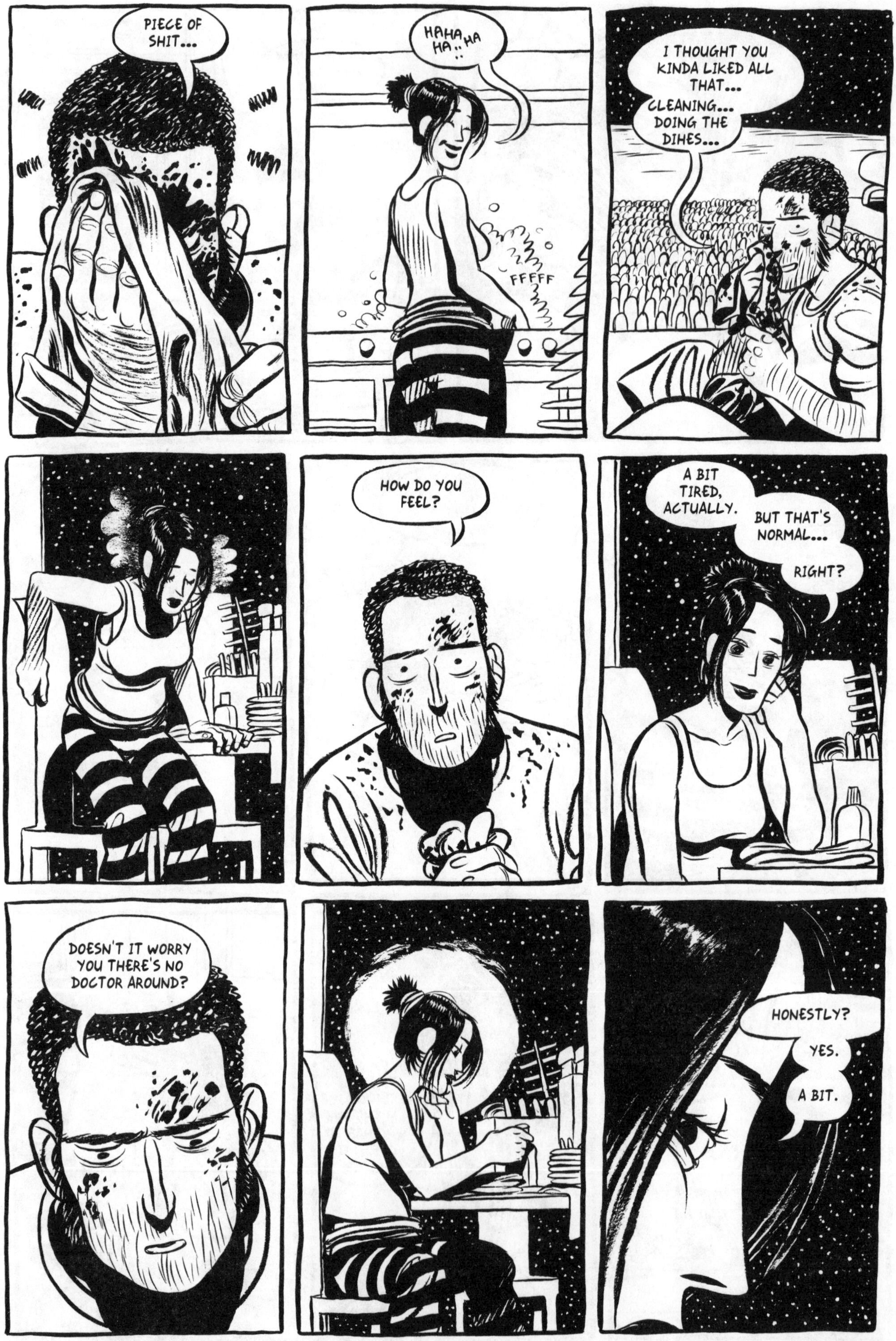
PIECE OF SHIT...
HAHA HA.. HA
FFFFF
I THOUGHT YOU KINDA LIKED ALL THAT...
CLEANING... DOING THE DIHES...
HOW DO YOU FEEL?
A BIT TIRED, ACTUALLY.
BUT THAT'S NORMAL...
RIGHT?
DOESN'T IT WORRY YOU THERE'S NO DOCTOR AROUND?
HONESTLY?
YES.
A BIT.

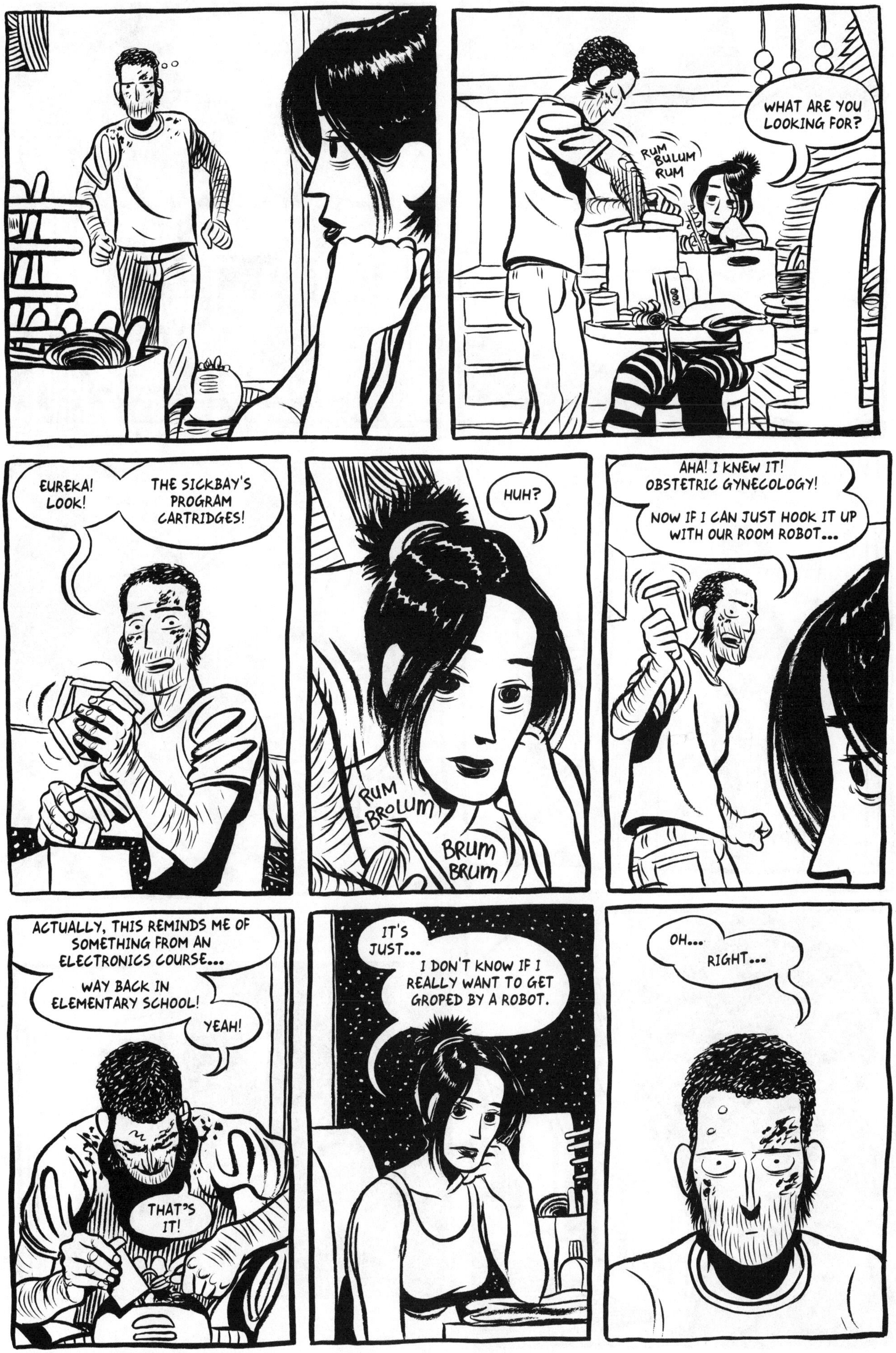
WHAT ARE YOU LOOKING FOR?
RUM BULUM RUM
EUREKA! LOOK!
THE SICKBAY'S PROGRAM CARTRIDGES!
HUH?
RUM BROLUM
BRUM BRUM
AHA! I KNEW IT! OBSTETRIC GYNECOLOGY!
NOW IF I CAN JUST HOOK IT UP WITH OUR ROOM ROBOT...
ACTUALLY, THIS REMINDS ME OF SOMETHING FROM AN ELECTRONICS COURSE...
WAY BACK IN ELEMENTARY SCHOOL!
YEAH!
THAT'S IT!
IT'S JUST...
I DON'T KNOW IF I REALLY WANT TO GET GROPED BY A ROBOT.
OH...
RIGHT...

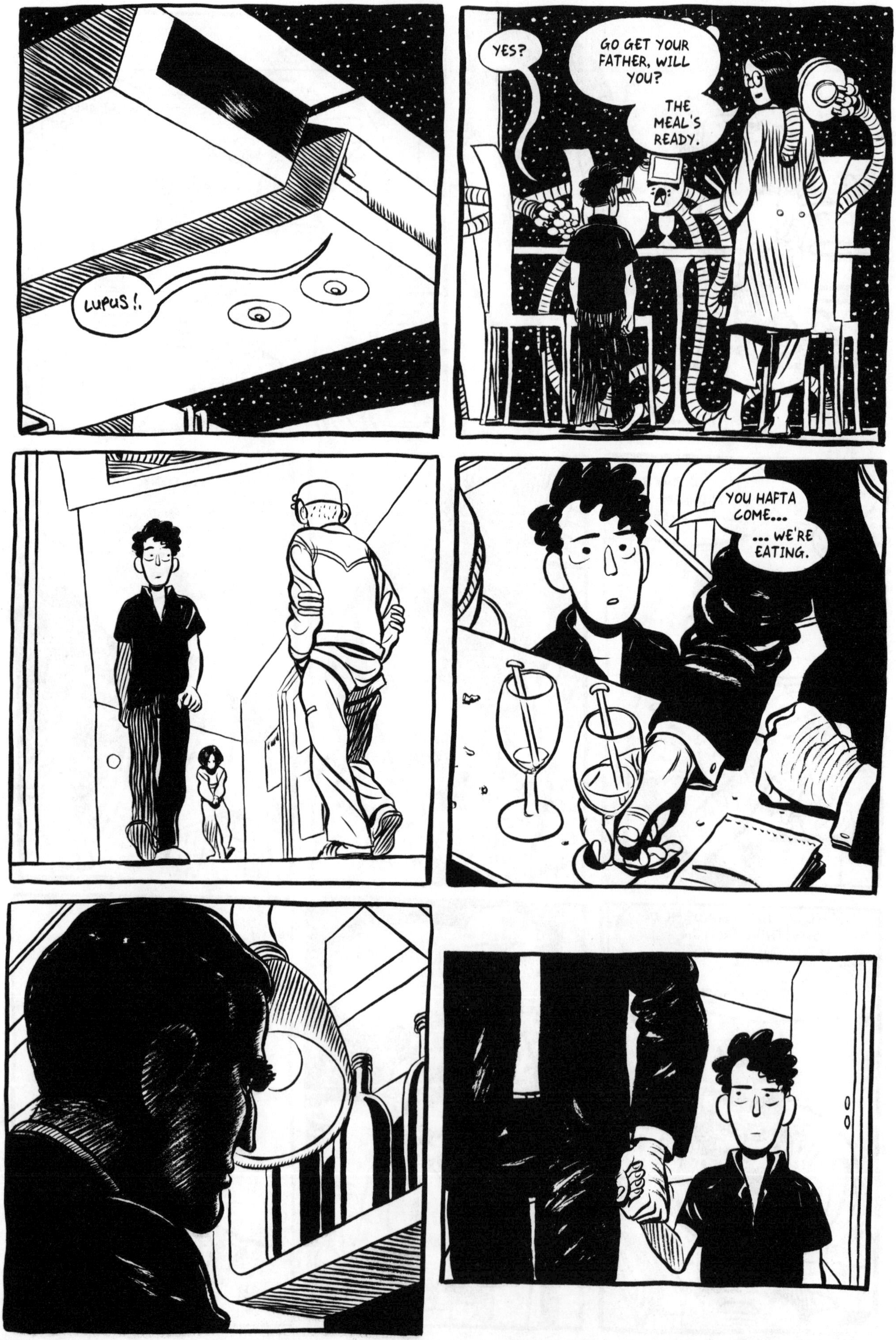
LUPUS !.
YES?
GO GET YOUR FATHER, WILL YOU?
THE MEAL'S READY.
YOU HAFTA COME...
... WE'RE EATING.

uuuuuuuuuuuuuuuuuuuu
?...
WHAT THE—?
WOOOO
NO WAY!

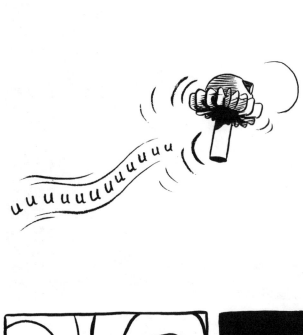

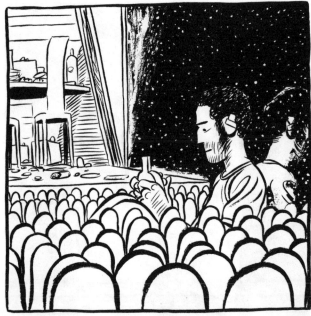

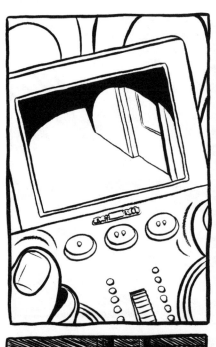

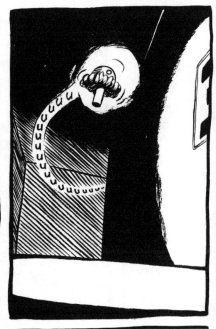

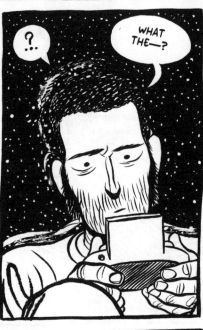

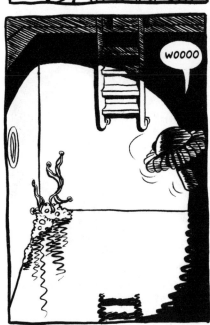

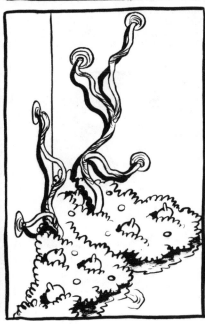

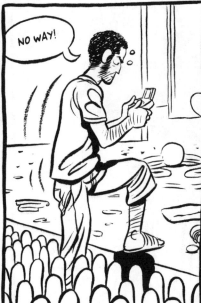

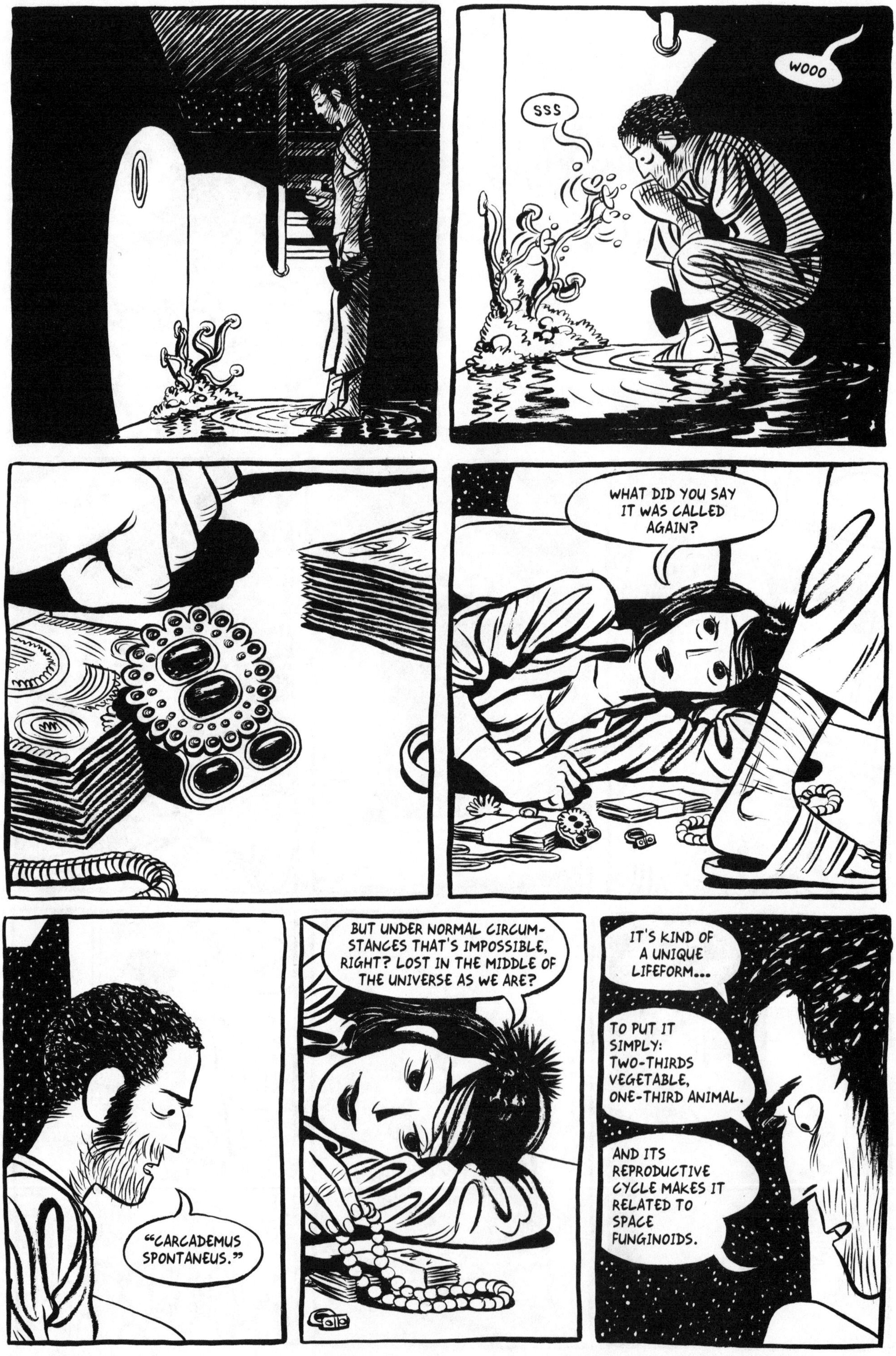
WOOO
SSS
WHAT DID YOU SAY IT WAS CALLED AGAIN?
"CARCADEMUS SPONTANEUS."
BUT UNDER NORMAL CIRCUMSTANCES THAT'S IMPOSSIBLE, RIGHT? LOST IN THE MIDDLE OF THE UNIVERSE AS WE ARE?
IT'S KIND OF A UNIQUE LIFEFORM...
TO PUT IT SIMPLY: TWO-THIRDS VEGETABLE, ONE-THIRD ANIMAL.
AND ITS REPRODUCTIVE CYCLE MAKES IT RELATED TO SPACE FUNGINOIDS.

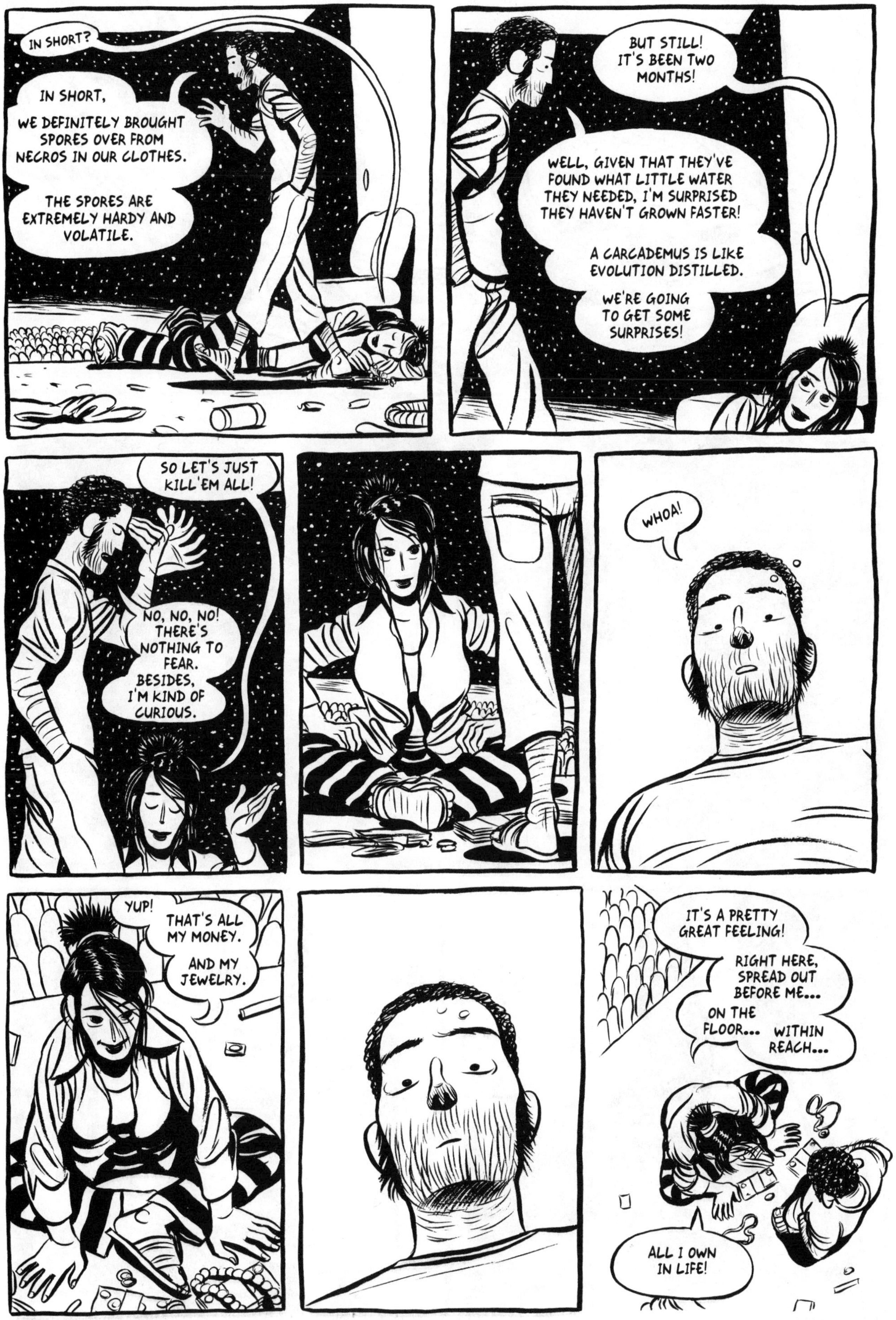
IN SHORT?
IN SHORT,
WE DEFINITELY BROUGHT SPORES OVER FROM NECROS IN OUR CLOTHES.
THE SPORES ARE EXTREMELY HARDY AND VOLATILE.
BUT STILL! IT'S BEEN TWO MONTHS!
WELL, GIVEN THAT THEY'VE FOUND WHAT LITTLE WATER THEY NEEDED, I'M SURPRISED THEY HAVEN'T GROWN FASTER!
A CARCADEMUS IS LIKE EVOLUTION DISTILLED.
WE'RE GOING TO GET SOME SURPRISES!
SO LET'S JUST KILL'EM ALL!
NO, NO, NO! THERE'S NOTHING TO FEAR. BESIDES, I'M KIND OF CURIOUS.
WHOA!
YUP!
THAT'S ALL MY MONEY.
AND MY JEWELRY.
IT'S A PRETTY GREAT FEELING!
RIGHT HERE, SPREAD OUT BEFORE ME...
ON THE FLOOR... WITHIN REACH...
ALL I OWN IN LIFE!

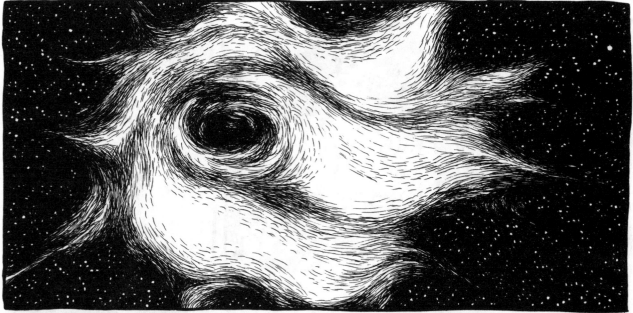

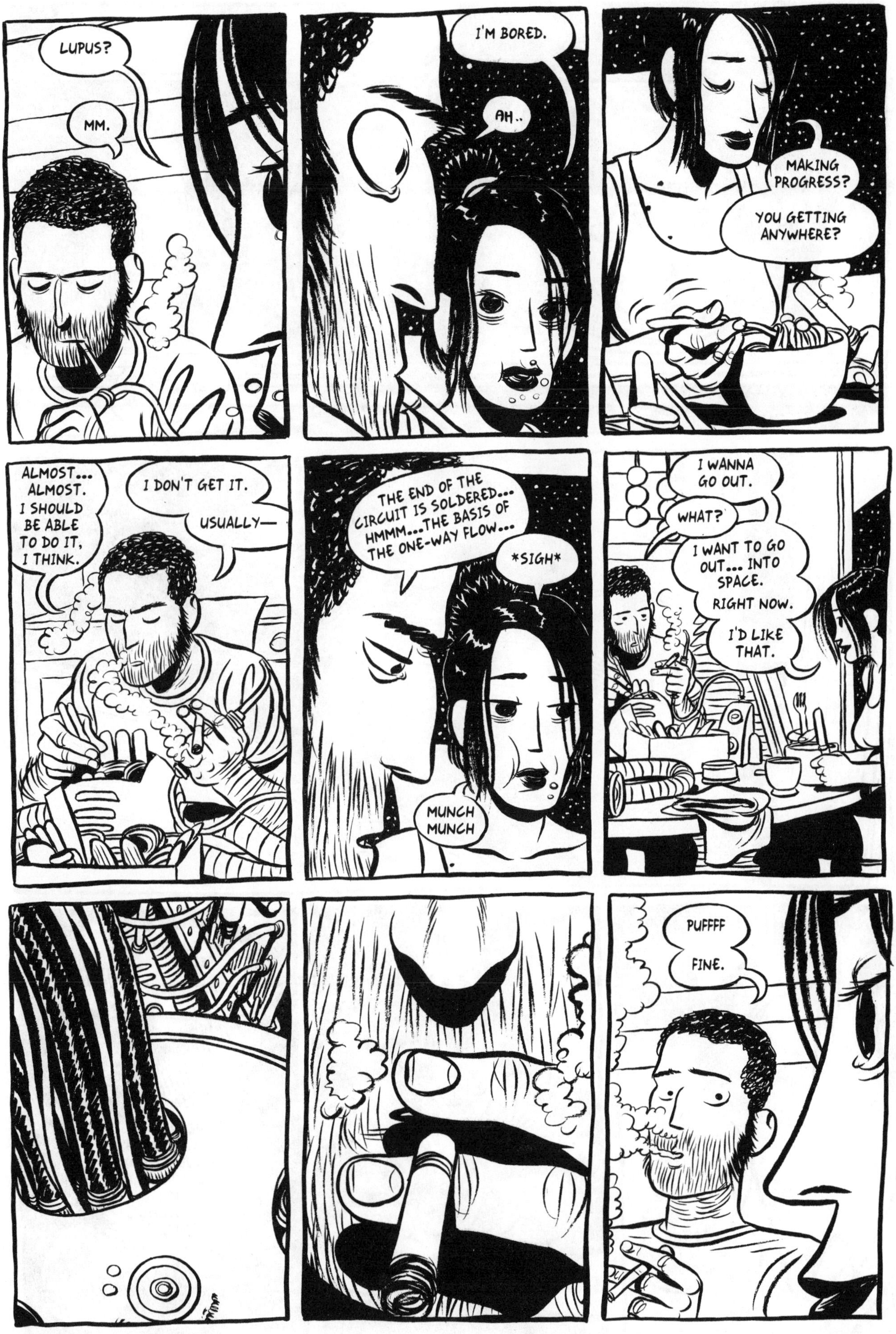

LUPUS?
MM.
I'M BORED.
AH..
MAKING PROGRESS?
YOU GETTING ANYWHERE?
ALMOST... ALMOST. I SHOULD BE ABLE TO DO IT, I THINK.
I DON'T GET IT.
USUALLY—
THE END OF THE CIRCUIT IS SOLDERED... THE BASIS OF HMMM... THE ONE-WAY FLOW...
SIGH
MUNCH MUNCH
I WANNA GO OUT.
WHAT?
I WANT TO GO OUT... INTO SPACE.
RIGHT NOW.
I'D LIKE THAT.
PUFFFF
FINE.

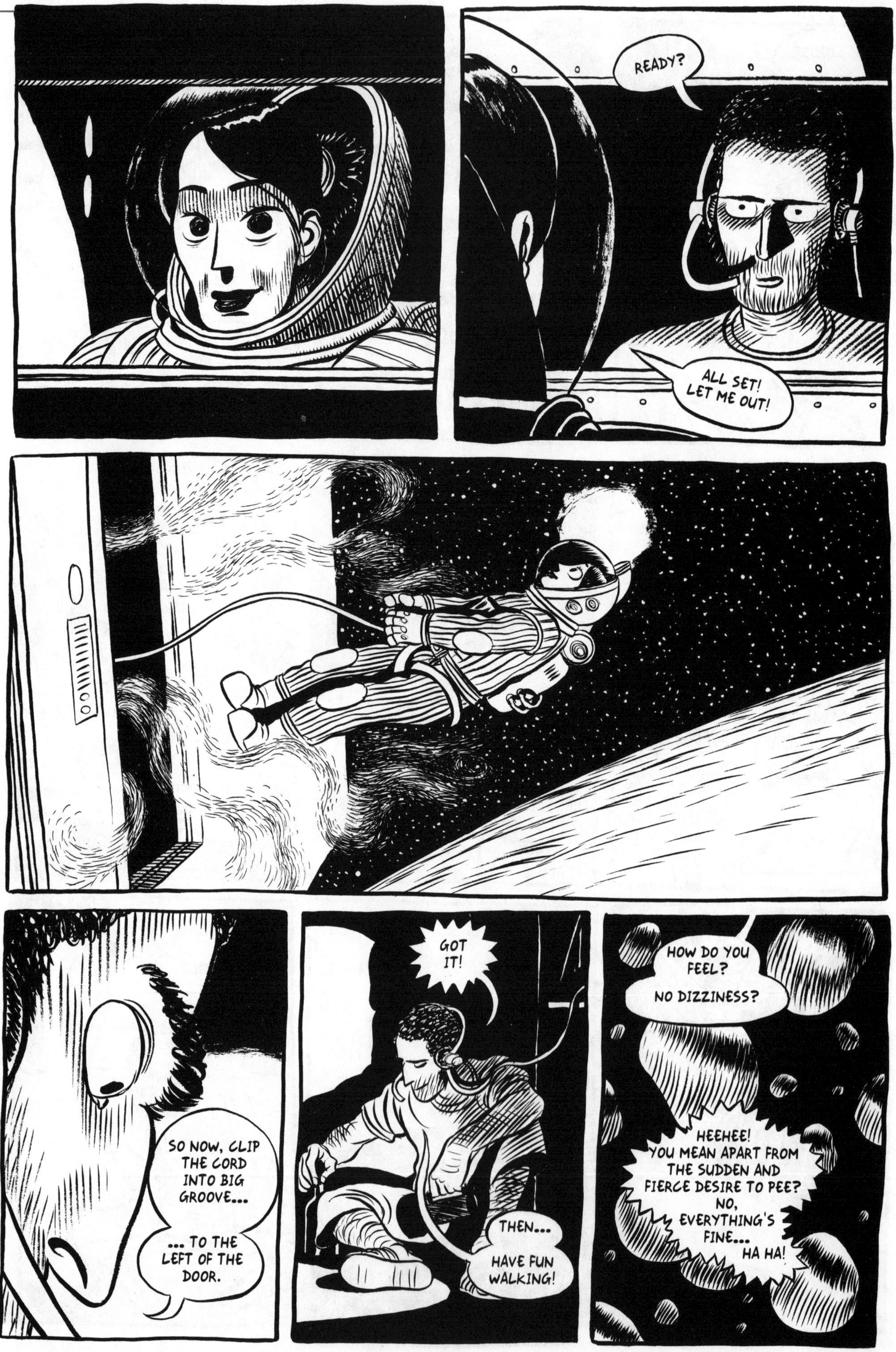
READY?
ALL SET! LET ME OUT!
SO NOW, CLIP THE CORD INTO BIG GROOVE...
... TO THE LEFT OF THE DOOR.
GOT IT!
THEN...
HAVE FUN WALKING!
HOW DO YOU FEEL?
NO DIZZINESS?
HEEHEE! YOU MEAN APART FROM THE SUDDEN AND FIERCE DESIRE TO PEE? NO, EVERYTHING'S FINE... HA HA!

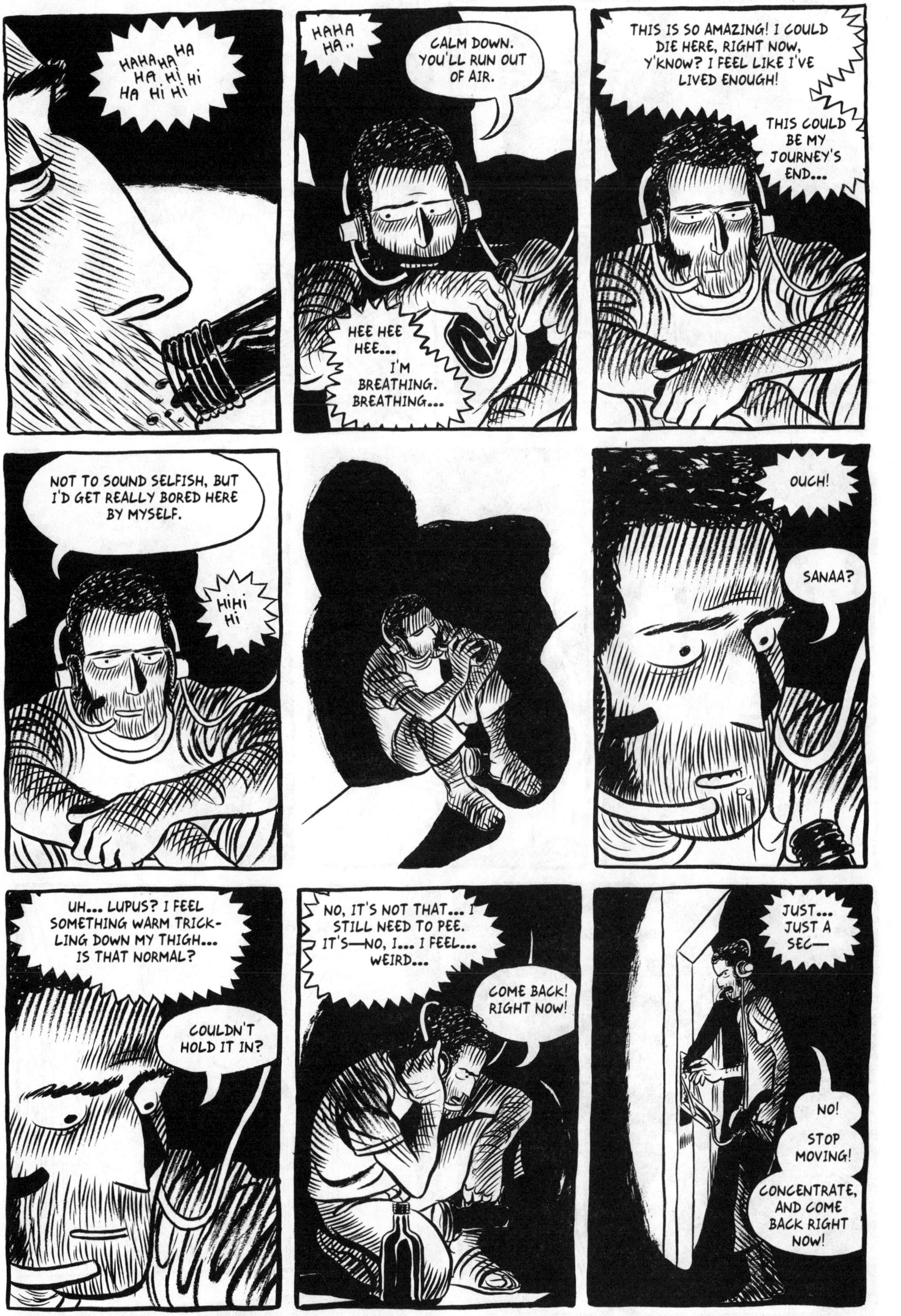
HAHAHA HA HA HI HI HA HI HI
HAHA HA..
CALM DOWN. YOU'LL RUN OUT OF AIR.
HEE HEE HEE... I'M BREATHING. BREATHING...
THIS IS SO AMAZING! I COULD DIE HERE, RIGHT NOW, Y'KNOW? I FEEL LIKE I'VE LIVED ENOUGH!
THIS COULD BE MY JOURNEY'S END...
NOT TO SOUND SELFISH, BUT I'D GET REALLY BORED HERE BY MYSELF.
HIHI HI
OUCH!
SANAA?
UH... LUPUS? I FEEL SOMETHING WARM TRICK-LING DOWN MY THIGH... IS THAT NORMAL?
COULDN'T HOLD IT IN?
NO, IT'S NOT THAT... I STILL NEED TO PEE. IT'S—NO, I... I FEEL... WEIRD...
COME BACK! RIGHT NOW!
JUST... JUST A SEC—
NO!
STOP MOVING!
CONCENTRATE, AND COME BACK RIGHT NOW!

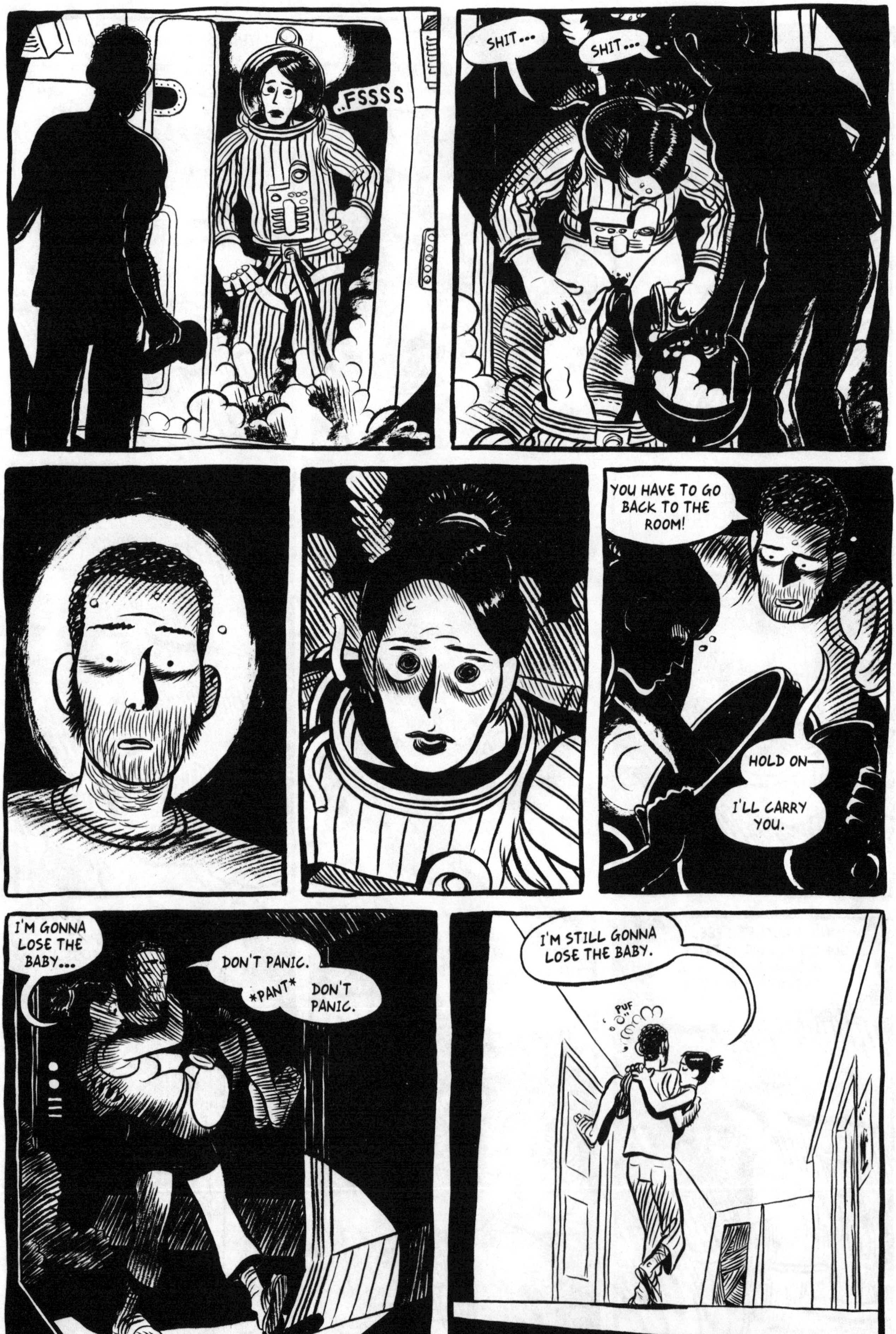
..FSSSS
SHIT...
SHIT...
YOU HAVE TO GO BACK TO THE ROOM!
HOLD ON—
I'LL CARRY YOU.
I'M GONNA LOSE THE BABY...
DON'T PANIC.
PANT DON'T PANIC.
I'M STILL GONNA LOSE THE BABY.
PUF

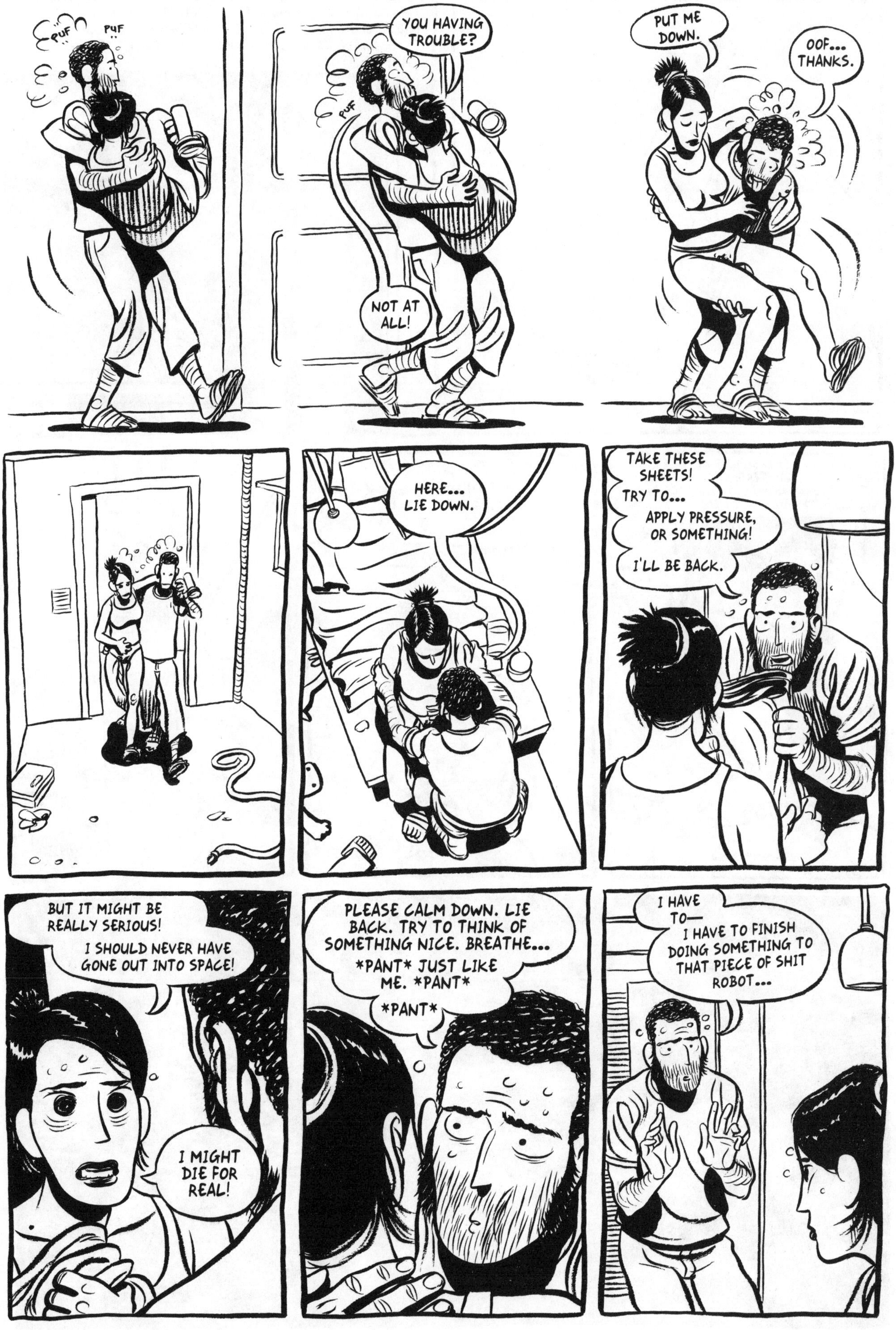
PUF
PUF
YOU HAVING TROUBLE?
PUF
NOT AT ALL!
PUT ME DOWN.
OOF... THANKS.
HERE... LIE DOWN.
TAKE THESE SHEETS!
TRY TO...
APPLY PRESSURE, OR SOMETHING!
I'LL BE BACK.
BUT IT MIGHT BE REALLY SERIOUS!
I SHOULD NEVER HAVE GONE OUT INTO SPACE!
I MIGHT DIE FOR REAL!
PLEASE CALM DOWN. LIE BACK. TRY TO THINK OF SOMETHING NICE. BREATHE...
PANT JUST LIKE ME. *PANT*
PANT
I HAVE TO—
I HAVE TO FINISH DOING SOMETHING TO THAT PIECE OF SHIT ROBOT...

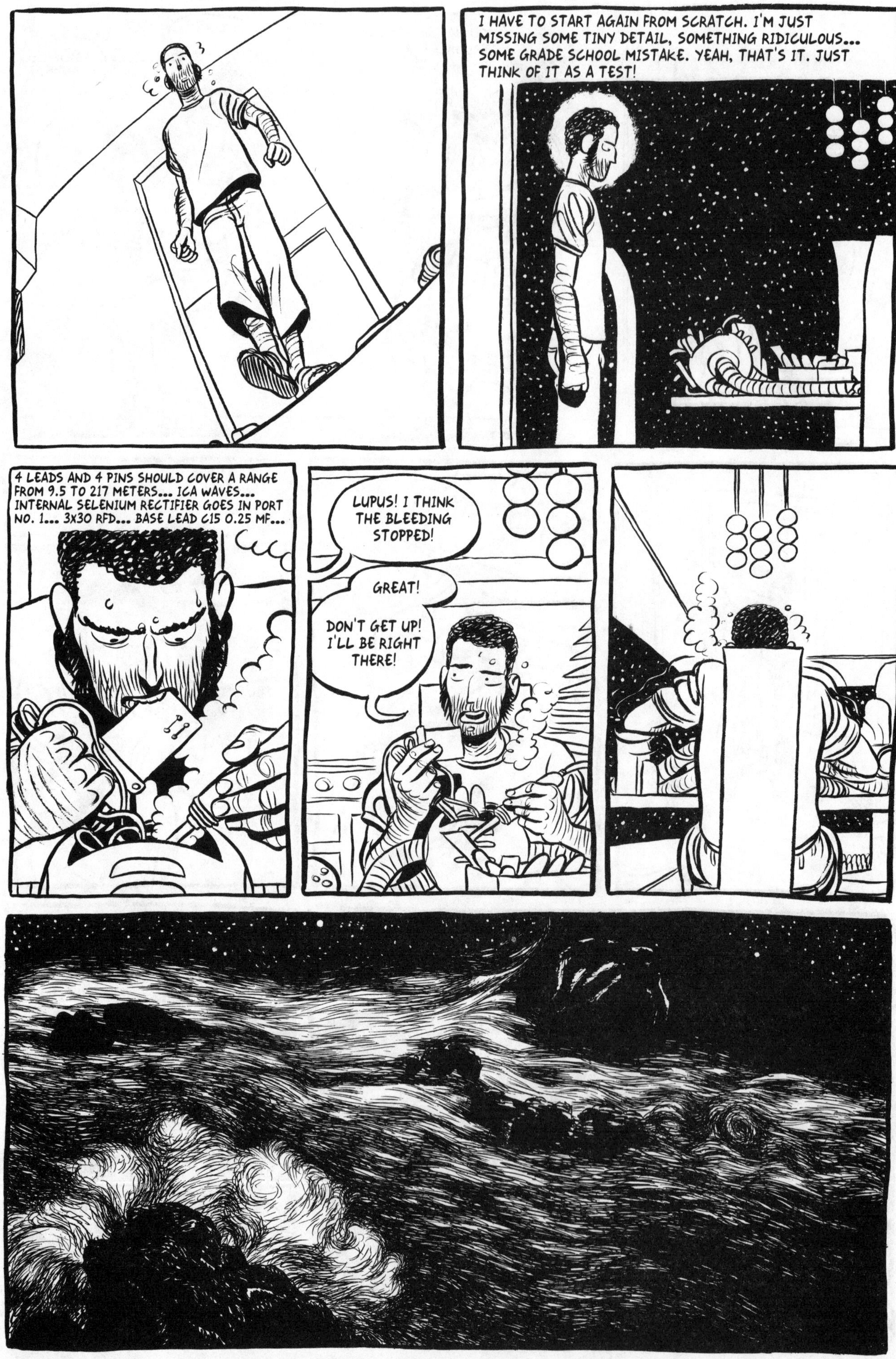

I HAVE TO START AGAIN FROM SCRATCH. I'M JUST MISSING SOME TINY DETAIL, SOMETHING RIDICULOUS... SOME GRADE SCHOOL MISTAKE. YEAH, THAT'S IT. JUST THINK OF IT AS A TEST!
4 LEADS AND 4 PINS SHOULD COVER A RANGE FROM 9.5 TO 217 METERS... ICA WAVES... INTERNAL SELENIUM RECTIFIER GOES IN PORT NO. 1... 3X30 RFD... BASE LEAD C15 0.25 MF...
LUPUS! I THINK THE BLEEDING STOPPED!
GREAT!
DON'T GET UP! I'LL BE RIGHT THERE!

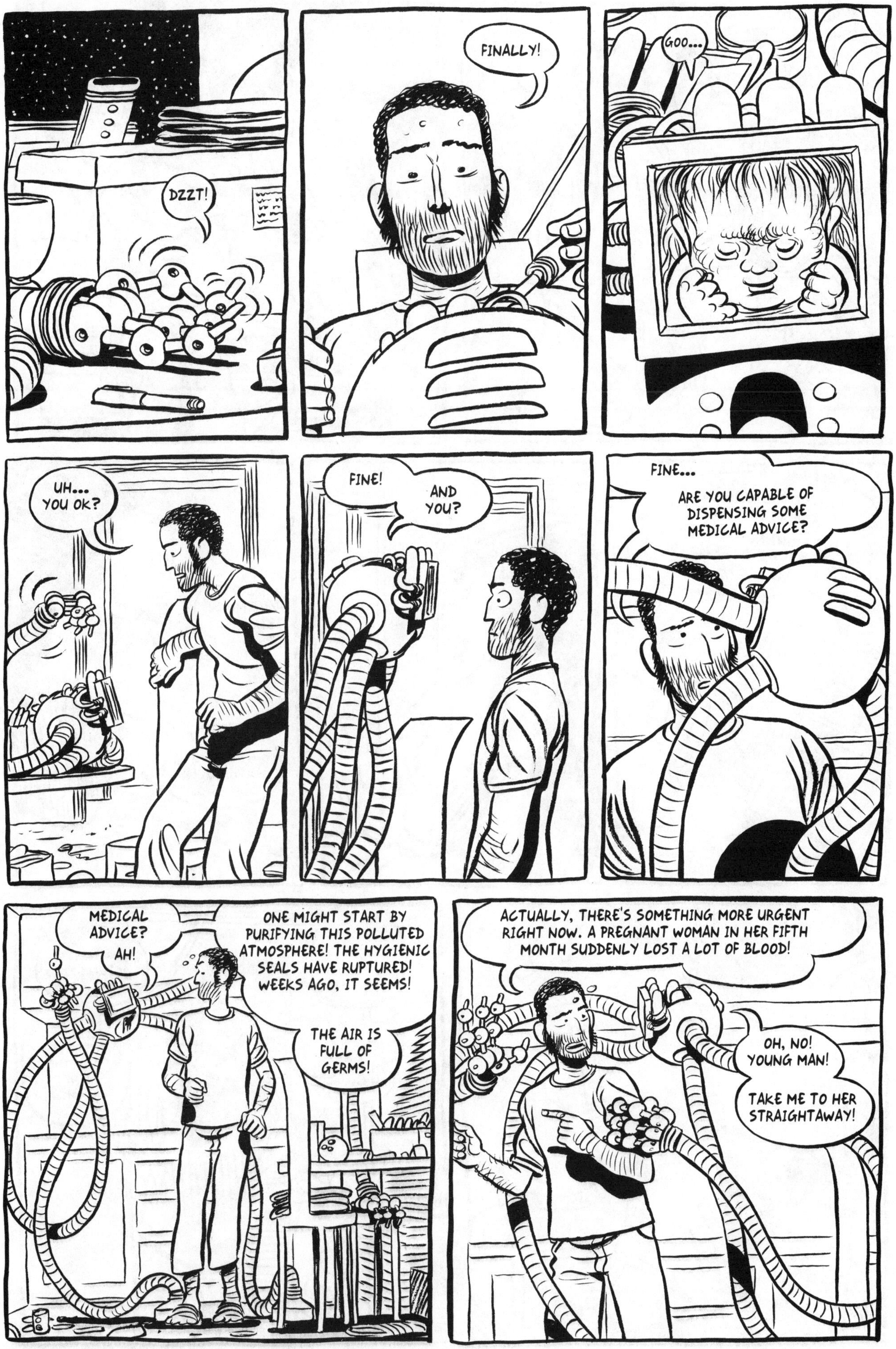
DZZT!
FINALLY!
GOO...
UH... YOU OK?
FINE!
AND YOU?
FINE...
ARE YOU CAPABLE OF DISPENSING SOME MEDICAL ADVICE?
MEDICAL ADVICE?
AH!
ONE MIGHT START BY PURIFYING THIS POLLUTED ATMOSPHERE! THE HYGIENIC SEALS HAVE RUPTURED! WEEKS AGO, IT SEEMS!
THE AIR IS FULL OF GERMS!
ACTUALLY, THERE'S SOMETHING MORE URGENT RIGHT NOW. A PREGNANT WOMAN IN HER FIFTH MONTH SUDDENLY LOST A LOT OF BLOOD!
OH, NO! YOUNG MAN!
TAKE ME TO HER STRAIGHTAWAY!

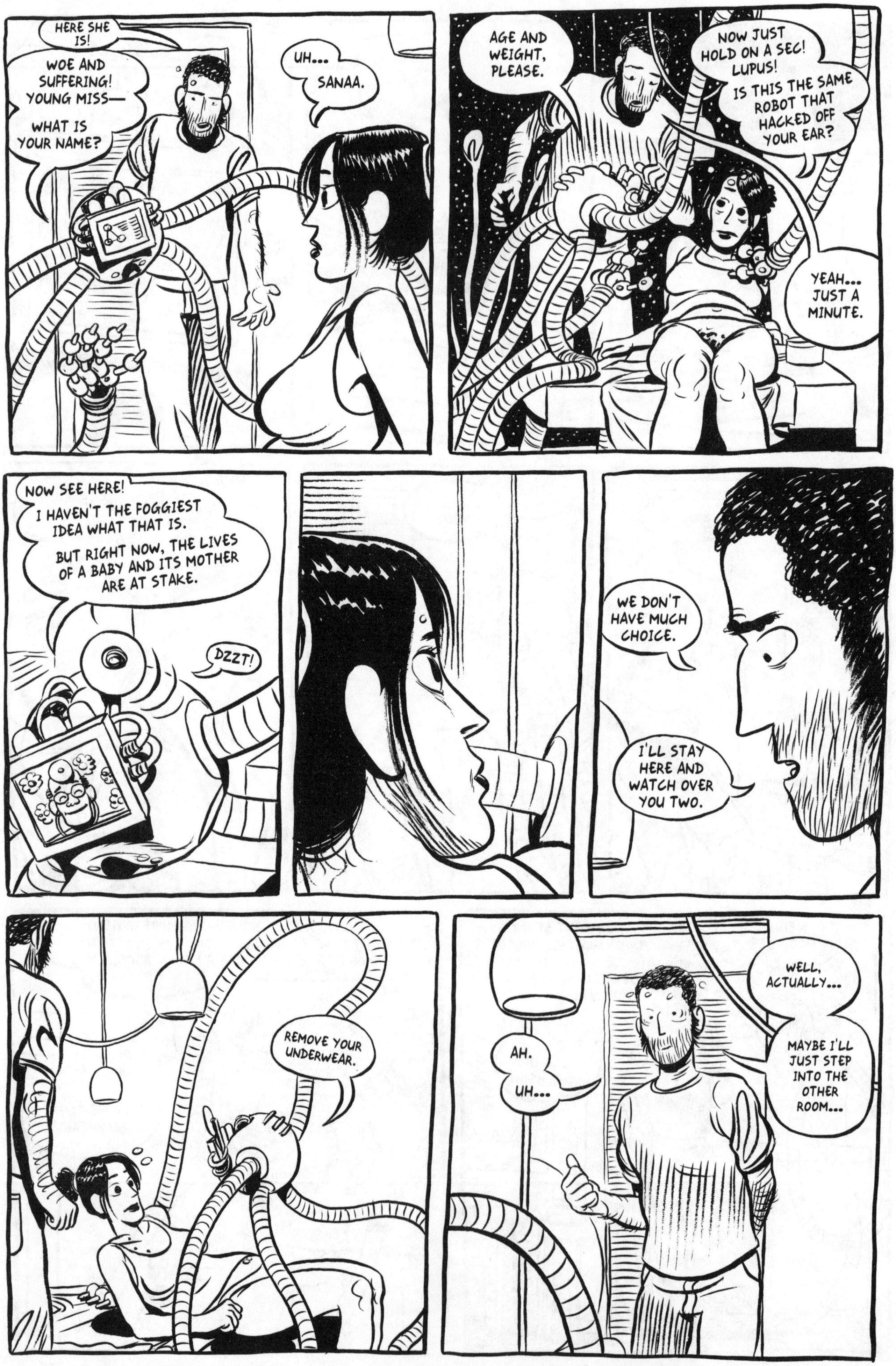
HERE SHE IS!
WOE AND SUFFERING! YOUNG MISS—
WHAT IS YOUR NAME?
UH...
SANAA.
AGE AND WEIGHT, PLEASE.
NOW JUST HOLD ON A SEC! LUPUS!
IS THIS THE SAME ROBOT THAT HACKED OFF YOUR EAR?
YEAH... JUST A MINUTE.
NOW SEE HERE!
I HAVEN'T THE FOGGIEST IDEA WHAT THAT IS.
BUT RIGHT NOW, THE LIVES OF A BABY AND ITS MOTHER ARE AT STAKE.
DZZT!
WE DON'T HAVE MUCH CHOICE.
I'LL STAY HERE AND WATCH OVER YOU TWO.
REMOVE YOUR UNDERWEAR.
AH.
UH...
WELL, ACTUALLY...
MAYBE I'LL JUST STEP INTO THE OTHER ROOM...

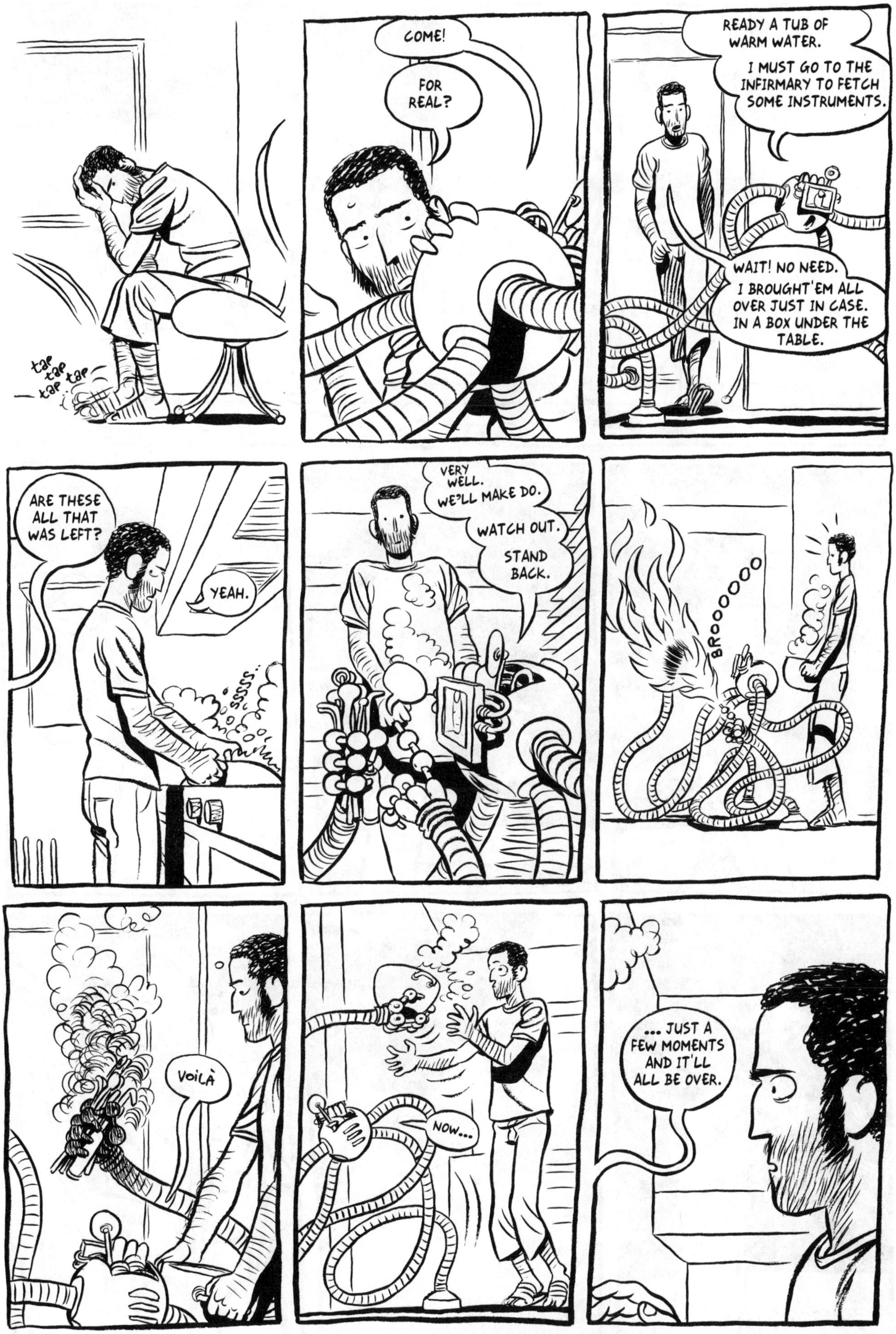
tap tap tap tap
COME!
FOR REAL?
READY A TUB OF WARM WATER.
I MUST GO TO THE INFIRMARY TO FETCH SOME INSTRUMENTS.
WAIT! NO NEED. I BROUGHT 'EM ALL OVER JUST IN CASE. IN A BOX UNDER THE TABLE.
ARE THESE ALL THAT WAS LEFT?
YEAH.
SSSSS..
VERY WELL. WE'LL MAKE DO.
WATCH OUT.
STAND BACK.
BROOOOOOO
VOILÀ
NOW...
... JUST A FEW MOMENTS AND IT'LL ALL BE OVER.

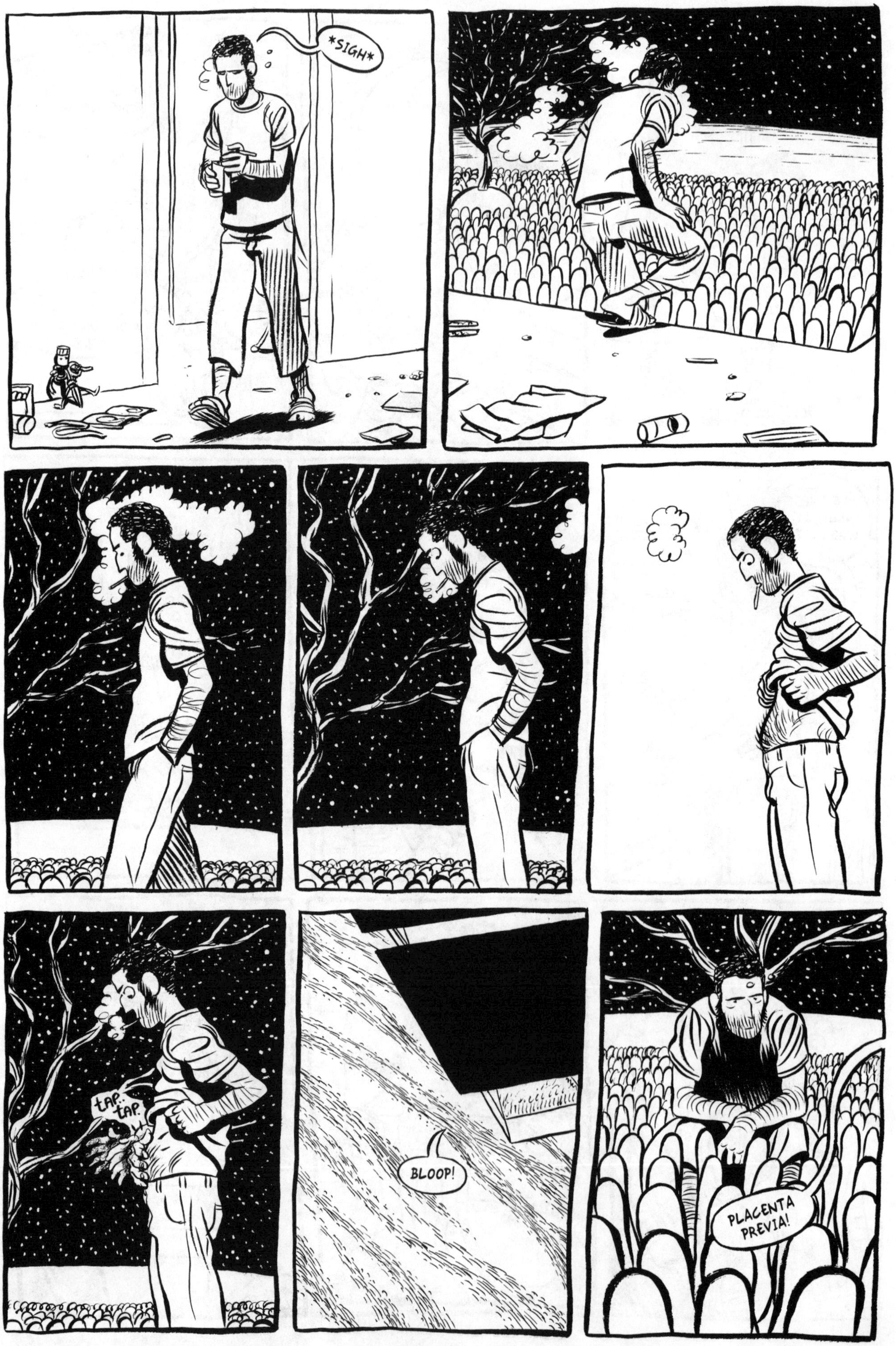
SIGH
TAP.. TAP..
BLOOP!
PLACENTA PREVIA!

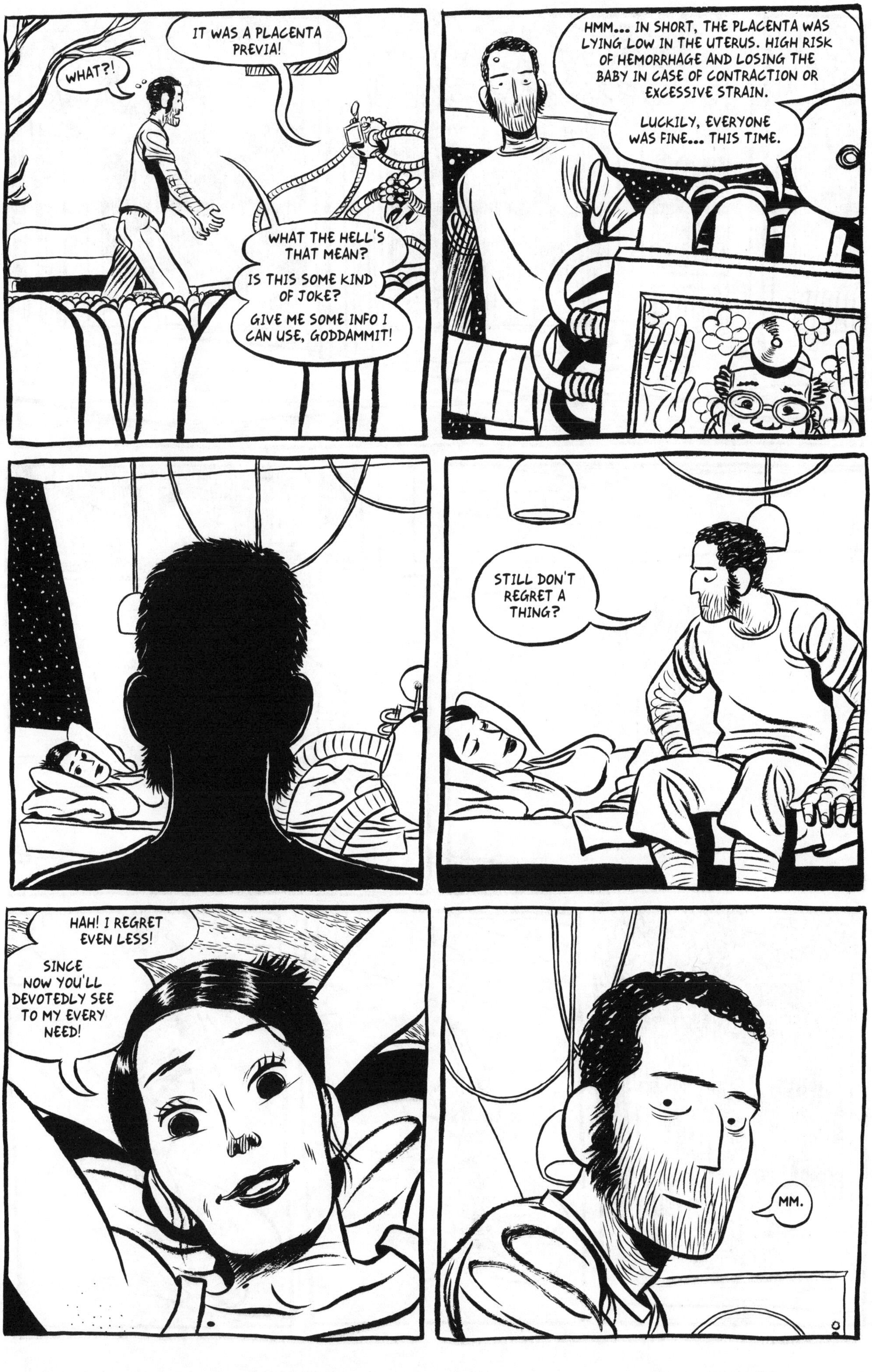

IT WAS A PLACENTA PREVIA!
WHAT?!
WHAT THE HELL'S THAT MEAN?
IS THIS SOME KIND OF JOKE?
GIVE ME SOME INFO I CAN USE, GODDAMMIT!
HMM... IN SHORT, THE PLACENTA WAS LYING LOW IN THE UTERUS. HIGH RISK OF HEMORRHAGE AND LOSING THE BABY IN CASE OF CONTRACTION OR EXCESSIVE STRAIN.
LUCKILY, EVERYONE WAS FINE... THIS TIME.
STILL DON'T REGRET A THING?
HAH! I REGRET EVEN LESS!
SINCE NOW YOU'LL DEVOTEDLY SEE TO MY EVERY NEED!
MM.

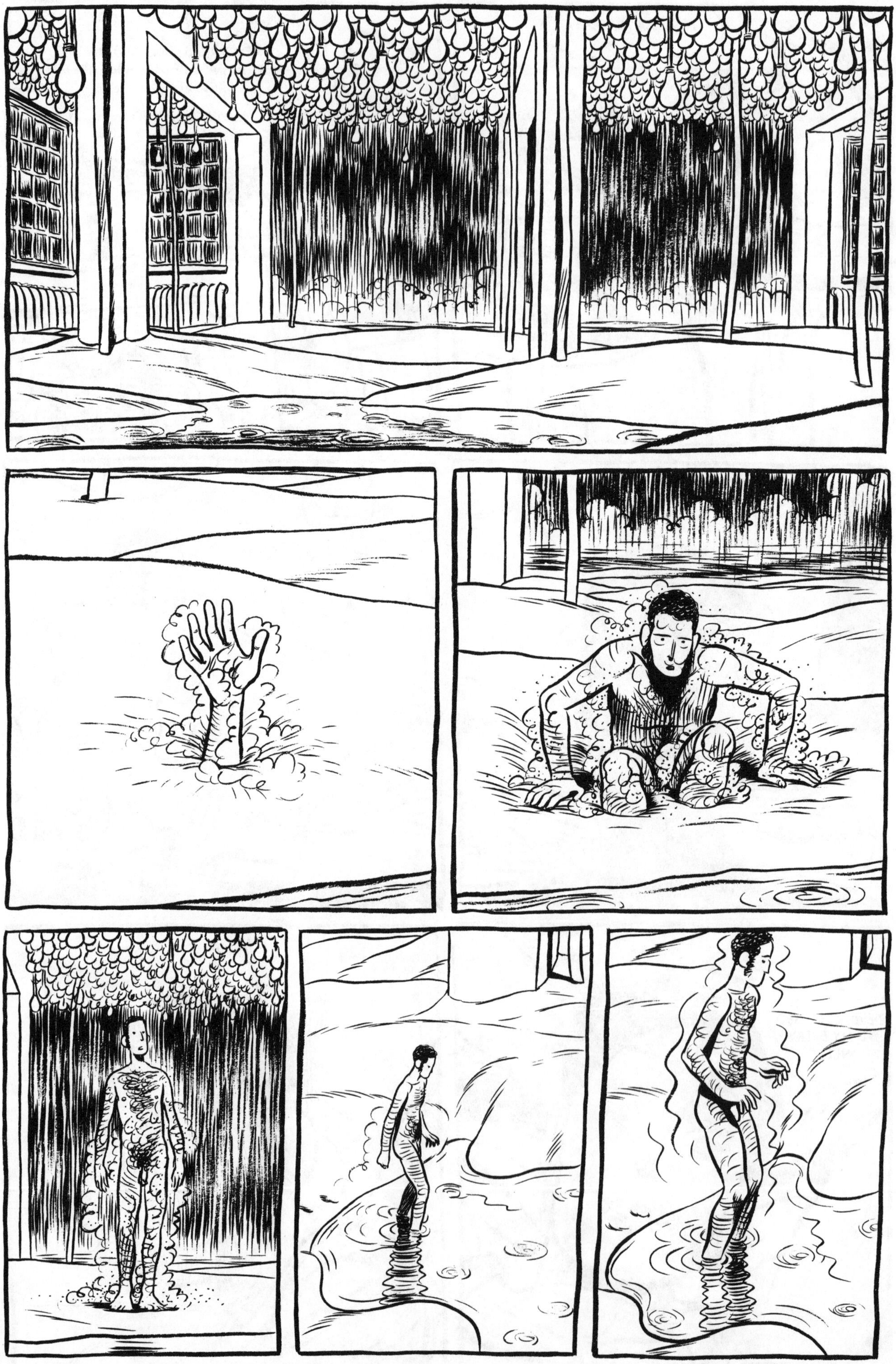

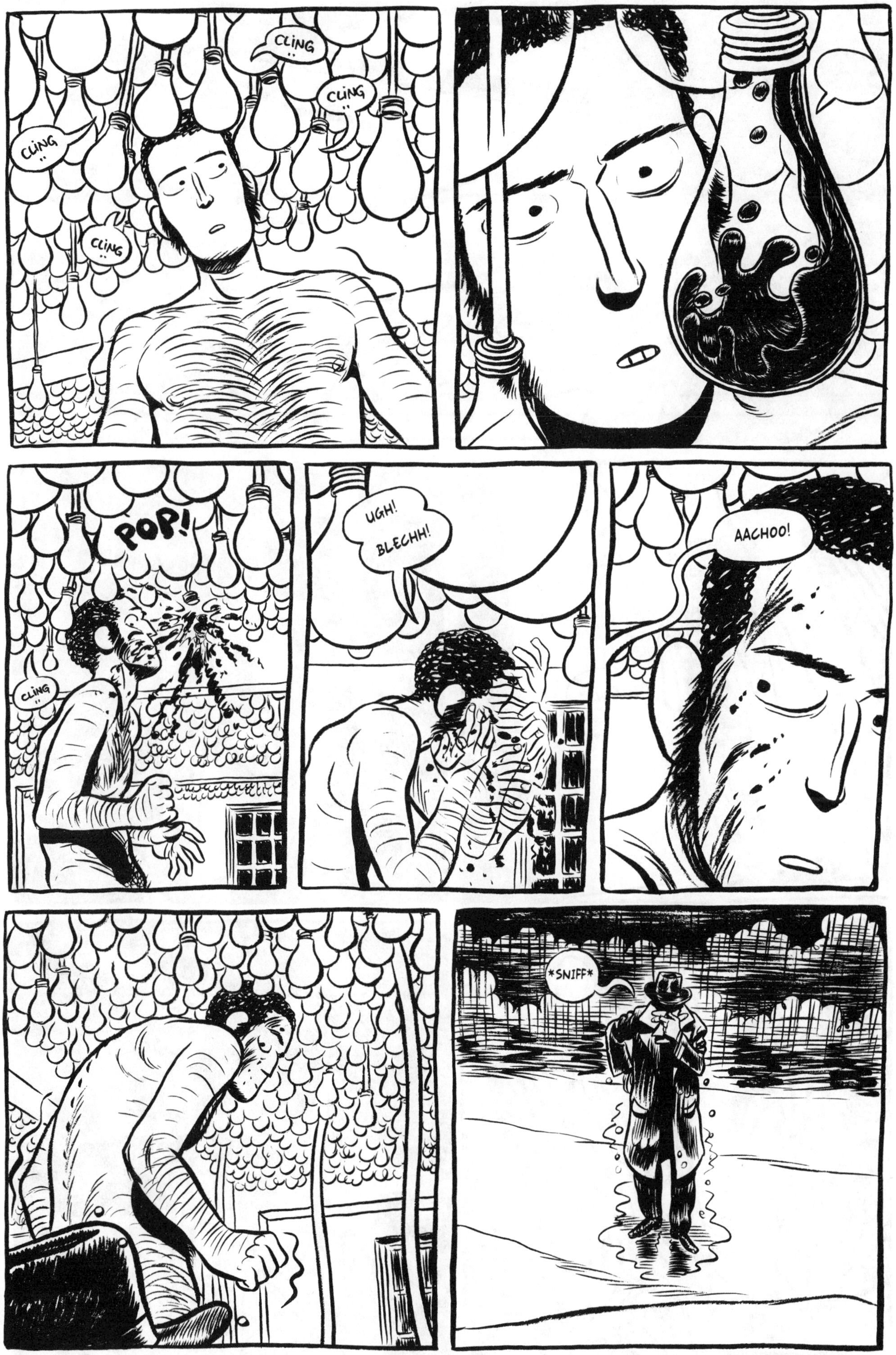
CLING
CLING
CLING
CLING
POP!
CLING
UGH! BLECHH!
AACHOO!
SNIFF

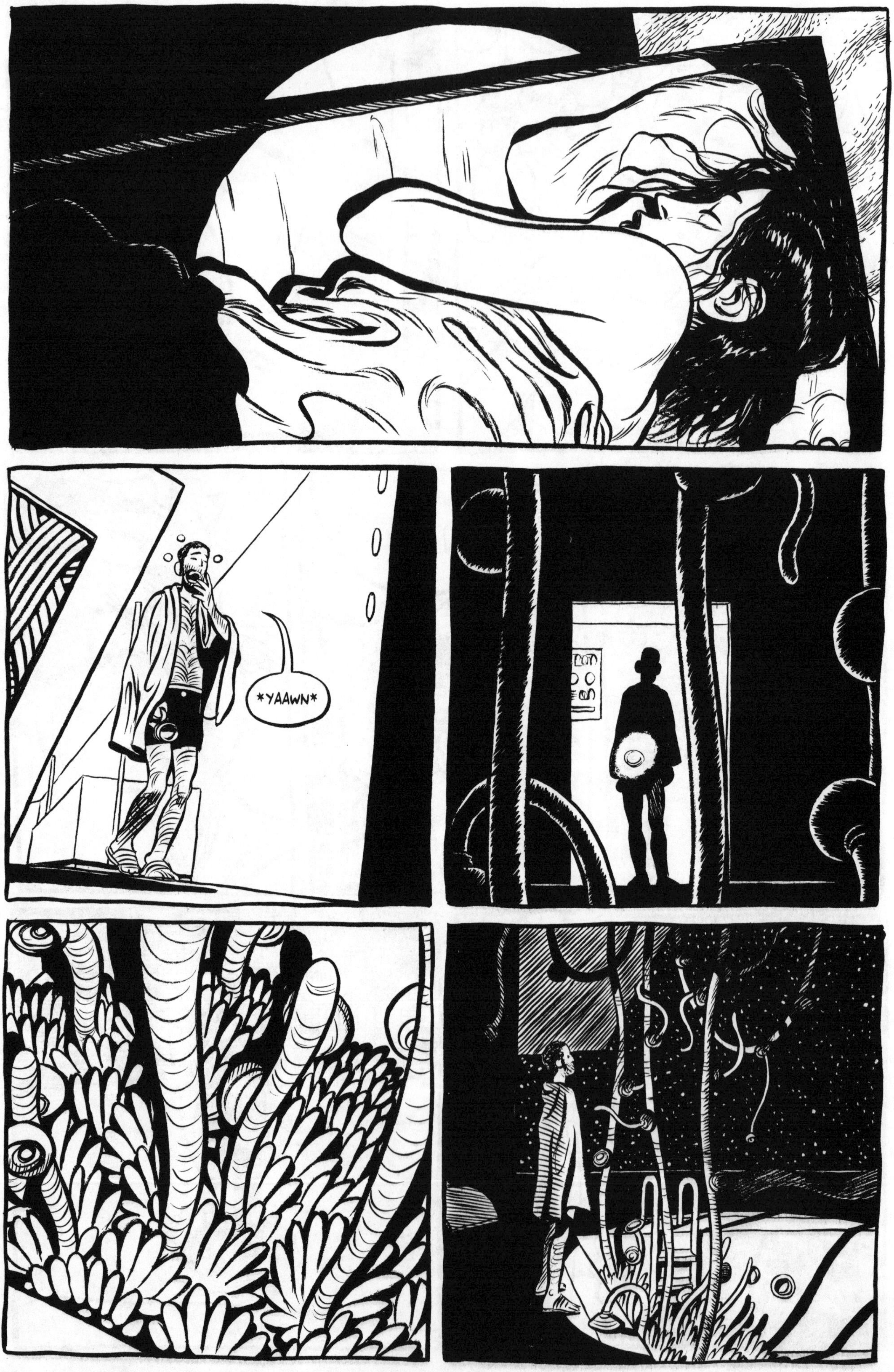
YAAWN

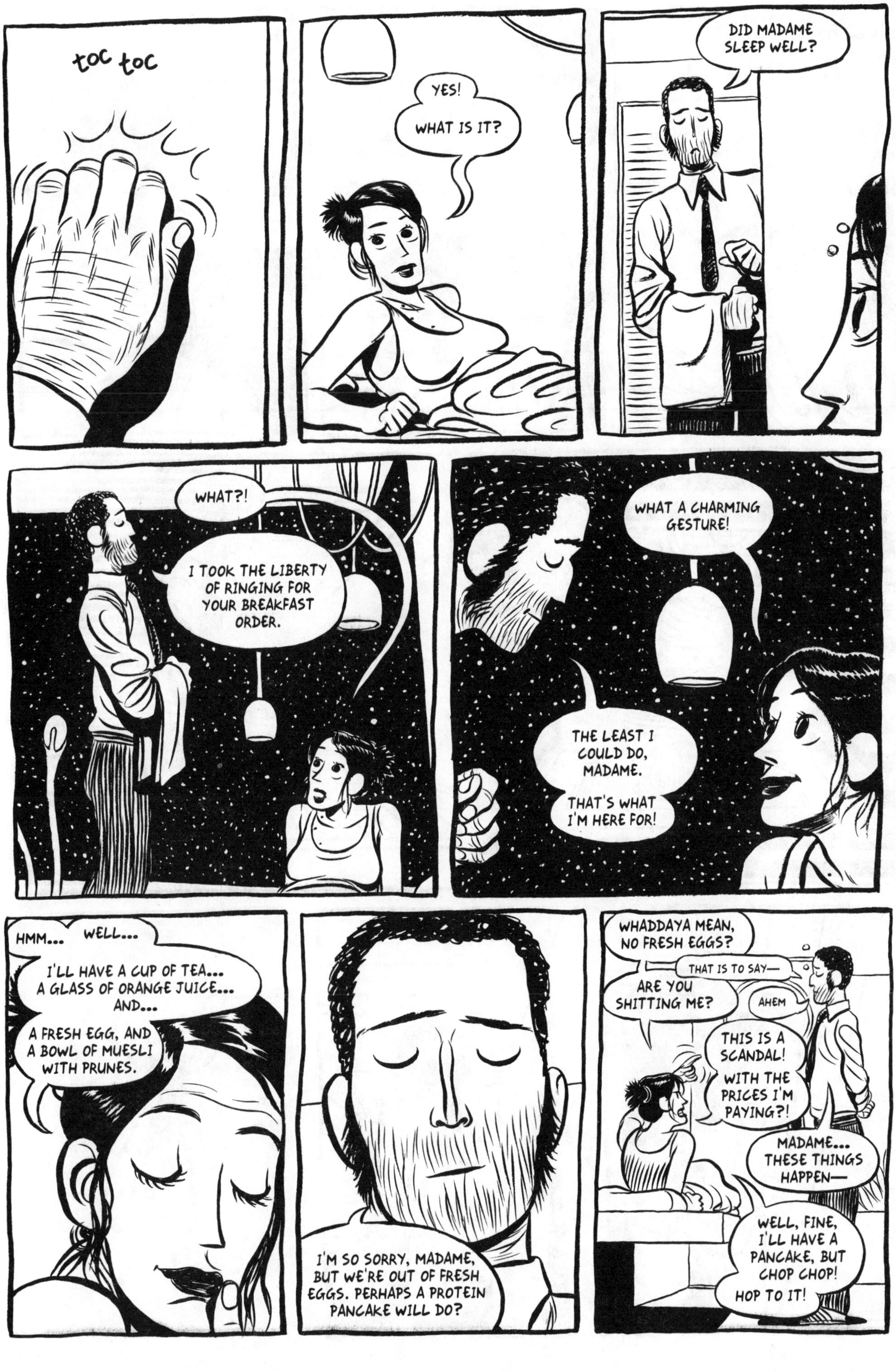
toc toc
YES!
WHAT IS IT?
DID MADAME SLEEP WELL?
WHAT?!
I TOOK THE LIBERTY OF RINGING FOR YOUR BREAKFAST ORDER.
WHAT A CHARMING GESTURE!
THE LEAST I COULD DO, MADAME.
THAT'S WHAT I'M HERE FOR!
HMM... WELL...
I'LL HAVE A CUP OF TEA... A GLASS OF ORANGE JUICE... AND...
A FRESH EGG, AND A BOWL OF MUESLI WITH PRUNES.
I'M SO SORRY, MADAME, BUT WE'RE OUT OF FRESH EGGS. PERHAPS A PROTEIN PANCAKE WILL DO?
WHADDAYA MEAN, NO FRESH EGGS?
THAT IS TO SAY—
ARE YOU SHITTING ME?
AHEM
THIS IS A SCANDAL!
WITH THE PRICES I'M PAYING?!
MADAME... THESE THINGS HAPPEN—
WELL, FINE, I'LL HAVE A PANCAKE, BUT CHOP CHOP!
HOP TO IT!

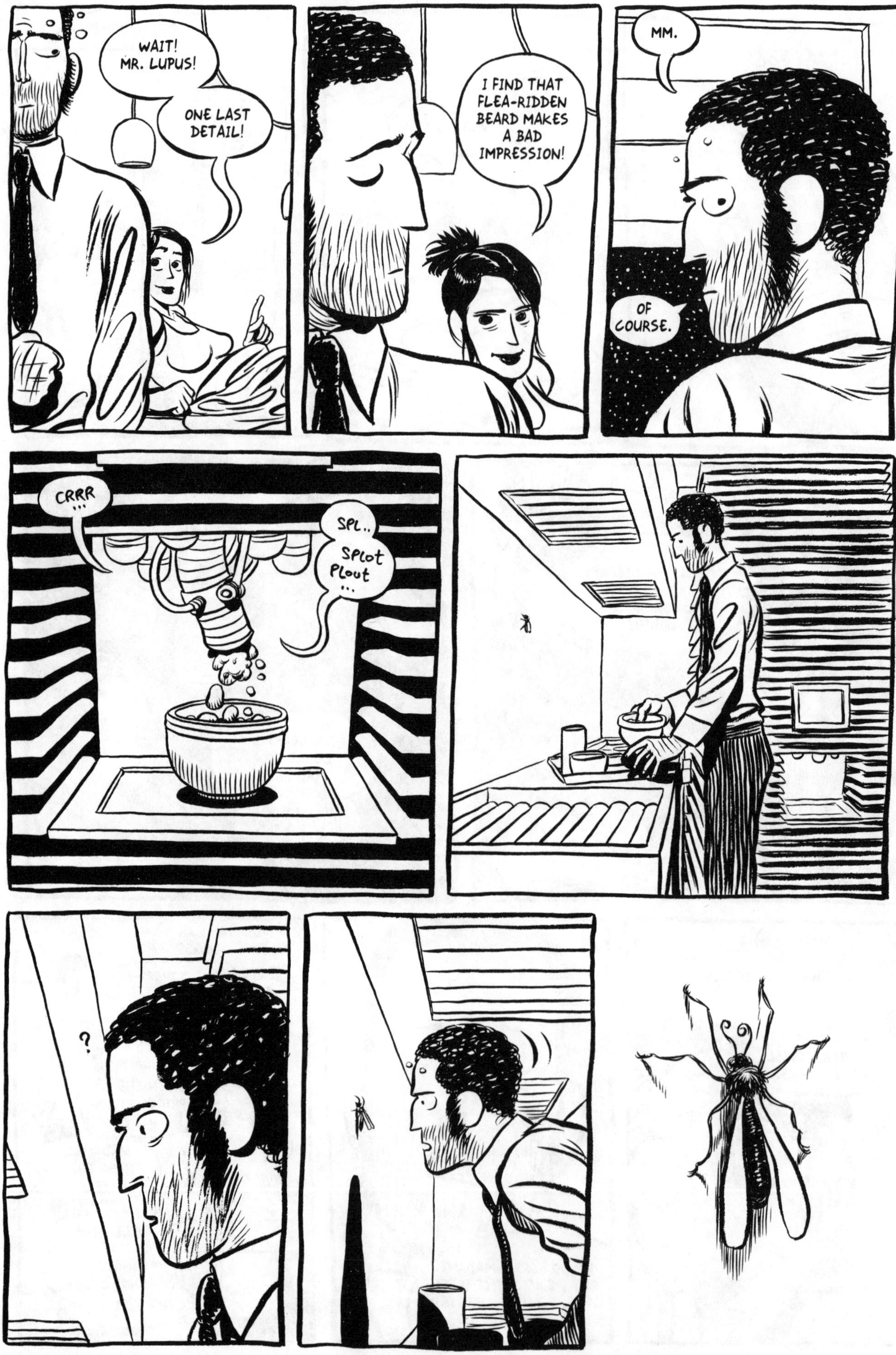

WAIT! MR. LUPUS!
ONE LAST DETAIL!
I FIND THAT FLEA-RIDDEN BEARD MAKES A BAD IMPRESSION!
MM.
OF COURSE.
CRRR ...
SPL.. SPLot PLout ...
?

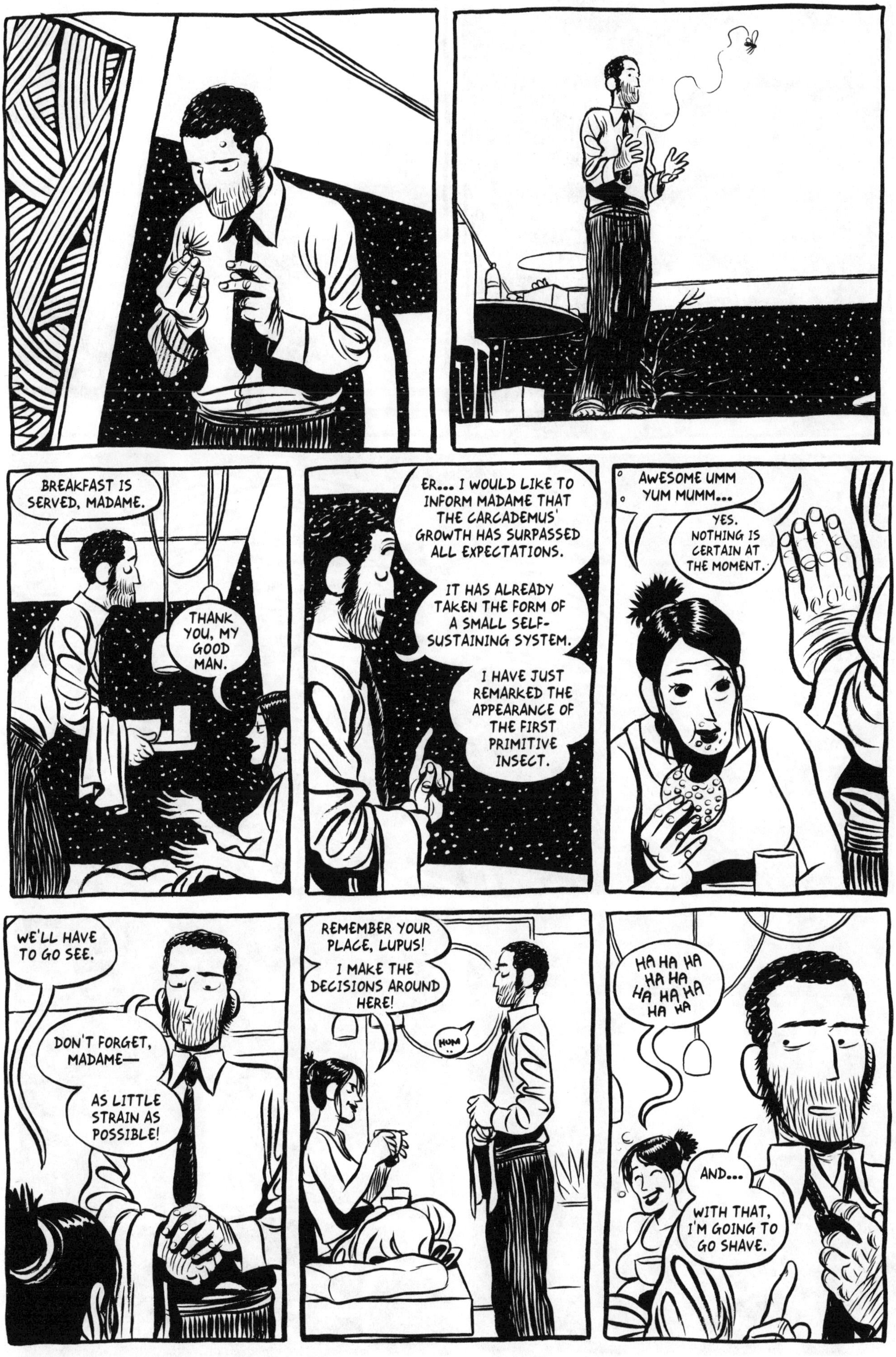
BREAKFAST IS SERVED, MADAME.
THANK YOU, MY GOOD MAN.
ER... I WOULD LIKE TO INFORM MADAME THAT THE CARCADEMUS' GROWTH HAS SURPASSED ALL EXPECTATIONS.
IT HAS ALREADY TAKEN THE FORM OF A SMALL SELF-SUSTAINING SYSTEM.
I HAVE JUST REMARKED THE APPEARANCE OF THE FIRST PRIMITIVE INSECT.
AWESOME UMM YUM MUMM...
YES. NOTHING IS CERTAIN AT THE MOMENT.
WE'LL HAVE TO GO SEE.
DON'T FORGET, MADAME—
AS LITTLE STRAIN AS POSSIBLE!
REMEMBER YOUR PLACE, LUPUS!
I MAKE THE DECISIONS AROUND HERE!
HUM
HA HA HA HA HA HA HA HA HA HA
AND...
WITH THAT, I'M GOING TO GO SHAVE.

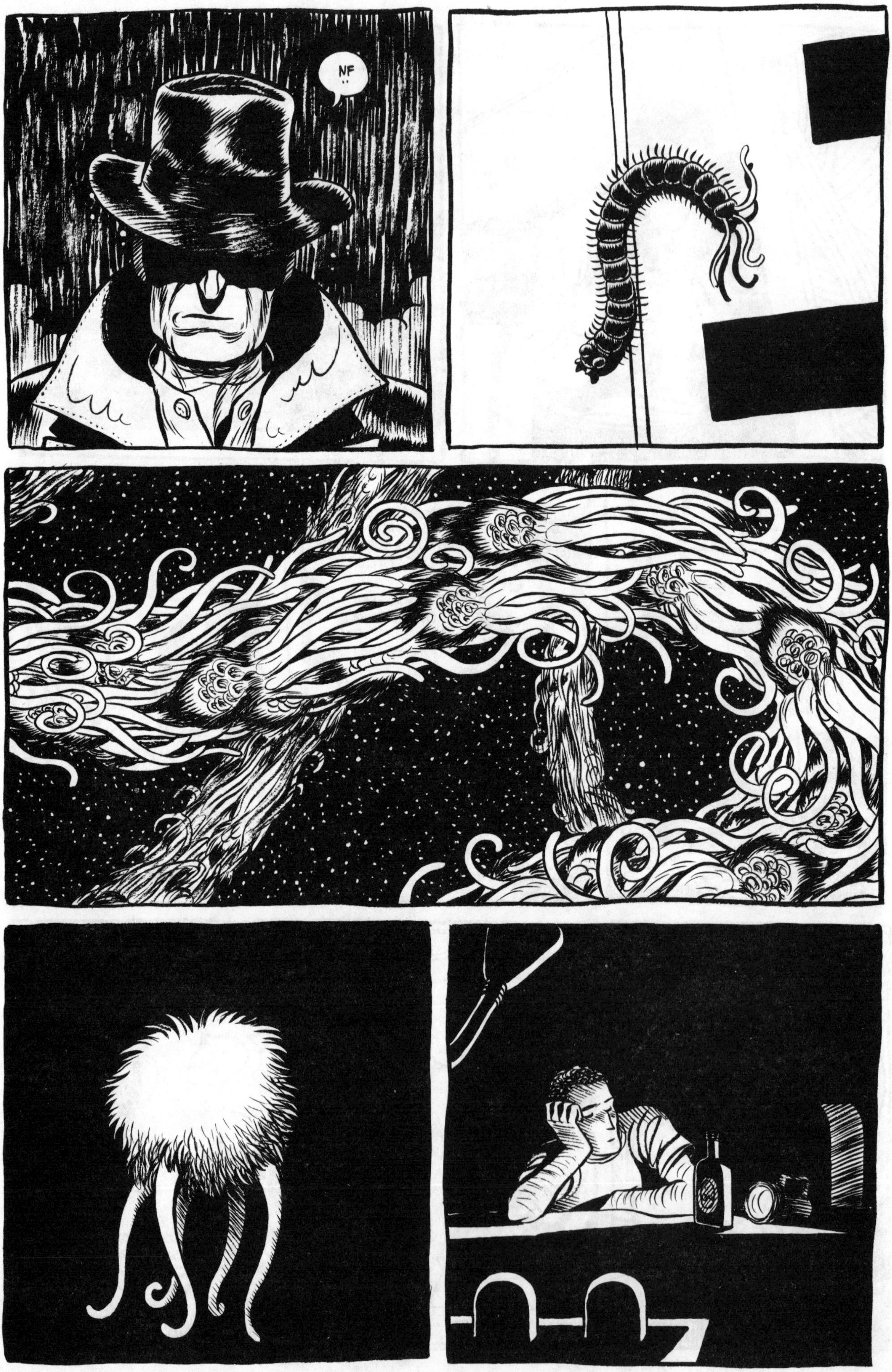
NF
..

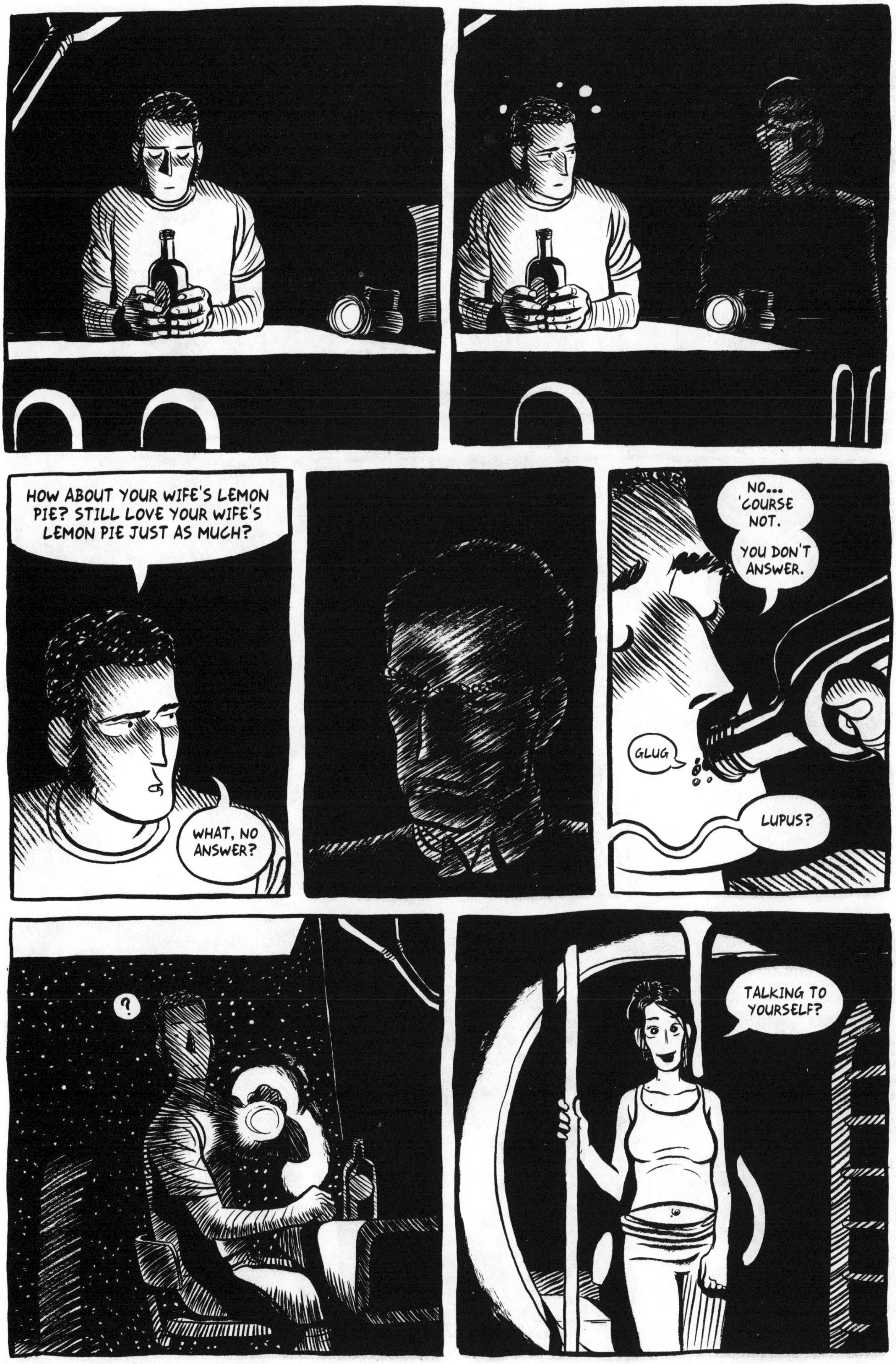
HOW ABOUT YOUR WIFE'S LEMON PIE? STILL LOVE YOUR WIFE'S LEMON PIE JUST AS MUCH?
WHAT, NO ANSWER?
NO... 'COURSE NOT.
YOU DON'T ANSWER.
GLUG
LUPUS?
?
TALKING TO YOURSELF?

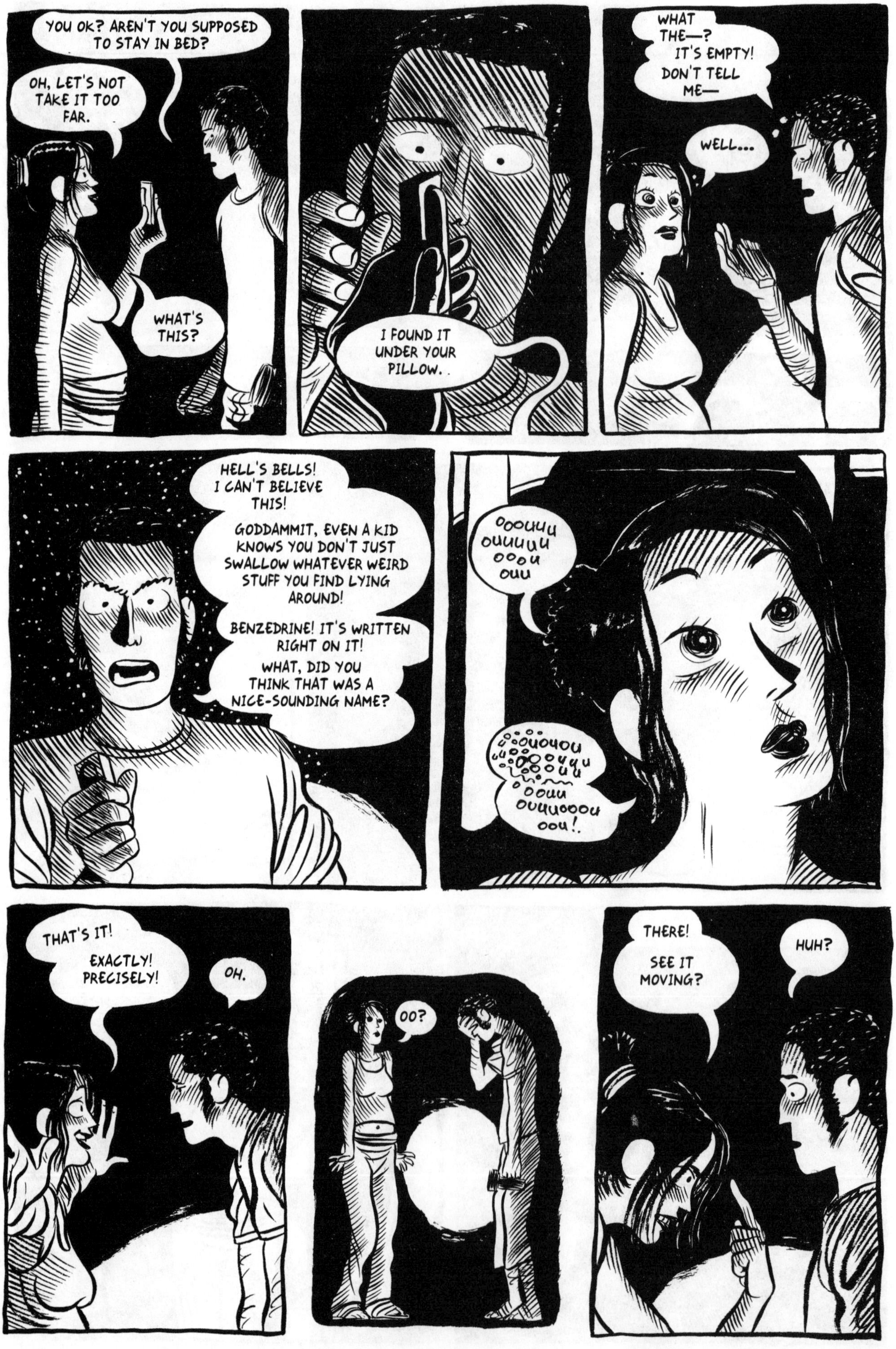

YOU OK? AREN'T YOU SUPPOSED TO STAY IN BED?
OH, LET'S NOT TAKE IT TOO FAR.
WHAT'S THIS?
I FOUND IT UNDER YOUR PILLOW. .
WHAT THE—? IT'S EMPTY! DON'T TELL ME—
WELL...
HELL'S BELLS! I CAN'T BELIEVE THIS!
GODDAMMIT, EVEN A KID KNOWS YOU DON'T JUST SWALLOW WHATEVER WEIRD STUFF YOU FIND LYING AROUND!
BENZEDRINE! IT'S WRITTEN RIGHT ON IT!
WHAT, DID YOU THINK THAT WAS A NICE-SOUNDING NAME?
OOOUUU OUUUUU OOOU OUU
OUUOUOU OOUUU OUUU OUUUOOOU OOU!.
THAT'S IT!
EXACTLY! PRECISELY!
OH.
OO?
THERE!
SEE IT MOVING?
HUH?

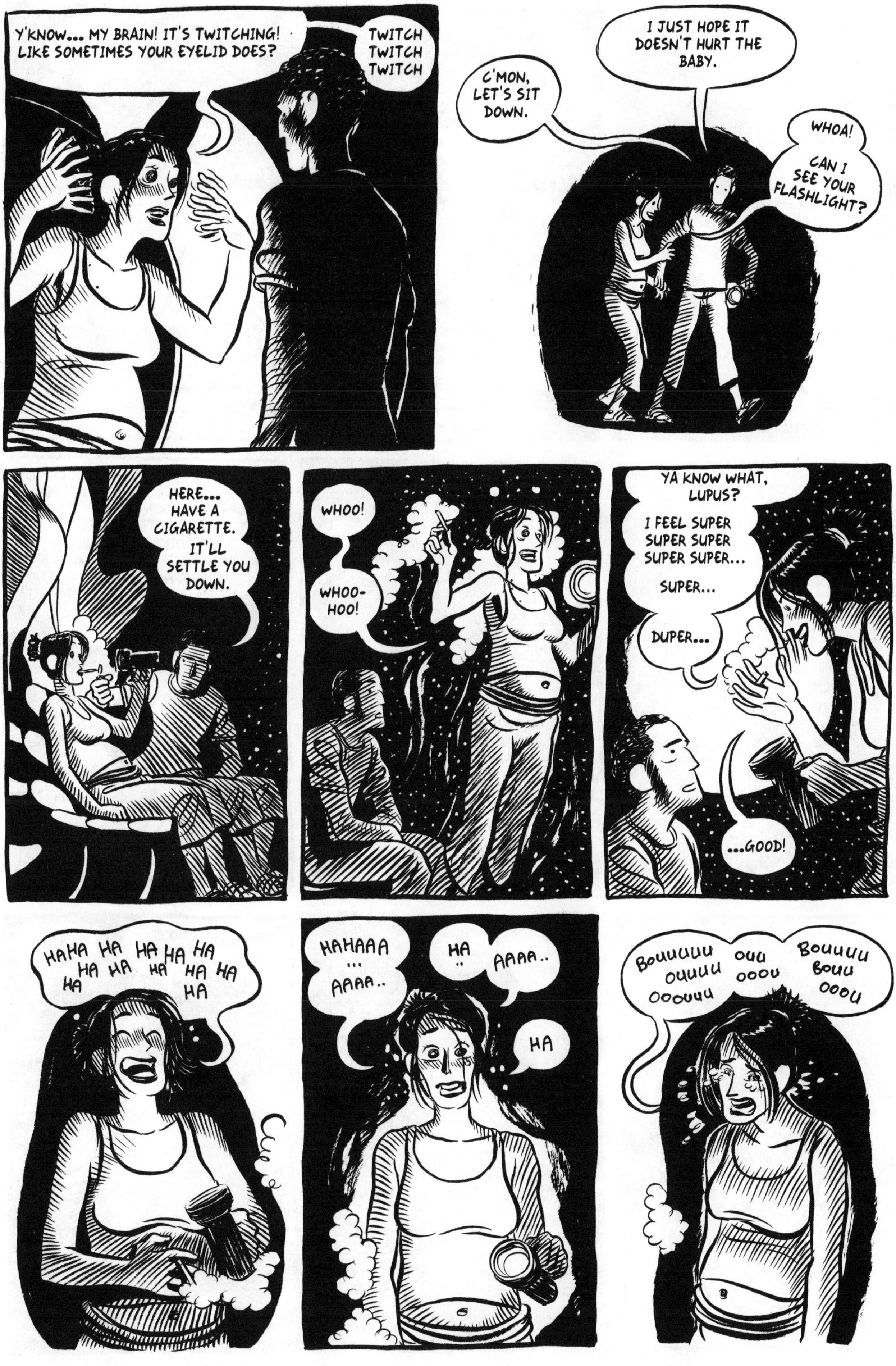

Y'KNOW... MY BRAIN! IT'S TWITCHING! LIKE SOMETIMES YOUR EYELID DOES?
TWITCH TWITCH TWITCH
I JUST HOPE IT DOESN'T HURT THE BABY.
C'MON, LET'S SIT DOWN.
WHOA!
CAN I SEE YOUR FLASHLIGHT?
HERE... HAVE A CIGARETTE.
IT'LL SETTLE YOU DOWN.
WHOO!
WHOO-HOO!
YA KNOW WHAT, LUPUS?
I FEEL SUPER SUPER SUPER SUPER SUPER...
SUPER...
DUPER...
...GOOD!
HAHA HA HA HA HA HA HA HA HA HA HA HA HA
HAHAAA ... AAAA..
HA ..
AAAA..
HA
Bouuuuu ouuuu ooouuu
ouu oooo
Bouuuu bouu oooo

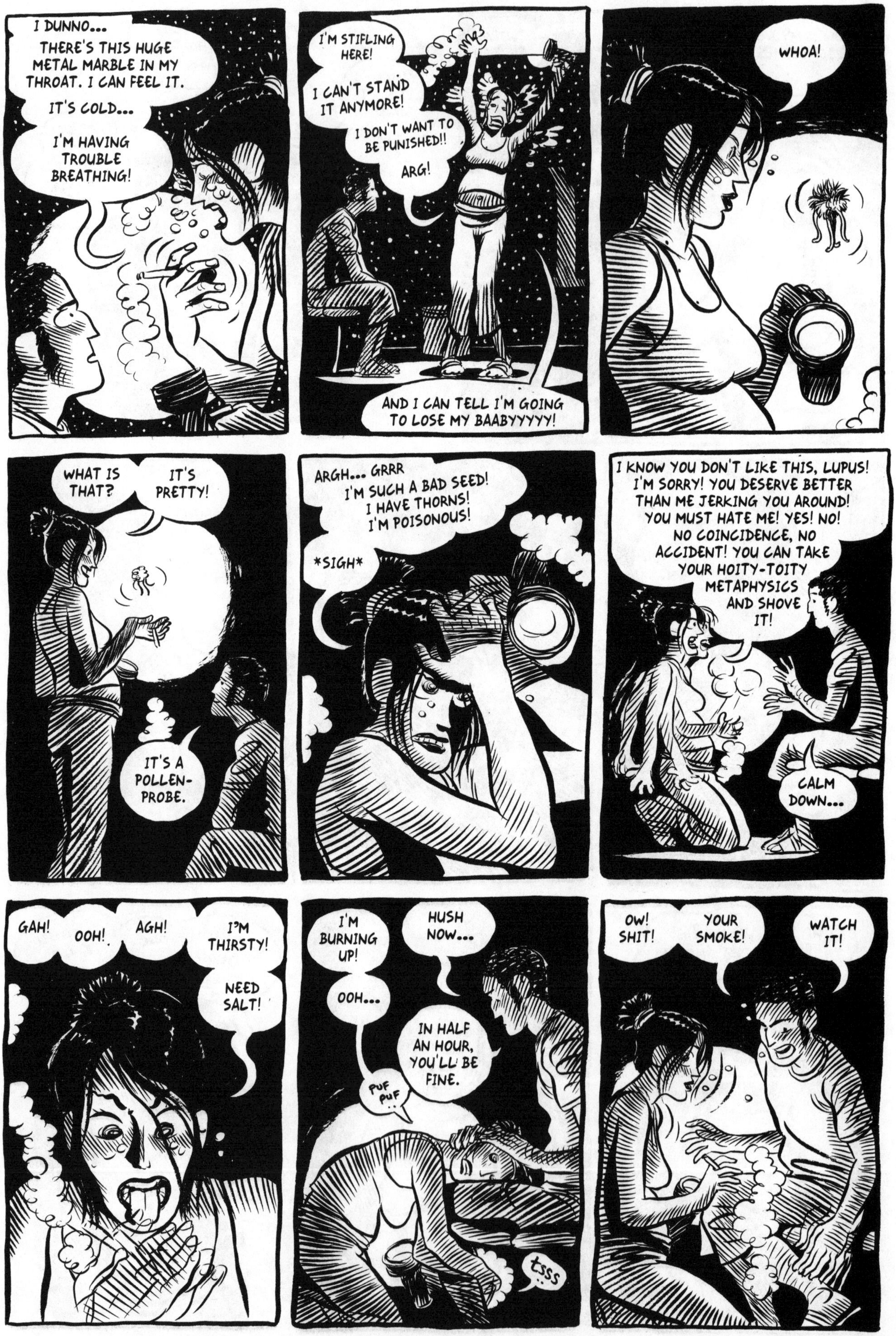
I DUNNO...
THERE'S THIS HUGE METAL MARBLE IN MY THROAT. I CAN FEEL IT.
IT'S COLD...
I'M HAVING TROUBLE BREATHING!
I'M STIFLING HERE!
I CAN'T STAND IT ANYMORE!
I DON'T WANT TO BE PUNISHED!!
ARG!
AND I CAN TELL I'M GOING TO LOSE MY BAABYYYYY!
WHOA!
WHAT IS THAT?
IT'S PRETTY!
IT'S A POLLEN-PROBE.
ARGH... GRRR
I'M SUCH A BAD SEED! I HAVE THORNS! I'M POISONOUS!
SIGH
I KNOW YOU DON'T LIKE THIS, LUPUS! I'M SORRY! YOU DESERVE BETTER THAN ME JERKING YOU AROUND! YOU MUST HATE ME! YES! NO! NO COINCIDENCE, NO ACCIDENT! YOU CAN TAKE YOUR HOITY-TOITY METAPHYSICS AND SHOVE IT!
CALM DOWN...
GAH!
OOH!
AGH!
I'M THIRSTY!
NEED SALT!
I'M BURNING UP!
HUSH NOW...
OOH...
IN HALF AN HOUR, YOU'LL BE FINE.
PUF PUF
TSSS
OW! SHIT!
YOUR SMOKE!
WATCH IT!

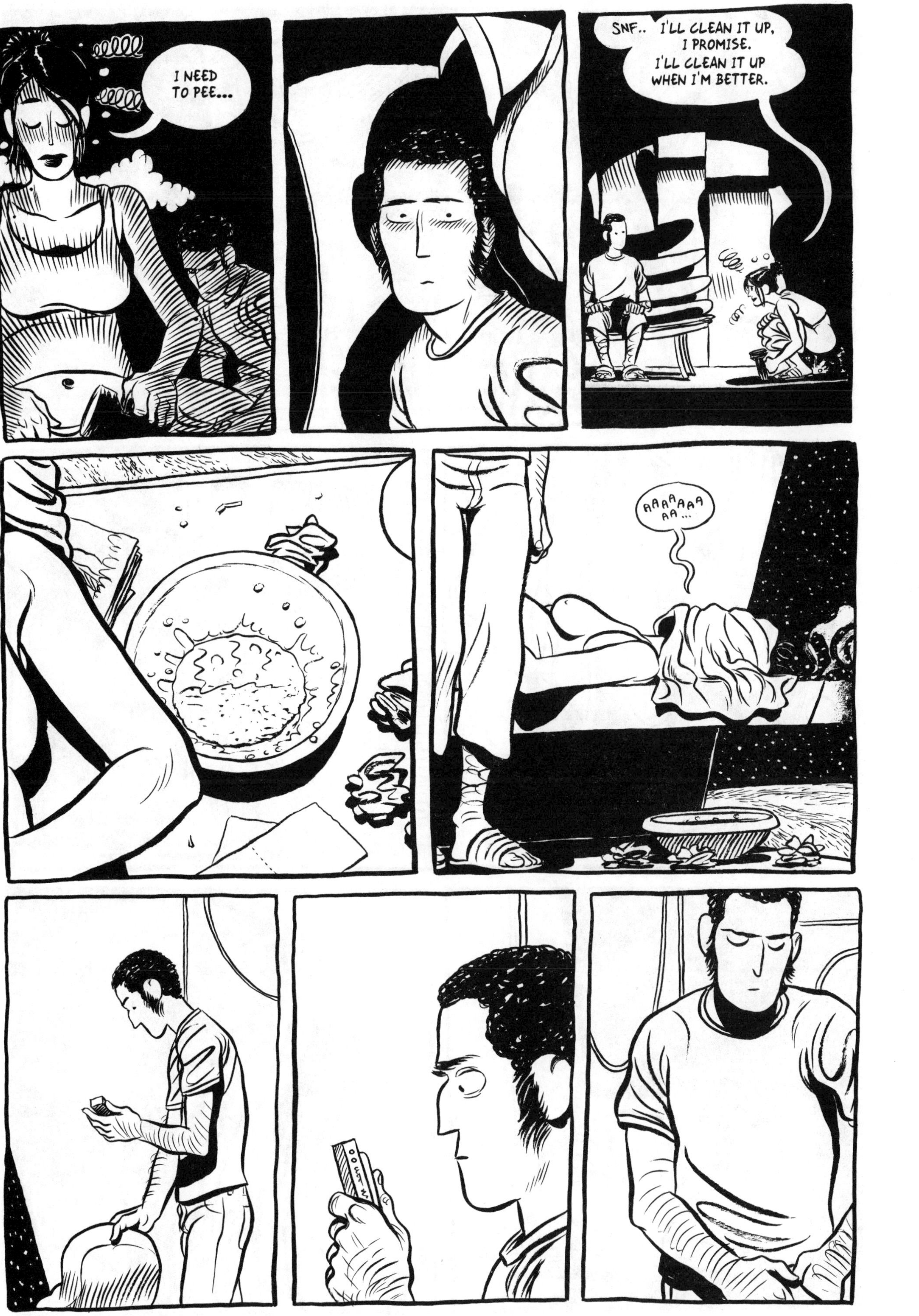
I NEED TO PEE...
SNF.. I'LL CLEAN IT UP, I PROMISE. I'LL CLEAN IT UP WHEN I'M BETTER.
AAAAAAA AA...

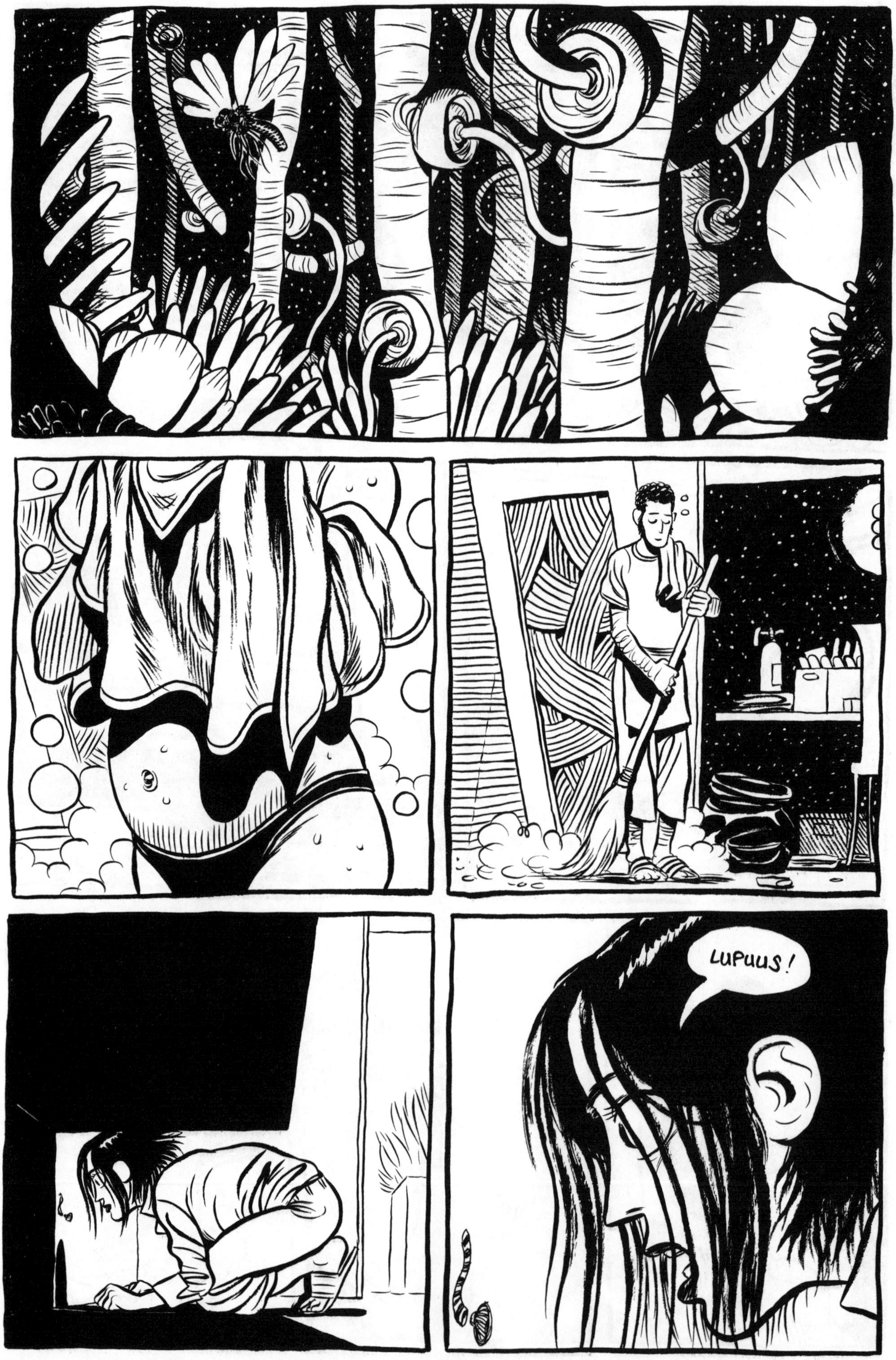
LUPUUS!

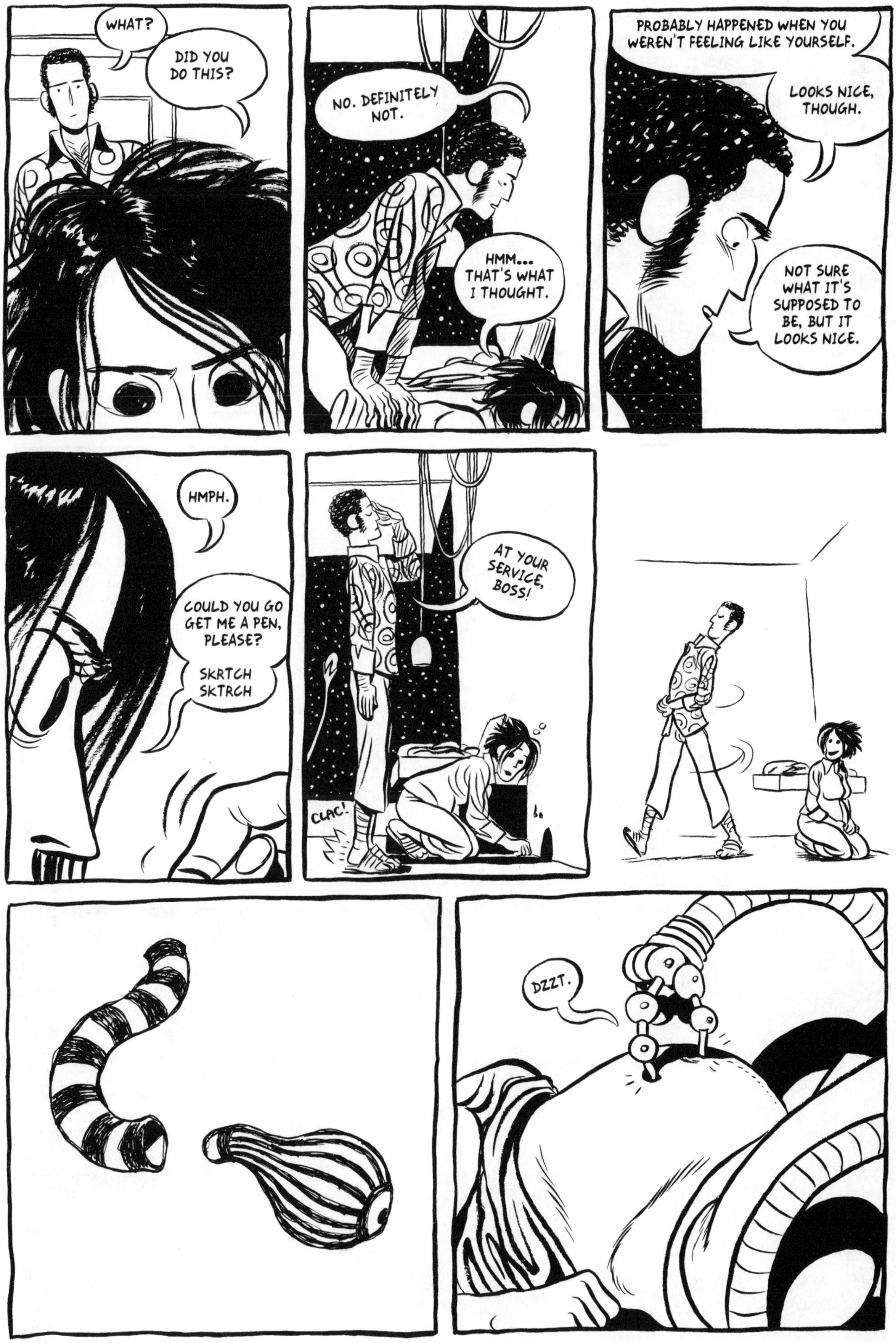
WHAT?
DID YOU DO THIS?
NO. DEFINITELY NOT.
HMM... THAT'S WHAT I THOUGHT.
PROBABLY HAPPENED WHEN YOU WEREN'T FEELING LIKE YOURSELF.
LOOKS NICE, THOUGH.
NOT SURE WHAT IT'S SUPPOSED TO BE, BUT IT LOOKS NICE.
HMPH.
COULD YOU GO GET ME A PEN, PLEASE?
SKRTCH SKTRCH
AT YOUR SERVICE, BOSS!
CLAC!
DZZT.

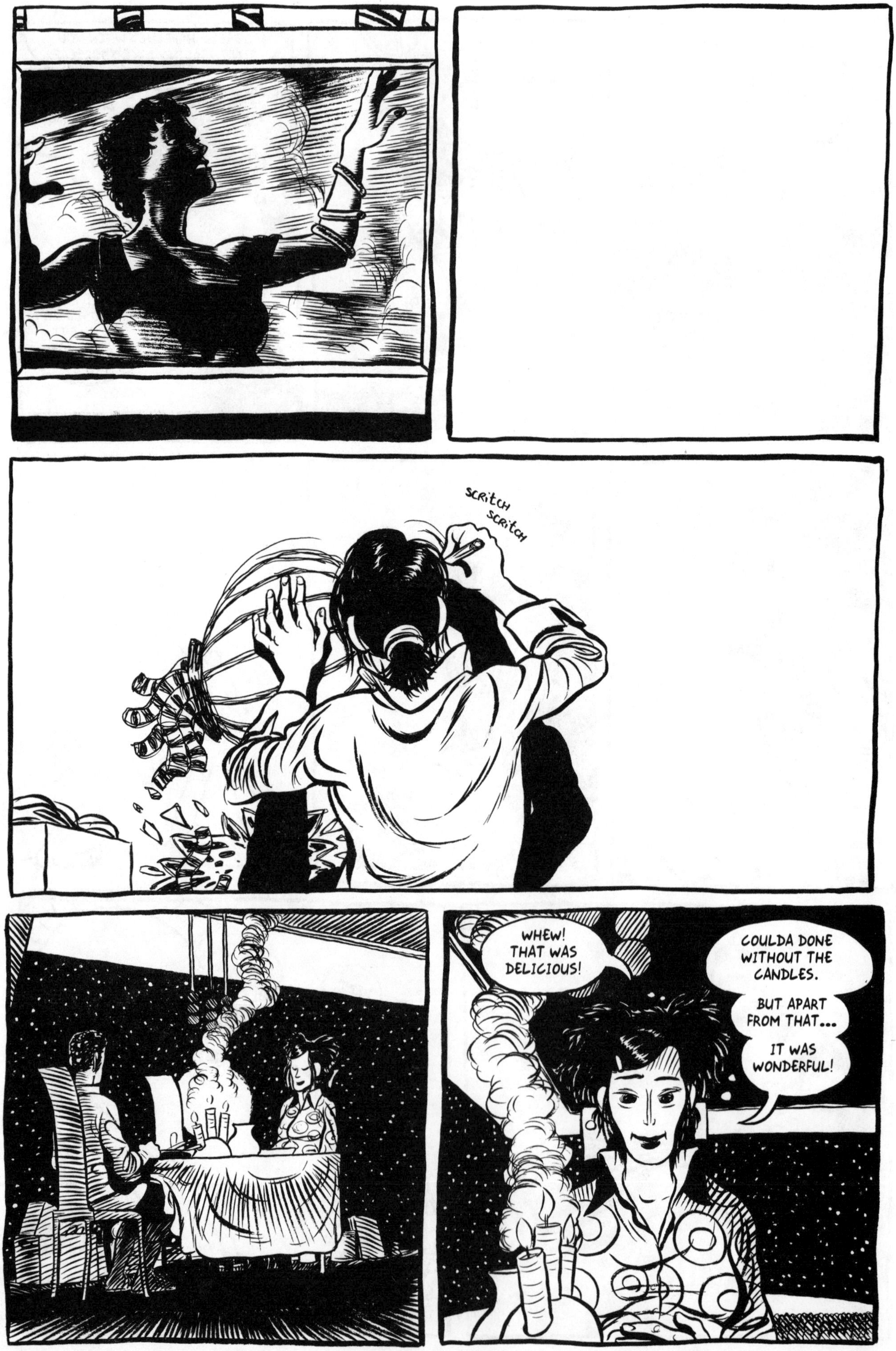
SCRITCH
SCRITCH
WHEW! THAT WAS DELICIOUS!
COULDA DONE WITHOUT THE CANDLES.
BUT APART FROM THAT...
IT WAS WONDERFUL!

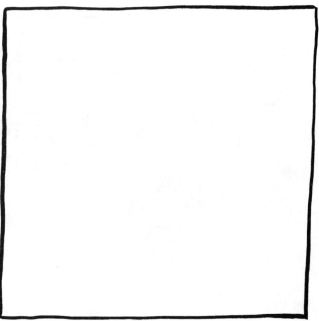

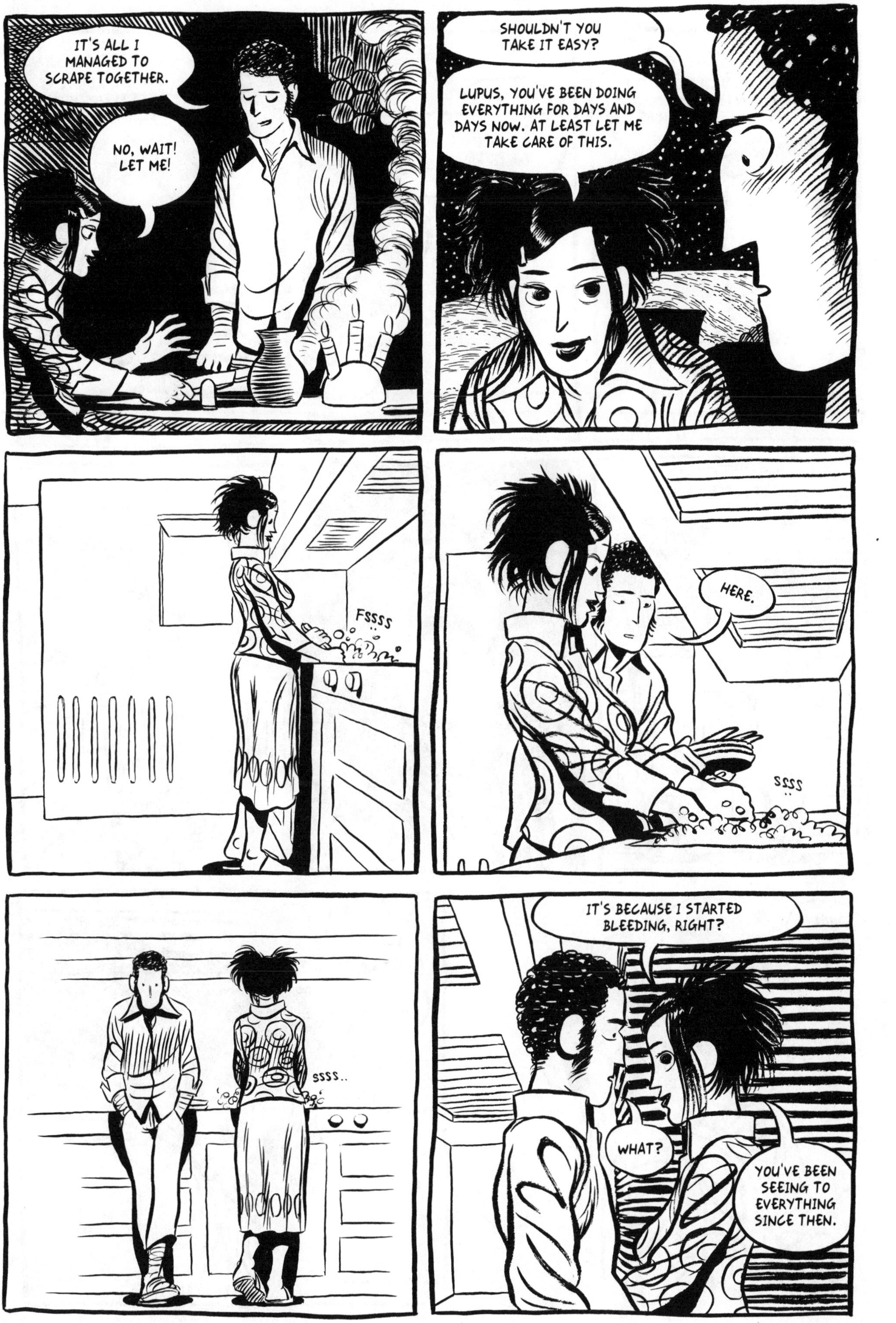
IT'S ALL I MANAGED TO SCRAPE TOGETHER.
NO, WAIT! LET ME!
SHOULDN'T YOU TAKE IT EASY?
LUPUS, YOU'VE BEEN DOING EVERYTHING FOR DAYS AND DAYS NOW. AT LEAST LET ME TAKE CARE OF THIS.
FSSSS
HERE.
SSSS
SSSS..
IT'S BECAUSE I STARTED BLEEDING, RIGHT?
WHAT?
YOU'VE BEEN SEEING TO EVERYTHING SINCE THEN.

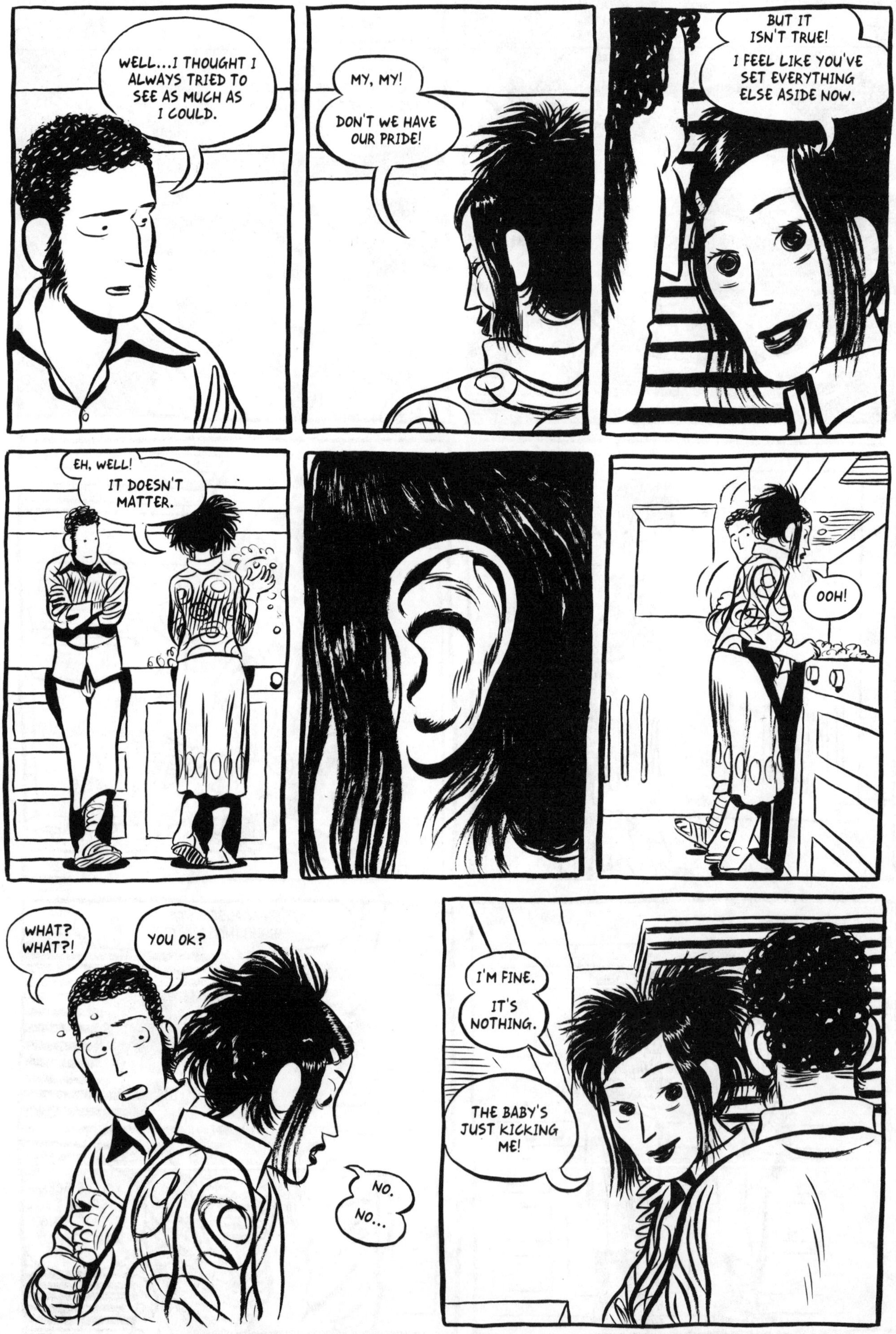
WELL...I THOUGHT I ALWAYS TRIED TO SEE AS MUCH AS I COULD.
MY, MY!
DON'T WE HAVE OUR PRIDE!
BUT IT ISN'T TRUE!
I FEEL LIKE YOU'VE SET EVERYTHING ELSE ASIDE NOW.
EH, WELL!
IT DOESN'T MATTER.
OOH!
WHAT? WHAT?!
YOU OK?
NO.
NO...
I'M FINE.
IT'S NOTHING.
THE BABY'S JUST KICKING ME!

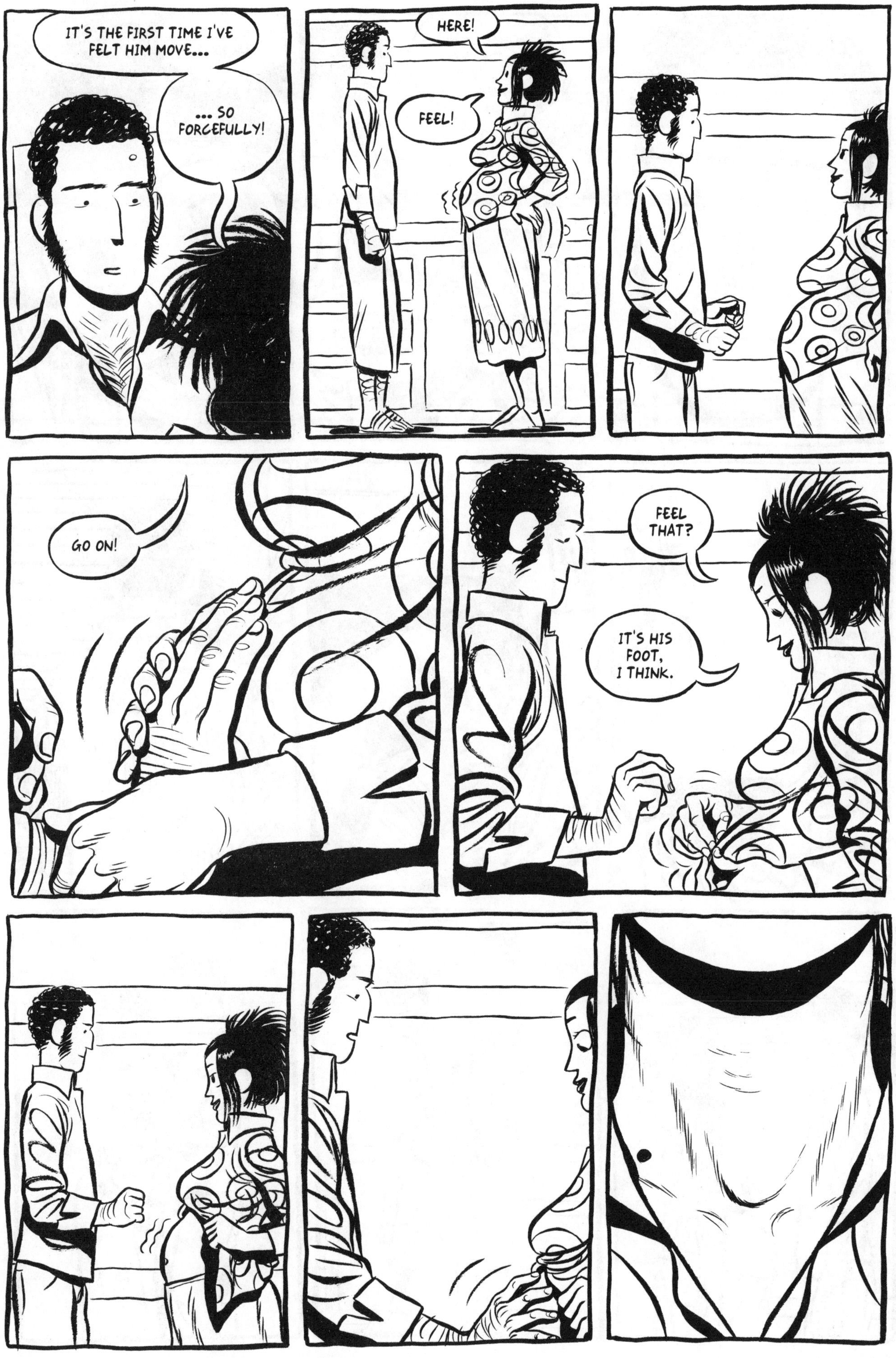
IT'S THE FIRST TIME I'VE FELT HIM MOVE...
... SO FORCEFULLY!
HERE!
FEEL!
GO ON!
FEEL THAT?
IT'S HIS FOOT, I THINK.

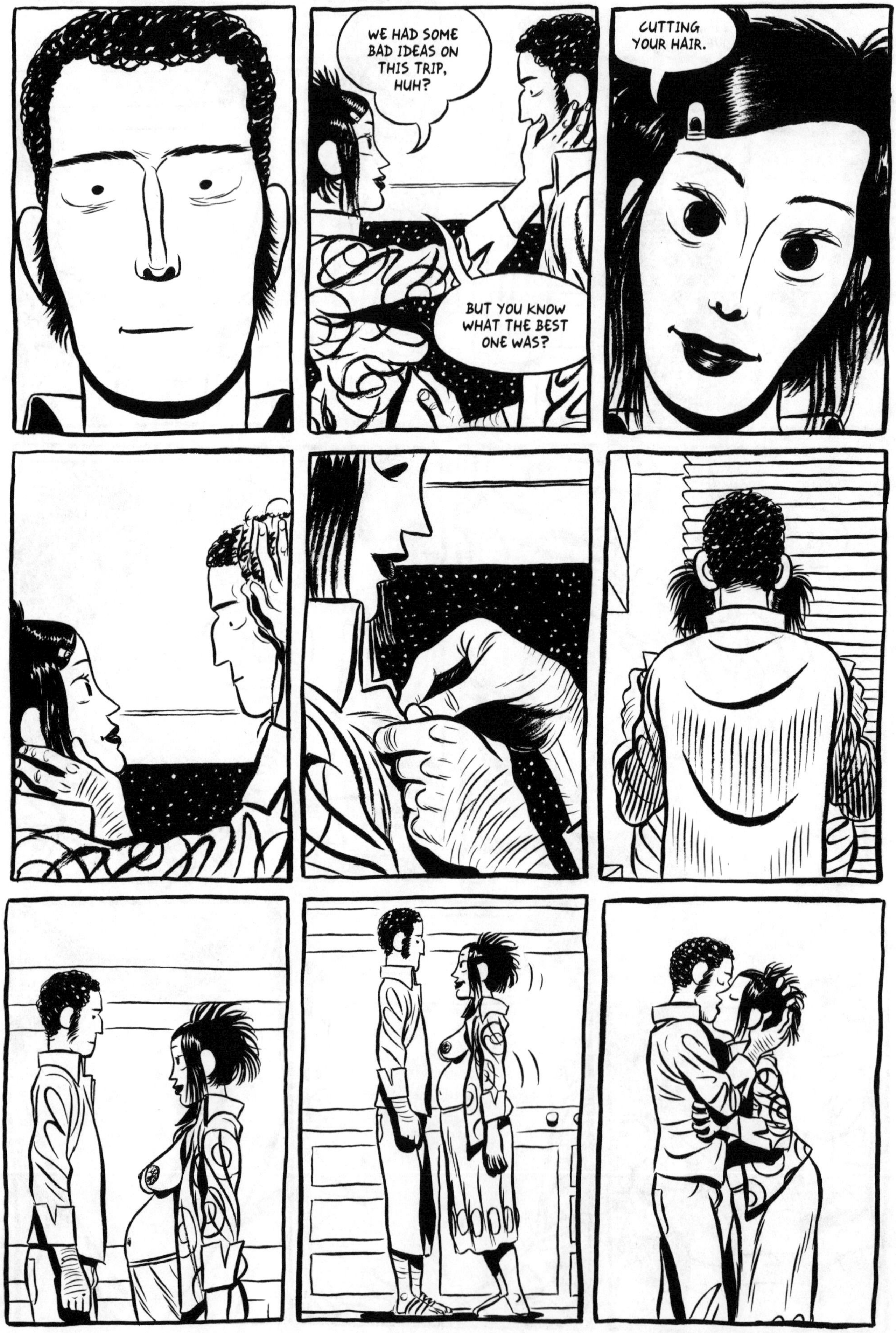
WE HAD SOME BAD IDEAS ON THIS TRIP, HUH?
BUT YOU KNOW WHAT THE BEST ONE WAS?
CUTTING YOUR HAIR.

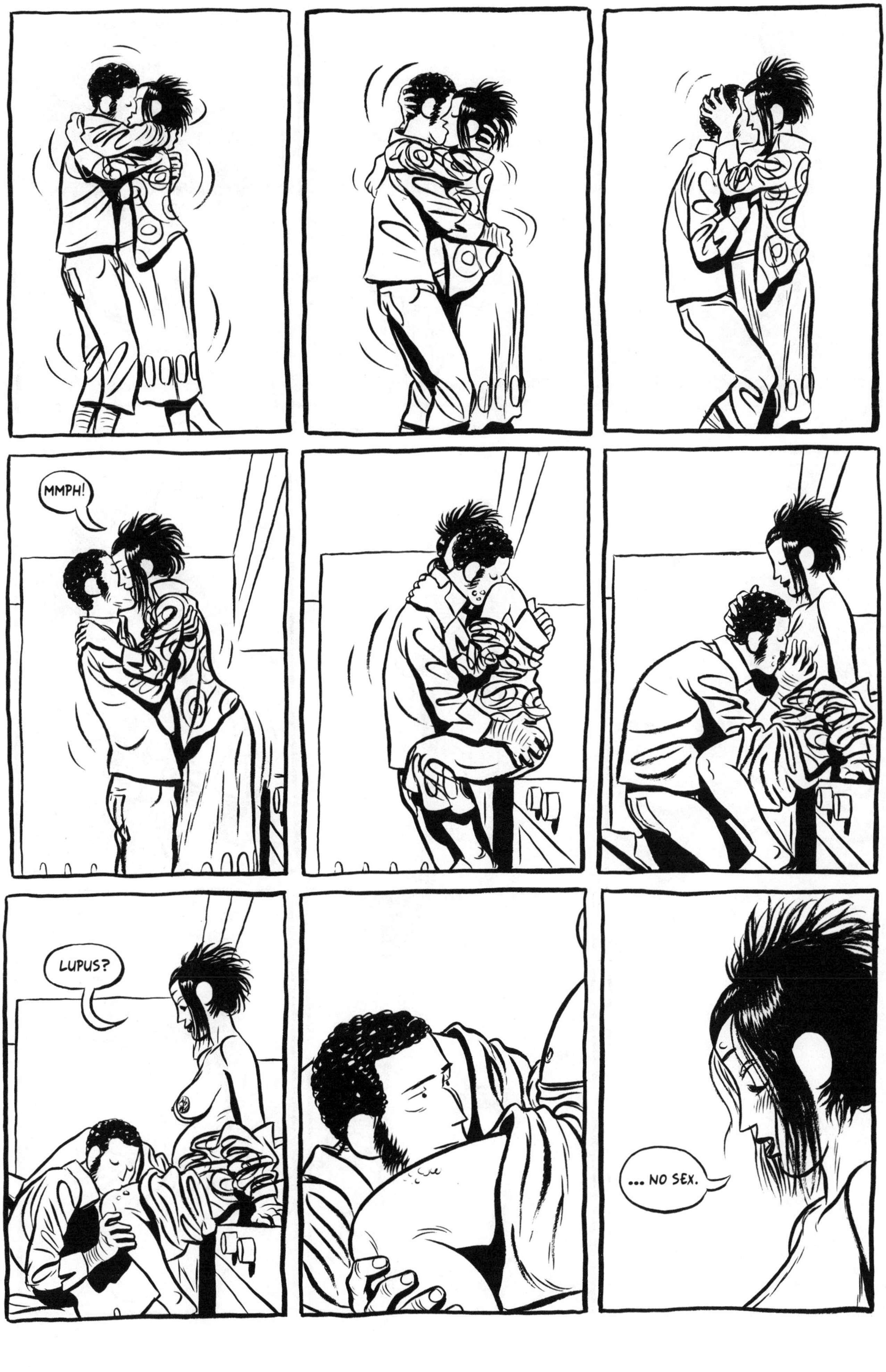
MMPH!
LUPUS?
... NO SEX.

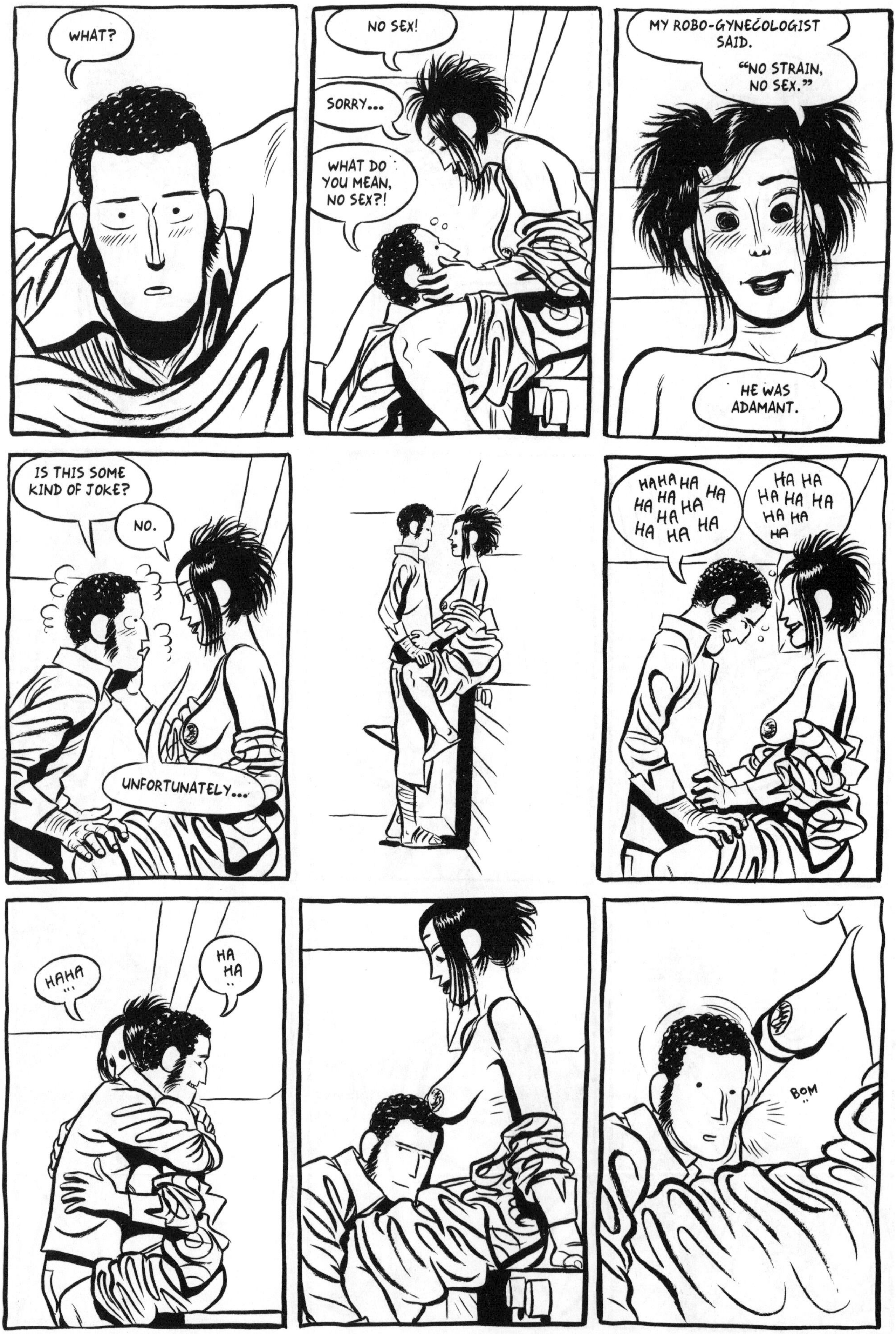
WHAT?
NO SEX!
SORRY...
WHAT DO YOU MEAN, NO SEX?!
MY ROBO-GYNECOLOGIST SAID.
"NO STRAIN, NO SEX."
HE WAS ADAMANT.
IS THIS SOME KIND OF JOKE?
NO.
UNFORTUNATELY...
HAHA HA HA HA HA HA HA HA HA HA HA
HA HA HA HA HA HA HA HA
HAHA ...
HA HA ..
BOM ..

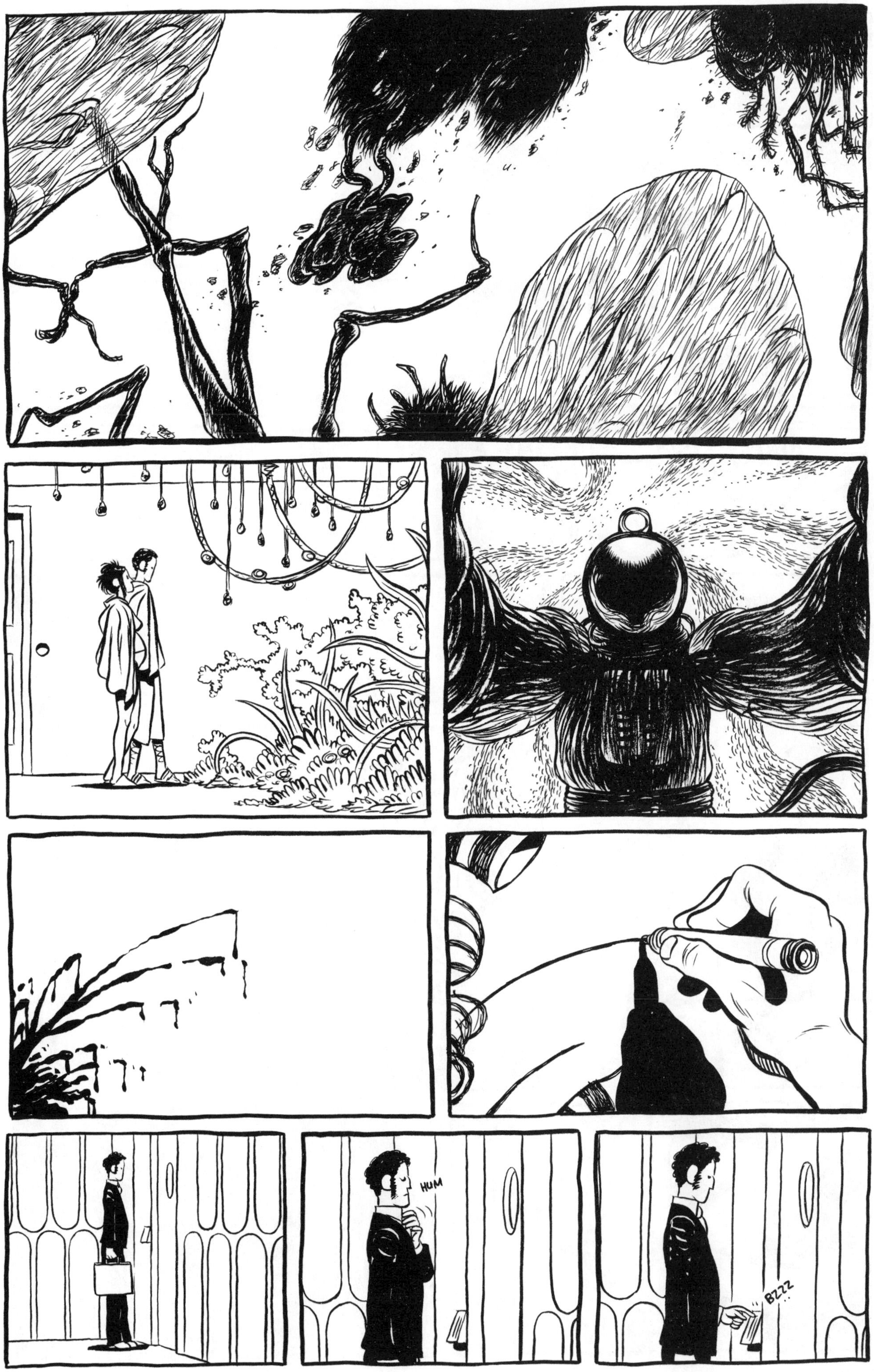
HUM
BZZZ

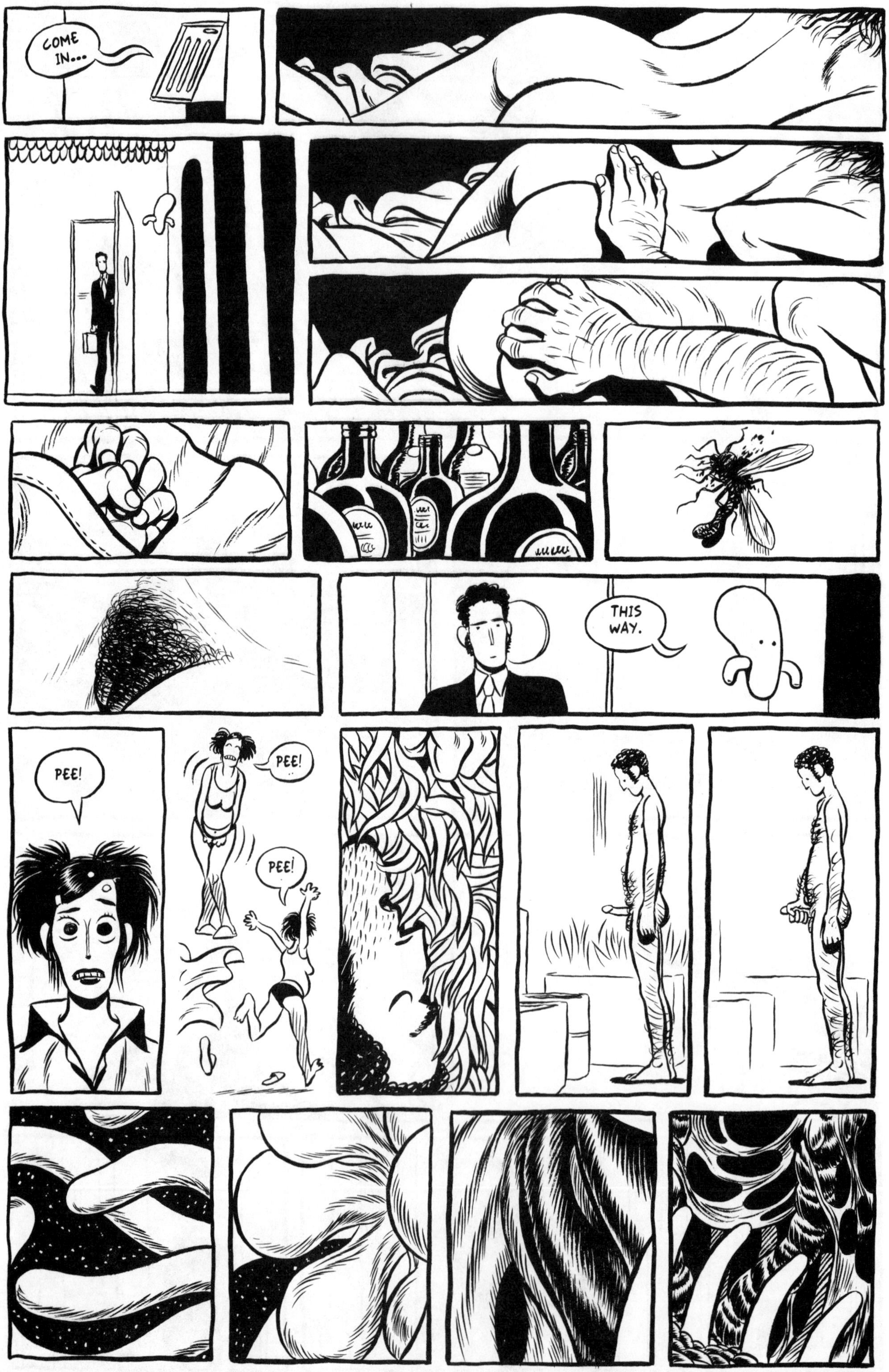
COME IN...
THIS WAY.
PEE!
PEE!
PEE!

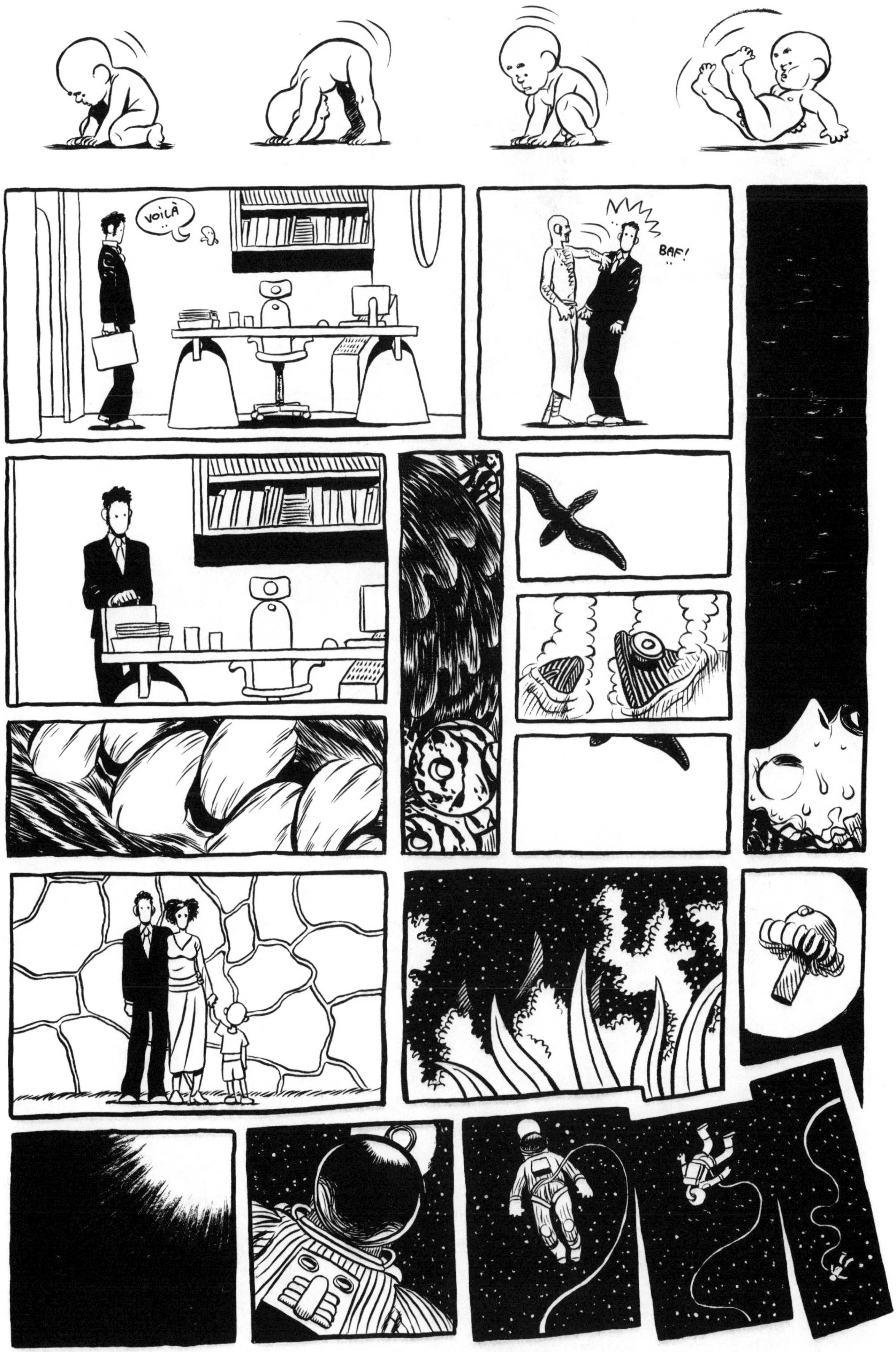
VOILÀ
BAF!

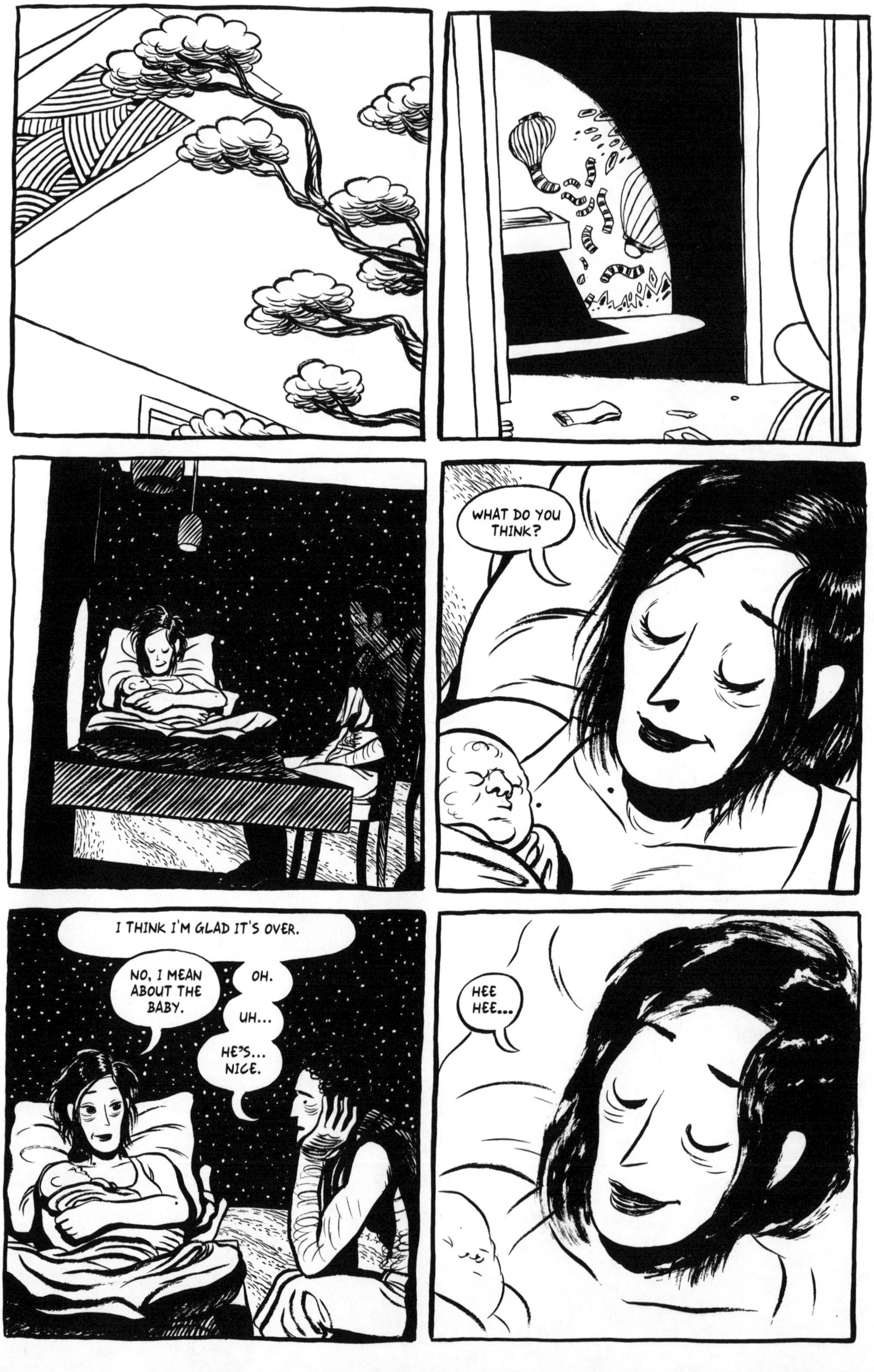
WHAT DO YOU THINK?
I THINK I'M GLAD IT'S OVER.
NO, I MEAN ABOUT THE BABY.
OH.
UH...
HE'S... NICE.
HEE HEE...

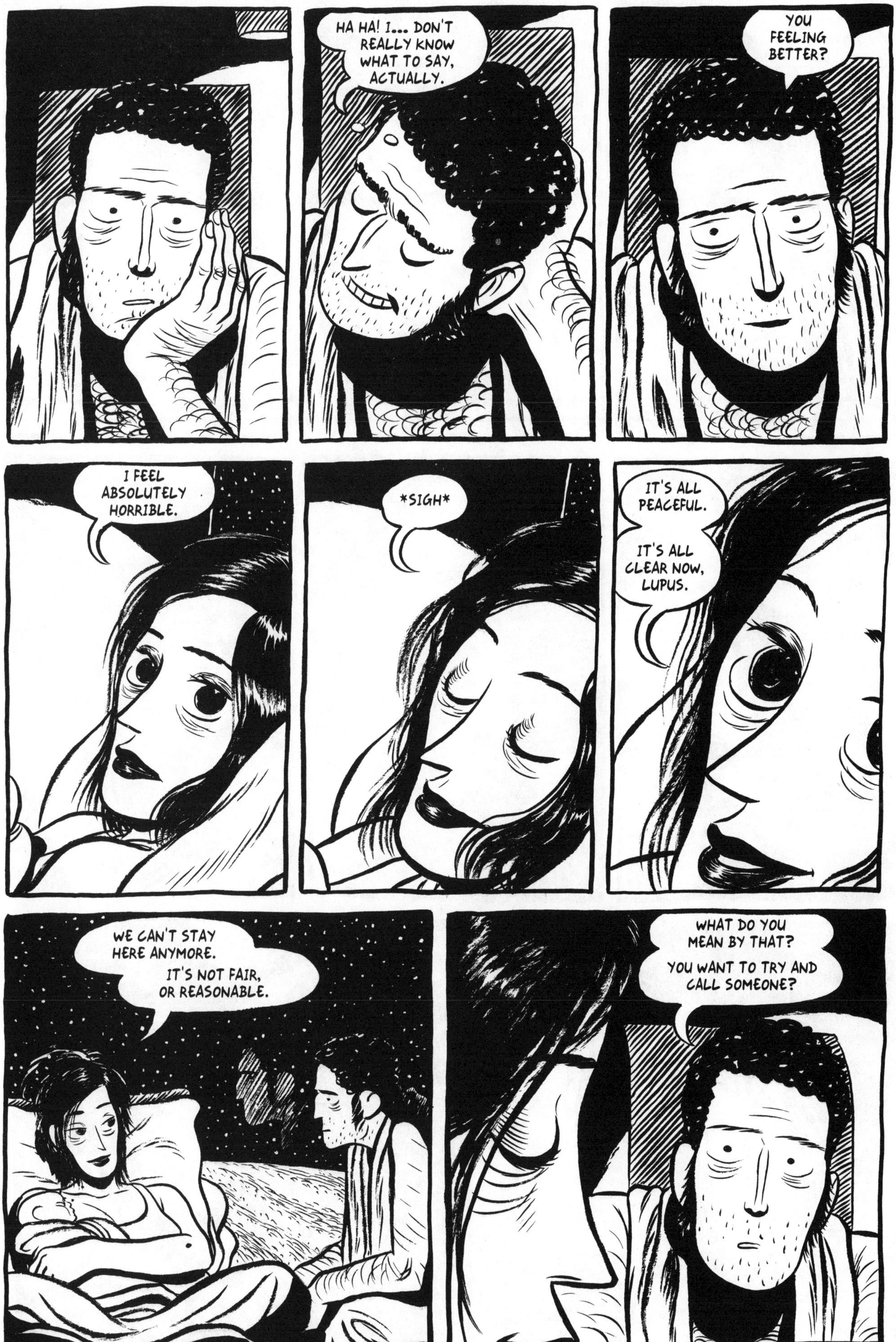

HA HA! I... DON'T REALLY KNOW WHAT TO SAY, ACTUALLY.
YOU FEELING BETTER?
I FEEL ABSOLUTELY HORRIBLE.
SIGH
IT'S ALL PEACEFUL.
IT'S ALL CLEAR NOW, LUPUS.
WE CAN'T STAY HERE ANYMORE.
IT'S NOT FAIR, OR REASONABLE.
WHAT DO YOU MEAN BY THAT?
YOU WANT TO TRY AND CALL SOMEONE?

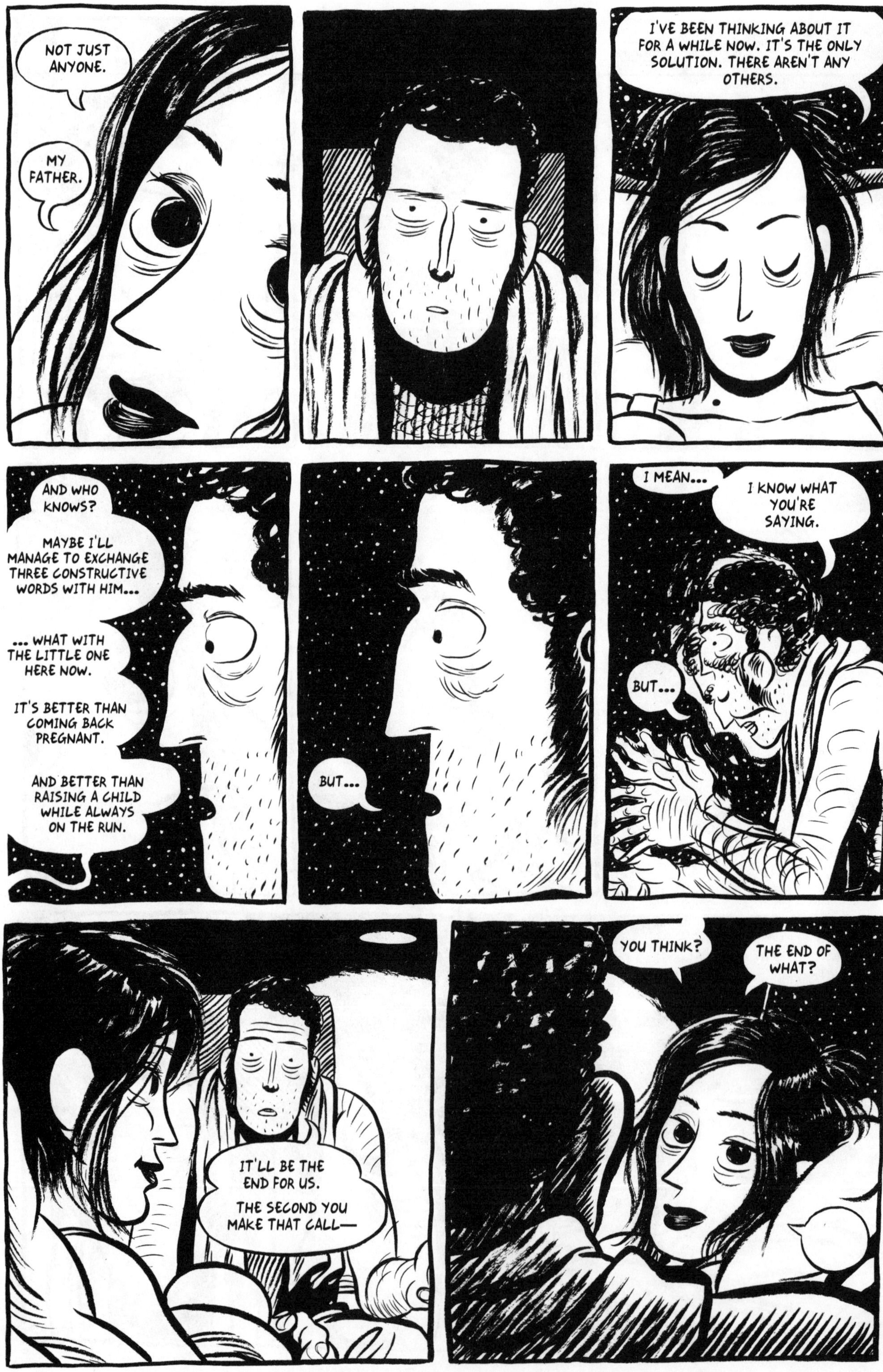

NOT JUST ANYONE.
MY FATHER.
I'VE BEEN THINKING ABOUT IT FOR A WHILE NOW. IT'S THE ONLY SOLUTION. THERE AREN'T ANY OTHERS.
AND WHO KNOWS?
MAYBE I'LL MANAGE TO EXCHANGE THREE CONSTRUCTIVE WORDS WITH HIM...
... WHAT WITH THE LITTLE ONE HERE NOW.
IT'S BETTER THAN COMING BACK PREGNANT.
AND BETTER THAN RAISING A CHILD WHILE ALWAYS ON THE RUN.
BUT...
I MEAN...
I KNOW WHAT YOU'RE SAYING.
BUT...
IT'LL BE THE END FOR US.
THE SECOND YOU MAKE THAT CALL—
YOU THINK?
THE END OF WHAT?

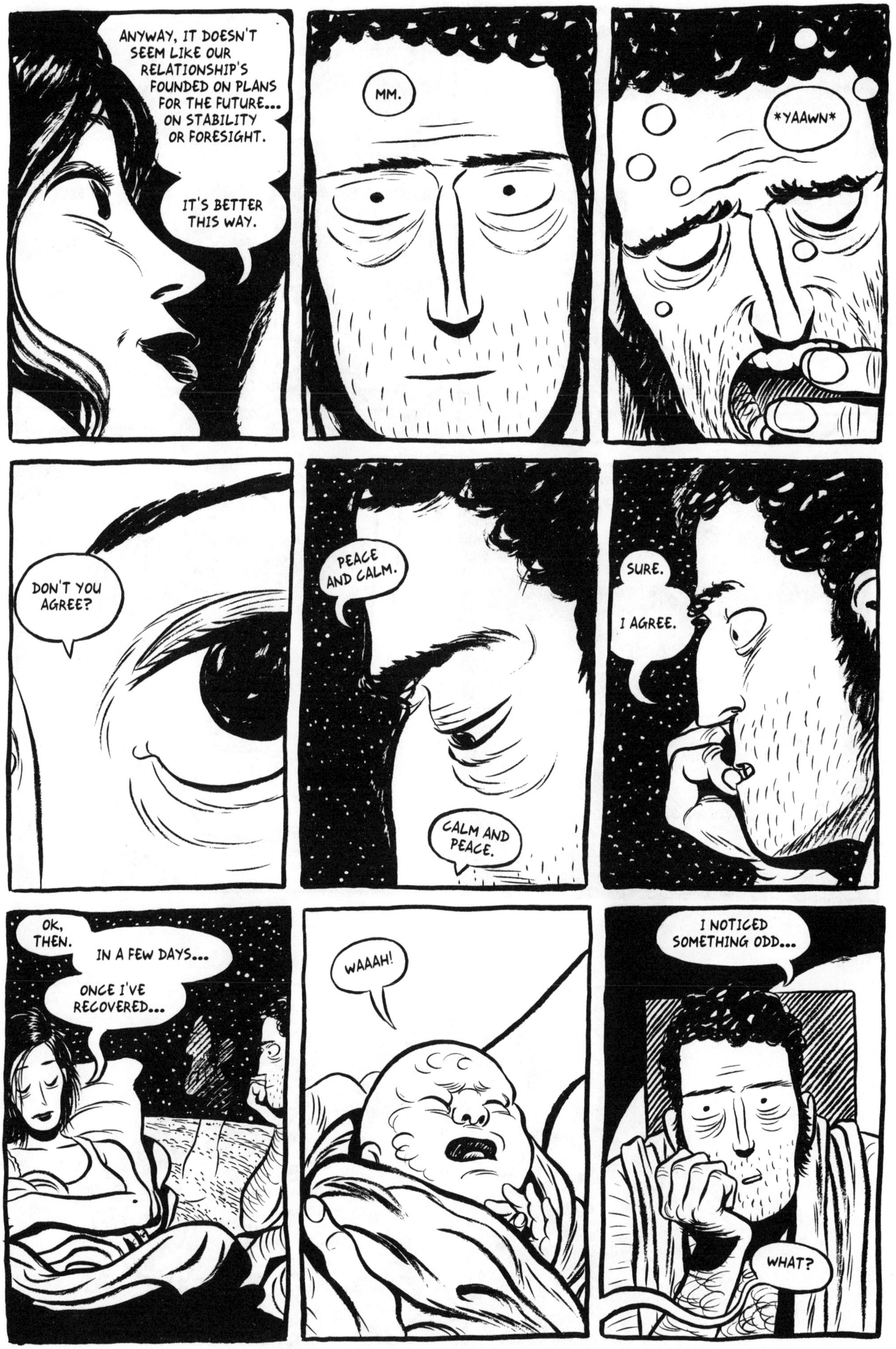
ANYWAY, IT DOESN'T SEEM LIKE OUR RELATIONSHIP'S FOUNDED ON PLANS FOR THE FUTURE... ON STABILITY OR FORESIGHT.
IT'S BETTER THIS WAY.
MM.
YAAWN
DON'T YOU AGREE?
PEACE AND CALM.
CALM AND PEACE.
SURE.
I AGREE.
OK, THEN.
IN A FEW DAYS...
ONCE I'VE RECOVERED...
WAAAH!
I NOTICED SOMETHING ODD...
WHAT?

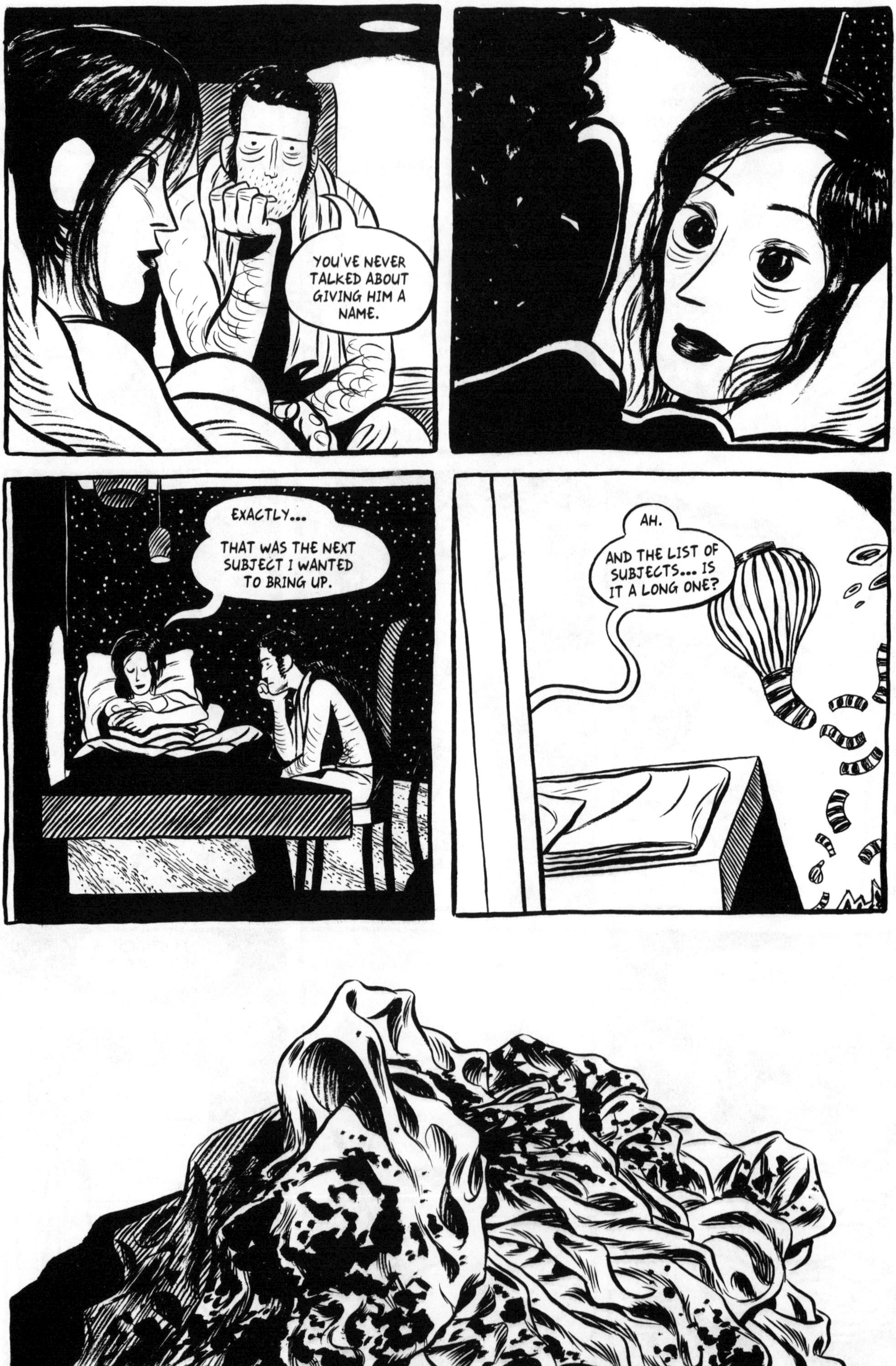
YOU'VE NEVER TALKED ABOUT GIVING HIM A NAME.
EXACTLY... THAT WAS THE NEXT SUBJECT I WANTED TO BRING UP.
AH. AND THE LIST OF SUBJECTS... IS IT A LONG ONE?

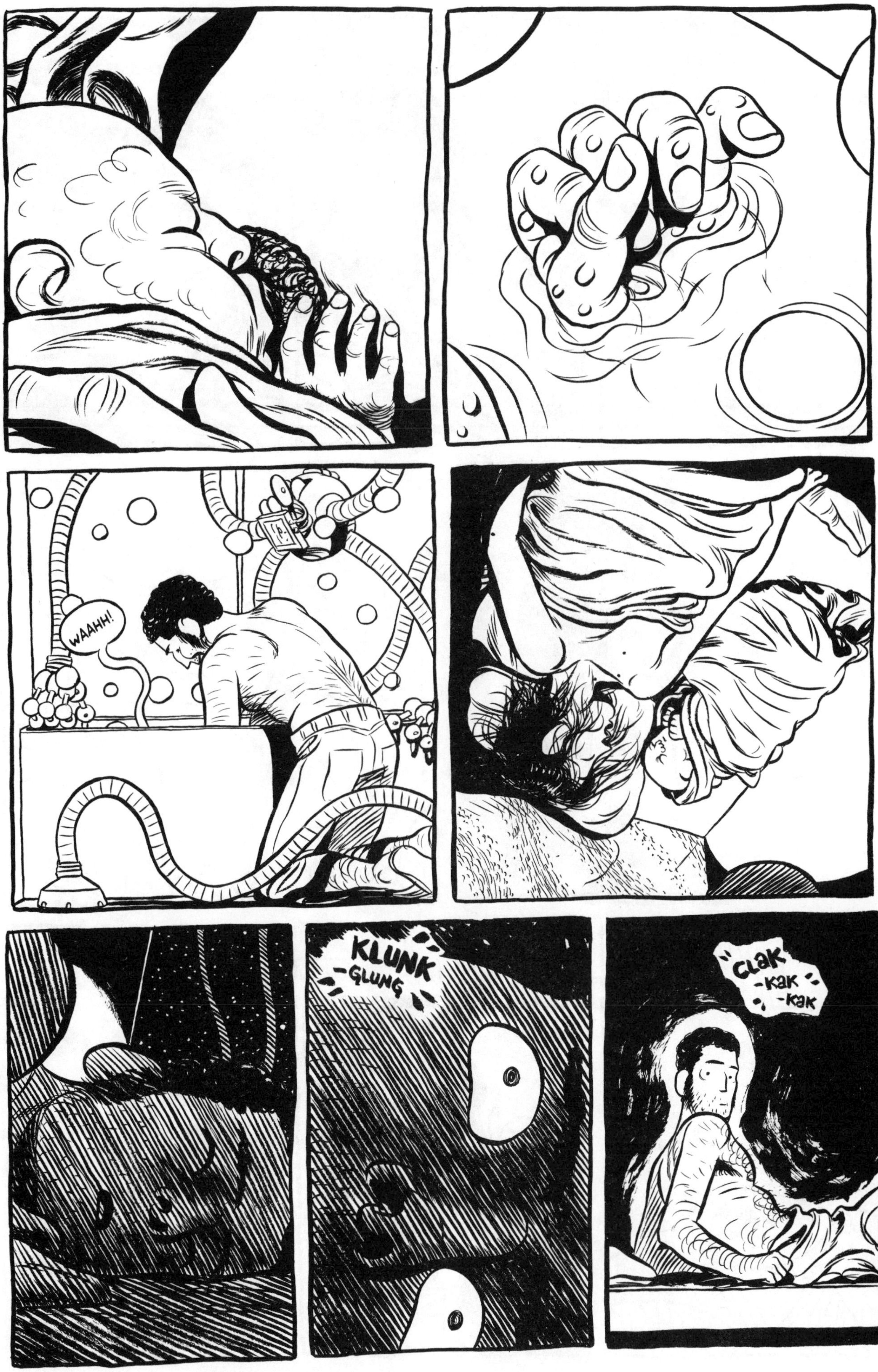
WAAHH!
KLUNK
-GLUNG
CLAK
-KAK
-KAK

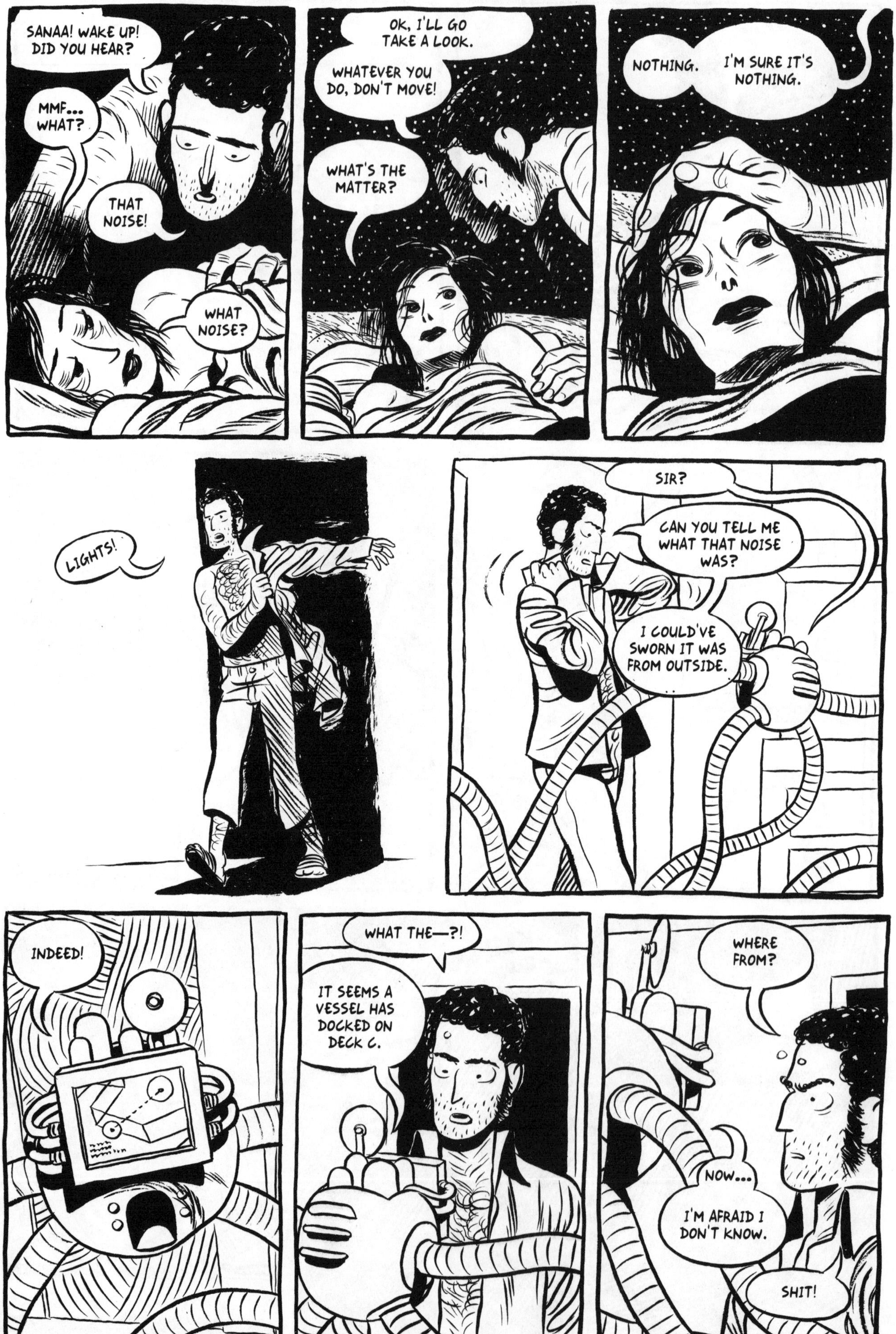
SANAA! WAKE UP! DID YOU HEAR?
MMF... WHAT?
THAT NOISE!
WHAT NOISE?
OK, I'LL GO TAKE A LOOK.
WHATEVER YOU DO, DON'T MOVE!
WHAT'S THE MATTER?
NOTHING.
I'M SURE IT'S NOTHING.
LIGHTS!
SIR?
CAN YOU TELL ME WHAT THAT NOISE WAS?
I COULD'VE SWORN IT WAS FROM OUTSIDE.
INDEED!
WHAT THE—?!
IT SEEMS A VESSEL HAS DOCKED ON DECK C.
WHERE FROM?
NOW...
I'M AFRAID I DON'T KNOW.
SHIT!

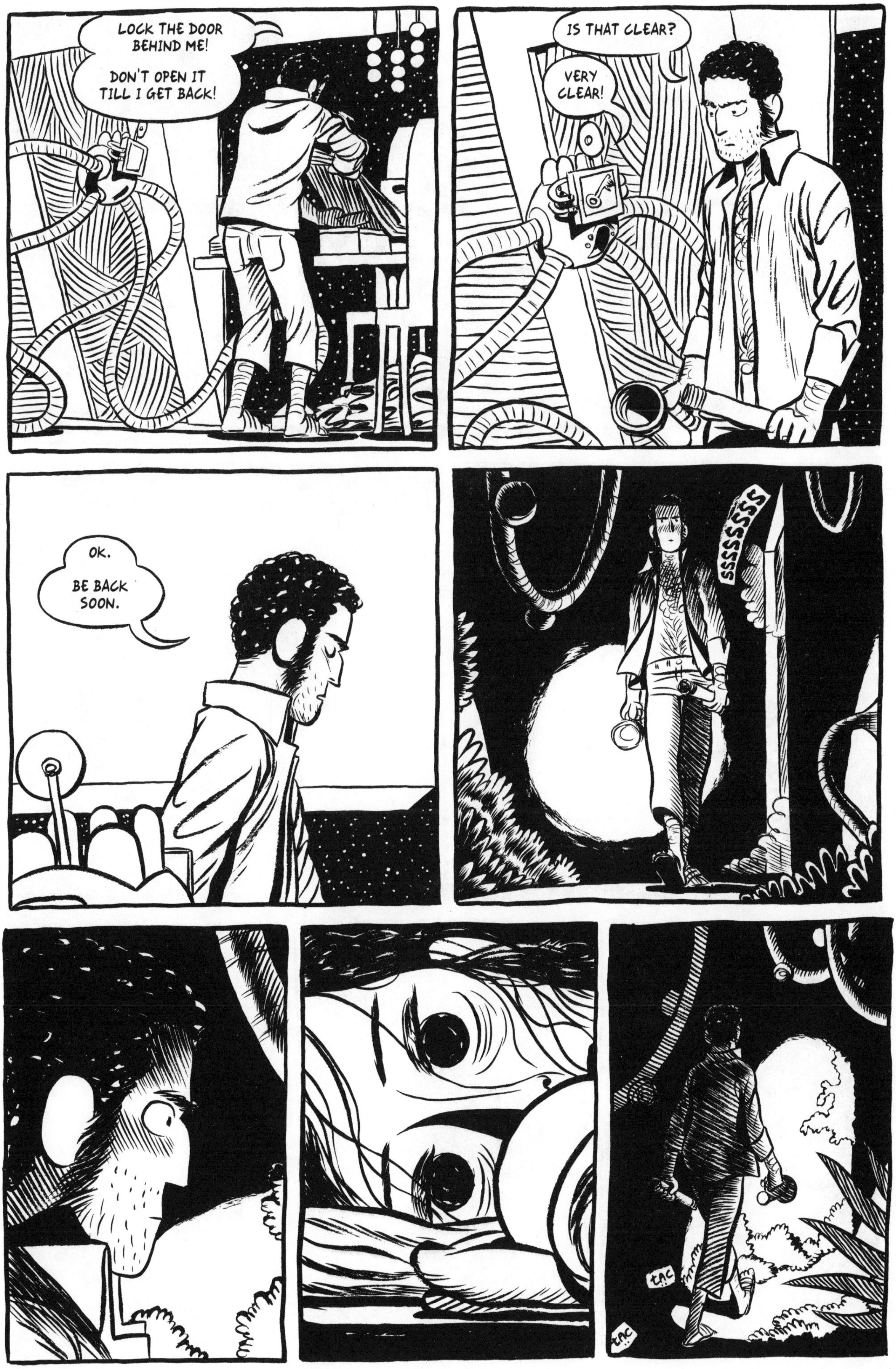

LOCK THE DOOR BEHIND ME!
DON'T OPEN IT TILL I GET BACK!
IS THAT CLEAR?
VERY CLEAR!
OK.
BE BACK SOON.
SSSSSSSS
TAC
TAC

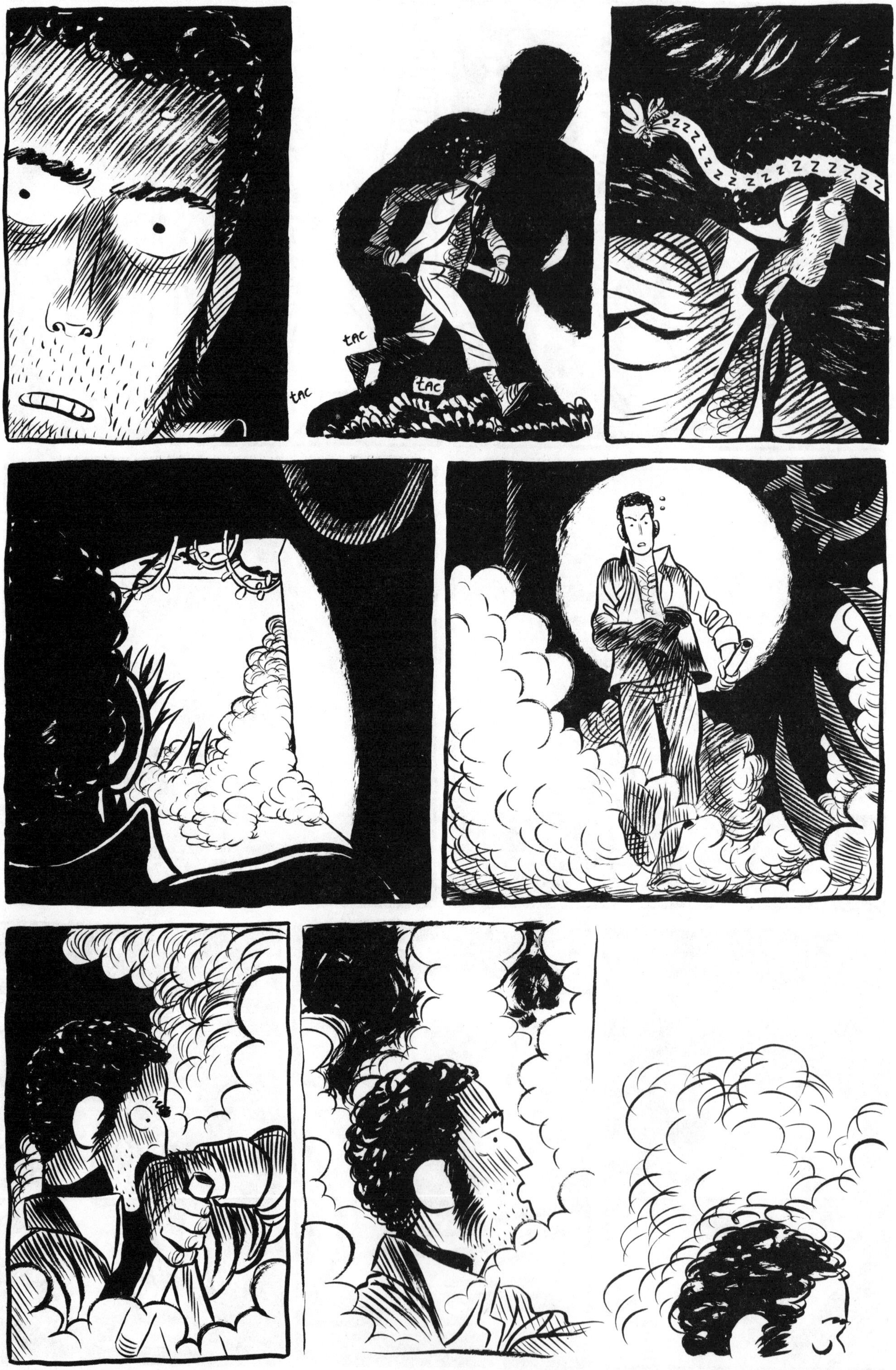
TAC
TAC
TAC

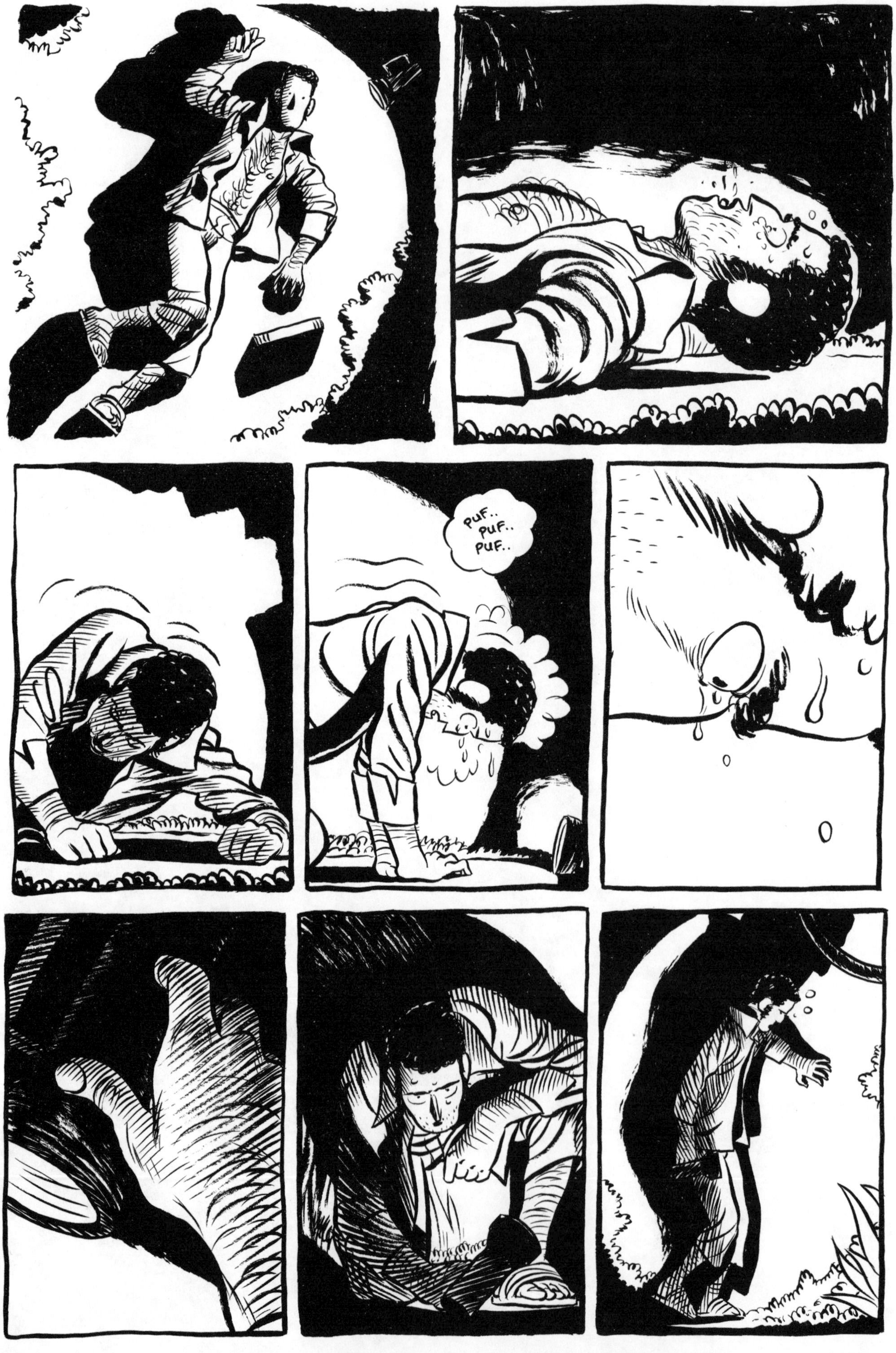
PUF.. PUF.. PUF..

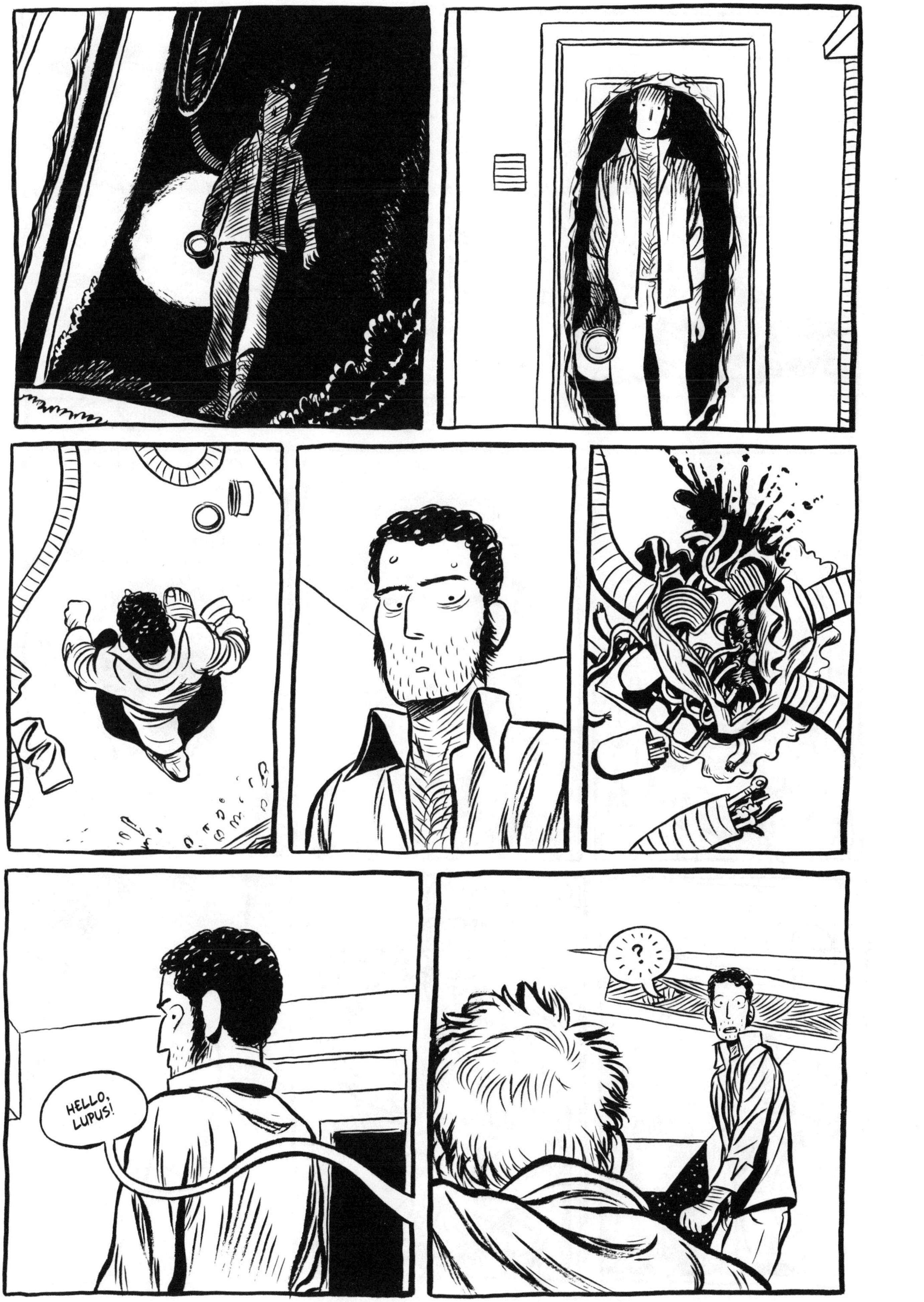
HELLO, LUPUS!
?

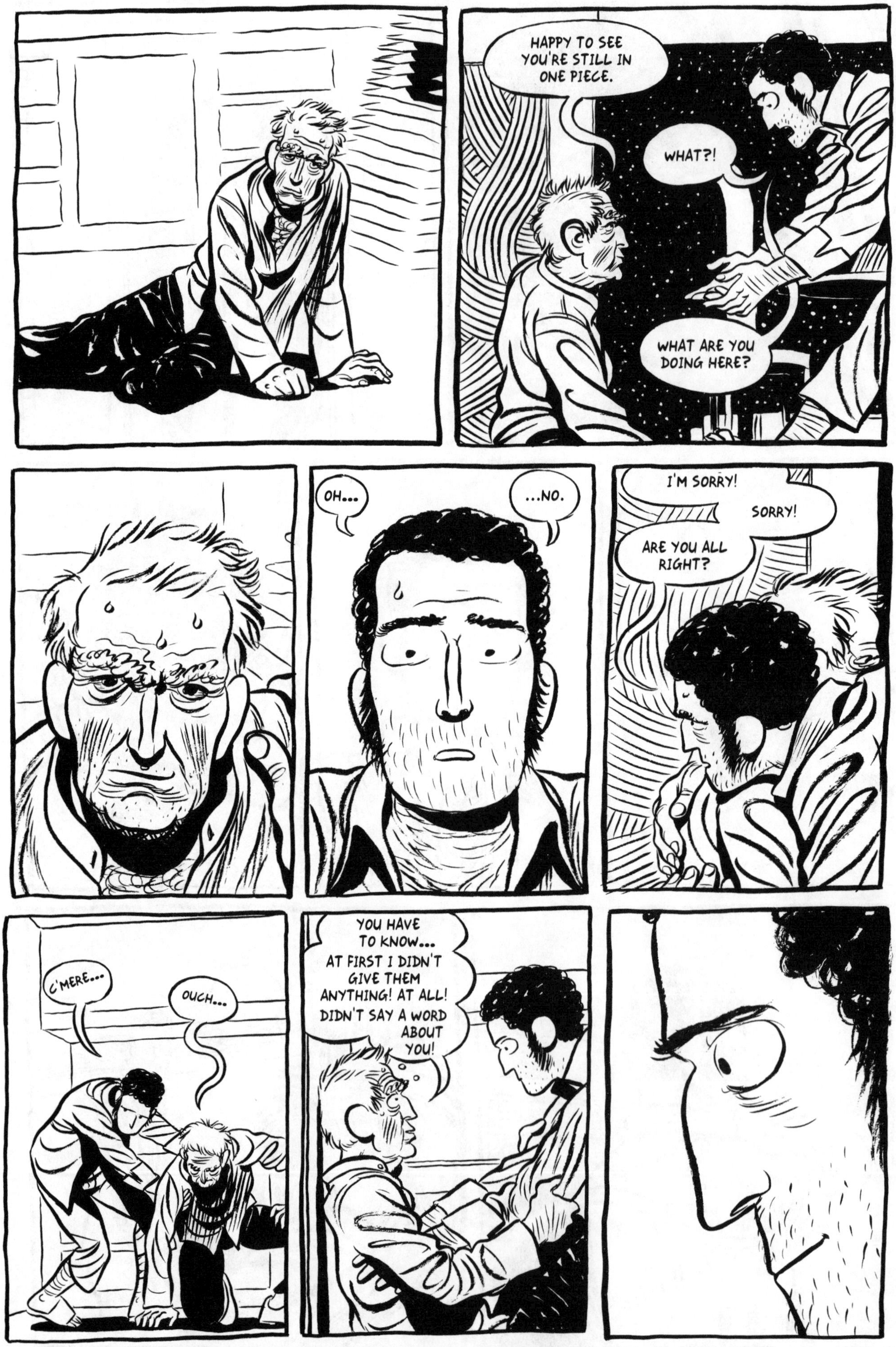
HAPPY TO SEE YOU'RE STILL IN ONE PIECE.
WHAT?!
WHAT ARE YOU DOING HERE?
OH...
...NO.
I'M SORRY!
SORRY!
ARE YOU ALL RIGHT?
C'MERE...
OUCH...
YOU HAVE TO KNOW... AT FIRST I DIDN'T GIVE THEM ANYTHING! AT ALL! DIDN'T SAY A WORD ABOUT YOU!

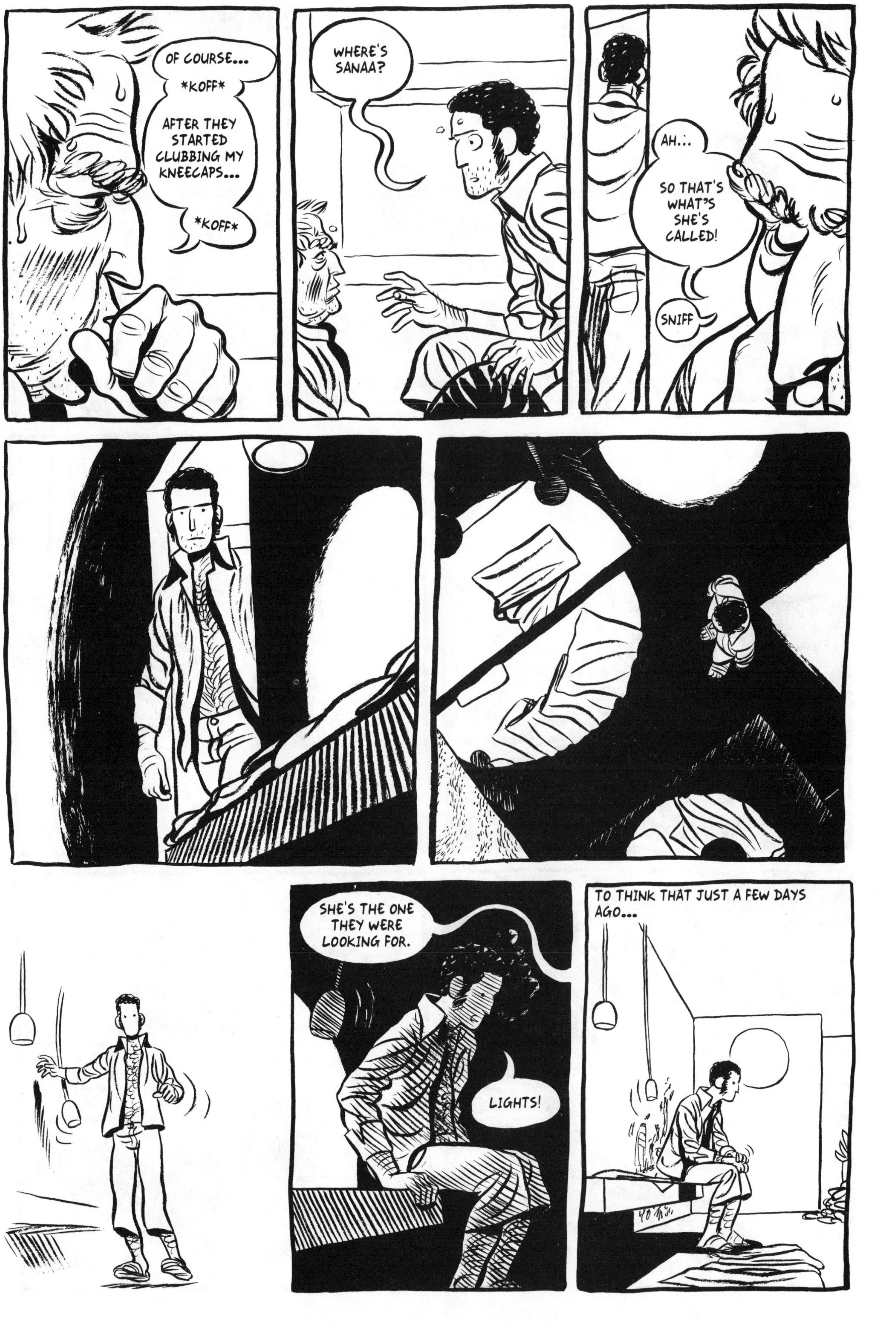

OF COURSE...
KOFF
AFTER THEY STARTED CLUBBING MY KNEECAPS...
KOFF
WHERE'S SANAA?
AH...
SO THAT'S WHAT'S SHE'S CALLED!
SNIFF
SHE'S THE ONE THEY WERE LOOKING FOR.
LIGHTS!
TO THINK THAT JUST A FEW DAYS AGO...

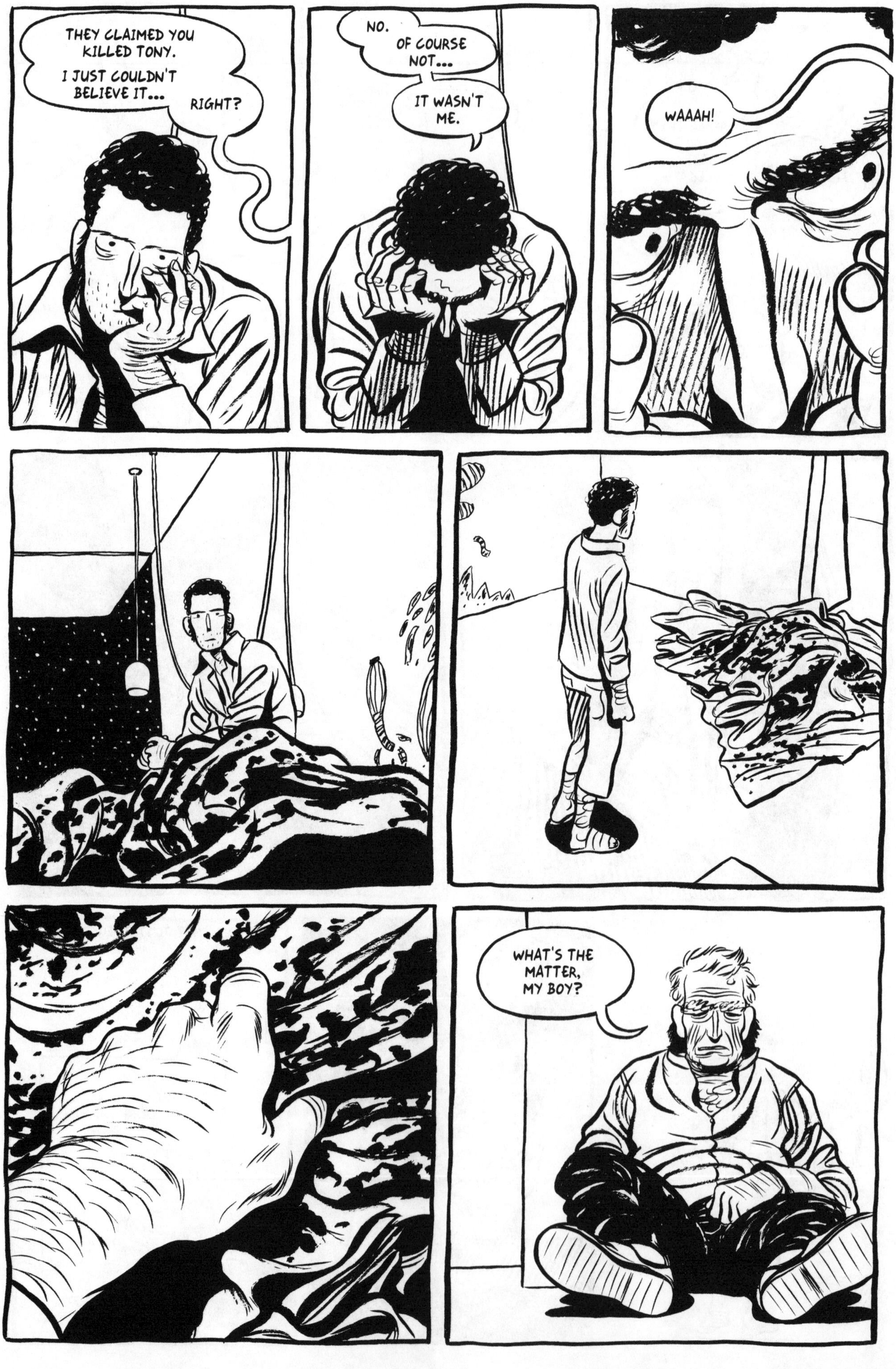
THEY CLAIMED YOU KILLED TONY.
I JUST COULDN'T BELIEVE IT...
RIGHT?
NO.
OF COURSE NOT...
IT WASN'T ME.
WAAAH!
WHAT'S THE MATTER, MY BOY?

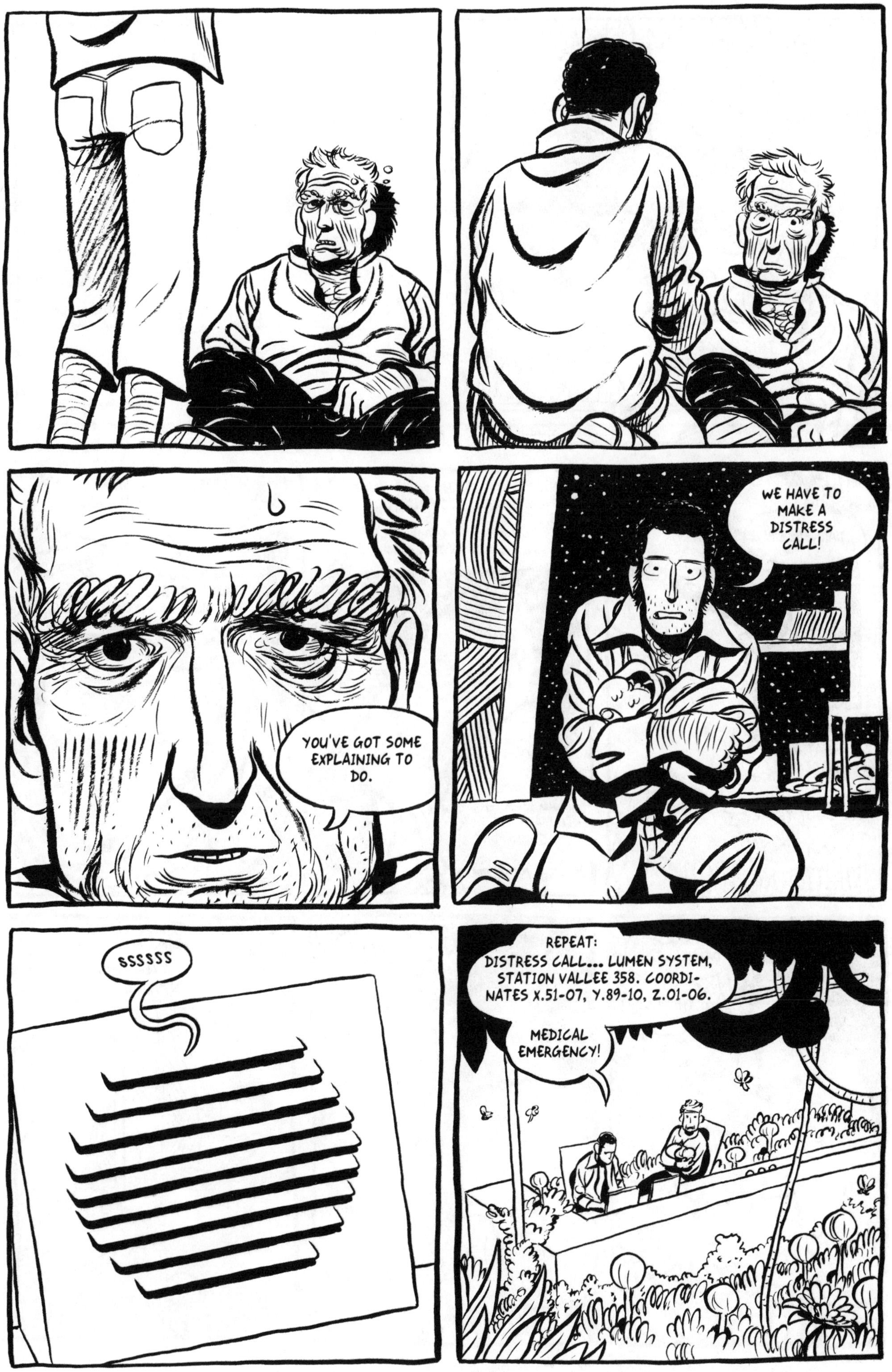
YOU'VE GOT SOME EXPLAINING TO DO.
WE HAVE TO MAKE A DISTRESS CALL!
SSSSSS
REPEAT: DISTRESS CALL... LUMEN SYSTEM, STATION VALLEE 358. COORDINATES X.51-07, Y.89-10, Z.01-06.
MEDICAL EMERGENCY!

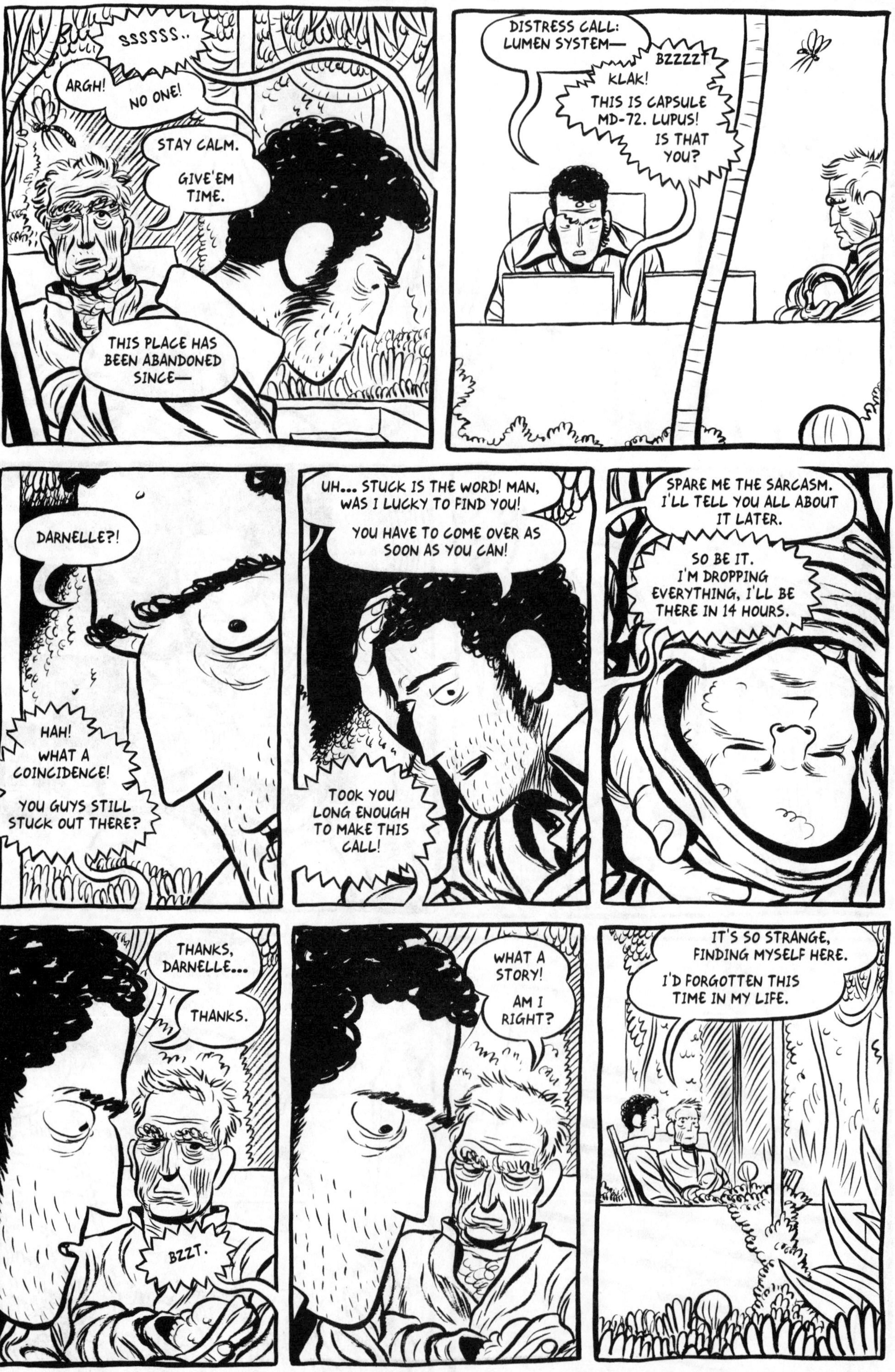
SSSSSS..
ARGH!
NO ONE!
STAY CALM.
GIVE'EM TIME.
THIS PLACE HAS BEEN ABANDONED SINCE—
DISTRESS CALL: LUMEN SYSTEM—
BZZZZT
KLAK!
THIS IS CAPSULE MD-72. LUPUS! IS THAT YOU?
DARNELLE?!
HAH! WHAT A COINCIDENCE!
YOU GUYS STILL STUCK OUT THERE?
UH... STUCK IS THE WORD! MAN, WAS I LUCKY TO FIND YOU!
YOU HAVE TO COME OVER AS SOON AS YOU CAN!
TOOK YOU LONG ENOUGH TO MAKE THIS CALL!
SPARE ME THE SARCASM. I'LL TELL YOU ALL ABOUT IT LATER.
SO BE IT. I'M DROPPING EVERYTHING, I'LL BE THERE IN 14 HOURS.
THANKS, DARNELLE...
THANKS.
BZZT.
WHAT A STORY!
AM I RIGHT?
IT'S SO STRANGE, FINDING MYSELF HERE.
I'D FORGOTTEN THIS TIME IN MY LIFE.

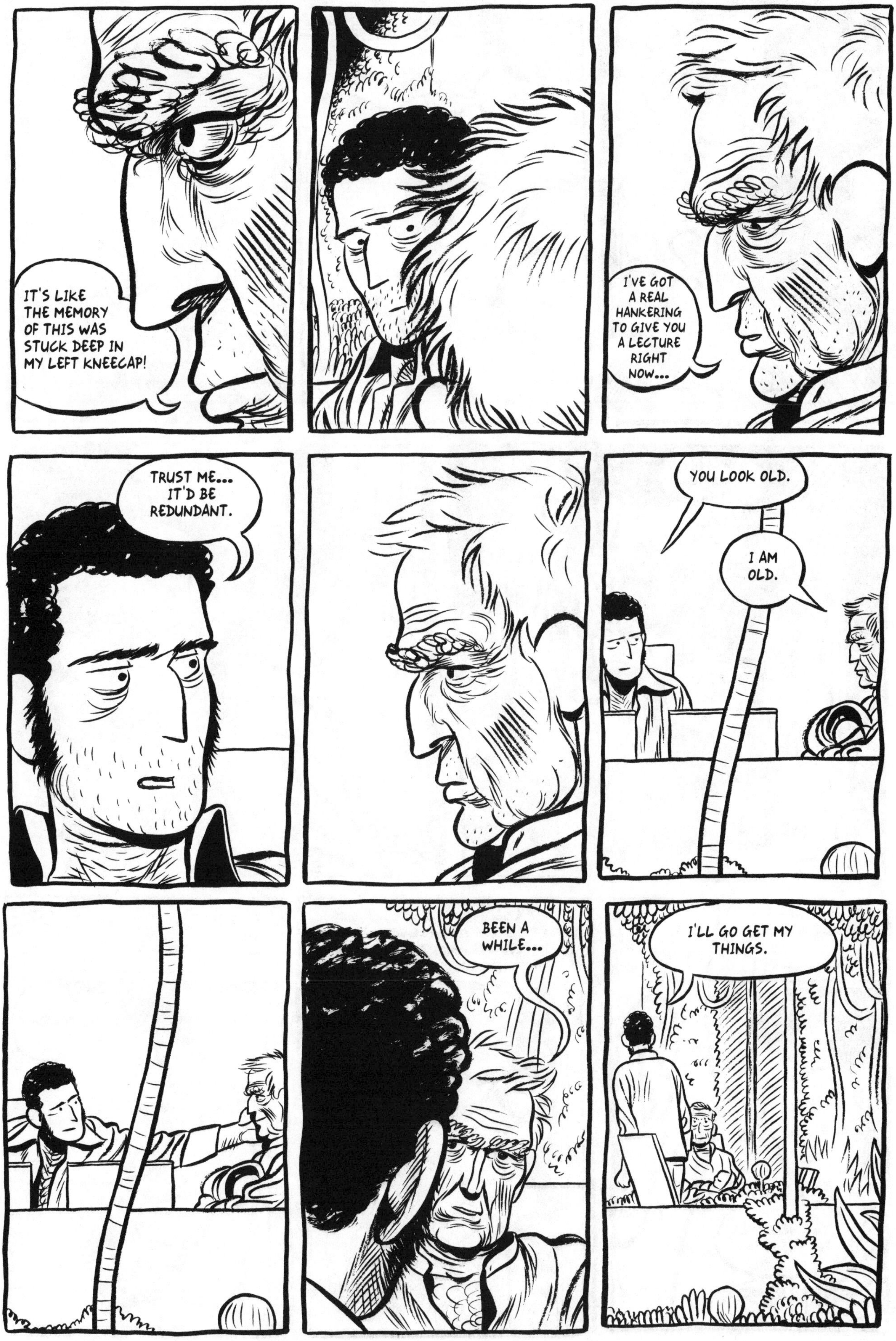
IT'S LIKE THE MEMORY OF THIS WAS STUCK DEEP IN MY LEFT KNEECAP!
I'VE GOT A REAL HANKERING TO GIVE YOU A LECTURE RIGHT NOW...
TRUST ME... IT'D BE REDUNDANT.
YOU LOOK OLD.
I AM OLD.
BEEN A WHILE...
I'LL GO GET MY THINGS.

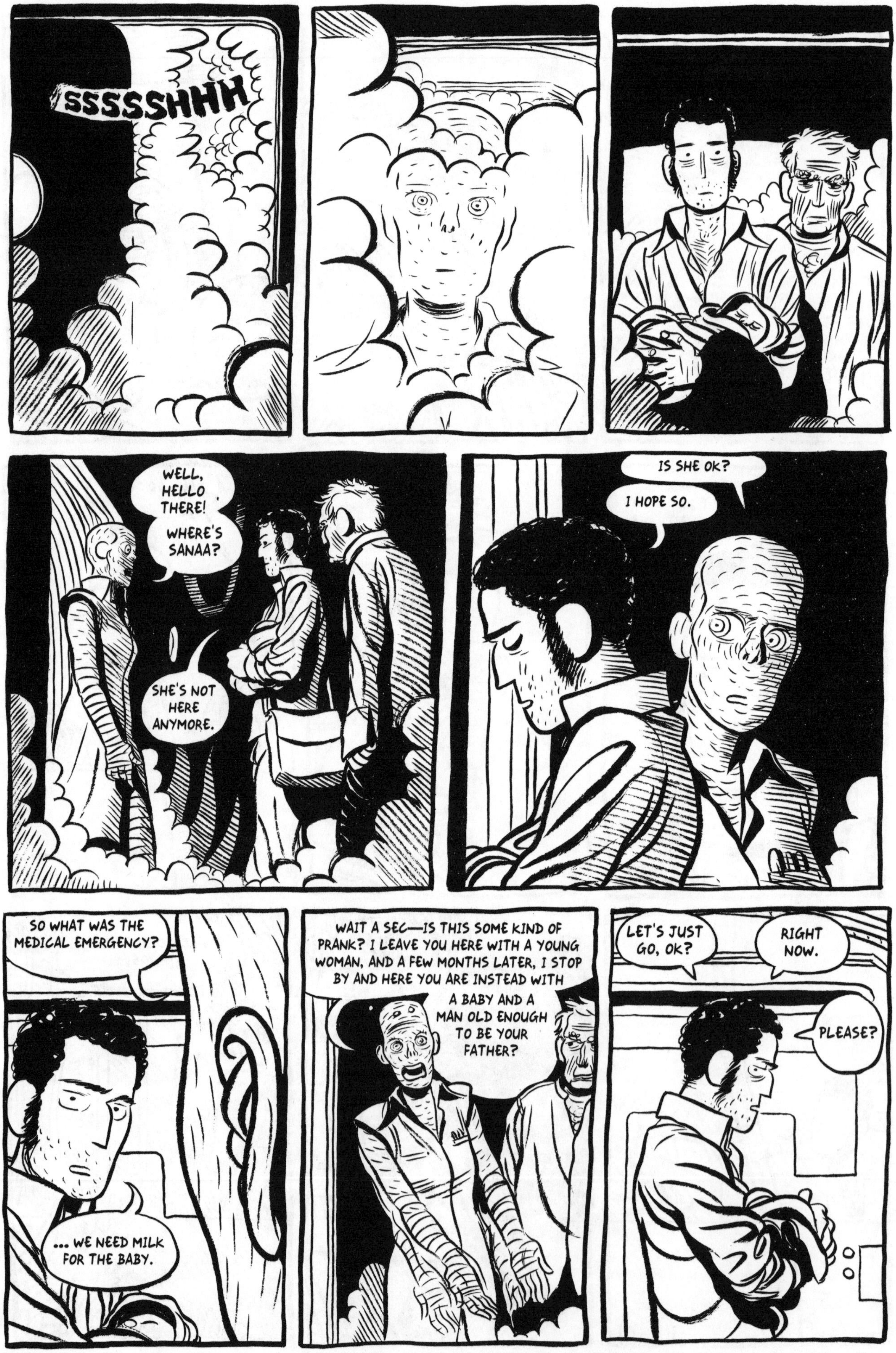
SSSSSHHH
WELL, HELLO THERE!
WHERE'S SANAA?
SHE'S NOT HERE ANYMORE.
IS SHE OK?
I HOPE SO.
SO WHAT WAS THE MEDICAL EMERGENCY?
... WE NEED MILK FOR THE BABY.
WAIT A SEC—IS THIS SOME KIND OF PRANK? I LEAVE YOU HERE WITH A YOUNG WOMAN, AND A FEW MONTHS LATER, I STOP BY AND HERE YOU ARE INSTEAD WITH
A BABY AND A MAN OLD ENOUGH TO BE YOUR FATHER?
LET'S JUST GO, OK?
RIGHT NOW.
PLEASE?

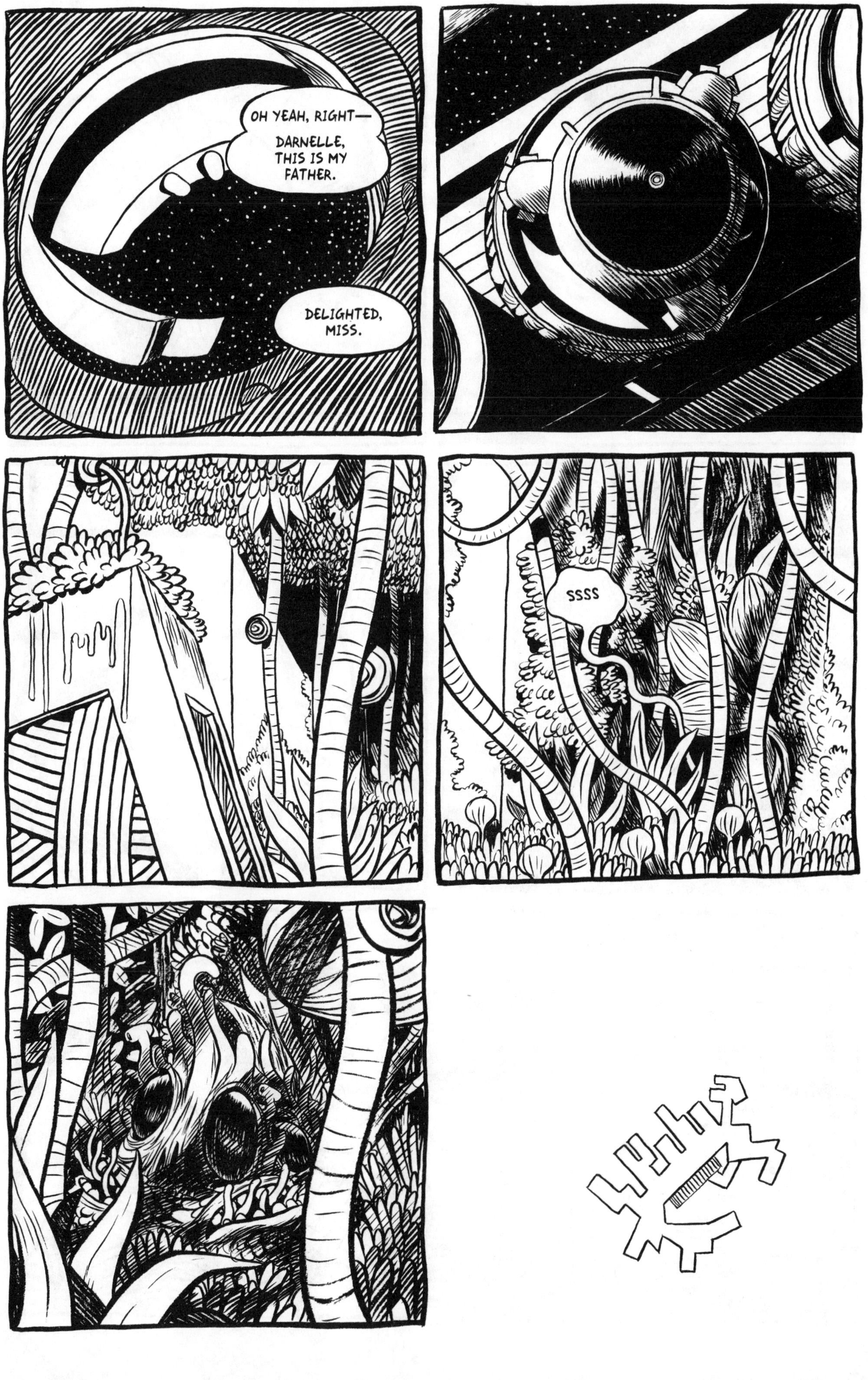
OH YEAH, RIGHT—
DARNELLE, THIS IS MY FATHER.
DELIGHTED, MISS.
SSSS

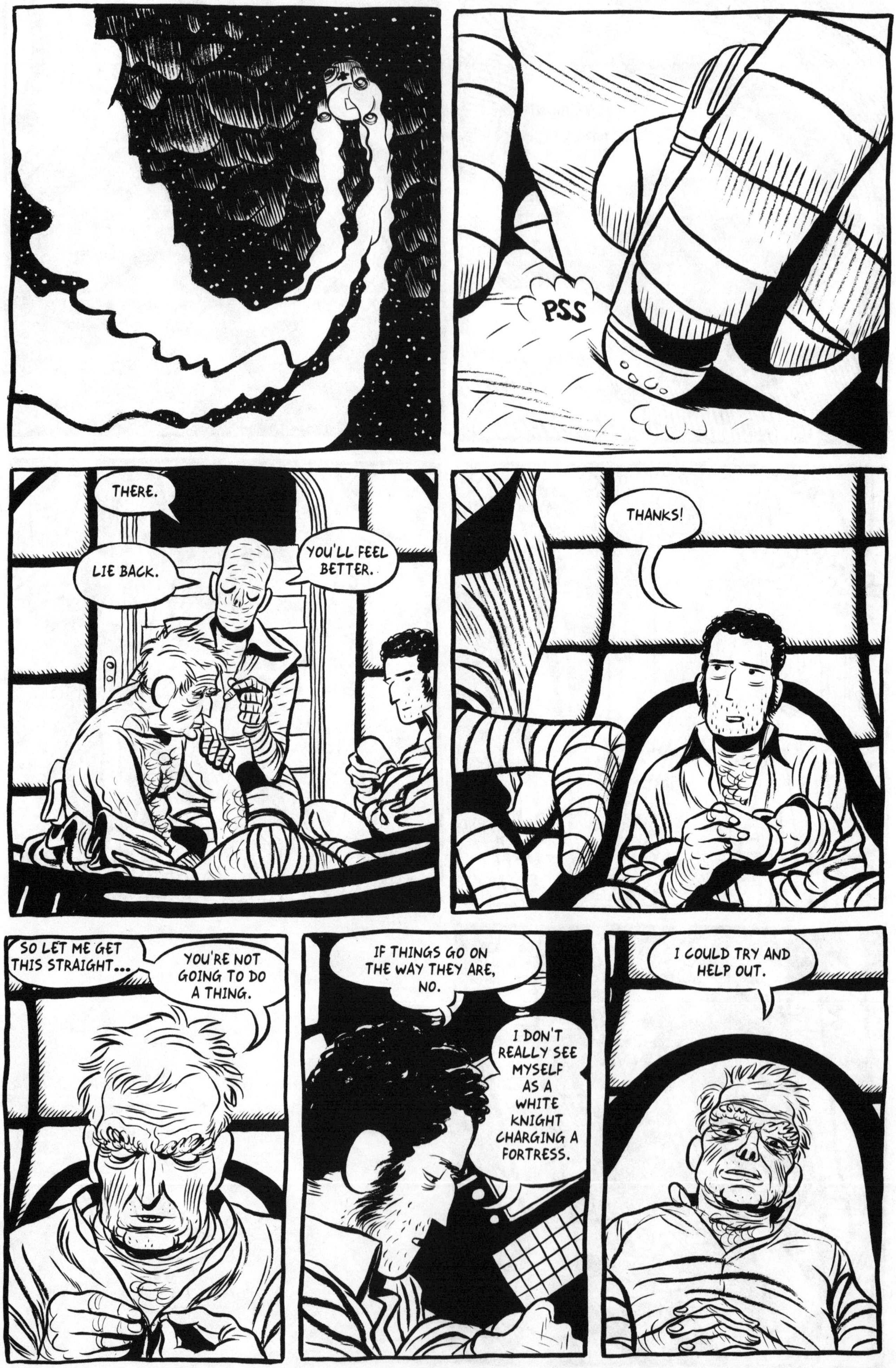
PSS
THERE.
LIE BACK.
YOU'LL FEEL BETTER.
THANKS!
SO LET ME GET THIS STRAIGHT...
YOU'RE NOT GOING TO DO A THING.
IF THINGS GO ON THE WAY THEY ARE, NO.
I DON'T REALLY SEE MYSELF AS A WHITE KNIGHT CHARGING A FORTRESS.
I COULD TRY AND HELP OUT.

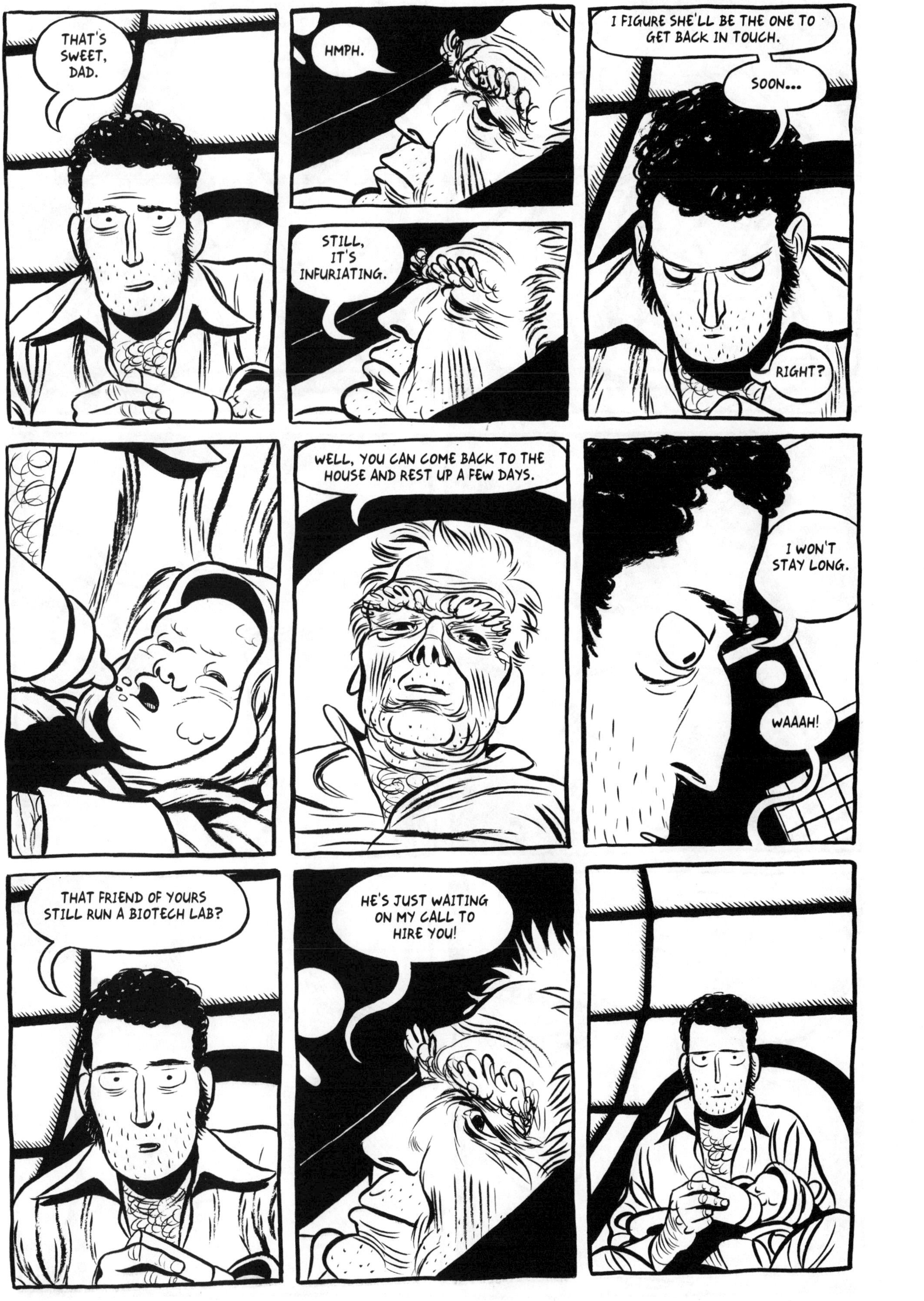
THAT'S SWEET, DAD.
HMPH.
STILL, IT'S INFURIATING.
I FIGURE SHE'LL BE THE ONE TO GET BACK IN TOUCH.
SOON...
RIGHT?
WELL, YOU CAN COME BACK TO THE HOUSE AND REST UP A FEW DAYS.
I WON'T STAY LONG.
WAAAH!
THAT FRIEND OF YOURS STILL RUN A BIOTECH LAB?
HE'S JUST WAITING ON MY CALL TO HIRE YOU!

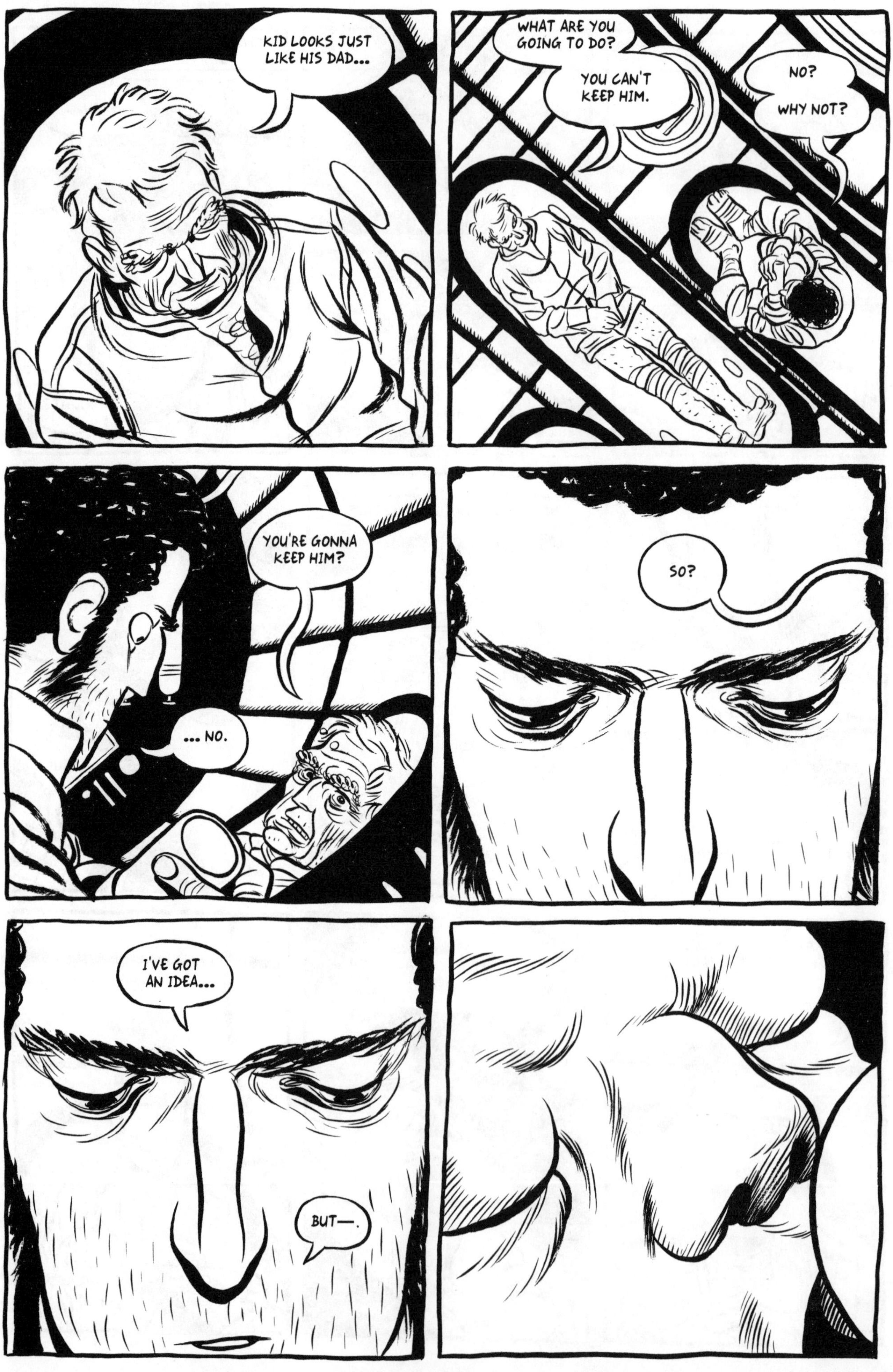
KID LOOKS JUST LIKE HIS DAD...
WHAT ARE YOU GOING TO DO?
YOU CAN'T KEEP HIM.
NO?
WHY NOT?
YOU'RE GONNA KEEP HIM?
... NO.
SO?
I'VE GOT AN IDEA...
BUT—.

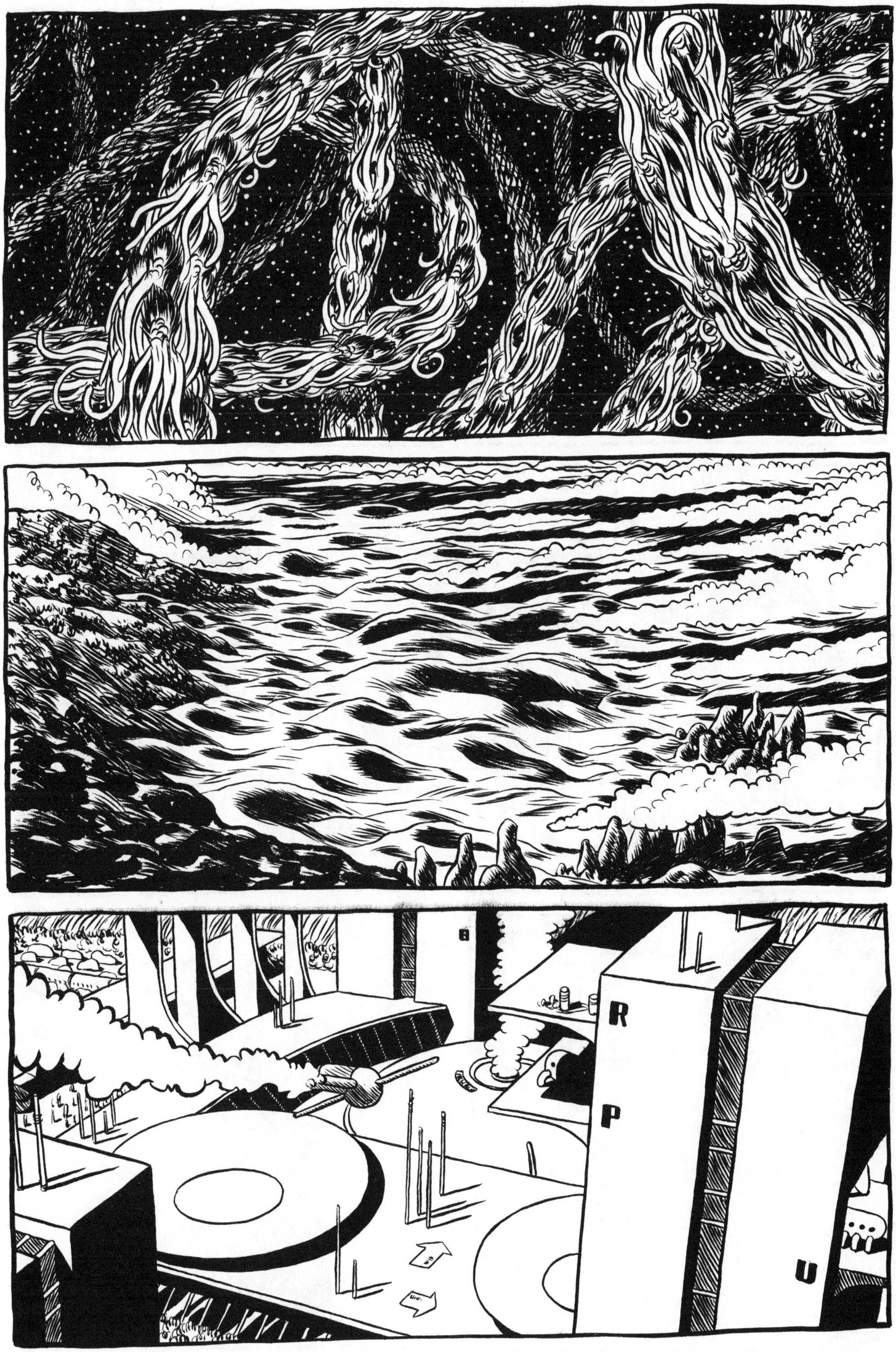
R
P
U

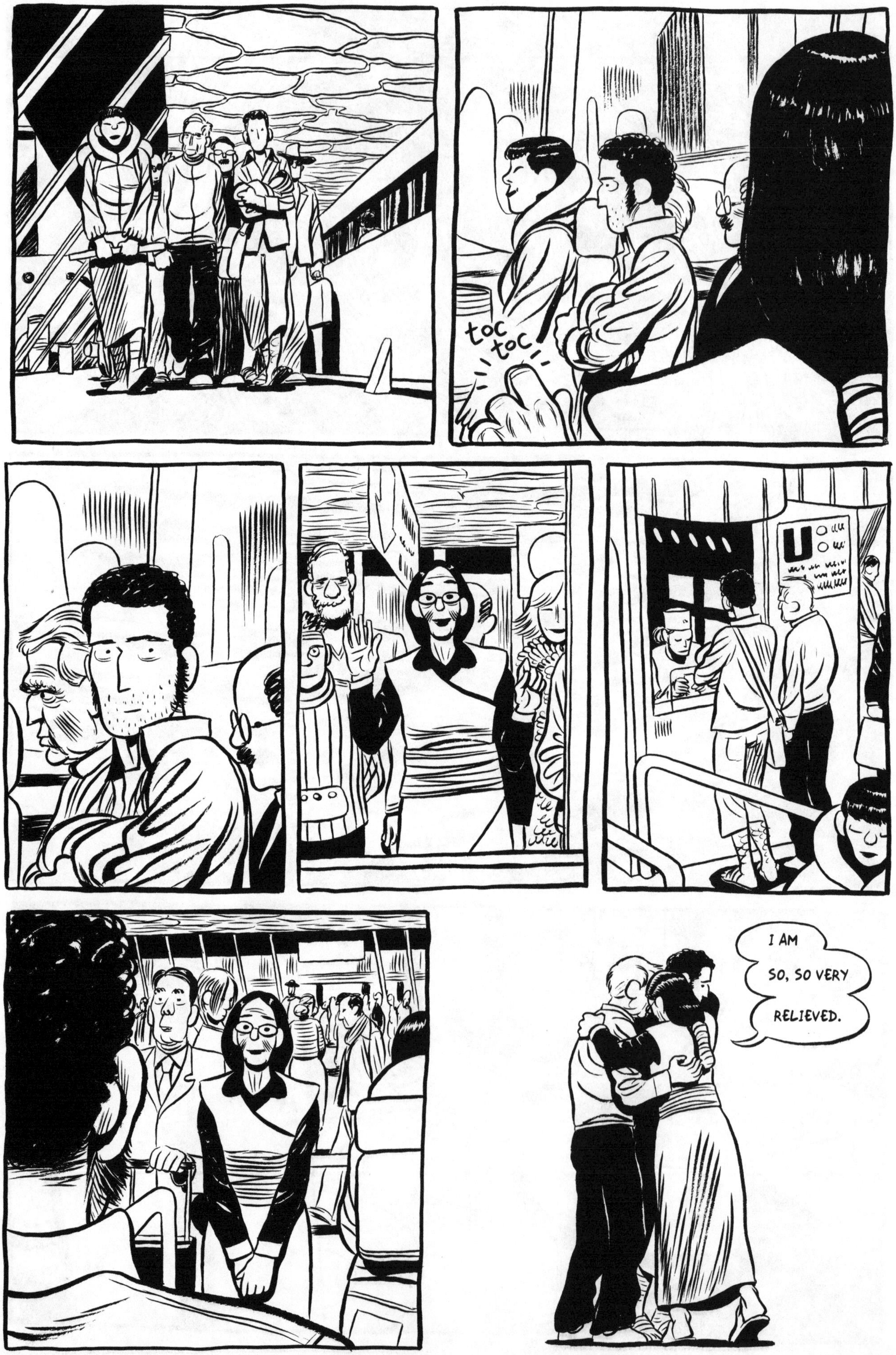
toc toc
I AM SO, SO VERY RELIEVED.

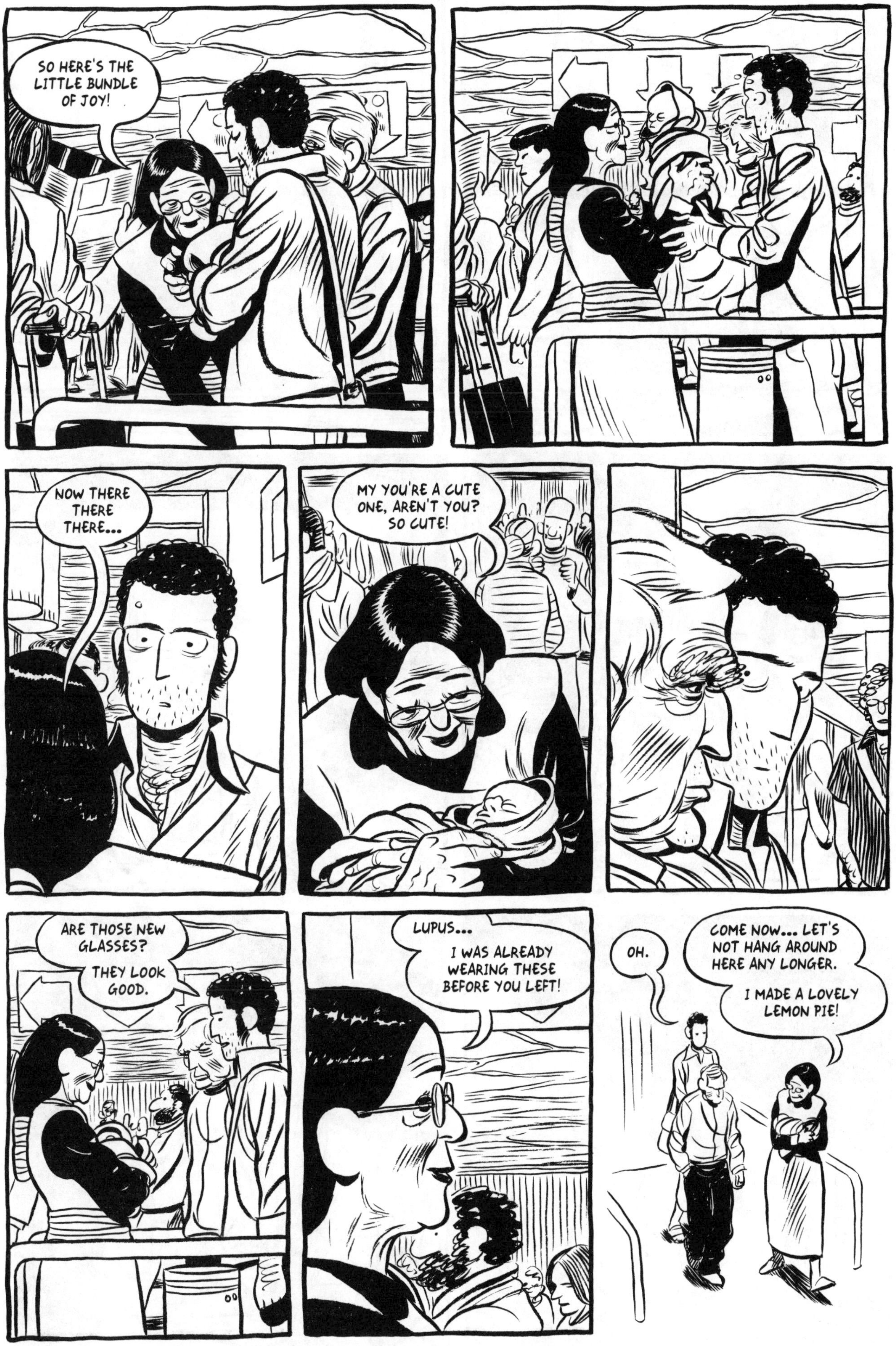
SO HERE'S THE LITTLE BUNDLE OF JOY!
NOW THERE THERE THERE...
MY YOU'RE A CUTE ONE, AREN'T YOU? SO CUTE!
ARE THOSE NEW GLASSES?
THEY LOOK GOOD.
LUPUS...
I WAS ALREADY WEARING THESE BEFORE YOU LEFT!
OH.
COME NOW... LET'S NOT HANG AROUND HERE ANY LONGER.
I MADE A LOVELY LEMON PIE!

SO, UH...
HOW ARE YOU?
OH, FINE!
FINE!
MMM...
FINE.
WELL.
WELL...

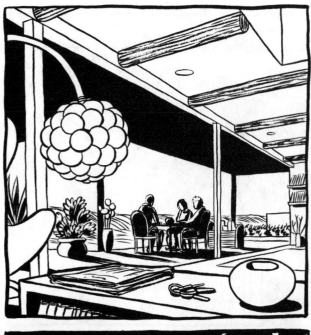

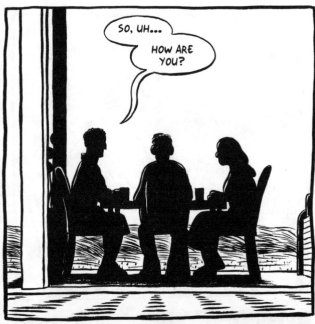

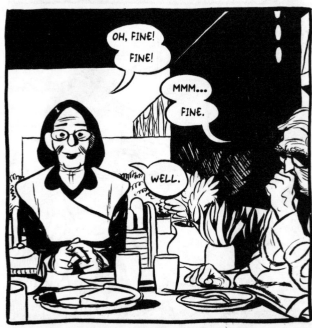

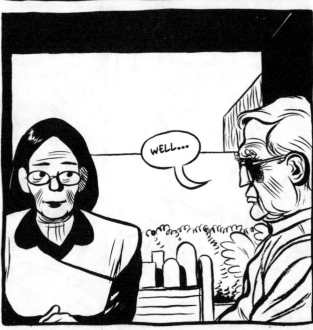

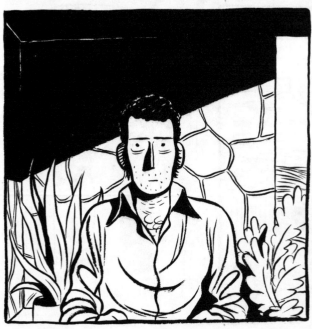

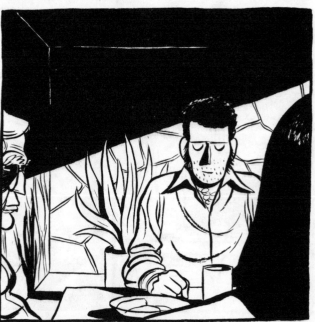

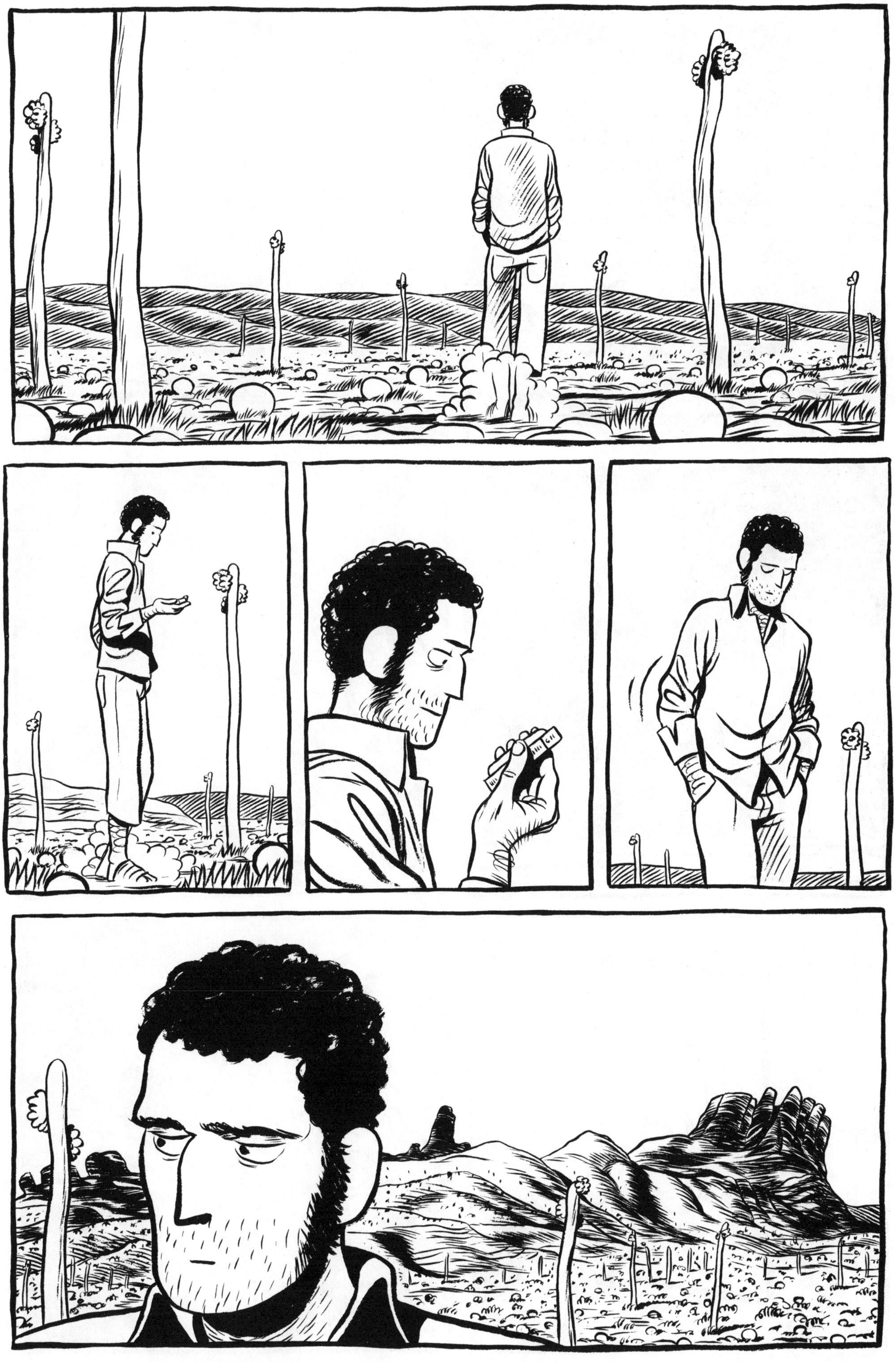

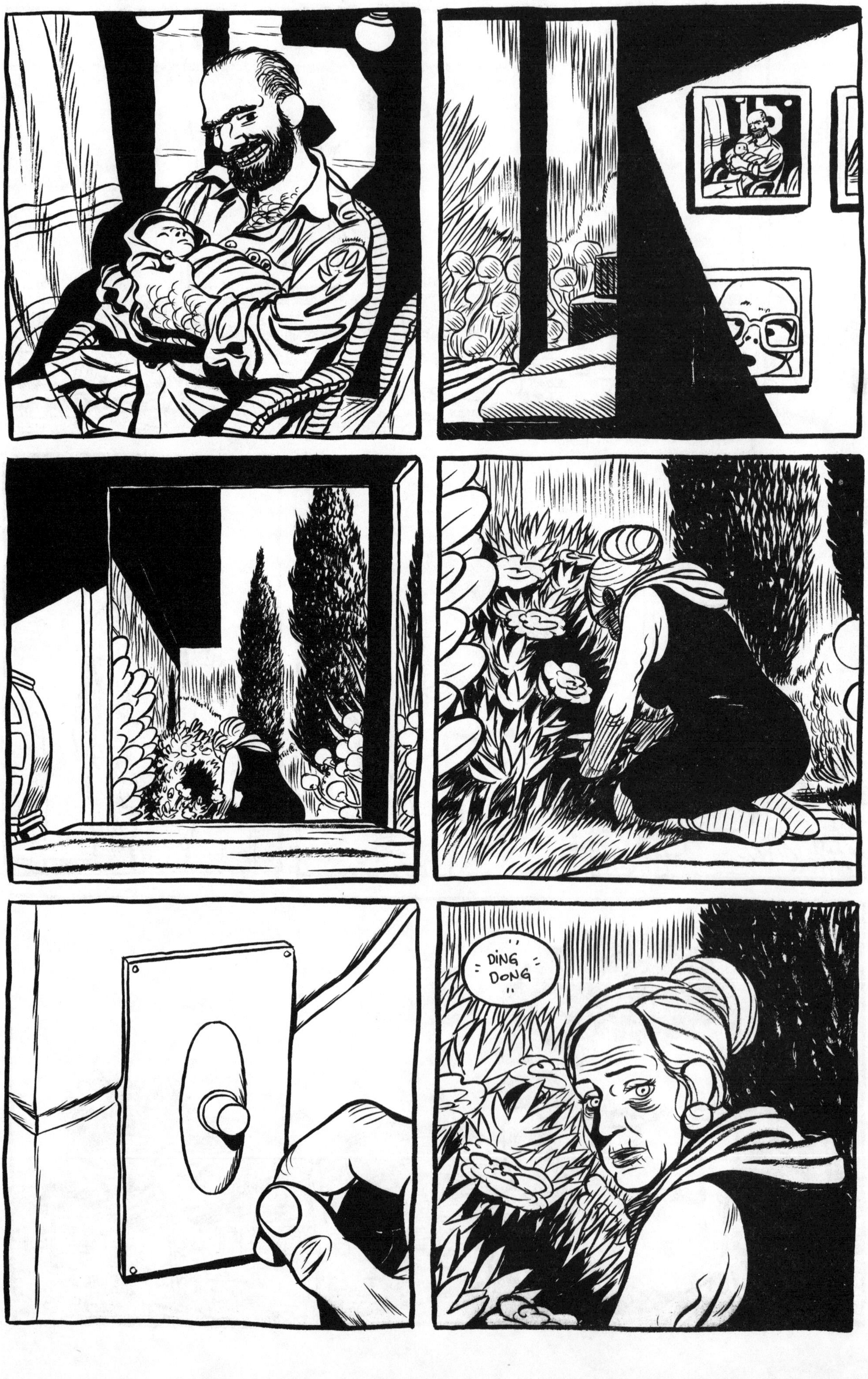
DING DONG

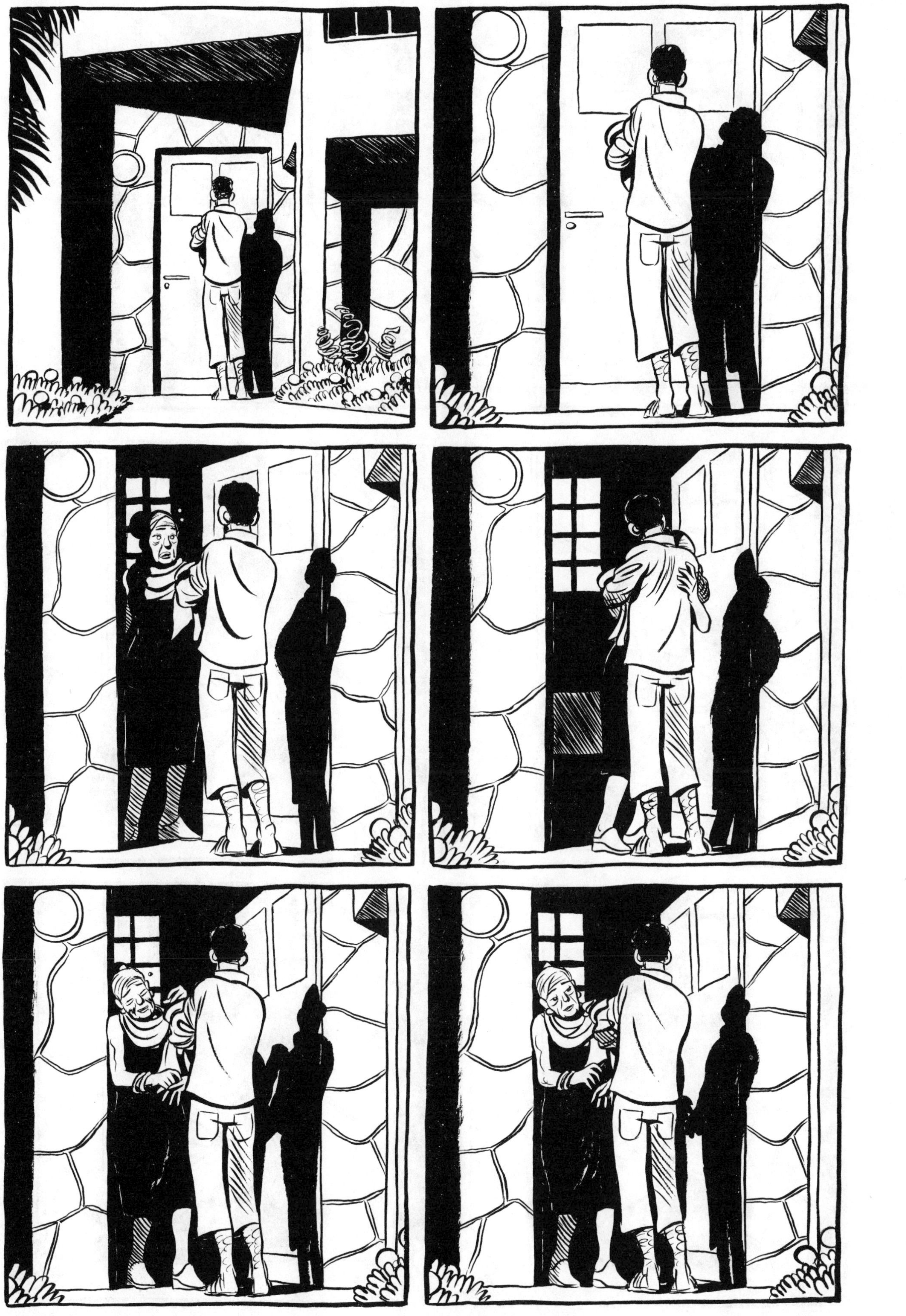

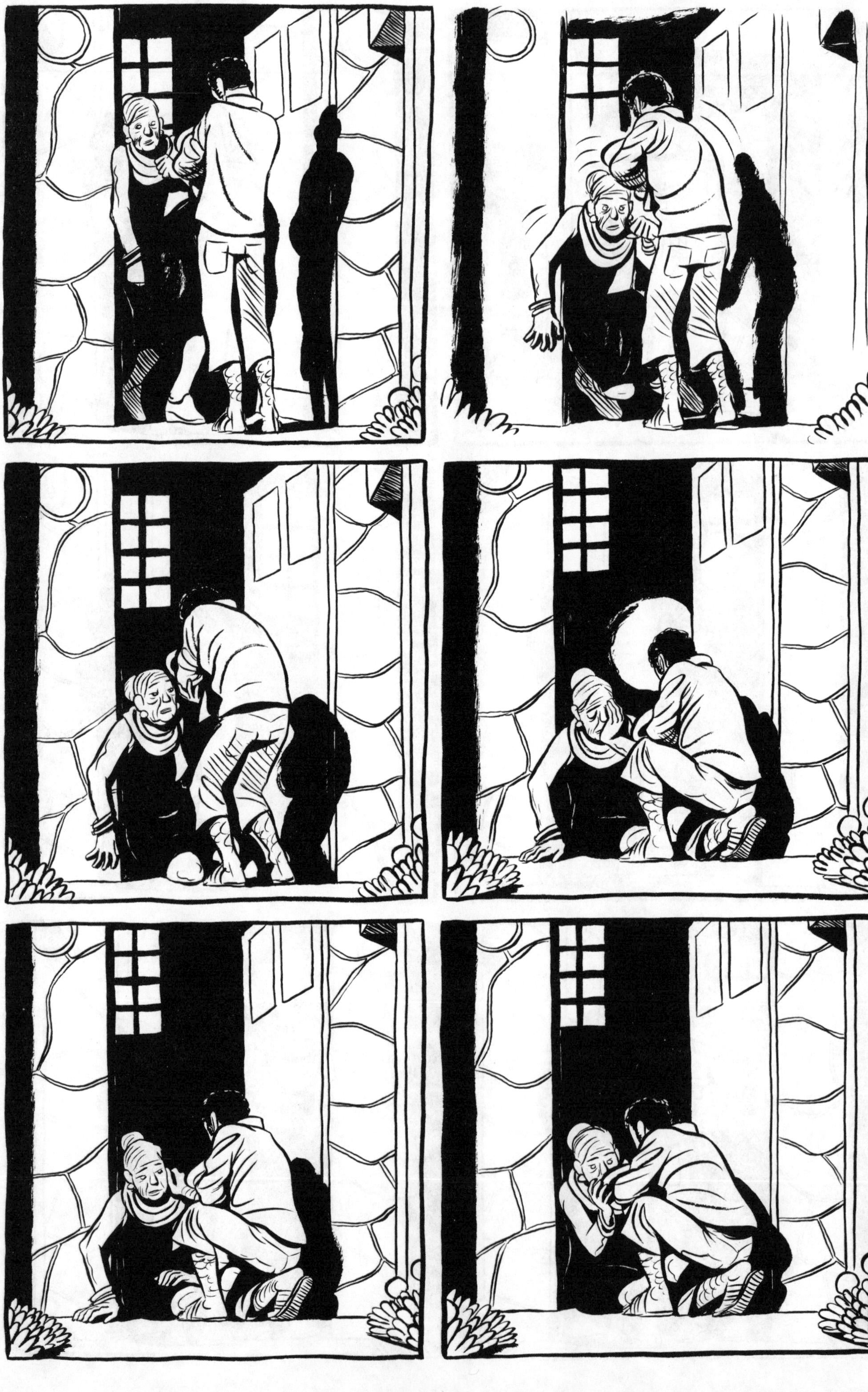

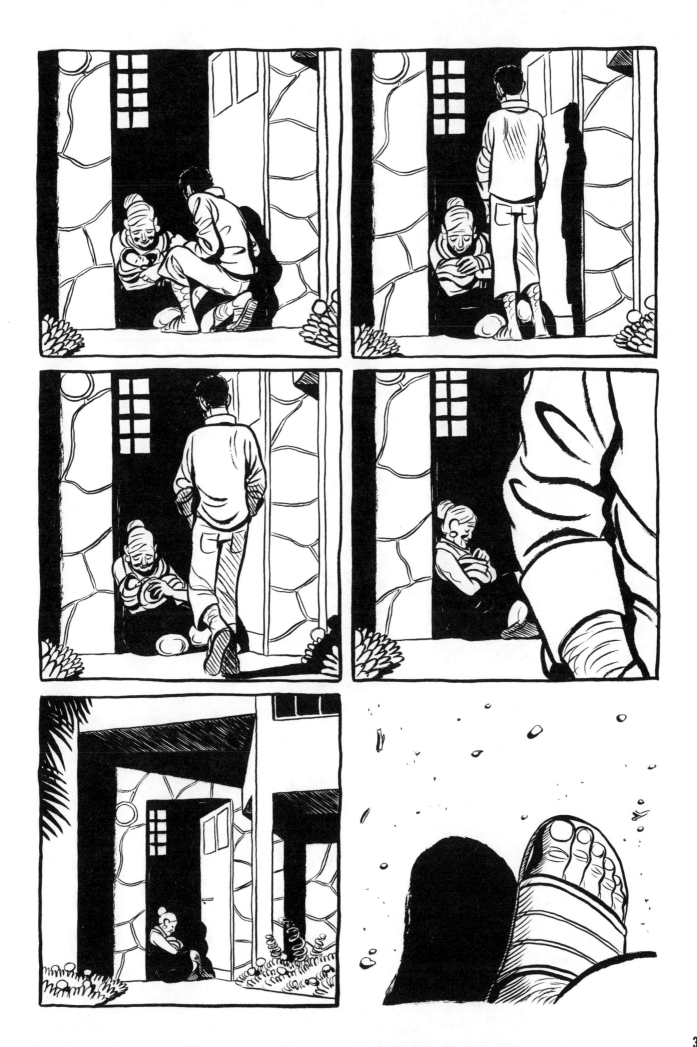

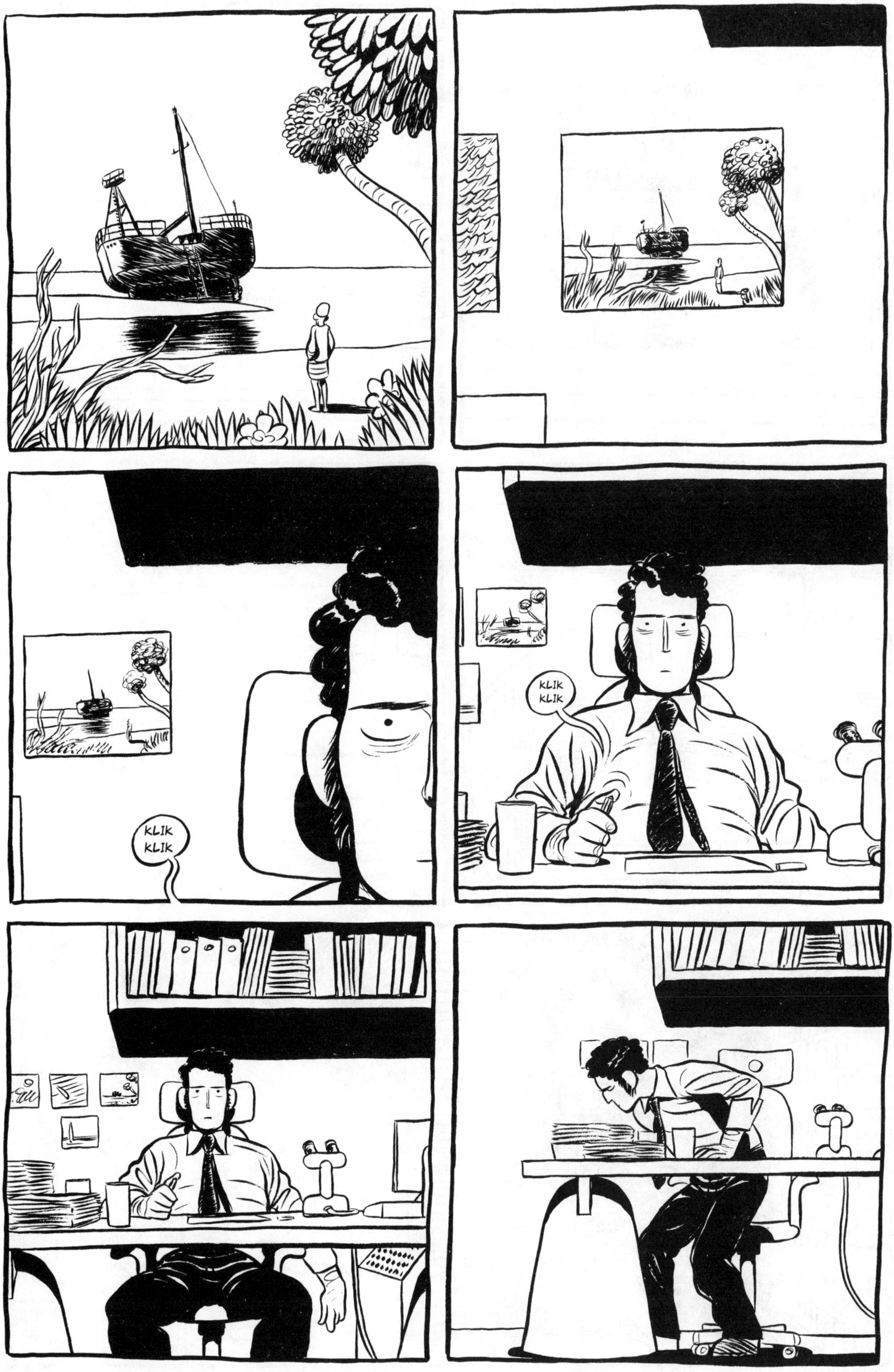
KLIK
KLIK
KLIK
KLIK

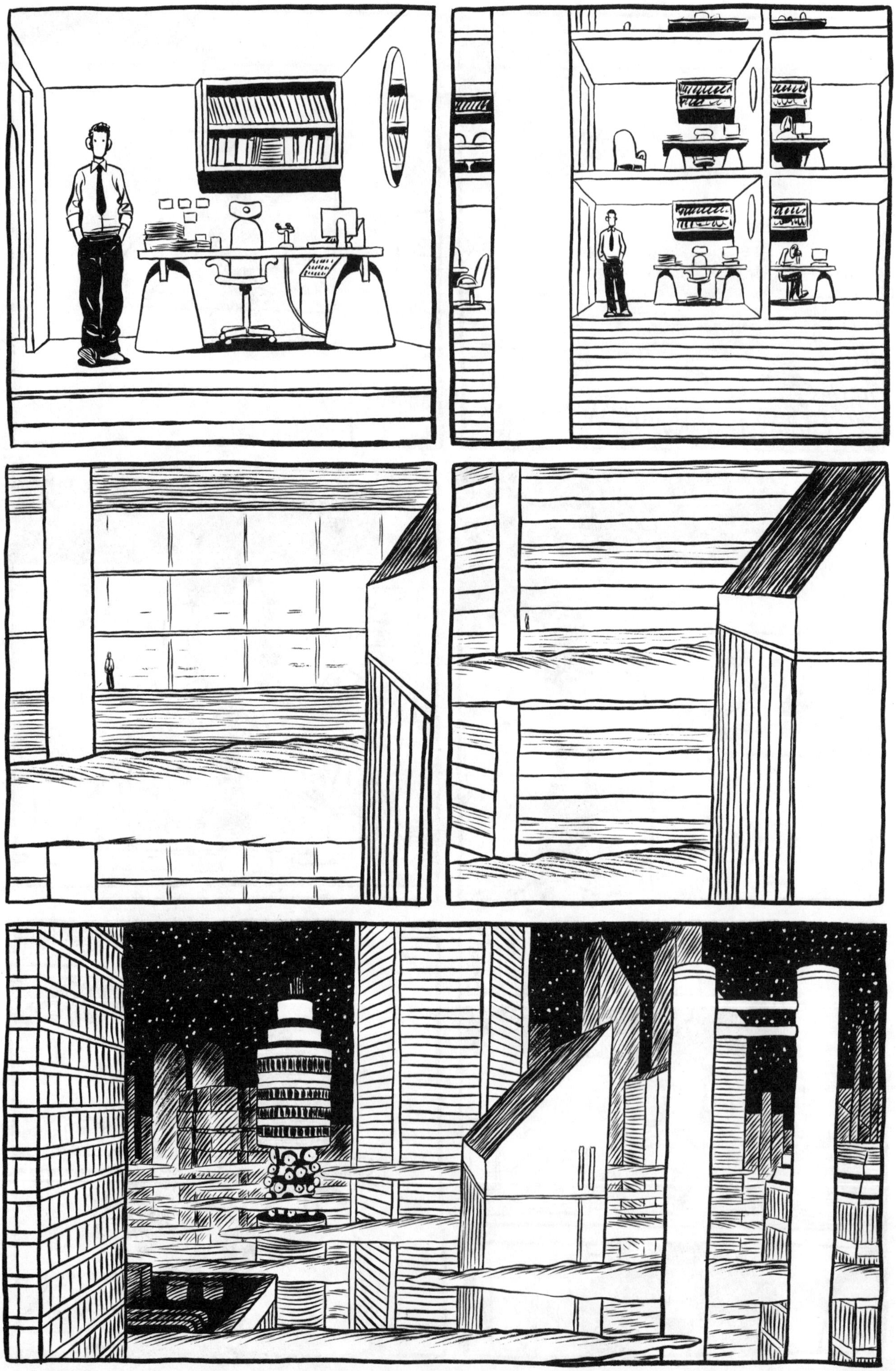

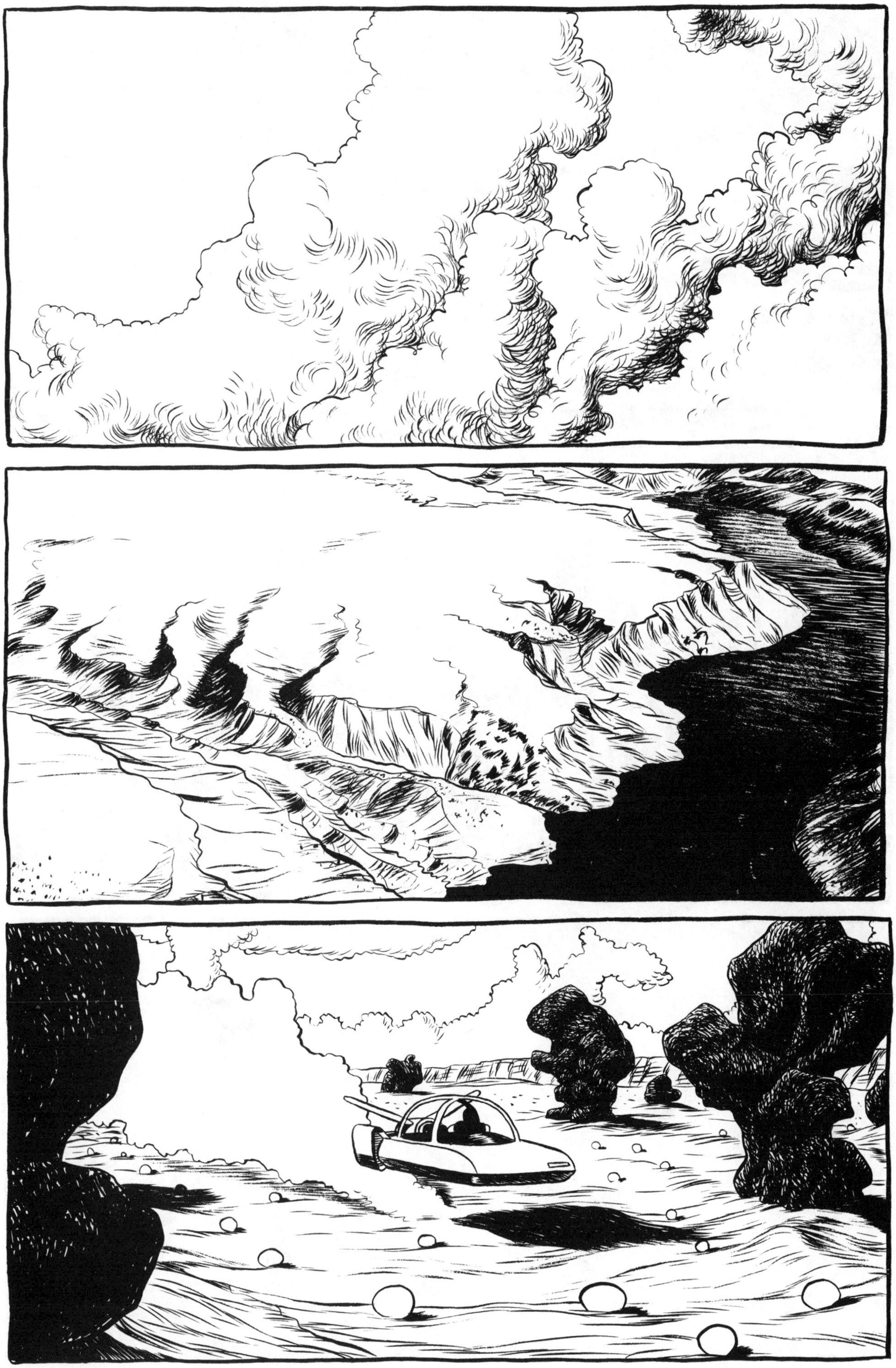

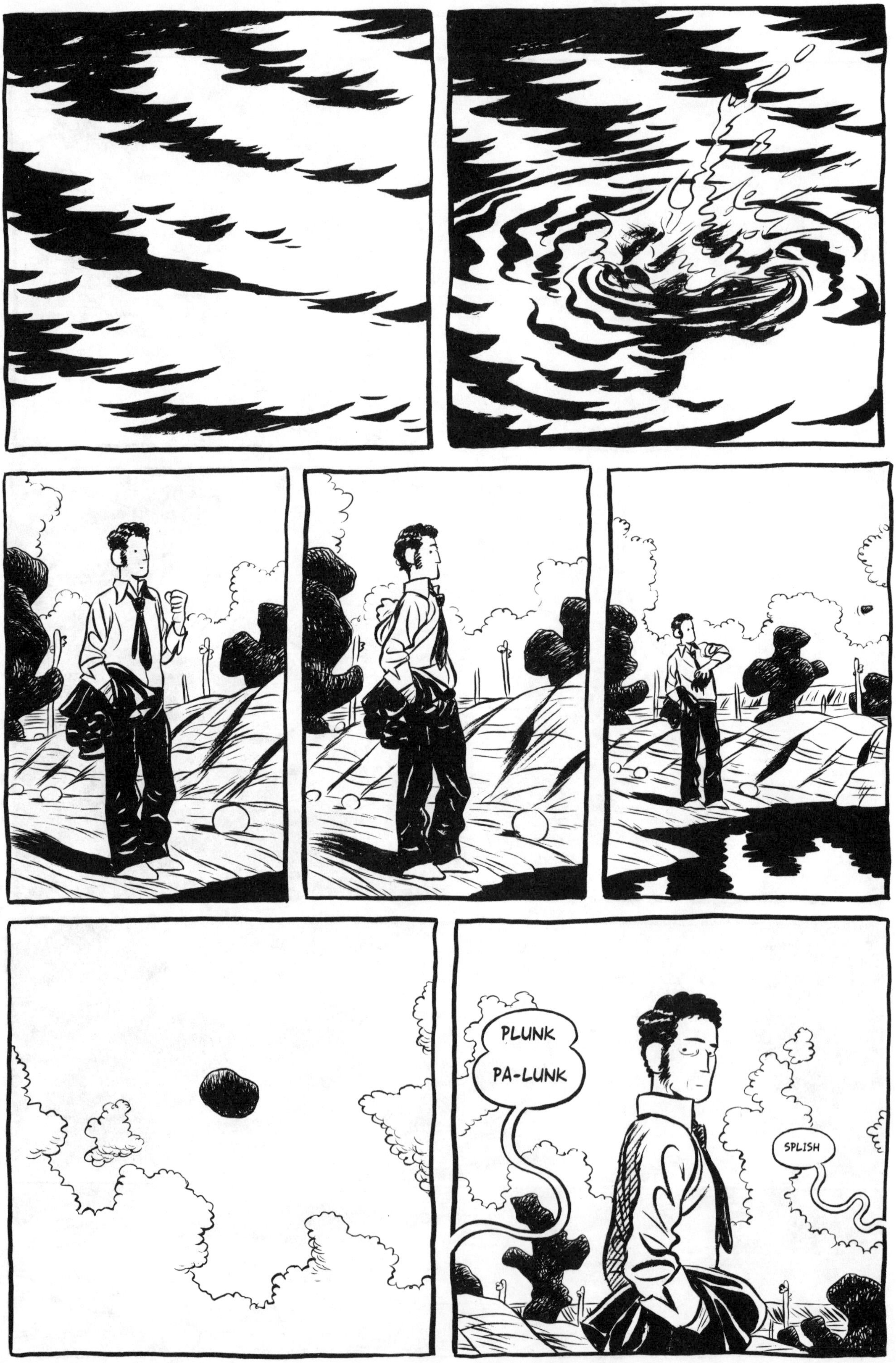
PLUNK
PA-LUNK
SPLISH

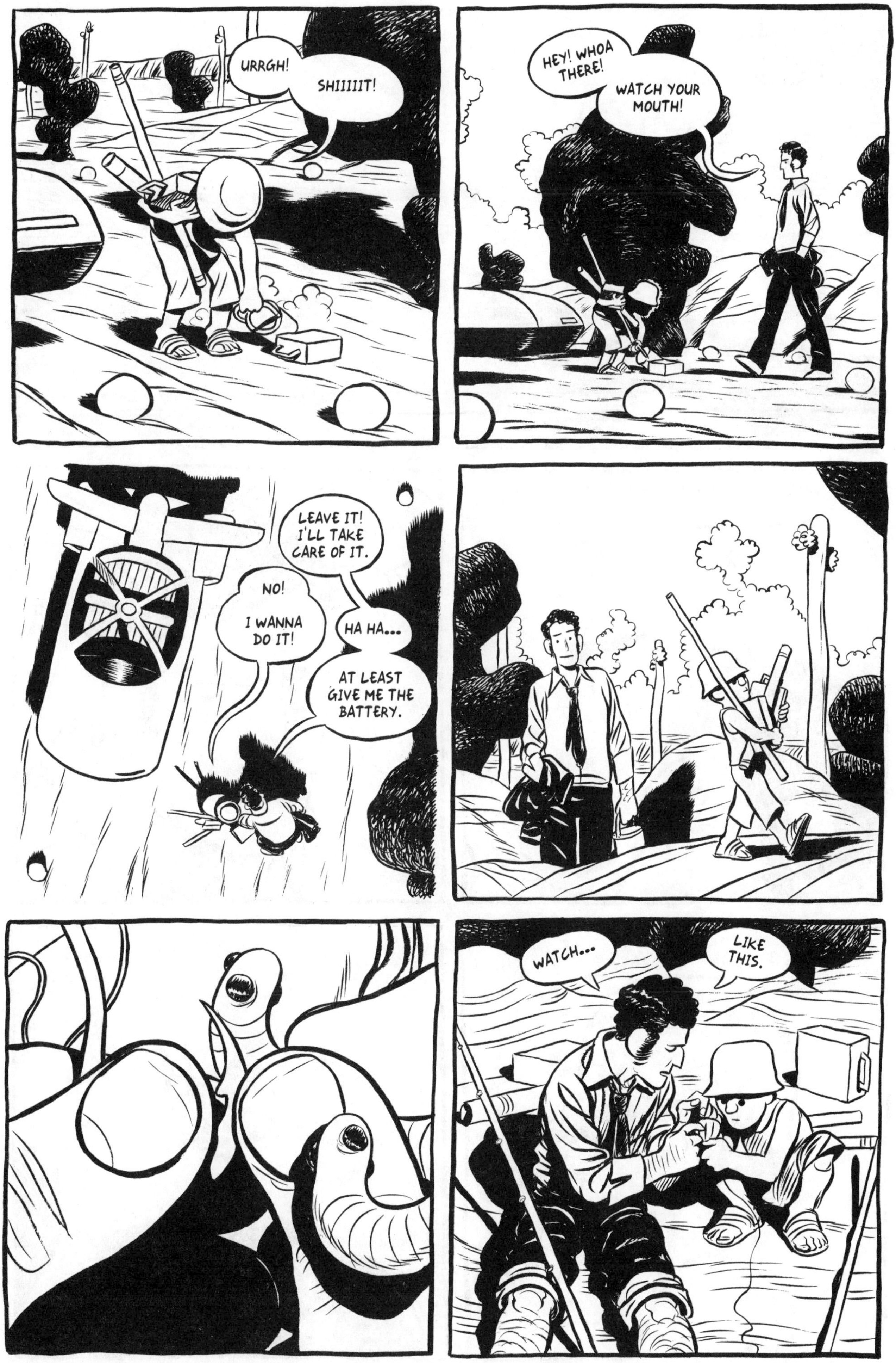
URRGH!
SHIIIIIT!
HEY! WHOA THERE!
WATCH YOUR MOUTH!
LEAVE IT! I'LL TAKE CARE OF IT.
NO!
I WANNA DO IT!
HA HA...
AT LEAST GIVE ME THE BATTERY.
WATCH...
LIKE THIS.

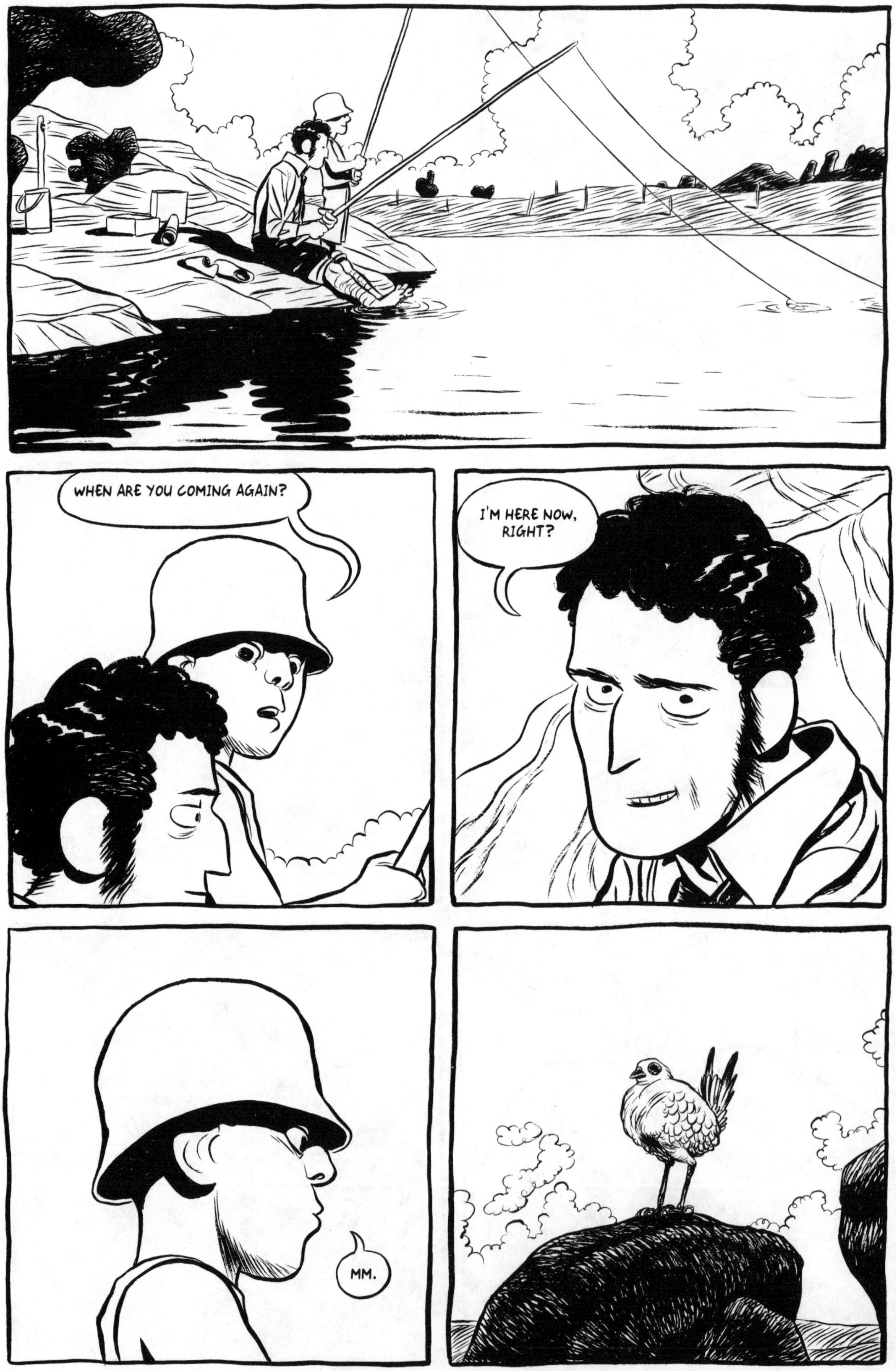
WHEN ARE YOU COMING AGAIN?
I'M HERE NOW, RIGHT?
MM.

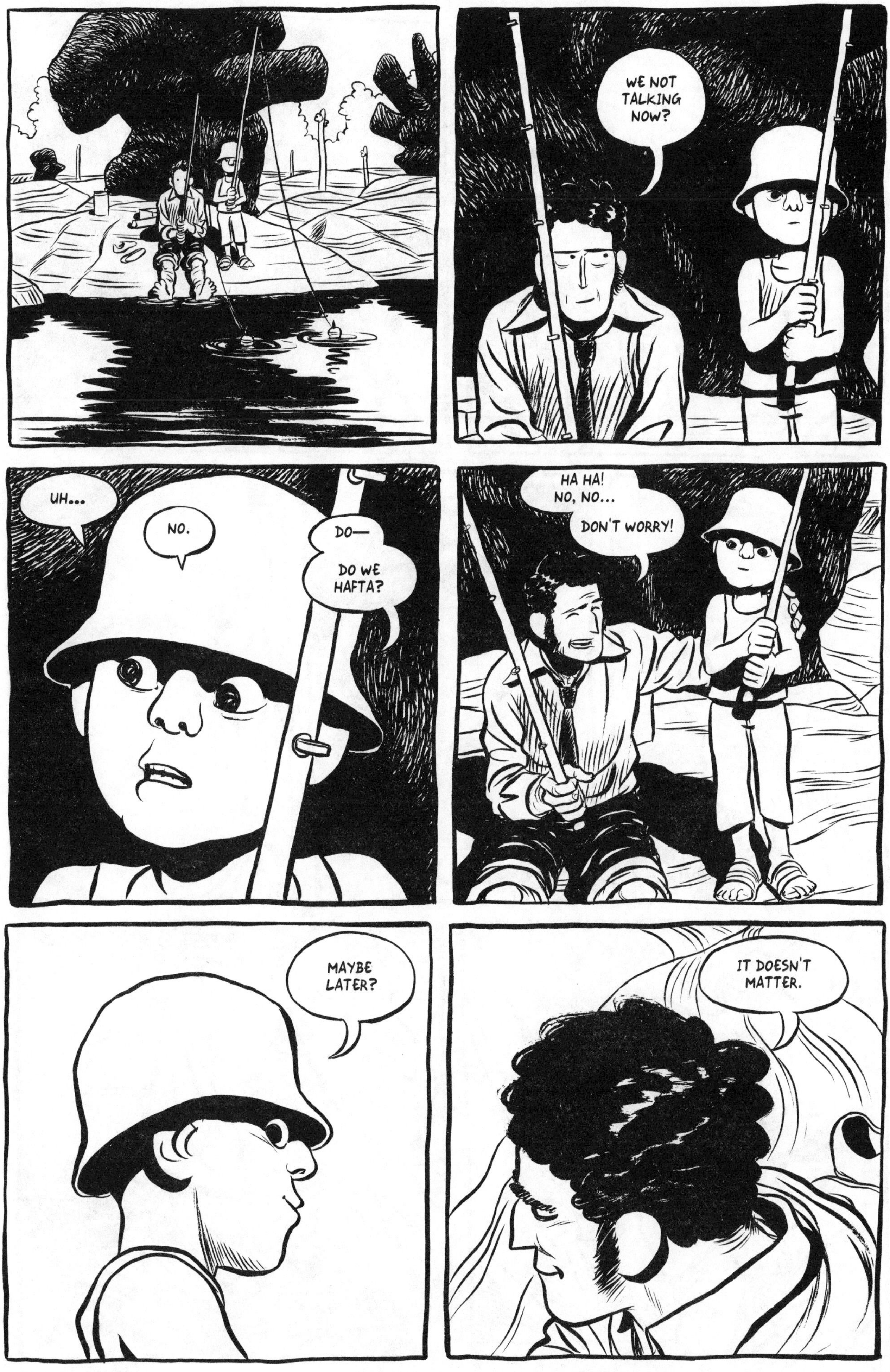
WE NOT TALKING NOW?
UH...
NO.
DO—
DO WE HAFTA?
HA HA! NO, NO...
DON'T WORRY!
MAYBE LATER?
IT DOESN'T MATTER.

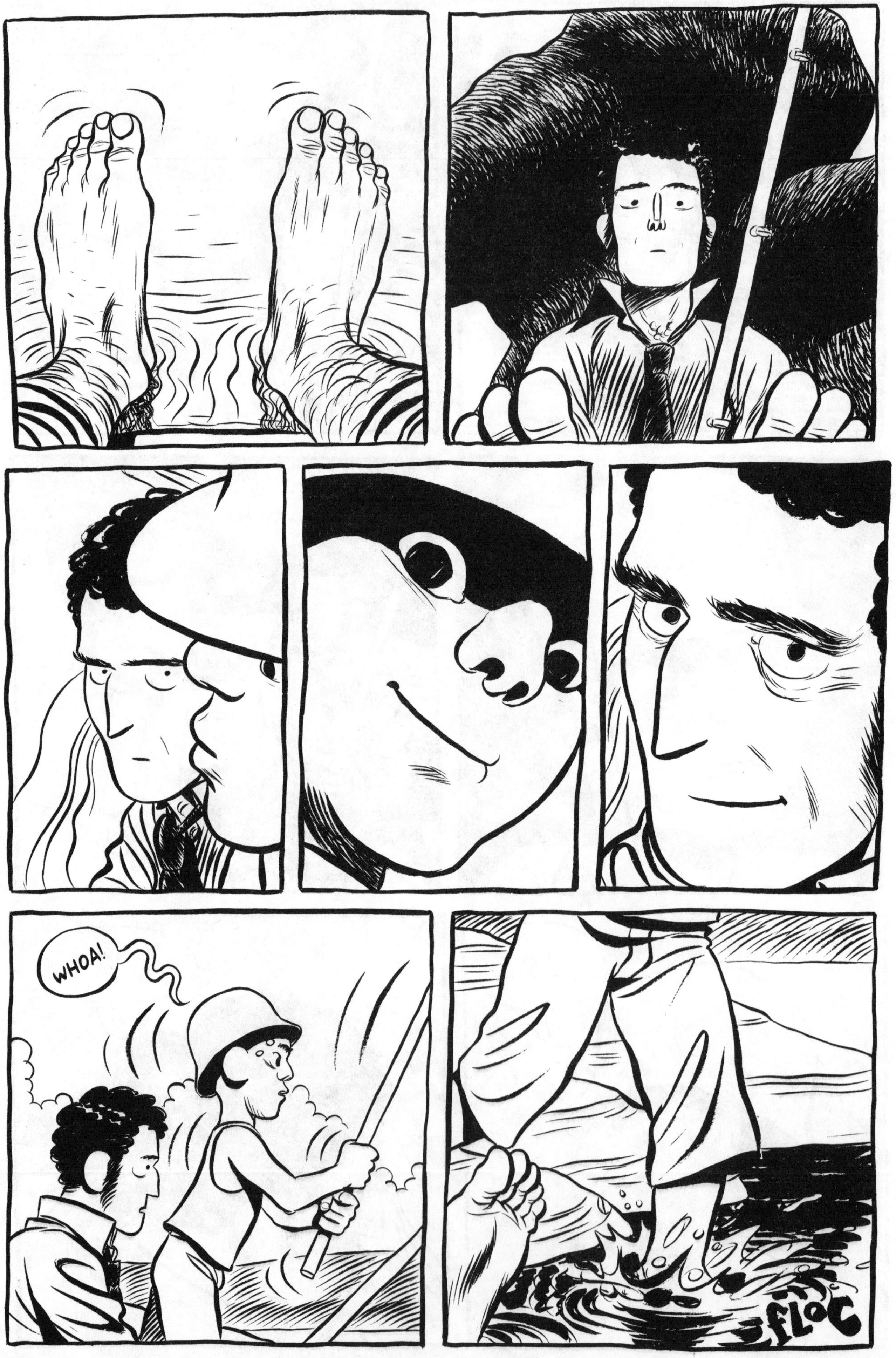
WHOA!
FLOC

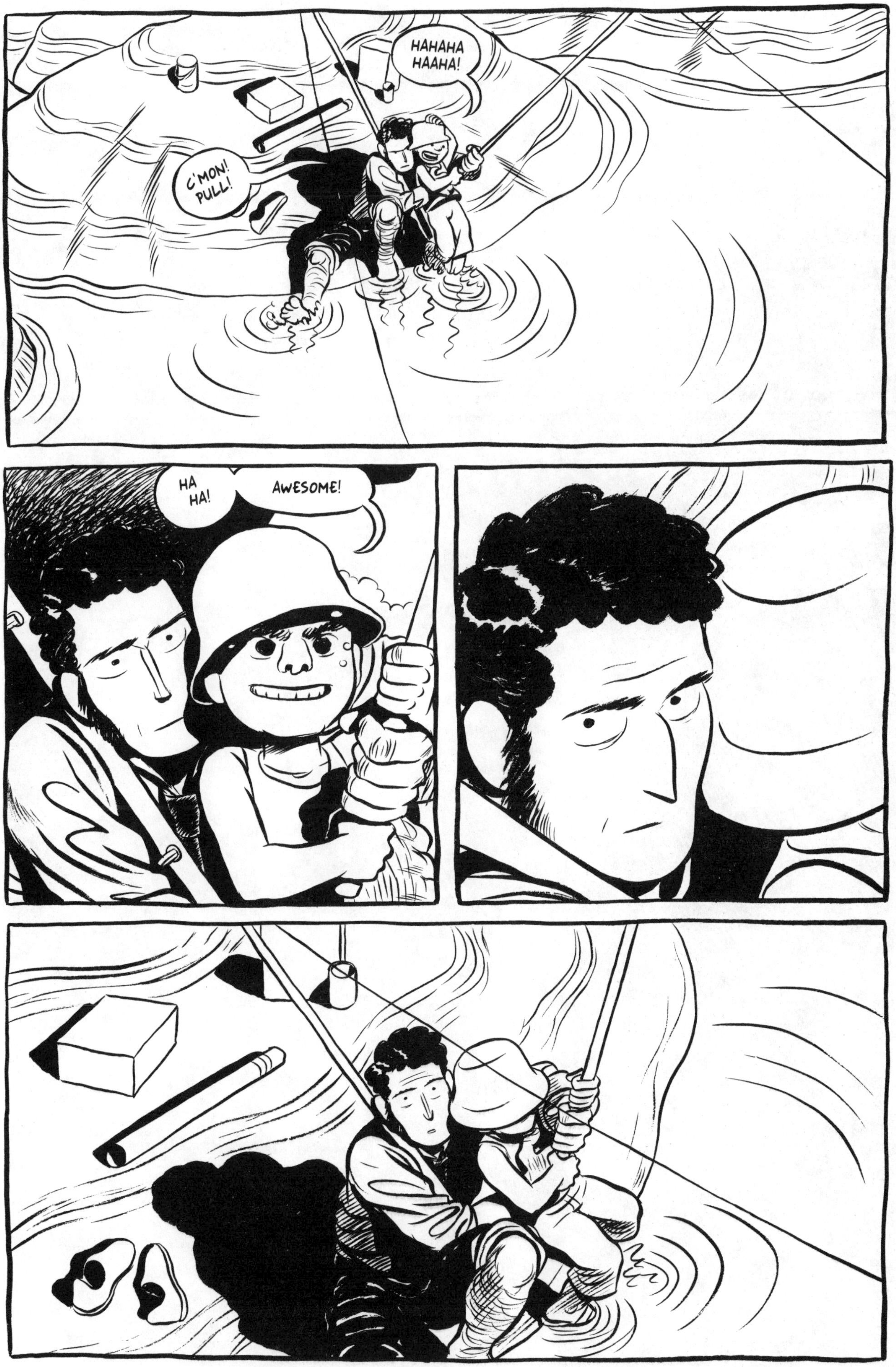

HAHAHA HAAHA!
C'MON! PULL!
HA HA!
AWESOME!

FIN

FREDERIK 05.02 - 10.05